T0396126

THE OXFORD HANDBOOK OF

# GREEK AND ROMAN MYTHOGRAPHY

# THE OXFORD HANDBOOK OF

# GREEK AND ROMAN MYTHOGRAPHY

R. SCOTT SMITH

*and*

STEPHEN M. TRZASKOMA

# OXFORD
## UNIVERSITY PRESS

Oxford University Press is a department of the University of Oxford. It furthers
the University's objective of excellence in research, scholarship, and education
by publishing worldwide. Oxford is a registered trade mark of Oxford University
Press in the UK and certain other countries.

Published in the United States of America by Oxford University Press
198 Madison Avenue, New York, NY 10016, United States of America.

© Oxford University Press 2022

Library of Congress Cataloging-in-Publication Data
Names: Smith, R. Scott, 1971- editor. | Trzaskoma, Stephen, editor.
Title: The Oxford handbook of Greek and Roman mythography /
[edited by] R. Scott Smith and Stephen M. Trzaskoma.
Description: New York, NY : Oxford University Press, [2022] |
Includes bibliographical references and index. |
Identifiers: LCCN 2022000719 (print) | LCCN 2022000720 (ebook) |
ISBN 9780190648312 (hardback) | ISBN 9780197642511 (epub) |
Subjects: LCSH: Mythology, Classical.
Classification: LCC BL723 .O94 2022 (print) | LCC BL723 (ebook) |
DDC 292.1/3—dc23/eng20220521
LC record available at https://lccn.loc.gov/2022000719
LC ebook record available at https://lccn.loc.gov/2022000720

DOI: 10.1093/oxfordhb/9780190648312.001.0001

1 3 5 7 9 8 6 4 2

Printed by Lakeside Book Company, United States of America

In memory of Ellie and Ezio.

# Contents

# PART III INTERPRETATIONS AND INTERSECTIONS

# PART IV MYTHOGRAPHY AND THE VISUAL ARTS

# Acknowledgments

We have many people to thank, the most prominent of whom are our colleagues Piero Garofalo (Italian, UNH) and Christopher Gregg (Art History, GMU), who gave us valuable guidance on several chapters. In addition, we are grateful to the John C. Rouman Classical Lecture Series for several grants that supported the work in these pages, as well as the Dion Janetos Fund for Hellenic Studies, which subsidized the building of our index. We also wish to thank the Office of the Dean of the College of Liberal Arts and the Office of the Provost at the University of New Hampshire for their support, including two sabbatical periods. The Undergraduate Research Team of the UNH Greek Myth Lab contributed to this work in sundry but important ways. Finally, we are tremendously grateful to our contributors who, despite past and current challenges, responded with outstanding scholarship that will doubtlessly frame future work in this field.

# LIST OF CONTRIBUTORS

**Daniel W. Berman** is Professor of Greek and Roman Classics at Temple University. His most recent book is *Myth, Literature, and the Creation of the Topography of Thebes* (Cambridge University Press, 2015). His interests lie primarily in the areas of myth and mythography, and specifically the representation of urban and built space in the Greek and Roman mythic traditions.

**Claude Calame** is Director of studies at the École des Hautes Études en Sciences Sociales in Paris (Centre AnHiMA: Anthropologie et Histoire des Mondes Antiques); he was Professor of Greek language and literature at the University of Lausanne. He taught also at the Universities of Urbino and Siena in Italy, and at Yale University in the US. In English translation he has published many books on Greek history, literature, and myth, including, *Greek Mythology. Poetics, Pragmatics and Fiction* (Cambridge University Press 2009). His latest book in French is *La tragédie chorale. Poésie grecque et rituel musical* (Les Belles Lettres 2018).

**Charles Delattre** is Professor of Ancient Greek Language and Literature at the University of Lille. His research focuses on ancient narrative practices involving the modern notion of "mythology." He devotes himself to the annotated edition of part of the mythographic corpus and to a reflection on contemporary definitions of "myth" from a perspective of literary theory and cultural anthropology.

**Ken Dowden** is Professor Emeritus of Classics at the University of Birmingham. He is well known for his work on mythology (*Death and the Maiden*, Routledge 1989; *Uses of Greek Mythology*, Routledge 1992; and, with Niall Livingstone, the *Companion to Greek Mythology*, Blackwell 2011), as well as on religion, Homer and latterday authors who contested Homer's veracity. For *Brill's New Jacoby* he has edited, translated and commented on many fragmentary Greek "historians" (from Aristeas of Prokonnesos and Diktys of Crete to Poseidonios and Dio Chrysostom), some of whom engaged in wilful mythographic activity. His interest in the ancient novel has focused mostly on Apuleius and Heliodoros, typically on their religio-philosophical aspects, a mythology of its own.

**Joseph Farrell** is Professor of Classical Studies at the University of Pennsylvania, where he has taught since 1984. The focus of his work is ancient Latin poetry, including its relationship to Greek poetry and to Greek and Roman literary scholarship, along with its reception from later antiquity to the present. His most recent book is *Juno's Aeneid: A Battle for Heroic Identity* (Princeton University Press, 2021).

**K. F. B. Fletcher** is Associate Professor of Classics at Louisiana State University. His research focuses primarily on the Roman use of Greek mythology, especially in mythography and Augustan poetry. In addition to articles and book chapters on a wide range of Roman poets and mythographers, he is the author of *Finding Italy: Travel, Nation, and Colonization in Vergil's* Aeneid and coeditor of *Classical Antiquity in Heavy Metal Music*.

**Christopher Francese** is Asbury J. Clarke Professor of Classical Studies at Dickinson College in Carlisle, Pennsylvania, USA. He is the author of *Parthenius of Nicaea and Roman Poetry* (2001), *Ancient Rome in So Many Words* (2007), and, with R. Scott Smith, *Ancient Rome: An Anthology of Sources* (2014). He is the project director of Dickinson College Commentaries (dcc.dickinson.edu).

**Benjamin Garstad** is Professor of Classics at MacEwan University in Edmonton, Alberta. His research concentrates on the literature of Late Antiquity, especially John Malalas and the origins of the Byzantine chronicle tradition, the *Alexander Romance*, and the integration of myth and history in Christian literature. He prepared an edition and translation of the *Apocalypse* of Pseudo-Methodius and the *Excerpta Latina Barbari* for the Dumbarton Oaks Medieval Library and is the author of *Bouttios and Late Antique Antioch: Reconstructing a Lost Historian* (forthcoming in the Dumbarton Oaks Studies series)

**Annette Harder** is emeritus Professor of Ancient Greek at the University of Groningen (The Netherlands). She has published on Greek tragedy, Greek literary papyri, and in particular on Hellenistic poetry. Since 1992 she has organized the biennial Groningen Workshops on Hellenistic Poetry, and edits the series *Hellenistica Groningana*. Her main publications are *Euripides' Kresphontes and Archelaos* (Brill, 1985); *Callimachus "Aetia"* (Oxford University Press, 2012). She has also published several mythographic papyri in *The Oxyrhynchus Papyri* and written articles on the *hypotheseis* of Euripides.

**Greta Hawes** is Research Associate at the Center for Hellenic Studies. She is author of *Rationalizing Myth in Antiquity* (Oxford University Press, 2014), *Pausanias in the World of Greek Myth* (Oxford University Press, 2021), editor of *Myths on the Map* (Oxford University Press, 2017), and codirector of MANTO (Mapping Ancient Narratives, Territories, Objects) and Canopos.

**William Hutton** is Professor of Classical Studies at William & Mary and the author of numerous publications on Pausanias, including the book *Describing Greece: Landscape and Literature in the "Periegesis" of Pausanias* (Cambridge University Press, 2005). He is currently completing a new annotated translation of Pausanias's *Description of Greece*.

**Hugo H. Koning** is a lecturer at Leiden University. His main interests are early epic, mythology, and reception. He is the author of *Hesiod: The Other Poet; Ancient Reception of a Cultural Icon* (Brill, 2010). He is currently working (with Glenn Most) on an edition of exegetical texts on the *Theogony* and has recently published (with Leopoldo Iribarren) a volume on Hesiod and the pre-Socratics.

**David Konstan** is Professor of Classics at New York University. He is the author of books on ancient comedy, the novel, friendship in the classical world, the emotions of the ancient Greeks, the classical conception of beauty and its influence, and Greek and Roman ideas of love and affection. His most recent book is *The Origin of Sin*. He is a fellow of the American Academy of Arts and Sciences and an honorary fellow of the Australian Academy of the Humanities.

**Eleanor Winsor Leach**[†] held the Ruth N. Halls Professorship in the Department of Classical Studies at Indiana University, Bloomington, until her death on February 16, 2018. She was an influential and wide-ranging scholar whose work treated Roman literary, social and cultural history through a variety of methodological and theoretical lenses, most notably by integrating the study of art—particularly painting—architecture and monumentality into her analyses. She authored four books and numerous articles over her lengthy career.

**Chiara Meccariello** is Lecturer in Greek Literature at the University of Cambridge. After obtaining a PhD in Classics from the University of Pisa, she held postdoctoral positions at the universities of Vienna, Oxford, Göttingen, and Cassino. Her research interests include papyrology, ancient education, Greek tragedy and satyr drama, and ancient scholarly and interpretive work on myth-based poetry.

**Zahra Newby** is Professor of Classics and Ancient History at the University of Warwick (UK). Her research interests focus on the reception of Greek culture in the visual arts of the Roman world. Her publications include *Greek myths in Roman art and culture: imagery, values and identity in Italy, 50 BC-AD 250* (Cambridge University Press, 2016) and *The Materiality of Mourning: Cross-Disciplinary Perspectives* (Routledge, 2019, co-edited with R. E. Toulson).

**Pura Nieto Hernández** is Distinguished Senior Lecturer in Classics at Brown University and Honorary Member of the Instituto de Estudios Medievales y Renacentistas y de Humanidades Digitales at the University of Salamanca. Her primary areas of research are the intersection of poetics and mythology in Homer and the archaic and Hellenistic poets, the history of the Greek language, and Philo of Alexandria. Among her most recent publications are "Philo of Alexandria on Greek Heroes," in *Philo of Alexandria and Greek Myth: Narratives, Allegories, and Arguments*, edited by Francesca Alesse and Ludovica De Luca (Brill, 2019), and "Mito y Poesía lírica," in *Claves para la lectura del mito griego*, edited by Marta González González and Lucía Romero Mariscal (Dykinson, 2021).

**Jennifer Nimmo Smith** is an independent scholar with close links to the School of History, Classics and Archaeology at the University of Edinburgh. After a MA Hons in Classics, she went on to Byzantine Studies in further degrees. Her PhD thesis on the Pseudo-Nonnus Commentaries on Sermons 4,5,39 and 43 by Gregory of Nazianzus was published in 1992, and she is currently working on an edition of the text of Gregory's Sermons 4 and 5.

**Joan Pagès** is Lecturer in Greek Philology at the Universitat Autònoma de Barcelona. He has published several articles and chapters of books on Greek mythography, myth, religion and Literature. In collaboration with Nereida Villagra he has recently published the collective volume *Myths on the Margins of Homer* for Trends in Classics (De Gruyter). He is currently preparing (with Nereida Villagra) an edition and commentary of the *Mythographus Homericus*.

**Irene Pajón Leyra** (Madrid, 1977) is assistant professor of Greek at the University of Seville. She has studied the Greek paradoxographic literature for her PhD, which is the topic of her book *Entre ciencia y maravilla: El género literario de la paradoxografía griega* (Zaragoza, 2011). Her fields of interest also include ancient Greek geography, history of Greek zoology, and papyrology. She has been a researcher at the universities of Oxford and Nice and at the Spanish High Council of Research.

**Jordi Pàmias** is professor at the Universitat Autònoma de Barcelona. His fields of interest are Greek mythology, mythography and religion, and their scientific reception. He is the editor of the reference text of Eratosthenes Catasterisms (Budé, 2013). His most recent works include "The Reception of Greek Myth", in L. Edmunds (ed.), Approaches to Greek Myth, 2014; and "Greek Mythographic Tradition", in R.D. Woodard (ed.), Cambridge History of Mythology and Mythography (forthcoming at Cambridge University Press).

**Lee E. Patterson** is Professor of History at Eastern Illinois University, where he teaches courses in ancient Greece, Rome, Armenia, Persia, and other areas. He is the author of *Kinship Myth in Ancient Greece* (University of Texas Press, 2010). Much of his current research focuses on Roman-Armenian relations, on which he is currently writing a book and has recent publications in *Revue des Études Arméniennes* and other venues.

**Ezio Pellizer†** held a chair in Greek literature at the University of Trieste from 1973 to 2010. He had wide ranging interests, including early archaic poetry, especially Semonides, on whom he published an edition with Gennaro Tedeschi (*Semonides: Testimonia et fragmenta* [Rome: Ateneo 1990]). He also published a number of articles and books on myth and mythography, with which he was centrally concerned in his later career. In 1990 he created and directed the Gruppo di Ricerca sul Mito e la Mitografia (GRIMM) and devoted great efforts toward a digital project, DEMGOL (Dizionario Etimologico della Mitologia On Line).

**Maria Pretzler** is Associate Professor in Ancient History at Swansea University (UK). Her interests in myth and geography started with Pausanias, leading to further research on travel writing and ancient geographers. She is author of Pausanias: *Travel Writing in Ancient Greece* (Duckworth, 2007). When she is not busy following ancient writers to the ends of the earth, she works on various aspects of Peloponnesian history, with a focus on small communities.

**Ilaria L.E. Ramelli** FRHistS holds two MAs, a PhD, a Postdoc, and Habilitations to Ordinarius. She has been Professor of Roman History, Senior Visiting Professor

(Harvard; Boston U.; Columbia; Erfurt), Full Professor of Theology and Endowed Chair (Angelicum), and Senior Fellow (Durham, twice; Princeton, 2017-; Sacred Heart U.; Corpus Christi; Christ Church, Oxford). She is also Professor of Theology (Durham, hon.; KUL) and Senior Fellow/ Member (MWK; Bonn U.; Cambridge). Recent books include *Apokatastasis* (Brill 2013), *Social Justice* (OUP 2016), *Lovers of the Soul* (Harvard 2021) and *Patterns of Women's Leadership* (OUP 2021).

**Manuel Sanz Morales** is Professor of Ancient Greek at the Universidad de Extremadura in Cáceres, Spain. He has published on Greek textual criticism, the transmission of classical texts, Greek mythography, Greek literature, and the classical tradition. His most recent publications include *Chariton of Aphrodisias' "Callirhoe": A Critical Edition* (Universitätsverlag Winter, 2020) and, co-authored with Manuel Baumbach, *Chariton von Aphrodisias "Kallirhoe": Kommentar zu den Büchern 1-4* (Universitätsverlag Winter, 2021).

**Evina Sistakou** is Professor of Greek Literature at the Aristotle University of Thessaloniki. She is the author of *Reconstructing the Epic: Cross-Readings of the Trojan Myth in Hellenistic Poetry* (Peeters 2008), *The Aesthetics of Darkness: A Study of Hellenistic Romanticism in Apollonius, Lycophron and Nicander* (Peeters 2012) and *Tragic Failures: Alexandrian Responses to Tragedy and the Tragic* (De Gruyter 2016). She has published articles on Apollonius, Callimachus, Lycophron, Euphorion, Greek epigram and Hellenistic aesthetics.

**R. Scott Smith** is Professor of Classics at the University of New Hampshire, where he has taught since 2000. His major field of study is ancient myth and mythography, with special focus on the intersection of mythography, space, and geography. He is currently co-director of a digital database and map of Greek myth, MANTO: https://manto.unh.edu. In addition, he is interested in how mythography operates in scholia and commentaries and is undertaking a student-supported project to translate mythographical narratives in the Homeric scholia. He also produces the podcast, *The Greek Myth Files*.

**Jon Solomon** holds the Robert D. Novak Chair of Western Civilization and Culture at the University of Illinois at Urbana-Champaign. Publications include *Ben-Hur: The Original Blockbuster* (2016), Boccaccio's *Genealogy of the Pagan Gods* (2011, 2017), *The Ancient World in the Cinema* (1978, 2001²), Ptolemy's *Harmonics* (1999), and six dozen articles/anthology chapters in classical studies, including ancient Greek music, medicine, poetry, Roman cooking, and reception of Hollywood Ancients and classical allusions in contemporary cinema

**Iris Sulimani** is Senior Lecturer at the Open University of Israel. She is the author of *Diodorus' Mythistory and the Pagan Mission: Historiography and Culture-heroes in the First Pentad of the "Bibliotheke"* (2011) and has published other works on historiography, mythography, and geography of the Hellenistic period. She is also interested in the utopian idea in antiquity and is currently working on Plutarch's biographies of mythical figures.

**Kathryn Topper** is Associate Professor of Classics at the University of Washington. Her publications include *The Imagery of the Athenian Symposium* (Cambridge University Press, 2012) and articles on a variety of issues in and related to Greek vase painting and myth. Her current research focuses on the Thalamegos of Ptolemy IV Philopator and its relationships to Dionysian cult and Egyptian religion

**Stephen M. Trzaskoma** is currently Dean of the College of Arts & Letters at California State University Los Angeles. Formerly, he served as Professor of Classics and Director of the Center for the Humanities at the University of New Hampshire. His two primary research areas are Greek prose fiction and ancient mythography, and he has published numerous studies in these areas, as well as translated key primary sources.

**Nereida Villagra** is Associate Professor at the Classics Department of the University of Lisbon, and member of the research Centre for Classical Studies of the same University. She obtained her PhD at the Autonomous University of Barcelona in 2012 and has published papers or chapters on mythography, textual criticism and Greek literature. She has just recently published  a a co-edited volume (with Joan Pàges) *Myths on the Margins of Homer* for Trends in Classics (De Gruyter) She is currently preparing a commented edition of the *Mythographus Homericus* in collaboration with Joan Pagès.

**Arnaud Zucker** is Professor of Classics at University Côte d'Azur (France), CNRS, Cepam. He received a Phd in Anthropology from the École Pratique des Hautes Études and a Habilitation thesis in Classics from University Aix-Marseille. His key research topics are ancient zoology, ancient astronomy, and mythography. *He is coauthor with J. Pàmias of *Ératosthène de Cyrène. Catastérismes* (Belles Lettres, 2013), coeditor of *Lire les mythes* (Septentrion, 2016), and author of *L'encyclopédie du ciel. Mythologie, astronomie, astrologie* (Laffont, 2016).

# INTRODUCTION

## R. SCOTT SMITH AND STEPHEN M. TRZASKOMA

## 1. GREEK AND ROMAN MYTHOGRAPHY TODAY

IN 1987 Albert Henrichs concluded an important article by noting that "[l]arge areas of the history of Greek mythography are still unexplored, and several important collections of myths lie ignored," further admonishing us that "[m]odern interpreters of Greek myths must constantly re-examine and strengthen the old foundations. If not, they build castles in the air" (1987: 267). This handbook is a testament to how different matters are today with regard to Henrichs's first assessment and how little they have changed with regard to his second. In the retrospect provided by the passage of some three decades, Henrichs's article seems to straddle a line that divides an earlier period, in which mythography—which for the moment we will define at a broad level as ancient writing about myth or the recounting of myth in prose with no pretensions to artistry—and the suriving mythographical works were seen as having interest only as sources of mythical data and variants, and our current scholarly era, when new approaches have advanced our understanding of the aims and motivations of the works themselves. Although mythography is yet firmly fixed in the minds of some classical scholars as a specialist's marginal enterprise, not only have mythographical works become the object of broader and more intense study, but the very nature of mythography has been investigated more thoroughly, and the extant texts have come to be seen both for their continuing value as sources for Greek myth and for the inherent interest in their role in intellectual and cultural life down to the end of antiquity and beyond. The various chapters in this handbook are intended to take stock of that progress by carefully examining the status of the scholarship on the subject, but also to cultivate additional advances by making more accessible to nonspecialists the important mythographical authors and works and the practical and theoretical questions that surround them—and, where possible, pointing to outstanding complexities and new avenues for research.

To get a sense of how the landscape has been altered, one need only do a quick scan of the entries in the "References" sections of the individual chapters in this book to see how much scholarship has appeared since the 1990s, especially in Catalan, English, French, German, Italian, and Spanish. The texts of most of the stand-alone mythographical collections have been re-edited (often multiple times, with productive results; for instance, for Ps.-Apollodorus we now have both Papathomopoulos 2010 and Cuartero 2010 and 2012), as have the fragmentary and dispersed texts, most notably, Fowler's edition of the remains of the earliest mythographers (2001), which is now supplemented by his fine commentary (2013). New translations have made most of the main mythographical sources much more accessible, and many are available in more than one language; for example, for Heraclitus the Allegorist's *Homeric Problems* we now have both the Italian of Pontani (2005) and an English version in Russell and Konstan (2005). The same period has seen the appearance of numerous articles, edited volumes (for instance, Pàmias 2017, on Apollodorus), and full commentaries on individual authors and texts (for example, Brown 2002, on Conon). There has also been a welcome turn to addressing broader questions about the nature of mythography and its methods. While it would be out of place to list all the recent contributions on this subject, we may point further not only to seminal monographs like those of Cameron (2004), *Greek Mythography and the Roman World*, and of Hawes (2014) on rationalizing, but also to collected volumes that take mythography as their only or main focus: Nagy (2013), Trzaskoma and Smith (2013), and Romano and Marincola (2019). There is also now an international network of scholars and a journal devoted specifically to mythography (*Polymnia*, https://polymnia-revue.univ-lille.fr/.). On the whole, we have both a clearer picture of the origins of mythography and its survival beyond antiquity, as well as its characteristics and development in the intervening eras.

Of course, much is still unknown or remains mysterious, and much is contested, but it is undeniable that headway has been made and that new pathways are being blazed by an international array of established and emerging researchers, many of whom have authored chapters of this handbook. Most importantly, the questions we ask today about mythography have moved beyond (but not abandoned) source criticism and transmission to querying the very nature of mythography and the place of the mythographical impulse and its methodological elaborations and presentations in the intellectual, artistic and cultural life of the ancient Greek and Roman worlds. This explains why this handbook contains chapters not only on authors traditionally deemed mythographers but also on ones that seek to connect mythographical thinking and activities with other domains of knowledge and life, from the visual arts to politics. In the next section, we discuss a broad intellectual rationale for the handbook and consider the boundaries of what we can call "mythography." In the third section, we then give a brief overview of the volume's organization and contents.

## 2.  THE NATURE(S) OF GREEK AND ROMAN MYTHOGRAPHY

At the center of Part I of the handbook is an attempt to sketch an overview of mythography across more than a millennium, from its initial impulses in oral poetry in the archaic period to the end of the western Roman empire. It will be immediately obvious that there is no simple definition of what constitutes "mythography," especially since responses to what we call the mythical story world constantly evolved along with political, literary, and cultural changes, sometimes upheavals, over the longue durée. As Bremmer (2013: 56) succinctly puts it, mythography is polymorphous, and its function "clearly varied according to the time and place of its production." Because of the many approaches to the mythical story world, establishing absolutely clear boundaries for a genre of mythography or defining a corpus of mythographers, even within a single era, is destined to fail. Even for the period from which we have the richest set of complete works that we call mythographical, the imperial period, we face a "complex ensemble of writing practices, whose borders with other practices remain porous" (Delattre in this volume, p. o-o-o).

We might pose the problem in another way: Is our definition of mythography simply a matter of convenience for modern scholars attempting to corral the wide-ranging responses to what *we* call myth? This is precisely the approach Pellizer took in the foundational article in which he defines mythography as the "activity of recording and transmitting in writing the narrative and descriptive material . . . that we normally call mythical" (1993: 283, with note 2). Although this runs the risk of making mythography, like myth (Delattre 2010; Edmunds 2021: xv–xxix), a "trash can category" (*catégorie poubelle*) or "dumping ground" (*fourre-tout*), such a generalizing view has one great advantage: it allows us to adopt our etic category and avoid confronting the details of the debates over the contested concept of "myth" itself, specifically when (if ever) "myth" became an emic category for the Greeks, a question of particular importance when we are trying to think strictly about the earliest period, when Acusilaus and Pherecydes—whom modern scholars often identify as the first mythographers—began transmitting "mythical" material in prose. To some degree, this handbook follows Pellizer's lead in casting our net widely over the various products that seem to emerge from what we (the editors) call "a mythographical mindset," which we will explore more below.

And yet, though there is hardly space here to cover such a complicated and probably insoluble problem, the question of whether mythography could exist in the earliest period is a pressing one—and an example of the productive disagreement and tension one will find in these pages precisely because consensus is impossible. If we are to imagine mythography as a *self-conscious* category of intellectual activity, this requires the pre-existence of an emic category of "myth." In other words, for a writer to know that he was producing mythography, even in the broadest sense, "myth" already had to be a recognizable category for the Greeks themselves. Few would vigorously argue against the notion that, after Thucydides, and certainly after Plato, myth had been decisively distinguished from history and had taken on a meaning that approaches our own conception of the word. Whether a category "myth"—and so "mythography"—can be pushed back in time is precisely the subject of two chapters in this handbook that come to different conclusions. Reviewing the activities of the earliest writers we regularly call mythographers and reminding us that the term *mythographos* does not occur before the 2nd century BCE (unless the occurrence in Palaephatus is original) and that *mythographia* is first found in Strabo, Calame in this volume (p. 464) concludes that "it is not possible to speak of 'mythography' as a genre or even as a critical activity before the end of the 4th century BCE." Since those who were cataloging the stories of the earliest periods had no conception of myth as separate from accounts of the past generally, their activity dealt with what we call the mythical story world but which they simply saw as events of the past.

Whether one agrees with Calame's position depends on whether one accepts myth as an early and "autonomous form of thought (*Denkform*)," as Pàmias champions as the triumph of modern scholarship on myth (p. 32). If this is correct, then even the Homeric epics are an "early form of appropriation and reception of myth," and myth was something that *could* be abstracted and set down into writing. We take such summary accounts for granted, but it should be remembered that abstracting stories typically belonging to the realm of poetry and committing them to prose "was an act of great intellectual imagination" (Fowler 2017: 18). Whether or not writers such as Pherecydes would have labeled themselves mythographers or conceived of themselves as producing what we call mythography, they "were already in possession of a category comparable to myth, being understood as a type of account that belongs to a heritage from which they were separated by a gap, and onto which they can cast an objective gaze" (Pàmias p. 34). If myth as *Denkform* existed in the archaic period, then we should not be surprised to find, already in the earliest poetic forms, "a good deal of explanation, commentary and interpretation" of stories that resembles later mythographical forms (Nieto Hernández p. 14). In other words, from the beginning, myth-making was self-reflective, and stories were understood as an object of analysis, redefinition, and, potentially, rejection. After all, for Pindar to actively reject a theologically inadmissible myth about Tantalus, Pelops, and the gods, that version of the myth not only had to be available and known but capable of being rejected in favor of a more palatable one.

If myth is one element of the compound *mythography*, the other is, of course, writing. Although the exact contours are hard to trace, the emergence of writing as a widespread technology in the archaic period was a necessary precondition both for recording and preserving stories and for serious collection, analysis, and comparison of them. In particular, as Pàmias demonstrates (pp. 38–42), the development of prose writing, removed from the performative context, opened up the path to the construction of the "author" as the locus of authority removed from the influence of the Muses. If the widespread use of writing was a precondition for the earliest mythographical writing, the evolution of a literary culture and a wider availability of books in the 4th century led to increasingly frequent critical activity around myth precisely because any piece of mythographical writing in turn became, alongside the underlying literary texts, a source for the next mythographer down the line, something that becomes obvious from the way in which later mythographers cite both poetic and prose mythographical writers as authorities, although the question of the nature, purpose, and meaning of such citations is a contested matter (see Cameron 2004: 88–123, esp. 93–94).

In considering the emergence of a literary culture that was establishing the material and cultural conditions making it possible for mythography and other forms of scholarship to evolve, we should not underestimate the special role of tragedy, not only as the object of study (for example, by Asclepiades of Tragilus, 4th c. BCE), but also for the way it was both influenced by and perpetuated mythographical conventions already in place—a twin process that Meccariello in this volume describes as a "coevolution of tragedy and mythography" (p. 300). Naturally, the Great Library of Alexandria and other academic centers, such as Pergamon, provided extensive material resources for mythographers, such as Lysimachus, and *grammatici*, such as Apollodorus of Athens (see Smith and Trzaskoma, "Hellenistic Mythography," in this volume) to conduct research, and for poets to mine as they created innovative poetry, much of which reflects what might be called a "mythographical mindset" (see Sistakou in this volume; we will return to this concept).

It is not uncommon to see a teleological view of mythography, where the proto-mythographical impulses (genealogical work, catalogs, narrative-as-history) gradually coalesce into a genre or separate discipline at some point in the Hellenistic period. Such a view, however, effaces the great variety of writing practices involving myth that we have been pointing to. Leaving aside the difficulty of saying anything about the Hellenistic period with certainty, from which there is but one extant text (Palaephatus, not unproblematic: see Koning in this volume), we encounter an immense range of mythographical products from the imperial period. We can point to the comprehensive *Library* of Ps.-Apollodorus; the rather wild revisionist histories of Dares and Dictys; the thematic collection of metamorphoses of Antoninus Liberalis; collections of narratives keyed to Homer (the *Mythographus Homericus*); and the Stoic theological work of Cornutus that allegorizes the gods. Even where form or technique overlap, there are also major differences of approach, which becomes even more obvious as more comparanda are added to the mix.

Given all of the above, it may seem unwise to propose a grand unifying theory that can contain the variety of responses to the mythical world, but even so, we can see critical responses to myth as they develop over time and through varying conditions. Literature-based educational practices took shape in the 4th century BCE, which is precisely the same time frame in which mythography as a generic activity became part of Greek intellectual life. As we show in the chapter on education, an elite child's education was built on a successive series of steps involving myth: learning, organizing, narrating, criticizing (rationalizing), defending (allegorical approaches), and finally creatively using it to demonstrate one's mental agility, interpretive skills, learning—or apparent learning—in creating coherent arguments. From the very beginning students are asked to start thinking "mythographically" by uniting like with like (for instance, who belongs to the Trojan War), and then later are asked to narrate stories. In the final stages, the advanced learner breaks them down to build them back up again. Although it is impossible to say whether mythographical practices led to the creation of such an educational structure, the practice of employing myth as a centerpiece of that system must have come from somewhere. And although not all students were trained to become mythographers, the net effect was that "the general intellectual atmosphere of the ancient world consisted of mythographical elements, and this formed an epistemological cycle" (Smith and Trzaskoma in this volume on education, p. 410).

Elsewhere, we have proposed, for convenience, the distinction between what we called "systematic" and "interpretive" mythography (Smith and Trzaskoma 2007: xiv–xv), which provides another axis along which to array the surviving texts. Systematic mythography is concerned with organizing and retelling the vast and chaotic mythical story world, which often contained contested and contradictory accounts, gaps, and other inconsistencies because of the various ways in which mythical traditions developed and proliferated among the Greeks. Interpretive mythography seeks to uncover the origins, function, and hidden meanings (often with attention to etymologizing) of the myths. This is a useful distinction, and those works that seem most purely mythographical tend to fall strongly in one category or the other rather than to mix modes, but ultimately both are part of the same intellectual enterprise, the taming of myth's complexities.

Such a focus not on the actual products of mythography, but on the mythographical *mentalité* that led to them, may also lend more insight into the "mythographical" expressions that are found in art, including the organization and composition of art in wall painting in Roman houses to the potentially symbolic meanings of myth on sarcophagi. Ultimately, artists may not be mythographers, as such, but their practices intertwine and interact with mythography as they treat their common subject, and these connections are of especial interest as we consider a broader cultural and intellectual response to the mythical storyworld. Mythography was not merely a limited activity of formal writing by a few; it was also an orientation woven into ancient life. In the pursuit of apprehending this wide scope and the specifics of interaction, some contributors to this handbook turn their attention to mythography's connections to topics as diverse as politics, geography, and Christianity.

## 3. A Brief Overview of the Contents

This book is divided into five parts, each with its own purpose and goals, and an overall aim of providing a clear statement of where the field is today, to push beyond that position where possible, and to limn some possible avenues for future study. Part I, "Mythography from Archaic Greece to the Empire" traces the key developments in myth criticism and mythographical impulses from the earliest period in Greek poetry (Nieto

Hernández) and prose (Pàmias) to the imperial period, from which the majority of our extant mythographical works come. Of particular importance is the Hellenistic period, which, as the authors (Smith and Trzaskoma) note, must have been crucial to the development of various forms but must be approached with caution given that nearly all of those works have been lost or survive only in fragmentary form. In an analysis of the vast extant mythographical output in Greek from the imperial period, Delattre suggests that we should approach the surviving works not as a closed category but as "open texts" (see also Fletcher on Hyginus), while at the same time testing the validity of the divisions between Hellenistic and imperial and even Greek and Roman. Smith provides an overview of the surviving mythographical texts in Latin and considers the rationale behind the production of mythographical material in Latin when so much was available in Greek.

Part II, "Mythographers," is meant to provide a complete overview of the authors and texts that are the main sources of mythography—a sort of handbook within a handbook that offers a survey of each in turn. One will of course find the systematic mythographers whose works are extant, including Apollodorus's comprehensive overview of the entire Greek mythical system (Trzaskoma), the more narrowly focused collections of Antoninus Liberalis (on metamorphoses: Delattre) and Parthenius (love stories gone wrong: Francese), and the less clearly organized collection of narratives by Conon (Sanz Morales) and Hyginus (Fletcher). But one will also find works that do not feature simple, straightforward narratives but offer interpretations of those stories, such the allegorical approaches in Cornutus (Ramelli) and Heraclitus's *Homeric Problems* (Konstan), or the rationalizing versions of Palaephatus (Koning) and Heraclitus the Mythographer (Hawes), although the latter also blends in allegory as well. Finally, there are the ludic, revisionist histories of Dictys and Dares (Dowden), whose inventive rewriting of Homeric myth hardly prevented them from becoming immensely popular in the Middle Ages and Renaissance.

At the same time, we recognize that not all mythographical thinking emerged in a self-contained prose works about myth. Indeed, the mythographical mindset is clearly at work in the poetic production of Hellenistic poets, as Sistakou systematically demonstrates in her chapter on Alexandrian verse, which can be seen as a pendant to Nieto Hernández' earlier chapter on early Greek poetry and a harbinger for Farrell's overview of mythography in Ovid. Broadly speaking, the same "universalizing macrostructures" that underpin Ovid's comprehensive treatment of myth from the beginning of time in the *Metamorphoses* can also be found earlier in the *Library of History* of Diodorus of Sicily, whose early books form a sort of compendium of the mythical story world. Even if they are drawing on earlier Hellenistic models, both Ovid and Diodorus are, like most mythographers, actively shaping their presentation of the mythical world (see especially, Sulimani on Diodorus). Another author who employs mythography, but in a larger matrix of topography and history, is Pausanias, whose view of the Greek landscape is decidedly linked to the mythical past, even if he tends to offer rationalized accounts of it (Hutton).

Rounding out this part is an overview of another important source of mythographical narratives, the so-called *Mythographus Homericus* (hereafter MH), an otherwise unknown author now seen as the source of a scattered but important group of narratives in the D-scholia to the *Iliad* and *Odyssey*. Because this collection has analogs in texts found on papyrus, the MH merits a separate essay (see Pagès), but similar mythographical narratives and notes are found in the extensive scholiastic traditions of other poets, not least Pindar, Euripides and Apollonius of Rhodes. As Villagra systematically demonstrates, a close reading of the scholia to each author often reveals subtle differences in aims and content, perhaps reflecting the commentators' perceived ideas of what aspects of the mythical story world needed emphasizing. A review of mythography in all its forms (exegetical, narrative, catalogic) would not be complete without a survey of the variety and massive amount of mythography that has been found on papyri (Harder)—the sheer volume of which is a strong indicator of how much mythography has been lost to us. One important collection of stories that has emerged from papyri is the so-called "Tales from Euripides," alphabetically arranged summaries that doubtlessly served as a convenient source for mythographers, though as Meccariello suggests, tragedy, especially the late plays of Euripides, was already taking part in mythographical conventions.

The reciprocal relationship between mythography and tragedy naturally leads us to Part III, "Interpretations and Intersections," which treats both interpretive approaches to myth and the ways in which mythography is naturally connected to or combined with other intellectual pursuits. In the former category, because of the importance of rationalizing and allegorizing approaches in the reception of myth in antiquity and beyond, there are two substantial chapters on the main developments and practitioners of each method (Hawes on rationalizing, Ramelli on allegorizing). Among the interpretive methods employed by Stoic allegorizers especially, but not limited to them, is the use of etymologies to reclaim the symbolic or deeper meaning of the myth, but etymologies were a frequent part of myth-building in other ways as well (Pellizer).

Since myth involves Greek heroes from the distant past, who move through a proto-Greek landscape, mythography is often found as part of geographical exposition, as we mentioned in regard to Pausanias. Pretzler's overview of mythography in geographical writing also includes a close analysis of Strabo's *Geography*, which, despite the geographer's early protests, includes a substantial amount of mythographical material. Myth is, of course, also part of the Greeks' conception of the past, and, again, Calame's analysis of the work of the earliest mythographers argues that what we call mythography in the earliest period is inseparable from historiography. Also focusing on the early period, Berman explores the blurred edges between local mythography and its Panhellenic counterpart, teasing out how one might think of "local mythography" as different from "local historiography," as Jacoby defines a group of writers in *FGrHist*. Local appropriation, especially of genealogical connections, through myth for political means is the focus of Patterson's chapter, which analyzes mythographical elements in charter myths and treaties, with additional focus on the authorial intent of the practitioners. Part III also contains explorations of how mythographical methods intersected with two other important intellectual trends in the ancient world: first, the cluster of issues surrounding the myths about the disposition of constellations (Zucker on catasterisms); second, the mythographical connections to be found in literature on wonders and rarities, a genre that arose formally and distinctly from the rest of historiography in the Hellenistic period (Pajón Leyra on paradoxography).

Part IV, "Mythography and the Visual Arts," features the first sustained attempt to view art—composition, organization, symbolism—from a mythographical point of view. Although the word mythography evokes the idea of writing, our three contributors take the view that representations of myth on vases, wall paintings, and sarcophagi can be viewed as texts—ones that reflect a mythographical mindset, guided by some of the same impulses that are found in literary or subliterary mythographical writing. From this point of view, Topper analyzes the 6th-century BCE François Vase and pendant images featuring the abduction of Helen, all of which "share narrative and rhetorical structures with texts that contributed to, or were appropriated into, the ancient mythographical tradition." Likewise, Leach considers the compositional and organizational strategies of wall painting that parallel mythographical writing, with an important look at Philostratus's *Imagines*, which dramatizes the viewer's engagement with paintings and offers a series of interpretive strategies one must bring to viewing a static image—reminding us that *paideia* was deeply steeped in mythographical training. Finally, Newby analyzes images of myth on Roman sarcophagi of the high empire as expressions of "interpretive" and "systematic" approaches of mythography (which reflects the Cumont-Nock controversy over the symbolic aspects of sarcophagi from the mid-20th century). In all, these essays provide a first look at the potential of viewing artistic products from a mythographical perspective.

Part V, "Christian Mythography," focuses on mythography in the forms it took after the rise of Christianity fundamentally shifted the role of myth in the wider culture. In a sweeping essay Nimmo Smith provides a chronological survey of the Christian authors that engaged with pagan myth, and in two separate chapters Garstad investigates the roles of mythography, first in the Byzantine world, which continued to have access to most of the Greek mythography from the previous periods, and again in the Latin West, which continued to need mythography to explain and interpret the pagan myths but which had lost direct access to Greek mythographical texts as bilingualism disappeared. Picking up in the 14th century with Bersuire, Petrarch, and Boccaccio, Solomon traces the further developments as Greek material were reintroduced to western Europe in the Renaissance, culminating in the massive and influential mythographical compilations such as those composed by Cartari and Conti in the 16th century.

## FURTHER READING

For an annotated bibliography on general and specific aspects of mythography, we invite you to consult our article on mythography in Oxford Bibliographies Online, which assembles and organizes the most important works on mythography up to 2010 (Smith and Trzaskoma 2011). For individual authors and broader topics, the best way to start is to consult the Further

Reading sections at the end the chapters. These will point you to the fundamental scholarship for each topic, organized in convenient fashion.

## References

Bremmer, Jan N. 2013. "Local Mythography: The Pride of Halicarnassus." In *Writing Myth: Mythography in the Ancient World*, edited by Stephen M. Trzaskoma and R. Scott Smith, 55–73. Leuven: Peeters.

Brown, Malcolm K. 2002. *The Narratives of Konon: Text, Translation and Commentary of the Diegeseis*. Munich and Leipzig: Saur.

Cameron, Alan. 2004. *Greek Mythography in the Roman World*. Oxford: Oxford University Press.

Cuartero, Francesc J. 2010/2012. *Pseudo-Apollodor. Biblioteca*. Vols. 1 and 2. Barcelona: Bernat Metge.

Delattre, Charles. 2010. "Introduction." In *Mythe et fiction*, edited by Danièle Auger and Charles Delattre, 11–19. Paris: Presses Universitaires de Paris Nanterre.

Edmunds, Lowell. 2021. *Greek Myth*. Berlin and Boston: De Gruyter.

Fowler, Robert L. 2000. *Early Greek Mythography*. Vol. 1: *Text and Introduction*. Oxford: Oxford University Press.

Fowler, Robert L. 2013. *Early Greek Mythography*. Vol. 2: *Commentary*. Oxford: University Press.

Fowler, Robert L. 2017. "Greek Mythography." In *A Handbook to the Reception of Classical Mythology*, edited by Vanda Zajko and Helena Hoyle, 15–27. Chichester, UK: and Malden, MA: Wiley-Blackwell.

Hawes, Greta. 2014. *Rationalizing Myth in Antiquity*. Oxford: Oxford University Press.

Henrichs, Albert. 1988. "Three Approaches to Greek Mythography." In *Interpretations of Greek Mythology*, 2nd ed., edited by Jan N. Bremmer, 242–277. London: Croom Helm.

Nagy, Joseph F., ed. 2013. *Writing Down the Myths*. Turnhout: Brepols.

Pàmias, Jordi, ed. 2017. *Apollodoriana*. Berlin and Boston: De Gruyter.

Papathomopoulos, Manolis, ed. 2010. *Apollodori Bibliotheca post Richardum Wagnerum recognita*. Athens: Aletheia.

Pontani, Filippomaria. 2005. *Eraclito: Questioni omeriche sulle allegorie di Omero in merito agli dèi*. Pisa, Italy: Edizioni ETS.

Romano, Allen J., and John Marincola, eds. 2019. *Host or Parasite? Mythographers and Their Contemporaries in the Classical and Hellenistic Periods*. Berlin and Boston: De Gruyter.

Russell, Donald A., and David Konstan. 2005. *Heraclitus: Homeric Problems*. Atlanta, GA: Society of Biblical Literature.

Smith, R. Scott, and Stephen M. Trzaskoma. 2007. Apollodorus' "Library" and Hyginus' "Fabulae": Two Handbooks of Greek Mythology. Indianapolis, IN: Hackett.

Smith, R. Scott, and Stephen M. Trzaskoma. "Mythography." Oxford Bibliographies Online, last modified 2011. doi:10.1093/OBO/9780195389661-0036.

Trzaskoma, Stephen M., and R. Scott Smith, eds. 2013. *Writing Myth: Mythography in the Ancient World*. Leuven: Peeters.

# PART I

# MYTHOGRAPHY FROM ARCHAIC GREECE TO THE EMPIRE

············································································

# CHAPTER 1

# THE MYTHOGRAPHICAL IMPULSE IN EARLY GREEK POETRY

············································································

## PURA NIETO HERNÁNDEZ

It is a curious fact that the romantic distinction between authentic myth and later re-elaborations should have been given a new life with the theory of oral composition as developed by Milman Parry and his successors, which established a boundary between archaic poetry and written texts. Indeed, some scholars, such as Havelock (1982), saw a fundamental change in human cognition in the transition from orality to literacy. From this perspective, the Homeric epics, Hesiodic poems, and other remnants of the archaic period in Greece were vehicles of myth *simpliciter*, whereas later treatments, above all, those in prose, had lost the original inspiration and were reduced to mere secondary compilations, "mythography" as opposed to "mythology," and frequently considered beneath the notice of serious scholarship. Cameron, in his massive study of Imperial mythography, writes of the so-called *Library of Myth* ascribed to Apollodorus, probably composed in the 1st or 2nd century CE:

> In the *Bibliotheca*'s defense, critics often confidently assert that it is "drawn from excellent sources," a claim based on its frequent direct citation of specific texts from archaic and classical poets and mythographers . . . The writer gives the *appearance* of an easy, firsthand familiarity with the entire range of relevant texts. But this is an illusion. In all probability he came by most of his citations at second (or third) hand and had never even seen an original copy of many of the texts he quotes. The same will usually apply to the scholiasts, however much we might like to think that some particular scholion bristling with plausible details and archaic citations was copied directly from one of the great Hellenistic critics. (Cameron 2004: vii–viii; see also Trzaskoma, this volume)

The early texts are the bearers of genuine myth, which is diluted, contaminated, or distorted in later compilations in the effort to create coherent and systematic narratives from the primitive accounts handed down in antiquity.

Nevertheless, by any reasonable definition of "mythography" and the features that presumably distinguish it from true myth, there are passages and, indeed, whole narratives in our very earliest sources—ones that we can read today even though Ps.-Apollodorus may have known them at fifth or sixth hand—that bear all the hallmarks of the mythographical tradition (Wendel 1935; Pellizer 1993; Alganza Roldán 2006; Smith and Trzaskoma 2011). Among other features, we may cite the catalogue sections of the epics (for example, the catalogue of Achaean ships in the second book of the *Iliad* or the list of heroines in Hades in the eleventh book of the *Odyssey*). This is not to say that Homer's epics have the same form and function as Ps.-Apollodorus's *Library*; they certainly do not. But this is a matter of genre or of the composition, reproduction, and transmission of the texts, not of date or nearness to the primary, creative period of Greek myth (Fowler 2006b; Calame 2006: 28–29). The works of mythography do not have the aesthetic aspirations and quality of poetry, and if some of them speculate about the meaning of the myths, they neither seek nor exhibit the plural significations of poetry. Broadly speaking, mythography simplifies the complexities and offers summaries rather than literary elaborations of the stories of myth (Calame 2015: 30). Consider, for instance, the brief resume that Ps.-Apollodorus gives us of the plot of the *Iliad*, condensing into one paragraph Books 5, 6, and 7 of the epic (*Epit.* 4.2):

> When Diomedes was dominating the battlefield, he wounded Aphrodite when she was helping Aineias. Coming face-to-face with Glaucos, he was reminded of their ancestral ties of friendship and swapped armor with him. When Hector challenged the best warrior to a duel, many wanted to fight him, but Aias was chosen by lot and fought. But heralds broke up their fight when night fell. (Smith and Trzaskoma 2007: 81)

Hesiod's *Theogony* bears a greater resemblance to Ps.-Apollodorus, not because it is necessarily later than the Homeric poems (indeed, some scholars have dated it earlier), but because it is a didactic work rather than a heroic epic poem.

Mythography is also often understood not only as an attempt to recount myths in an orderly and extensive fashion, but also to explain the absurdities that many myths contain, to cleanse them of irrationalities, and to interpret the true meaning hidden behind their apparent contradictions and immoralities. But, again, the texts of archaic poetry already contain a good deal of explanation, commentary, and interpretation. This seems to have been part of the oral tradition from the beginning; even the earliest texts that survive contained obscurities that required clarification, and the poets felt obliged to provide it. As Graziosi and Haubold (2015: 7) have recently observed, a critic might well begin by asking "where composition of the Homeric text ends and explanation of its meaning begins. The question quickly reveals that even the earliest text of the *Iliad* we can possibly reconstruct is shaped by attempts to explain and comment on an earlier poetic tradition. Some epic expressions, for example, must have sounded obscure even to the earliest audiences of Homeric poetry, because internal glosses attempt to explain their meaning." It is a testimony to the enduring influence of the distinction between oral and written composition that so fine a critic as Glenn Most can write, in the introduction to his Loeb Classical Library edition of Hesiod:

> [N]ot only does Hesiod use writing: he also goes to the trouble of establishing a significant relation between his poems that only writing could make possible. In various passages, the *Works and Days* corrects and otherwise modifies the *Theogony*: the most striking example is *WD* 11, "So there was not just one birth of Strifes after all," which explicitly rectifies the genealogy of Strife that Hesiod had provided for it in *Th.* 225. Thus, in his *Works and Days* Hesiod not only presupposes his audience's familiarity with his *Theogony*, he also presumes that it might matter to them to know how the doctrines of the one poem differ from those of the other . . . Hesiod's announcement depends upon the dissemination of the technology of writing. For in a context of thoroughgoing oral production and reception of poetry, a version with which an author and his audience no longer agree can be dealt with quite easily, by simply replacing it: it just vanishes together with the unique circumstances of its presentation. (2006: xxi)

In a similar vein, West writes that the author of the *Odyssey* "was trained as an oral performer of epic, but he resolved to create an *Odyssey* that would emulate the *Iliad* in scale and be likewise stabilized in writing . . . Like the *Iliad* poet, he made many insertions in what he had already written, in a few places adding a whole scene" (West 2014: 2–3). Self-correction, interpolation, auto-allusion are taken as necessary features of literate composition, impossible in a strictly oral tradition. In the same way, mythography proper has been closely identified with prose and writing and so regarded as entirely alien to the culture of oral poetry, which is the proper repository of pure myth, and the great majority of scholars, who today regard archaic Greek poetry as principally oral in nature, have neglected to identify the features of this corpus that not only anticipate the later, systematizing style but are evidence that mythography in all likelihood is as ancient as mythology itself. As Fowler (2006b: 43) puts it:

> Hesiod and the mythographers both provide a great deal of information in conveniently accessible form. But Hesiod lived in a world in which the work of the Muses meant poetic performance. The first mythographers lived in an emerging new world, in which many texts were circulating at a distance among a select, highly literate few.

Even as Fowler (2006b: 44) notes the interaction between mythography and oral poetry in the early classical period, he proposes that mythological narratives were circulating in written form at an earlier time than most scholars believe and so rescues the distinction between an oral and a written tradition.

What, then, is mythography? We may subsume the most relevant features under two broad headings. First, there is the organization and systematization of myths by way of lists, catalogues, genealogies, indications of contrasting versions of the same story, corrections of other versions, and the like. This set of features is often labeled *systematic* mythography (Smith and Trzaskoma 2011), and indeed, according to some scholars (for instance, Pellizer 1993: 284), this alone is characteristic of mythography proper. Second, there is the interpretation of myths by means of rationalization, etymological explanation, glosses, and more elaborately, allegory, an approach known as *interpretive* mythography. Mythography, then, in contrast to mythological narrative, requires a categorization or ordering (temporal, hierarchical, geographical) of dispersed myths and the operation of linking them together. It provides a certain degree of consistency or coherence within what in the poetic tradition appears to be a relatively chaotic, when not utterly contradictory, mass of diverse stories. At the same time, some mythographical works provide analyses and interpretations of the deeper, not always evident, meanings of myths. In the Greek tradition, both strands may be detected in the earliest poets and prose writers, who are sometimes identified as historians, genealogists, logographers, and mythographers proper, since these were not distinct genres or disciplines at the time (Alganza Roldán 2006: 5–6; Calame 2015: 79).

In what follows, I identify some of the main compositional resources that are characteristic of mythography and show how they are found in Homer (that is, the poet or poets of the *Iliad* and the *Odyssey*), Hesiod, and other archaic poets. I first discuss the systematizing and ordering of scattered stories and their incorporation into a larger narrative framework, beginning with two well-known resources of archaic composition that mythographers regularly employ—that is, catalogues and genealogies (the latter are a subset of catalogues, but have their own function and structure). I then turn to examples of the way the poets acknowledge different versions of a story and correct what they regard as erroneous or impious elements. In the second part, I take up the interpretive aspect of mythography and illustrate etymological explanations of words or names and other glosses and then conclude with examples of full-blown allegory. These categories frequently overlap, and I do not mean to suggest that the archaic poets were necessarily aware of these features as constituting distinct mythographical modes (though they may well have been). But the above typology should suffice to show that mythography is coeval with what we understand by mythology, and readers will readily supplement the examples provided below.

# 1. CATALOGUES AND GENEALOGIES

Lists are an important aid to memory in both the oral and written traditions (Calame 2006: 25) because they impose order on a large number of items and thus constitute an important means of organizing materials in early poetry and prose. Occasions for such catalogues within the poems are large gatherings of individuals, such as contests for the hand of a woman or games honoring the death of a hero, with their lists of competitors, gifts, and prizes, and armaments; major weddings; and great expeditions and wars, representing wide areas of the Greek world. These lists entail a selection and recombination of elements deriving from what we can assume to have been a considerable amount of geographically and chronologically dispersed stories. After all, catalogues make a show, at least, of being exhaustive or including as much information as possible, and they present that information in some kind of coherent arrangement.

Poets use catalogues not only for the enumeration of simple lists of objects, such as the flowers mentioned in the prologue of the Homeric *Hymn to Demeter* (ll. 6–8) or other items that might have constituted virtuoso exhibitions of knowledge and memory in an oral performance (for example, the catalogue of thirty-three Nereids in *Iliad* 18.38–49), but also as an important aid in the creation and transmission of a cultural patrimony. For instance, the catalogue of the Achaean ships in the second book of the *Iliad* is an extraordinary record of the map of Greece at the end of the Mycenaean period, or, rather, of the semi-mythic world that was associated with the end of the heroic age but retained traces of a genuinely archaic geography. By placing the various peoples from the several regions of Greece together, united in this collective expedition, the *Iliad* represents the Trojan War as a Panhellenic enterprise; in Benjamin Sammons's words, the purpose is "to emphasize the huge numbers involved in the expedition, and to represent the conflict as a kind of 'world war'" (2010: 139). But the Homeric *Catalogue of Ships* includes as well, to be sure, a great deal of genealogical commentary on the heroes mentioned in it (Larson 2001: 121–126).

The war, then, is an opportunity to relate and confirm the lineages of the major families of the Greek world. If for us the Trojan War is the most familiar instance, archaic poetry (much of it lost) also recounted the several expeditions against Thebes, the wars between the Lapiths and Centaurs and between the Calydonians and Curetes, and many others. Itemizing the suitors for the hand of Helen or of Hippodameia, or of the guests attending the weddings of Cadmus and Harmonia, Thetis and Peleus, and Helen and Menelaus, again allowed for orderings that might reflect social hierarchy, geographical distribution, or other principles of selection, and at the very least picked out and brought together figures representing a wide range of myths and stories. So, too, a great voyage, such as the expedition of the Argonauts, which was doubtless the subject of an early epic since Homer himself refers to it, or the returns of the heroes from Troy, of which the only surviving example is that of Odysseus in the *Odyssey*, assembled a variety of episodes under an umbrella narrative not essentially different from what later mythographers attempted. Games and poetry contests, such as the competitions in honor of Pelias or the poetical contests in honor of Amphidamas, also offer this opportunity. Catalogues listing the participants in such social occasions, who come from lineages all over the Greek world, contributed to the creation of a common Panhellenic cultural patrimony. The catalogue form was so appreciated by poets and their publics in the archaic period that several entire poems were basically nothing but catalogues. So, too, the first historians were especially interested in the genealogical connections among great families, to the extent that many today are simply dubbed "genealogists."

In the Greek tradition, the intersection between catalogue and genealogy is omnipresent. Genealogies provide a chronological framework because each generation brings with it a new stage or epoch, and because they signal the passage of time; they also establish important links between lines of descent within and among families and link historical aristocratic clans with heroes and gods. Genealogical catalogues are, for these reasons, a fundamental factor in the creation of the Panhellenic ideology in the archaic period. What is more, as Higbie (2008) writes, "catalog poetry also provided both material and a structuring principle to later prose works."

Such genealogical lists may well have been in circulation quite early and available to those engaged in cultural production, whether poets and early prose writers or plastic artists (on catalogues and genealogies in the plastic arts, see Jaccottet 2006). In this respect, poets and mythographers were drinking from the same wells: Greek genealogies are "not pure oral tradition untouched by writing but the product both of written coordination and oral tradition" (Thomas 2009: 155).

Hesiod, in all of his works but especially in the *Theogony*, offers a wide array of genealogies, some involving landscape elements, such as seas, mountains, rivers, and other features of the natural world such as sky, day, and night, but also, and primarily, of gods and heroes and a good number of personified abstractions. Genealogies structure the pseudo-Hesiodic and very influential *Catalogue of Women*, which organizes Greek myths around descent from the mother, and they also inform the *Library* of Ps.-Apollodorus, the very model of formal mythography. Thus, the systematization of myths, their grouping into integrated overarching narratives, and the self-conscious reference to earlier mythic materials which are recombined and reorganized—all these features that we take to be the hallmarks of mythography— are already there in the catalogue form, as deployed by Homer and Hesiod. There is no reason not to count instances of this device as genuine examples of the mythographical method. Indeed, the most read books of the *Iliad* in schools in the Imperial period were the first and second (that is, the catalogue of ships), to judge by papyrus fragments; this was the training ground for mythographers steeped in the rhetorical tradition.

## 2. TREATMENT OF VARIANT VERSIONS

Works of mythography often mention several versions of a story. For example, Ps.-Apollodorus's *Library* reports:

> After Althaia died, Oineus married Periboia daughter of Hipponoos. The author of the *Thebaid* says that he took her as a war-prize after the city of Olenos was attacked, but Hesiod says that after she was seduced by Hippostratos son of Amarynceus, her father Hipponoos sent her from Olenos (in Achaia) to Oineus because he lived far away from Elis and commanded him to kill her. But there are those who say that Hipponoos upon discovering that his daughter had been seduced by Oineus, sent her off to him carrying his child. Oineus fathered Tydeus with her. Peisandros says

that his mother was Gorge because Oineus fell in love with his own daughter in accordance with Zeus' will. (1.74–75 [1.8.4–5]; trans. Smith and Trzaskoma 2007: 10)

Here the *Library* is contrasting the testimony of the cyclic *Thebaid* (or possibly a poem by Antimachus on the same topic) regarding the circumstances of the marriage of Periboea to Oeneus with Hesiod's more sinister version. Ps.-Apollodorus then adds yet another account, ascribed simply to "some," of the marriage and the problematic stance of the maiden, and, finally, after explaining that the girl was the mother of Tydeus, he adds the testimony of still another epic author, Peisandros, to the effect that Tydeus's mother was in fact Gorge.

We do not find anything quite like this in archaic poetry, but our earliest texts nevertheless indicate recognition of other versions, sometimes produced by the same poet. Such alterations represent a special type of variant, in which two versions of a myth are juxtaposed and evaluated for their accuracy or propriety. I mention here two well-known cases. One of Hesiod's most famous self-corrections occurs in *Works and Days*, in which he rectifies the narrative he related in the *Theogony* regarding Eris, as Most has pointed out (cited in my introduction to this chapter). Whereas in the *Theogony* (225) only one Eris is mentioned, in the *Works and Days* Hesiod speaks of two (*Op.* 11)—"So there was not just one birth of Strifes after all"—and he develops this new conception at length (lines 11–25), which indicates its importance. According to the genealogy of Strife that Hesiod related in the *Theogony*, Strife is an irremediably bad thing, born from Night and mother of:

> Toil and Forgetfulness and Hunger and tearful Pains, and Combats and Battles and Murders and Slaughters, and Strifes and Lies and Tales and Disputes, and Lawlessness and Recklessness, much like one another, and Oath, who indeed brings most woe upon human beings on the earth, whenever someone willfully swears a false oath.
>
> (*Theog.* 225–232, trans. Most).

In the *Works and Days*, however, there is also a good Strife that is the source of the healthy competition that causes human beings to strive harder and advance beyond their neighbors.

Another famous example of auto-correction among the archaic poets is Stesichorus's *Palinodia* or *Recantation*. The story (told in Plato, *Phdr.* 243a; see also Isocrates *Helenae Encom.* 64) goes that he composed this palinode after he was blinded for having offended Helen by recounting her story as we read it in Homer, where she is represented as the unfaithful wife of Menelaus who eloped to Troy with Paris, who, in turn, committed a gross violation of hospitality. In the recantations (there seem to have been two), Stesichorus avers that there were in fact two Helens, or rather, as a papyrus (*P.Oxy.* 29.2506) of the poem that includes a commentary explains, "he reproaches Homer for having set Helen in Troy and not her phantom (*eidōlon*), and in another he reproaches Hesiod." The brief fragment that survives runs:

> No, that tale isn't true,
> you did not step in the well-benched ships
> nor did you reach the citadel of Troy.

The palinode, as this poetical resource is commonly known, does not in fact eliminate one version by substituting another (Bassi 1993). This very brief fragment of Stesichorus sets both versions together and does not really erase the condemned story, leaving both versions side by side. In this respect, as Carruesco (2017: 193) suggests, Stesichorus's *Palinode* exhibited "the double ways of the poem and the poet's ability to master both," and was the model for the double treatment of Neoptolemus's death in Pindar and indeed "the precedent to Parmenides's two alternative ways, that of *Aletheia* and that of *Doxa*, and Empedocles's "double tale" (*dipl' ereō*).

There are also cases in which a poet corrects others. Pindar is not averse to altering traditional accounts of myths or even to self-correction. For instance, in *Nemean 7* Pindar seems to rectify the version of the death of Neoptolemus that he had offered in *Paean* 6. According to the scholia, Aristarchus and Aristodemus had a theory that the version of this death presented in *Pae.* 6, according to which Neoptolemus had gone to the temple to rob it, had offended the Aeginetans, and so Pindar composed *Nem.* 7, in which Neoptolemus dies in a dispute over sacrificial meats, as an apology to them (see, most recently, Pòrtulas [2018, with bibliography]). Certainty, however, is difficult since *Nem.* 7 is a particularly challenging poem and scholia are characteristically unreliable, and the difference between the two versions may be due to their respective genres, which is tantamount to saying the distinct occasions of their performance (see Rutherford 2001: 321–323). In the passage I have chosen to comment on here, however, Pindar is clearly amending a version of myth related by other poets that he regards as false. In narrating the story of Tantalus and his son Pelops in the first *Olympian Ode*, Pindar explains that Pelops's ivory shoulder was a congenital feature of his beautiful body (lines 25–27), and that his sudden disappearance from earth was due to Poseidon, who fell in love with him and snatched him away (as Zeus snatched Ganymedes). The more usual tale had it that Tantalus had cooked his son and served him to the immortals, who became aware of the deception only after Demeter had bitten a morsel of his shoulder. Pindar concludes his amended version of the myth of Pelops with the following words, making clear, among other things, that he is responding to those who accuse the gods of gluttony (in context, evidently a euphemism for "cannibalism"; so Race 1997: 53 n. 14) and other "impious" beliefs:

> Son of Tantalus, of you I shall say, contrary to my predecessors,
> that when your father invited the gods
> to his most orderly feast and to his friendly Sipylus,
> giving them a banquet in return for theirs,                                    40
> then it was that the Lord of the Splendid Trident seized you,
> his mind overcome by desire, and with golden steeds              Ant. 2
> conveyed you to the highest home of widely honored Zeus,

where at a later time  
Ganymede came as well                                                   45  
for the same service to Zeus.  
But when you disappeared, and despite much searching  
no men returned you to your mother,  
one of the envious neighbors immediately said in secret  
that into water boiling rapidly on the fire  
they cut up your limbs with a knife,  
and for the final course distributed your flesh                         50  
around the tables and ate it.  
But for my part, I cannot call any of the blessed gods                  Ep. 2  
a glutton—I stand back:  
impoverishment is often the lot of slanderers.

(*Ol.* 1.36–53, trans. Race)

Some lines earlier in the same ode, Pindar again reveals his awareness of other versions of stories, which he qualifies as "lies":

Yes, wonders are many, but then too, I think, in men's talk  
stories (*mythoi*) are embellished beyond the true account            28b  
and deceive (*exapatōnti*) by means of  
elaborate lies

(*Ol.* 1. 28–29, trans. Race)

We can observe in Pindar, as in Stesichorus, that the "rejected" version is still present (and so is transmitted, not omitted) in the many details that the poet includes and that evoke Pelops's dismemberment and boiling by his father, Tantalus, and the latter's sacrilegious sin against the gods. On the one hand, Pelops is extracted from a "purifying cauldron" (*Ol.* 1.26), and he has a shoulder of ivory (*Ol.* 1.27). On the other hand, we are told later on that Tantalus had offered his human friends the nectar and ambrosia that he himself could eat because of his special connection with the gods, thereby committing, even in Pindar's "true" version, the sort of food-related violation he had in the rejected version, in which he had cooked and fed his own child to the gods (see, further, Nagy 1990: 131–136). As usual, poetry recounts even the stories that are rejected with artistic embellishment and allusive suggestion, whereas full-blown mythographical texts generally adopt a crisp, summary style.

## 3. Etymological Analysis and Glosses

There are many words and names in the Homeric language whose meanings were embedded in inherited formulaic expressions and were no longer understood, and poets often felt the need to include a gloss to explain the obscure term. This procedure, which is not uncommon in Homer (see Werner 2018: 193–195; and, esp., Graziosi and Haubold 2015) and Hesiod, is similar in intention and function to the explanatory etymologies of the names of the gods or other opaque terms by later mythographers; it finds a particularly sophisticated expression in the allegorical interpretations of the Stoics, but also in such eclectic works as Heraclitus's *Homeric Problems* (see Konstan this volume) and in the rationalizations of myths by Palaephatus and Euhemerus (see Koning, this volume; Smith and Trzaskoma, this volume [on Hellenistic Mythography]; for a more detailed discussion of mythographical etymologizing, see Pellizer, this volume).

Glosses are, then, another feature common to archaic poetry, from Homer to Pindar, and later mythographical writers, and are motivated by the same impulse to explain. In addition, although such glosses have a basis in the grammatical and linguistic intuitions of the poets (they often provide, or are based on, popular etymologies), they are often also moralizing, and in this regard, too, they anticipate later mythographical practices.

In a recent article challenging the radical division commonly accepted between composition and commentary (or, to put it differently, between textual criticism and reception), Barbara Graziosi and Johannes Haubold examine some Homeric expressions that "must have sounded obscure even to the earliest audiences of Homeric poetry" and hence required or invited glosses (Graziosi and Haubold 2015: 7). An example is the meaning of the adjective *daiphrōn* because the *Iliad* betrays some uncertainty about its significance. Two popular etymologies are suggested in the text: one points to the meaning "warlike" (*en daï*, "in battle"); the other, to "wise" (*daēmōn* = "knowledgeable, understanding"). According to Graziosi and Haubold, the evidence of the Homeric text itself suggests "live explanation in performance" ranging from elementary issues, such as pronunciation, to highly complex ones, like "the framing of controversial speeches" (27).

Homeric etymologizing explanations or glosses can also convey a subtle moralizing commentary on myth, which is yet another dimension of mythographical interpretation in our early texts. For example, in the well-known lines in the *Iliad* in which Patroclus accuses Achilles of not being the son of Peleus and Thetis but rather of mount Pelion and the sea, on account of his harsh, pitiless heart, Patroclus proceeds in a way parallel to that employed by etymologists: to find its origins in order to understand the "true" meaning of a word. Then, by playing on his parents' names and identities, he underscores the hero's lack of pity: he is born of the harsh rock and the wild sea (Peleus readily recalls Pelion, and Thetis is a sea nymph; see Most [1993, with bibliography]). The implicit allegorical treatment that reduces Peleus and Thetis to natural phenomena anticipates later interpretations in which they simply represent the union of earth and water (for example, Fulgentius, *Myth.* 3.7).

Another notable gloss in Homer involves the name of a people called Abioi, mentioned in the *Iliad* (13.5–6: "and the Mysians that fight at close-quarters, and the proud Hippemolgoi, drinkers of milk, and the Abioi, most righteous of men"). The Homeric scholia and the lexicographical tradition both attest that Abioi (whether taken as a noun or an adjective) was interpreted as deriving either from an alpha privative prefixed to *biē* (force), thus meaning "without violence" (this seems to be the Homeric interpretation) or from *bíos*, "life, means of life," thus meaning "without means of existence;" others derived it in turn from *biós* "bow" with either a privative or copulative alpha and so giving the opposite senses of "bowless" or "archers" (see Janko 1994; Reece 2001; Ivančik 1996). The lines "had inspired intense debate among ancient scholars of Homer and geography" (Kim 2010: 193). But these later interpreters (as well as Philo of Alexandria; see Nieto 2014) had a model for this type of speculation already in Homer's own text. To say that the Hippemolgoi (literally, "Horsemilkers") and Abioi are the "most just of men," implicitly explains the name Abioi as deriving from an alpha privative and *biē*, and so accounts for the moral quality of the Hippemolgoi: they are by nature nonviolent and therefore the most just of men (even the collocation of *hippēmolgoi* and *glaktophagoi*, or "milk-drinkers," suggests a self-conscious gloss; see Reece 2001: 466). The idealized and peaceful Hippemolgoi are in radical contrast to the military violence of the Achaeans and Trojans that dominates the Iliadic book these lines introduce, and so suggests a moral commentary on the theme of the epic itself.

The *Odyssey* offers various examples. The poet plays on the name Odysseus by relating it to the verb *odyssomai* (feel wroth with someone, hate) in 1.60–62:

> Did Odysseus not
> please you by the Argive ships, making sacrifice
> in wide Troy? Why are you now so angry at him, Zeus (*ōdysao, Zeu*)?

These words are pronounced by Athena in her response to Zeus (1.45–62) and reflect her desire to call attention to Odysseus's situation and initiate his rescue from Calypso's island and homecoming. The last few words of line 62 not only connect the name Odysseus etymologically to Zeus's apparent antagonism to him, but the collocation *odysaoZeu* both sounds like *Odysseus* and sets the name of Zeus within that of the hero. The same union of Odysseus's name with *odyssomai* is also present in book 19 (406–408), in the narrative of the history of the Odysseus's scar. There, it is explained that his maternal grandfather Autolycus had given him the name Odysseus (19.409), in memory of the hatred that gods and men felt for Autolycus himself (*odyssamenos*, 19.407; see the related discussion in Pellizer, this volume).

There are several well-known cases of this kind of etymologizing gloss in Hesiod too. For example, in *Theog.* 207–210, Hesiod introduces the Titans as follows:

> As for those children of great Heaven, their father who begot them railed at them and gave them the surname of Titans, saying that straining *tight* (*titainontas*) in wickedness they had done a serious thing, and that he had a *title* (*tisin*) to revenge for it later
>
> (trans. West).

As we see, Hesiod connects the name *Titēnes* with both the verb *titainō* (stretch, strain) and the noun *tisis* (revenge, retribution). The proposed etymologies are intended to reveal something essential in the Titans' nature: their wickedness and their future defeat in the battle against the Olympians and Zeus. It is precisely the victory over the Titans that constitutes the beginning of Zeus's supremacy over the world. This is, again, clearly moral commentary.

Another famous example in Hesiod involves Aphrodite's name and her epithet *philomeidēs* (*Theog.* 195–200), which by relating her to the sea foam and to genitals, also provide information about her function in sexual unions, not only in the reference to genitals but also, I suspect, in the image of foam. Chrysaor and Pegasus are both explained (*Theog.* 281–283) via the etymology of their names (the former as he who has "a sword of gold," the latter as "born by the springs (*para pēgas*)."

The Homeric Hymns continue the tradition of this type of etymologizing. In the *Hymn to Aphrodite*, the goddess, in the address to Anchises in which she informs him of the birth of their son, Aeneas, produces two interesting cases, by punning on (and explaining etymologically) the names of both Anchises and his child. Aphrodite begins by addressing Anchises in the vocative (*Anchisē*), at the start of the line (192). After explaining the name he must give to their child and his future role in Troy (193–199), she proceeds to indicate that the reason Anchises's family has been so favored by the gods (Ganymede was snatched away by Zeus, and Tithonus was the lover of Eos, the Dawn) is that they are "close to the gods." This is expressed in the text with the adjective *anchitheoi*, a word that is also placed in the first position in the line and nicely echoes the name of Anchises (van der Ben 1986: 24; Faulkner 2008). Aphrodite is simultaneously extenuating her own behavior: she is not the only divinity to have fallen for the beauty and charm of the men in this family. Since the real reason for her affair with Anchises is Zeus's revenge against Aphrodite, giving the goddess, who constantly provokes love in others, a taste of her own medicine, she seems here to be putting herself on a par with Zeus. That her lapse in fact causes her only pain and shame is insisted on throughout the poem, but it is neatly expressed in the name she assigns to her child: he will be called *Aineias*, because "I suffered a terrible (*ainon*) pain (*achos*), because I fell in the bed of a mortal man" (198–199). This play on Aeneas's name is found already in the *Iliad* (13.481–2; see Olson 2012), but the use here has another component. The word *ainon* (here, a neuter adjective) is identical to the accusative of the noun *ainos* (story, tale, riddle, often with a moral), apart from a change of accent. The child's name thus both defines his future character as one who causes "dreadful pain" and is himself associated with suffering, and calls attention to itself as a riddle.

There is a similar case concerning the name of Helen in Aeschylus, *Ag.* 689–690, where her name is associated with the root *\*hel-* "destroy, eliminate"—hence the compounds the poet creates in *Ag.* 689, *helenas, helandros, heleptolis*, meaning "destroyer of ships," "man-killer," and "ruin of the city." Once again, the deeper meaning of the name reveals the moral character of its bearer.

In Pindar, the name of King Pelias is related to the old man's white hair (*polias*; for an extensive list of other possible cases, see Adorjáni 2013: 361, n. 4). The procedure is common to many other authors, such as the Hellenistic poet Callimachus, who, in his *Hymn to Apollo* (esp. 69–70) seems to analyze the god's name as an alpha privative and the root *polys*, "many," hence indicating the god's unity and uniqueness. In fact, several other derivations were common. Many texts relate Apollo's name with *apollymi*, "to ruin, kill," thus identifying him as the "destroyer." Plato (*Cra.* 405b6–506b) connects it with *apolousis*, "purification"; *apolysis*, "liberation, redemption"; *haploun*, "simple, straight-forward" (the Thessalian form of the god's name was *Apploun*); and *ballō* "shoot," which, taken together, allude to Apollo's various functions as god of medicine, purification, prophecy, and archery. The Roman historian Tacitus (*Histories* 5.2–5) presents the Jews as originating in Crete by explaining their name, *Judaei*, as a deformation of *Idaei*—that is, those who live on the Cretan mountain Ida.

These are, then, not just instances of folk etymologies, which are clever enough in their own right, but also subtle rationalizations, because they give sense to other-wise arbitrary and meaningless terms, as proper names commonly are (many Greek names derive from the pre-Greek language of the earlier inhabitants of the region), and in expressing and proclaiming the moral features, circumstances, and functions of characters (a common procedure in the speaking names of folk-tales), they constitute proto-allegorical exegeses of the sort found in later Stoic texts, such as Cornutus's trea-tise on theology (see Ramelli, this volume, on Cornutus). Incidentally, such derivations might also serve as a mnemonic technique, helping people to memorize the many names that occur in Greek myth.

Theagenes of Rhegium (6th c. BCE) is commonly credited with having been the first to apply allegorical criticism to the Homeric texts. But, as Ford (1999: 35) suggests, it is possible that instead of being the first, Theagenes was simply the most famous exponent of the method, just because the time in which he lived was especially receptive to alle-gorical interpretation. Ford even ventures that Theagenes might have been a rhapsode-cum-explicator of Homer, performing, as well as explicating, his poems (1999: 37). This is in line with what we have been suggesting: composition and interpretation go hand in hand in the Homeric tradition. Even if, as Feeney (1991: 9) affirms, all Theagenes did was to suggest elementary etymological analyses of divine names, such as interpreting Hera (in Greek, (H)ēra*) as "Air" (in Greek, aēr), the tradition already offered not only the possibility but, in fact, multiple examples of the method.

Finally, there are more complex allegories in the texts of Homer that go beyond simple etymological explanation. Probably the passage most often cited as an example of full-blown allegory in Homer is the account of the *Litae*, personifications of prayers, which Phoenix recounts in *Iliad* 9.502–512. The *Litae*, who are lame, are contrasted with *Atē*, "folly," who is strong and fast; in due course, however, the *Litae* follow upon *Atē* and heal the damage she has caused. To take another, subtler example, in the Battle of the Gods, an episode in the *Iliad* that offended later critics for its frivolous and impious rep-resentation of the deities at war with one another, Xanthus, the river of Troy, engages in conflict with the god Hephaestus. Achilles in his fury had saturated the river with Trojan corpses, and the river, in retaliation, comes close to drowning Achilles. Hera, al-ways a supporter of the Achaeans, sends her son Hephaestus to rescue Achilles, and as the smithy god, he sets the river on fire. As Konstan (2015: 9–11) proposes, the interlude, like the Battle of the Gods itself, is clearly comic in design, not intended to be taken as proper theology, and any reader or auditor, not just the most alert among them, would have understood this fight as symbolically opposing water and fire, and as providing a moment of relief and humor before Achilles's carnage continues.

The Greek poetic medium, especially in the archaic period, presupposes live performance (often in a ritual context and almost always with musical accompaniment), before a public that also participates in its composition and (re-)production. The mythographical texts as we know them were composed to be read at any time and moment: unlike archaic poetry, they are not linked to concrete live, public events (Fowler 2006: 41). Nevertheless, it would be wrong to draw too sharp a distinction between the two modes. Indeed, the living interaction between poets and the audience, both implicitly inclined to organize and interpret traditional stories, may have constituted part of the impulse to collect and systematize such traditions, as well as to reinterpret them critically. It is entirely plausible to suppose that the audiences of the poets included thinkers such as Xenophanes, Theagenes, Pherecydes, and Hecataeus, who developed their own genres in verse and prose, which, in turn, inspired the poets to embrace features we associate with mythography. We may well imagine that it was just such circumstances of recitation and response that created the conditions for the development of mythography as we understand it.

I hope to have shown in these pages how self-aware the poetic tradition of the ancient Greeks was, and that it contained, from the beginning as far as we can judge, the keys to its own interpretation, bearing within itself the stimulus to expand, control, organize, rationalize, and reflectively interpret its contents, stories, and characters. In this way, archaic poetry already embodies the kernel of mythography.

## FURTHER READING

On mythography in general, the annotated bibliography by Smith and Trzaskoma (2011) is an excellent starting point. Pellizer (1993), Alganza Roldán (2006), and Higbie (2008) also offer good overviews. On oral and written cultures in Greece, apart from the classic study by Havelock (1982), see the thoughtful account in Ford (2002); on the association of oral versus written composition with mythology and mythography, respectively, see Calame (2006), Higbie (2008), and Calame (2015). For the early historians (including genealogists, chronographers, and mythographers) and their relation to myth, Fowler (2006, 2006a), Higbie (2008), and Thomas (2009) are especially rich.

## REFERENCES

Adorjáni, Zsolt. 2013. "A Poetic Etymology of a Name in Pindar *P.* 4. 156–158." *Philologus* 157: 361–363.

Alganza Roldán, Minerva. 2006. "La mitografía como género de la prosa helenística: Cuestiones previas." *Florentia Iliberritana* 17: 9–37.

Bassi, Karen. 1993. "Helen and the Discourse of Denial in Stesichorus' Palinode." *Arethusa* 26: 51–75.

Calame, Claude. 2006. "Logiques catalogales et formes généalogiques: Mythes grecs entre tradition orale et pratique de l'écriture." *Kernos* 19: 23–29.

Calame, Claude. 2015. *Qu'est-ce que la mythologie grecque?* Paris: Éditions Gallimard.

Cameron, Alan. 2004. *Greek Mythography in the Roman World.* New York: Oxford University Press.

Carruesco, Jesús. 2017. "The Invention of Stesichorus: Hesiod, Helen, and the Muse." In *Authorship and Greek Song: Authority, Authenticity, and Performance; Studies in Archaic and Classical Greek Song*, vol. 3, edited by Egbert J. Bakker, 178–196. Leiden and Boston: Brill.

Faulkner, Andrew. 2008. *The Homeric Hymn to Aphrodite: Introduction, Text and Commentary.* Oxford: Oxford University Press.

Feeney, Denis C. 1991. *The Gods in Epic: Poets and Critics of the Classical Tradition.* Oxford: Clarendon Press.

Ford, Andrew. 1999. "Performing Interpretation: Early Allegorical Exegesis of Homer." In *Epic Traditions in the Contemporary World: The Poetics of Community*, edited by Margaret Beissinger, Jane Tylus, and Susanne Wofford, 33–53. Berkeley: University of California Press.

Ford, Andrew. 2002. *The Origins of Criticism: Literary Culture and Poetic Theory in Classical Greece.* Princeton, NJ: Princeton University Press.

Fowler, Robert. 2006a. "Herodotus and His Prose Predecessors." In *The Cambridge Companion to Herodotus*, edited by Carolyn Dewald and John Marincola, 29–45. Cambridge, UK: Cambridge University Press.

Fowler, Robert. 2006b. "How to Tell a Myth: Genealogy, Mythology, Mythography." *Kernos* 19: 35–46.

Graziosi, Barbara, and Johannes Haubold. 2015. "The Homeric Text." *Ramus* 44: 5–28.

Havelock, Eric A. 1982. *The Literate Revolution in Greece and Its Cultural Consequences.* Princeton, NJ: Princeton University Press.

Higbie, Carolyn. 2008. "Hellenistic Mythographers." In *The Cambridge Companion to Greek Mythology*, edited by Roger D. Woodard, 237–254. Cambridge, UK: Cambridge University Press.

Ivančik, Askold. 1996. "Die hellenistischen Kommentare zu Homer Il. 13, 3–6. Zur Idealisierung des Barbarenbildes." In *Hellenismus: Beiträge zur Erforschung von Akkulturation und politischer Ordnung in den Staaten des hellenistischen Zeitalters: Akten des Internationalen Hellenismus-Kolloquiums 9.–14. März 1994 in Berlin*, edited by Bernd Funck, 671–692. Tübingen: J.C.B. Mohr Paul Siebeck.

Jaccottet, Anne-Françoise. 2006. "L'objet narratif ou le *mythos* matérialisé: Généalogies et catalogues sans paroles au sanctuaire d'Olympie." *Kernos* 19: 215–228.

Janko, Richard. 1994. *The Iliad, a Commentary.* Vol. 4, Bks. 13–16. Cambridge, UK: Cambridge University Press.

Kim, Lawrence. 2010. *Homer between History and Fiction in Imperial Greek Literature.* Cambridge, UK: Cambridge University Press.

Konstan, David. 2015. "Homer Answers His Critics." *Electryone* 3: 1–11.

Larson, Jennifer. 2001. *Greek Nymphs: Myth, Cult, Lore.* Oxford: Oxford University Press.

Most, Glenn W. 1993. "Die früheste erhaltene griechische Dichterallegorese." *Rheinisches Museum für Philologie* 136: 209–212.

Most, Glenn W. 2006. *Hesiod.* Vol. 1: *Theogony, Works and Days, Testimonia.* Loeb Classical Library. Cambridge, MA: Harvard University Press.

Nagy, Gregory. 1990. *Pindar's Homer: The Lyric Possession of an Epic Past.* Baltimore, MD: John Hopkins University Press.

Nieto, Pura. 2014. "Philo of Alexandria and Greek Poetry." *Studia Philonica Annual* 26: 135–149.

Olson, S. Douglas. 2012. *The "Homeric Hymn to Aphrodite" and Related Texts: Text, Translation and Commentary.* Berlin: De Gruyter.

Pellizer, Ezio. 1993. "La mitografia." In *Lo spazio letterario nella Grecia antica*. Vol. 1.2 *L'Ellenismo*, edited by Guiseppe Cambiano, Luciano Canfora, and Diego Lanza, 283–303. Rome: Salerno Editrice.

Pòrtulas, Jaume. 2018. "Parménide et les traditions de la palinodie poétique." In *La poésie archaïque comme discours de savoir*, edited by Marie-Laurence Desclos, 219–244. Paris: Classiques Garnier.

Race, William, ed. and trans. 1997. *Pindar*. Vol. 1: *Olympian Odes: Pythian Odes*. Loeb Classical Library. Cambridge, MA: Harvard University Press.

Reece, Steve. 2001. "The Ἄβιοι and the Γάβιοι: An Aeschylean Solution to a Homeric Problem." *American Journal of Philology* 122: 465–470.

Rutherford, Ian. 2001. *Pindar's Paeans: A Reading of the Fragments with a Survey of the Genre*. Oxford: Oxford University Press.

Sammons, Benjamin. 2010. *The Art and Rhetoric of the Homeric Catalogue*. Oxford: Oxford University Press.

Smith, R. Scott, and Stephen M. Trzaskoma. 2007. *Apollodorus' "Library" and Hyginus' "Fabulae": Two Handbooks of Greek Mythology*. Indianapolis, IN: Hackett.

Smith, R. Scott, and Stephen M. Trzaskoma. 2011. "Mythography." In Oxford Bibliographies Online. doi:10.1093/obo/9780195389661-0142.

Thomas, Rosalind. 2009. *Oral Tradition and Written Record in Classical Athens*. Cambridge, UK: Cambridge University Press.

van der Ben, Nicolaas. 1986. "Hymn to Aphrodite 36–291: Notes on the Pars Epica of the Homeric Hymn to Aphrodite." *Mnemosyne* 39: 1–41.

Wendel, Carl. 1935. "Mythographie." In *RE XVI*.2, cols. 1352–1374.

Werner, Christian. 2018. *Memórias da Guerra de Troia: A performance do passado épico na "Odisseia" de Homero*. Coimbra, Portugal: Imprensa da Universidade de Coimbra.

West, Martin L., trans. 1988. *Hesiod: Theogony: Works and Days*. Oxford: Oxford University Press.

West, Martin L. 2014. *The Making of the "Odyssey."* Oxford: Oxford University Press.

# CHAPTER 2

# THE ORIGINS OF MYTHOGRAPHY AS A GENRE

JORDI PÀMIAS

## 1. THE PROBLEM OF THE GENRE: WHAT IS MYTHOGRAPHY?

HISTORIES of Greek literature tend to assign a marginal role to the "mythographical" genre. This is in part because mythography has been considered a minor discourse—producing mere compilations lacking in literary merit. In part it can also be explained because scholars do not agree on a criterion by which it would be possible to decide what is and is not a mythographical work. Related to this terminological problem is the challenge of delimiting the borders of mythography with other literary genres, since the genres we call local history, universal history, and ethnography, despite having superficial differences, overlap at the base. In late archaic and classical Greece, among the large group of authors we recognize as historians, ethnographers, mythographers, genealogists, or even "pre-Socratic" philosophers, are many who practice more than one genre. Nor did the Greeks make a distinction: for them, these activities were known by generic terms such as *historiē* or, simply, *logoi* (Fowler 2001: 96–97). The word *historiē*, in fact, indicates an intellectual activity rather than a particular field in which it would operate (Hartog 2001: 27). We can therefore say that mythography is an exogenous category, with the term remaining completely unattested until the 4th century BCE. The first attestation dates back to Palaephatus's treatise *On Unbelievable Tales*. And it may have first appeared in a Peripatetic context (Alganza Roldán 2015: 14, 20). Given the lack of specificity of the mythographical genre and inconsistent terminology, different strategies have been deployed to conceptualize mythography:

> One convenient solution is to restrict the genre chronologically. It is probably a *vérité acquise* to consider mythography as a typically Alexandrian bookish product, and to

view mythographical manuals as collections, from the Hellenistic period onward, created in a "world of libraries, official texts, and institutionalised research" (Fowler 2000: xxxiii). In his fundamental article "Mythographie" in the *Realencyclopädie*, Carl Wendel (1935: 1353–1354) wrote that mythography is ushered in with the *Tragodoumena* by Asclepiades of Tragilus (4th century BCE). Mythography will find its natural expression in compilatory and scholarly literature arranged either thematically (by metamorphosis, constellations, amorous episodes, and so on) or as supplementary and exegetical material for a better understanding of the great poets. (On mythography as a scholarly activity, see Meliadò 2015: 1067–1089.)

The second solution is to expand the concept in order to define mythography in terms of activity, regardless of how it might fit into this or that literary genre. Pellizer (1993: 284) describes mythography as the "activity involving the registration and written transmission of narrative and descriptive materials that, by secular convention and empirically shared, we usually call mythical." Along the same lines, Detienne and Calame understood mythography as written mythology and as a means of transcribing an oral tradition (see Alganza Roldán 2006: 11). Viewed this way, mythography goes well beyond the framework of ancient treatises and manuals.

The third strategy for containing the mythographical genre in stable terms consists of turning it into an appendage of history. In the modern conception of mythography, Felix Jacoby's studies and his monumental edition of the *Fragmente der griechischen Historiker* have been instrumental. Mythography is tied to the origins of early historical prose. And local history would be the last of the historical genres to develop. Captured by Jacoby's *entwicklungsgeschichtliches Prinzip*, the writings of the so-called mythographers or genealogists (Hecataeus of Miletus, Acusilaus of Argos, Pherecydes of Athens, Hellanicus of Lesbos) are considered the first rudimentary but necessary phase in the development of Western historiography, whose greatest exponent will be Herodotus of Halicarnassus. By excluding the mythical period of his *historiē*, Herodotus emerges as the father of history.

An instructive account of Dionysius of Halicarnassus (1st century BCE) stands in clear contrast to Jacoby's teleological and "progressive" view. Although Dionysius primarily confines himself to analyzing style and composition, in his description of the forerunners of Herodotus, he assumes an intense historiographical activity, in particular, local historiography, by a group of ancient writers (*archaioi syngrapheis*):

> The old writers, then, were many and came from many places; among those living before the Peloponnesian War were Eugaion of Samos, Deiochos of Prokonnesos, Eudemos of Paros, Demokles of Phygela, Hekataios of Miletos, the Argive Akousilaos, the Lampsakene Charon, the Chalkedonian <. . . and the Athenian> Amelesagoras; born a little before the Peloponnesian War and living down to the time of Thukydides were Hellanikos of Lesbos, Damastes of Sigeion, Xenomedes of Keos, Xanthos the Lydian and many others. These writers had a similar plan in respect of subject matter and did not differ greatly from one another in ability. Some wrote about Greece, others about barbarians, not joining their inquiries together into a continuous whole, but separating them by nations and cities and bringing them out individually, with one and the same object in view, that of bringing to the attention

of the public traditions [*mnēmai*] preserved among the local people, written records preserved in sacred or profane archives, just as they received them, without adding or subtracting anything. Among these sources were to be found occasional myths, believed from time immemorial, and dramatic tales of upset fortunes, which seem quite foolish to people of our day. The style which they all employed was for the most part the same (at any rate among those who used the same dialect): clear, ordinary, unaffected, concise, suited to the subject and displaying none of the apparatus of professional skill; nonetheless a certain grace and charm attends their works, some more than others, and this has ensured their preservation. (Dion. Hal. *Thuc.* 5.1, trans. Fowler 1996: 63, slightly modified)

This text raises problems of a different nature (such as the dating of these historians or the obscure reference to "written records preserved in sacred or profane archives") that have provoked scholarly discussions (Gozzoli 1970–1971; Toye 1995; Porciani 2001; Breglia 2012; Tufano 2019: 439-444). Yet it has the merit of grouping under the same heading an array of authors from the 6th and 5th centuries BCE who would, in retrospect, be anachronistically labeled mythographers (with the surprising omission of Pherecydes of Athens). In Greek, these authors are categorized as different sorts of writers: given that quotations of their words and references to their works are usually found in much later authors, it is difficult to know what contemporary term would have described them. Indeed, as Robert Fowler has put it, the term *mythography* could not have existed before it was possible to distinguish it from historiography, in other words, until "myth" was distinguished from "history" (Fowler 2006: 35). The question at this point is if, and how, these late archaic authors whom *we* call mythographers contributed to the conception and consolidation of myth as a particular kind of account—that is, one different from history.

## 2. MYTH AND *MYTHOS*

For this fundamental distinction to come about, the appropriation and reception of mythical traditions had to adopt a specific and exclusive form that falls outside the scope and the interests of historians, which allows them to focus on other objects. In this context are usually mentioned the programmatic statements of the authors who represent the pinnacle in the evolution of historiographical thought: Herodotus and Thucydides. In this choice, which is no coincidence, there is an echo of the teleological-developmental concept imposed by Jacoby, which is a product of 19th-century evolutionism and of the assumption of "progress" from myth to science—a narrative to which the two great historians of the 5th century lend themselves easily (Humphreys 1997: 207–208).

Thus, for example, when Herodotus criticizes the *mythos*, understood as an implausible account, in order to reject the theories about the sources of the Nile (Hdt. 2.23) or the heroic deeds of Heracles (2.45), he recognizes a different category of stories (see section 7, "The Time of the Mythographers"). When he describes the thalassocracy of Polycrates as the first of the so-called time of men as opposed to the thalassocracy of Minos (Hdt. 3.122.2), he differentiates between divine and human generations and defines a specific field for "mythology." In the preface of Thucydides, the division of time is based on the same principle when he contrasts the present with "past events" and with a remote past, "which cannot be known with certainty because of the remoteness of the time" (Thuc. 1.1.3). In contrast, Thucydides defends his written history and rejects *to mythōdes* "the mythical," understood as an ornament of oral discourses (1.22.4). What is perhaps even more significant is the fact that the plots of tragedies are, almost without exception, related to the mythical period, suggesting that the bulk of stories that *we* label as myths were recognized in the 5th century BCE as a well-defined category of story.

All this shall lead us to reconsider the correspondences between our concept of myth and the ancient *mythos*, and to challenge the current consensus that tends to deny any relationship between these two terms: this wide agreement appears to be a side effect of late 20th-century criticism of enlightened rationalism (Fowler 2011). Indeed, research by specialists in Greek myth during the last decades of the century raised the suspicion that the modern concept of myth had no equivalent in the Greek world. According to such critics, myth would be nothing less than a modern construction, projected onto Greek antiquity only after the fact. In other words, the appropriation and study of ancient myths, as practiced in the 18th century, would have resulted in the very concept of myth (Pàmias 2014: 44–45). Along these lines, Marcel Detienne (1981) tracked the origins of "myth" in the mythology of the Enlightenment—that is, the scientific study of myth, which begins with Bernard de Fontenelle's *De l'origine des fables* (originally published in 1724).

The contemporary scientific study of myth, however, has achieved a triumph that, in my view, ought to be reckoned an accepted truth: the 20th century has been able to recognize in myth an autonomous form of thought (*Denkform*), with a meaning that goes beyond the textual support by which a particular myth has come down to us. The distinction between myth and its expression in poetic, choral, dramatic, and visual form seems fundamental. This contrast is the basis of the definition of myth proposed by Fritz Graf (1993: 2):

> A myth is a peculiar kind of story. It does not coincide with a particular text or literary genre. For example, in all three major genres of Greek poetry the story of Agamemnon's murder and of Orestes' subsequent revenge is told: in epic (at the beginning of the *Odyssey*), in choral lyric (e.g., in Stesichorus' *Oresteia*), and in the works of all three tragedians. A myth is not a specific poetic text. It transcends the text: it is the subject-matter, a plot fixed in broad outline and with characters no less fixed, which the individual poet is free to alter only within limits.

Insofar as myth can be accommodated in an expressive vehicle such as poetry, Homeric epics should be considered as an early form of appropriation and reception of myth.

Since each retelling of the same story has a particular motivation, it has a new focus and new perspectives. Leaving aside the fact that myth may be taken as a collective expression of the beliefs of a society, it can be said that every new performance, under new conditions and for new purposes, constitutes a particular reception of myth (see Edmunds 2005: 31–32).

A crucial episode in the history of the reception of myth in archaic and classical Greece begins with the rapid spread of a new technology: alphabetic writing, particularly from the 6th century BCE on (see section 4, "A New Technology: Writing"). For Hecataeus of Miletus, Pherecydes of Athens, or Hellanicus of Lesbos, writing is a means to address an abstract public, independent of particular places or times (Jacob 1994: 172–173). Collections of stories, as "autonomous intellectual objects," are equidistant from the reading public and from the mythical traditions the "mythographer" draws upon. Writing has thus opened a breach, now forever impassable, between the author and his mythical heritage, which will generate multiple opportunities for its appropriation and reception. In this context, the prologue of Hecateus of Miletus is often cited:

> Hecataeus of Miletus speaks as follows. I write these things, as they seem to me to be true. For the tales (*logoi*) of the Greeks are many and ridiculous, as they seem to me. (Hecat. fr. 1 Fowler, trans. Pownall)

Not only the ironic laughter aroused by the stories of the Greeks but, above all, their colorful multiplicity, confirm the distancing of the author from an unattainable and singular *alētheia* "truth." In his programmatic text, Hecataeus does not limit himself to criticizing the content of the tradition; he also, as suggested by Robert Fowler, "comes close to problematising stories *qua* stories" (Fowler 2001: 101). In his methodological program, and in practice, Hecataeus proves to already be in possession of a category of story that corresponds to the notion of myth in the sense of a traditional story—regardless of the term he used to refer to it.

The reception of the mythical tradition, marked by a methodological and ironic detachment in the case of Hecataeus of Miletus, can take several forms. The *Histories* of Pherecydes of Athens seem to me a new case. The surviving fragments show that he often introduced the origin of a place name (or ethnonym) by showing that it went back to a character of heroic mythology:

> Pherecydes says in Book Nine that Elatus son of Icarius married Erymede daughter of Damasiclus whose son was Taenarus, for whom the city and the promontory and the harbor of Taenarum are named. (Pherecyd. fr. 39 Fowler, trans. Morison)

The willingness to make the objective nature of the story evident can be seen in the linking of the myth with a place name, to the extent that the author relates it to a specific, physical geographical place (Dolcetti 2000: 30–31). But above all, by using a well-codified formula (*aph' hou kaleitai*, "from whom it takes the name"), Pherecydes establishes a connection between both names, that of the hero and that of the place—whose relationship is one, not of identity, but of nominal derivation (compare Taenarus and Taenarum). The awareness of the detachment from the mythical heritage (see section 7) allows the mythographer to draw on the inexhaustible repository of local and Panhellenic traditions to anchor a physical reality, which he knows from his own experience, in a reality that is different from and alien to it: that of myth.

To sum up: the investigation into the reception of myth by "mythographers" suggests that these authors were already in possession of a category comparable to myth understood as a type of account that belongs to a heritage from which they are separated by a gap, and onto which they can cast an objective gaze (Pàmias 2014: 47–50). Assuming the challenge of the circular argument, we can state that it is the authors from the late archaic period whom we call mythographers who have, precisely, set the conditions so that the mythographical genre is constituted as such.

# 3. MYTH AND MYTHOGRAPHY

The consolidation of the notion of myth—understood as a particular kind of account— affords a mirror image in the concept of history, which will be defined, as a result, as an account other than myth. The conditions that led to the formation of mythography are therefore the same as those that enabled the emergence of historiography. In the same way, for example, the analysis of the different labels (historian, logographer, mythographer, and so on) that ancient authors applied to Hecataeus of Miletus demonstrates that the use of one term or another—in our case, "myth" or "history"—is not neutral but, rather, emerges in a context of controversy and often appears in a specular relation to another term (see Alganza Roldán, 2012, for Hecataeus's labels).

If the terms *mythos, logos,* or *epos* appeared in archaic epic to be used interchangeably to describe what the poet was singing (*mythos* was not a specific kind of story), with the advent of new subjects to write about and new fields of inquiry—the philosophical discourse with the so-called pre-Socratics and, especially, the historical discourse—these terms tended to specialize semantically from the late archaic age on (Graf 2002: 2); thus in the 5th century BCE, *mythos* is equivalent to fictitious and false speech to be rejected, whereas *logos*, a written account, indicates true and real discourse (Vernant 1990: 203– 208; the term *epos*, on the other hand, was used to refer specifically to epic poetry). The consolidation of historiography as a new genre would occur at the price of projecting a different program of truth onto mythography. Indeed, as long as the difference between fiction and reality is not objective and does not belong to the thing itself but, rather, depends on whether one believes in it or not, the truthfulness of a statement may change according to different criteria or programs (Veyne 1988: 21–22). As a result, the new genre, historiography, would acquire the value of historical truth. As parallels provided by anthropology show, in oral cultures (but also in literate ones) the decision to observe traditions as a source of historical truth or purely as fiction is closely related to genre. As a genre, fairy tales, for example, are fictions: they are transmitted and retold, but they are not considered historically true. The distribution of different kinds of memory in different genres and the various levels of accuracy or authority the group assigns to these genres are reflections of social and cultural practices, and do not necessarily indicate where the historical truth lies (Fentress and Wickham 1992: 78).

It is, therefore, in relation to historiography that a genre such as mythography must be defined so as to indicate a particular production in prose by a number of authors prior to the Hellenistic period—even though, as was pointed out above, the term *mythography* did not come into existence until much later. For a tentative definition of mythography as a genre, I have followed Marincola's considerations, according to which, instead of eliminating the notion of genre, we need to redefine it: genre is not a fixed and static recipe but, rather, a dynamic concept that should be viewed as a "strategy of literary composition" (Marincola 1999: 281–282).

If the analysis of the fragmentary texts does not deceive us, the authors of the late archaic period whom we label as mythographers offer a variety of characteristics that may not be reducible to a fixed category. We shall apply Wittgenstein's notion of *Familienähnlichkeit* to the group of texts in question. In his research the German philosopher introduces the concept of "family resemblance," which involves similarities among different members of a family that overlap without there being an observable trait that they all share. In what follows, I propose to explore and describe some of these traits, which may help define the mythographical genre as dynamic and as an "open concept"—that is, without establishing necessary preconditions for membership in a particular group.

# 4. A New Technology: Writing

As noted in section 2, "Myth and *Mythos*," an epochal turning point in the history of the reception of myth in antiquity occurred with the rapid expansion of a new technology—alphabetic writing—particularly from the end of the Archaic period onward. Although alphabetic writing was well known in Greece from the 8th century BCE, it was in the 6th century that it would begin to spread, in increasingly diversified applications—such as for recording literary works like epic poetry, medical treatises, philosophy, and so forth. It seems convenient to locate and describe the production of the first mythographers within a context of change: a period of evolving social and political mutation coinciding with a technological revolution brought about by the dissemination of a new tool in a basically preliterate society.

An influential article by Jack Goody and Ian P. Watt (1963) contributed to the belief that "technological revolutions" such as writing have unavoidable consequences. According to this interpretation, whose intellectual precedents can be traced back to the theories of Marshall McLuhan ("the medium is the message"), alphabetic writing had an influence, not only on the transmission of knowledge, but also on the capacity for abstraction that was associated with the new medium. Ultimately, this deterministic view is based on the notion that a binary opposition separates oral cultures from literate ones—a "Great Divide" between orality and literacy such as that propagated by Eric Havelock or Walter Ong—from which scholars have distanced themselves in recent years (Schmitz 2007: 99–104).

In fact, the hypothesis that argues that such a technical innovation mechanically triggered the progress from the domain of myth to the domain of history has been severely contested, especially from the 1980s on (Andersen 1987; Thomas 1992: 15–28; Porciani 1994). The written word seems to conspire, along with other factors, toward a development that society has already embarked on. It is not only writing that contributed to the innovativeness in speculative thought and self-distancing from tradition that made it possible for Greeks to "invent" history, mathematics, the sciences, and philosophy: for many scholars, the critical knowledge needs to be located against the background of the sociopolitical and legal changes that were occurring; and a crucial factor must have been the communal life at the heart of the polis and the use of speech in public meetings (see, for instance, Lloyd 1995: 70–82, 101). One should therefore be cautious on this point: although writing exerts powerful effects (for instance, on the storage capacity of human memory), it is not enough, in itself, to modify the cognitive abilities of human thought—as Goody and Watt optimistically believed, relying on the technological determinism of a "graphical reason." Nor is there agreement on the degree of credibility and accuracy that can be attributed to oral transmission: confrontation oscillates between "optimists," who consider that oral memory can be reliable over several generations, and "sceptics," for whom memory is, above all, fiction (Thomas 1989: 4–5). In this context, some anthropologists have issued a warning against the functionalist perspective and have insisted that the traditions of the past cannot be treated as a simple mirror of the present, because societies do not reshape the past every day so that it agrees with the present (Luraghi 2001: 14; for critique of functionalism, see Geertz 1973). Rather, "intentional history," as an amalgamation of "myth" and "history," has given prominence to the "social surface" of tradition—that is, to the ideological significance of the past for the self-understanding of a particular group (Gehrke 2001: 286).

Either way, though it is not the sufficient cause for the historiographical development in Greece, writing was a necessary instrument for fostering a new attitude toward tradition. It has been pointed out that a performance within the framework of a strictly oral culture reproduces a statement, whereas a written culture tends to look for external control on the validity of what is said. At the risk of simplifying, it can be said that orality recognizes the authority of utterances within a living tradition, whereas writing objectifies tradition and attempts to distance itself from it. And this is the case not because the alphabetic application of the Greek alphabet of Phoenician origin has inherent conceptual and logical virtues of abstraction, as Havelock (1982) suggested. It is, rather, because oral expression acquires authority from its social context—as Richard Martin puts it, the *mythos* of Homeric heroes is an "authoritative utterance" (Martin 1989: 10–26). In contrast, written discourses assert their authority independently of such contexts (Fowler 2001: 100).

Writing will also affect the ways of storing and constructing memory. The archaic poet surrendered his voice to the Muses to produce or reproduce the song in such a way that memory was inseparable from the process of creation: it was the Muses who guaranteed the *alētheia* "truth." In archaic Greece, the language in which the gods speak through human voices is, in general, one of metrical verse (Most 1999: 353). Firmly anchored in an oral tradition, the archaic epic poet invoked the Muse to recall the events of the past that belong to the collective memory. Thus, before reciting the *Catalogue of Ships*, the bard requests the assistance of the Muses to be able to remember all the names of the troops taking part in the Trojan War:

> And now, O Muses, dwellers in the mansions of Olympus, tell me . . . who were the chiefs and princes of the Danaans? As for the common soldiers, they were so that I could not name every single one of them though I had ten tongues, and though my voice failed not and my heart were of bronze within me, unless you, O Olympian Muses, daughters of aegis-bearing Jove, were to recount [*mnēsaiato*] them to me.
>
> (Hom. *Il.* 2.484–492, trans. Butler)

In this context, the word *mnēsaiato* means "mention," but also "remember" (ancient Greek makes no distinction between the two meanings). The word of the poet is consistent with the religious power of the Muse—or the Muses, daughters of *Mnemosyne* "Memory" and, originally, a religious group of three divinities. Epic poetry cannot be understood without taking into account the mnemonic resources, since behind inspiration, the invocation to the Muses reveals an intense mastery of poetic techniques. That said, the poets' memory is not a historical memory properly speaking, since it has no oriented function nor does it aim to reconstruct the past according to a temporal perspective. In other words: memory is not material support for the sung word, but rather indicates an omniscience of a divinatory kind that involves the ability to see "what is, what will be and what has been" (Hes., *Theog.* 38; see Detienne 1996: 39–52; Velardi 2014). Poetic memory is not therefore a repository for storing the oral heritage; rather, it is a way of penetrating the unfathomable and of accessing the truth and formulating it: in the Hesiodic formula (*Theog.* 28), the poet is endowed with the ability to *alēthea gērysasthai*, "proclaim the truth."

In contrast, truth for the mythographers is not revealed but must be established by entirely different procedures, which could be described as intellectual and critical ones. Truth is therefore indebted to a writing activity that selects, rejects, and transcribes preexisting *logoi* "stories"—although these critical operations are less clear in the case of Pherecydes of Athens, who does not reveal divergences in his sources and adopts a pragmatic, just-the-facts style (Fowler 2013: 706–710). Poetry and oral traditions can, indeed, more easily accommodate inconsistencies than can a written text, which will tend to highlight them. As Rosalind Thomas has noted, the correction of inconsistencies and of chronological implausibility among the genealogist mythographers presupposes a written study (Thomas 1989: 179–184; Möller 1996: 26). With the renouncing of the mantic-religious truth with which epic poetry was traditionally invested, the strong connection between *mnēmosynē* (memory) and *alētheia* (truth) of the older poets has now been shattered: our authors have seized the tradition from the authority of the Muses to surrender it to human judgment. And the artificialization of memory relies on a new technology, writing—and writing in prose, which emerges as an innovative medium to claim the truth (see Asper 2007: 91–92).

Finally, it is worth examining one configuration of memory that does seem to be specific to the written culture: complete and comprehensive genealogies, an exclusively literary product because they presuppose the use of writing. Known as "full genealogy," it is a kind of nonsegmented genealogy—that is, a sequence of fathers and sons without any mixing of parallel lines and often without wives or sisters. Whereas family traditions do not normally extend beyond the third or fourth generation, a full genealogy can be traced much further back in time.

A paradigmatic example is attributed by a later source to Pherecydes of Athens—although Hellanicus of Lesbos is also cited. Through an unbroken succession of generations, the genealogist goes back from his immediate past to the heroic world, which for the Greeks ended with the fall of Troy and the return of the fighting heroes to their homeland. Through the parent-child relationship, Pherecydes goes through the thirteen generations of offspring that come between the epic hero Ajax and Miltiades the Elder, the colonizer of the Chersonese in the middle of the 6th century BCE.

> Philaeus son of Ajax lived in Athens. From him was born Aeclus, whose son was Epilycus, whose son was Acestor, whose son was Agenor, whose son was Oulius, whose son was Lyces, whose son was Tophon (?), whose son was Philaeus, whose son was Agamestor, whose son was Tisandrus, during his archonship in Athens (text missing), whose son was Miltiades, whose son was Hippoclides, during whose archonship the Panathenaea was established, and his son was Miltiades, who colonized the Chersonese (Pherecyd. fr. 2 Fowler, trans. Morison).

In this way it was possible to establish the link with the past and bridge the memory gap that opened up after the collapse of the Mycenaean civilization and that separates the heroes of the Bronze Age from the recent past, the time of the polis (see section 7). Unlike orally transmitted genealogies, Pherecydes's text reveals a new attitude: like genealogies reported by modern anthropologists, the distinctive characteristic of genealogies written by mythographers is their comprehensive and all-encompassing projection (Thomas 1989: 180–195).

# 5. The Construction of the Author and the "Mythographical" Reason

The formal vehicle that these authors chose is revealing. Following the practice of some philosophers, mythographers, too, use prose instead of the metrical form typical of poetry and particularly of the oral epic tradition. In the beginning this decision was not a choice between two formal alternatives but a proper revolution. The emergence of prose entails such a severe rupture that the earlier notion that written prose somehow grew out of oral poetry needs to be abandoned (Asper 2007: 68–69). The use of prose is associated, as mentioned earlier, with the conditions of production and reception of the mythographical work, deracinated from the festive context of oral performance (see Martin 2013: 64). This is why all traces of the Muses have disappeared in the programmatic statements of the early mythographers, something that distances them from the Homeric tradition—as can be seen from the comparison with the quoted text from the *Iliad* (see section 4).

Renouncing the Muses, and the mantic-religious truth they guarantee, has profound consequences. It is now the mythographer—or rather the *logos*—who occupies the space that the goddesses have left empty. And he takes the floor to construct himself as an author. It is thus not surprising that some scholars have seen in Hecataeus's prologue ("Hecataeus of Miletus speaks as follows. I write these things. . . ") the inaugural act of historiography and, in its egotism, the immediate forerunner of Herodotean research (Bertelli 1996: 68; Hartog 1990: 181).

By means of the name itself, the author constructs a character, a new space in which to "dwell." This entails the use of the third person—that is, the distanced "he" or even, according to Benveniste's classification, the register of the nonperson (1971: 198). Thus, by mentioning himself, the historian is inscribed in the place of the "absent one of history" (*absent de l'histoire*). This development will reach a climax with Pherecydes, an Athenian mythographer active in Cimon's circle, as it appears, around 470 BCE (see Dolcetti 2001; Pàmias 2017a; see also below section 6, "Oral Sources, Written Communication: An Extra-institutional Memory"). Yet the dearth of biographical details is conspicuous, and it is difficult to believe that this was not a deliberate decision by the author to efface his personality from the text (Fowler 2006: 44). There is no trace of personal information in the fragments or the testimonies of his work—which has even led some scholars to question the identity of Pherecydes, an Athenian mythographer, as distinct from another author of the same name, a theologian of Syros (see Toye 1997, whose arguments are refuted by Fowler 1999). In his work, a collection of myths in ten books, he lays the foundations for later mythography: Eratosthenes of Cyrene (in the Alexandrian period) or Ps.-Apollodorus (in the imperial age)—equally impersonal—owe a debt to Pherecydes's *Histories*. Consistency of style in mythographical texts (pragmatic tone, matter-of-factness) is, indeed, an element of continuity between archaic and late-antiquity mythography (Fowler 2006).

The mythographer has opened a gap that will separate the narrated from the narrator, and it is in this interstitial space that he can adopt a critical attitude toward the traditional material (section 2). Indeed, this detachment is a crucial condition for attaining the stage, typical for the Greek experience, that Jan Assmann called "agonistic intertextuality," based on a triangular dynamics that connects the author to his predecessor and to the content itself (Assmann 2011: 257–263). Discrepancies between authors and the willingness to be controversial regarding their predecessors, which we see in Hecataeus's "foundational" text, is a topic with a long tradition in Greek literature (see Hes., *Theog.* 24–28; Pind., *Ol.* 1.28–29; see Nieto Hernández, this volume). These discordances and disputes attracted the attention of non-Greek authors (see, for instance, Herenn. Phil. *BNJ* 790F1 = Eus., *PE* 1.9.27). Thus, Christian apologists would see in the Greeks' stories the perfect example of a culture full of contradictions and dissonance. A good example is the Jewish historian Flavius Josephus, who argues that Acusilaus developed genealogies in contrast to Hesiod, as did Hellanicus in contrast to Acusilaus. Josephus confronts Greek dissonance with the greater antiquity and superiority of Jewish monism, which possesses a single holy book:

> Can one not easily discover from the authors themselves that they wrote without re-liable knowledge of anything, but on the basis of their individual conjectures about events? Indeed for the most part they refute each other in their books, and do not hes-itate to say the most contradictory things on the same topics. It would be superfluous for me to instruct those who know more than I how much Hellanicus disagreed with Acusilaus on the genealogies, how often Acusilaus corrects Hesiod, or how Ephorus proves Hellanicus to have lied on most matters, and how Timaeus did the same to Ephorus, and Timaeus' successors to him, and everyone to Herodotus. (*Ap.* 1.15–16, trans. Barclay)

In his apologetic text, Josephus emphasizes that Greeks tended to assert their authority by criticizing their predecessors (Marincola 1997: 217–236, 282). This is condemned by the Jewish author as a sign of confusion and ignorance: for him, "[I]t is evidence of true history if everyone both says and writes the same things about the same events" (*Ap.* 1.26). On the other hand, for Greek authors, who feel comfortable with an agonistic cul-ture, controversy is an indication of a critical spirit in the search for the truth, as this pas-sage of Diodorus Siculus shows (Sulimani 2011: 132–133):

> But on such matters as these it is not easy to set forth the precise truth, and yet the disagreements among historians must be considered worthy of record, in order that the reader may be able to decide upon the truth without prejudice. (Diod. Sic. 1.56.6; trans. Oldfather)

Greek historiography is therefore inaugurated under the sign of criticism and contro-versy. While it is true, as Schepens has pointed out, that ancient historians hardly ever mention their precursors except to attack them, it is also true that, in general, they prefer to not cite their names, so the authors of the earliest historiography often remain anony-mous (1997: 166). Moreover, in a context of quite repetitive topics (such as cosmogonies and divine or heroic genealogies), identifying adversaries mattered less than completely canceling the muddle of old, contradictory alternatives before stating one's own new and unique truth. Either way, the construction of the historiographical narrative rests on the foundations of what has been called the "hypoleptic horizon." "Hypolepsis" suggests a discourse that does not begin from the beginning, anew each time, but takes everything that has preceded it as its starting point (Assmann 2011: 257).

This strategy is fundamental for understanding an aspect of Greek rationality. Of course, any assumption based on a transhistorical notion of reason is risky, but as Ambaglio (2007: 685) has pointed out, one of the most common aspects of "rationalism" over the ages has been "correctivism," or the desire to straighten out mistaken opinions, remove prejudices, and resolve apparent contradictions. As a result, a controversial projection of any form of rationalism emerges, which becomes a hallmark of Greek mythographical "reason." For example, when the mythographer Ps.-Apollodorus in the 2nd century CE produced a story about Proetus's daughters, he compared two variants concerning the cause of their insanity (West 1985: 79):

> When these girls grew up, they went mad, as Hesiod says, because they would not ac-
> cept the rites of Dionysus. But Acusilaus says that it was because they disparaged the
> wooden image of Hera. (Acus. fr. 28 Fowler = Apollod. 2.26 [2.2.2], trans. Toye)

The confrontation in this passage between Acusilaus's variant and the Hesiodic one does not seem to have been produced by Apollodorus himself but rather to already be explicit in Acusilaus's work (see Fontana 2012: 404–411). Indeed, although there is no reason to assume that the sources mythographers used were exclusively drawn from epic poetry (section 6), parallels with other Acusilaus's fragments seem to suggest that this mythographer critically revised some of the poet's genealogical variants (see Acus. fr. 34 and 42 Fowler). This would confirm Josephus's aforementioned judgment that it would be futile to point out "how often Acusilaus corrects Hesiod."

Critical intertextuality, when a text responds dialectically to preexisting texts, is consolidated with the transcription of myths by mythographers. It has been pointed out that an element of Greek written culture is a new form of intertextual relation-ship: it is not a case of speakers reacting to speakers but of texts reacting to texts. The writings of early mythographers respond to the tradition as long as they place the canonical texts of ancient poetry on the same level as the opinion of an ordinary private individual who expresses himself in simple, secular prose: mythical stories and genealogies in prose replace one authority with another. In this context, the written word has acquired prestige, and can, if necessary, be taken as an accredited and reputable source. A telling example of this is precisely Acusilaus of Argos, who, according to the late testimony transmitted by a Byzantine lexicographer, claimed to have transcribed the divine and heroic genealogies from some bronze tablets that his father had unearthed somewhere in his house (see Pàmias 2015; for another view: Lanzillotta 2010). This account most probably appeared in the proem to his *Genealogies* (Pàmias 2019a):

> Acusilaus was the son of Kabas. He was Argive from the city of Kerkas, which is near
> Aulis. He was the most ancient of historians. He wrote *Genealogies* based on bronze
> writing-tablets which, according to one account, his father discovered after he had
> dug up some place in his house. (*Sud.* s.v. Akousilaos ed. Adler = Acus. test. 1 Fowler,
> trans. Toye)

As Christian Jacob points out, the anecdote about the bronze tablets "stamps Acusilaus' *Genealogies* with the seal of intertextuality," and underlines the fundamental value of reading and writing at the end of the archaic period. Based on his father's "epigraphic" discovery, Acusilaus opens a new horizon of textual production, grounded in the authority of a preexisting text, its guaranteed antiquity, and the critical operations of rewriting (1994: 181). Moreover, by mentioning the story of the bronze tablets, Acusilaus is refusing at the outset to invoke the Muses as a source of authority—as was customary among the mythographers, as we have seen (section 4). Yet, at the same time, by using this strategy, Acusilaus is attempting to avoid any type of criticism (Fowler 2001: 104–105).

In addition to the triangular dynamics of author, predecessor, and content, agonistic intertextuality is based on a triple reference in the text itself: to previous texts, to the subject matter; and to the criteria used to evaluate the veracity of this text (Assmann 2011: 261). One criterion, it seems, is probability or plausibility (*to eoikos*). Thus when Pausanias recalls the reinterpretation Hecataeus advanced about the myth of Cerberus, he says that Hecataeus produced (*heuren*, "found" or "invented') a plausible account:

> Some Greek poets have said that here (in Taenarum) Hercules dragged up the hound of hell. But no road leads underground through the cave, nor is it easy to believe that gods have an underground abode in which the souls of the dead assemble. Hecataeus, the Milesian, hit on (*heuren* "invented" or "found) a likely explanation (*logon eoikota*): he said that Taenarum was the home of a dreadful snake called the hound of hell, because its bite was instantly fatal (Paus. 3.25.5, trans. Frazer = Hecat. fr. 27a Fowler).

Whether the terms *logon eoikota*, "plausible story," go back to Pausanias or were already present in Hecataeus, the expression accurately describes a critical perspective toward the traditional stories (see more on the account of Cerberus in section 6). In full agreement with the proem to his *Genealogies*, Hecataeus of Miletus expresses a sense of discomfort with myths, as well as the need to find a principle of universal application that will allow him to require that the stories meet standards of truthfulness in accordance with particular previously established rules. The *logos* needs to accommodate certain objective criteria from outside the discourse itself, such as, in this case, verisimilitude and plausibility (Fowler 2001: 101).

# 6. Oral Sources, Written Communication: An Extra-institutional Memory

As has been established (sections 4 and 5), the impact of technology such as writing on the ways of appropriating the past is huge. And the effects of writing on the nascent historiography would be irreversible. However, this should not obscure a crucial means of communication in archaic and classical Greece, which was still a primarily oral culture—or, perhaps more accurately, an aural one. If classical scholarship had traditionally neglected orality when interpreting the works of ancient authors (generally considered merely as texts), this began to change, notably in the 1950s (Schmitz 2007: 98–99)—and today one can say that the interest in orality as a category for interpreting Greek culture is not yet extinguished. In contrast, this oral revolution reached historiography after a delay (Luraghi 2001: 3). Indeed, a fundamental notion must be emphasized: in the second part of the 5th century BCE, historians like Herodotus and Thucydides were still mainly relying on oral traditions in building their literary monuments. The neglect of written records shows that written sources were not primarily considered suitable material for reconstructing the past. Such indifference to documents needs to be explained, not by any absence of written records, but rather as a cultural choice, as Momigliano argued (1990: 29–53; see also 1966).

In 1987, Oswyn Murray marked a special milestone in the new direction in historiographical studies with his analysis of the oral background of Herodotean historiography. On this point, the application of modern studies on oral history, especially African oral history, to the Greek tradition is clear (see Vansina 1961; Finnegan 1970; for a comparison of Herodotus with American folklore traditions, see Stadter 1997). This change of perspective implies a more peripheral view of history, and it can, in fact, be easily explained in a postcolonial context. The interest in individuals or groups that are further from the center of power or the economy attracted the historians' attention to a knowledge of a more ambiguous past—a past that at the same time does not reflect an institutional perspective.

Indeed, lacking official status and a mandate, the mythographer arrogated to himself the right to shape the memory of the past, just as Greek citizens took the floor of the assembly to participate in the debates on the common affairs of the polis (Jacob 1994: 173). It has been pointed out that the concept of *doxa*, "opinion," that Hecataeus uses for the intellectual operation leading to the *alētheia*, "truth," indicates a conjectural knowledge of the same order as the opinion that emerges from public deliberation. As with the philosopher Xenophanes of Colophon, in Hecataeus, *doxa* is not the word for illusion or appearance: just as in the agora, according to the introductory formula, a decree "seemed (best) to the people" (*edoxe tōi dēmōi*), Hecataeus uses the same formula "as they seem true to me" (*hōs moi dokei alēthea einai*, Hecat. fr. 1 Fowler) to present a credible, from his point of view, story to his readers (Detienne 1981: 140–141). Indeed, his account is the tentative result of deliberating and pondering the story's truthfulness or plausibility. Significantly, the term Hecataeus used to introduce the story of the myth of Cerberus was *dokein*, "think, expect." The discovery of a papyrus in Cairo has made it possible to reconstruct the text of that interpretation in the first person, which, as we have seen (section 5), Pausanias attributed to Hecataeus:

> I think (*dokeo*) that it was a snake, not so large or monstrous [as in the standard version], but more terrible than other snakes. (Hecat. fr. 27b Fowler, trans. Pownall)

Because they fall outside the margins of public and political control, we can expect the myths transcribed by mythographers to reflect a less institutional, less official, and more fluid reality. To fully appreciate this "submerged literature," it seems advisable to abandon the notion that there is a single public sphere. Next to the institutional sphere (which in classical times would have been the assembly or council, etc.), a more informal, extra-institutional public sphere exists whose most visible manifestations for us today are the various kinds of groupings and associations in the ancient city (*phratry, dēmos, orgeones, eranoi, thiasoi, hetaireiai*, and so on). These spheres coexisted in time, but the latter is clearly more inclusive and amorphous (see Gottesman 2014: 20). If the standard myths of the great Panhellenic festivals thrive within the ambit of the high civilization of the polis (epics and tragedy, above all), then one can wonder about the nature of the myths transcribed by the mythographers—oral accounts from different sources and subjected to a different propagation and reception.

In the process of establishing the texts of our authors, the nature and the form of mythographical fragments as we can read them today have often been overlooked by modern philology. Indeed, the ways and vehicles of transmission for these texts have fatally conditioned our perception of them. In other words, the material contexts of preservation of the fragmentary mythographers shape our way of approaching them. The very process of the reception of epic poetry by the exegetical and grammatical tradition distorts our point of view and induces us to see these authors as dependent on, or engaged with, Homer and Hesiod. When quoting from these texts, grammarians, lexicographers, and scholiasts have filtered out aspects that are irrelevant to them. And this often creates the impression that the mythographers' interests are merely antiquarian (Schepens 1997: 167 n. 66; on the Atthidographers, see McInerney 1994: 22–23). Thus, for example, if Pherecydes is cited by Homeric scholiasts up to seven times to illustrate certain terms used by Homer, this does not necessarily entail, as Fowler (2013: xvi, 706–707) assumes, that the grammarians would see Pherecydes as the source of this piece of exegetical information. Instead, the fact that Pherecydes is cited with regard to a passage from the *Iliad* or the *Odyssey* is what leads the modern scholar to believe that Pherecydes was referring to, or giving an opinion of, Homeric words or passages. There is very little indication that, if the Homeric scholiast were to turn to Pherecydes to provide a variant of the text from the *Iliad* or the *Odyssey*, the Athenian mythographer would mention the poet explicitly in order to correct, discuss, or explain it (one exception would be Pherecyd. fr. 169 Fowler; see Pàmias 2017a). As it will be argued, besides the epic background, mythographers used largely other sources of information, such as local and family traditions.

By contrast, classical scholarship has emphasized, since at least the 17th century, the relationship of dependence between these authors and archaic epic poetry (for Pherecydes, see Saumaise 1629: 846; for Acusilaus and Hesiod, see section 5, "The Construction of the Author and the 'Mythographical' Reason"). It is usually taken for granted that the earliest mythographical prose developed in direct continuity with the Homeric tradition, which it attempted to supplement, correct, adapt, comment on, or interpret. Furthermore, in the reception history of myths, mythographers' contributions seem to fit comfortably into the chronological gap between Homer, Hesiod, and the cyclic epics, on the one hand, and history and tragedy, on the other (see Fowler 2013: 5). It should be noted that this evolutionary and teleological discourse, which assumes the secondary nature of mythographical prose compared to the venerable epic tradition, has its forerunners in ancient erudition. For example, Strabo sees in the earliest Greek prose a simple *mimesis* of poetry:

> For poetry, as an art, first came upon the scene and was first to win approval. Then came Cadmus, Pherecydes, Hecataeus, and their followers, with prose writings in which they imitated the poetic art, abandoning the use of metre but in other respects preserving the qualities of poetry. (Str. 1.2.6 [18]; trans. Jones)

The knowledge of archaic and classical mythography we have gained in recent years, above all, thanks to the publications and commentaries by Robert Fowler (2000, 2013), has provided us with more accurate details of the context of production and the purposes of the fragmentary works by Hecataeus of Miletus, Acusilaus of Argos, Pherecydes of Athens, and Hellanicus of Lesbos. For example, Pherecydes's *Histories* seem firmly rooted in the Athens of the first third of the 5th century BCE—specifically, in the circle of Cimon and the Philaedae family (Dolcetti 2001; Pàmias 2017a; to be precise, Pherecydes's work can be dated to the early 470s: see also Huxley 1973). The work of this Athenian mythographer places him comfortably in the intellectual and artistic entourage (with Polygnotus, Sophocles, Ion, Bacchylides, and the elegists Archelaus and Melanthius) that surrounded the Philaedae, and helped to strengthen the identity and political aspirations of this clan, as we will see. This prompts us to reappraise the mythographers' contribution to the process of appropriating myth. They transcribed both family memories and stories from the Greek mythical heritage from a particular perspective; each had his own agenda and program, which must be explained within its context and not, from a purely historical-literary perspective, as an appendix, a continuation, or an exegesis of epic tradition.

A second factor should also be considered—relative chronology, which seems to make mythographical prose fatally dependent on epic poetry. A century ago, philologists dated the *Iliad* and the *Odyssey* to the 10th and 9th centuries BCE. Throughout the 20th century, there was a sustained tendency to move down the date of composition of Homeric epics, to the extent that dates as late as the mid-sixth century have been proposed (West 2012: 224). But perhaps even more important is the displacement of the relative chronology of epics and lyric poetry: today the fact that epic poetry *must* come before lyric poetry, as well as iambic and elegiac poetry, cannot be taken as an axiom. For example, in the *Cambridge Companion to Greek Mythology*, Nagy's chapters on lyric poetry and on Homer appear in an "inverted" order (Woodard 2007). In parallel to this phenomenon, we should note the efforts made in recent years to better adjust the dating of some mythographers, and specifically the chronology of Acusilaus of Argos. Following an intuition of Mazzarino (1966: 58–70), some philologists consider Acusilaus to be an author of the late archaic period and bring his production back to the sixth century. As a result of both tendencies, the chronology of epic and lyric poetry and of mythography will tend to be constrained within much narrower time limits. For example, if we accept the later date of the *Catalogue of Women* proposed by West (1985: 136)—maybe around 540–520 BCE— it would mean that this genealogic poem was contemporary with works by earlier mythographers.

This invites us to consider mythographical production as a project that is—at least in part—independent of epic poetry. In addition to poetic sources, we should also consider an oral tradition running parallel to the epic one and leaving much weaker traces than the great epic poetry institutionally consolidated by the spread of Panhellenism. We are accustomed to thinking of the Greek oral tradition as a homogeneous body of transmitted accounts in a fixed poetic form. The existence of mythographical oral traditions in prose may find support in the figure of the *logios*, who is the depositary of those oral traditions in prose, separate from the oral traditions of epic poetry (for which the *aoidos* is competent). The poet Pindar seems to assume this distinction when he declares that the posthumous glory attests the lives of men of the past by means of the *logioi* and the *aoidoi*:

> for the posthumous acclaim of fame
> alone reveals the life of men who are dead and gone
> to both chroniclers and poets (*kai logiois kai aoidois*)

(Pind. Pyth. 1.92–94, trans. Race)

Despite not necessarily denoting a specific type of "master of oral traditions in prose" as Nagy (1987) wished, the term *logioi* can designate those competent though not institutionalized figures whose knowledge or wisdom imbued their statements with authority (Luraghi 2009: 454). In a world in which truth was established primarily through speech, not everybody's words carried the same weight. The term *logioi* is the unmarked member in an opposition between this word and *aoidoi*, which is the marked term— just as everyday speech is the unmarked term of the opposition to "song," which is the marked one (Nagy 1990: 224, n. 54). In fact, there are no clear indications that professional remembrancers existed in Greece, as there did in other societies with restricted literacy. From a Greek perspective, it is perhaps interesting to point out that such memorialists seem characteristic of collectives in which a centralized government tends to monopolize the past.

Besides the imposing institutionalized and authorized epic poetry, less official and institutional oral traditions in prose should also be examined—for example, local sources, from which the first mythographers drew and which have a long history in ancient historiography and in other genres (Marincola 1997: 283–285; see Verdin 1970). These may be the oral epichoric traditions of which we have some evidence, as, for example, in the passage of Dionysius that mentions the memories (*mnēmai*) used by the first authors of mythographical prose (section 1). Thucydides also uses *mnēmē* to refer to the sources of local traditions about the Peloponnese:

> Those who have preserved most clearly the traditional lore [*mnēmēi*] of the Peloponnese say that first of all Pelops . . . (Thuc. 1.9.2, trans. Hammond)

Although there is disagreement about the meaning of the term *mnēmēi*, it seems clear that it cannot be any kind of written record or archive. It is, rather, a way of describing the chain of transmission of oral traditions through learned men who passed on the memories. Individuals who communicate and receive information orally, like the ones that Thucydides himself mentions a little further below, may be referred to (Thuc. 1.20.1: "oral traditions handed down to them"; see Porciani 2001: 117–124). Epichoric narrators, *logioi*, existed in archaic Greece, and before the emergence of mythography they may have transmitted local and family memories (*mnēmēi dedegmenoi*), even though they did not constitute an official professional group, which would explain why they left few institutional traces. Figures such as Hippias of Elis, who was able to delight a public in Sparta that was fond of hearing about genealogies, foundations of cities, and "ancient stories in general" (*pasēs tēs archaiologias*; Pl. *Hp.Mai.* 285d), may resemble these local *logioi* (Porciani 2001: 122). Ultimately, Herodotus may be seen as the heir to these storytellers, who absorbed their traditions into a new mold (Murray 2001: 34).

If oral epichoric and family traditions were indeed at the base of the earliest mythographical prose, this better explains the perspective with which these authors proceeded: works of the first mythographers had an intrinsic value to those social groups who were convinced that they descended from heroes of divine ancestry. It is therefore to be expected that the genealogical versions they produced favored the interests of their own cities or particular groups or families by echoing the *kleos* "glory" of their ancestors. We saw a good example of this with the full genealogy of the Philaedae as transmitted by Pherecydes of Athens (section 4). The lineage of this family is different in some ways from a parallel source of Herodotus, and some of the differences seem relevant. Pherecydes does not limit himself to extolling the glory of the Philaedae. When he advances the line of descent, he omits members of the family past they may find uncomfortable or embarrassing, Cypselus, for example, perhaps because of his connection with the Corinthian tyranny; or Miltiades, whose archonship under the tyrant Hippias is left out, whereas Hippoclides's archonship is included (Thomas 1989: 168–169). In the same vein, Hellanicus traced the genealogy of the Codridae, descendants of Codrus and founders of Ionian cities, up to Deucalion (Hellanic. fr 125 Fowler). And Acusilaus discussed the lineage of a contemporary group, the Homeridae (Acus. fr. 2 Fowler), and a family, the Priamidae (Acus. fr. 39 Fowler) .

The new written genealogies established a sort of family glory (*kleos*) based more on mythographical writing and on the authority conferred by from the literary research of the author—and less on ancestral graves, shrines, or family cults. The praise a citizen obtained in this way was substantially different from the traditional authority they might have by being an official of a local cult—that is, the authority of old cults based on kinship and locality (Frost 1996: 87–89). In addition, the mythographers' works, and their authority vis-à-vis epic traditions, could have broader purposes. Acusilaus's innovative development of Argive genealogies, for example, has a direct connection, it seems, to the Peloponnesian politics of the 6th century. And contrary to the precedent epic tradition (the Hesiodic *Catalogue of Women* and Asius's epics), Pelasgus is not the autochthonous progenitor of the Arcadian people. Instead, by turning Pelasgus into the son of Niobe and Zeus like Argos, Acusilaus is disparaging Arcadian claims for autochthony and at the same time subordinating their hero to the Argive genealogical tree (Lanzillotta 2004: 52–53).

> To Niobe (the daughter of Phoroneus)—the first mortal woman with whom Zeus had intercourse—and Zeus, the child Argos was born, and Pelasgus, according to Acusilaus, from whom the Pelasgians who inhabit the Peloponnese were named. But Hesiod says that Pelasgus was sprung from the land itself. (Acus. fr. 25 Fowler = Apollod. 2.2 [2.1.1], trans. Toye)

Unlike the epic inspired or dictated by the Muse (section 4), which is placed under the authority of the divine, prose books are the work of individuals who have something to say and who introduce and legitimize themselves in the book's preface or the introductory sentence (Jacoby 1947: 45). And more important, they appeal to a reading public that is potentially Panhellenic. To the extent the mythical repertoires of the mythographers are abstracted from the conditions of oral communication, they become autonomous objects. The books of Hecataeus, Pherecydes, Acusilaus, and Hellanicus are a means of targeting an abstract audience, regardless of a particular time or place (see section 2; Jacob 1994: 172–173). In fact, authors like Acusilaus of Argos or Pherecydes of Athens would have had no reason to use the Ionian dialect in their books unless they had an "international" readership.

We have a good example in a fragment of Pherecydes. When the mythographer traces the mythical origins of the Athenian deme of the Daedalidae, he adds a telling detail informing us that it is in Athens—which would have been a superfluous piece of information for an Athenian reader:

> The reference is to Daedalus, about whom Pherecydes says as follows: "Born to Metion son of Erechtheus and Iphinoe was Daedalus, from whom the deme is called Daedalidae in Athens." (Schol. Soph. *OC* 472 = Pherecyd. fr. 146; trans. Morison)

If the detail "in Athens" was in Pherecydes's work (and not added by a later commentator or scholiast), it proves that the original text was conceived to be read beyond Athens, and its perspective was therefore Panhellenic (Fowler 2001: 111). If the mythographical texts do in fact reflect, as we said above, a less institutional and more fluid and marginal reality than the epic myths of the high civilization of the polis, dissemination of the books aspires to a Panhellenic readership. A more international reception for (more) local material guarantees, precisely, a less institutionalized and controlled transmission.

Parallels with other cultures suggest, as Finkelberg reminds us, that oral transmission is more restricted and more appropriate for the elites to exercise control over the spread of information and the forms that this takes. Dissemination of written texts, on the other hand, guarantees a mass circulation that is less controlled and more "democratic" (Finkelberg 2007: 302–303).

This may add a new dimension to a reassessment of the tension between localism and Panhellenism in archaic Greece, and specifically, the relationship of priority between local or universal history. In contrast to what Felix Jacoby believed, local and Panhellenic history predate Herodotus, developed in parallel, and defined each other. A Panhellenic tradition had once been local. Moreover, as Clarke has emphasized, local histories of Greece are not purely an expression of parochial pride; they are intended to introduce the polis as an integral part of a wider world (Clarke 2008: 230). Although they tend to focus on local genealogies and myths of their own polis (for example, Acusilaus focuses on the primordial character of Argos, and Pherecydes on Athenian autochthony), the early mythographers take as potential material Greek mythology as a whole—the *polloi logoi*, "many stories," of Hecataeus of Miletus. Local histories and a Panhellenic history have long coexisted, insists Fowler, and constitute an inseparable pair of terms: semiotically, one provides meaning to the other (Fowler 2001: 96; 2013: xiii; critical: Porciani 2009: 178–179, with n. 10; and particularly, Rengakos 2015). In contrast to the strict opposition between localism and Panhellenism, more relevant to us seems the distinction between one past subjected to public control and another, that of the mythographers, which is extra-institutional, less formal, and more fluid. To go even further: that rigid divide is undermined by the latest concepts from network theory and connectivity, which supersede hierarchical notions of center and periphery (see Malkin 2011). A decentralized network defines the Greek Mediterranean in contrast to the modern image of the uniform and symbolically central nation-state. As Bromberg (2021: 11) reminds, "scholars have not yet disentangled classics from national borders in a satisfying way".

## 7. THE TIME OF THE MYTHOGRAPHERS

In addition to ensuring the dissemination of a less institutional memory, the use of writing to transcribe myths has multiple effects, as we have seen (section 4). A final aspect to point out, which seems common to the earliest mythographical authors, is a new perception of time. In accordance with the determinist vision attributed to writing technology, Goody and Watt assumed that writing helped to conceive the past as being qualitatively different from the present (Goody and Watt 1963: 325, 333). Nonetheless, it has been pointed out that no qualitative distinction existed between a *spatium mythicum* and a *spatium historicum* for mythographers. Not even for Herodotus is the distinction between the *temps des dieux* and the *temps des hommes* clear, as Pierre Vidal-Naquet (1986: 39–59) wished (see the criticism by Williams 2002: 155–161). Rather, what the father of history does is to distinguish that period for which he has reliable, first-hand information from that which is unfathomable: what sets one time in opposition to another is not, in short, substantive difference, but rather an epistemological criterion (Saïd 2007: 79; Leyden 1949–1950: 95). What is innovative for the mythographers, and in this one can see the effect of the written product, is the effort to bridge the gap in order to weave an uninterrupted continuity between the past and the present.

In this way, and in contrast to the genealogies of oral epics, mythographers bridge the memory gap between the *spatium mythicum* and the *spatium historicum*—in other words, the floating gap that anthropologists have identified in "oral" societies: a hiatus between the accumulation of traditions and memories about the distant past, on the one hand, and the more recent past, on the other (Vansina 1985: 23). Despite the number of eponyms it mentions, the *Catalogue of Women* does not seem to establish direct connections between ancient genealogies and contemporary aristocratic families, as would have been common among early mythographers. Thus, Acusilaus of Argos (fr. 2 Fowler) discussed the lineage of a contemporary family, the Homeridae (section 6; see also Pàmias 2019b on the Priamidae). Hecataeus of Miletus (*FGH* 1F300 = Hdt. 2.143), who claimed that his sixteenth forefather had been a god, attempted to offer a clear idea of the extent of Greek history from the time of the gods to the present. Hellanicus traced the lineage of the family of Andocides back to Odysseus and Hermes (Hellanic. *FGH* 4F170 = 323aF24). Pherecydes's full genealogy (section 4) is a good demonstration of how the Athenian mythographer strives to produce tools to deal with the memory gap. And as noted earlier, Pherecydes often establishes an explicit connection between a toponym (or ethnonym) and a character from the heroic past (see also the discussion of Pherecydes's fragments in section 2, on Taenarum; and in section 6, on the Daedalidae):

> Lycaon was born from Pelasgos and Deianeira; this man marries Cyllene the water nymph, after whom Cyllene Mountain is named. (Pherecyd. fr. 156 Fowler, trans. Morison)

Awareness of the time gap from the mythical heritage allows the mythographer to make use of the inexhaustible repository of traditions to tie up a physical entity, which is his own, to a reality that is detached from it: that of the myth. However, one should not see in this connection "a logical operator between two universes considered as heterogeneous, a bridge between two worlds", as will be typical of the etiological discourse of the Alexandrian poets and scholars (Delattre 2009: 288–289). Rather, Pherecydes appropriates myth in an attempt to accommodate it without rupturing his own temporal dimension. The use of the same verb form (the present tense of the indicative: *ginetai*, "is born," . . . *kaleitai* "takes the name") to describe both the time of the myth and the phenomenal time, present and stable, is significant. It suggests that the author does not require any grammatical device to mark a heterogeneity of these two statements. This synoptic vision of the past announces and advances the account of the causes, the genesis of the facts—and not only of men!—that is to say, the procedure which properly constitutes the new *historiē*, the history of Herodotus. By transcribing myths synoptically, the genealogies of the mythographers, as a structuring form, have thus contributed to the emergence of a historical temporality (see Jacob 1994: 171).

The authors we are dealing with have helped, in different ways, to reconstruct a history of mankind up to the present time. If Hecataeus, with a lineage that dated back sixteen generations to the divinity, translated generations into years, one can say that he innovated with a chronological genealogy (see Bertelli 2001: 89–94; critical: Fowler 2013: 663–664). No doubt Hellanicus of Lesbos made a crucial step forward, however, becoming the "inventor" of chronography in Greece. For his universal history, this mythographer uses the list of priestesses of Hera at Argos as a reference point:

> The compiler of the *Priestesses at Argos* [Hellanicus] and the events during the tenure of each of them says that Aeneas . . . (Hellanic. fr. 84 Fowler = D.H. 1.72.2. trans. Pownall).

The annalistic pattern used by Hellanicus consisted, it seems, in combining the time of the events with the name and year of office of a priestess of Hera:

> The Sicel people in this way migrated from Italy, as Hellanicus of Lesbos says, in the third generation before the Trojan War, and in the twenty-sixth year of Alcyone's tenure as priestess at Argos. (Hellanic. fr. 79b Fowler = Dion. Hal. 1.22.3, trans. Pownall)

But Hellanicus began as a genealogist before undertaking his chronographical work. In his *Deucalionea*, *Phoronis*, *Asopidis*, and *Atlantis*, he reduced the mass of mythological stories and genealogies to only four ancestors. And he related the myths of the four lineages in a parallel and synchronous way, taking them down to the generation of the Trojan war, which he described in *On Troy*. And he did so by lengthening and shortening genealogies and constructing synchronisms between them (Möller 2001: 250).

We are, without a doubt, facing a new way of understanding temporality. Some Hellenists have emphasized the notion that, with the end of the archaic period, a new way of looking at the present time began to develop (on innovation and novelty in this new conception of time, see Dunn 2007; and D'Angour 2011). It is perhaps no coincidence that, at the same moment, thinkers like Anaxagoras, Protagoras, or Democritus were formulating theories on the evolution of humanity from primitivism to civilization (Corcella 2006: 42; particularly, see Democr. *FVS* 68B5). In effect, the understanding and the significance of the past have undergone a mutation: if the archaic Greeks projected their regard into the past in search of models and values, the present, as a result, was not so much placed on a linear continuum extending indefinitely between past and future, but rather in a belated and "postlapsarian" position after the generations of gods and heroes (see the classical study of Groningen 1953). In contrast, the literature of the classical age provides testimonies of a new regime of temporality, a temporality that now hovers over the present (see Csapo and Miller 1998: 100; for the detachment from the exemplary past in Herodotus and Thucydides, see Grethlein 2014: 327–328). The development of Herodotus's and especially Thucydides's historiography, which leans toward the author's present, would hardly be imaginable without a new conception of time, which early mythographers have helped to devise.

## FURTHER READING

Early Greek mythography has received increasing attention from classical scholarship in the last decades. Robert Fowler brought about a paradigm shift. With his papers (1996, 2001) and, notably, the collection of fragmentary *Early Greek Mythography* (2000, text; and 2013, commentary), he demolished earlier conceptions based on Jacoby's developmental view of Greek historiography (critical: Rengakos 2015). Fowler's standard edition supersedes the edited fragments under the rubric "Genealogie und Mythographie" in Jacoby's *Die Fragmente der griechischen Historiker* (1923). Jacoby's monumental edition has now been replaced by *Brill's New Jacoby*, which is nevertheless organized along the same lines (Hecataeus: Pownall 2013; Acusilaus: Toye 2009; Pherecydes: Morison 2011; Hellanicus: Pownall 2016). Monographic editions of the earliest mythographers have also been published: Hecataeus (Nenci 1954); Acusilaus (Andolfi 2019); Pherecydes (Dolcetti 2004; Pàmias 2008); Hellanicus (Ambaglio 1980; Caerols 1991). Theoretical issues surrounding the edition of fragmentary historians are addressed by Schepens (1997).

The old RE chapter (Wendel 1935) established that the genre does not come into existence prior to the 4th century bce. (On the notion of genre as a dynamic concept to be applied to mythography, see Marincola 1999; on the interaction between mythography and other genres, see Romano and Marincola 2019). On Greek accounts dealing with "Eastern" history, see Pearson (1939); Drews (1973). More recent contributions have explored the mythographic activity among early logographers: Pellizer (1993: 285–289); Jacob (1994); Toye (1995); Bertelli (1996); Fowler (2006); and the first chapters on the origins and development of Greek mythography in Trzaskoma and Smith (2013). On the relationship between mythography and historiography, see Saïd (2007). For an overview of these early writers see Meliadò (2015: 1058–1066); Alganza Roldán (2015); Fowler (2016); Andolfi (2017), who focuses on Hecataeus and Acusilaus; Pàmias (2017b); and Tufano (2019), who focuses specifically on Boeotia.

There are monographic contributions dealing with particular authors: on Hecataeus, see Lasserre (1976); Nicolai (1997); Bertelli (2001); Alganza Roldán (2012); on Acusilaus, see Pellegrini (1973–1974); Calame (2004); Lanzillotta (2009); Fontana (2012); Pàmias (2015, 2019a, 2019b); on Pherecydes, see Jacoby (1947); Dräger (1995); Dolcetti (2000); Blakely (2007); Pàmias (2017a); Pàmias (2020); on Hellanicus, see Joyce (1999); Möller (2001); Alpers (2002); Ottone (2010); on Xenomedes, see Huxley (1965).

On the coextensiveness of "myth" and ancient *mythos*, see the seminal book by Detienne (1981). A critical view in Fowler (2011; see also 2017). On the "oral revolution" and its relationship to Greek genealogy and mythography, see Andersen (1987); Thomas (1989); Murray (2001). On the oral background of Athenian history, see Raaflaub (1988). On mythographic accounts to be seen as plot lines abstracted from speech-acts, see Martin (2013). On the origins of Greek prose, see Asper (2007); Müller (2006); Laks (2001). On "submerged literature" (where mythography, and its extra-institutional background, can be included), see Colesanti and Giordano (2014); and Colesanti and Lulli (2016). On the relationship between local history and Panhellenism, see Porciani (2001); Clarke (2008); Goldhill (2010); Tober (2017); Tober (2019); Thomas (2019); Beck (2020). On the ancient conception of time, see the classical study of Groningen (1953). More recent investigation of memory and temporality is found in Marincola, Llewellyn-Jones, and Maciver (2012). "Intentional history" as the history in a group's own understanding has been studied by Gehrke (2001, 2014) and Foxhall, Gehrke, and Luraghi (2010). Relationship between (fragmentary) mythography and the shaping of Greek identity or identities is addressed by Skinner (2020). A critique of the oppositional Greek-barbarian paradigm has been recently raised by some authors (see Vlassopoulos 2013).

## REFERENCES

Alganza Roldán, Minerva. 2006. "La mitografía como género de la prosa helenística: Cuestiones previas." *Florentia Iliberritana* 17: 9–37.

Alganza Roldán, Minerva. 2012. "Hecateo de Mileto, 'historiador' y 'mitógrafo.'" *Florentia Iliberritana* 23: 23–44.

Alganza Roldán, Minerva. 2015. "Historiadores, logógrafos o mitógrafos? (Sobre la recepción de Hecateo, Ferécides y Helánico)." *Polymnia* 1: 3–24.

Alpers, Klaus. 2002. "Hellanikos von Lesbos: Apollodor und die mythographische frühgriechische Epik." *Abhandlungen der Braunschweigischen Wissenschaftlichen Gesellschaft* 52: 9–35.

Ambaglio, Delfino. 1980. *L'opera storiografica di Ellanico di Lesbo*. Pisa, Italy: Giardini.

Ambaglio, Delfino. 2007. "Quale razionalismo negli scrittori greci pretucididei?" *Athenaeum* 95: 685–691.

Andersen, Øivind. 1987. "Mündlichkeit und Schriftlichkeit im frühen Griechentum." *Antike und Abendland* 33: 29–44.

Andolfi, Ilaria. 2017. "An Ambiguous Literary Genre: The Origins of Early Greek Mythography." *Mnemosyne* 70: 183–201.

Andolfi, Ilaria. 2019. *Acusilaus of Argos' Rhapsody in Prose. Introduction, Text, and Commentary*. Berlin & Boston: De Gruyter.

Asper, Markus. 2007. "Medienwechsel und kultureller Kontext: Die Entstehung der griechischen Sachprosa." In *Philosophie und Dichtung im antiken Griechenland: Akten der 7. Tagung der Karl und Gertrud Abel-Stiftung am 10. und 11. Oktober 2002 in Bernkastel-Kues*, edited by Jochen Althoff, 67–102. Stuttgart: Franz Steiner.

Assmann, Jan. 2011. *Cultural Memory and Early Civilization: Writing, Remembrance, and Political Imagination*. Cambridge, UK: Cambridge University Press.

Barclay, John M.G. 2007. *Flavius Josephus. Volume 10. Against Apion. Translation and Commentary*. Leiden & Boston: Brill.

Beck, Hans 2020. *Localism and the Ancient Greek City-State*. Chicago and London: The University of Chicago Press.

Benveniste, Émile. 1971. *Problems in General Linguistics*. Translated by Mary Elizabeth Meek. Coral Gables, FL: University of Miami Press.

Bertelli, Lucio. 1996. "'C'era una volta un mito . . .': Alle origini della storiografia greca." In *De tuo tibi: Omaggio degli allievi a Italo Lana*, 49–85. Bologna: Pàtron.

Bertelli, Lucio. 2001. "Hecataeus: From Genealogy to Historiography." In *The Historian's Craft in the Age of Herodotus*, edited by Nino Luraghi, 67–94. Oxford: Oxford University Press.

Blakely, Sandra. 2007. "Pherekydes' Daktyloi: Ritual, Technology, and the Presocratic Perspective." *Kernos* 20: 43–67.

Breglia, Luisa. 2012. "Dionigi di Alicarnasso, la nascita della storiografia e le *Politeiai* aristoteliche." In *Istituzioni e costituzioni in Aristotele tra storiografia e pensiero politico*, edited by Marina Polito and Clara Talamo, 263–288. Tivoli: Tored.

Bromberg, Jacques A. 2021. *Global Classics*, London and New York: Routledge.

Butler, Samuel. 1898. *The Iliad of Homer*. London, New York and Bombay: Longmans, Green, and Co.

Caerols, José J., ed. 1991. *Helánico de Lesbos. Fragmentos*. Madrid: Consejo Superior de Investigaciones Científicas.

Clarke, Katherine. 2008. *Making Time for the Past. Local History and the Polis*. Oxford: Oxford University Press.

Colesanti, Giulio, and Manuela Giordano, eds. 2014. *Submerged Literature in Ancient Greek Culture. An Introduction*. Berlin and Boston: De Gruyter.

Colesanti, Giulio, and Laura Lulli, eds. 2016. *Submerged Literature in Ancient Greek Culture. Case Studies*. Berlin and Boston: De Gruyter.

Corcella, Aldo. 2006. "The New Genre and its Boundaries: Poets and Logographers." In *Brill's Companion to Thucydides*, edited by Antonios Rengakos and Antonios Tsakmakis, 33–56. Leiden and Boston: Brill.

Csapo, Eric, and Margaret Miller. 1988. "Towards a Politics of Time and Narrative." In *Democracy, Empire, and the Arts in Fifth-Century Athens*, edited by Deborah Boedeker and Kurt A. Raaflaub, 87–126. Cambridge, MA: Harvard University Press.

D'Angour, Armand. 2011. *The Greeks and the New: Novelty in Ancient Greek Imagination and Experience*. Cambridge, UK: Cambridge University Press.

Delattre, Charles. 2009. "Αἰτιολογία: mythe et procédure étiologique." *Métis* 7: 285–310.

Detienne, Marcel. 1981. *L'invention de la mythologie*. Paris: Gallimard.

Detienne, Marcel. 1996. *The Masters of Truth in Archaic Greece*. Foreword by Pierre Vidal-Naquet. Translated by Janet Lloyd. New York: Zone Books.

Dolcetti, Paola. 2000. "Ἀφ᾽ οὗ καλεῖται . . .: Ordinamento genealogico e definizione degli spazi geografici in Ferecide di Atene." *Quaderni del Dipartimento di filologia, linguistica e tradizione classica "Augusto Rostagni"* 14 : 23–32.

Dolcetti, Paola. 2001. "Le genealogie di Ferecide di Atene e i Θησεῖα cimoniani." *Quaderni del Dipartimento di filologia, linguistica e tradizione classica «Augusto Rostagni»* 17 : 67–75.

Dolcetti, Paola, ed. 2004. *Ferecide di Atene: Testimonianze e frammenti*. Introduzione, testo, traduzione e commento. Alessandria: Edizioni dell'Orso.

Dräger, Paul. 1995. *Stilistische Untersuchungen zu Pherekydes von Athen: Ein Beitrag zur ältesten ionischen Prosa*. Stuttgart: Franz Steiner.

Drews, Robert. 1973. *The Greek Accounts of Eastern History*. Washington: Center for Hellenic Studies.

Dunn, Francis M. 2007. *Present Shock in Late Fifth-Century Greece*. Ann Arbor: University of Michigan Press.

Edmunds, Lowell. 2005. "Epic and Myth." In *A Companion to Ancient Epic*, edited by John Miles Foley, 31–44. Malden, MA: Blackwell.

Fentress, James, and Chris Wickham. 1992. *Social Memory*. Oxford and Cambridge, UK: Blackwell.

Finkelberg, Margalit. "Elitist Orality and the Triviality of Writing." In *Politics of Orality*, edited by Craig Cooper, 293–305. Leiden and Boston: Brill 2007.

Finnegan, Ruth. 1970. *Oral Literature in Africa*. Oxford: Oxford University Press.

Fontana, Federica. 2012. "Sul metodo storiografico di Acusilao di Argo." *Historia* 61 : 383–413.

Fontenelle, Bernard de. 1989. "De l'origine des fables." In *Oeuvres Complètes*, vol. 3, edited by Alain Niderst, 187–202. Paris: Fayard. (Original work published in 1724).

Fowler, Robert L. 1996. "Herodotos and His Contemporaries." *Journal of Hellenic Studies* 116 : 62–87.

Fowler, Robert L. 1999. "The Authors Named Pherekydes." *Mnemosyne* 52 : 1–15.

Fowler, Robert L., ed. 2000. *Early Greek Mythography*. Vol. 1. *Texts*. Oxford: Oxford University Press.

Fowler, Robert L. 2001. "Early *Historiē* and Literacy." In *The Historian's Craft in the Age of Herodotus*, edited by Nino Luraghi, 95–115. Oxford: Oxford University Press.

Fowler, Robert L. 2006. "How to Tell a Myth: Genealogy, Mythology, Mythography." *Kernos* 19 : 35–46.

Fowler, Robert L. 2011. "*Mythos* and *Logos*." *Journal of Hellenic Studies* 131 : 45–66.

Fowler, Robert L. 2013. *Early Greek Mythography*. Vol. 2. *Commentary*. Oxford: Oxford University Press.

Fowler, Robert L. 2016. "Hekataios, Pherekydes, Hellanikos: Three Approaches to Mythography." In *Lire les mythes. Formes, usages et visées des pratiques mythographiques de l'Antiquité à la Renaissance*, edited by A. Zucker, J. Fabre-Serris, J.-Y. Tilliette, and G. Besson, 25–41. Villeneuve d'Ascq: Presses Universitaires du Septentrion.

Fowler, Robert L. 2017. "Greek Mythography." In *Blackwell Companion to the Reception of Classical Myth*, edited by Vanda Zajko, 15–28. Oxford and Malden: Blackwell.

Foxhall, Lin, Hans-Joachim Gehrke, and Nino Luraghi, eds. 2010. *Intentional History. Spinning Time in Ancient Greece*. Stuttgart: Franz Steiner.

Frazer, James G. 1898. *Pausanias's Description of Greece. Translated with a Commentary*. Vol. I. Translation. London: Macmillan and Co.

Frost, Frank J. 1996. "Faith, Authority, and History in Early Athens." In *Religion and Power in the Ancient Greek World. Proceedings of the Uppsala Symposium 1993*, edited by Pontus Hellström and Brita Alroth, 83–89. Uppsala: Almqvist & Wiksell International.

Geertz, Clifford. 1973. *The Interpretation of Cultures. Selected Essays*. New York: Basic Books.

Gehrke, Hans-Joachim. 2001. "Myth, History, and Collective Identity: Uses of the Past in Ancient Greece and Beyond." In *The Historian's Craft in the Age of Herodotus*, edited by Nino Luraghi, 286–313. Oxford: Oxford University Press.

Gehrke, Hans-Joachim. 2014. *Geschichte als Element antiker Kultur. Die Griechen und ihre Geschichte(n)*. Berlin and Boston: De Gruyter.

Goody, Jack, and Ian Watt. 1963. "The Consequences of Literacy." *Comparative Studies in Society and History* 5 : 304–345.

Goldhill, Simon. 2010. "What is Local Identity? The Politics of Cultural Mapping." In *Local Knowledge and Microidentities in the Imperial Greek World*, edited by Tim Whitmarsh, 46–68. Cambridge: Cambridge University Press.

Gottesman, Alex. 2014. *Politics and the Street in Democratic Athens*. Cambridge, UK: Cambridge University Press.

Gozzoli, Sandra. 1970–1971. "Una teoria antica sull'origine della storiografia greca." *Studi classici e orientali* 19/20: 158–211.

Graf, Fritz. 1993. *Greek Mythology. An Introduction*. Translated by Thomas Marier. Baltimore, MD: Johns Hopkins University Press.

Graf, Fritz. 2002. "La génèse de la notion de mythe." In *Mitos en la literatura griega arcaica y clásica*, edited by Juan Antonio López Férez, 1–15. Madrid: Ediciones Clásicas.

Grethlein, Jonas. 2014. "The Value of the Past Challenged: Myth and Ancient History in the Attic Orators." In *Valuing the Past in the Greco-Roman World. Proceedings from the*

*Penn-Leiden Colloquia on Ancient Values VII*, edited by James Ker and Christoph Pieper, 326–354. Leiden and Boston: Brill.

Groningen, Bernhard Abraham van. 1953. *In the Grip of the Past: Essay on an Aspect of Greek Thought*. Leiden: Brill.

Hammond, Martin. 2009. *Thucydides. The Peloponnesian War*. With an Introduction and Notes by P. J. Rhodes. Oxford: Oxford University Press.

Hartog, François. 1990. "Écritures, généalogies, archives, histoire en Grèce ancienne." In *Mélanges Pierre Lévêque. 5. Anthropologie et société*, edited by Marie-Madeleine Mactoux and Evelyne Geny, 177–188. Paris: Les Belles Lettres.

Hartog, François. 2001. *Le Miroir d'Hérodote: Essai sur la représentation de l'autre*. Rev. and expanded ed.. Paris: Gallimard.

Havelock, Eric A. 1982. *The Literate Revolution in Greece and its Cultural Consequences*. Princeton, NJ: Princeton University Press.

Humphreys, Sally C. 1997. "Fragments, Fetishes and Philosophies: Towards a History of Greek Historiography after Thucydides." In *Collecting Fragments / Fragmente sammeln*, edited by Glenn W. Most, 207–224. Göttingen: Vandenhoeck and Ruprecht.

Huxley, George. 1965. "Xenomedes of Keos." *Greek, Roman and Byzantine Studies* 6: 235–245.

Huxley, George. 1973. "The Date of Pherekydes of Athens." *Greek, Roman and Byzantine Studies* 14: 137–143.

Jacob, Christian. 1994. "L'ordre généalogique: Entre le mythe et l'histoire." In *Transcrire les mythologies*, edited by Marcel Detienne, 169–202. Paris: Albin Michel.

Jacoby, Felix, ed. 1923. *Die Fragmente der griechischen Historiker. Erster Teil: Genealogie und Mythographie*. Berlin: Weidmann.

Jacoby, Felix. 1947. "The First Athenian Prose Writer." *Mnemosyne* 13: 13–64.

Jones, Horace L. 1917. *The Geography of Strabo. Volume I*. London and Cambridge, MA: William Heinemann Ltd-Harvard University Press (Repr. 1960).

Joyce, Christopher. 1999. "Was Hellanikos the First Chronicler of Athens?" *Histos* 3: 1–17.

Laks, André. 2001. "Écriture, prose et les débuts de la philosophie grecque." *Methodos* 1: 131–151.

Lanzillotta, Eugenio. 2004. "Patriottismo e tradizioni mitiche: Le origini della storiografia locale in Grecia." In *Historia y mito: El pasado legendario como fuente de autoridad*, edited by José M. Candau Morón, Francisco J González Ponce, and Gonzalo Cruz Andreotti, 47–55. Málaga, Spain: Centro de Ediciones de la Diputación de Málaga.

Lanzillotta, Eugenio. 2009. "Acusilao di Argo, il mito di Atlantide in Platone e gli inizi della storia dei Greci." In *Tradizione e trasmissione degli storici greci frammentari: In ricordo di Silvio Accame*, edited by Eugenio Lanzillotta, Virgilio Costa, and Gabriella Ottone, 43–56. Tivoli: Tored.

Lanzillotta, Eugenio. 2010. "Gli *archaioi syngrapheis* nella *Suda*. Acusilao." In *Il lessico Suda e gli storici greci in frammenti. Atti dell'incontro internazionale, Vercelli, 6–7 novembre 2008*, edited by Gabriella Vanotti, 57–63. Tivoli: Tored.

Lasserre, François. 1976. "L'historiographie grecque à l'époque archaïque." *Quaderni di storia* 4: 113–142.

Leyden, Wolfgang M. von. 1949–1950. "Spatium Historicum (The Historical Past as Viewed by Hecataeus, Herodotus, and Thucydides)." *Durham University Journal* 11: 89–104.

Lloyd, Geoffrey E. R. 1995. *The Revolutions of Wisdom: Studies in the Claims and Practice of Ancient Greek Science*. Berkeley: University of California Press.

Luraghi, Nino. 2001. "Introduction" to *The Historian's Craft in the Age of Herodotus*, edited by Nino Luraghi, 1–15. Oxford: Oxford University Press.

Luraghi, Nino. 2009. "The Importance of Being λόγιος." *Classical World* 102: 439–456.

Malkin, Irad. 2011. *A Small Greek World. Networks in the Ancient Mediterranean*. Oxford: Oxford University Press.

Marincola, John. 1997. *Authority and Tradition in Ancient Historiography*. Cambridge, UK: Cambridge University Press.

Marincola, John. 1999. "Genre, Convention, and Innovation in Greco-Roman Historiography." In *The Limits of Historiography: Genre and Narrative in Ancient Historical Texts*, edited by Christina Shuttleworth Kraus, 281–324. Leiden: Brill.

Marincola, John, Lloyd Llewellyn-Jones, and Calum Maciver, eds. 2012. *Greek Notions of the Past in the Archaic and Classical Eras: History without Historians*. Edinburgh: Edinburgh University Press.

Martin, Richard P. 1989. *The Language of Heroes: Speech and Performance in the Iliad*. Ithaca, NY: Cornell University Press.

Martin, Richard P. 2013. "The 'Myth before the Myth Began.'" In *Writing Down the Myths*, edited by Joseph F. Nagy, 45–66. Turnhout: Brepols.

Mazzarino, Santo. 1966. *Il pensiero storico classico. 1*. Bari: Laterza.

McInerney, Jeremy. 1994. "Politicizing the Past: The *Atthis* of Kleidemos." *Classical Antiquity* 13: 17–37.

McLuhan, Marshall. 1964. *Understanding Media: The Extensions of Man*. New York: McGraw-Hill.

Meliadò, Claudio. 2015. "Mythography." In *Brill's Companion to Ancient Greek Scholarship*. Vol. 1: *History: Disciplinary Profiles*, edited by Franco Montanari, Stephanos Matthaios, and Antonios Rengakos, 1057–1089. Leiden and Boston: Brill.

Möller, Astrid. 1996. "Der Stammbaum der Philaiden. Über Funktionen der Genealogie bei den Griechen." In *Retrospektive: Konzepte von Vergangenheit in der griechisch-römischen Antike*, edited by Martin Flashar, Hans Joachim Gehrke, and Ernst Heinrich, 17–35. Munich: Biering and Brinkmann.

Möller, Astrid. 2001. "The Beginning of Chronography: Hellanicus' *Hiereiai*." In *The Historian's Craft in the Age of Herodotus*, edited by Nino Luraghi, 241–262. Oxford: Oxford University Press.

Momigliano, Arnaldo. 1966. "Storiografia su tradizione scritta e storiografia su tradizione orale: Considerazioni generali sulle origini della storiografia moderna." In *Terzo contributo alla storia degli studi classici e del mondo antico*, 13–22. Roma: Edizioni di Storia e Letteratura.

Momigliano, Arnaldo. 1990. *The Classical Foundations of Modern Historiography*. Berkeley: University of California Press.

Morison, William S. 2011. "Pherekydes of Athens (3)." In *Brill's New Jacoby*, edited by Ian Worthington. Leiden: Brill. https://referenceworks.brillonline.com/entries/brill-s-new-jacoby/pherekydes-of-athens-3-a3.

Most, Glenn W. 1999. "The Poetics of Early Greek Philosophy." In *The Cambridge Companion to Early Greek Philosophy*, edited by Anthony A. Long, 332–362. Cambridge, UK: Cambridge University Press.

Müller, Carl Werner. 2006. "Zur Frühgeschichte der erzählenden Prosaliteratur bei den Griechen." In *Legende–Novelle–Roman: Dreizehn Kapitel zur erzählenden Prosaliteratur der Antike*, edited by Carl Müller, 1–54. Göttingen: Vandenhoeck & Ruprecht.

Murray, Oswyn. 2001. "Herodotus and Oral History." In *The Historian's Craft in the Age of Herodotus,* edited by Nino Luraghi, 16–44. Oxford: Oxford University Press.

Nagy, Gregory. 1987. "Herodotus the *Logios*." *Arethusa* 20: 175–184.

Nagy, Gregory. 1990. *Pindar's Homer: The Lyric Possession of an Epic Past*. Baltimore, MD: Johns Hopkins University Press.

Nenci, Giuseppe, ed. 1954. *Hecataei Milesii Fragmenta*. Florence: Nuova Italia.

Nicolai, Roberto. 1997. "*Pater Semper incertus*. Appunti su Ecateo." *Quaderni urbinati di cultura classica* 56: 143–164.

Oldfather, C.H. 1933. *Diodorus of Sicily. I. Books I and II, 1–34*. London and Cambridge, MA: William Heinemann Ltd-Harvard University Press (Repr. 1968).

Ottone, Gabriella. 2010. "L'Ἀττικὴ ξυγγραφή di Ellanico di Lesbo: Una *Lokalgeschichte* in prospettiva eccentrica." In *Storie di Atene, storia dei Greci: Studi e ricerche di attidografia*, edited by Cinzia Bearzot and Franca Landucci, 53–111. Milan: Vita e Pensiero.

Pàmias, Jordi, ed. 2008. *Ferecides d'Atenes, Històries*. Vols. 1 and 2. Introducció, edició crítica, traducció i notes. Barcelona: Fundació Bernat Metge.

Pàmias, Jordi. 2014. "The Reception of Greek Myth." In *Approaches to Greek Myth*. 2nd ed., edited by Lowell Edmunds, 44–83. Baltimore, MD: Johns Hopkins University Press.

Pàmias, Jordi. 2015. "Acusilaus of Argos and the Bronze Tablets." *Harvard Studies in Classical Philology* 108: 53–75.

Pàmias, Jordi. 2017a. "Coon or Cimon? Pherecydes' Homer: The Mythographic Possession of an Epic Past." *Mnemosyne* 70: 131–139.

Pàmias, Jordi. 2017b. "La recepción de los mitos en la primera mitografía." In *La mitología griega en la tradición literaria. De la Antigüedad a la Grecia contemporánea*, edited by Minerva Alganza and Panagiota Papadopoulou, 23–33. Granada: Centro de Estudios Bizantinos, Neogriegos y Chipriotas.

Pàmias, Jordi. 2019a. "El proemio a las *Genealogías* de Acusilao de Argos." *Quaderni urbinati di cultura classica* 122: 69–73.

Pàmias, Jordi. 2019b. "The Plan of Aphrodite: Helen between *Heldendämmerung* and Social Engineering." *La parola del passato* 74: 143–155.

Pàmias, Jordi. 2020. "Pherekydes von Athen: Struktur der *Historiai* (oder: Der längere Weg von Athen bis Alexandria)." *Classica & Mediaevalia* 68: 1–13.

Pearson, Lionel. 1939. *Early Ionian Historians*. Oxford: Clarendon Press.

Pellegrini, Daniela. 1973–1974. "Sulle 'Genealogie argive' di Acusilao." *Atti e memorie dell'Accademia Patavina di Scienze* 86 (3): 155–171.

Pellizer, Ezio. 1993. "La mitografia." In *Lo spazio letterario della Grecia antica*, vol. 1.2: *L'Ellenismo*, edited by Giuseppe Cambiano, Luciano Canfora, and Diego Lanza, 283–303. Rome: Salerno Editrice.

Porciani, Leone. 1994. "Oralità, scrittura, storiografia." In *Ἱστορίη: Studi offerti dagli allievi a Giuseppe Nenci in occasione del suo settantesimo compleanno*, edited by Salvatore Alessandrì, 377–397. Galatina: Congedo.

Porciani, Leone. 2001. *Prime forme della storiografia greca: Prospettiva locale e generale nella narrazione storica*. Stuttgart: Franz Steiner.

Porciani, Leone. 2009. "Il problema della storia locale." In *Aspetti dell'opera di Felix Jacoby*, edited by Carmine Ampolo, 173–184. Pisa: Edizioni della Normale.

Pownall, Frances. 2013. "Hekataios of Miletos (1)." In *Brill's New Jacoby*, edited by Ian Worthington. Leiden: Brill. https://referenceworks.brillonline.com/entries/brill-s-new-jacoby/hekataios-of-miletos-1-a1.

Pownall, Frances. 2016. "Hellanikos of Lesbos (4)." In *Brill's New Jacoby*, edited by Ian Worthington. Leiden: Brill. https://referenceworks.brillonline.com/entries/brill-s-new-jacoby/hellanikos-of-lesbos-4-a4.

Raaflaub, Kurt A. 1988. "Athenische Geschichte und mündliche Überlieferung." In *Vergangenheit in mündlicher Überlieferung*, edited by Jürgen von Ungern-Sternberg and Hansjörg Reinau, 197–225. Stuttgart: Teubner.

Race, William H. 1997. *Pindar. Olympian Odes. Pythian Odes*. Cambridge, MA and London: Harvard University Press.

Rengakos, Antonios. 2015. "Felix Jacoby, Robert Fowler und die Änfange der griechischen Geschichtsschreibung." *Gymnasium* 122: 233–248.

Romano, Allen J., and John Marincola, eds. 2019. *Host or Parasite? Mythographers and Their Contemporaries in the Classical and Hellenistic Periods*. Berlin and Boston: De Gruyter.

Saïd, Suzanne. 2007. "Myth and Historiography." In *A Companion to Greek and Roman Historiography*, vol. 1, edited by John Marincola, 76–88. Malden, MA: Blackwell.

Saumaise, Claude. 1629. *Claudii Salmasii Plinianae exercitationes in Caii Iulii Solini Polyhistora. Pars altera*. Paris: Apud Hieronymum Drouart.

Schepens, Guido. 1997. "Jacoby's *FGrHist*: Problems, Methods, Prospects." In *Collecting Fragments: Fragmente sammeln*, edited by Glenn W. Most, 144–172. Göttingen: Vandenhoeck and Ruprecht.

Schmitz, Thomas A. 2007. *Modern Literary Theory and Ancient Texts. An Introduction*. Malden, MA: Blackwell.

Skinner, Joseph E. 2020. "Writing Culture: Historiography, Hybridity, and the Shaping of Collective Memory." In *Shaping Memory in Ancient Greece: Poetry, Historiography, and Epigraphy*, edited by Christy Constantakopoulou & Maria Fragoulaki, 189–234. Newcastle upon Tyne: Newcastle University.

Sulimani, Iris. 2011. *Diodorus' Mythistory and the Pagan Mission. Historiography and Culture-heroes in the First Pentad of the Bibliotheke*. Leiden and Boston: Brill.

Stadter, Philip. 1997. "Herodotus and the North Carolina Oral Narrative Tradition." *Histos* 1: 13–41.

Thomas, Rosalind. 1989. *Oral Tradition and Written Record in Classical Athens*. Cambridge, UK: Cambridge University Press.

Thomas, Rosalind. 1992. *Literacy and Orality in Ancient Greece*. Cambridge, UK: Cambridge University Press.

Thomas, Rosalind. 2019. *Polis Histories, Collective Memories and the Greek World*. Cambridge, UK: Cambridge University Press.

Tober, Daniel 2017. "Greek Local Historiography and Its Audiences." *Classical Quarterly* 67: 460–484.

Tober, Daniel 2019. "Greek Local History and the Shape of the Past." In *Historiography and Identity I. Ancient and Early Christian Narratives of Community*, edited by Walter Pohl and Veronika Wieser, 133–155. Turnhout: Brepols.

Toye, David L. 1995. "Dionysius of Halicarnassus on the First Greek Historians." *American Journal of Philology* 116: 279–302.

Toye, David L. 1997. "Pherecydes of Syros: Ancient Theologian and Genealogist." *Mnemosyne* 50: 530–560.

Toye, David L. 2009. "Akousilaos of Argos (2)." In *Brill's New Jacoby*, edited by Ian Worthington. Leiden: Brill. https://referenceworks.brillonline.com/entries/brill-s-new-jacoby/akousil aos-of-argos-2-a2.

Trzaskoma, Stephen M., and R. Scott Smith, eds. 2013. *Writing Myth: Mythography in the Ancient World*. Leuven: Peeters.

Tufano, Salvatore 2019. *Boiotia from Within. The Beginnings of Boiotian Historiography*, Münster: Universitäts- und Landesbibliothek.

Vansina, Jan. 1961. *De la tradition orale*. Tervuren, Belgium: Musée royal de l'Afrique centrale.

Vansina, Jan. 1985. *Oral Tradition as History*. Madison: University of Wisconsin Press.

Velardi, Roberto. 2014. "Presente, futuro, passato: Il sapere del mantis e il sapere dell'aedo." *Quaderni urbinati di cultura classica* 107: 27–44.

Verdin, Herman. 1970. "Notes sur l'attitude des historiens grecs à l'égard de la tradition locale." *Ancient Society* 1: 183–200.

Vernant, Jean-Pierre. 1990. *Myth and Society in Ancient Greece*. Translated by Janet Lloyd. New York: Zone Books.

Veyne, Paul. 1988. *Did the Greeks Believe in Their Myths? An Essay on the Constitutive Imagination*. Translated by Paula Wissing. Chicago: University of Chicago Press.

Vidal-Naquet, Pierre. 1986. *The Black Hunter: Forms of Thought and Forms of Society in the Greek World*. Translated by Andrew Szegedy-Maszak. Foreword by Bernard Knox. Baltimore, MD: Johns Hopkins University Press.

Vlassopoulos, Kostas. 2013. *Greeks and Barbarians*. Cambridge: Cambridge University Press.

Wendel, Carl. 1935. "Mythographie." *RE XVI*/2, 1352–1374. Stuttgart: Alfred Druckenmüller Verlag.

West, Martin L. 1985. *The Hesiodic Catalogue of Women: Its Nature, Structure, and Origins*. Oxford: Clarendon Press.

West, Martin L. 2012. "Towards a Chronology of Early Greek Epic." In *Relative Chronology in Early Greek Epic Poetry*, edited by Øivind Andersen and Dag T. T. Haug, 224–241. Cambridge, UK: Cambridge University Press.

Williams, Bernard. 2002. *Truth and Truthfulness: An Essay in Genealogy*. Princeton, NJ: Princeton University Press.

Woodard, Roger D., ed. 2007. *The Cambridge Companion to Greek Mythology*. Cambridge, UK: Cambridge University Press.

CHAPTER 3

....................................................................................................

# HELLENISTIC MYTHOGRAPHY

....................................................................................................

## R. SCOTT SMITH AND STEPHEN M. TRZASKOMA

Mʏᴛʜᴏɢʀᴀᴘʜʏ of the Hellenistic era is like a dim star you see out of the corner of your eye and know is there, but it vanishes when you shift your gaze to look at it directly. Mythography of the period exists, and we can see a precious few examples of it— Palaephatus is the rare author whose work is not entirely fragmentary (see Koning, this volume, for more on Palaephatus; we do not treat him in detail in this chapter)—but when we look closer at what we have, the notion of "Hellenistic mythography" all but fades into mysterious darkness. The period is bracketed by the original mythographical writings from the late archaic and classical period produced by such figures as Acusilaus and Pherecydes, which are now left in sadly fragmentary form, and the fuller remains from the imperial period, which are the preoccupation of much of the rest of this handbook and, more generally, of research into mythography. However, nearly everything that we know about Hellenistic mythographical writers is mediated through later sources, whose presentation may, consciously or unconsciously, misrepresent their subjects and, therefore, impair our attempts to reconstruct their original aims, methods, and intentions. Often, we have nothing more than a suggestive title or a few fragments. In short, we know that mythography existed in the Hellenistic period, and must have been crucial for its development, but the proof of that is mostly by inference, and specific arguments are frustratingly difficult to make.

As an index of the general predicament, one can consider the excellent chapter in Higbie (2007) "Hellenistic Mythographers." Although it is taken as axiomatic that mythography emerged in the 4th century ʙᴄᴇ alongside paradoxography, very little space is given over to Hellenistic authors, and significantly greater attention is paid to those who are, in fact, *imperial* mythographers: Ps.-Apollodorus, Parthenius, Antoninus Liberalis, Conon, and the *Mythographus Homericus* (likewise, Lightfoot 1999: 224–240, though her interest is in finding parallels for Parthenius). Similarly, Meliadò's (2015) treatment moves seamlessly from the emergence of scientific mythography in the 4th century ʙᴄᴇ to Ps.-Apollodorus, as if the *Bibliotheca* is an inevitable outgrowth or a culmination of practices and forms that emerged in the Hellenistic period (see the section "Apollodorus of Athens: A Mythographer?" below). There is little else to do. We are faced with a methodological leap of faith that requires us to assume that a direct line can be traced from the extant imperial collections back to nonextant Hellenistic predecessors, so we also imagine that what we have from the imperial period is representative of, analogous to, or otherwise derivative of lost works.

We want to stress that we mention these examples not as criticism of those studies but out of sympathetic camaraderie with their authors. The challenges of saying almost anything certain are immense. Not only do we face the methodological problems that are inherent in dealing almost exclusively with lost or fragmentary authors; we also encounter a pair of related difficulties: establishing what we mean by "mythography" and then applying that definition to the varied output of the Hellenistic period. As Alganza Roldán (2006) lays out in detail, on our current evidence, Hellenistic works that deal with myth are not at all homogenous and seem to utilize a wide array of formats and approaches. Without claiming to be exhaustive, we can, on the systematic side of mythography, point to works—none, unfortunately, fully extant—focusing on myths in tragedy (Glaucus of Rhegium, Asclepiades, Dicaearchus); collections of star myths (Eratosthenes, Hermippus of Smyrna); and compilations of "surprising" myths (Lysimachus). On the interpretive side, in addition to the surviving systematic rationalization of myth (Palaephatus), we also have the remains of revisionist accounts of the gods and other myths by Euhemerus and his successors, not least Dionysius Scytobrachion, an author whose works one study rates as "prose romance" (Lightfoot 1999: 224; see also Gutzwiller 2007: 189–190). Finally, we cannot forget that mythography was conducted in relation to other scholarly pursuits and deployed to different ends, for example, in the interpretation of Homer, especially in relationship to the *neōteroi* (see Nünlist 2019; Schironi 2018: 661–708), and in historiography (Philochorus, Xenomedes of Ceos, Atthidographers), including *ktisis* (city-foundation) accounts set in the mythical past (Philostephanus, Istrus). Any survey, then, is likely to be diffuse, misleading, or, like Wendel's (1935) foundational article on mythography, formulated to fit a narrative that ends up displaying more confidence and coherence than our lack of evidence truly permits.

In other words, defining a corpus of either mythographers or mythographical works in the Hellenistic period remains problematic, and the results will vary depending on where the boundaries of mythography are drawn. Even Wittgensteinian *Familienähnlichkeit* (family resemblance), used to great effect by Pàmias in the previous chapter, seems less helpful here. For instance, it is difficult to delineate with precision how Asclepiades and Euhemerus belong to the same intellectual pursuit at anything but the broadest level, or how the local histories of Xenomedes of Ceos and the Lindian Chronicle can be categorized with either the mythical exegesis of Aristarchus or the work on the catalog of ships by Apollodorus of Athens and Demetrius of Scepsis. And yet, if we limit the discussion to, say, systematic mythography aimed at compiling and organizing disparate traditions, we not only face the dearth of directly relevant evidence almost immediately; we are also omitting methodological responses to the mythical storyworld that treated myth as a separate category, but in a fundamentally different way, such as through rationalization and allegory. In fact, these approaches are perhaps our best proof that myth was now a separate category that could be seen as a topic worthy of study in its own right, whether to assemble and systematize or interpret and correct.

Other chapters in this handbook treat various texts or approaches that are found in the period under discussion: mythographical collections with Palaephatus (Koning) and Eratosthenes and other catasteristic works (Zucker); mythographical texts on papyrus, including some Hellenistic ones (Harder); the mythographical connoisseurship of the Alexanderian poets (Sistakou); and myth-critical approaches such as rationalization, including that of Euhemerus and Philochorus (Hawes); and allegorizing, together with its Hellenistic philosophical origins (Ramelli). Rather than rehearse these again here or attempt an inadequate survey, after a brief sketch of the material and intellectual developments that emerged just before the Hellenistic period and their importance for the rise of mythography, we will consider three case studies of "Hellenistic mythographers" to help frame the challenges to understanding the development of mythography in this period, as well as how some assumptions may lead to misleading conclusions about these works.

# 1. Developments in the 5th and 4th Centuries bce

By the time the Hellenistic period began after the death of Alexander the Great, mythographical writing had already emerged as a practice that regarded *mythoi* as something conceptually distinct. As Pàmias, this volume, systematically lays out, by the late 5th century, what we call myth was a recognizable, if still-debated category. If Meccariello is right to see in Euripides's late works a response to mythographical practices in the prologues of tragedies, then by 400 bce, systematic mythography itself seems to be a self-conscious activity (see Meccariello, this volume). In this case, then, the first phase of mythographical writing in the 6th and early 5th centuries, facilitated by the rapid spread of writing practices and circulation, was followed soon after by a second phase as written texts began to proliferate (Pfeiffer 1968: 25–32). Among these texts would have been epic and lyric poetry, the work of mythographers like Pherecydes, and, of course, tragedies, which were almost exclusively devoted to the mythical world. We do not need to go as far as Wilamowitz does, who suggested that tragedies were the first true *biblia*, to recognize that texts of the tragedies were made more widely available to an educated readership during this period than previously (Wilamowitz 1907: 120–127; Pfeiffer 1968: 29, for discussion). We can catch a glimpse of this in Aristophanes's *Frogs* (405 bce), when the god Dionysus mentions that he has been reading the *Andromeda* (presumably, Euripides's version, produced in 413 bce). It also stands to reason that comic parody of this sort thrives, both in responding to written texts and in being disseminated through them, as, more generally, does the culture of quotation (for example, in the direct quotations of Aeschylus and Euripides in the famous battle in the *Frogs*).

The move from a culture of orality to one based on literature was not linear and uniform, but the emergence of educational practices bound to writing, along with the appearance of major libraries, indicates a progressive reliance on writing as a cultural phenomenon for at least some segments of society. Such reliance seems to have increased dramatically in the 4th century BCE. Isocrates's role in collecting books— though the evidence is circumstantial and based partly on his wide excerpting of other authors—is doubtless a reflection of the increased number of books that were available and symptomatic of an emerging interest in collecting books into a library (Pinto 2013). Given Isocrates's longevity and role as an educator, his influence may have led to an increase in collecting and using written texts. Of course, we cannot be certain how common written texts were at any specific point of time, and our guesses about literacy rates are mere conjecture. Still, by 400 BCE, papyrus rolls had been depicted on red-figure vases for nearly a century and were being exported as far as away as the Black Sea (Pfeiffer 1968: 28; Pinto 2013: 94–95, argues for a library in Heraclea in the first half of the 4th c. BCE), giving some indication of increased literacy in the Greek-speaking world. It is equally unclear who owned or otherwise had access to texts (and to which texts). Yet it seems undeniable that the development of an intellectual culture dependent on *written* texts progressed unabated from the 5th century until the establishment of the Library and Mouseion in Alexandria.

Given the increase of written documents, one might reasonably expect that mythographical activities would evolve in response to such material and social changes. If early mythography sought to organize oral traditions through the new medium of writing, it stands to reason that the wider availability of various written texts—especially those that were focused specifically on the mythical storyworld—would present new opportunities for inquiry, especially if they offered innovative or variant versions of otherwise established traditions. The emergence of tragedy, not only as mimetic performance, but also as a literary genre, should not be underestimated, for tragedies offered a new target, one based on *genre*, for organizing and potentially analyzing mythical traditions. Writing now served two functions for the mythographical impulse: it made possible an ever-increasing material record from which to draw, and it was itself the medium in which to transmit myth, and every new piece of mythographical writing became a resource for future mythographers.

If mythography—in the sense of documentation, systemization, and analysis of the mythical storyworld—shifts in response to the increase in written documents, we also cannot ignore the important contributions of other intellectual currents, especially in philosophy, that affected responses to the stories of the distant past. Although there is hardly space here to consider all of these, it is worth emphasizing the important role of the Peripatetics in setting the stage for further developments in the Hellenistic period. What follows is deeply indebted to a recent article by Fowler (2019). First, in contrast to Plato, Aristotle, who often rejected *mythoi* as fictitious, nonetheless could accept an account that was consistent with his theoretical presuppositions—in other words, if it fit in as reputable of received opinions (*endoxa*) that could, by critical review, be somehow preserved (Johansen 1999: 283–285). Recently, Fowler (2019) has taken Johansen's basic idea and applied it systematically to the Peripatetics, arguing that they allowed for the legitimization of myths as useful knowledge, one that aimed not to neutralize through *demythologization*, but to rework traditional materials in a process of *remythologization*. If this is correct, "it lent the highest philosophical respectability to the idea that myth may, after all, be true, and gave the green light to multitudinous Hellenistic historians to include myth in their histories, no doubt yielding happily to natural inclination" (Fowler 2019: 51; see also Veyne 1983: 41–57, for the idea that the whole fabric of myth could not be a "gratuitous lie"). This position that myths have value no doubt gave validation to universal historians like Dicaearchus and Diodorus of Sicily—but it may even motivate authors who outwardly reject using material from the mythical storyworld to give it considerable space when it fits their narrative (Ephorus: Clarke 2008: 98–106; Polybius: Clarke 2007: 94–97; Strabo: Patterson 2017; also Patterson 2013).

Second, and more briefly, the Peripatetics seemed particularly interested in collecting and organizing myths in their own right as a separate subject—perhaps in part, as Fowler (2019: 44) suggests, to "assemble the *endoxa*" for further analysis. A number of titles indicate a focus on the myths in the tragedians (notably, Philochorus [about 340–261 BCE], who was also an Atthidographer), but there is also at least one collection of star myths by Hermippus of Smyrna (active 3rd c. BCE) and the tantalizing title "On Myths" by one Hieronymus of Rhodes (about 290–230 BCE), which at least treated Heracles and Tithonus in the three fragments that have been preserved for us. Whether or not the Peripatetics' collecting of myths was part of a wider cultural phenomenon or whether they were the first to introduce the practice is impossible to document, but certainly, "myth collecting was in the air" at the dawn of the Hellenistic period (Fowler 2019: 45).

## 2. ASCLEPIADES: THE FIRST MYTHOGRAPHER?

Since Wendel (1935: 1353–1354), it has been traditional to view Asclepiades (*BNJ* 12) as the first mythographer. A student of Isocrates (436–338 BCE), alongside Theopompus and Ephorus, Asclepiades was the author of a work entitled *Tragodoumena*, in six books, from which we have thirty-two fragments and a handful of testimonia. Asclepiades's importance is assumed from his citation by later authors as an authority (for example, in Apollod. *Bibl.* 2.6 and 3.7, and with some frequency in the scholia to Homer, Apollonius Rhodius, and Euripides). Asclepiades has been seen as representing the first flower of a Hellenistic scholarly mindset, whereby the approach to the mythical traditions represented by epic, lyric, and now tragic poetry was "of a philological nature and scientifically based" (Meliadò 2015: 1067; cf. Wendel 1935: 1353). It is often claimed either that Asclepiades "gathered mythological stories from the tragedians" (Higbie 2007: 245), or, more analytically, that he "examined myths treated by tragedians and compared them with well-known versions of archaic poetry and even earlier mythographers" (Meliadò 2015: 1067; Wendel 1935: 1353, more cautiously states that his reference to Pherecydes proves that he did not confine his work to tragedians). Such judgments then become part of the *communis opinio* (for instance, in Smith and Trzaskoma 2007: xxii–xxiii). But in fact, we do not have any explicit statement by Asclepiades, or any ancient authority, about his methodological approach, and the surviving miscellaneous fragments do not offer a clear picture of the organizational principles or structure of the overall work. This has led the editor of a recent edition and commentary on the fragments to state bluntly, "One cannot even be certain of what his work consisted" (Villagra Hidalgo 2012a: 290; see also 2012b: xii–xxiii), and this should be considered the proper *status quaestionis*. As the supposed first (Hellenistic) mythographer, Asclepiades offers us a test case for our presuppositions about our knowledge. The results show that our assumptions come up short.

If, for instance, we consider Asclepidaes's revelation of the Sphinx's riddle (fr. 7a–b; see Meccariello, this volume, sec. 2.1), we might assume that the work was aimed at clarifying allusions in tragedies—a sort of exegetical text to help with reading of their texts. Several other fragments, meanwhile, are found in *Zitatennester* (citation nests), where Asclepiades, alongside others, is named as an authority for a genealogical detail, giving the impression, perhaps misleadingly, that he was interested in collecting such variants himself. We also encounter rationalized interpretations of myths, for instance, that of the Thessalian women drawing down the moon (they just knew about eclipses, fr. 20; see also fr. 19, where Boreas is simply a king of the Celts). In addition, we find a surprising allegorical explanation attributed to Pherecydes in a supposed direct quotation of Asclepiades's words (fr. 3), but as has been pointed out, the language in the quotation is decidedly postclassical and probably does not belong either to Pherecydes or Ascelpiades (Villagra Hidalgo 2012a: 291). These inconsistencies, which on their face point to an extraordinarily motley work, may be some true refraction of the original nature of the work, but they may also simply owe to the vagaries of the transmission of mythological data. We are unable to judge between these or potential other possibilities based on our current knowledge.

When we consider the longer *historiai*, for instance, those recounted in the Homeric scholia in the style of the *Mythographus Homericus* (fr. 13–14, fr. 27–31), we come away with a completely different impression of the work. From these it appears that Asclepiades was interested in recording and transmitting full stories in self-contained narratives. We face here the added complexity that we must be on guard for such "blanket references," which may originally may have been attached to a single detail but then haphazardly applied to the whole narrative (on this phenomenon in mythography generally, see Cameron 2004: 93–94; for Asclepiades specifically, Villagra Hidalgo 2012a: 159–163). In Wendel's (1935: 1353) view these represented the continuous narrative that characterized the work. And yet, even if we suppose that they do belong to Asclepiades, it remains unclear exactly whether they are based on the content of tragedies themselves or other traditions, whether they are part of a larger discussion or comparison, and how they fit together with the other sorts of fragments mentioned above. Scholarly approaches to these narratives differ as well, and the same critic can offer varying opinions. For instance, we find the following interpretations in the commentary to fragments 27–31 of Asclepiades in *Brill's New Jacoby* (#12, Asirvatham 2014). Some narratives are seen as recording the basic plot of a tragedy. For instance, in this view fr. 27 is a recapitulation of Euripides's *Heracles* but with some additional details, whereas fr. 28 cannot come from the extant *Hippolytus* of Euripides, so it must be a plot summary of another of Euripides's plays or Sophocles's *Phaedra*. By contrast, the presentation of the myth in fr. 31, a lengthy narrative of Phineus with background stories for both Phineus and Jason, cannot be a summary since it provides mostly *background* material and only some material from a play (though we can't say which play). What we come away with, unless we have some a priori idea of what Asclepiades's work must have looked like, is rather vague; as Villagra Hidalgo (2012a: 290) summarizes, it may have been "some sort of compilation of myths used—or susceptible of being used—in tragedies."

Because tragedies were becoming more widely available to an elite public in this period, it is tempting in any case to view Asclepiades's *Tragodoumena* as the first mythographical treatment that accorded myth status *as a separate subject*—that is, as "myth" separate from the historical record of the past. And yet, Asclepiades was apparently not the first to write on the myths of a tragedian. A century or so earlier Glaucus of Rhegium (*FHG* 2.23–24 Müller)—if not a later Hellenistic Glaucus (see Jacoby 1910: 1418)—had composed *On the Myths of Aeschylus*, of which two meager fragments survive; these suggest that the work had to do with sources (fr. 1) and comparisons between lyric, epic, and tragic offerings. It may be simply because of availability bias that we highlight Asclepiades's contribution over that of someone like Glaucus. In that case, Asclepiades might not have been as innovative or as foundational as he has been made out to be. In the end, we are in aporia. If we grant Asclepiades status as *a* mythographer, which we are happy to concede, we still know essentially nothing about the nature of his mythography aside from its being tied, somehow, to the single genre of tragedy.

## 3. LYSIMACHUS: USING LIBRARIES AND COMPILATION

Lysimachus of Alexandria (probably early 2nd c. BCE; perhaps 1st c. BCE) seems to have been, from the twenty-two fragments that have been passed down to us (*BNJ* 382), an Alexandrian collector par excellence, who was interested not in canonical versions but in more obscure material that was made accessible through the accumulation of texts at the library of the Alexandrian Mouseion. Author of the *Theban Paradoxes* and *Nostoi*, Lysimachus apparently focused his work solely on the stories and genealogies of the mythical storyworld. If that impression is correct, then it is evident that myth was by this point firmly established as a separate area of inquiry and was so in the practices of the intellectual tradition. Because of the manner of composition, which we will treat presently, Jacoby argued that Lysimachus was not a historian, but a *grammatikos* involved in *peri*-literature (for instance, an essay or a monograph on a particular subject). Why Lysimachus chose to focus on Thebes and Trojan War narratives is not clear, and the structure of neither work can be readily determined from the attested fragments. This issue is complicated by the fact that Radtke (1893) scoured the scholia and produced another 116 potential unnamed fragments and that Jacoby admitted that of these a "great number is perhaps from Lysimachos." Here, we will content ourselves with those that are securely attested.

We are fortunate in the case of Lysimachus to have an indication of his methodological principles, which seem directed at bringing together disparate materials on the same subject (F1 *BNJ* = *FGrHist* 382):

> Concerning Europa and Cadmus's arrival at Thebes, Lysimachos has assembled in his first book of *Theban Paradoxes* a great deal of contradictory material (*hylēn diaphōnousan*).

Other fragments bear out Lysimachus's interest in digging out variant traditions and collecting them in one place, and he seems to have have taken great care to identify his sources, most of which are obscure to us. For instance, in a scholion from the *Argonautica* of Apollonius of Rhodes, we find a direct quotation that gives us a glimpse of the number and the kind of sources Lysimachus cites (fr. 8 = Schol. Ap. Rhod. 1.558):

> Apollonius follows the post-Homeric poets (*neōteroi*), saying that Achilles was raised by Cheiron. Some disagree also concerning the mother of Achilles, as Lysimachus of Alexandria says in the second book of the *Nostoi*, and I quote: "Souidas, Aristotle (the one who wrote *On Euboia*), the author of the *Phrygian Tales*, Daimachus, and Dionysius of Chalcis all have not allowed the widely circulated version concerning Achilles to stand, but instead some think that he was born of Thetis daughter of Cheiron, others of Philomela daughter of Actor."

In a manner that seems typical of the Alexandrian spirit of ferreting out curiosities (see Sistakou, this volume), Lysimachus was invested in recording unconventional versions of traditional myths, an approach captured in the title *Theban Paradoxes*, a work that reached at least thirteen books. The unexpected versions that Lysimachus reports, however, are firmly historicizing—no marvels of a fantastic sort. Heracles sacks Oechalia because the town demanded thirty talents of silver for Iphitus's death (fr. 3), and the Sphinx is simply a daughter of Laius (fr. 4). Remarks about Lysimachus's views, however, mask the fact that Lysimachus did not seem to offer his own assessment but was content to gather together the various views of others, which either reflects or helps to set the fashion for the style of noncommittal reference, which is found in later mythographers. The original text of the *Theban Paradoxes* may have also contained considerable narrative material. A good example of this involves a lengthy quotation from an otherwise unknown variant myth by an obscure writer, Arizelus (F2, our translation):

> There are even those who say that Oedipus' tomb is in the sacred enclosure of Demeter in Eteonus, after people transferred him from a certain unmarked place in Ceos. This is what Lysimachus says Arizelus narrates (*historein*) in the 13th book of his *Thebaika*: "When Oedipus died and his friends were planning on burying him in Thebes, the Thebans stopped them because of the misfortunes they had encountered earlier because Oedipus was accursed. So they took him to a spot in Boeotia (the region Thebes is in) called Ceos and buried him there. After this was done and some of the inhabitants were suffering some misfortunes, they figured that this was happening because of Oedipus' burial, and so they asked his friends to remove him from the land. Though puzzled at what was going on, they removed him and carried him to Eteonus. They wanted to bury him in secret, so they did so at night, in the sacred enclosure of Demeter, though they did not know that at the time. When it became clear what happened, the inhabitants of Eteonus sent an embassy to ask the god (Apollo) what they should do. The god said not to disturb the suppliant of the goddess, so this is where Oedipus was buried, and his shrine is called the Oedipodeion.

Lysimachus's other work was the *Nostoi*, in at least three books and perhaps as many as eleven (fr. 12). As we saw in the quotation on Achilles's mother (fr. 8), the content was not entirely focused on the aftermath of the Trojan War but seems to have treated other parts of the Trojan legend. From what we can glean from the fragments, the work mostly treated the returns and family genealogies of not only the Greek heroes but also the Trojans. In terms of the latter, one fragment from the scholia of Euripides's *Andromache* informs us that Lysimachus recorded the opinions of those who wrote that Astyanax did not die in Troy but went on to found several cities, ending with a lengthy excerpt from Dionysius of Chalcis (F9; see F6 on the fate of the Antenoridai). Other fragments—mostly from scholia to tragedies—cover the contested offspring of Neoptolemos, Hermione and Andromache (fr. 10, citing Proxenos's *Epirote History* and Nicomedes's *Macedonian History*), of Helen (fr. 12), Odysseus's sister (fr. 11), and his numerous offspring (fr. 15).

In the end, we have good reason to securely place Lysimachus among mythographers. His subject matter is explicitly myth of the systematizing sort, and he demonstrates at a relatively early period the typical mythographical citation practices we find in later mythographers. At the same time, it is difficult to get any sense of the overall texture of his attested works or to determine their precise intellectual aims or imagined audience. The mixture we find in the fragments of the recording of mythical data, especially genealogical information, with lengthier and fuller narrative finds no precise parallels in later imperial mythography, even if they are recognizably of the same tradition. So, while he was clearly a source eventually mined for scholia, his interests—aside from a fascination with obscure variants—are hard to trace as direct influences on subsequent mythographers.

# 4. APOLLODORUS OF ATHENS: A MYTHOGRAPHER?

Our last case study involves a figure whose intellectual output was certainly influential but whose role as a mythographer has been, in our view, misunderstood. Apollodorus of Athens—so called to distinguish him from Ps.-Apollodorus, author of the *Bibliotheca*—lived in the 2nd century BCE and in antiquity was identified as a *grammatikos*. He was a student of the famed Homeric scholar Aristarchus, a good indication that he was active in Alexandria, probably in the period before Ptolemy VIII drove out the scholars in 145 BCE. Thereafter, he almost certainly settled in another academic center, Pergamon, where he would dedicate his *Chronica*, a chronological work that starts with the fall of Troy, to his patron Attalus II in 143 BCE. He likely returned to Athens at the end of his life, perhaps after the death of Attalus III in 133 BCE. In addition to learning at the feet of Aristarchus and plying his trade at the two great libraries in the Greek world, he was the student of the Stoic Diogenes of Babylon, whose influence may have helped shape his approach to the theological work *On the Gods* (*Peri Theon*). In addition to the two works already mentioned, Apollodorus authored a major study of Homeric geography entitled *On the Catalog of Ships*, other geographical works, etymological studies, literary essays on Epicharmus and Sophron, and a compilation about courtesans.

Although Apollodorus's other works engaged tangentially with myth from time to time, the range of his scholarly activity is an important indication that Apollodorus did not conceive of himself as solely a Homeric scholar or a mythographer. In this context, however, we will focus on *On the Gods* (*BNJ* 244 fr. 88–153; see also fr. 352–357) because this fragmentary work and its subject matter have led to the frequent inclusion of Apollodorus in surveys of Hellenistic mythography (see Meliadò 2015: 1074–1077; Wendel 1935: 1356–1357) and to his mention as a mythographer. Modern scholars, moreover, have regarded *On the Gods* as an especially rich source of mythological material that was mined by later mythographers. In its most extreme form, this view sees *On the Gods* as the primary source behind the imperial mythographical text, the *Bibliotheca*, which has been passed down to us as the work of one Apollodorus (see Trzaskoma, this volume). Despite the vast differences in the nature of the fragments of the Hellenistic Apollodorus's work and the surviving *Bibliotheca*, that view continues to crop up: Obbink (2004: 201) judges the *Bibliotheca* to be a Roman-era epitome, while Bremmer (2011: 529) views it as mostly dependent on the Hellenistic work of Apollodorus of Athens, a sort of pale, pedestrian reflection of it, lacking the brilliance of the original work of the *grammatikos* who was, in Pfeiffer's view, one of the epigoni of the great Alexandrian scholars (1968: 252–266). As Henrichs (1987: 242) vividly and confidently puts it, Apollodorus of Athens was "one of the most knowledgeable authorities on Greek mythology in the Hellenistic period" and "searched the remotest corners of Greek literature for significant myths that would highlight the characteristics of individual gods and heroes." In line with the generally pessimistic tone we have adopted throughout this chapter, our judgment is that this says a lot on little evidence. Apollodorus has, like so many lost intermediaries, become somewhat outsized in the scholarly imagination in the absence of clarity. Although we in general agree with Henrichs that Apollodorus was likely well-versed in mythology and, like other Alexandrian scholars, took advantage of the reference resources at his disposal, it is unclear to what extent narrative myths were employed in *On the Gods*, and there is little indication that heroes were centrally important to it. Even if we are to understand from Photius's remarks that *On the Gods* did treat heroes (more below), it seems that it only treated a selection of them. However, when we look at the *Bibliotheca,* we find the opposite; only a small portion of it focuses on divine figures (Apollod. *Bibl.* 1.1–44); the bulk of the narrative is devoted to heroic lineages and individuals. If this is a reflection of *On the Gods,* then it is a massively distorted one.

Unlike in the case of Asclepiades's *Tragodoumena,* we can say more about the content of *On the Gods* because we have a greater number of fragments and testimonials about it. Still, as with Asclepiades's work, we are woefully ignorant of its structure and uncertain about its overall aims. With regard to purpose, however, we have enough to say that *On the Gods* was clearly theological in nature and was concerned with divinities, their names, epithets, and cult titles, as well as with some rituals (though it is unclear how these were connected to the work on the divinities). There are also indications that *On the Gods* was oriented, at least in part, to Homeric scholarship, and it is clear that Apollodorus compiled lists, sometimes adding quotations from poetic sources (more on this below). What is not obvious, however, is how all the material was organized or whether the work included any systematic presentation of narrative myths, such that it could serve as the source for the later imperial work's form of presentation. To anticipate our conclusion, there is little to suggest it did. In other words, while *On the Gods* was a theological text, in our view it was not necessarily a mythographical one, even if it proved to be an excellent source for mythographers.

What do we know of *On the Gods*? Let us consider a reference to Apollodorus's work as the source for the excerpts of the sophist Sopater, found in Photius's *Bibliotheca* (161 p. 103a18 = *BNJ* 244 T11, our translation):

> The first book—which has been excerpted from the third book of Apollodorus' *On the Gods*—treats the gods that are mythologized in Greek culture (*peri tōn par' Hellēsi mythologoumenōn theōn*). Apollodorus was Athenian, a *grammatikos* by training . . . [Photius notes that this material does not come only from Book 3 but from several books of *On the Gods*.] In this collection he [Sopater] has incorporated both the details that have been mythically invented about the gods (*ta te mythikōs peri theōn diapeplasmena*), including if anything has been told in the form of a story, and material about the heroes among the gods—both the Dioscuri and those in Hades—and all such things.

There is much uncertainty about this excerpt, in particular, about what it means for the gods to be "mythologized." Meliadò interprets it as "the first [book], then, deals with Greek theology expressed in the myths," and then says, "this sylloge embraced . . . the invented myths about the gods" (2015: 1075). The translation in *BNJ* goes further in seeing this as involving narrative accounts: "In this collection are the mythic tales that were fashioned about the gods." But the Greek itself resists such a totalizing interpretation; instead, it targets the *aspects* of stories or elements that have been invented because of an improper understanding of the true etymologies, which have in turn led to misunderstandings of the true nature of the gods. In fact, the addition of "including if anything has been told in the form of a story" emphasizes that the previous mention of details does not necessarily mean "stories" of any sort and indicates that narrative was the exception rather than the rule.

Critics have also tended to assume that the early part of Sopater's work is basically equivalent to the work of Apollodorus, which may be true, but we must be cautious. After all, Photius notes two additional sources for the first book, Juba's *On Painting* and Athenaeus's *Deipnosophistae*, and in any case, we do not have any real indication of Sopater's method of excerption. He certainly selected material from Apollodorus, but in the process must have left material out, just as he added and commingled material from his other sources. Whether the narrative material Photius saw was largely or entirely derived from Apollodorus is simply unclear. Moreover, regarding the mention of "heroes" at the end, it is worth pointing out that the fragments of Apollodorus that have been passed down to us are devoid of any mention of the heroes, and, Photius seems to indicate, if we understand the phrase *par' autois* (among them) correctly as meaning "among the gods," then whatever heroic discussion was in Sopater was apparently limited to heroes that were objects of cult practices. Moreover, when we consider the surviving fragments of Apollodorus, we find that mythical stories or, better, *elements of stories*, are provided in only the briefest compass and used as a foil for an alternative interpretation, usually based on an etymology that offers a clue to the nature of the god rather than a correction to a narrative. For instance, after briefly mentioning (fr. 130) that in myth (*mythikōs*) Hermes was called Cyllenian because he was born on Mt. Cyllene, Apollodorus gives the interpretation based on an etymology that indicates his true nature: as the giver of sleep, he holds the reins of the under-eye parts (*kyl-* or *kylad-*). Here, the broader mythical narrative is only implied; Apollodorus, for his part, is taking issue with one element of the myth, not the entire myth or its broad narrative.

Another important testimony to *On the Gods* comes from a papyrus fragment from Herculaneum that has been identified as part of Philodemus's *On Piety* (fr. 103a = T9):

> Apollodorus, who composed the twenty-four books on the gods and included nearly everything in them (*ta panta schedon eis tauta analōsas*), even if he occasionally fights back against the "unifiers," he does not . . .

The fragment is without context, and the text breaks off at the column end, but it confirms the number of books and hints at the interpretive approach connected to the Stoic "unifiers," who attempted to connect different divinities under one nature (see Henrichs 1975: 14–15). However, it it is not entirely certain what the phrase *ta panta . . . analōsas* exactly means. It seems sufficiently clear that the writer meant that Apollodorus was exhaustive. But does this mean exhaustive in the sense that he "put all of his energy toward this purpose," as Henrichs would have it, or in the sense of providing a comprehensive set of mythical narratives that are associated with the gods, as Schober rendered it (Henrichs 1975: 15, with n. 59, citing Schober's unpublished dissertation)?

We get a revealing look into Apollodorus's methods in another papyrus that seems to be taken directly from his own work (*P.Köln* 5604 = *BNJ* 244 fr. 105d). In it we find extensive discussion of Athena's epithet Pallas. At the beginning, the author repeats what he had said elsewhere in a treatment of Epicharmus, which involves a very short quotation of the poet describing how Athena leapt out of the head of Zeus, destroyed Pallas, the foremost of those who were fighting alongside Cronus, and wrapped his skin around her. But from this point on we encounter first-person language, when the author remarks that he had fallen upon (*periepesomen*) an anonymous poem with the title *Meropis*. In this work, the flaying episode took place not during the Titanomachy, but in Heracles's war against the Coans, one of whom, named Asterus, was invulnerable to Heracles's attacks. Athena comes to Heracles's aid, kills Asterus and, recognizing the usefulness of his skin, wraps it around her feet and hands. The writer further tells us that the poem seemed post-Homeric, and that the peculiarity of the content (*idiōma tēs historias*) had prompted him to excerpt it, though the papyrus breaks off here and we do not know the extent of the excerpting.

This episode offers a testimony to what must have been a common practice in Alexandria and Pergamum, where *grammatici* and other writers would have reduced a poetical work to a prose summary that could then be taken over by later authors with or, more often, without attribution. But it is not entirely clear that this one example of narrative—entirely unparalleled as it is in other fragments—is proof positive that Apollodorus systematically included narratives as a methodology. Critics who assume that he did overlook an important fact: Apollodorus introduced the narrative—in brief compass, at that—precisely because it was a surprising and unique version. The way it is introduced strongly suggests that Apollodorus did not regularly include narratives for narrative's sake but only in the service of other aims. A survey of the preserved fragments shows that very few of them even assume a narrative, much less provide a full version of one, and because of the nature of citation, it is not always clear that Apollodorus is the source. See fr. 94 (Areopagus); fr. 111b (Tauropolos); fr. 119 (Zeus deflowers Hera on Samos in secret, which is why the Samians sleep with their wives in secret before the public ceremony); fr. 122 (Naxians call Amphitrite Poseidonia because Poseidon carried her off from there); fr. 133a (*aition* for the Choes festival during the Anthesteria).

In the vast majority of fragments, Apollodorus is primarily focused on the etymological interpretation of the gods' natures, epithets, and cult titles, and he tends to reject explanations that are based on narratives from the mythical storyworld (as we saw in fr. 130), preferring to show how they indicate the natures of the gods. For instance, Zeus Dodonaeus was named based on the fact that he gives (*didōmi*) us good things (fr. 88); the Charites come from "joy" (*chara*, fr. 90); Leto is from *eleētō* because she is kind and gentle (fr. 121); the name of the sun (Helios or Iēios) is derived from its movements (*iesthai* or *ienai*) through the heavens (fr. 95a, b; see also the 29 fragments under fr. 99 on Apollo's name and epithets, with no reference to a narrative myth). If anything, it appears that Apollodorus's intent is to ignore as much of the mythical storyworld involving the gods as possible.

It may be that the fragments are misleading and that further discoveries might reveal that *On the Gods* was a rich work that blended narratives, continuous genealogies, and analysis of epithets and rituals—such that it could have been the basis for the later author of the *Bibliotheca* and a model for narrative mythography more generally. But on balance, our current evidence suggests that this is an overoptimistic view of the work—and it certainly is not enough to insist that the imperial *Bibliotheca* is a direct descendant of or heavily dependent on the work of Apollodorus the Athenian. In sum, it is difficult to argue at all that *On the Gods* is work of mythography; it has the character more of a theological study that only occasionally engages with the mythical world, when the theological aspects merit it.

# 6. Some Conclusions

From the late 4th century to the beginning of the imperial period, we have one somewhat intact mythographical work (that of Palaephatus) and a dizzying array of fragments and testimonia from authors we regularly think of as mythographers or, at least, as engaging in related work. Although it is tempting to flesh out our record by drawing lines of influence from the late Classical period through these Hellenistic writers, and to attribute to them much of the shape and material found in the later surviving mythographies, this is a hazardous venture. We have tried to indicate here some of the ways in which Hellenistic work has been assessed that go beyond what the evidence allows. Our three case studies could easily be multiplied many times over, especially through the investigation of just how little we know about the vast majority of such writers—writers for whom we have nothing like the evidence we have for a Lysimachus or an Apollodorus. There is much to be gained from new, fresh studies of mythographical activity in the Hellenistic period, but such inquiry must proceed from a more skeptical initial orientation and take into account the limits of the evidence. Mythography, as this entire handbook makes clear, is a complex and heterogeneous category, and simple assumptions about what Hellenistic mythography must have looked like are to be avoided.

## Further Reading

Although there is no comprehensive survey of mythography and myth criticism from the 4th-century to the imperial period, there are several good starting points. Wendel (1935) surveys the period from the "inception" of mythography (Asclepiades) down through the imperial period, although the narrative for the Hellenistic period presents a neater picture than the evidence allows. Other general studies that include the Hellenistic period are Lightfoot (1999) and Meliadò (2015). Higbie (2007), despite her title, focuses less on the Hellenistic period than on the extant texts from the imperial period. Alganza Roldán (2006) provides a good overview of the difficulties of defining mythography and a corpus of texts for the Hellenistic period.

Individual mythographers are included in Jacoby's *Fragmenta der Griechischen Historiker*, now with an updated translation and commentary, in *Brill's New Jacoby* (*BNJ*), which is available behind a paywall. For studies of Asclepiades (*BNJ* 12), see Villagra Hidalgo (2012a, 2012b). For Lysimachus, see *BNJ* 382, with Jacoby's commentary at *FGrHist* 382, with Radtke (1893) as an important study for possible further evidence for him in the scholia and in Alexander Polyhistor. For Apollodorus of Athens (*BNJ* 144) most of the studies are likewise from the 19th century; at present Pfeiffer (1968: 252–266) is a good starting point for Apollodorus generally; on the mythography of *On the Gods*, see Meliadò (2015: 1074–1077); for a detailed argument for how the catalogs in Philodemus's *On Piety* relate to Apollodorus's *On the Gods*, see Henrichs (1975).

On the approach of Aristarchus, Apollodorus's predecessor, to myth in his exegesis of Homeric poetry, see Nünlist (2019) and Schironi (2018: 265–339 on *historiai*, and 661–708 on Homer and the *neoteroi*). Pfeiffer (1968) and Fraser (1972) are useful general discussions of Alexandrian scholarship. For broader studies on the period, see Easterling (1985); Gutzwiller (2007); Sistakou, this volume; Préaux (1978, a general account). Other valuable material can be found in the other chapters in this handbook on texts related to the Hellenistic period.

## References

Alganza Roldán, Minerva. 2006. "La mitografía como género de la prosa helenistica." *Florentina Iliberritana* 17: 9–37.

Asirvatham 2014 = Asclepiades of Tragilos *BNJ* #12.

Bremmer, Jan N. 2011. "A Brief History of the Study of Greek Mythology." In *A Companion to Greek Mythology*, edited by Ken Dowden and Niall Livingstone, 527–547. Chichester, UK and Malden, MA: Wiley-Blackwell.

Cameron, Alan. 2004. *Greek Mythography in the Roman World*. Oxford: Oxford University Press.

Clarke, Katherine. 2007. *Between Geography and History: Hellenistic Constructions of the Roman World*. Oxford: Oxford University Press.

Clarke, Katherine. 2008. *Making Time for the Past: Local History and the Polis*. Oxford: Oxford University Press.

Easterling, Patricia E. 1985. "Book and Readers in the Greek World." In *The Cambridge History of Classical Literature*, edited by Patricia E. Easterling and Bernard M. W. Knox, 1–41. Cambridge, UK, and New York: Cambridge University Press.

Fowler, Robert. 2019. "Myth(ography), History and the Peripatos." In *Host or Parasite: Mythographers and Their Contemporaries in the Classical and Hellenistic Periods*, edited by Allen J. Romano and John Marincola, 29–52. Berlin and Boston: De Gruyter.

Fraser, Peter M. 1972. *Ptolemaic Alexandria*, 3 vols. Oxford: Oxford University Press.

Gutzwiller, Kathryn. 2007. *A Guide to Hellenistic Literature*. Malden, MA: Blackwell.

Henrichs, Albert. 1975. "Philodemos *De Pietate* als mythographische Quelle." *Cronache Ercolanesi* 5: 5–38.

Henrichs, Albert. 1987. "Three Approaches to Mythography." In *Interpretations of Greek Mythology*, edited by Jan N. Bremmer, 242–277. London and Sydney: Croom Helm.

Higbie, Carolyn. 2007. "Hellenistic Mythographers." In *The Cambridge Companion to Greek Mythology*, edited by Roger D. Woodard, 237–254. Cambridge, UK: Cambridge University Press.

Jacoby, Felix. 1910. "Glaukos von Rhegion." In *Realencyclopädie der classischen Altertumswissenschaft (RE)* 7.1: 1417–1420.

Johansen, Thomas K. 1999. "Myth and Logos in Aristotle." In *From Myth to Reason? Studies in the Development of Greek Thought*. Edited by Richard Buxton, 279–291. Oxford: Oxford University Press.

Lightfoot, Jane L. 1999. *Parthenius of Nicaea. The Poetical Fragments and the Ἐρωτικὰ Παθήματα*. Oxford: Oxford University Press.

Meliadò, Claudio. 2015. "Mythography." In *Brill's Companion to Ancient Greek Scholarship*, vol. 1, edited by Franco Montanari, Stephanos Matthaios, and Antonios Rengakos, 1057–1089. Leiden and Boston: Brill.

Nünlist, René. 2019. "Questions of Mythology as Seen through the Eyes of a Hellenistic Critic." In *Host or Parasite: Mythographers and Their Contemporaries in the Classical and Hellenistic Periods*, edited by Allen J. Romano and John Marincola, 53–74. Berlin and Boston: De Gruyter.

Obbink, Dirk. 2004. "Vergil's *De Pietate*: From *Ehoiae* to Allegory in Vergil, Philodemus, and Ovid." In *Vergil, Philodemus, and the Augustans*, edited by David Armstrong, Jeffrey Fish, Patricia A. Johnston, and Marilyn B. Skinner, 175–209. Austin: University of Texas Press.

Patterson, Lee. 2013. "Geographers as Mythographers: The Case of Strabo." In *Writing Myth: Mythography in the Ancient World*, edited by Stephen M. Trzaskoma and R. Scott Smith, 201–221. Leuven: Peeters.

Patterson, Lee. 2017. "Myth as Evidence in Strabo." In *The Routledge Companion to Strabo*, edited by Daniela Dueck, 276–293. London and New York: Routledge.

Pfeiffer, Rudolf. 1968. *History of Classical Scholarship from the Beginnings to the End of the Hellenistic Age*. Oxford: Oxford University Press.

Pinto, Pasquale M. 2013. "Men and Books in 4th-Century BC Athens." In *Ancient Libraries*, edited by Jason König, Katerina Oikonomopoulou, and Greg Woolf, 85–95. Cambridge, UK: Cambridge University Press.

Préaux, Claire. 1978. *Le monde hellénistique*. 2 vols. Paris: Presses Universitaires de France.

Radtke, Guilelmus. 1893. "De Lysimacho Alexandrino." Diss. Strasbourg.

Schironi, Francesca. 2018. *The Best of the Grammarians: Aristarchus of Samothrace on "The Iliad."* Ann Arbor: University of Michigan Press.

Smith, R. Scott, and Stephen M. Trzaskoma. 2007. *Apollodorus' "Library" and Hyginus' "Fabulae."* Indianapolis, IN: Hackett.

Veyne, Paul. 1983. *Did the Greeks Believe in Their Myths? An Essay on the Constitutive Imagination*. Translated by Paula Wissing. Chicago: University of Chicago Press.

Villagra Hidalgo, Nereida. 2012a. "Commenting on Asclepiades of Tragilos: Methodological Considerations on a Fragmentary Mythographer." In *Estudiar el passado: Aspectos metodológicos de la investigación en Ciencias de la Antigüedad y de la Edad Media*, edited by Ainoa Castro Correa, Daniel Gómez Castro, Gerard González Germain, Katarzyna K. Starczewska, Joan Oller Guzmán, Arnald Puy Maeso, et al., 289–296. Oxford: BAR International.

Villagra Hidalgo, Nereida. 2012b. "Τραγῳδούμενα: Edición crítica, traducción y comentario de los fragmentos atribuidos a Asclepíades de Tragilo." Diss. Barcelona.

Wendel, Carl. 1935. "Mythographie." In *RE* 16.2 (1935): 1352–1374.

Wilamowitz-Moellendorff, Ulrich von. 1907. *Einleitung in die griechischen Tragödie*. Berlin: Weidmann.

...................................................................................

# CHAPTER 4

# IMPERIAL MYTHOGRAPHY

...................................................................................

### CHARLES DELATTRE

To speak of "Greek mythography in the imperial period" implies the existence of two preconditions: first, that mythography constitutes an identifiable corpus that one can delimit with precision;[1] and second, that the imperial period is a chronological stratum appropriate, in particular, for the study of this corpus. For various reasons, neither of these two premises seems completely operational. We will thus speak here of Greek mythography, not as a genre, but rather as a complex ensemble of writing practices, whose borders with other practices remain porous. Similarly, the Imperial period does not constitute an autonomous block between the Hellenistic period and late antiquity—even if historians of antiquity normally adopt this division—and should take into account regional microhistories, which each have their own dynamics. Even the use of the Greek language is susceptible to new interpretations in a space where "being Greek" or "being Roman" does not have a stable or unequivocal meaning (see also Smith, this volume, on Latin Mythography).

## 1. WHAT IS IMPERIAL IN IMPERIAL GREEK MYTHOGRAPHY?

.......................................................................................

The eruption of Rome into Greek affairs and the development of the province of Asia in the 2nd century BCE led to the integration of Greek language and culture into the Roman system of government. The political and social crises of the first century BCE, from the Athenian revolt in 88 BCE to the conquest of Alexandria in 30 BCE, and to the organization of new provinces (for example, Achaea, Creta-Cyrenaica), placed into question the relations between Greek populations and the Roman power. The Augustan pacification,

---

[1] This chapter was translated by Alexander Brock.

followed by imperial administration, imposed a new order. Do the mythographic texts from this period carry the trace of these developments?

The first effect of the new imperial order is a change in the world's dimensions, in particular toward the west and the north. After the Roman expansion toward the east following the conquests of Alexandria, Greek texts take into greater account the western regions of Europe: Italy, of course, but also Gaul and Hispania. Strabo's *Geography* (3: Iberian Peninsula; 4: Gaul, Britain, and the Alps; 5–6: Italy and Sicily; 7: north, east, and central Europe) shows the possible extent of the Greek view toward the west. One can nevertheless compare this space opened in the west with the more limited references to it in Ps.-Plutarch's *De Fluviis* (6: Gaul; 16: Hispania), in which the author follows the interest in the east that had been developed by the lists of rivers of the Hellenistic period (for example, *P.Berol.* 13044, col. 11–12, from the 2nd c. BCE). The example from the western Mediterranean coast is, of course, an exception, given the presence of Greek populations in the region since the end of the Archaic period.

Certain Greek mythographers fully adapt to these modifications: Ps.-Plutarch's *Parallela minora* (more fully known as *Synagōgē historiōn parallēlōn Hellēnikōn kai Rhōmaikōn*) offers in Greek a catalogue of stories, principally situated in Greek and Roman regions, which were constructed in parallel. Hellenocentric anecdotes are taken from the mythic and historical tradition (the epic and tragic cycles, the cycles of Heracles and Theseus, the story of Midas of Phrygia, the Persian Wars, the wars of Philip, the Gallic wars). Romanocentric anecdotes mainly refashion the Roman mythic and historical tradition (Romulus, Decius, the Punic Wars, and so on) while also mentioning neighboring peoples (Falerii in Etruria, Segesta in Sicily). On the other hand, Ps.-Apollodorus in his *Library* omits any reference to Rome, even though the inclusion of the characters Aeneas, Odysseus, or Heracles gave him the opportunity to do so (Fletcher 2008). Ps.-Apollodorus thus contributes to the Hellenocentric and classicizing framework of Greek mythology (Trzaskoma and Smith 2008). Through the choice of referring only to traditions from the archaic and classical periods, or of introducing into their texts regions thenceforth politically administrated by Rome, mythographers reflect less the new Mediterranean space in which they live than the diverse cultural choices that are available in this space. In many instances, there is no direct correlation between the elites' nationality and the Greek or Roman identity of their adopted cultural referents. The Roman elite, for example, do not necessarily choose specifically Roman legends for the decorative programs in their villas, whether under the republic or under the empire (Zanker 1995: 27–28; Newby 2016).

Through their geographical choices, mythographers take part in a debate concerning what it means to be Greek or Roman in the Imperial period. Spawforth (2012), following Wallace-Hadrill (2008), has shown how certain decisions of the Augustan administration could be understood as expressions of a cultural politics aimed at integrating Greek culture into the new Roman order. The result of these politics may have been a new Greek identity, defined in terms, not of geographic division or historical continuity, but of language and culture. Being Greek would no longer mean being associated with a city-state or dominion, but rather, being able to demonstrate a *paideia*, an *ethos*, and a linguistic control, independently from national, provincial, and familial origins. In the words of Whitmarsh (2005: 15), "To practice paideia was to strive for a very particular form of identity, a fusion of manliness, elitism and Greekness." The mythographic corpus is one of the promoters of this *paideia*, whose contents it helps to construct. It is also one of its consequences, since it is this *paideia*, redefined in the terms of the elite who were in power—whether at a local level or in the large imperial cities—that gives the mythographic corpus its specific form and distinguishes it from texts of the Hellenistic period and their themes. As a result, the distinction between Greek and Latin texts should not lead one to forget their convergences, such as borrowings, translations, or hybridizations. One could cite the texts of Hyginus or Dictys of Crete as possible results of this phenomenon.

## 2. SOURCES: INCREASED DOCUMENTATION

Compared to classical and Hellenistic times, the Roman period presents us with a significantly larger number of surviving texts. This increase could be the result of chance in terms of what sources survive; it could also bear witness to an increased production of mythographic works, whether this be limited to a specific body of work or extends to neighboring textual practices (history, paradoxography, and so forth).

The nature of the extant texts also changes from the preceding period. First, an abundant quantity of papyrological material is available and reflects the diversity of writing practices. Certain mythographic texts are summaries of other works (for example, dramatic *hypotheseis*) that transform poetic texts into a plot centred on the characters' actions. Other texts are lists of names (*P.Oxy.* 61.4097–4099, from the beginning of the Roman period) or dictionaries, such as *P.Mich.* 1447 (end of the 2nd c. or beginning of the 3rd c. CE). The only column preserved from this latter papyrus contains five items, arranged in alphabetical order, devoted to characters who have undergone a metamorphosis (Renner 1978; van Rossum-Steenbeck no. 70). *P.Oxy.* 62.4308 is a mixed example: this papyrus from the 2nd century CE reformulates a catalogue from Hesiod's *Theogony* into the form of a list of names (van Rossum-Steenbeck 1998: no. 58; see Hesiod, *Th.* 975–1018).

Though some of these papyri were written with care for a learned public who used them as documentary sources for their own works, the majority were written in cursive, sometimes quickly or negligently, and are interpreted as documents from a school environment. One can contrast two texts that are nevertheless similar: that of *P.Mich.* 1315, from the end of the 2nd or beginning of the 3rd century CE (van Rossum-Steenbeck 1998: no. 36), written by an experienced hand and which could have served as a reading companion to the *Iliad*; and that of *P.Mich.* 1319, from the end of the 3rd or beginning of the 4th century CE (Cribiore 1996: no. 301; van Rossum-Steenbeck 1998: 13), which contains a "narrative exercise" (*diēgēma*) modeled on the *hypothesis* of the Euripides's

*Temenides* or *Temenos*, and written down (or recopied) in two versions by two different individuals.

In an educational setting, mythographic texts have clearly documentary and pedagogical functions, and can be considered a secondary textual product: the texts are used as an aid for interpreting a text, or for mastering a writing exercise (see Smith and Trzaskoma on education in this volume). The mythographic production from Roman-era academic settings does not significantly differ in kind from what was practiced in the Hellenistic period. A witness to this is the "school book" from the 3rd century BCE (*P.Cair.* LV 445), in which the practice of borrowing words from the poetic tradition (nouns, adjectives, etc.) is used to construct rules and examples of declination. Certain texts transmitted by Roman-era papyri could indeed have been written, in one form or another, at any time starting from the Hellenistic period. Yet the fact that they were still in use, that they were rewritten and read in the Imperial period, makes them products of that era as well.

Another difference between the Hellenistic and Imperial periods is that substantial texts that were written in the latter period have survived. Our interpretation of mythographic information no longer depends on fragmentary texts but can take into account works that are complex in form and can include questions about order and structure. The simple fact of possessing complete texts allows us to determine authorial strategies with greater certainty and eliminates the necessity of passing through the prism of citations and distortion. Admittedly, the medieval manuscripts that transmit these texts are not themselves direct witnesses to the Imperial period and could contain significant modifications compared to the state of the text at its moment of composition and diffusion. Thus, the last books of Ps.-Apollodorus's *Library* are only conserved in the form of a compendium, transmitted in two diverging versions by *Vat. gr.* 950 and *Sabb. Hierosol.* 366. These compressed texts contrast with the abundance of details and structural complexity of the first three books. The text of Conon, and, even more, that of Ptolemy Chennus, are only available through the summaries provided by Photius in the 9th century CE (*Bibl.*, [Cod. 186], 130b–142b and [Cod. 190], 146a–b). Nor did the mythographic texts themselves necessarily exist in an individual state from their beginning: multiple versions could have been distributed when they were first recopied, complicating any attempt to identify an individual mythographic text. This is the case for the *Mythographus Homericus*, passages of which are known both from papyrological fragments and from the D-scholia to Homer (see Pagès Cebrián 2007, who usefully compares the different versions of the text from two documentary traditions, as well as Pagès in this volume). Nonetheless, it remains the case that our documentation is, under the Empire, in part composed of stable texts identified by a title and, in most cases, by an author's name. In some instances, the name seems authentic, but the individual is unknown (Antoninus Liberalis); at other times, the name designates an otherwise known author: the identification should be sometimes accepted (Parthenius of Nicaea, Plutarch) and sometimes rejected (hence "Ps. Plutarch", as opposed to "Plutarch"). It is these texts that have attracted editors' attention since the Renaissance, and which form the heart of projects for scholarly editions today.

Within this group of texts, one must undoubtedly set apart the *Palatinus Graecus* 398 from the second half of the 9th century CE. Without this manuscript, three complete mythographic treatises from the Imperial period would have remained unknown: the *Disastrous Love Stories* by Parthenius of Nicaea (*Erōtika Pathēmata*), the *Collection of Metamorphoses* (*Metamōrphōseōn Synagōgē*) by Antoninus Liberalis, and *On Rivers* (*Peri Potamōn kai Orōn Epōnymias*, more usually known as *De Fluviis*) by Ps.-Plutarch. And yet, an analysis of this manuscript as a whole is still wanting. The *Palatinus Graecus* 398 presents itself as a compilation of texts that are themselves compilations, which are organized around questions of geography, mythography, paradoxography, and biography. Our analysis of mythography from the Imperial period depends in part on the editorial practices that this scribe adopted for his (still to be defined) well-educated audience in Byzantium.

Finally, our documentation can include epigraphic documents that follow strategies created during the Hellenistic period. Certain inscriptions allude to or partially reproduce mythographic texts that were written by local or itinerant scholars and which are used by the city that erects the stela as a means of recognizing the scholar. This is the case for P. Anteius Antiochus, a native of Aegae in Sicily in the 2nd century CE, whom the city of Argos honored for his role in renewing the bonds of friendship between Argos and Aegae. The honorific inscription employs the example of Perseus, prince of Argos, who passed through Aegae in the course of his adventures (*SEG* 1.69 = *BCH* 101 (1977) 120–132; see Clarke 2008: 359). The state of the stone does not permit greater elucidation of Perseus's actions. Nevertheless, it is adequate to reveal the example of Perseus as a hybrid text, mythographic in its form, historical in regard to its mention of a far-off past that the inhabitants of Argos accept as true, and transactional within the framework of a diplomatic negotiation.

We arrive here at the limits of mythography, whose borders with historiography, in particular, are fluid. Nothing indeed forbids us from including in our Imperial period corpus extracts from historians (for example, Dionysius of Halicarnassus, *Rom. Ant.*, 1–2) or from authors who include historico-mythographic texts in their own work, such as the periegete Pausanias (for example, 4.2.2–3, 8.15.6–7) and the geographer Strabo. Numerous local histories (*Argolika*, *Lakonika*, for example.) could also be included, which historians and periegetes claim to be the documentary sources they consulted, whether they were actually written and fixed in a text or produced in conversation. With these last extensions, the mythographic corpus explodes and expands into the entirety of written practices during the Imperial period.

# 3. DIVERSITY OF MYTHOGRAPHIC PRACTICES

By comparing these different types of documents, we can gain an idea of the diversity of mythographic practices in the Imperial period. The fundamental unity in the mythographic project, whose function A. Westermann described in his 1843 edition as telling "the plot of the poems" (*historia poetica*), is not derived from notions of "character," "story," and "myth," but rather from specific narrative functions.

## 3.1. Secondary Literature and Commentary

First, following Westermann's definition, a large portion of mythographic texts can be understood as secondary literature and, more specifically, as commentary literature. They could thus be included under the third section of grammar defined by Dionysius of Thrace (*Ars grammatica*, 1 Lallot = pp. 5–6 Uhlig), which has as its aim "the easily accessible clarification of stories and rare words" (*glōssōn te kai historiōn prokheiros apodosis*). In this way, mythographic texts fulfil a twofold function. On one hand, they give access to the texts that they summarize, simplify, reorganize, and possibly help to understand. This is evidently the case for the *Mythographus Homericus* and the dramatic *hypotheseis*, whose texts constitute coherent and homogenous entities that, even when read for their own sake, are intended to reference a preexisting text. The epigram that Photius found in his copy of Ps.-Apollodorus pushes this logic to an extreme through its proposal of replacing the summarized works with the summary itself. It is unnecessary for the reader to refer to Homer, the elegiacs, or the tragedians: he will find in the *Library* "everything the world contains" (*panth' hosa kosmos ekhei*; Photius, *Library*, 186, 142a–b). Imperial mythography is a form of exegesis.

On the other hand, the mythographic text, though defined as secondary in relation to the primary text, should serve as an access path that is both quick and effective. It transmits information that should be accessible; it is a guide and an interpreter in the service of the reader. For this reason, many imperial mythographic texts conserved in their entirety have a remarkable internal architecture. This organization creates a reading grid that helps the reader easily find his place in the work and memorize, if not the facts themselves, then at least their location (see Delattre 2013a: 147–149, 155–158, for Heraclitus and Ps.-Plutarch, *De Fluviis*; for Ps.-Apollodorus, see Delattre 2017). A documentary interpretation of mythographic writing seems particularly applicable for dictionaries (for example, *P.Mich.* 1447) and catalogues (for example, *P.Oxy.* 61.4099) and for general summaries and protracted mythographic works (Ps.-Apollodorus's *Library*), but also for summaries of general works or of specific passages. These summaries can serve as a tool for memorization or for finding one's place when one next reads the work (for example, *P.Oxy.* 62.4308 reformulates lines 975–1018 of Hesiod's *Theogony*). Mythography is a form of memory aid and reading guide, or, following Cameron (2004: viii), a "companion".

Including the mythographic corpus in the vast field of exegesis shows the continuity between imperial practices and earlier eras. The tools of analysis that were developed during the Classical period and systematized in Alexandria, Pergamum, and in philosophical schools are commonly used in imperial mythographic texts. The practice of *hypotheseis* and *historiai* already has a counterpart in Aristotle's *Poetics* (17, 1455b1–22); allegory as used by Heraclitus also has a long history; and the insertion and discussion of multiple references, in the work of Pausanias or Dionysius of Halicarnassus, is already explicit in a conserved passage from Apollodorus of Athens, where a discussion on the birth of Athena and the names of Pallas and Tritogenia (fr. 354bis Mette = *P.Köln* 5604) is accompanied by a citation of Epicharmus (fr. 85a Austin).

The evolutions in exegesis specific to the Imperial period, such as have been studied in most recent years in papyrological documentation, have not yet been compared with the mythographic texts available to us. The distinction between "companions" (*hypomnēmata*) and "treatises" (*syngrammata*), in spite of the difficulties it presents, could explain one part of our corpus: Parthenius uses the term *hypomnēmation* in his preface to describe his work. The evolution of media, with the passage from the *volumen* to the *codex* and the still later creation of medieval scholia and scholarly commentaries (Eustathius, Tzetzes), which contain a great deal of information from autonomous Hellenistic and imperial commentaries, is another subject for investigation.

## 3.2. Autonomous Treatises

The autonomy of certain mythographic texts, contrasting with the general notion of the corpus as secondary literature, is an important factor to consider. Though these texts show a form of intertextuality, given their close relationship to local traditions or the works of the Archaic, Classical, and Hellenistic periods, a certain number seem to be fully independent. They do not appear to refer to any single work, mention any single text, or even openly take on an exegetic function. If they maintain a purpose as commentary, it is only in a very general sense.

Considered to be documentary sources until recently, only useful to provide information for the creation of contemporary dictionaries of mythology, these treatises call for re-evaluation, both as a specific group of texts and individually. In a first approach, one can define them negatively. Unlike Ps.-Apollodorus, they do not offer a general panorama of classical stories. They are not organized in a continuous narration, but as a collection of chapters. Positively, one can notice that each work follows complex narrative strategies that create a unique grid for reading each text. They refer, whether explicitly or not, to works from the Hellenistic period, not only to archaic and classical poetic works. The titles given to them in the medieval manuscript tradition most often reflect a single unifying theme: the *Disastrous Love Stories* by Parthenius of Nicaea; the *Onomastics of Rivers and Hills* (or *De Fluviis*) by Ps.-Plutarch; the *Parallela Minora*, also by Ps.-Plutarch; *Collection of Metamorphoses* by Antoninus Liberalis; the *Refutation or Cure of Traditional and Unnatural Tales* (*Anaskeuē ē Therapeia Mythōn tōn para Physin Paradedomenōn*) by Heraclitus (now known as *De incredibilibus*); *Women's Virtues* (*Gynaikōn Aretai*, known as *De Mulierum Virtutibus*); and *Love Tales* (*Erōtikai Diēgēseis*, known as *Narrationes Eroticae*) by Plutarch. One can also include here treatises of a philosophical nature: the *Summary of Traditions Relating to Greek Theology* (*Epidromē tōn kata tēn Hellēnikēn Theologian Paradedomenōn*) by Cornutus, and *The Gods and the Universe* (*Peri Theōn kai Kosmou*) by Sal(l)ustius. That these works are compilations with a repetitive structure connects them with Palaephatus's treatise, *Incredible Tales* (*Peri Apistōn*), which could date from as early as the 4th century BCE, but which could also, in its current state, be the result of a reformulation during the Imperial period. This could explain the obvious formal resemblances that link these works.

Remarkably, each treatise contains not only a collection of tales, but also a specific mythographic problem, hermeneutic in nature. In this way, they can be considered as reflexive treatises that offer interpretations of the stories they tell, or that create an interpretive process inside the story itself. If the allegorical process proposed by Heraclitus is not necessarily original (one need only consult Palaephatus), one can, nonetheless, note more original structures in works such as Ps.-Plutarch's *De Fluviis*, in which the text is organized around questions of eponymy; Ps.-Plutarch's *Parallela Minora*, which link a narration from the Greek world to a second narration from the Latin world, in the tradition of the "comparison" (*synkrisis*); and Antoninus Liberalis's *Metamorphoses*, which undoubtedly reuses the same principle of earlier compilations, but also constitutes an essay whose prose is meant to rival Hellenistic Greek and Augustean Latin poetry.

We do not have any similar examples from the Hellenistic or Classical periods. Should we thus consider these characteristics to be distinctive of the Imperial period? At the very least, one can notice in many of these treatises (in particular, those transmitted in the *Palatinus Graecus* 398, in addition to Conon, Plutarch, and Ps.-Plutarch) the frequent omission of any Archaic or Classical past, as well as of characters and contexts that are characteristic of epic poetry, tragedy, and the Hesiodic cycle. Even when these characters appear, they are systematically refashioned and placed with new actors and in new plots. Most of all, in these treatises the reader discovers new names, previously documented infrequently or not at all. Narcissus appears for the first time both in Conon and in a composition of elegiac distichs (*P.Oxy.* 69.4711, papyrus from the 4th c. CE) that Henry, the papyrus's editor, associates with the *Metamorphoses* by Parthenius of Nicaea (see also Hutchinson 2006). As for Byblis, she is present in Parthenius (11), Antoninus Liberalis (30), and Conon (2). The tale of Polycrite is given both by Parthenius (9) and Plutarch, *De Mulierum Virtutibus*, 17.254b–f; one can also find it in Polyaenus, *Strategemata*, 8.36, and, allusively, with a reference to Aristotle, in Aulus Gellius, 3.15.1 (Aristotle, fr. 511 Rose). Even if it is possible that these names appeared in earlier poetic works in the Hellenistic or even Classical periods, it is because of these treatises of the Imperial period that they acquire the identity by which we know them today. One can compare, for example, the Daphnis of Theocritus's first and sixth *Idylls* with the Daphnis of Parthenius, *Erōtika Pathēmata* 29 (with a marginal reference to Timaeus), of Diodorus, 4.84.4, and of Aelianus, *Varia Historia* 10.18, without, of course, forgetting the poetic rendition offered by Ovid, *Metamorphoses* 4.276. Can we see in these treatises a mythography that is cognizant of its heritage from previous centuries, and aims to provide a mythology that is no longer founded on the archaic epic cycle and classical tragedy but is rather fully Hellenistic and imperial?

With this new definition, imperial mythography becomes the recipient and the producer of a Hellenistic mythology, a fact that is clear in certain cases: the insertion of anecdotes about Romans from the Republican period in Ps.-Plutarch's *Parallela*

*Minora* makes it obvious that this work is from a later era. More generally, the setting constructed around the characters can confirm this new relationship, which turns the Hellenistic world into the new point of reference: whether urban or rural, the setting is rarely that of the wars from the epic cycle (Thebes, Troy), and it does not match the world of the tragic heroes. The slaves and nurses that inhabit these stories have greater resemblance to those in Menander's comedies. It may be that a comparison with the Greek novel would yield fruitful results for one or more of our mythographic texts.

# 4. From Heterogeneity to Heterogenericity: Mythography as Open Text

When we are confronted with one of these documents, whether it is complete or fragmentary, we can too easily treat it as a fixed text that reveals its full meaning through the intention of a transparent author who himself identifies with what he has written. This is most prominently the case of Parthenius, whose preface seems to give a single objective to the compilation the author addresses to Cornelius Gallus. Yet it is also possible to object to reading the text of Parthenius as a representation of his own thoughts: see Lightfoot (1999: 222–223), who even suggests that the preface may be "a showy appendage to published work." We can, further, try to apply what we know generally about textual creation in antiquity to these mythographic texts: the practice of diffusion rather than publication; the multiplication of possible versions of a single text, whether through its avowed author or through its successive copyists and readers; the inadequacy of notions of originality and authenticity in our conception of ancient authorship. Mythographic texts are open to interpretation, precisely because they are "open texts."

A reappraisal of the notion of "literary genre" also belongs here. We have already seen how mythography and historical writing sometimes overlapped, whether it be local historiography or universal history, and how geography and periegesis borrow parts of their texts from mythography. Sophistic performances, through their *exempla*, can be interpreted as discourses that include mythographic elements, or even as reflexive mythographic texts in the case of complex performances, such as the *Trojan Discourse* by Dio Chrysostom or Philostratus's *Heroicus*. Libanius's rhetorical manual, the *Progymnasmata*, also includes mythographic elements, in his compilation of "Diegemata" (see also Smith and Trzaskoma, this volume, on education).

These phenomena of hybridization can also be found in earlier eras and thus do not offer any particular points of originality. There nonetheless exist three imperial corpora with which the mythographic corpus has such tight relations that generic distinction between these types of writing loses all relevance. This is the case for the paradoxographical corpus, first identified for academics by Westermann four years before his edition of the "mythographers" (Westermann 1839, 1843). The use of the title *De Incredibilibus* (*Peri Apistōn*) for Palaephatus's and Heraclitus's texts demonstrates the relevance of the categories *paradoxon*, *apiston*, and *thaumaston* (amazing, unbelievable, and surprising) for analyzing that part of the mythographic corpus that employs rationalizing allegories. The same can be said for the other various "Anonymi Paradoxographoi" whom Westermann identifies in his 1839 volume, who would also have fit well in his 1843 edition (see also Pajón Leyra, this volume).

A second, less expected corpus also has strong connections with mythography. In question here are texts that describe works of art, or that transpose these artworks, whether real or fictional, into the form of a text that aims to both provide information about the artwork and, as a work in its own right, replace it. Philostratus's and Callistratus's works, as well as the descriptions of the *periegetai* (Pausanias, Polemon), enter into this category. It is remarkable, for example, that the description Pausanias provides for a painting by Micon in the Theseion of Athens is in all respects identical to a passage in Hyginus's *Astronomy*: one must assume that a Greek mythographic text is the source for these two passages (Pausanias, 1.17.3; Hyginus, *Astronomy*, 2.5.3; see Delattre 2009: 144–146; 2012: 319–323). The prose texts in Book 3 of the *Greek Anthology* can also be considered mythographic in regard to their theme as well as to their function. They describe the nineteen bas-reliefs with mythological subjects on the columns of the temple of Apollonis, wife of Attalus I of Pergamum, at Cyzicus, and explain the anonymous epigrams that are themselves the poetic transposition of these bas-reliefs. It is quite possible to reconsider certain mythographic texts as the reformulation of paintings, whether fictional or real.

The third corpus is gigantic, since it consists both of Hellenistic Greek poets, who give imperial mythography its distinctive character, and contemporary Greek and Latin poets. The links between Ovid's *Metamorphoses* and mythography are well known, but one cannot simply make mythography a source of inspiration for the poet. The example provided by the *Ibis* shows how certain poetic works can be considered, independently of the goal the poet assigns to the work and its generic constraints, as mythography in verse (see Smith, "Latin Mythography," this volume). On the opposite side, the *Erōtika Pathēmata* of Parthenius of Nicaea can be read as a poem in prose that includes versified sections. To define mythography solely by its mythological themes does not suffice to differentiate it from poetic productions, from Callimachus to Nonnus of Panopolis via Ovid.

If mythography is identified with any mythological production, it will become the equivalent of the "cultural knowledge" that Cameron likens to mythology in the imperial period (2004: xii). It would thus be a vague category without academic relevance. Among the ways to restore specificity to mythographic writing, we could privilege the evaluation of specific authorial practices, in particular, the question of fiction writing, such as it has been recently defined in literary criticism. This question is pertinent, first and foremost, for those mythographic works considered marginal or extravagant, such as Ps.-Plutarch's *De Fluviis* or the *Kainē Historia* by Ptolemy Chennus. These writers appear to construct an alternative mythology, another world of myth, without, however, adopting a novelistic form and staying firmly within what we think of as mythography (see Delattre 2011, 2013b). Yet the question also importantly concerns works that are in close relation to poetic fiction, such as the texts of Antoninus Liberalis and Parthenius, or even the texts of Apollodorus and Hyginus, which are generally considered documentary. The divergences of these texts from the tradition they avow to reproduce could receive new evaluations and cease to be considered as errors or aberrant variants. Just as poets begin to innovate in the Hellenistic period as a response to philological problems, in a complex intertextual network, mythographers fill in the empty spaces of their sources and participate by offering versions that are unattested anywhere else. As Pausanias wrote, "[A]ncient narratives, without the support of poetry, have given rise to all kinds of inventions, particularly with respect to the genealogies of heroes" (1.38.7; see also Sluiter 1999: 188). Mythography is therefore about not only describing but also inventing and proposing new directions.

# 5. Mythography, Erudition, Society

Considered broadly, imperial mythography is the rewriting of material, of a theme, and, sometimes, of a plot; it is the reinterpretation and reformulation of texts from the poetic and mythographic corpus of the archaic, classical, Hellenistic, and even imperial periods. It equally helps give form to a cultural knowledge of importance to the imperial period: it includes elements that had become traditional, were known by a large number of individuals, even those with no access to literacy, and which served to construct a shared cultural identity. It also integrates into this same mold several new elements, in particular those linked to the new geographic extension of the Greek and Roman gazes. The different educational systems are fundamental in this process, whether at the level of learning language and writing under the schoolmaster, of reading poets under the *grammatikos*, or of developing complex texts under the rhetor. Even if there is no unified school system (Cribiore 2001: 3, 8), schools nonetheless ensure the transmission of a common and general cultural knowledge (see also Smith and Trzaskoma, this volume).

Nonetheless, it remains the case that these mythographic texts, which may be the transcriptions of an elitist culture, but which might also correspond to interpretations belonging to other social circles, are now largely inaccessible. What we do have, either in extant texts or those that we can reconstruct with some certainty, is a written expression that characterizes only one part of antique culture, and which occurred in minority social practices—those of the socioeconomic elite and the *pepaideumenoi* (educated). In a world where only a minority achieve full literacy, and where access to the written production of the past is never easy or complete, literate people such as mythographers evidently gain access to elite society. Even if mythographers might be neither rich nor powerful themselves, their works, and perhaps they as individuals, were connected to those who are, either at a very local level or in the large imperial cities.

Once again, a few distinctions are necessary so as not to create a too simplistic pic-ture: there is no strict equivalence between members of the elite and individuals benefiting from a large and reflexive culture. Seneca's attacks against Calvisius Sabinus, an extremely rich Roman of indecent behavior, is solid proof of this: Sabinus compensated for his failing memory—and thus flagrant lack of culture—through the employment of slaves who were specially trained to serve as a nomenclator of the clas-sical tradition (*Ep.* 27.5). A man who loved a good laugh, Satellius Quadratus advised him to use *grammatici analectes* (27.7): professors, commentators, and mythographers, who could both "read" for him (*legere*) and, in a wordplay with the Greek, "pick up the crumbs" of his feasts (*analegein*). In Petronius's *Satyricon* (48, 52, and 59), the rich and vulgar Trimalchio himself reformulates the epic cycle, adding one error and confusion to the next. He is without any doubt a poor mythographer—unless one deems that he pushes the practice of mythography as fiction to the absurd.

We know little about the life of imperial mythographers (Parthenius perhaps being the only exception). Certain mythographers could have been part of the elite by right, through their family, social status, and behavior. Others may have mingled with the elite without becoming part of it and could have depended on rich Greeks or Romans for their survival. In both cases, mythographers assured the promotion of a knowledge and erudition that helped define a Greek identity based on *paideia*. Members of a network defined by erudition, writing, and the borrowing of books (see also *P.Berol.* 21849, 2nd half of the 5th c. CE), mythographers constituted an informal society, a group without a recognized social identity, but, through its interests and practices, significantly linked to the socially defined group of the rich *papaideumenoi*.

It is particularly tempting to create links between mythographic practices and the rhetorical works summarized under the label "Second Sophistic," as Bowie (1970: 23–24) has already done for Ps.-Apollodorus. For Bowie, the approach of mythographers, as that of the sophists, results from "the Greeks' preoccupation with their past [and] their dissatisfaction with the political situation of the present" (1970: 4). Yet one can also turn to the new definitions of Greek identity defended by Whitmarsh (2010, fol-lowing Swain 1996). Mythography would thus no longer be merely an antiquarian search, the construction of a knowledge that is detached from political, social, or eco-nomic preoccupations. It would be both a symptom of an imperial society that was in the middle of refashioning multiple identities—Greek, Roman, the rulers, the elite, and so on—and one of the ways to arrive at this reconfiguration.

If social competition is one of the paths to distinction, mythography is one of the fields in which this competition is engaged. The anecdote about the emperor Tiberius interrogating (and bullying) learned professors (*grammatici*) so that they reveal—or invent—the name of Hecuba's mother, or the name Achilles used when he was disguised in King Lycomedes's court, pushes to the extreme this agonistic rivalry, in which participants confront each other in a social game, where mythographic erudi-tion, enigma, and riddle define statuses and relations (Suetonius, *Tib.* 70). In this regard, mythography from the imperial period no longer plays the same role it played in the Hellenistic period. The imposition of the imperial regime, the reorganization of political power, and the reconfiguration of identities now give a new meaning to the world's order. The establishment of rhetorical knowledge as the basis of culture—including the philosophical cosmopolitanism; the references, implicit or explicit, to imperial authority; the elite's performance of cultural affiliations in order to define itself as elite; the reconstruction of the hierarchy of disciplines; the value placed on the textual object as an instrument of knowledge; the development of textual techniques such as cataloguing and itemization; and even the use of the *codex* instead of the *volumen*, which for König and Whitmarsh (2007) are the signs of an "ordering knowledge" specific to the imperial period—all this could also help us in defining the mythography of this era.

# 6. Mythographers, Mythographies

No study of mythography from the imperial period can be complete without taking into account what remains stable and what mutates, which both modern historians and the actors of the era use to define the characteristics of the period. One must make a special place here for the authors' possible consciousness of their own works. In the general absence of prefaces and facts concerning the mythographers' biographies—Parthenius of Nicaea and his *Erōtika Pathēmata* being the sole exception—we can rely only on preserved texts. This, of course, makes our job more difficult. If one accepts the authenticity of the poem transmitted by Photius (*Library*, 186, 142a–b) for Ps.-Apollodorus, the affirmation of the *paideia* defining the author (*ap' emeio—paideiēs*), and the claim that Ps.-Apollodorus' book will replace all others (*eis eme d' athrōn—heurēseis en emoi*) establish a mythographic consciousness. This consciousness is different from the generic indecision apparent in, for example, Diodorus or Strabo when they refer to *mythographoi* (Diodorus 1.23.8; 3.62.2; 3.62.7; 3.66.4; Strabo 1.2.8; finally, see Alganza Roldán 2015: 18–19). In this case, mythography could also be defined as a specific activity, the mark of a certain learned approach, the sign of a specific authorial and intellectual activity.

At the end of this journey, many questions remain unanswered. For the imperial period, we are left uncertain as to the authors' identities and the character of their readers (contemporary, late antique, medieval, and others). More generally, the possible uses of imperial mythographic texts are under evaluation, as entities of autonomous meaning, as intertextual semantic operators, and as agents interacting with iconographic systems or social practices.

Papyrologists include precise textual and material details in their editions, but such is not the case with mythographic editions. The omission of significant details in the medieval manuscripts (for instance, tables of contents, marginal reference signs, commentaries) can modify our perception of the texts. Even the delimitation of these texts with the inclusion of each version that had been transmitted with its own specificity and uses, would allow a revaluation of the act of writing that is at the center of our corpus. The analyses developed for medieval scholia in recent years might usefully be reversed for the study of imperial mythography.

Mythographers' language has only been evaluated in exceptional circumstances, whether in the terminology of ancient rhetoric or in that of contemporary linguistics. Yet the adoption of a particular register, the use of *koine*, the recourse to Atticisms, and the borrowings from poetic vocabulary could be distinctive signs of a Greek identity in the imperial period. The stylistic revaluation of the prose written by each imperial mythographer and the determination of different writing styles are promising axes, following in the footsteps of that which has been developed for the Byzantine world: "to go beyond the dichotomies spoken—written, real—artificial, mixed—pure and living—dead" (Manolessou 2008: 79; see also Toufexis 2008: 213–215). Nor should one forget an interlinguistic study that would identify the Latinisms in the Greek mythographic corpus or the possible presence of other languages (Celtic, Phrygian, Aramaic, and others).

It goes without saying that drawing on other disciplines—cultural anthropology, subaltern studies, gender studies, or memory studies, to name a few—advances this investigation. The imperial period is rich in practices that involve the mythographic corpus and which call for interdisciplinary approaches, with different questions for each author. That is to say, there are as many imperial mythographies as there are mythographers.

## FURTHER READING

There exists no published collection devoted uniquely to mythographers from the imperial period. It is therefore necessary to use the dated edition by Festa (1902) and that of Giannini (1966) devoted to paradoxographers to read certain less studied mythographic texts, as well as those editions devoted to well-known authors of the time. Jacoby's *Fragmente der griechischen Historiker* (Volume 3b; see now *Brill's New Jacoby* online) contains a number of fragments from imperial-era mythographers (for the problems posed by the evaluation of ancient "fragments," see the warning of Brunt 1980). Particularly interesting is the corpus of the apologetes and Christian polemicists, who engage in a war of erudition with the pagans by using as examples for their attacks elements that originate in mythographic treatises, lists, or narrations (for example, Tatian, *Ad Gr.* 39.3; Clement of Alexandria, *Strom.* 1.21.103.2–4).

A lot of material that has seldom been taken into consideration until now is found in papyrological and epigraphic collections. One cannot forgo consulting the editions and commentaries of Cribiore (1996) and van Rossum-Steenbeek (1998), complementing them with new editions and papyrus studies in specialized reviews.

An analysis of the corpus's materiality, of its form and layout on the page, is important for determining the exegetic nature and function of mythographic practices. For this reason, for both papyri and manuscripts, one should refer to studies on specific writing practices in antiquity (for example, van Groningen 1963, to be complemented by Small 1997: 26–40; Dorandi 2000:19–22; and Gurd 2012), on the material evolution of commentary (Maehler 2000), and on medieval collections.

The epigraphic corpus also provides, through relations between heroes, an interesting complementary material. Any analysis of it should be made in the context of diplomatic relations between cities (Jones 1999; Ma 2003) and would belong to the question of national identities (Curty 1995; Price 2005; Patterson 2010).

General definitions of mythography never outline its particularities in the imperial period (Henrichs 1987; Pellizer 1993; Alganza Roldán 2006). A synthesis on this topic is still lacking. Nevertheless, neighboring fields of study that do not treat mythography per se can shed light on certain of its features. The bibliography on commentary offers useful information (Most 1999: vii; Montanari 1995; Dorandi 2000; Schironi 2012) for defining mythography as a form of knowledge and a practice of learning (Jacob 1994; Cameron 2004; Too 2010: 116–142; Huys 2013; König and Woolf 2013). The connections between mythography and historiography are analyzed in the context of local city life by Clarke (2008), and links between mythography, knowledge, and power can be studied through König and Whitmarsh (2007).

A frequently encountered problem resides in the distinction between mythography and my-thology: even recent monographs on myth do not recognize the specificity of the mythographic corpus (see for example Johnston 2018). The use of rationalization (Hawes 2014) and, more generally, of allegory (Long 1992: 42–43; Richardson 1992; Ramelli and Lucchetta 2004) in the imperial period helps further the distinction by examining in what way mythography is fore-most an activity of reflection and writing (see also Pàmias 2015, to be compared with Fisher 2012). See also Hawes, this volume, on rationalizing and historicizing; and Ramelli, this volume, on allegoresis.

Mythographic studies, like other fields of research, reflect evolution in human sciences and literary theory. One notable evolution in recent studies on mythography has been the re-evaluation of the place of the author: formerly a compiler, the mythographer has now become a man of letters, capable of reorganizing his material to offer new formulas (for ex-ample, Trzaskoma 2013). Yet it is not the author but the text that has gained the greatest im-portance: following Foucault (1969; see also Bennett 2005: 29–54, 94–107), the mythographer, like other ancient authors, is becoming a voice (Taub and Doody 2009; Hill and Marmodoro 2013) rather than a personality, the product of his work rather than its creator. Questions of authorship and authenticity characteristic of the *Quellenforschung* join together with new interrogations of intertextual practices (Fabre-Serris 2015), polyphonic writing (Fletcher 2013; Smith 2013), and operations of adaptation and translation (Zucker 2015).

The status of the mythographer as author and his role in the creation of an autonomous universe, with its own characters and rules, have not yet been considered systematically. Studies on Homer (Kim 2010), Theocritus (Payne 2007), or the novel (Morgan 1993) show the path that must still be tread in order to define an imperial mythographic work as a fictional creation or possible world, in line with work done by Pavel (1986), Doležel (1998), and Schaeffer ([2010]; see Delattre 2013b). Similarly, the borders of mythographic discourse in prose are generally analyzed from the outside, through poetic practices (Jolivet 2014), historiographic practices (Clarke 1999: 245–336), or paradoxographical practices (Pajón Leyra 2011). Comparisons between text and image, narration and iconography, will certainly benefit in the future from new inquiries on the Roman gaze (Elsner 2007; Squire 2009, 2016; Newby 2016).

The renewal of studies on the Second Sophistic (Whitmarsh 2005) and, more generally, on impe-rial culture (Wallace-Hadrill 2008; Spawforth 2012) contains many lessons. The debate between Bowersock (1969) and Bowie (1970) on the relation of Roman-era Greeks to their past had al-ready included references to mythography, in particular to Ps.-Apollodorus. As men of letters, mythographers were part of a privileged social world (Eshleman 2012), where culture could serve as a path to power (Schmitz 1997) and forge new identities (Swain 1996; Whitmarsh 2010; Schmitz and Wiater 2011). Mythography thus becomes one of the ways in which cultural memory (Alcock 2002: 37–98) constructs itself, lives, and dies in the imperial period.

# References

Alcock, Susan E. 2002. *Archaeologies of the Greek Past: Landscape, Monuments, and Memories.* Cambridge, UK: Cambridge University Press.

Alganza Roldán, Minerva. 2006. "La mitografía como género de la prosa helenística." *Florentia iliberritana* 17: 9–37.

Alganza Roldán, Minerva. 2015. "¿Historiadores, logógrafos o mitógrafos? (Sobre la recepción de Hecateo, Ferécides y Helánico)." *Polymnia* 1: 4–24. https://polymnia-revue. univ-lille.fr/pdf/2015/1.Alganza-Polymnia-1_2015.pdf.

Bennett, Andrew. 2005. *The Author.* London: Routledge.

Bowie, Ewan L. 1970. "Greeks and Their Past in the Second Sophistic." *Past & Present* 46: 3–41.

Bowersock, Glen W. 1969. *Greek Sophists in the Roman Empire.* Oxford: Clarendon Press.

Brunt, Peter A. 1980. "On Historical Fragments and Epitomes." *Classical Quarterly* 30: 477–494.

Cameron, Alan. 2004. *Greek Mythography in the Roman World.* Oxford: Oxford University Press.

Clarke, Katherine. 1999. *Between Geography and History: Hellenistic Constructions of the Roman World.* Oxford: Clarendon Press.

Clarke, Katherine. 2008. *Making Time for the Past: Local History and the Polis.* Oxford: Oxford University Press.

Courrier, Cyril. 2014. *La plèbe de Rome et sa culture (fin du II$^e$ siècle av. J.-C.–fin du I$^{er}$ siècle ap. J.-C.).* Rome: École française de Rome.

Cribiore, Raffaella. 1996. *Writing, Teachers and Students in Graeco-Roman Egypt.* Atlanta, GA: Scholars Press.

Cribiore, Raffaella. 2001. *Gymnastics of the Mind: Greek Education in Hellenistic and Roman Egypt.* Princeton, NJ: Princeton University Press.

Curty, Olivier. 1995. *Les parentés légendaires entre cités grecques: Catalogue raisonné des inscriptions contenant le terme SUGGENEIA et analyse critique.* Geneva: Droz.

Delattre, Charles. 2009. *Le cycle de l'anneau: De Minos à Tolkien.* Paris: Belin.

Delattre, Charles. 2011. *Nommer le monde: Ps. Plutarque, De fluviis.* Lille: Presses du Septentrion.

Delattre, Charles. 2012. "Pausanias, une description sans objet." In *La trame et le tableau: Poétiques et rhétoriques du récit et de la description dans l'Antiquité grecque et latine,* edited by Michel Briand, 317–326. Rennes: Presses Universitaires de Rennes.

Delattre, Charles. 2013a. "Pentaméron mythographique: Les Grecs ont-ils écrit leurs mythes?" *Lalies* 33: 77–170.

Delattre, Charles. 2013b. "Du commentaire à la pratique fictionnelle: L'exemple de Ptolémée Chennos." In *Théories et pratiques de la fiction à l'époque impériale,* edited by Christophe Bréchet, Anne Videau, and Ruth Webb, 193–203. Paris: Picard.

Delattre, Charles. 2017. "Apollodorus' Text: Experimental Layout and Edition." In *Apollodoriana,* edited by Jordi Pàmias, 176–203. Berlin and New York: De Gruyter.

Doležel, Lubomír. 1998. *Heterocosmica: Fiction and Possible Worlds.* Baltimore, MD: Johns Hopkins University Press.

Dorandi, Tiziano. 2000. *Le stylet et la tablette: Dans le secret des auteurs antiques.* Paris: Belles Lettres.

Dorandi, Tiziano. 2012. "Le commentaire dans la tradition papyrologique: Quelques cas controversés." In *The Social World of Intellectuals in the Roman Empire: Sophists,*

*Philosophers, and Christians*, edited by Kendra Eshleman, 15–27. Cambridge, UK: Cambridge University Press.

Elsner, Jaś. 2007. *Roman Eyes: Visuality and Subjectivity in Art and Text*. Princeton, NJ: Princeton University Press.

Eshleman, Kendra. 2012. *The Social World of Intellectuals in the Roman Empire. Sophists, Philosophers, and Christians*. Cambridge, UK: Cambridge University Press.

Fabre-Serris, Jacqueline. 2015. "La pratique mythographique de Parthénius de Nicée et l'usage des *Erotika Pathemata* chez Gallus, Properce et Ovide." *Polymnia* 1: 61–82. http://polymnia. recherche.univ-lille3.fr/revue/eng/.

Festa, Nicola, ed. 1902. *Mythographi graeci*. Vol. 3.2. Leipzig: Teubner.

Fisher, Matthew. 2012. *Scribal Authorship and the Writing of History in Medieval England*. Columbus: Ohio State University Press.

Fletcher, Kristopher F. B. 2008. "Systematic Genealogies in Apollodorus' *Bibliotheca* and the Exclusion of Rome from Greek Myth." *Classical Antiquity* 27: 59–91.

Fletcher, Kristopher F. B. 2013. "Hyginus' *Fabulae*: Toward a Roman Mythography." In *Writing Myth: Mythography in the Ancient World*, edited by Stephen M. Trzaskoma and R. Scott Smith, 133–164. Leuven: Peeters.

Foucault, Michel. 1969. "Qu'est-ce qu'un auteur?" *Bulletin de la Société française de philosophie* 3: 73–104.

Giannini, Alessandro, ed. 1966. *Paradoxographorum graecorum reliquiae*. Milan: Istituto Editoriale Italiano.

Gurd, Sean A. 2012. *Work in Progress: Literary Revision as Social Performance in Ancient Rome*. Oxford: Oxford University Press.

Hawes, Greta. 2014. *Rationalizing Myth in Antiquity*. Oxford: Oxford University Press.

Henrichs, Albert. 1987. "Three Approaches to Greek Mythography." In *Interpretations of Greek Mythology*, edited by Jan Bremmer, 242–277. London: Routledge.

Hill, Jonathan, and Anna Marmodoro, eds. 2013. *The Author's Voice in Classical and Late Antiquity*. Oxford: Oxford University Press.

Horsfall, Nicholas. 2003. *The Culture of the Roman Plebs*. London: Duckworth.

Hutchinson, Gregory O. 2006. "The Metamorphosis of Metamorphosis: P.Oxy. 4711 and Ovid." *Zeitschrift für Papyrologie und Epigraphik* 155: 71–84.

Huys, Marc. 2013. "Traces of Scholarship and Erudition in Greek Mythographic Papyri from the Roman Period." In *Writing Myth: Mythography in the Ancient World*, edited by Stephen M. Trzaskoma and R. Scott Smith, 115–131. Leuven: Peeters.

Jacob, Christian. 1994. "Le savoir des mythographes (note critique)." *Annales. Histoire, Sciences Sociales*: 419–428.

Johnston, Sarah Iles. 2018. *The Story of Myth*. Cambridge, MA: Harvard University Press.

Jolivet, Jean-Christophe. 2014. "Exégèse homérique et fiction dans la poésie augustéenne." *Lalies* 34: 7–74.

Jones, Christopher P. 1999. *Kinship Diplomacy in the Ancient World*. Cambridge, MA: Harvard University Press.

Kim, Lawrence. 2010. *Homer between History and Fiction in Imperial Greek Literature*. Cambridge, UK: Cambridge University Press.

König, Jason, and Tim Whitmarsh, eds. 2007. *Ordering Knowledge in the Roman Empire*. Cambridge, UK: Cambridge University Press.

König, Jason, and Greg Woolf, eds. 2013. *Encyclopaedism from Antiquity to the Renaissance*. Cambridge, UK: Cambridge University Press.

Lightfoot, Jane L., ed. 1999. *Parthenios of Nicaea. Poetical Fragments and the Erōtika Pathēmata*. Oxford: Clarendon Press.

Long, Anthony A. 1992. "Stoic Readings of Homer." In *Ancient Homer's Readers: The Hermeneutics of Greek Epic's Earliest Exegetes*, edited by Robert Lamberton and John J. Keaney, 42–66. Princeton, NJ: Princeton University Press.

Ma, John. 2003. "Peer Polity Interaction in the Hellenistic Age." *Past and Present* 180: 9–39.

Maehler, Herwig. 2000. "L'évolution matérielle de l'*hypomnèma* jusqu'à la basse époque: Le cas du *P.Oxy.* 856 (Aristophane) et *P.Würzburg* 1 (Euripide)." In *Le commentaire entre tradition et innovation*, edited by Marie-Odile Goulet-Cazé, 29–36. Paris: Vrin.

Manolessou, Io. 2008. "On Historical Linguistics, Linguistic Variation and Medieval Greek." *Byzantine and Modern Greek Studies* 32 (1): 63–79.

Montanari, Francesco. 1995. "Gli *Homerica* su papiro: Per una distinzione di generi." In *Studi di filologia omerica antica II*, edited by Francesco Montanari, 69–85. Pisa, Italy: Giardini.

Morgan, John R. 1993. "Make-Believe and Make Believe: The Fictionality of the Greek Novels." In *Lies and Fiction in the Ancient World*, edited by Christopher Gill and Timothy P. Wiseman, 175–229. Exeter, UK: University of Exeter Press.

Most, Glenn. 1999. Preface to *Commentaries-Kommentare*, edited by Glenn Most, vii–xv. Göttingen: Vandenhoeck and Ruprecht.

Newby, Zahra. 2016. *Greek Myths in Roman Art and Culture: Imagery, Values and Identity in Italy, 50 BC–AD 250*. Cambridge, UK: Cambridge University Press.

Pagès, Joan. 2007. "*Mythographus Homericus*: Estudii edició comentada." Diss. Universitat Autònoma de Barcelona.

Pajón Leyra, Irene. 2011. *Entre ciencia y maravilla: El género literario de la paradoxografía griega*. Zaragoza: Prensas Universitarias de Zaragoza.

Pajón Leyra, Irene. 2014. "Little Horror Stories in an Oxyrhynchus Papyrus: A Re-edition and Commentary of *P.Oxy.* II 218." *Archiv für Papyrusforschung* 60 (2): 304–330.

Pàmias, Jordi. 2015. "Acusilaos of Argos and the Bronze Tablets." *Harvard Studies in Classical Philology* 108: 53–75.

Patterson, Lee E. 2010. *Kinship Myth in Ancient Greece*. Austin: University of Texas Press.

Pavel, Thomas. 1986. *Fictional Worlds*. Cambridge, MA: Harvard University Press.

Payne, Mark. 2007. *Theocritus and the Invention of Fiction*. Cambridge, UK: Cambridge University Press.

Pellizer, Ezio. 1993. "La mitografia." In *Lo spazio letterario nella Grecia antica*, vol. 1.2, edited by Giuseppe Cambiano, Luciano Canfora, and Diego Lanza, 283–303. Roma: Salerno.

Price, Simon. 2005. "Local Mythologies in the Greek East." In *Coinage and Identity in the Roman Provinces*, edited by Christopher Howgego, Volker Heuchert, and Andrew Burnett, 115–124. Oxford: Oxford University Press.

Ramelli, Ilaria, and Giulio Lucchetta. 2004. *Allegoria, I: L'età classica*. Milan: Vita e Pensiero.

Renner, Timothy. 1978. "A Papyrus Dictionary of Metamorphoses." *Harvard Studies in Classical Philology* 82: 277–293.

Richardson, Nicholas J. 1992. "Aristotle's Reading of Homer and its Background." In *Ancient Homer's Readers: The Hermeneutics of Greek Epic's Earliest Exegetes*, edited by Robert Lamberton and John J. Keaney, 30–40. Princeton, NJ: Princeton University Press.

Schaeffer, Jean-Marie. 2010. *Why Fiction?* Translated by Dorrit Cohn. Lincoln: University of Nebraska Press.

Schironi, Francesca. 2012. "Greek Commentaries." *Dead Sea Discoveries* 19: 399–440.

Sluiter, Irene. 1999. "Commentaries and the Didactic Tradition." In *Commentaries-Kommentare*, edited by Glenn Most, 173–205. Göttingen: Vandenhoeck and Ruprecht.

Schmitz, Thomas. 1997. *Bildung und Macht: Zur sozialen und politischen Funktion der zweiten Sophistik in der griechischen Welt der Kaiserzeit*. Munich: Beck.

Schmitz, Thomas, and Nicolas Wiater, eds. 2011. *The Struggle for Identity: Greeks and their Past in the First Century BCE*. Stuttgart: Steiner.

Small, Jocelyn. P. . *Wax Tablets of the Mind: Cognitive Studies of Memory and Literacy in Classical Antiquity*. London and New York: Routledge 1997.

Smith, R. Scott. 2013. "Mythographic Material and Method in the So-Called 'Statius Scholia.'" In *Writing Myth: Mythography in the Ancient World*, edited by Stephen M. Trzaskoma and R. Scott Smith, 165–200. Leuven: Peeters.

Spawforth, Antony J. S. 2012. *Greece and the Augustan Cultural Revolution*. Cambridge, UK: Cambridge University Press.

Squire, Michael. 2009. *Image and Text in Graeco-Roman Antiquity*. Cambridge, UK: Cambridge University Press.

Squire, Michael, ed. 2016. *Sight and the Ancient Senses*. London: Routledge.

Swain, Simon. 1996. *Hellenism and Empire: Language, Classicism, and Power in the Greek World, AD 50–250*. Oxford: Clarendon Press.

Taub, Liba Ch., and Aude Doody, eds. 2009. *Authorial Voices in Greco-Roman Technical Writing*. Trier: WVT Wissenschaftlicher Verlag Trier.

Too, Yun Lee. 2010. *The Idea of the Library in the Ancient World*. Oxford: Oxford University Press.

Toufexis, Notis. 2008. "Diglossia and Register Variation in Medieval Greek." *Byzantine and Modern Greek Studies* 32 (2): 203–217.

Trzaskoma, Stephen M. 2013. "Citation, Organization and Authorial Presence in Ps.-Apollodorus' *Bibliotheca*." In *Writing Myth: Mythography in the Ancient World*, edited by Stephen M. Trzaskoma and R. Scott Smith, 75–94. Leuven: Peeters.

Trzaskoma, Stephen M., and R. Scott Smith. 2008. "'Hellas' in the *Bibliotheke* of Apollodorus." *Philologus* 152: 90–96.

Trzaskoma, Stephen M., and R. Scott Smith, eds. 2013. *Writing Myth: Mythography in the Ancient World*. Leuven: Peeters.

van Groningen, Bernhard A. 1963. "EKDOSIS." *Mnemosyne* 16: 1–17.

van Rossum-Steenbeek, Monique. 1998. *Greek Readers' Digests? Studies on a Selection of Subliterary Papyri*. Leiden: Brill.

Wallace-Hadrill, Andrew. 2008. *Rome's Cultural Revolution*, Cambridge, UK: Cambridge University Press.

Westermann, Anton. 1839. *Scriptores rerum mirabilium Graeci*. Brunswick: G. Westermann.

Westermann, Anton. 1843. *ΜΥΘΟΓΡΑΦΟΙ. Scriptores poeticae historiae Graeci*. Brunswick: G. Westermann.

Whitmarsh, Tim. 2005. *The Second Sophistic*. Oxford: Oxford University Press.

Whitmarsh, Tim, ed. 2010. *Local Knowledge and Microidentities in the Imperial Greek World*. Cambridge, UK: Cambridge University Press.

Zanker, Paul. 1995. *The Power of Images in the Age of Augustus*. Translated by Alan Shapiro. Ann Arbor: University of Michigan Press.

Zucker, Arnaud. 2015. "Hygin et Ératosthène: Variation mythographique ou restitution d'un original perdu." *Polymnia* 1: 83–125. https://polymnia-revue.univ-lille.fr/pdf/2015/4.Zucker-Polymnia-1_2015.pdf.

# CHAPTER 5

## MYTHOGRAPHY IN LATIN

### R. SCOTT SMITH

THE most remarkable aspect of Alan Cameron's lengthy list of mythographical texts from the late Hellenistic and Imperial periods is that only four of the entries are written in Latin: the *Fabulae* and *On Astronomy* (*De Astronomia*), both ascribed to someone named Hyginus; the anonymous Ovidian *Narrationes*; and the equally anonymous Germanicus scholia (Cameron 2004: 27–32). Any views, then, that we may have about "Latin mythography" are based on a minuscule sample. That sample, moreover, is hardly diverse; two of these Latin works, *On Astronomy* and the Germanicus scholia, are quite similar and are essentially translations or adaptations of the same Greek work. The *Fabulae*, too, owes much to Greek mythographical sources (if the original language of the *Fabulae* was not in fact Greek; see Cameron 2004: 35–37). But if it was composed, as seems probable, by the author of the *De Astronomia*, then we may have four Latin mythographical texts, but only three authors are represented. Obviously, the vast majority of the output of ancient authors, including that of any unknown Latin mythographers, has been lost, but when one compares the Latin corpus to the Greek, it is difficult not to conclude that mythographical collections were seen as a particularly Greek phenomenon.

Even so, we *do* have a fairly substantial amount of mythography in Latin, especially when we take into consideration the large corpus of mythographical material in the commentaries and other ancillary texts to help understand Latin poets, in particular Vergil but also Ovid and Statius—the same material that will be substantially mined as a source for Greco-Roman myth by later collectors in the West, for example, the Vatican mythographers (see Garstad, "Mythography in the Latin West," this volume). If, then, mythography was for the most part seen as something to do in Greek, it will be imperative to interrogate these Latin collections from the imperial period and late antiquity not only for what they contain, but the reasons these might have been transmitted in Latin and how they might have operated in the literary or cultural contexts of the Empire—contexts in which dichotomies like Greek/Roman and Greek/Latin can either be blurred or kept distinct depending on the time or situation.

For this reason, it is important to keep in mind that all of this material, like mythographical collections in Greek, was focused entirely on elaborating the *Greek* mythical tradition, which the Romans came to adopt rather early on. Whatever stories the early Romans may have told about themselves and their origins, and there were likely rather few, they were quickly supplanted by the traditions from the Greek world. The essays in Bremmer and Horsfall (1987) show how little survives of archaic Roman and Italic storytelling ("myth") and how difficult it is to tease out the original stories, or rather some original elements of those stories, beneath the later mythographical reshaping of narratives, which were themselves often modeled on Greek narratives ("secondary myth" in their phrasing). Whatever accounts for the "failure" of native Roman/Italic peoples to create a rich body of myths, the fact is that myths of the Greeks almost entirely displaced the native Italic product (Bremmer and Horsfall 1987: 1–5).

With the constant introduction of Greek myth into the Roman consciousness through Greek-language sources, it is no great leap to think that mythographical texts, written in Greek, would have naturally accompanied them, although the pace and timing of such an introduction is impossible to determine because of the nature of the evidence. While it is clear, for instance, that Nigidius Figulus, a contemporary of Cicero (who himself translated Aratus's *Phaenomena*: see Gee 2001), drew on a Greek work on catasterisms in his Latin work on astronomy and the constellations (*Sphaera*), we simply cannot know the number or nature of the Greek mythographical works that were available to Latin speakers at any given time, or whether Nigidius's Latin adaptation was unique for its time or part of a broader attempt to render Greek mythographical works in Latin. The former is far more likely; soon after, Parthenius would provide for Cornelius Gallus his prose summaries of love affairs gone wrong—in Greek (see Francese, this volume).

Even if we cannot see the exact process, over time Latin speakers came to accept Greek myth as a cultural legacy for themselves, and knowledge of the mythical system became an important component of their cultural capital (Cameron 2004: 217–252). It is likely that the process included a combination of repeated exposure to the literary adaptations of Greek literature and drama and the adoption of Greek educational practices, which, as we argue in another chapter (see Smith and Trzaskoma on education, in this volume), was a systematic introduction to "mythographical thinking." But if a having a command of Greek mythology was a necessary requirement for elite Roman life, it remains unclear whether native Latin speakers gained this knowledge in Greek or Latin, or both. And we should not assume that there was complete consistency over some four centuries and across a sprawling empire. In a bilingual society like that of elite imperial Rome, however, instruction would have presumably been in both languages. Certainly, by Quintilian's day, and very likely before, students—at least those aspiring to be orators—would start with Homer before moving to the Latin authors. Preparation for reading Homer, in turn, presumably would have included short Greek passages that explained the background of the story, and during the (slow) reading of the poem, students would have read or heard, and possibly written, short narratives explaining references in Homer's text. In other words, students would certainly have been exposed to mythographical material in Greek, whether in written form or indirectly through oral delivery during instruction.

By the empire, a large body of helpful tools had already been built up around Greek literary and school texts: commentaries, lists, *peri*-literature, and so on. These exegetical materials would not only have provided content to be mined or remembered by industrious commentators, but the forms of these materials also served as models for the production of specifically Latin versions of them. Yet there was no widespread attempt to produce specifically mythographical manuals in Latin form, leading to two interconnected questions that will frame the rest of this chapter, even if the answers are not always evident: Why did they not produce more mythography in Latin, and what were the motivations when they did do so?

One answer to the first has already been hinted at: a number of Greek mythographical texts were available, and mythography in Greek was, by and large, easy to comprehend. Summary narratives were written in clear, concise language; lists and catalogues, in turn, would hardly have been challenging for someone who knew even the rudiments of Greek. In other words, in the bilingual world of elite Roman culture there would have been little need to translate Greek mythographical collections that could be read with relative ease into correspondingly easy Latin. The emergence of Latin mythographical material, then, must have been motivated by an increased need to appeal specifically to a Latin-speaking audience that needed access to the world of Greek myth but not necessarily through the Greek language itself. The exact reasons for appealing to this audience, however, need not have been the same in every case. For instance, the choice to use Latin in mythographical narratives in the commentaries and scholia to Roman poets seems obviously motivated by the desire to match the language of the text. A collection such as the star-myths in Hyginus's *On Astronomy* is embedded in a larger work, but similar material was also found as scholia to Germanicus's adaptation of Aratus— two separate approaches to the same material, one of which was aimed at explicating and directly tied to a poetic text. And finally, there is the work known as Hyginus's *Fabulae*, which remains somewhat enigmatic, not only because it underwent numerous alterations in antiquity (itself perhaps a clue to its usefulness), but also because there exists no mythographical manual quite like it, either in Greek or in Latin. Its very comprehensiveness, if that was part of the original format, may suggest that it was meant to be a compendium of useful knowledge for Latin readers specifically. It may be stretching things to characterize it as an attempt to democratize access to these mythical stories, but it certainly does provide a new avenue for such material.

Before surveying the prose mythographical material in detail, we should remind ourselves of the obvious fact that Roman poets and other authors were influenced by the Greek mythographical tradition, whether in written form or in conversations with literary scholars. One such scholar, already mentioned, was the Greek Parthenius, who was the author of the mythographical compilation *Erotica Pathemata* and served as Cinna's and Vergil's "literary collaborator" (as Francese, 1999, defines *grammaticus*; see also his contribution in this volume; Cameron 2004: 255–260; Horsfall 1991). Parthenius, then, is a key example of how an active poet can also be a mythographer and a *grammaticus*, reinforcing the idea that there is no hard and fast line between literary, scholarly, and pedagogical projects and that the same person can be engaged in all three. It also reminds us that, for all our attention to written sources, conversations about myth were also important ways knowledge of myth could be transmitted (see Tiberius's grilling of his *grammatici*, Suet. *Ti.* 70.3). As for Ovid, his work is clearly indebted to various types of mythographical texts (Farrell 2013, and this volume; Cameron 2004: 261–303), as well as to other scholarly projects involving the mythical world, such as Castor of Rhodes's *Chronicle* (Cole 2004, 2008) and Eratosthenes's *Catasterisms* (Robinson 2013). As we will see, Ovid's *Ibis* is also organized on mythographical lines. Poets of the Flavian era were no different. Zissos (2008: xxiv–v) has argued that Valerius Flaccus engaged with mythographical writing; and Smith (2017) makes the case that Statius likely consulted mythographical texts—and was actively thinking mythographically—in the construction of his catalogs of Argive and Theban fighters.

# 1. Mythographical Collections: Two Texts by Hyginus

The only two substantial mythographical collections that have come down to us in Latin are both ascribed to someone named Hyginus. First, we have a collection of nearly 250 narratives and lists known today as the *Fabulae*, though that is probably not the original title (for a full treatment of the *Fabulae*, see Fletcher, this volume). It contains summaries of various myths in narrative form and list form, but we also, surprisingly, find lists of, for example, the seven wise men (*Fab.* 221), the seven wonders of the world (223), and really big islands (275)—reminiscent of Lucius Ampelius's *Reminder-Book* (*Liber Memorialis* 6.12, 8.1–25), which also contains a smattering of mythographical material. The title and the attribution of the *Fabulae* to Gaius Julius Hyginus may be the invention of the first editor, Micyllus, in 1535; the original title was almost certainly *Genealogies*, as it was called by an excerptor of a portion of our text for a schoolbook, the *Hermeneumata Pseudodosithieana Leidensia*, in 207 CE (3.4, pp. 103–104 Flammini).

The other mythographical collection bearing the name Hyginus is the second book of *On Astronomy* (*De Astronomia*), which is a compilation of mythological stories connected to forty-one constellations, with two additional chapters on the planets and the Milky Way, primarily drawn from Eratosthenes's *Star Myths* (*Catasterisms*; for catasteristic mythography, including the *De Astronomia*, see Zucker in this volume). Since Eratosthenes's work survives only in a heavily abridged form, Hyginus's *On Astronomy* is a valuable witness to the original form of the Greek work on which it depends. As for its author, we have a prefatory letter from a Hyginus to one M. Fabius, but since that name is extremely common, it is of little to no help in identifying our Hyginus or dating the text.

In considering these two texts as works of Latin mythography, we should note that there is general agreement that both were written by the same Hyginus, although caution is warranted. There is a possible cross-reference at *Astr.* 2.12.2, which points to a discussion of the Graeae and Gorgons that "we wrote about this in the first book of the *Genealogies*." Since, as we have seen, the original name of the *Fabulae* was *Genealogies*, it seems likely that we are dealing here with the same author. Unfortunately, the text of the *Fabulae* that has come down to us does not include anything about Perseus and the Gorgons, so it is impossible to be sure. Yet, because a few narratives show close correspondence (Marshall 2002: ix–x) and the language of the two works is similar in nature, the most plausible scenario is that the story of the Gorgons simply dropped out of the *Fabulae* as it was transformed into a new, likely abridged, form. In any case, it seems rather improbable that the Hyginus of *On Astronomy* was referring to second, wholly unknown work entitled *Genealogies* in Latin. If these two texts were written by the same author, we have what appears to be a concerted effort by one ambitious author to bring Greek cultural material of some importance to a specifically Latin-speaking audience.

Although a few scholars maintain that our Hyginus can be identified with the Palatine librarian of Augustus (La Boeuffle 2002: xxxi–xxxvi; Expósito 2003), our author's sometimes awkward language seems to speak against attributing them to a *grammaticus* who rubbed shoulders with the likes of Ovid. Of course, this does not mean that the works were not composed in the Augustan period, only that our desire to link virtually anonymous works to a known figure cannot be sustained without pressing the evidence. The *Fabulae*, at least, must have been composed before parts of it were excerpted in the *Hermeneumata*. The compiler of that work claims that Hyginus was at the time "world famous." Given that remark, it seems prudent to suppose that the work had not been written long before that time, perhaps a few years for it to circulate and find success; it is hard to believe that an Augustan-period text circulated for some two hundred years, only to achieve fame so late. A reasonable guess, then, is that our Hyginus lived sometime between 150 and 200 CE.

Although the texts of Hyginus we have are written in Latin, both are clearly indebted to Greek models to a greater or lesser extent, although we are quite uncertain as to the exact nature of the Greek sources for the *Fabulae*. This is due, in part, to the state of the extant collection, which obscures the original text in terms of form, intention, and even language. Recent studies have asserted that Roman sources had a greater influence than has previously been recognized, even if they remain rare. These include Vergil and Ovid (see Fletcher 2013, and this volume), but it is also possible that Latin tragedy, particularly that of Pacuvius, lies behind some of the narratives (Fantham 2003; Schierl 2006: 22–25), though the fragmentary nature of Pacuvius's plays and the loss of much Greek tragedy make this a tentative hypothesis. If it is correct, however, it shines an important light on the *Latin* nature of the collection, and it seems hardly credible that an original Greek composition would have looked to Pacuvius as a source.

At the same time, it can be demonstrated in some places that the author of the *Fabulae* was translating Greek sources, sometimes awkwardly (see Fletcher, this volume). It is also clear that the collection features numerous entries that seem to derive from summaries of Greek tragedies; Greek papyri have also provided clear parallels for Hyginus's catalogs and in some cases confirmed otherwise unattested names found previously only in Hyginus. The question then remains: was the *Genealogies/Fabulae*, unparalleled in its combination of potted narratives and lists set side by side, originally made in Greek and then translated into Latin by someone named Hyginus? Or was the collection itself the product of a Latin speaker, who translated or adapted Greek sources as he compiled them alongside some Latin sources? Or, is the best we can say that the text we have is the result of a long series of modifications, additions, abridgments, and alterations—a sort of "open" text, meant to be reframed for different audiences, which was originally based on Greek sources but fundamentally an act of Romanization through translation (Fletcher 2013)? However that may be, the work seems to have been operative only as a Latin text, and it was seen as an authoritative source—a well-indexed and rather comprehensive one at that—for later collections and commentaries in Latin (though less than we might expect, see Marshall 2002: x–xii). And its success may well have owed to the fact that a Latin speaker felt the need to produce a volume that brought together different forms of Greek mythography to produce a culturally relevant omnibus of the Greek mythical system in one place.

By contrast, the collection of star myths that forms book 2 of *On Astronomy* is an obvious act of translation, meant to bring a Greek work to a Latin-speaking audience. If, as suggested above, the Hyginus of the *On Astronomy* is the same as that of the *Fabulae*, then it is a reasonable conclusion that the latter text was seen, to some extent, as an act of translation too. Any claim about *Astr.* 2, however, must also take into account the overall work in which it is embedded. The prefatory letter to one Fabius, prominently evoking the *ars grammatica* and *historiae*, indicates that the author sees the work as something of an aide-de-memoire for his already well-educated (*scientissimum*) dedicatee, but a wider audience was certainly intended. The star myths, for their part, are included in an introductory work about the heavens that aimed to be comprehensive, covering basic astronomical definitions (book 1), the positions of the constellations (book 3), and the movements of the heavenly bodies (book 4). As the author expressed it, one of its goals was to offer a clearer and more accurate exposition than had Aratus (around 310–245 BCE), whose *Phaenomena* achieved great popularity and was the "subject of a vast amount of commentary," both in Greek and Latin (Dickey 2007: 56).

For the second (and third) book it is obvious that Hyginus drew mainly from Eratosthenes's *Star Myths*, since *On Astronomy* and the surviving epitome of the Greek text correspond in structure, language, and (most significantly) the citation of sources, which are always met in the same order (Zucker 2015). We do not need to go so far as to accept Martin's exclusivity thesis—that Eratosthenes was the only source for Hyginus, and conversely, that Hyginus can be used to reconstruct Eratosthenes's original text—to recognize that the Hellenistic text served as the primary model for the organization and much of the content (Zucker 2015, esp. 86; Martin 2002: 17, reprising Martin 1956).

Hyginus's version, however, has been deliberately Latinized, resulting in a "we–they" opposition, but it is not systematically applied. The "lead" language in the headings varies: under the Latin heading "Olor," Hyginus points out that the Greeks call this constellation Cycnus (2.8); but we also have Greek headings like "Heniochus," which is immediately followed by Hyginus's clarification that "we" call it Auriga (2.13). Arctos and Cetus, meanwhile, are kept in Greek without Latin translation (2.1, 31, possibly reflecting Latin poetic usage), yet Ophiuchus is kept as a header, with Hyginus quickly pointing out that it was called *Anguitenens* by Latin writers (2.14, *apud nostros scriptores*; it is found in Cicero's translation of Aratus and Manilius, who also uses Ophiuchus). Meanwhile, Lepus and Canis are given without any indication of any Greek equivalent (2.34, 35). One gets the impression that a familiarity with both the Latin and Greek forms, which are variously privileged in Latin astronomical poetry, is expected—and needed—from a reader of Latin texts, both astronomical and poetic.

From a mythographical point of view, a comparison of the accounts of the same myth (Phrixus and the Golden Fleece) will reveal some major differences in the approach, organization, and goals of the *Fabulae* and *On Astronomy* 2. First, let us consider *Fabula* 3, which tells the myth in a straightforward, narrative style: Liber drives Phrixus and Helle mad, whereupon the golden ram arrives and takes them to Colchis; Helle, as she must, falls off on the way, while Phrixus reaches Colchis, sacrifices the ram, and sets up its fleece in a temple. This story, in turn, is part of a series of narratives that explain the origin of the Golden Fleece, focusing Athamas (*Fab.* 1–5), as well as the genealogical thread from the foundation of Thebes to Pelias and Jason (6–13)—which all serve as a prelude to the Argonaut adventure and its aftermath (14–27). Although it is not always easy to detect a coherent organizational pattern in the *Fabulae*, there are some connected groupings such as this, whether organized by mythical arc or thematic coherence, especially up to *Fabula* 175 (see Smith and Trzaskoma 2007: xliv–xlvi). The Phrixus entry, then, is part of a longer chain of narrative events.

The same basic story—though the motivation for the arrival of the ram is different—is found at the beginning of the entry on *Aries* at 2.20.1, but it focuses not so much on the narrative as on the image of the "ram" itself. As Zucker in this volume (section 3) notes, the ram is an "open" figure to which several myths could be attached. One is that of the golden ram that carried off Phrixus and Helle. While the author does provide an extended narrative, specific details are highlighted to connect it to the constellation. For instance, Ino's parching of the grain as part of the plot to kill Phrixus explains the season of Aries's ascendancy, and the removal of the ram's fleece during the sacrifice and the ram's subsequent ascension into the heavens explain the faintness of the constellation. But Hyginus, presumably following Eratosthenes, offers further accounts. These include an alternative explanation for why Athamas wanted to punish Phrixus—basically a mythical variant without a connection to the constellation—as well as the introduction of a different mythical ram, the one that led Liber (Dionysus) to water in Africa. The latter story is also found in Hyginus's *Fabulae* (133), but there it is placed in a cycle involving the god Liber (129–134). Because the story in the *Fabulae* includes a star myth, as does the entry on Icarius and Erigone (130), while the others do not, it is clear that the author of the *Fabulae* was drawing from multiple kinds of sources when compiling this section, at least. That the *Fabulae* contains a number of star myths (see 14.33, 177, 192,

194–197) may be a further indication that the authors of the *Fabulae* and *On Astronomy* are one and the same, despite the different goals of the works.

## 2. Scholia to Germanicus

Hyginus's *On Astronomy* is not the only surviving collection of star myths in Latin. The so-called Scholia to Germanicus are not scholia in the normal sense of the word, but a collection of narrative star myths organized according to the order found in Germanicus's *Aratea*. These also derive, at some remove, from the *Star Myths* ascribed to Eratosthenes. The complicated tradition—they are transmitted to us in three recensions—need not concern us here (see Zetzel 2018: 269–270, Dickey 2007: 59). Generally speaking, the narratives, though they are shorter and reduce the number of potential mythical candidates for the images in the sky, overlap with those presented in *On Astronomy*, and the two texts often contain the same source references. In addition, the Germanicus scholia occasionally cite and relate versions attributed to the 1st-century BCE polymath Nigidius Figulus, whose lost *Sphaera*—like Hyginus's, an astronomical work—included catasteristic entries that were evidently based on Eratosthenes's work, though he seems to have added details drawn from other sources. In particular, Nigidius seems interested in including additional geographical details; for example, he locates the scorpion's attack on Orion on Mt. Pelinaeum on Chios, and notes that the shrine built where the ram showed Liber the water is a "nine-day journey from Alexandria" (see Breysig 1867: 63–64, 80, details confirmed in Lucius Ampelius's *Liber Memorialis* 2.1 and 2.8). Nigidius's astronomical work, then, may have contained the earliest mythographical collection written in Latin.

To conclude our discussion of mythographical collections in Latin, it is worth stressing that, when we include Nigidius's lost work, three of the four known collections of Latin mythography concern star myths. This is unsurprising given the interest in Aratus's *Phaenomena*, which was rendered in Latin no fewer than three times in antiquity: by Cicero in a "youthful" composition, by Germanicus (if he is the author) around 17 CE, and by Avienus in late antiquity (4th c. CE)—interest that would continue into the Middle Ages with the prose Aratus Latinus (7th c. CE). And yet star myths themselves seem to have been of great interest to the Romans: in his translation Germanicus more than doubled the number of catasteristic myths provided by Aratus (Possanza 2004: 172–198), integrating the original poetic text and mythographical exegesis to create a new form.

## 3. Exegesis on Poetic Works

The largest body of mythographical stories in Latin, however, is not to be found in separate collections, but is rather embedded in commentaries, scholia, and other exegetical texts that accompanied Latin literary texts. As may be expected, the commentaries to Vergil's works are a valuable source, containing hundreds of potted mythical stories and other, more expansive interpretations of the mythical tradition. But one can also find many similar examples in the so-called scholia to Statius's *Thebaid*. There is also substantial mythographical material in various forms to be found in the Ovidian *Narrationes* and in the scholia to Ovid's *Ibis*; the occasional mythographical story may be found in other exegetical works, such as those on Juvenal and Horace. In each case, there is an attempt to explicate the Greek mythical story world in the target language of the poems themselves—no differently than the Germanicus Scholia, which provides Latin versions of star myths to explicate Germanicus's *Aratea*.

## 3.1. The Commentary Tradition on Vergil's Works

Although we have references to several ancient scholars who were producing studies and commentaries on Vergil's works continuously from the 1st century BCE into the high empire, we are woefully uninformed about the nature and content of these works (for an overview: Zetzel 2018: 131–142, 262–267). Because of this, it is even unclear whether any of these reflected the "variorum" type of commentary exemplified by Servius's major work, and, presumably, that of his predecessor Donatus, who surveyed "nearly every" scholarly work on Vergil and made excerpts, though he self-consciously omitted references to his sources (Donatus, *Ep. ad Mun.* 1 Brugnoli and Stok). The commentaries and other exegetical texts that we do have are all late, though only Servius's school text, written in the early 5th century CE, can be securely dated. But without a doubt, they all draw on the mass of material in earlier works; by the time Servius composed his commentary, there were four centuries of material on Vergil that he could consult.

All the extant commentaries and scholia include mythographical material to a greater or lesser extent, depending on the needs or desires of each commentator or scholiast, not to mention the amount of space that was available for comments. For example, the *Scholia Veronensia* from the late 5th century CE contain, among other forms of exegesis, a small number of mythographical notes, often shortened, presumably because of space. The commentary known as Ps.-Probus (on the *Eclogues* and the *Georgics*), by contrast, has a higher proportion of mythographical stories compared to other sorts of exegesis. Both of them, in turn, preserve more source references than Servius, who includes a number of potted stories and other interpretative notes. Servius's commentary, in turn, was at some point (probably in the 7th century) supplemented by an unknown person, who seems to have drawn on another commentary that is now lost, resulting in the so-called Servius Auctus, also called Servius Danielis. It, too, features several potted stories, some bizarre, supplementing Servius's own collection. It remains a source of contention whether this second commentary was in fact one of Servius's own sources, Donatus's variorum commentary (see Zetzel 2018: 131–136; Stok 2012; Daintree 1990). For the sake of completeness, we may also mention here the related exegetical texts known as the two

*Explanationes* (also called Philargyrius I and II), the *Scholia Bernensia*, and the *Brevis Expositio* (Funaioli 1930; Daintree 1993; Zetzel 2018: 137–138).

Where does all this mythographical material come from? On the one hand, it could be the result of individual commentators collecting stories as they engaged in other exegesis, grammatical, linguistic, and interpretive. On this reading, the collections of stories littered throughout these Vergilian commentaries would be the result of multiple layers of mythographical material accumulated over time, some drawn from Greek mythographical material (manuals or scholia), whether by consulting them directly or from memory, others taking over now-existing Latin versions. On the other hand, following Cameron's (2004: 184–216) provocative thesis, an earlier *grammaticus*—or three, one for each book—may have, on the model of the *Mythographus Homericus* (hereafter *MH*; see Pagès, this volume), created a mythographical handbook that was drawn from specifically Greek sources and focused singularly on providing potted stories keyed to Vergil's texts, each with a "telltale" source citation. This supposed handbook, dubbed the *Mythographus Vergilianus* (*MV* hereafter), would have served as the source for the majority of stories in preserved Vergilian exegesis, most of the citations being omitted as the stories were recopied into different forms.

This theory, which Cameron (2004: 190) calls a "suggestion," has gained traction in scholarly literature, despite a lack of evidence, acknowledged by Cameron himself, and without the independent verification of corresponding papyri, such as we have for the *MH* (Delvigo 2012; Longobardi 2016; Deremetz 2016; Clément-Tarantino 2016; but compare the contrary opinion of Ziolkowski 2013: 96). While it is attractive to think that the *MH* would have been an "an obvious, inescapable model" and that there was "an obvious incentive to produce a Latin equivalent of the MH" (Cameron 2004: 190; but see also Farrell 2008), the evidence that we have does not support the existence of such a figure in Vergilian scholarship (Smith, 2022). Rather, the evidence points to scholars drawing on different sorts of sources, including the works of their predecessors, which were likely amalgamations of earlier work. According to this model, Vergilian exegesis would have been modeled on Greek commentaries and, in the early period, would have drawn on Greek sources. As Latin material built up, later commentators could draw either on that increasing body or still turn to Greek sources if they were available.

Before moving on from the Vergilian commentaries, we may briefly note here that recent studies have discerned a fundamental difference in approaches to mythographical material in Servius and in the additional material of the compiler of Servius Auctus. For instance, one study (Clément-Tarantino 2016) shows that Servius is less interested in providing a basic account of the storyline than in showing students methods of reading and interpretation (often allegorizing) that could also be applied in other contexts, such as philosophy and natural science. The later compiler, by contrast, was left to add narrative summaries and rarely engaged in rationalization and allegory. Further attention to the methods of providing mythographical narratives in these commentaries would prove fruitful.

## 3.2 The Scholia to Statius's *Thebaid*

Less well known than the Servian commentaries is the exegetical material on Statius's *Thebaid*, commonly known as the "Statius Scholia" and ascribed, falsely, to one Lactantius Placidus. This body of work as transmitted is Carolingian or later, reassembled from marginal scholia into a cohesive whole, but much seems to owe to a single earlier commentary. The date of that original commentary is unknown, but it is now generally placed in the second half of the 4th century (Smith 2013: 166–168; Jakobi 2004: 4–6) or around 450 CE (Cameron 2004: 13–14), both times that could be seen as coinciding with the resurgence of Statius and other Silver Age poets. Although some, following Klotz (1908: 510), have asserted that Statius's *Thebaid* was never a school text, Statius does appear on a list of school authors in a bilingual work from Gaul dated by its latest editor to the 4th and perhaps late 3rd century CE (Dionisotti 1982: 122–124). Furthermore, Servius (ca. 410 CE) included citations of Statius and Lucan in his Vergilian commentary, whereas earlier commentaries, as far as we can tell, did not. It is possible that Servius single-handedly made Statius and Lucan relevant, however, it is more likely that Servius was simply responding to the growing importance of these authors, whether in schools or among the literati. If this is correct, the original *Thebaid* commentary would have been "composed to meet the needs of a growing readership of Statius' *Thebaid* during this resurgence" (Smith 2013: 168), and so the earlier date seems more likely.

Of course, readers would benefit from mythographical notes to help them understand Statius's challenging poem. All told, there are over eighty notes with substantive mythographical information, some 50 of which are of extended narrative character (list at Smith 2013: 194–198). These notes draw on both Greek (perhaps at some remove) and Latin sources. The most identifiable source is Hyginus's *Fabulae*, which accounts for about a third of the narrative summaries preserved in the scholia, but it is not clear where the other thirty or so narratives come from. Only two full-length stories can definitively be said to draw on Vergilian scholarship and are related to material found in the additions of Servius Auctus, not to Servius himself; if the compiler of the expanded Servian corpus was using Donatus's commentary, this is perhaps another indication that the Statius scholia, which drew on the same source, date to the late 4th century (Smith 2013: 176). For other mythographical items, while it is not always possible to identify a specific source, we can glean the sorts of sources the commentator used: Greek encyclopedias (especially geographical), mythographical collections (perhaps some Greek), and Vergilian scholarship. In addition, it seems clear that the Statius commentator, like most, would also have encountered mythographical exegesis when reading Homer and Latin poets, which would have informed his commentaries later (on Homer and the Statius scholia, see Smith 2011).

## 3.3 The Ovidian *Narrationes*

The only major form of exegesis for Ovid's *Metamorphoses* that has survived comes in the form of the *Narrationes* ("Stories," also called *Argumenta* in the manuscripts; thus Otis

1936), an anonymous collection of prose summaries of the poet's transformation stories, ascribed to a variety of persons in the manuscripts, none worth considering, least of all the nonexistent "Lactantius" (Otis 1936: 132; Cameron 2004: 4, 313–316). In our earliest manuscripts, the stories for the first fourteen books (180 of them) are either inserted into the text of the poem (before Ovid's account begins) or found in the margins at a similar point. It is only in the later manuscripts, which also contain the fifty-one entries for book fifteen, that these stories are found continuously presented and transmitted separately from the text of the *Metamorphoses*. Whether or not the *Narrationes* originally circulated as a work independent of the poem cannot be determined. Based on comparisons to the Callimachean *Diegeseis*, Cameron (2004: 78) has asserted that it did, but the case remains open. It is worth pointing out here that, while the vast majority of the stories are understandable without the Ovidian context, some of them are obviously dependent on the text, sometimes simply restating what is found in the poem. For instance, at one point (p. 636 Magnus) we find the brief but separate note, "Jupiter sends Mercury to kill the above-mentioned Argus in the appearance of a shepherd" (on *Met.* 1.668–681). This serves only to denote that a metamorphosis is recorded in Ovid, perhaps to index the poem; it does not point to the wider mythographical tradition.

For a long time, the *Narrationes* was regarded as the very late (6th c. CE) remnants of a more scholarly commentary, now lost. And yet, as Cameron has persuasively shown, the *Narrationes* cannot be later than the end of the 4th century. This is consistent with Tarrant's (1995: 96–100) evaluation of the language and the style, which belong to late antiquity. Tarrant further shows that a stylistic change from book 1 onward suggests that the *Narrationes* may have gone through some abridgment. Cameron's attempt to push the date back to the mid-3rd century CE or earlier (2004: 18–19), which is based on a single vague echo in the Germanicus scholia, is less convincing. He is more successful in dislodging the notion that the *Narrationes* is but the mangled remains of a fuller commentary. Instead, these "Tales from Ovid," which resemble other collections of simple summaries of poetic texts, such as "Tales from Euripides" and the Callimachean *Diegeseis*, belong to a mythographical tradition focused on a combination of summary and expansion of the tales in a poetic text.

Thus, the *Narrationes* has a dual function: to denote metamorphoses in the text (perhaps as an index in a complicated web of storylines), and at the same time, to provide additional help to the reader. In many cases, the author, termed "Narrator" by Cameron, adds details drawn from other sources to supplement Ovid's narrative, which is frequently allusive. For instance, where Ovid only mentions one of the five Sparti in Thebes (*Met.* 3.126), Narrator provides the other four names, perhaps taken from Hyginus *Fab.* 178. At the beginning of the account of Actaeon that appears later in the same book, Ovid avoids naming him directly, calling him "Cadmus' grandson" or *Hyantius*, an obscure ethnonym meaning "Boeotian" (*Met.* 3.138, 147). By contrast, the entry in the *Narrationes* (p. 643 Magnus) starts by naming him and adding his genealogy (son of Aristaeus and Autonoe), which was a frequent practice. Despite these sorts of additions, some of which contradict the Ovidian original, the *Narrationes* generally try to follow Ovid's narrative and make it comprehensible, not always successfully. One illustrative example, in Ovid's account of the Tyrrhenian sailors' attempt to abduct Liber, seems to involve the Narrator's misunderstanding of Ovid's reference to Libys's hands turning into *pinnas* (3.678), commonly meaning "feathers" but here meaning "fins." Narrator—if the error is his and not a later scribe's—tells us that the sailors "turned into dolphins and *birds*" (p. 645 Magnus).

The cases where the *Narrationes* add contextual information could be multiplied hundreds of times over, and one gets the impression that one of the main goals of this ancillary text is to help the reader make sense of the allusive nature of Ovid's poetry. Let us take a single example from the ninth book (*Met.* 9.407–417), where Themis predicts the outcome of the march of the Seven against Thebes, culminating in the story of Alcmaeon.

As is typical, Ovid's deeply allusive approach relies on the reader's understanding of myth to fill in the gaps. The poet does not name Alcmaeon, his mother Eriphyle, or his father Amphiaraus. He references a "Phegean sword," but are we are not told about Alcmaeon's earlier relationship with Phegeus and his daugther in Arcadia. Ovid's focus is, of course, on the transformation of Alcmaeon's sons by Callirhoe into men, but the reader is expected to fill in the background for himself. The account in the *Narrationes* attempts to give the nonexpert reader some help (pp. 681–682 Magnus):

> Callirhoe, the daughter of the river Achelous, was wife of Alcmaeon who, tainted with his mother's blood, had gone to Acarnania to be purified < . . .Callirhoe> got married and had two sons by him. When he was killed in an ambush by Phegeus, whose daughter he had been married to before, she asked Jupiter to add years to her sons so that they could be their father's avengers. So that they could achieve that, by the will of the god it happened that they passed from boys to young men.

What this *narratio* chooses to add, and what it leaves out, may help us understand the purpose of this text. Narrator does not provide the full myth from top to bottom. Although he mentions that Alcmaeon had been married to Phegeus's daughter—motivation for his revenge—we do not get her name or where they lived. Nor is the fact that Alcmaeon had killed his mother on his father's order made explicit. Rather, Narrator adds just enough detail to make the Ovidian references understandable *in the immediate context of the metamorphosis.* In other words, the *Narrationes* is keyed to help one read Ovid, not to provide a comprehensive narrative or widen the reader's knowledge about the whole fabric of the myth. A systematic study of selection of additional mythographic details in the *Narrationes* could potentially expose the purpose of the *Narrationes* more fully.

## 3.4 The *Ibis* and Its Scholia

In addition to the Ovidian *Narrationes*, there is the mass of notes, some of which are surely from ancient sources but mixed with much nonsense, to Ovid's challenging poem, the *Ibis*, an extended attack against an unnamed enemy. Ovid's poem is itself an example of mythography. After an initial 250 lines of general invective, Ovid turns to the mythological world, "so that you'll also be tortured in the manner of the previous age" (251). Thus begins a nearly 400-line catalog of the horrible fates experienced by mythological figures, but none of the references use the character's name. As one study of the work (Krasne 2012) puts it, the result, for both the ancient and the modern reader, is "a prolonged exercise of scholarly research and investigative cross-references." Here is a sample from the beginning of the catalog:

> I hope you suffer as great a wound in your poisoned leg
> > as did Poeantius, the heir to club-wielding Hercules.
> I want your pain to be as much as the man who drank from a deer's teat,
> > receiving a wound from an armed man, aid from the unarmed,
> or he who fell headlong from his horse in the Aleian field,
> > and whose beauty nearly brought an end to himself. (253–258)

Here we encounter, in order, references to Philoctetes (son of Poeas, received Hercules's bow), Telephus (raised by deer, wounded and then cured by Achilles), and Bellerophon (fell from Pegasus and landed in Alea, and was almost killed when he rejected the queen's advances). As one immediately realizes, these examples all involve horrific leg injuries, and this is typical of the structure, which features "mini-catalogs" that are organized thematically—in other words, Ovid's poem is itself a kind of mythographical text. For instance, the following lines (259–272) are a catalog of mythical figures who were blinded: Phoenix, Oedipus, Tiresias, Phineus, Polymestor, and Phineus's sons. A recent study of the mythographical aspects of the work has outlined the ways in which these catalogs mirror thematic lists found in Hyginus's *Fabulae* (Krasne 2013: 71–75). For example, the list of three people who were eaten by dogs (477–480) corresponds to one at *Fab.* 247 entitled "People Consumed by Dogs," and two of the names overlap. The catalog of people struck by lightning (769–776) has a matching entry in the table of contents at *Fab.* 264, although that portion of the *Fabulae* itself is unfortunately missing.

The scholia to the *Ibis*, which feature both errors and false testimonies of poets (including invented names such as Lupertius, a mashup of Lucretius and Propertius), nonetheless try to make sense of Ovid's allusions. At times, we encounter a full story, even if the details are not always correct. For instance, for the Bellerophon reference, the B-scholion begins: "Bellerophon was the son of Proetus (!), who was the brother of king Acrisius (the father of Danae). His mother-in-law (!) fell in love with him because of his beauty and propositioned him for an affair." The account continues along known lines until we get to the end: "falling onto the plains of Lycia, they say he injured his legs, as Propertius says concerning a girl." The trouble is, the following six verses, which reuse some language from the story, are nowhere to be found in Propertius's elegies and are clearly invented (similar for citations of "Callimachus" and other poets). It is no wonder that one editor of the scholia (La Penna 1959) states, "Few scholiastic traditions offer such a difficult task to separate the pearls from the crap as the scholia to the Ibis." And yet, some of the material derives from ancient sources (Cameron 2004: 180–182; Zetzel 2018: 269), including possibly pre-Servian Vergilian exegesis (see, for example, the bizarre version of the Philoctetes myth at line 253, which closely resembles Serv. at *Aen.* 3.402). All things considered, an assessment of this body of material as an indicator of a Latin mythography in antiquity is rendered difficult, possibly hopeless, by the present chaotic state of the text.

# 4.  CONCLUSION

While we have only a few Latin mythographical works—which probably reflects their actual proportion relative to those in Greek—Greco-Roman mythographical material was intertwined with Latin literature in a number of ways. First, there are the Latin poets themselves, who looked not only to Greek poets as models, but also to prose works that helped them to organize mythical material in various ways. Second, there are the ancient commentaries and scholiastic texts on those literary works, which transmitted that Greco-Roman material in Latin to match the target language of the poets. Third, there are the works of Hyginus, who apparently sought to offer mythical lore specifically to meet the needs of a specifically Latin-speaking audience. And yet, it cannot be entirely known whether the appearance of (say) the *Fabulae* indicated a decline in available Greek mythographical works, heralded a need to accommodate Latin speakers by using less Greek, or functioned as an exercise in translation or adaptation that happened to find a large audience. If the date of Hyginus is the late 2nd century CE, perhaps we are witnessing a transition in a Roman world in the west that was decreasingly connected to Greek literature, but such a proposal is vitiated both by our inability to date Hyginus and by the assumption that this period was marked somehow by a decline. In any case, the mythographical material—less Hyginus than the Latin commentaries—became an important source for the Latin West, providing a valuable link to the Greco-Roman mythological data that presumably remained an important body of knowledge.

## FURTHER READING

There is no good introduction to mythographical material in Latin, though now see Hays (2017), which offers an overview. Recently, interest in Roman mythography has blossomed since Cameron's provocative monograph appeared in 2004. This monograph takes the Ovidian *Narrationes* (chs. 1–2) as its starting point, but also covers other topics that focus on Greek myth in Roman culture, in chapters on Servius and the so-called Mythographus Vergilianus (ch. 8), on myth in Roman society (ch. 9), and on myth and the Roman poets (ch. 10, mostly on Ovid). Since Cameron there have been a number of highly specialized studies in other languages on mythography in the Servian commentaries: Delvigo (2012), Longobardi (2016), Deremetz (2016), and Clément-Tarantino (2016). For a review of the evidence for and arguments against the existence of the Mythographus Vergilianus, that is, a collection of myths keyed to Vergil's texts, see Smith (forthcoming). A good and accessible overview of Donatus and Servius and of the relationship between Servius and Servius Danielis is Stok (2012). Zetzel (2018) is an indispensable handbook for the commentaries and exegesis on Vergil and Latin literature in general. For mythographical method in the Statius scholia, one may consult Smith (2013; also 2011). While there is no good introduction in English to the scholia to Ovid's *Ibis* (see the Italian edition of La Penna 1959), the mythographical aspects of the poem itself have been well studied by Krasne (2012, 2013). For further reading on Hyginus, I refer the reader to the chapters by Fletcher and Zucker in this volume.

## References

Bremmer, Jan N., and Nicholas Horsfall. 1987. *Roman Myth and Mythography*. Oxford: Oxford University Press.

Breysig, Alfredus. 1867. *Germanici Caesaris Aratea cum scholiis*. Berlin: Georg Reimer.

Brugnoli, Giorgio, and Fabio Stok. 1997. *Vitae Vergilianae Antiquae*. Rome: Typis Officinae Polygraphicae.

Cameron, Alan. 2004. *Greek Mythography in the Roman World*. Oxford: Oxford University Press.

Clément-Tarantino, Séverine. 2016. "Servius mythographe? Réflexions à partir du commentaire au chant 1 de l'Énéide." *Polymnia* 2: 120–162.

Cole, Thomas. 2004. "Ovid, Varro, and Castor of Rhodes: The Chronological Architecture of the *Metamorphoses*." *Harvard Studies in Classical Philology* 102: 355–422.

Cole, Thomas. 2008. *"Ovidius Mythistoricus": Legendary Time in the "Metamorphoses."* Frankfurt: Peter Lang.

Daintree, David. 1990. "The Virgil Commentary of Aelius Donatus—Black Hole or 'Éminence Grise'?" *Greece and Rome* 37: 65–79.

Daintree, David. 1993. "Scholia Bernensia: An Edition of the Scholia on the Eclogues of Virgil in Bern Burgersbibliothek Manuscript 172." Diss. University of Tasmania.

Delvigo, Maria L. 2012. "*Secundum fabulam, secundum veritatem*: Servio e il mito." *Prometheus* 38: 179–193.

Deremetz, Alain. 2016. "La mythographie dans le 'Commentaire aux Bucoliques' de Servius: Quelques réflexions." In *Lire des Mythes*, edited by Arnaud Zucker, Jacqueline Fabre-Serris, Jean-Yves Tilliette, Gisele Besson, 161–175. Lille: Presses du Septentrion.

Dickey, Eleanor. 2007. *Ancient Greek Scholarship: A Guide to Finding, Reading, and Understanding Scholia, Commentaries, Lexica, and Grammatical Treatises, from Their Beginnings to the Byzantine Period*. Oxford: Oxford University Press.

Dionisotti, Anna C. 1982. "From Ausonius' Schooldays? A Schoolbook and Its Relatives." *Journal of Roman Studies* 72: 83–125.

Expósito, Guadalupe M. 2003. "Caius Iulius Hyginus, Mitógrafo." *Anuario de Estudios Filológicos* 26: 267–277.

Fantham, Elaine. 2003. "Pacuvius: Melodramas, Reversals and Recognitions." In *Myth, History and Culture in Republican Rome: Studies in Honour of T. P. Wiseman*, edited by David Braund and Christopher Gill, 98–118. Exeter, UK: University of Exeter Press.

Farrell, Joseph. 2008. "Servius and the Homeric Scholia." In *Servio: Stratificazioni esegetiche e modelli culturali* [Servius: Exegetical stratifications and cultural models], edited by Sergio Casali and Fabio Stok, 112–131. Brussels: Collection Latomus 317.

Farrell, Joseph. 2013. "Complementarity and Contradiction in Ovidian Mythography." In *Writing Myth: Mythography in the Ancient World*, edited by Stephen M. Trzaskoma and R. Scott Smith, 223–251. Leuven: Peeters.

Flammini, Giuseppe, ed. 2004. *Hermeneumata Pseudodositheana Leidensia*. Munich and Leipzig: Teubner.

Fletcher, K. F. B. 2013. "Hyginus' *Fabulae*: Toward a Roman Mythography." In *Writing Myth: Mythography in the Ancient World*, edited by Stephen M. Trzaskoma and R. Scott Smith, 133–164. Leuven: Peeters.

Francese, Christopher. 1999. "Parthenius 'Grammaticus.'" *Mnemosyne* 52: 63–71.

Gee, Emma. 2001. "Cicero's Astronomy." *Classical Quarterly* 51: 520–536.

Funaioli, Gino. 1930. *Esegesi Virgiliana antica*. Milan: Società editrice Vita e Pensiero.

Hays, Gregory. 2017. "Roman Mythography." In *A Handbook to the Reception of Classical Mythology*, edited by Vanda Zajko and Helena Hoyle, 29–41. Chichester and Malden, MA: Wiley-Blackwell.

Horsfall, Nicholas. 1991. "Virgil, Parthenius and the Art of Mythological Reference." *Vergilius* 37: 31–36.

Jakobi, Rainer. 2004. "Textgeschichte als Kulturgeschichte: Der sogennante Lactantius Placidus Kommentar zur 'Thebais' des Statius." In *Der Kommentar in Antike und Mittelalter*, vol. 2, edited by Wilhelm Geerlings and Christian Schulze, 1–16. Leiden: Brill.

Klotz, Alfred. 1908. "Die Statiusscholien." *Archiv für lateinische Lexikographie und Grammatik* 15: 485–525.

Krasne, Darcy. 2012. "The Pedant's Curse: Obscurity and Identity in Ovid's *Ibis*." *Dictynna* 9: 1–52. doi.org/10.4000/dictynna.912.

Krasne, Darcy. 2013. "Starving the Slender Muse: Identity, Mythography, and Intertextuality in Ovid's *Ibis*. In *Writing Down the Myths*, edited by Joseph F. Nagy, 67–85. Turnhout: Brepols.

La Boeuffle, André. 2002. *Hygin "L'Astronomie."* Paris: Les Belles Lettres.

La Penna, Antonio. 1959. *Scholia in P. Ovidi Nasonis Ibin: Introduzione, testo, apparato critico e commentario*. Florence: Nuova Italia.

Longobardi, Concetta. 2016. "*Sic Servius Magister Exposuit*: L'*auctoritas* mitografica di Servio e le interconnessioni fra i commentatori tardi." In *Fragments d'érudition: Servio e le savoir antique*, edited by Alessandro Garcea, Marie-Karine Lhommé, and Daniel Vallat, 479–497. Hildesheim, Germany: Georg Olms Verlag.

Magnus, Hugo. 1914. *Metamorphoseon Libri XV: Lactanti Placidi qui dicitur Narrationes fabularum Ovidianarum*. Berlin: Weidmann.

Marshall, Peter K. 2002. *Hyginus "Fabulae." Editio Altera*. Munich: Teubner.

Martin, Jean. 1956. *Histoire du texte des "Phénomènes" d'Aratos*. Paris: Klincksieck.

Martin, Jean. 2002. "Sur le sens réel des mots "catastérisme" et "catastériser."" In *Palladio Magistro: Mélanges Jean Soubiran (= Pallas 59)*, edited by Mireille Armisen-Marchetti and Maximilien Monbrun, 17–26. Toulouse: Presses Universitaires du Mirail.

Otis, Brooks. 1936. "The Argumenta of the So-Called Lactantius." *Harvard Studies in Classical Philology* 47: 131–163.

Possanza, D. Mark. 2004. *Translating the Heavens: Aratus and the Poetics of Latin Translation*. New York: Peter Lang.

Robinson, Matthew. 2013. "Ovid and the *Catasterismi* of Eratosthenes." *American Journal of Philology* 134: 445–480.

Schierl, Petra. 2006. *Die Tragödien des Pacuvius: Ein Kommentar zu den Fragmenten mit Einleitung, Text und Übersetzung*. Berlin and New York: De Gruyter.

Smith, R. Scott. 2010–2011. "Homer in the Late Antique Commentary to Statius' Thebaid." *Illinois Classical Studies* 35–36: 175–194.

Smith, R. Scott. 2013. "Mythographic Material and Method in the Late Antique Commentary to Statius' Thebaid." In *Writing Myth: Mythography in the Ancient World*, edited by Stephen M. Trzaskoma and R. Scott Smith, 165–200. Leuven: Peeters.

Smith, R. Scott. 2017. "Mythographical and Literary Notes on the Catalogs of Argive and Theban Allies in Statius' *Thebaid*." *Mnemosyne* 70: 240–261.

Smith, R. Scott. 2022. "The Myth of the Mythographus Vergilianus." In *Myths on the Margins of Homer. Prolegomena to the Mythographus Homericus*, edited by Joan Pagès and Nereida Villagra, 157–194. Berlin and Boston: de Gruyter.

Smith, R. Scott, and Stephen M. Trzaskoma. 2007. *Apollodorus' "Library" and Hyginus' "Fabulae": Two Handbooks of Greek Mythology*. Indianapolis, IN: Hackett.

Stok, Fabio. 2012. "Commenting on Virgil, from Aelius Donatus to Servius." *Dead Sea Discoveries* 19: 464–484.

Tarrant, Richard J. 1995. "The *Narrationes* of 'Lactantius' and the Transmission of Ovid's *Metamorphoses*." In *Formative Stages of Classical Tradition: Latin Texts from Antiquity to the Renaissance*, edited by Oronzo Pecere and Michael D. Reeve, 83–115. Spoleto: Centro italiano di studi sull'alto medioevo.

Zetzel, James E. 2018. *Critics, Compilers, and Commentators: An Introduction to Roman Philology, 200 BCE–800 CE*. Oxford: Oxford University Press.

Ziolkowski, Jan. 2013. "Medieval Latin Mythography as Death and Resurrection of Myth." In *Writing Down the Myths*, edited by Joseph F. Nagy, 87–106. Turnhout: Brepols.

Zissos, Andrew. 2008. *Valerius Flaccus' "Argonautica" Book 1*. Oxford: Oxford University Press.

Zucker, Arnaud. 2015. "Hygin et Ératosthène: Variation mythographique ou restitution d'un original perdu." *Polymnia* 1: 83–125.

# PART II

# MYTHOGRAPHERS

# CHAPTER 6

# MYTHOGRAPHY IN ALEXANDRIAN VERSE

## EVINA SISTAKOU

IMAGINE the Alexandrian Museum of the 3rd century BCE as an ancient version of a Cabinet of Curiosities. These cabinets displayed a collection, primarily of objects, representing the entire scope of human civilization—science, natural history, archaeology, art. Introduced in the late Renaissance, such cabinets flourished throughout the Baroque, and aspired to offer spectators a "theatre of the world." The aspiration to collect, categorize, and exhibit—albeit among small circles of connoisseurs—objects representing the totality of human knowledge and achievements was the driving force behind the passionate engagement of the Ptolemies with culture and science. It is not without significance that apart from the Library, where books from the entire known world were collected, acquired sometimes by cunning or force, scientific data were collected to help researchers in the various branches of physical sciences. It may be that the Alexandrian Museum was primarily a research institution modeled on Aristotle's Lyceum rather than a static collection of "objects," yet the idea that it could preserve and put on display the cultural heritage of the whole world through its collections made it akin to a modern-era museum.

But where does mythography, the writing down of myths in their infinite variations, fit into this scheme, and what was the role played by the scholars, who were also active poets, in its making? Seen from a literary-historical viewpoint, mythography can be divided into an early stage of development, when it was inseparable from historical writing; a more mature phase, connected with the collective zeal of the Peripatetics; and a final stage, when it was eventually recognized as a discipline per se. Hellenistic scholarship, originating at the Museum of Alexandria but then spreading to other cultural institutions of the Hellenistic kingdoms, saw the potential of mythography in its numerous applications. First, mythography was recognized as a valuable tool for the explanation of the grand literature of the past, including Homer, Hesiod, the lyric tradition, and the tragedians, and hence formed an essential part of the Hellenistic scholiastic corpora. Second, the concept of collecting and classifying all kinds of data fascinated scholars, all the more so because myths were seen as the building material of poetry and historiography, as the quintessence of Greek culture itself. Third, omnipresent in their research and writings is the scholars' desire for rare stories with local coloring or of archaeological interest, their desire for curiosities—in effect, paradoxography was a most popular philological genre in the Hellenistic age—and their desire for exotic names, which are found in abundance in the genealogies and catalogues of mythical narratives. These trends led gradually to the creation of mythographical compilations and anthologies of myths on the basis of thematic criteria. The oldest such collection is Eratosthenes's *Catasterisms*—that is, narratives on the stars—compiled in the second half of the 3rd century. During the following centuries, thematic mythographies such as Parthenius's *Sufferings in Love* and Antoninus Liberalis's *Metamorphoses* stood side by side with more general mythographical works such as Conon's *Narrations* and Apollodorus's *The Library*.

The mythographical treatises written in prose emerged from the quasi-scientific spirit of authors who were less concerned with originality and more obsessed with the idea of unearthing and bringing together mythical narratives drawn from written and oral sources of all sorts, archaeological remains, works of art. Between the early mythographers, whose method approached that of the logographers and the historians and who worked against the background of local tradition, and the scholars, who did research in the library and drew on the textual corpus preserved from the past, the learned poets of the first decades of the 3rd century took a different path. The challenge faced by the poets Hermesianax of Colophon, Alexander of Aetolia, Euphorion of Chalcis, Callimachus of Cyrene, Apollonius of Rhodes, and "Lycophron," the author of the *Alexandra*, was how to channel scholarship and learning into poetry and how to achieve this, not in a pedantic manner, but in a highly artistic one. These poets were also collectors and scholars, and in their poems, they spoke through the persona of the connoisseur. If we use the Cabinet of Curiosities as a metaphor, then the learned poem is such a cabinet. The wealth of strange and rare material that is worked into these poems resembles the curious objects that are put on display in the *Wunderkammer*. In blending mythography with neoteric poetics, the various Hellenistic poets gave their personalized responses. In what follows, I will sketch out four strategies by which they poeticized mythography to demonstrate the aesthetic impact of mythography as poetry.

# 1. Working Mythography into Learned Poetry: From Antimachus to Euphorion

Collections of rare myths were integrated into poetry early on, on the one hand, through the catalogue-form mythological poetry of the Hesiodic tradition and, on the other, through the recherché stories about heroes brought to light by the lyric poets, especially Pindar and Bacchylides (see Nieto Hernández, this volume). But these early poets did not depend on scholarship in writing their poetry. Antimachus of Colophon (active about 400 BCE) and Philitas of Cos (340–285 BCE) first introduced the idea that poetry should be the product of philology. Even if based on stylistic criteria (at least, as understood by Callimachus in the *Aetia*-Prologue fr. 1.7–12 Pf.), Philitas is a more elegant and sophisticated poet than Antimachus, it appears that both showcased their learnedness by creating poetry that relied largely on glossography and mythography. The latter became the raw material of their poetry.

Antimachus, in particular, appears to have been an expert in compiling episodes from different myths to achieve novel artistic effects. So, instead of elaborating on a single mythical narrative, as he did in his epic *Thebaid*, which was formed around the Theban cycle, he also wrote the narrative elegy *Lyde*, where he put together a wealth of stories from the entire range of Greek mythology (Matthews 1995; for the testimonia, see 3–5, and for the fragments, 207–264). Against a quasi-biographical background, since Lyde was the name of the poet's beloved, and the poem was written as a consolation for her death, Antimachus collected myths revolving around unhappy love affairs and other gloomy subjects—the wanderings of Demeter and the fate of Oedipus are telling examples of the latter—and reproduced them with meticulous detail (Matthews 1995: 26–39). As the scant testimonies about this work suggest, the tone of the poem was lugubrious (according to Hermesianax fr. 7.41–46 Powell, Antimachus filled the books of *Lyde* with tears), whereas its subject matter was the sorrows of the heroes (*hērōikas symphoras*, as clearly stated by Ps.-Plut., *Cons. ad Apoll.* 9.106c).

Philitas, an even more obscure figure, must have made broad use of recondite mythology in his poems, although the extant testimonies and fragments do not allow us a clear insight into their content. His narrative elegy *Demeter* focused on the local cults of the goddess and their etiologies, and allusions to various mythical narratives cannot be excluded; whether *Bittis* was a catalogue poem with erotic mythological content in the manner of Antimachus's *Lyde* is still an open question (see Sbardella 2000). Scholars have also assumed that his *Hermes* could not have dealt exclusively with the love affair of Odysseus and Polymele on the island of Aeolus and was actually a catalogue-like poem that drew heavily on mythology for the narration of lesser-known episodes from the life of gods and heroes (Spanoudakis 2002: 223–243 on *Demeter*, and 126–137 on *Hermes*).

Lack of evidence prevents us from assessing Antimachus and Philitas's contribution to the scholarly revival of the catalogue poem, as introduced by Hesiod's *Catalogue of Women*, through which mythography found its way into Alexandrian poetry (on the Hellenistic adaptation of the catalogue form, see Asquith 2005). However, with other scholar-poets, we are in a better position to judge. Following in Antimachus's footsteps, his fellow-countryman Hermesianax wrote a catalogue-formed elegy in three books, entitled *Leontion*. Hermesianax (active in the early 3rd century BCE) was mainly active on the periphery of the Greek world—he was born in Colophon, but he is also known as a pupil of Philitas, probably on Cos—and it is likely that he never went to Alexandria. Yet he is one of the predecessors of Alexandrian aesthetics (Lightfoot 2009: 147–187). Writing in the literary tradition of Colophon that begins with the *Nanno* of Mimnermus and extends to the *Lyde* of Antimachus, Hermesianax is considered the Hellenistic predecessor of mythographical erotic elegy that may sometimes have struck a more personal, subjective tone (Asquith 2005: 279–286). Unrequited love was the thematic core around which legendary and fictional episodes, drawn not only from the realm of mythology but also from history and biography, were assembled in the *Leontion*. Among the love stories retold by Hermesianax were two emblematic ones for Hellenistic, in particular, bucolic poetics: that of Cyclops and Galateia, reworked by Theocritus in *Idyll* 11, and perhaps that involving Daphnis and Menalcas.

With a penchant for Alexandrianism, Hermesianax also recounted heartbreaking love affairs: the story of a certain Arceophon and his beloved Arsinoe that ended in metamorphosis; a story of incest between Leucippus and his sister leading to her death; and the romantic narrative about Nanis, the supposed daughter of Croesus, who betrayed her city out of love for Cyrus. The story of Arceophon and Arsinoe figured among the mythological metamorphosis narratives collected by the mythographer Antoninus Liberalis. The other two stories were later reworked by Parthenius in the *Sufferings in Love* (Parth. 5 and 22), where Hermesianax is also named as Parthenius's source in the manchettes introducing the narrations (however, the marginal source citations in Parthenius and Antoninus Liberalis may not originate from the authors themselves but may be later additions: on this problem, see Cameron 2004: 321–327). It is therefore highly probable that Parthenius and Antoninus Liberalis viewed the *Leontion*, a collection of mythological rarities, as a poem that matched their own conception of mythography.

Alexander of Aetolia (born around 315 BCE) comes from a different cultural milieu. He is known for his philological activity in the Library of Alexandria, where he was appointed by Ptolemy II Philadelphus as an editor of Greek tragedies and satyr plays, and for his participation in the Pleiad, the official group of tragedians of Alexandria (Lightfoot 2009: 99–145). Alexander's interest in the minutiae of Greek mythology is evident even in the scant remains of his poetry (for a cultural portrayal of Alexander and a discussion of his poetry, see Magnelli 1999: 9–56). One of his tragedies (or, in the opinion of other scholars, one of his satyr plays) was entitled *Astragalistae* "The Dice Players." Based on a Homeric para-narrative (*Il.* 23.85–88), Alexander dramatized an episode from Patroclus's youth, when the hero had, as a boy, killed the son of Amphidamas in a rage over a dice game. Alexander's method was to fill in the gaps of a Homeric "footnote" with scholarly details, such as the dispute over the name of the murdered boy or the reference to Patroclus's schoolteacher (see fr. 10 Powell and the reconstruction of the plot by Spanoudakis 2005).

To choose such subject matter for dramatization reflects Alexander's penchant for mythological rarities. Two of his fragments demonstrate an interest in alternative genealogies. According to the ancient sources, Alexander of Aetolia agreed with Stesichorus and Euphorion that Iphigenia was the daughter of Theseus (fr. 12 Powell), and Hector, the son of Apollo (fr. 13 Powell). Other poems with mythological content were probably *Circe*, of which only one couplet survives (fr. 2 Powell), and the elegy *Apollo* (fr. 3 Powell). The latter was perhaps a catalogue poem in the vein of the amatory, multinarrative elegies of Antimachus and Hermesianax, as is suggested by its sole extant fragment (fr. 3 Powell). Alexander, like Philitas and Hermesianax, served as a source for Parthenius's *Sufferings in Love* for the recherché story of Antheus, a romance of secret love and tragic death (Parth. 14). In Parthenius's summary thirty-four verses of the original survive, from which we may infer that the poem was written as a prophetic discourse, probably uttered by Apollo. It is worth noting that apart from Alexander of Aetolia, the manchette to Parthenius's summary expressly names Aristotle and the authors of *Milesiaca* as his co-sources for the story of Antheus, suggesting that Alexander made use of prose sources in his poems. In other words, the subject matter of his poetry must have been the product of scholarly research, a method that underlies pure mythographical works as well.

The gathering of different mythical narrations in one poem by focusing on their trivia rather than their plots gradually became a dominant trend in Alexandrian poetics. Apart from the masterwork in this area, Callimachus's *Aetia*, which will be discussed separately, numerous poets followed in the tradition of Antimachus, Hermesianax, and Alexander of Aetolia. Some poets insisted on grouping rare or lesser-known stories from mythology in thematically organized poems. Phanocles's *Erotes or Beautiful Boys* and verse collections of myths ending in metamorphosis fall into this category. Phanocles's erotic elegy focuses on a theme that became popular mainly through the epigrammatic tradition—namely, love for fair youths (for a recent overview of the poem, see Gärtner 2008). But in contrast to the personalized tone of the homoerotic epigrams, the *Erotes or Beautiful Boys* substantiates its core idea based on mythological evidence, drawn from the love affairs of both gods and heroes (see the only extensive surviving fragment [fr. 1 Powell] on the love of Orpheus for Calais).

Alongside love—and etiology, as will be evident from the case of Callimachus—metamorphosis was the other key theme of Hellenistic catalogue poems. A certain Boios, known only for his poem *Ornithogonia* ("On the Birth of Birds"), and the 2nd-century poet Nicander of Colophon, who wrote *Heteroioumena* ("Transformations"), collected and narrated stories of metamorphosis in verse. They, in turn, became a point of reference for the making of the mythographical literature (they are systematically mentioned as sources for the corpora of the ancient scholia and the later mythographer Antoninus Liberalis) and also created a poetic trend that developed into the core idea of Ovid's *Metamorphoses* (Forbes Irving 1990: 19–37).

This overview cannot be complete without a brief reference to the mythographical poet par excellence, Euphorion of Chalcis (Lightfoot 2009: 189–427). Euphorion (born around 275 BCE) is connected to another cultural center of the Hellenistic world: he was appointed librarian in the Library of Antioch, but his spiritual connections to the Alexandrians and their literary taste are beyond dispute. Following in the footsteps of Callimachus and being recognized as a model for the Roman avant-garde, the so-called *cantores Euphorionis*, he cultivated a poetic style that was both learned and obscure. Mythology played a key role in his poetry, although he seems to have been less concerned with narrative per se than with the accumulation of rare details, genealogies, and a wealth of obscure names (for a comprehensive account, see Cusset, Prioux, and Richer 2013). He only wrote hexametric poems, which may be classified as epyllia (*Philoctetes, Anius, Hyacinthus*) and especially catalogue poems (*Mopsopia, Chiliades, Curses* or *Cup-Thief, Thrax*). What can be inferred from most of what remains is that Euphorion's poems were a mélange of various stories told in a fragmentary (that is, selective and incomplete) style, yet precious for the ancient scholars for the bulk of the mythographical information they contained. It is hardly surprising that the *Mythographus Homericus*, the anonymous commentator of Homeric mythology, attributes six of his recondite stories to Euphorion: the myth of the giant Ophion, the myth of the giant Eurymedon, the story of Orion, the *aetion* of the *aegis*, the story of Thersites, and that of Niobe (Pagès Cebrian 2013). Euphorion was so notorious for the amount of scholarly material in his poetry that Clement of Alexandria once wrote about him (*Stromat.* 5.8.50): "Euphorion the poet and the *Aetia* of Callimachus and the *Alexandra* of Lycophron and similar works constitute a veritable playground for grammatical exegesis" (trans. Lightfoot).

## 2. The Aesthetics of Mythography in Callimachus's *Aetia*

Callimachus of Cyrene (around 310–240 BCE) is the leading figure of Alexandrian aesthetics, and his elegy *Aetia* is the most innovative and influential work of the Hellenistic age. In Callimachus's poetry, the interaction between literature and scholarship is complex and sustained. The *Suda* article on Callimachus lists numerous scholarly works that not only reveal his penchant for collecting oddities from all types of sources—archaeological, textual, literary—but also highlight his talent in offering organized material in bulk for poets and grammarians to exploit (Blum 1991: 124–137). It is obvious from the surviving titles that Callimachus was keen to list any type of material (*On the Rivers of the World, On Birds, On Contests, The Customs of the Barbarians, On Nymphs*) and was specifically interested in onomastics (*Foundations of Islands and Cities and Changes of their Names, Dialectal Names, The Names of Months, On the Names of Fishes*) and paradoxography (*Selection of Natural Curiosities* or *Collection of the Marvels of the World*); on the other hand, his major work in the Library, the *Pinakes* "Lists of Greek Authors and Their Works," attests to his profound knowledge of previous literature.

Seen against this background, the miscellaneous and unconventional content of his magnum opus, the *Aetia*, should not come as a surprise. The *Aetia* is an elegiac poem in four books on customs, names, works of art, and cults explained on the basis of events from the distant past, where the boundaries of mythology and history are blurred. The material gathered in the *Aetia* falls outside the range of mainstream mythology. Both geographically and chronologically, the *Aetia* expands the reader's horizon beyond the Panhellenic Greek tradition and leads him or her to the untrodden paths of local and archaic myths from the entire Mediterranean region. Callimachus could not have created his spatiotemporal heterotopia, this alternative poetic world of recondite legends, had he not had access to a wealth of textual sources (for these alibis in Callimachus's poetry, see Selden 1998).

The motto by which Callimachus is usually interpreted is his famous saying *amartyron ouden aeidō* ("I sing nothing unattested," fr. 612 Pf.). The recourse to sources for the making of poetry is not only an undercurrent sensed throughout his poems; the very process of transforming a chronographical work or an oral tradition into a sophisticated narrative is dramatized repeatedly in the *Aetia* (Meyer 1993). Books 1–2 are designed as an extended dialogue where the poet poses etiological questions and the Muses respond by providing a bulk of mythological information, whereas in books 3–4 the narrator draws directly upon all possible sources of knowledge. A much-discussed example of this is the romance of Acontius and Cydippe, a love story whose two protagonists are marginal, almost fictional, figures in the Greek mythical tradition (fr. 67–75 Pf.). In a mythographical digression on the local legends of Ceos, Callimachus directly quotes his source—namely, the fifth-century logographer Xenomedes of Ceos (fr. 75.53–55 Pf.): "We heard about this love of yours [sc. Acontius] from ancient Xenomedes, who once set down the whole island in a mythological record" (trans. Harder). The quotation clearly reflects how Callimachus, qua mythographer, draws on earlier mythographers for material; the term *mythologos mnēmē*, "mythological memory," points to a prose mythological account that Callimachus translates into poetry (Harder 2012: 2.635–636).

Even if it is not explicitly stated, the *Aetia* exploits a wealth of prose authors whose work fluctuates between mythography and historiography: Hecataeus, Herodotus, Pherecydes, Hellanicus, the Argive authors Agias and Dercyllus, the author of the Sicilian antiquities Timaeus, Thucydides, and eventually Aristotle. Moreover, mythological rarities are collected from the most demanding Greek poets, such as Homer, Hesiod, and Pindar. Not coincidentally, the *Aetia* has been characterized a "poem of knowledge" in the sense that the thread binding together this discontinuous poem is the recourse to erudition—divine, human or plainly scientific, historical and philological (Hutchinson 2003).

Callimachus conceived the *Aetia* as a Hellenistic response to the archaic catalogue poetry of Hesiod and the elegiac tradition of the *Kollektivgedicht* introduced by Mimnermus and later developed by Antimachus and Philitas. The myths collected here would not be connected thematically, as in the Hellenistic poems revolving around "love" or "metamorphosis." Instead, Callimachus opted for a metaliterary theme, the idea of the *aetion*, the explanation of any question by reference to an authority. The mythical stories in the *Aetia*, however, are never thoroughly recounted. Their fragmentariness results from their very scholarly nature since the genealogical detail or the geographical catalogue or the emphasis on exotic onomastics is more important than storytelling per se (Sistakou 2009b: 394–401). In effect, the *Aetia* is a mythographical encyclopedia offering a panorama of the adventures of gods, heroes, and humans in the broader Greek world, in Asia Minor, Sicily, and, eventually, Egypt. The time span covered by the etiological stories extends from the beginning of the heroic age (major mythical cycles such as the Argonautic and the Trojan and heroic enterprises like that of Heracles are broadly represented) through the obscure past of the Greek cities (here local cults and myths of foundation play a major role) until the present-day world of Ptolemaic Alexandria. The *Aetia* monitors, although not linearly, the progress of civilization from the era of Minos until the Hellenistic world through the narrations of hundreds of local myths and legends; many scholars have seen the work as a sequel to the Hesiodic *Theogony*, which begins with the creation of the world, extends to the establishment of the Olympian pantheon, and concludes with the catalogue of the heroes (for an overview of its contents, see Harder 2012: 2.15–21).

Yet the *Aetia* is much more than a remake of Hesiodic mythological poetry. Through its nonlinear structuring and digressive style, the amassing of alternative names, genealogies, and legendary anecdotes, and the appeal to various authorities for the acquisition of specialized knowledge, the reader is constantly reminded of the act of reading, collecting, and rewriting of mythography in the *Aetia*. Not unjustly later authors criticize Callimachus's obsession with mythography as poetry. The satiric comments against him highlight his pedantry in the quest for mythographical detail: to investigate in the books whether Cyclops had dogs (Philippus of Thessalonica, *A.P.* 11.321) or to dedicate several verses to the minutiae of Tantalus and Ixion's tortures in the Underworld (Lucian, *How to Write History* 57) is a typical feature of Callimachus and his imitators. Even his most severe critics, however, cannot deny the erudition of the *polyhistor*, the "well-read" Callimachus. The anonymous epigrammatist of *A.P.* 7.42 hails the *Aetia* as the poem that can teach mythology to its readers:

> O great and widely known dream of the clever Battiad,
> truly you were of horn and not of ivory;
> for such things you showed us, which we men did not know before,
> about the immortals and about half-gods,
> when you lifted him up from Libya and brought him to Mt. Helicon,
> placing him in the middle of the Pierian Muses;
> and they told him in answer to his questions the *Aetia* about
> the ancient heroes and the blessed gods.

(trans. Harder)

# 3. Weaving Mythography into Epic Saga: Apollonius's *Argonautica*

Apollonius of Rhodes (active during the 3rd century BCE) was a distinguished Homeric scholar and was appointed chief librarian in Alexandria during the reign of Ptolemy II Philadelphus. His scholarly work, now lost, was oriented primarily toward glossography and the textual interpretation of Homer and other archaic poets, and it may have served as a basis for later commentators. Apollonius's mythographical interests are particularly evident in his *ktisis* poetry, a collection of poems where the founding of a city is explained on account of its mythical past. Like Callimachus, Apollonius drew on previous prose writers for etiological material and foundation stories. Most prominent among his sources were Hecataeus, Hellanicus, Herodotus, and Ephorus, all of whom belonged to the tradition of the Ionian logographers and local historians also extensively exploited by Callimachus in his poetic oeuvre, especially the *Aetia*. Apollonius's *ktisis* poems—on the founding of Naucratis, Alexandria, Cnidus, Caunus, Rhodes, Lesbos, and perhaps Canobus—combine all the features found in other "mythographical" poems: thematic emphasis on unlucky love and metamorphosis, genealogical details, explanations of names, etiology (Krevans 2001; Sistakou 2008a, 2008b). Three of these stories were later collected by Parthenius in his mythographical compilation *Sufferings in Love*. Several verses survive from the love story of Pisidice and Achilles that took place during the siege of Methymna (fr. 12 Powell = Parthenius 21). About the stories of Lyrcus and Byblis, we are only indirectly informed by the introductory manchette of Parthenius's summaries, where it is expressly stated that they were treated in Apollonius's foundation poem on Caunus (Parth. 1 and 11).

Yet it is his magnum opus, the epic poem *Argonautica* in four books, which opened up a world of possibilities for the rewriting of mythography as poetry. *Argonautica*'s main plot follows the storyline of the Argonautic saga that records the journey of Jason and the Argo to Colchis, the romance of Jason and Medea, the acquisition of the Golden Fleece, and, finally, the safe return of the Argonauts to Iolcus. Apollonius had many sources to provide him with mythological material, most of which belong either to archaic epics and other poetic accounts of the Argonautic myth or to the corpus of mythography, local history, and geography, because the *Argonautica* is first and foremost a voyage epic written against a semi-mythical, semi-historical background. The first category constitutes the pre-Homeric Argonautic epic, known only from a Homeric passage on the *Argō pasimelousa* "most sung-of Argo" (*Od.* 12.69–72), the lost epics Eumelus's *Corinthiaca*, the *Naupactia* by an unknown author, and, probably, Epimenides's account of the Argonautic journey, as well as lyric poems such as Pindar's *Pythian* 4 and Stesichorus's *Funeral Games for Pelias*. In particular, Pindar served as the source for several episodes of the *Argonautica*, such as the background of Jason's myth (*P.* 4.70–168), the passage through the Wandering Rocks (*P.* 4.169–187), and the events in Colchis (*P.* 4.213–250), but also for some of the critical stages of the voyage, including Lemnos, Calliste, and Cyrene. There is also solid basis for supposing that Apollonius made extensive use of the Greek tragedies about the Argonautic myth, which, with the exception of Euripides's *Medea*, survive only in fragments (Aeschylus's *Hypsipyle*, *Argo*, *Lemnians*, and *Phineus*; Sophocles's *Lemnians*, *Colchides*, and *Root-cutters*; Euripides's *Phrixus* and *Hypsipyle*). Even more impressive is the range of prose authors Apollonius exploited in making the Argonautic universe: Hecataeus, Acusilaus, Pherecydes, Hellanicus, Herodotus, Herodorus, Timagetus, Euphorus, Timaeus, Nymphodorus. In combining legends and data from all these authors, Apollonius strove to counterbalance the mythographical and paradoxographical accounts of the Argonautic voyage by adding historical and geographical details (for a detailed survey of the poetic and prose sources used by Apollonius in the *Argonautica*, see Scherer 2006: 10–42).

Despite the realistic light Apollonius cast on the saga, learned mythology remains at the core of the *Argonautica*. The dominance of mythology in Apollonius's epic is reflected primarily in the blending of different mythical cycles into the Argonautic story. An obvious starting point in investigating Apollonius's mythographical interests is to look at how he integrates the Trojan War myth into his plot. From the viewpoint of mythical chronology, the Argonautic expedition predates the Trojan War by one heroic generation; that is, the Argonauts are the fathers of the Trojan heroes. The latter are present at key stages of the Argonautic plot as an indication of the genealogical continuity between the two mythological cycles. This is especially evident in the catalogue of the Argonauts, where the names of the heroes recall various Iliadic patronymics. The most striking examples are the special appearance of Achilles as a baby bidding Peleus farewell during the departure of the Argo (*Arg.* 1.553–558) and the episode recording how Thetis abandoned Peleus after her failed attempt to make Achilles immortal (*Arg.* 4.866–879). The Odyssean *nostos* is also part of the Homeric mythography that has been integrated into the Argonautic story. Although Apollonius eschews making any straightforward reference to Odysseus and his adventures, it is beyond doubt that the return of the Argonauts is modeled on the *Odyssey* and its mythographical tradition (Sistakou 2008b: 88–100).

But Apollonius's penchant for mythography reaches far beyond Homer. A plethora of mythical cycles of events, of heroic narratives of Panhellenic or local provenance, and of genealogical associations between mythical personalities create a broader canvas on which the Argonautic expedition takes place. Apollonius's sources include poems such as Hesiod's *Theogony* and *Catalogue of Women* and archaic epics that are now lost (the *Titanomachy* and epics on the Theban cycle, on Theseus, and especially, Heracles). Following the patterns of catalogue poetry and the narrative techniques introduced by Callimachus's *Aetia*, Apollonius opts for fragmentation—that is, for selective and incomplete narratives of mythical episodes. He makes extensive use of this narrative strategy in the *Argonautica*, not in the narration of the main storyline (in dramatizing the Argonautic myth, Apollonius strives for linearity and wholeness), but in the inclusion of stories from other mythical cycles (Sistakou 2009b: 386–394).

The catalogue of the Argonauts and the *ecphrasis* of Jason's cloak offer ample opportunities for integrating fragmented stories into the main thread of the Argonautic plot. Unlike the Catalogue of Ships from the *Iliad*, which strictly follows the formula of archaic lists of names, each entry of the Catalogue of the Argonauts is enriched with mythographical material: the identity of the hero, his genealogy, his geographic provenance and narratives about his family, his special talents, his relation to the gods, and his past and future life (*Arg.* 1.23–233). Slightly different is the structuring of the description of Jason's cloak, which consists of seven fragmented episodes drawn from cyclic myth (*Arg.* 1.721–768): the Cyclopes fabricate a thunderbolt for Zeus; Amphion and Zethus lay the foundations of the city of Thebes; Aphrodite has a love affair with Ares; a fight erupts between the Teleboans and the sons of Electryon; Pelops and Oenomaus participate in a chariot race; Apollo shoots Tityus; and Phrixus meets with the speaking ram (for the mythological background of these scenes and their symbolism in Apollonius's narrative, see Merriam 1993 and Bulloch 2006). Moreover, during the voyage to Colchis and on the return journey, the Argonauts encounter various heroes, occasioning a glimpse into their mythological background. The episode with Hypsipyle motivates the digression on the slaughtering of the Lemnian men by their wives (*Arg.* 1.609–639); the encounter with Prometheus bound on the rock of Caucasus evokes the Aeschylean account of the hero's punishment by Zeus (*Arg.* 1.1247–1261); through the participation of Heracles in the Argonautic expedition, two of his Labors, the killing of the Erymanthian Boar (*Arg.* 1.122–129) and the stealing of the Apples of the Hesperides (*Arg.* 4.1393–1449), are retold by Apollonius.

The list of mythical events introduced in the *Argonautica* through digressions, etiologies, and *ktisis* stories is endless. Beyond the detailed narration of the Argonautic myth, Apollonius's epic may also be read as a mythographical commentary on the cosmos of a distant past, a world of gods, heroes, and ordinary men, where the lines between fantasy, legend, and reality are blurred.

## 4. Mythography as Key to Solving Riddles in the *Alexandra*

Lycophron of Chalcis, the scholar and tragedian of early 3rd-century Alexandria, owes his legacy to a monodrama surviving under his name, the *Alexandra*. Because of the internal criteria of chronology—the poem probably alludes to historical events of the 2nd century BCE—modern scholars tend to doubt the authorship of the play. Whether Lycophron, the member of the tragic Pleiad and the learned scholar who edited Greek comedy in the Alexandrian Library, and the author of the *Alexandra* were the same person is of limited relevance to the critical question of the mythographical quality of this poem. The plot of the *Alexandra* covers the Trojan War myth, the *nostoi*, and its aftermath in an ambitious storyline that embraces events from the foundation of Troy to the historical present of the author. Dramatically, the *Alexandra* is designed as a prophetic monologue by the Trojan princess Cassandra, who foretells the fates of the Trojan and Greek heroes. Not only the wide range of myths and stories treated in the *Alexandra*, but also the highly sophisticated manner of presentation and diction, account for the use of a plethora of textual sources. The *Alexandra* draws heavily on the *Odyssey*, the Epic Cycle, Hesiod's *Catalogue of Women*, Stesichorus, Pindar, Bacchylides, and classical drama. But the author of the *Alexandra*, like his Hellenistic predecessors, also extracts a barrage of detail from mythographers and local historians, among whom Hellanicus, Pherecydes, Herodotus, and Ephorus figure prominently (Hornblower 2015: 7–36).

The interaction between the *Alexandra* and mythography seems to have been two-way. On the one hand, the Trojan War myth, with its rich documentation in archaic and classical poetry, and the numerous foundation stories associated with the veterans of the war that were collected by historians belongs to material firmly based on previous literature. "Lycophron" was acutely aware that he had chosen to dramatize the most popular subject matter of Greek literature, one that bridges myth and history over the perpetual conflict between Asia and Greece. Furthermore, he was conscious of the fact that the Homeric epics, supplemented by a series of cyclic epics that recounted the events before, between, and after the *Iliad* and the *Odyssey* were widely known to ancient audiences. In essence, "Lycophron" had little freedom in retelling of the Trojan adventure: he should either align himself with the popular stories of Homer and reproduce them in his poem or experiment with alternative versions and hidden details of the story as told by Homer. On the other hand, Lycophron proved to be very inventive in combining variants of the Trojan myth from the Epic Cycle, the lyric poets, and tragedy and in rewriting a well-known myth against a historical-geographical background (Sistakou 2008b: 100–120).

In effect, the *Alexandra* not only incorporates rich mythographical material from a wide body of texts; moreover, the knowledge of mythography itself becomes the key for understanding this extremely obscure poem. Indeed, the author of the *Alexandra* was already notorious in antiquity for his enigmatic style.

A striking example is the substitution of rare epithets or periphrases for all the common mythical names. Onomastics forms the core of mythographical writing because it is through the dense web of names and their genealogical associations that the vast territory of myth can be charted. In reading the *Alexandra*, one has to use one's mythographical expertise as a compass to orient oneself in the narrative. The simplest naming strategy consists in the use of an animal metaphor instead of the proper name of a hero: thus, Heracles is called "the lion" in lines 459 and 697; Hector, a "bull" in line 269; Helen, a "female dog" in 87 and 851; and Clytemnestra, a "lioness" in 1107, and a "viper" in 1121. Other periphrases highlight the genealogical associations between the heroes and their ancestors; Neoptolemus, for example, is named after his mother, Iphigenia, and is thus indirectly linked to her dark past as a priestess who performed human sacrifices in Aulis (*Alex.* 324–325: "the sullen lion, child of Iphis, imitating his dark mother's lustrations"; compare Iphigenia as "the one who cuts the throats of the Greeks" in line 187). But in the majority of cases, a hero is designated through reference to one of his characteristic adventures in mythology: Heracles is "the three-evening lion" (*Alex.* 33), an allusion to Zeus's making love to Alcmena for three nights, and Achilles is negatively characterized as "the corpse-seller" (*Alex.* 276), a reference to the exchange of Hector's corpse for its weight in gold between Priam and Achilles (Sistakou 2009a). Exotic names or cult epithets are usually accumulated to identify a deity; in the region of divine onomastics "Lycophron" draws equally on mythographical texts and epigraphic evidence in pursuit of alternative names and mythical details (Hornblower 2015: 62–93).

The *Alexandra* demands mythographical knowledge from its reader and, at the same time, imparts it. "Lycophron's" cryptographical style obscures the popular aspects of Greek mythology, whereas a plethora of mythological variants offer new insights into the Trojan War myth. Lycophronian obscurity is a commonplace since antiquity when it was widely acknowledged that a reading of the *Alexandra* without a mythographical and glossographical explanation was impossible. To solve the riddles of this cryptic poem, scholars from antiquity and Byzantium wrote extensive commentaries on it; among them Eustathius, who constantly draws on "Lycophron" to support his mythographical commentary on the Homeric epics, and John Tzetzes, whose guide to the *Alexandra* enlightens readers about mythological matters (Berra 2009). The first riddle is in the title. Tzetzes gives two etymological explanations for why Cassandra appears under the name Alexandra in the poem (Sch. Lyc. *genus* 85–87): "She is called *Alexandra* either from the verb *aluxai*, which suggests that she avoids intercourse with men, or from the verb *alexein*, in the sense that she helps men, that is the people, through her prophecies." Knowledge of the heroine's mythological background is a prerequisite for understanding the title. Conversely, the poet acquires the persona of the mythographer through whom alternative stories about the Trojan myth survive; in effect, "Lycophron" appears to be the only extant source for many of these stories (on "Lycophron" as a mythographer, see Berra 2009: 280–292).

The alternative narratives about the Trojan War heroes are either stories connected with the archaeology of Troy, the background of the Priamid family, and the prehistory of the war or foundation stories that put mythology under a reality-based, historical perspective (for the first class of myths, see Wathelet 2009; for the latter, Hornblower 2015: 53–62). Indeed, the *Alexandra* explores the boundaries between myth and history in encompassing the whole range of stories from the first foundation of Troy by Heracles until the dominion of the Romans in the Mediterranean, who are marked as descendants of the Trojans through the line of Aeneas. Tzetzes describes the content of the *Alexandra* as follows (Sch. Lyc. *hypoth.* 8–10): "The poem contains divinations and narrations that range from the story of Heracles until the sovereignty of the Romans (which is introduced to the narrative from the outside) and other various history." The *Alexandra* is a mythographical poem that gradually develops into world history and, conversely, a universal history explained mythologically (see Sulimani, this volume). One of the critical passages in "Lycophron's" narrative is the account of the clash between Europe and Asia (*Alex.* 1283–1450), a turning point marking the transition from mythical to historical time already since Herodotus's famous introduction to the *Histories*. But whereas Herodotus demythologizes the confrontation, "Lycophron" restores the mythical by retelling the legendary abductions of Io (1291–1295), Europa (1296–1311), Medea (1309–1321), Antiope (1322–1340), and Helen (1362–1365), thus explaining universal history on the basis of mythical cycles—the Argonautic, the Trojan, the ones concerning Heracles, Theseus, and the other heroes (West 2009). Thus, the phrase *Lykophrōn historei* (Lycophron tells the story) becomes almost proverbial: it suggests that the *Alexandra* and the scholarly exegesis that accompanied "Lycophron's" text were replete with recondite knowledge (on this citation denoting "the book of Lycophron," which includes both the poem and the scholia on it, see Pagès, this volume).

It was because of such authors that mythography grew into sophisticated poetry during the Hellenistic period, and it was through works like the *Aetia*, the *Argonautica* and the *Alexandra* that the Alexandrian Cabinet of Mythographical Curiosities could exhibit its treasures for an elite group of learned readers. The scholar-poets of the Museum had discovered a plethora of hidden knowledge in the writers of the past. Apart from collecting and commenting on the mythographical stories they found in the most unexpected sources, these learned poets creatively reworked legends, fables, and folklore into refined poetry. From this trend originated a neoteric aesthetic that has certain similarities and significant differences from the mythographical works in prose. The most common similarities include their thematic categorization (such as myths about metamorphoses or recherché love stories) and the deluge of genealogical and geographical data that are incorporated into the poems. Yet Alexandrians strove to achieve much more than setting mythography into verse. Elimination of the common mythical versions and insistence on the lesser-known episodes which are rewritten in new generic forms and retold through bold narrative strategies are part of an experimentation with content and form by the Hellenistic poets. Essentially, these poets drew upon all kinds of learning, gathered not only from mythography but also from historiography, geography, and scientific treatises, to demonstrate that the aesthetic impact of poetry is largely irrelevant to its "content." On the other hand, *qua* scholars and researchers, they ameliorated the methods of mythographers and enriched the mythographical corpus by bringing attention to a bulk of material from past literature and local sources. The interaction between poetry and scholarship, the ways in which Alexandrian poetry transformed mythographical knowledge into art and, conversely, the influence of this poetry in the compilation of mythographical anthologies by later authors opens up a field for meticulous research in the future.

## FURTHER READING

The scholarly foundation underlying the development of learned poetry with mythographical content presupposes an acquaintance with Alexandrian scholarship (Pfeiffer 1968; Blum 1991) and especially Hellenistic mythography (Higbie 2007; Trzaskoma and Smith 2013; and Smith and Trzaskoma on Hellenistic mythography in this volume). Catalogue poetry, whose origins can be traced back to Hesiod, becomes the vehicle for the transformation of mythography into poetry in the Hellenistic period: on the matter see Asquith (2005). Since Alexandrian poets do not deal with traditional or well-known mythical stories but instead record alternative myths, genealogical variants, and geographical details, it is essential to search for mythographical data in general studies of myth in Hellenistic poetry. The variations on the Trojan War myth, the Greek myth par excellence, across the entire spectrum of Hellenistic poetry are discussed by Sistakou (2008b). For the texts and a basic introduction and commentary on the catalogue poems of Alexander of Aetolia, Hermesianax, and Philitas, see Lightfoot (2009); catalogue poems dealing specifically with metamorphosis are explored by Forbes Irving (1990). Antimachus is thoroughly discussed by Matthews (1995); for Philitas's mythological learnedness there is also a systematic analysis by Spanoudakis (2002); for Euphorion and his myths, it is essential to consult the collective volume by Cusset, Prioux, and Richer

(2013). Although there is no comprehensive study of Callimachean myth, the mythographical impetus as exhibited in the *Aetia* is meticulously recorded in the commentary of the poem by Harder (2012). The mythographical emphasis of Apollonius's *ktisis* poetry is highlighted by Krevans (2001) and Sistakou (2008a). There is, however, no large-scale survey of the myth in the *Argonautica*; the introduction (especially on myth) and detailed commentary in the three volumes by Vian (1976–1996) is a good starting point for researchers; see also the recent overview of myths and their sources in the *Argonautica* by Scherer (2006: 9–56). The treatment of myth and the reception of mythography in the *Alexandra* have been extensively discussed in numerous commentaries and articles, among which the collective volume Cusset and Prioux (2009) offers valuable insights into every aspect of Lycophronean mythography; the most recent in-depth commentary with an introduction that highlights the literary sources, the foundation myths and myths of origin in the poem is owed to Hornblower (2015).

## References

Asquith, Helen. 2005. "From Genealogy to Catalogue: The Hellenistic Adaptation of the Hesiodic Catalogue Form." In *The Hesiodic Catalogue of Women: Constructions and Reconstructions*, edited by Richard Hunter, 266–286. Cambridge, UK: Cambridge University Press.

Berra, Aurélien. 2009. "*Obscuritas lycophronea*: Les témoignages anciens sur Lycophron." In *Lycophron: Éclats d'obscurité*, edited by Christophe Cusset and Évelyne Prioux, 259–318. Saint-Étienne: Presses Universitaires de Saint-Étienne.

Blum, Rudolf. 1991. *Kallimachos: The Alexandrian Library and the Origins of Bibliography*. Translated by Hans H. Wellisch. Madison: University of Wisconsin Press.

Bulloch, Anthony. 2006. "Jason's Cloak." *Hermes* 134: 44–68.

Cameron, Alan. 2004. *Greek Mythography in the Roman World*. Oxford: Oxford University Press.

Cusset, Christophe, and Évelyne Prioux, eds. 2009. *Lycophron: Éclats d'obscurité*. Saint-Étienne: Presses Universitaires de Saint-Étienne.

Cusset, Christophe, Évelyne Prioux, and Hamidou Richer, eds. 2013. *Euphorion et les mythes*. Naples: Centre Jean Bérard.

Forbes Irving, Paul M. C. 1990. *Metamorphosis in Greek Myths*. Oxford: Clarendon Press.

Gärtner, Thomas. 2008. "Die hellenistische Katalogdichtung des Phanocles über homosexuelle Liebesbeziehungen: Untersuchungen zur tendenziellen Gestaltung und zum literarischen Nachleben." *Mnemosyne* 61: 18–44.

Harder, Annette. 2012. *Callimachus "Aetia": Introduction, Text, Translation, and Commentary*. Oxford: Oxford University Press.

Higbie, Carolyn. 2007. "Hellenistic Mythographers." In *The Cambridge Companion to Greek Mythology*, edited by Roger D. Woodard, 237–254. Cambridge, UK: Cambridge University Press.

Hornblower, Simon. 2015. *Lykophron: "Alexandra."* Oxford: Oxford University Press.

Hutchinson, Gregory O. 2003. "The *Aetia*: Callimachus' Poem of Knowledge." *Zeitschrift für Papyrologie und Epigraphik* 145: 47–59.

Krevans, Nita. 2001. "On the Margins of Epic: The Foundation-Poems of Apollonius." In *Apollonius Rhodius*, edited by Annette Harder, Remco Regtuit, and Gerry Wakker, 69–84. Leuven: Peeters.

Lightfoot, Jane L., ed. and trans. 2009. *Hellenistic Collection*. Cambridge, MA: Harvard University Press.

Magnelli, Enrico. 1999. *Alexandri Aetoli: Testimonia et fragmenta*. Florence: Università degli Studi di Firenze.

Matthews, Victor J. 1995. *Antimachus of Colophon*. Leiden, New York, and Cologne: Brill.

Merriam, Carol U. 1993. "An Examination of Jason's Cloak (Apollonius Rhodius *Argonautica* 1.730–768)." *Scholia* 2: 69–80.

Meyer, Doris. 1993. "'Nichts Unbezeugtes singe ich': Die fiktive Darstellung der Wissenstradierung bei Kallimachos." In *Vermittlung und Tradierung von Wissen in der griechischen Kunst*, edited by Wolfgang Kullmann and Jochen Althoff, 317–336. Tübingen: Gunter Narr Verlag.

Pagès Cebrian, Joan. 2013. "Euphorion dans les scholies mythographiques à l'*Iliade*." In *Euphorion et les mythes*, edited by Christophe Cusset, Évelyne Prioux, and Hamidou Richer, 247–264. Naples: Centre Jean Bérard.

Pfeiffer, Rudolf. 1968. *History of Classical Scholarship: From the Beginnings to the End of the Hellenistic Era*. Oxford: Oxford University Press.

Powell, Iohannes U. 1925. *Collectanea Alexandrina*. Oxford: Clarendon Press, repr. 1970.

Sbardella, Livio. 2000. "Βιττίδα . . . θοήν: Il problema dell'elegia erotica in Filita." In *La letteratura ellenistica*, edited by Roberto Pretagostini, 79–89. Rome: Quasar.

Scherer, Burkhard. 2006. *Mythos, Katalog und Prophezeihung: Studien zu den "Argonautika" des Apollonios Rhodios*. Stuttgart: Franz Steiner Verlag.

Selden, Daniel L. 1998. "Alibis." *Classical Antiquity* 17: 290–412.

Sistakou, Evina. 2008a. "In Search of Apollonius' *Ktisis* Poems." In *Brill's Companion to Apollonius Rhodius*. 2nd rev. edited by Theodore Papanghelis and Antonios Rengakos, 311–340. Leiden and Boston: Brill.

Sistakou, Evina. 2008b. *Reconstructing the Epic: Cross-Readings of the Trojan Myth in Hellenistic Poetry*. Leuven: Peeters.

Sistakou, Evina. 2009a. "Breaking the Name Codes in Lycophron's '*Alexandra*'." In *Lycophron: Éclats d'obscurité*, edited by Christophe Cusset and Évelyne Prioux, 237–257. Saint-Étienne: Presses Universitaires de Saint-Étienne.

Sistakou, Evina. 2009b. "Fragments of an Imaginary Past: Strategies of Mythical Narration in Apollonius' *Argonautica* and Callimachus' *Aitia*." *Rivista di Filologia e di Istruzione Classica* 137: 380–401.

Spanoudakis, Konstantinos. 2002. *Philitas of Cos*. Leiden, New York, and Cologne: Brill.

Spanoudakis, Konstantinos. 2005. "Alexander Aetolus' *Astragalistai*." *Eikasmos* 16: 149–154.

Trzaskoma, Stephen M., and R. Scott Smith, eds. 2013. *Writing Myth: Mythography in the Ancient World*. Leuven: Peeters.

Vian, Francis. 1976. *Apollonios de Rhodes, "Argonautiques."* Bk. 1: *Chants I–II*. Paris: Les Belles Lettres.

Vian, Francis. 1993. *Apollonios de Rhodes, "Argonautiques."* Bk. 2: *Chants III*. Paris: Les Belles Lettres.

Vian, Francis. 1996. *Apollonios de Rhodes, "Argonautiques."* Bk. 3: *Chants IV*. Paris: Les Belles Lettres.

Wathelet, Paul. 2009. "L'apport de Lycophron à la connaissance des mythes troyens." In *Lycophron: Éclats d'obscurité*, edited by Christophe Cusset and Évelyne Prioux, 331–345. Saint-Étienne: Presses Universitaires de Saint-Étienne.

West, Stephanie. 2009. "Herodotus in Lycophron." In *Lycophron: Éclats d'obscurité*, edited by Christophe Cusset and Évelyne Prioux, 81–93. Saint-Étienne: Presses Universitaires de Saint-Étienne.

CHAPTER 7

......................................................................................................................

# ANTIHOMERICA

*Dares and Dictys*

......................................................................................................................

KEN DOWDEN

Dares of Phrygia and Dictys of Crete are fictions invented by those who wished to play games with this most famous war.

—Joan Lluís Vives of Valencia, *De Disciplinis* (1532: 360)

## 1. Background and Context

......................................................................................................................

THE Trojan story was placed at the heart of Greek culture by Homer. Although there were other mythic cycles, through Homer the war gained its special presence in Greek mythology, marking a turning point in "history." The classical author was not, however, beyond challenge. Homer's views on theology and ethics had been disputed, for instance, by Xenophanes around 500, and by Plato in the first half of the 4th century. And Plato's younger contemporary, the sophist Zoilos, wrote an *Against the Poetry of Homer* comprising no fewer than nine books, earning the nickname "Scourge of Homer" (*Homeromastix*) thanks to the ridicule to which he subjected the Poet's implausibilities.

The creation of the Library at Alexandria around 290 BCE catalyzed the identification of the authors who mattered in each genre. These were the authors whose texts required study, and therefore explanation by experts. This sort of expertise inevitably led to a scholarship that was centered on "problems," and it rendered Homer more problematic than most. One outgrowth of this was the notion cultivated by some writers that Homer had been *wrong*, particularly on matters of historical fact. For us, Homer is recognized as a poet, and it seems strange to treat him as recording historical events blow by blow. It was harder, however, for Greeks, who recognized no firm dividing line between history and mythology. For them, Troy, the Trojan War, and the characters named by Homer had a claim to be real and historical—except the gods, of course, because no one witnesses what the gods think, say, or do.

*Antihomerica* is not an ancient term but a modern one, employed beginning in the late 19th century to refer to accounts of the Trojan War whose purpose was to dispute Homer's factual accuracy. Although we also hear of a "Sisyphus of Cos," a companion of Teucer, whose work was used by Homer and a "Corinnus of Ilion," who wrote a contemporary history of the Trojan War (John Malalas 5.29, Souda s.v. Korinnos), there are two principal surviving examples, both of them "eyewitness" accounts of the Trojan War: first, perhaps in the 70s CE, is the *Diary of the Trojan War* (*Ephemeris Belli Troiani*) of Dictys of Crete (a companion of Idomeneus and, of course, a Greek); the second, of uncertain date, is the *History of the Sack of Troy* (*Historia de Excidio Troiae*) by Dares of Phrygia—Phrygia is where Troy was, on this view, and Dares is a priest glimpsed in Homer's *Iliad*. Both these texts are in Latin translation in the form we have them.

These are the texts I look at here, but there were others, each with a rather distinctive character. Of Ptolemy Chennus's *Anthomeros* (probably toward the end of the 1st century CE), we know that it was in twenty-four books, like the *Iliad* itself, and from its name we can tell that it set out to counter Homer, to respond and refute (like Caesar's *Anti-Cato*, a response to Cicero's *Cato*). Ptolemy was a controversialist who set out to stun and amaze. We know him best from a summary of his lost work, the *Novel History*, which contained some alarming rewriting of the history of legendary times, including at Troy. There is also a report that "Dares" wrote "the Phrygian *Iliad*," which is hard to square with our little prose text in Latin and could be a different work altogether. Dio Chrysostom, like Dictys, toward the end of the 1st century CE, among his many orations, wrote one called the "Trojan discourse," which survives and preposterously asserts that Homer had gotten the war all wrong: the Trojans had not been defeated, but, quite the contrary, lived happily ever afterward! Continuing interest in this antihomeric sort of composition in later centuries is shown not only by the few papyri of the Greek Dictys we have recovered, evidence in themselves that his work was copied and read in the 2nd and 3rd centuries, but also by the "Heroic discourse" of Philostratus (toward 220 CE). Philostratus seems to know the *Diary* of Dictys—there could even be a sort of Dictys revival at this time. The *Heroicus* has a Phoenician merchant arrive at Elaious, on the Thracian Chersonese, a peninsula looking out from Europe across the Hellespont to the Troad. There he encounters a person who works on vines and to whom Protesilaus, the first Greek to die at Troy, appears and talks. This is the eyewitness from whom the impressions gained from Homer and the poets can be "corrected."

## 2. The Mythography of Dictys

Dictys's *Ephemeris* is an eyewitness account of the Trojan War, from Paris's seizure of Helen to the none-too-happy returns of the heroes from Troy. It was originally written in Greek (the discovery in the 20th century of papyrus fragments of that original put to rest the common 19th-century view that there had never been a Greek version). It was quite substantial, covering nine or ten books in the Greek, reduced by its Latin translator to six books (about 130 pages of Latin) by bundling books 6 onward into a single final book. The Greek of Dictys is deliberately simple and vivid, to convey the impression of a straightforward reporter of events. The Latin translation, by one L. Septimius, is quite elegant and, where we can judge it, faithful to the Greek without being overly literal.

Dictys is for those "who want to know the real story" (*avidos verae historiae*, according to Septimius's prefatory letter) and tells the story "truthfully." Thus, readers conspire in the fiction that Homer is a second-hand authority, from hundreds of years after the Trojan War, who poetically adjusts the material to create his epic. Of course, if Homer had never existed, there would be no point in this—you need to know Homer and the epic tradition well to enjoy this cultural game. The simple-seeming narrative is, in fact, a virtuoso stunt, imagining what a real history behind Homer might have looked like.

So, like Lucan's Latin epic, the *Pharsalia* (perhaps only twenty years earlier), it is *demythologized*, and no event can be ascribed unambivalently to a god, except in the same way a historian would. If the kings of Greece who assemble in Crete at the outset to carve up the estate of Atreus descend from "Minos born of Zeus" (1.1), the location points us to the Zeus of the arch-rationalist Euhemerus: this was a real king, in Crete, later acclaimed as a god. There is no Judgment of Paris—Paris is just "captivated" (*captus*) by Helen while in Sparta (1.3). Gods exist simply to be worshiped at the shrines that figure in the narrative, none looming larger than the shrine of Apollo of Thymbra, where Achilles catches sight of Polyxena and "is captivated" (3.2), just as Agamemnon is later "captivated" by Cassandra, at 5.13. The Trojan Horse is not a vehicle for warriors: the point of the horse, when built, is solely that the walls will have to be breached to get it into the city, and the Trojans themselves then do so (5.9, 11). The breaching, does indeed, go back to the Cyclic Epic (the *Little Iliad*, with a horse 120 feet long and 30 feet wide! [fr. 1 West]), but now there are no warriors sitting implausibly and rather redundantly inside the horse. Later, Cassandra is seized by Locrian Ajax from her asylum at the temple of Athene (5.12), but the storm in which Ajax dies (6.1) is not sent by Athene or by any god—it is just bad weather. The only intervention is that of Nauplius, who avenges his son Palamedes by showing misleading light signals (again, based on material in the Cyclic epic, the *Returns of the Heroes* in this case).

There *are*, of course, still prophets: on the Greek side, Calchas (and, at Aulis, a miscellaneous woman in delirium); on the Trojan side, Helenus and Cassandra. They all seem to have genuine skills. And there are also some portents: sacrifices that will not burn after crimes in Apollo's temple (5.7–8), and a quite spectacular close to book 1 concerning grim skies, the near-sacrifice of Iphigenia, and the miraculous substitution of a deer for her at Aulis. So long as events are focalized and evidenced through human beings, they pass the test of Dictys's new mythography.

The text of Dictys is studded with names: names are important facts in this *record*. One needs to read it with the grammarian's eye. The *Iliad* opens with the issue of abducted maidens. The first is Chryseis, by her name the "daughter of (the priest)

Chryses" (according to Dictys and other ancient commentators), whom Agamemnon is obliged to return to her father. The second is Briseis, the daughter of a "Brises"; this is the girl assigned to Achilles, of whom he is fond, and who is taken away rudely by Agamemnon. Though "Chryseis" and "Briseis" identify the girls, we grammarians will still be left asking *what are their actual names?* Obligingly, Dictys includes this detail: they are called Astynome and Hippodamia respectively (2.19). And it only takes a moment's thought to realize that Paris and Helen, in ten years, must have had children. Their names too are known to Dictys: Bunimus, Corythus (usually a child by his earlier wife, the nymph Oenone), and Idaeus (5.5). Other grammarians of the time told us Achilles's name when he was brought up amid the girls on Scyrus, and which iTune the Sirens sang when they were luring Odysseus.

But what strikes us above all is the *realism*. We learn about politics at Troy—the war party and the peace party. We learn how Achilles was treacherously murdered (his mind romantically distracted by the thought of Priam's daughter Polyxena), and how Hector was killed in an ambush. This is real, gritty history.

## 3. THE MYTHOGRAPHY OF DARES

Dares's *De Excidio Troiae* begins with a dedicatory letter, in which the historian Cornelius Nepos (roughly 110–25 BCE) writes to the historian Sallust (86 to about 35 BCE) to the effect that he has translated the text from Dares's alleged original, presumably Greek (rather than Trojan!). We can be sure that this letter is part of the fiction, and not real; it is not even wholly clear that there *was* a Greek original text, unlike in the case of Dictys (see Bretzigheimer 2008). The letter represents the original as written "truthfully and straightforwardly"—that is, in a simple style like that of Dictys, representing his honesty and credibility as a witness—in contrast to Homer, who was even, this letter assures us, put on trial for insanity at Athens because he had claimed that gods fought with men. The Latin text, supposedly a verbatim translation, strives to achieve the sort of simplicity that rhetoric prescribed for telling the facts of the case in lawcourts (the *narratio* of a speech) but has generally been judged as quite poor. It is much shorter than Dictys, only fifty pages of Latin—probably because it is abridged from a much longer Greek original (see Schetter 1988).

Dares is quirky, less convincing than Dictys, but clearly solving problems as he goes. The preliminaries are more complex: Dares chooses to begin by revamping a relatively unfamiliar myth in which the Argonauts are now so badly received at Troy that Hercules takes revenge by raiding the city, killing King Laomedon and abducting his daughter Hesione (sections 2–3)—thus integrating the story of the first sack of Troy with the story of the Trojan War. The Judgment of Paris, eliminated by Dictys because it assigns a role to the three *goddesses*, is given a different explanation by Dares: it was a *dream*, which Paris adduces as evidence of divine favor for his hawkish views (7). When Paris and Helen fall in love with each other (10), and Helen elopes with Paris, she nonetheless diplomatically becomes the counterweight to Hesione, and Priam recounts the wrongs suffered at the hands of the Argonauts (17).

Agamemnon and his forces convene at Athens (14) and Calchas's prophecy that the war would last ten years is instead a Delphic oracle (15). It is in fact at Delphi that Calchas joins them—how else would a prophet from southeast Asia Minor come to be among the Greeks? On Calchas's instructions the fleet will meet at the traditional location, Aulis. The length of the war had been a problem since Thucydides and was addressed as a sequence of delays by Dictys (1.16–2.9), including a period of five years to get the Greek fleet together for the invasion (1.18). Dares prefers fighting that is so fierce that Agamemnon successfully proposes a three-year truce to Priam to rebuild their strength (22)! This is followed, after further bouts of fighting, by a six-month truce and by a thirty-day truce (23). We now see why the war took so long.

Where, occasionally, Dictys would pause to mention, for instance, that Telephus was a tall man (2.4) or to describe the appearance (tall, attractive), youth, and strength of Achilles (1.14), Dares presents, or has picked up, a whole series of descriptions, rather like a group photograph. So, he finds out what Castor and Pollux looked like from the Trojans themselves: "They were both similar to each other—blond hair, big eyes, perfect face, well-shaped, lean body. Helen shapely like them, charming with straightforward mind, superb legs, with a mark between her two eyebrows, and a small mouth."

## 4. Conclusions

There is only space here to give a taste of some of the mythographic moves of Dictys and Dares. The overwhelming impression is of a clever game played by literary scholars. By setting as their objective a real, historical account of events that Homer and the epic tradition had told, they are able to devise solutions to newly observed problems and reshuffle events and incidents to improve plausibility, though the effect is of moves on a literary chessboard. There was always an underlying Greek sense that their mythology *did* in fact tell a history, but it was an intellectual game to reconstruct it. The new age of Alexandrian scholarship provided the tools for bravura displays of ingenuity, which, in turn, sat well in an age now dominated by rhetoric. This was partly formal: rules existed for "plausibility" when "narrating" alleged facts (simple style, lots of names and details, careful sequencing of events). More broadly, rhetoric knew its audience and the new Troy was in harmony with the mood of an age when clever performance was privileged, nowhere more so than in the specimen declamations of professionals. These latter were remembered, and recorded, by the Elder Seneca, and the *Suasoriae* (speeches commending a course of action), in particular, often involved stepping back in history and recreating that history (for example, Alexander decides whether to head West and capture Rome). So, mythography took on this rhetorical character and dared you to unpick the narrative, say, of Dictys, one that was so plausible in an age of learning.

Such writing arises from real learning, like that of Demetrius of Scepsis (near Troy) in the 2nd century BCE, who identified the geography of the Troad as described by Homer, taking thirty books to do so in his *Catalogue of the Trojans*. Such work was meant seriously and incorporated into the *Geography* of Strabo (died about 25 CE). The work that took issue with Homer was, in a way, an offshoot of this industry.

But eventually, there were also writers who took the ludic mythography at face value. This quickly found its way into the tradition of commentary on texts that became our scholia (notes in the margins of manuscripts of, especially, Homer). And in the end for Byzantine chroniclers from the 6th century CE and for the western Middle Ages, the accounts of Dictys and Dares had become the real history of early times. This may have been a category mistake, but it populated times that otherwise had no history so that they could be set alongside biblical history. It also dominated the imagination when Troy was the issue: it is visible as late as Shakespeare's *Troilus and Cressida* (1602), where the myth has evolved in medieval hands: just as, previously, in Chaucer's *Troilus and Criseyde* (1380), Shakespeare's Cressida (that is, Chryseis) is the daughter of Calchas (!), a Trojan priest who has signed up with the Greeks (as Dares had explained). This can be traced back via Boccaccio to Benoit de Ste. Maure's *Roman de Troie* (line 13261) in the 12th century, though he called her Briseïda. This is just a tiny sample of the power of the Trojan story once it is liberated from Homer.

## FURTHER READING

The first task is to read and enjoy the various texts. They and, in particular Dictys and Dares, are not easy to find in English, but the *Bibliography* below lists what there is, including some web resources.

Something of the climate surrounding Homer and his accuracy amongst writers of the first centuries CE is presented by Kim (2010; esp. ch. 1). The sense of gamesmanship and problem-based study of Homer emerges from Dowden (2017: Commentary on F 1b) and more accessibly in Dowden (2009).

Turning to Dictys and Dares specifically, there is still much to be said for Griffin (1907) as an introductory book to both texts, their nature and their reception in later European literature. But see now Clark (2020), which offers a detailed overview of Dares' work and later reception of it.

Authors coming from the study of the ancient novel have found little to say about Dictys and Dares. Holzberg (1995: 22) briefly raises key issues and with good reason divorces these Troy texts from the novel, and Hägg's few pages (1983: 143–147) are principally concerned with the important influence they had on medieval literature. Merkle has been most concerned to advance the understanding of Dictys: his 1994 piece has interesting things to say about Achilles and his doomed love for Polyxena (in book 4), though Dictys's account is perhaps less literature than spoof journalism. His 2003 piece seeks to deliver "a proper appreciation of the text's literary conception" (2003: 567) of Dictys and then of Dares (see also Bradley 1991), raising fruitful and challenging issues in this uphill battle.

In German, Beschorner (1992, edition and discussion) is indispensable for Dares. But Schetter (1988) argues powerfully for the Latin Dares as an abridgement of a longer Greek text, unlike Beschorner.

My own study of Dictys's Greek original, as far as we know it, in *BNJ Second Edition* 49, aims to be comprehensive in placing this work in a mythographic and playful context (and dating it), while at the same time trying to understand the use Byzantine chroniclers made of his text and what we can learn from them about his original text.

Other texts by bigger names—such as Dio Chrysostom's *Trojan Discourse* and Philostratus's *Heroikos logos*—are more comfortably discussed given how much else we know of their author's works: for Dio see Kim (2010, ch. 4); for Philostratus, Kim (2010, ch. 6), Hunter (2009); Maclean and Aitken (2002).

## References

### Abbreviations

*BNJ* = Ian Worthington, ed. 2007–2019. *Brill's New Jacoby*. Brill online.
*BNJ Second Edition* = Ian Worthington, ed. 2016-date. *Brill's New Jacoby – Second Edition*. Brill online.
*FGrHist* IV/V = Hans-Joachim Gehrke and Felix Maier, with Veronica Bucciantini, *Die Fragmente der griechischen Historiker Part V*. Brill online.


### Texts and Translations

Cyclic epic: Martin L. West, ed. and trans. 2003. *Greek Epic Fragments* (with English translation). Loeb Classical Library. Cambridge, MA: Harvard University Press.
Dares (in English): Richard M. Frazer Jr. 1966. *The Trojan War: The Chronicles of Dictys of Crete and Dares the Phrygian*. Bloomington: Indiana University Press. Also available at www.theoi.com. See Beschorner (1992) below for Latin text and (German) translation.
Demetrius of Scepsis (fragments): Anna M. Biraschi. 2011. "Demetrio di Skepsis (2013)" (with Italian translation and commentary). In *FGrHist* IV/V. Brill online.
Dictys (in Latin): Werner Eisenhut. 1973. *Dictys Cretensis*. 2nd ed. Leipzig: Teubner. For English translation, see Dares.
Dictys (in Greek, fragments): Ken Dowden. 2020. "Diktys of Crete (49)" (with English translation and commentary). In *BNJ Second Edition*. Brill online.
Dio Chrysostom. *Troikos Logos*. Translated by James W. Cohoon, 1932. *Dio Chrysostom*. vol. 1 (with English translation). Loeb Classical Library. Cambridge, MA: Harvard University Press.
Philostratus. *Heroikos logos*: Edited and Translated by Jeffrey Rusten and Jason König. 2014. *Philostratus*. Vol. 4: "Heroicus, Gymnasticus: Discourses 1 and 2" (with English translation). Loeb Classical Library. Cambridge, MA: Harvard University Press. Also, Jennifer K. B. Maclean and Ellen B. Aitken, trans. *Flavius Philostratus: On Heroes* (English translation with introduction and notes). Atlanta, GA: Society of Biblical Literature, 2002.

Ptolemy Chennus. *Novel History* (summary): Photius, *Library*, cod. 190. Available in English translation at http://www.tertullian.org/fathers/photius_copyright/photius_05bibliotheca. htm#190.

Zoilos (fragments): Mary F. Williams. 2013. "Zoilos of Amphipolis (71)" (with English translation and commentary). In *BNJ*. Brill online.

*Discussion*

Beschorner, Andreas. 1992. *Untersuchungen zu Dares Phrygius*: *Classica Monacensia*, 4. Tübingen: Narr.

Bradley, Dennis R. 1991. "Troy Revisited." *Hermes* 119: 232–246.

Bretzigheimer, Gerlinde. 2008. "Dares Phrygius: Historia Ficta: Die Präliminarien zum Trojanischen Krieg." *Rheinisches Museum* 151: 365–399.

Clark, Frederic. 2020. *The First Pagan Historian: The Fortunes of a Fraud from Antiquity to the Enlightenment*. Oxford: Oxford University Press.

Dowden, Ken. 2009. "Reading Diktys: The Discrete Charm of Bogosity." In *Readers and Writers in the Ancient Nove: Ancient Narrative*, Suppl. 12, edited by Michael Paschalis, Stelios Panayotakis and Gareth Schmeling, 155–168. Groningen: Barkhuis.

Dowden, Ken. 2017. "Antipater of Akanthos (56)." In *BNJ Second Edition*. Brill online.

Griffin, Nathaniel E. 1907. *Dares and Dictys: An Introduction to the Study of Medieval Versions of the Story of Troy*. Baltimore, MD: J. H. Furst. Also available at www.archive.org.

Kim, Lawrence. 2010. *Homer between History and Fiction in Imperial Greek Literature*. Cambridge, UK: Cambridge University Press.

Hägg, Tomas. 1983. *The Novel in Antiquity*. Translated by Tomas Hägg. Oxford: Blackwell.

Holzberg, Niklas. 1995. *The Ancient Novel: An Introduction*. Translated by Christine Jackson-Holzberg. London and New York: Routledge.

Hunter, Richard. 2009. "The *Trojan Oration* of Dio Chrysostom and Ancient Homeric Criticism." In *Narratology and Interpretation: The Content of Narrative Form in Ancient Literature*, edited by Jonas Grethlein and Antonios Rengakos, 43–61. Berlin: De Gruyter.

Merkle, Stefan. 1989. *Die Ephemeris belli Troiani des Diktys von Kreta*. Frankfurt: Peter Lang.

Merkle, Stefan. 1994. "Telling the True Story of the Trojan War: The Eyewitness Account of Dictys of Crete." In *The Search for the Ancient Novel*, edited by James Tatum, 183–196. Baltimore, MD: Johns Hopkins University Press.

Merkle, Stefan. 1999. "News from the Past: Dictys and Dares on the Trojan War." In *Latin Fiction: The Latin Novel in Context*, edited by Heinz Hofmann, 155–166. London and New York: Routledge.

Merkle, Stefan. 2003. "The Truth and Nothing but the Truth: Dictys and Dares." In *The Novel in the Ancient World*, 2nd ed., edited by Gareth Schmeling, 563–580. Leiden: Brill.

Schetter, Willy. 1988. "Beobachtungen zum Dares Latinus." *Hermes* 116: 94–109.

# CHAPTER 8

## ANTONINUS LIBERALIS, *COLLECTION OF METAMORPHOSES*

### CHARLES DELATTRE

THE *Collection of Metamorphoses* (*Synagōgē Metamorphoseōn*) by Antoninus Liberalis is composed of forty-one short chapters, in Greek.[1] Each chapter contains an exclusively prose narration that centers on a character or a group of characters and that normally ends with the metamorphosis of that character or characters. This thematic unity—despite of the diversity of the narrations—justifies the title that the manuscript tradition gives to this collection.

## 1. DEFINITION OF THE TEXT

Concerning the manuscript tradition, only one manuscript is responsible for the transmission of Antoninus Liberalis's *Synagōgē*, the *Palatinus Graecus* 398. This manuscript is noteworthy in two respects. First, it is the only witness, aside from Antoninus Liberalis, of Parthenius of Nicaea's *Erōtika Pathēmata* and of pseudo-Plutarch's *De Fluviis*. Furthermore, it was written in a scriptorium in Constantinople at a very early date in the second half of the 9th century, and may even belong to the *Collectio Philosophica*, a collection of manuscripts intended for a wealthy and erudite patron with an interest in classical Greek philosophy (Ronconi 2012).

Questions about how we interpret—and present and publish—the manuscript are determined to some degree by the presence of Antoninus's text within, which, as noted, is found only here (and without any indirect tradition whatsoever). And the

---

[1] Translated by Alexander Brock.

overall contents of the manuscript create a context in which one reads and receives the collection—a context from which it cannot be isolated without consequences.

The three mythographical texts were chosen by the copyist (or his patron) because of their formal resemblances to one another and were later copied, with Antoninus Liberalis's *Synagōgē* at the end (ff. 189r–208v). In all three, the text is a collection of chapters, contains a unique thematic unity, and includes references that include authors' names (*historei* X—*hē historia para* X; that is, "X relates" or "the story is in X") that introduce or conclude each chapter. The ensemble of the manuscript, which also contains paradoxographical, geographical, and pseudo-epistolary texts, is itself clearly organized as a compilation, as was characteristic of the Byzantine culture of *syllogē* described by Paolo Odorico (1990, 2011). Yet the *Palatinus Graecus* 398, by the nature of the texts that it transmits, constitutes a unique example in comparison to the rest of the *Collectio philosophica*, whose thematics are heavily marked by Platonism. It is not possible, therefore, to identify the patron, a potential reader of Antoninus Liberalis's text, with certainty.

The *Synagōgē* remained largely unknown until the Renaissance, even though other parts of the manuscript had been copied earlier (the geographical texts were copied in the *Vatopedinus* 655, at the beginning of the 14th century). The acquisition of the manuscript by Ivan Stojković (John of Ragusa) and its transfer first to Basel in 1443, then in 1553 to Heidelberg, changed this situation. Thirty years after the *Erōtika Pathēmata* and the *De Fluviis*, edited by Cornarius, in 1531 and 1533, a Greek teacher in Heidelberg, Xylander, published from the same manuscript the *editio princeps* of Antoninus Liberalis with Thomas Guarini in Basel in 1568.

## 2. Date and Authorship

The author's name is given twice in the *Palatinus Graecus* 398, at the beginning and at the end of the text. It is a name of Latin origin, transcribed into Greek capitals. The *nomen* Antoninus is attested beginning in the 1st century CE and becomes particularly frequent in the 2nd and 3rd centuries of our era. Liberalis is also not rare, and one finds it among all strata of Roman society. We have knowledge of a M. Vibius Liberalis, suffect consul in 166 CE, but also of numerous freed slaves and soldiers with the same *cognomen*. One M. Antonius Liberalis, *latinus rhetor*, is also mentioned in the *index* of Suetonius' *De grammaticis et rhetoribus*.

Because the name is of no help in identifying the author, one must rely on the text to learn more about him. He is evidently a man of letters who masters the codes of scholarly writing. If his syntax does not present any difficulties, he uses an at times sophisticated vocabulary, borrowed from classical and Hellenistic poetry or based on the model of these (for example, the word *therapes* in 18.3 can be found in Eur., *Ion*, 94; *Supp.*, 762; Ion, fr. 27 West; Straton, *Anthol. Gr.* 12.299). Recent editors generally agree on placing him in the 2nd or 3rd century of our era, without being able to offer greater precision. Yet is he a Greek with Roman citizenship, like Plutarch? A Roman who masters the Greek language and culture, like Cornutus, Musonius Rufus, or even Marcus Aurelius (and maybe the *rhetor* M. Antonius Liberalis)? Or is he even an inhabitant of the empire, neither Greek nor Roman, but mastering the codes and customs of one or the other culture? It is impossible to say with certainty.

# 3. CONTENTS

The title the manuscript gives to the text is at the same time a definition: the text is a *synagōgē*, highlighting the author's work in compiling it. The redaction into clearly distinct chapters underlines this as well. The manuscript emphasizes the nature of the text as a compilation via the insertion of titles in the margin and the addition of references (*historei*) at the head or foot of the pages for thirty-four of forty-one chapters. Nonetheless, the term *synagōgē* can be used to describe a collection of excerpts (*eklogē*) as much as to describe a personal recomposition (see Zucker 2012: sections 2–3). Antoninus Liberalis's work of rewriting, both stylistic and thematic, should not be underestimated.

The manuscript's copyist took special care to make the *Synagōgē* into a text that was easy to consult. He reproduced a table of contents and a partial thematic index of the manuscript (see Delattre 2013: 150–151). He included in the margins signs to draw readers' attention (*sēmeiōsai*), sometimes accompanied by a brief summary. He created a numbering system, which he applied to the table of contents, thematic index, and chapters, thus offering different possibilities for reading the text (Delattre and Hawes 2020). The chapters follow one another in no clear order, yet there still exist several organizational principles. For example, excluding chapters 28 and 37, all metamorphoses into birds are told in chapters 1 to 24. Up until chapter 33, the only authors mentioned as references (sometimes with the mention of a secondary author) are Nicander and Boeus, whereas the names of Pherecydes, Menecrates, and Hermesianax only appear in chapters 33 to 41. The organization of the stories is therefore not random, even if the logic remains difficult to explain in greater detail.

Each chapter is an autonomous narration, coherent and contained within itself (see Delattre 2017). The majority of the stories offer the etiology of an animal species. Chapter 18, for example, concerns a Theban named Eumelus and his son, Botres. During a sacrifice, Botres commits a sacrilege that provokes his father's anger. When his father strikes him too violently, the young man dies, provoking the despair of his family. Apollo intervenes at this point and transforms Botres into a bird, the bee-eater.

Contrary to what can be said of the *De Fluviis* of Ps.-Plutarch or of Heraclitus the Mythographer's writings, the chapters are not organized into sequences that correspond to a strict repetitive grid for reading (see Delattre 2013: 147–149, 155–158). The length and the complexity of the episodes vary. It is only the mention of emotions (for example, anger and shame) and the concluding metamorphoses of the stories that gives coherence to the array of narrations. Ultimately, the metamorphoses determine the unity of the collection. They are often caused by a god who at times manifests his anger, and at other times, his pity. The gods intervene directly rather than in the form of an anonymous providence (*pronoia*).

The idea of metamorphosis is nevertheless ambiguous in that it includes many different kinds of cases: if a transformation into a bird concerns 19 of 41 chapters, one can find 7 metamorphoses into a rock; 5 into a divinity, nymph, or cult statue; 4 into a tree; 3 into a terrestrial or aquatic animal; and several unique cases (fountain, 8; gender, 17; catasterism, 25; echo, 26). Chapter 28 is set apart by its narration of a temporary metamorphosis of the divinities. One can see this diversity as the result of the author's sources as well as of his own selection; catasterisms, the object of Eratosthenes's text, are virtually absent from this collection.

In the end, the text escapes any general typology. In contrast to Conon, the selection is defined by a thematic unity. Unlike Hyginus or Apollodorus, it contains stories that do not summarize the epic cycle or the Athenian tragedies; but one should not confuse it with a dictionary of metamorphoses (such as, from the same period, *PMich.* inv. 1447) because it is not intended to be exhaustive or to serve as a reference.

# 4. NETWORK STRATEGIES

By taking metamorphoses as the principal motif of his text, Antoninus Liberalis offers a work that is less original than Parthenius's or Ps.-Plutarch's. The theme is already well attested in the 5th century, both in texts and in images. In the Hellenistic era, Nicander, in his *Heteroioumena*, and Boeus, in his *Ornithogonia*, had already provided a systematic treatment of the material. If the text does indeed date from the 2nd or 3rd centuries, one cannot exclude the possibility of Ovid as an influence, even if it is indirect. An older date for Antoninus Liberalis does not exclude a relationship with Ovid either. Both authors clearly draw from the same sources and adopt complementary narrative strategies.

The *Synagōgē* is thus a prose text with close connections to Hellenistic poetry. Not only the themes but also the language that Antoninus Liberalis adopts render his text the rival of anterior Hellenistic productions. The author has a relationship of emulation with, in particular, Nicander and Boeus—if, indeed, it is with them that his text is in dialogue—and without a doubt with other authors who are not explicitly mentioned in the margins. An intertextual relationship with Ovid is also a possibility and is currently under investigation (see, for example, Delattre 2019).

The references with an author's name that the manuscript gives in the margins play a crucial role in the re-evaluation of Antoninus Liberalis's work. A comparison with other compilations that contain the same type of indications (Parthenius, Ps.-Plutarch, the *Mythographus Homericus*) shows that the expression "*historei* X" invites the reader to use the author X as an element of comparison (see Delattre 2016, against Papathomopoulos 1968: xi–xxi, and Cameron 2004: 106–116, 321–327). Though the mentioned author could certainly have been Antoninus Liberalis's direct source, Liberalis does not simply provide a summary of the author. The formula underlines the separation and re-elaboration that the mythographer enacts. The reference defines the author in prose as a successor concerned with emulation, in an intertextual relationship in which the specific act of recalling the Hellenistic text might be less important than the knowledge that this text has been replaced by a new version. In a counterintuitive manner, the presence of Nicander's, Boeus's, or Euphorion's names in the manuscript invites the reader to turn away from their texts in order to appreciate Antoninus Liberalis's work in prose.

The references, furthermore, serve to hide other intentional parallels: chapter 1 (Ctesylla) distinctly alludes to Callimachus, while chapter 30 (Byblis) holds a relation with Apollonius of Rhodes and his *Foundation of Caunus*. The presence of the story of Byblis in the work of Parthenius (*Erōtika Pathēmata*, 11), Conon (2), and Ovid (*Met.* 9.441–665) or that of Leucippus in the *Synagōgē* (17, with Galatea), in the work of Parthenius (15, with Daphne), Pausanias (8.20.2–4), and Ovid (*Met.* 9.666–797) demonstrates that Antoninus Liberalis is part of a network of rewriting and intertextuality that was characteristic of his era. It is in this sense that one must interpret Antoninus Liberalis's originality. Chapter 11, for example, is a rewriting of the story of Philomela and Procne, where the name of Aedon, daughter of Pandareus, is a reference to Homer (*Od.* 19.518); where that of her husband Polytechnos is a playful commentary on his activity as a carpenter (*Polytekhnos ho tektōn*); and where that of her sister Chelidon, already attested in the 7th century BCE (*LIMC*, s.v. Prokne et Philomela, no. 1), announces the final metamorphosis. Antoninus Liberalis's mythographical writing could be considered a dynamic game of treasure hunt. Each chapter is a crossroads where different references—archaic, classical, or Hellenistic—are summoned together. Antoninus Liberalis sets himself the task of harmonizing and recomposing these references in order to provide a new version that contains, comments, and, finally, goes beyond them.

Unfortunately, the manuscript offers no foreword: contrary to Palaephatus and Parthenius, the author does not state a precise aim for this work of rewriting. Should we consider it simply a work of prosaic recomposition? A succession of thematic proposals for future works in poetry? A literary proposal that rivals in prose the productions in verse? The *Synagōgē* admits of many uses, provided one considers it in relation to the poetic production of which it is the heir and, in its particular way, the continuator.

## 5. AN AUTONOMOUS STATUS?

The care with which Antoninus Liberalis wrote might tip the balance in favor of a nondocumentary reading of the *Synagōgē*. Each chapter can be defined as an autonomous composition with its own internal logic. In the absence of a general framework for reading, each story defines its own narration. Aside from the intertextual relationships described earlier, the author focuses his writing around onomastic echoes that favor a paradigmatic reading of each chapter, for example, conventional etiological constructions (animal names, such as the *meleagrides* in 2, or place names, such as *Meropis* in 15.1, among others), assonances and wordplay (for example, *Mismē—memisētai* in 24.1), or networks of meaning that appear with transparency (for example, 20.4: *Lykios* (Wolf) and *Harpasos* (Kidnapper [masculine]) are the children of *Harpē* (Kidnapper [feminine]) or, in the same paragraph, the names of *Ortygios* and *Artemikhē*, which recall the names of Artemis and of Ortygia—Delos). The whole collection might even seem to be a constructed entity if one pays attention to the phenomena of concatenations through the reuse of notable expressions or the presence of uncommon words that could invite the reader to approach the text as if it were a network (for instance, the mention in 39 and 40 of *Phoinikes—Phoinix*).

If one follows these indications, the *Synagōgē* does not simply tell stories. It is a collection of autonomous narrative fictions that borrows its themes, part of its vocabulary, and its characters from Hellenistic poetry and, through Hellenistic poetry, from classical poetry, all while transforming these. Antoninus Liberalis's choice of an ornate prose could be a sign of an assumed rivalry with the poetic tradition or even of a claimed innovation. In the corpus of mythographers, one could consider him, because of his stylistic attentiveness, to be a close cousin to Libanius, though the absence of any pedagogical project nonetheless distinguishes Antoninus' work from Libanius' *Diegemata*; to Plutarch, particularly in *Narrationes Eroticae*; and possibly to Conon, even if a precise comparison with the latter is impossible, given that Conon's text is only accessible in Photius's summarized version. Given Antoninus' suggested relationship to poetry, in the end it is to Parthenius that Antoninus Liberalis is closest, even if he does not go so far as to offer his own verses in his compositions.

## FURTHER READING

The *editio princeps* of Antoninus Liberalis by Xylander (1568), which includes both the Greek text and a Latin translation, has been regularly reused and expanded, whether in an isolated manner (van Berkel 1674 ; Muncker 1675; Verheyck 1774), or in association with other texts from the mythographical corpus (Gale 1675; Westermann 1843).

Martini's scientific edition (1896, without translation) has been replaced by the translations of Cazzaniga (1962), Papathomopoulos (1968, with a translation into French), and Almirall i Sardà and Calderón Dorda (2012). Translations without scholarly apparatus are offered by Mader (1963, German); Ozaeta Gálvez (1989, Spanish); Celoria (1992, English); and Braccini and Macrì (2018, Italian). Excerpts have been translated by Trzaskoma, Smith, and Brunet (2016: 9–16, English).

To these, one can add detailed studies for the establishment of the text provided by Cessi (1921–1922); Sellheim (1930); Papathomopoulos (1962); Giangrande (1987); and Delattre (2010).

These editorial analyses should be henceforth associated with a re-evaluation of the manuscript. Unfortunately, the manuscript tradition of the "philosophical collection" identified by Allen (1893), to which one attaches the *Palatinus Graecus* 398, is still highly debated. One will find a fairly complete overview of the question in Ronconi (2012) and Marcotte (2014).

At present there is no modern general study devoted specifically to Antoninus Liberalis. Discussions on mythography (Pellizer 1993; Alganza 2006) include only a few general remarks on the subject. Detailed analyses are scattered throughout the important work of Cameron (2004), but are orientated by a general interpretation of mythographical treatises from the imperial era as "companions," memory aids or reading guides. A new interpretation of anthological treatises is outlined by Delattre (2013: 102–110, 131–137, 143–153) and should lead to a new commentary destined for the "Mythographes" collection of Presses du Septentrion.

Studies on metamorphoses sometimes include quick discussions of the *Synagōgē*, without nevertheless emphasizing its specificity, for example in Forbes Irving 1990: 20–24, and Buxton 2009: 111–115. The *Synagōgē*, which for a long time has served as a source for dictionaries of mythology, most often serves as a point of comparison for detailed analyses of Ovid's *Metamorphoses*. Partial studies of the *Synagōgē* are thus frequently found in the Ovidian bibliography or in thematic studies (Létoublon 2004 on *Ant. Lib.* 11; Bettini 2013: 1.1.5 on *Ant Lib.* 29).

## References

*Editions and Translations (in chronological order)*

For a complete list before 1968, see Papathomopoulos (1968: xxvi).

Xylander, Guilielmus, ed. and trans. 1568. *Antonini Liberalis Transformationum congeries. Phlegontis Tralliani de Mirabilibus et longaevis libellus. Ejusdem de Olympiis fragmentum. Apollonii Historiae mirabiles. Antigoni Mirabil. narrationum congeries. M. Antonini, . . . de Vita sua libri XII. Ab innumeris quibus antea scatebant mendis repurgati et nunc demum vere editi. Graece latineque omnia, Guil. Xylandro, . . . interprete, cum annotationibus et indice.* Basel: Thomas Guarini.

van Berkel, Abraham, ed. and trans. 1674. *Antonini Liberalis Metamorphoses, Graece et Latine. Abrahamus Berkelius emendavit.* Leyden and Amsterdam: Daniel Gaasbeek.

Muncker, Thomas, ed. and trans. 1675. *Antonini Liberalis transformationum congeries, interprete Guilielmo Xylandro. Thomas Munckerus recensuit et notas adjecit.* Amsterdam: Jansson-Waesberg.

Gale, Thomas, ed. and trans. 1675. *Historiae Poeticae Scriptores Antiqui. Apollodorus, . . . Conon, . . . Ptolemaeus, . . . Parthenius, . . . Antoninus Liberalis, graece et latine cura T. Gale.* Paris: F. Muguet.

Verheyk, Hendrik, ed and trans. 1774. *Antonini Liberalis transformationum congeries, interprete Guilielmo Xylandro, cum Thomae Munckeri notis, quibus suas adjecit Henricus Verheyk.* Leyden: Sam. and Joan. Luchtmans.

Westermann, Anton, ed. 1843. *ΜΥΘΟΓΡΑΦΟΙ. Scriptores poeticae historia Graeci.* Brunswick, Germany: G. Westermann.

Martini, Edgar, ed. 1896. *Mythographi Graeci.* Vol. 2. Pt. 1. Leipzig: Teubner.

Cazzaniga, Ignazio, ed. 1962. *Antoninus Liberalis. Metamorphoseon Synagoge.* Milan: Cisalpino.

Mader, Ludwig, ed. and trans. 1963. *Griechische Sagen. Apollodoros, Parthenios, Antoninus Liberalis, Hyginus. Aus dem Nachlass herausgegeben und ergänzt von Liselotte Rüegg.* Zürich: Artemis.

Papathomopoulos, Manolis, ed. and trans. 1968. *Les Métamorphoses d'Antoninus Libéralis.* Paris: Belles Lettres.

Ozaeta Gálvez, María Antonia, trans. 1989. *Heráclito, Alegorías de Homero. Antonino Liberal, Metamorfosis.* Madrid: Gredos.

Celoria, Francis, trans. 1992. *The Metamorphoses of Antoninus Liberalis*. London: Routledge.

Calderón Dorda, Esteban, ed. 2012. *Antoní Liberal. Recull de metamorfosis*. Translated by Jaume Almirall i Sardà. Barcelona: Fundació Bernat Metge.

Trzaskoma, Stephen M., R. Scott Smith, and Stephen Brunet, trans. 2016. *Anthology of Classical Myth. Primary Sources in Translation*. 2nd ed. Indianapolis, IN: Hackett.

Braccini, Tommaso, and Sonia Macrì, trans. 2018. *Antonino Liberale: Le metamorfosi*. Milan: Adelphi.

## Studies

Alganza Roldán, Minerva. 2006. "La mitografía como género de la prosa helenística." *Florentia iliberritana* 17: 9–37.

Allen, Thomas W. 1893. "Palaeographica III: A Group of Ninth-Century Manuscripts." *Journal of Philology* 21 (41): 48–65.

Bettini, Maurizio. 2013. *Women and Weasels: Mythologies of Birth in Ancient Greece and Rome*. Translated by Emlyn Eisenach. Chicago: University of Chicago Press.

Buxton, Richard. 2009. *Forms of Astonishment: Greek Myths of Metamorphosis*. Oxford: Oxford University Press.

Cameron, Alan. 2004. *Greek Mythography in the Roman World*. Oxford: Oxford University Press.

Cessi, Camillo. 1921–1922. "Gli indici delle fonte di Partenio e di Antonino Liberale." *Atti dell'Istituto Veneto di Scienze, Lettere ed Arti* 81: 345–350.

Delattre, Charles. 2010. "Le renard de Teumesse chez Antoninus Liberalis (*Mét.*, XLI): Formes et structures d'une narration." *Revue des Études grecques* 123: 91–111.

Delattre, Charles. 2013. "Pentaméron mythographique: Les Grecs ont-ils écrit leurs mythes?" *Lalies* 33: 77–170.

Delattre, Charles. 2016. "Référence et corpus dans les pratiques de commentaire: Les emplois de *historia*." *Revue de philologie* 90: 90–110.

Delattre, Charles. 2017. "Récit mythographique et intrigues: Le cas d'Antoninus Liberalis." In *La mitología griega en la tradición literaria: De la Antigüedad a la Grecia contemporánea*, edited by Minerva Alganza Roldán and Panagiota Papadopoulou, 99–120. Granada: Centro de Estudios Bizantinos, Neogriegos y Chipriotas.

Delattre, Charles. 2019. "Duplications, réécritures et intertextualité chez Antoninus Liberalis: Céphale, Procris et le renard de Teumesse." *Polymnia* 4: 64–96. https://polymnia-revue.univ-lille.fr/pdf/2019/Polymnia-4-2019-3-Delattre.pdf.

Delattre, Charles, and Greta Hawes. 2020. "Mythographical Topography, Textual Materiality, and the (Dis)ordering of Myth: the Case of Antoninus Liberalis." *Journal of Hellenic Studies* 140: 106–119.

Forbes Irving, Paul M. C. 1990. *Metamorphosis in Greek Myths*. Oxford: Clarendon Press.

Giangrande, Giuseppe. 1987. "On the Text of Antoninus Liberalis." In *Athlon: Satura grammatica in honorem F. Rodríguez-Adrados*, edited by Pedro Bádenas de la Peña, Alfonso Martínez Díez, María Emilia Martínez Fresneda, and Esperanza Rodríguez Monescillo, 363–372. Madrid: Gredos.

Létoublon, Françoise. 2004. "Le rossignol, l'hirondelle et l'araignée: Comparaison, métaphore et métamorphose." *Europe* 904–905: 73–102.

Marcotte, Didier. 2014. "La 'collection philosophique': Historiographie et histoire des textes." *Scriptorium* 68: 145–165.

Odorico, Paolo. 1990. "Cultura della συλλογή." *Byzantinische Zeitschrift* 83: 1–21.

Odorico, Paolo. 2011. "Cadre d'exposition / cadre de pensée: La culture du recueil." In *Encyclopedic Trends in Byzantium?*, edited by Peter Van Deun and Caroline Macé, 89–108. Leuven: Peeters.

Papathomopoulos, Manolis. 1962. "Notes critiques au texte d'Antoninus Liberalis." *Revue de Philologie* 36: 245–251.

Pellizer, Ezio. 1993. "La mitografia." In *Lo spazio letterario nella Grecia antica*, vol. 2, edited by Giuseppe Cambiano, Luciano Canfora, and Diego Lanza, 283–303. Rome: Salerno.

Ronconi, Filippo. 2012. "La collection brisée: La face cachée de la 'collection philosophique': Les milieux socioculturels." In *La face cachée de la littérature byzantine: Le texte en tant que message immédiat*, edited by Paolo Odorico, 137–166. Paris: École des hautes études en sciences sociales.

Sellheim, Rudolf. 1930. "De Parthenii et Antonini fontium indiculorum auctoribus." Diss. Vereinigte Friedrichsuniversität Halle.

Zucker, Arnaud. 2012. "Qu'est-ce qu'épitomiser: Étude des pratiques dans la *Syllogé* zoologique byzantine." *Rursus* 7. https://journals.openedition.org/rursus/961.

# CHAPTER 9

# APOLLODORUS THE MYTHOGRAPHER, *BIBLIOTHECA*

## STEPHEN M. TRZASKOMA

## 1. AUTHOR AND AUDIENCE

THE *Bibliotheca* (*Library*) ascribed to Apollodorus is a connected and summary account of Greek myth from the reign of Uranus and Gaea to the death of Odysseus, and it is widely regarded as the finest surviving work of ancient mythography. This judgment on its quality, however, masks a number of issues, for it is notably unhelpful to us in assessing either its own nature and ambition or the wider activity or genre of mythography, especially because no other mythographical work that survives from the ancient world attempts such a complete overview (Cuartero 2017). Customarily, the author of the *Bibliotheca* is, rather too precisely, referred to as *Pseudo*-Apollodorus because whoever he was, he was not, as some Byzantine writers thought (Robert 1873), Apollodorus of Athens, the 2nd-century BCE author of *Peri Theon*, and it has been supposed that Apollodorus's name became mistakenly attached to the *Bibliotheca* (Diller 1935). I say "too precisely" with full awareness that this convention is followed in this handbook, outside this chapter; but it is, at least, possible that the author was actually named Apollodorus, a common enough name, and that this otherwise unknown Apollodorus had his work eventually credited to his once more famous Athenian namesake. Fame and fortune, however, are now reversed, and the author of the *Bibliotheca* is both better known and better studied than the other. We ought, therefore, to distinguish between Apollodorus the Mythographer and Apollodorus of Athens rather than between the latter and a "Pseudo," particularly because the Athenian was not, on our current evidence, a mythographer (on this point, see Smith and Trzaskoma, this volume, on Hellenistic mythography). The supposed problems that come from simply calling our author Apollodorus are exaggerated.

We know essentially nothing about Apollodorus aside from the fact that he produced the *Bibliotheca*. As for date, a mention of "the chronicler Castor" in 2.5 gives us a *terminus post quem* of 61 or 60 BCE, the date down to which Castor of Rhodes brought his *Chronological Tables*. However, whether the *Bibliotheca* was written in 60 BCE or 260 CE cannot be determined, and scholarly opinion varies dramatically. For instance, Zuntz (1955: 138) leaned toward the 1st century BCE, while Carrière and Massonie (1991: 11) favor a date as late as 235 CE. Other scholars have proposed almost everything in between. We have no clear ancient *terminus ante quem* because we cannot even tell with certainty when information and language from the *Bibliotheca* became incorporated into scholiastic traditions or whether such coincidences depend on mutual sources or there is some other explanation (for some discussion, see Pagès 2017; Fowler 2013: 378–384). Nevertheless, no one has seriously suggested a date after the 3rd century CE. The desire to pin down the date of composition is understandable, for having the date would allow us to connect the work with broader social, literary, and intellectual trends, but there is a danger of circularity in this approach (Bowie 1970: 23–24, writes of a sort of "amnesia" about Rome that reinforces a 2nd-century date; Fletcher [2008] connects the *Bibliotheca* in more detail to larger currents of that century and the wider Second Sophistic, but if the work is from 50 BCE, this is mere illusion). Similar hazards are intertwined with conjectures about the author's political stance (Scarpi 1999; Fletcher 2008) and geographic origin (Hard 1997: xiii: "We can surely conclude that it is most unlikely that he came from Italy or the west").

We have no reason to doubt that the title of the *Bibliotheca* is original, and it accords well with the text we actually have, a kind of universal mythical history along the lines of the universal history of Diodorus Siculus's *Bibliotheca* (see Sulimani, this volume).. Both *Libraries* likewise share a technique of distilling preexisting sources into a new form, although the exact nature of those sources and the authors' respective techniques for handling them have exercised scholars considerably. One mystery surrounding the mythographical *Bibliotheca* is the question of its purpose and audience, and the answer hinges, at least to a degree, on an introductory epigram that the 9th-century patriarch Photius found at the head of his copy:

> By gathering the coils of time from my learning, come to know the myths of ancient times.
> Look not into the pages of Homer or of elegy, nor to the tragic Muse or the lyric,
> nor seek clamorous verse of Cyclic poets. Look into me and you will find in me all the cosmos holds.
>
> (Trans. Trzaskoma, in Smith and Trzaskoma 2007)

If the poem is genuinely by the author, then it points us to a broad purpose and audience—literally anyone who wanted to learn about myths but preferred or necessarily had to do so without recourse to the vast tradition of literature across multiple genres that engaged with myth. It is also a clear methodological statement that a prose mythographical work of this sort is a better way to acquire mythological data than are the specifically poetic alternatives. One potential key here is the mention of clamorous (*polythroun*) verses, which I take as a pointed reference to the many (*poly-*) contradictory accounts represented in the indistinct voices (*-throun*) of various little-read poets. Apollodorus, meanwhile, as we will see, generally reconciles mythological variants, or, at least, at most points chooses a favored version, giving his audience a supposedly complete, single, and straightforward account (Fowler 2017: 162–163). That audience, meanwhile, contains anyone literate enough to make their way through a linear account written in a relatively simple style. This does not mean only those barely capable of reading such a text but everyone, up to and including the highly educated. Less charitably, Maurice Croiset (1899: 690) characterized the audience as "all those who would have been frightened by long research," although it is unclear whether by that he meant the reading the original literary texts or more erudite mythographical works.

There has been much speculation about a narrower intended audience than I have posited above. For instance, the idea that the *Bibliotheca* is a text for schools was first mooted by Robert (1873: 35), and then picked up by Wagner (1926: xxxiii) and, particularly, Van der Valk (1958: 102). But while it may have been read by students (or their teachers—see Trzaskoma in Smith and Trzaskoma 2007: xxxi), there is no good reason to limit the audience to them, and the introductory epigram militates against doing so. Moreover, the positive argument for student readership is weak (van Rossum-Steenbeek 1997: 168–169; Cameron 2004: 170). Carrière and Massonie (1991:15) likewise point to an undefined and inclusive audience (although within the particular period of the Second Sophistic). Fowler points out that this audience would have included the elite, to judge by the "the number of *unique* details" (2017: 165–166, emphasis original; see also Acerbo 2019: 8–9) in the *Bibliotheca*. Pàmias (2017: 3) neatly sums it up: "Different levels of readership may be envisaged." The fact that in later antiquity and in the Byzantine Middle Ages the *Bibliotheca* is cited as a work of scholarship gives us no indication of its reputation in the period of its composition, but it at least points to an eventual audience of some sophistication, however we imagine the author's intentions or its original reception.

## 2. THE CONTENTS AND ORGANIZATION OF THE *BIBLIOTHECA*

The *Bibliotheca* presents in summary form a single narrative of Greek myth from the primeval reign of Uranus and Gaea to the period immediately after the Trojan War. There is no account of creation or of any figures before Uranus. In terms of presentation, the level of detail accorded to different myths and mythical figures varies considerably, but the effect is not disorienting at any given moment because the narrative style is otherwise quite uniform throughout and the organization of sections is neat and clear, though we do not have a clear picture of how audiences consumed it or oriented themselves to the work as a whole (but now see Delattre 2017, which gives new perspective on this issue). The bulk of the narrative survives complete, but after 3.218 it is known only from two Byzantine epitomes.

Modern editions are broken into three books that are followed by material recovered from these two other sources, which, combined, is often referred to loosely as "the" Epitome, although it is not, in fact, a single entity (see further the section "The Text and Its Transmission" below). The contents can be schematized as follows:

> **Book 1:** 1–44 Myths of the Gods; 45–147 Lineage of Deucalion
>
> **Book 2:** 1–180 Lineage of Inachus
>
> **Book 3:** 3.1–95 Lineage of Agenor; 3.96–109 Lineage of Pelasgus; 3.110–155 Lineage of Atlas; 3.156–176 Lineage of Asopus; 3.177–218 Athenian Myth
>
> **Epitome:** 1.1–24 Continuation of Athenian Myth; 2.1–16 Lineage of Pelops; 3.1–7.40 The Trojan War and Its Aftermath

Of course, we could divide this material differently, or break it into smaller units, but even in what is presented here one should be able to see the basic genealogical arrangement of the whole, at least until the Epitome. Attendant upon genealogy, however, are chronology and geography since, on the one hand, parents come before children and families and, on the other, mythical personages and groupings are connected to specific places in the imaginary and real landscape. Because of the complexity of the underlying material, Apollodorus sometimes abandons strict genealogical presentation, as at 1.87 with Perieres, whom he treats with the Aeolids but then delays the account of his offspring until later because "many say that Perieres was not the son of Aeolus, but that his father was Cynortas son of Amyclas," introducing not merely genealogical variation but also a change in location. The result is that while he may mention a particular figure in their appropriate genealogical place, he will sometimes reserve a fuller narrative of that figure for a more appropriate time in another lineage's narrative.

The *Bibliotheca* is decidedly a work of systematic mythography; it is interested in retelling and organizing mythical narratives rather than critiquing or interpreting them. While he does employ methodologies such as the etymologizing we see in the Telephus episodes, he avoids allegoresis, rationalizing, and other interpretive strategies. This seems to confirm the promise of the initial epigram that Apollodorus's intent is primarily informational (Delattre 2017).

Crafting a single narrative out of the massive and confusing traditional accounts was a Herculean task, of course, and there are signs, too, of either carelessness or inconsistencies that were allowed to remain. It is difficult to decide between these alternatives, and it may be that there is a combination of them throughout the *Bibliotheca*, but the slight repetitions of information one finds may be natural because so many myths overlap. In a case like that of Auge, who appears among the tales of Heracles, in a short narrative in Book 2 as the mother of Telephus (2.146–147), and again in a brief mention in the same capacity in a catalog not much later (2.166), and then again in a brief passage in her "proper" place in the Pelasgid genealogy (3.102–103), we can suspect something is a bit amiss since she is not merely mentioned in multiple places but the two narratives are of equal length and repeat some of the same information, including the etymology of Telephus's name. On the other hand, the passage in Book 3 is focused more on Telephus and his fate after his miraculous salvation as an infant than on his mother, so perhaps Apollodorus decided the repetition made sense so as not to leave the beginning of the son's story truncated because it had been told earlier.

To return to the subject of organization, in places geography supersedes strict genealogy; we see this, for example, with autochthonous figures, who, by definition, have no lineage behind them (on autochthony in Apollodorus, see Trzaskoma 2013: 91–93). The peculiar needs of the pan-Hellenic myth of the Trojan War—the narrative culmination of the entire *Bibliotheca*—also means that in Book 3 and the epitomized material we see Apollodorus bring stray figures together to set the stage for his summaries of the epic cycle and the Homeric poems, and genealogy retreats before other imperatives. Apollodorus has carefully thought through the arrangement of the whole, and this can be seen in narrative signposts throughout, particularly in the forward-looking references early in the narrative, as well as in forward- and backward-pointing ones later. These are presented in the narrator's voice, and while the prose of the *Bibliotheca* is generally unadorned and strictly focused on mythical events and figures rather than commentary or interpretation, this only makes the authorial remarks and other markers stand out, giving a clear impression of an author who is taking credit in his narrative voice for the organization (Trzaskoma 2013).

Before leaving the topic of the content of the *Bibliotheca* and its presentation, it is worth pointing out that despite the apparent inevitability of a book of its nature and form, there is nothing else at all like it from the ancient world. Modern scholars and popularizing authors have produced handbooks and manuals of Greek myth, sometimes weaving the complex material into a single connected narrative as Apollodorus did. This has perhaps made it easier for some scholars, as we have seen, to theorize not only that there were other such manuals in antiquity but, further, that Apollodorus must have been copying one of them from an earlier time. If they did exist, we have no evidence for them. The closest analog is perhaps Hyginus's *Fabulae* (on which see Fletcher, this volume, along with the chapter by Smith, this volume, on mythography in Latin), and it is not close at all, at least in its present form. It is not nearly as exhaustive; the presentation of myths is dramatically different in it; and above all, the material is not fused into a single narrative. One cannot imagine an epigram of the sort that Photius read in this copy of the *Bibliotheca* standing at the head of the *Fabulae*. Other mythographical works select myths because they fit some criterion or a small set of criteria. Parthenius's stories are all about unhappy love. Antoninus Liberalis's are about metamorphoses. We have not yet discerned what Conon's unifying theme may have been, but however he chose his myths, he chose only a small subset of all those he might have, and he did not aim for anything like an overall summary.

At the same time, we should be clear that Apollodorus's claim to completeness, whether taken implicitly or stated explicitly if the epigram is genuine, is an illusion, an authorial assertion he could never have lived up to. Any presentation of all the myths and all their variants would have looked nothing like the *Bibliotheca*. And even where our author could have included more, he did not; for instance, he excluded most Italian and all Roman material and did not include any primordial theogonic material of the sort we are familiar with from the early sections of Hesiod's *Theogony*. What is not in the *Bibliotheca* could fill volumes, and we must acknowledge with Fowler (2017: 162) that this is due not to shoddiness but to choice: "His purpose was therefore not to include absolutely everything . . . and his reason for including variants at all was not scholarly but literary or cultural."

## 4. The Text and Its Transmission

What follows does not presume to be a complete and technical description of the transmission of the *Bibliotheca*, which would be out of place in a handbook of this sort. At the same time, it is perhaps longer and more detailed than might be expected because it is designed to make clear some of the complexities in dealing with the contents of the work and the problems of assessing its nature and the specifics of the information found within it. While we sometimes lapse into thinking that Apollodorus's work comes to us complete with few problems, in fact, the situation is rather more complex. Apollodorus's text comes to us through three sources. First and most important is a family of manuscripts, all of which are descended from the extant *Parisinus Gr.* 2722, to which the siglum **R** is assigned. **R** contains an assortment of texts, among which was an incomplete, difficult to read, and heavily abbreviated text of the *Bibliotheca* that cut off at 3.218 and was then further damaged by the loss and reordering of several folia. It does not contain any trace of the epigram that Photius found in his copy in the 9th century. Copies were produced before the loss and displacement, but in this manuscript the text never seems to have been complete, so all of its descendants have an incomplete text as well. Wilson (1977: 238–239) dates **R** to the last half of the 12th century. Two partial apographs of **R** (**M** and **O**) were produced before the loss of the additional folia and their disordering. The Renaissance humanist Politian produced **M** (*Monacensis Gr.* 182), which can now be supplemented by a few additional excerpts from another of Politian's manuscripts, *Monancensis Lat.* 754 (to which Michels has assigned the siglum **F** and which has not been used by any editor to date; see Michels 2014: 13–18, building off Lo Monaco 1991). We have several additional minor manuscripts that are of slight interest for their conjectures but have no independent value otherwise.

Better manuscripts must still have been in circulation before and after the production of **R**, as we can deduce not only from Photius's evidence but, more directly, from our second major source, the epitomes. We have a lengthy epitome, the Vatican Epitome ([**E**]; Wagner 1891), which was produced by the 12th-century scholar John Tzetzes, and another collection of reworked excerpts made before the middle of the 13th century, the Sabbaitic Fragments (**S**). These overlap differently with parts of the *Bibliotheca* that survive in **R** and its descendants—the Vatican Epitome has material from across the whole, while the Sabbaitic Fragments only excerpt Book 3—but have the most value because they were produced from manuscripts that were both manifestly not **R** and were complete, including all the material after 3.218 to the end. Our knowledge of this portion of the *Bibliotheca* derives almost entirely from them.

Finally, we have a significant tradition of indirect transmission. Most importantly, our earliest (but still undatable) evidence consists of five *historiai* in the D-Scholia to Homer (see Pagès 2017, for a detailed discussion) that have subscriptions to Apollodorus, including, in some cases, references to Books 1, 2, and 3, although none of the extant manuscripts have unambiguous indications of book divisions, which appear, however, already in the the *editio princeps* of Aegius (1555). Four of these have close verbal correspondences to the *Bibliotheca*. Several other *historiai* also overlap in language and content with the *Bibliotheca* but do not contain subscriptions. There are also two subscriptions to Apollodorus that do not seem to refer to our mythographer but to Apollodorus the Athenian. The nature of the relationship between these scholia and the *Bibliotheca* is difficult to determine (van Rossum-Steenbeek 1997: 108–111; Fowler 2013: 378–384; and, especially, Pagès 2017, with earlier bibliography). For additional sources of indirect transmission (other scholia, paroemiographical collections, and so on), the edition of Cuartero (2010: 42–51) and the dissertation of Michels (2014: 27–39) contain the most up-to-date full discussions.

One important line of research stemming from this indirect transmission has less to do with trying to establish the text of Apollodorus and think about the ways in which his mythographical work exists in an ongoing and evolving network of mythography that extends into medieval Byzantium (Kenens 2012; Kenens 2013; Levrie 2018).

## 5.  Sources

Scholarship of the 19th and 20th centuries was fixated on the question of Apollodorus's sources, and most scholars viewed the *Bibliotheca* as a relatively uncritical repository for mythological data derived from earlier mythographical works rather than from a direct reading of archaic and classical literary texts (Van der Valk [1958] is an exception, arguing for Apollodorus as a diligent original researcher). The view of the nature and extent of such intermediary sources varies widely in detail, with the most extreme position being that the *Bibliotheca* is essentially an epitome of a single earlier and presumably "better" mythographical manual (beginning with Bethe 1887 and continuing with others through to Dräger 2005: 887–889. Most have held more nuanced views. Even Van der Valk (1958: 146–151) saw Apollodorus's original research as possibly being underpinned by such a manual, and Cameron (2004: 93–104), who views Apollodorus as primarily dependent on earlier mythographical works that he used uncritically, does not imagine that our author had no firsthand knowledge of any classical literature. What unites many of the more recent opinions on the subject (besides, perhaps,

Cameron's) is a growing realization of Apollodorus as a creative force as an author and narrator, even if these opinions do not always credit him with an original genius or methods that involved reading the oldest sources (the desire for which is more a reflection of the modern desire to value the oldest sources of myth than a reflection on what makes for good mythographical writing). These see greater sophistication in how the *Bibliotheca*'s narrative shapes mythology and presents it in particular ways for particular purposes (Trzaskoma 2013). Calame (1987: 168), for instance, writes of Apollodorus's intentional manipulation of Messenian myth. Scarpi (1999) and Fletcher (2008) discuss the *Bibliotheca* as expressing and constructing its author's worldview and attitudes toward Rome (see Edmunds 2017: 95–97, for a brief contrary opinion that nevertheless acknowledges Apollodorus's "inventiveness"). Even for scholars who are interested in the—still interesting and important—question of sources, it is no longer a matter of trying to trace a straightforward and unimaginative descent of information from good classical or Hellenistic origins. We will return to this matter briefly here in section 5 of this chapter.

From early in the modern study of Apollodorus (Robert 1873; Söder 1939), the main questions have fallen into two large groups: What were his sources and did he consult them directly? And, how do his citations reflect answers to the questions in the previous group? Alongside generic citations of the "some say" type, Apollodorus cites several authorities by name in the *Bibliotheca*, favoring ancient and authoritative poets (Homer, Hesiod, the tragedians) and early prose mythographers (Acusilaus, Hellanicus, Herodorus, Pherecydes). Other figures appear only a few times: Telesilla the poet, for instance, or Asclepiades of Tragilos and Peisander.

The bibliography on these is so now so enormous that it is impossible to summarize these controversies adequately in the space available here. The dominance of this early preoccupation with *Quellenforschung* can be traced through the annotated bibliographies of Huys and Colomo (Huys 1997: 226–338; Huys and Colomo 2004: 223–229), which demonstrate the interest in determining where Apollodorus got his information and whether he got it directly, or not, from its ultimate source. This search included, therefore, the question of whether Apollodorus's organization was itself an inheritance from an earlier model or models. For instance, the Hesiodic *Catalog of Women* is sometimes taken as a direct model or, at least, an inspiration for the *Bibliotheca*'s genealogical and geographical arrangement (Robert 1873; West 1985), although having too much confidence in our current evidence is a danger here. While work on the *Bibliotheca*'s relationship to earlier texts is still of interest, the approaches have become more creative, and the questions have become contextualized differently by looking at Apollodorus (or parts of his narrative) as nodes in a mythographical network that extends both backward and forward. This is a necessary shift in perspective because, frankly, whatever his sources were, we know that most of them are not now extant, and with regard to the relationships between the text of the *Bibliotheca* and other imperial mythographical writings, we are usually unable even to establish what the direction of influence was—a natural consequence of being unable to date most of this material.

# 6.  CONCLUSION

The *Bibliotheca* is our most important surviving ancient mythographical work from Greek and Roman antiquity. Its value derives in part from its systematic and comprehensive nature—even if it is neither as systematic in places as it seems nor as comprehensive as it pretends. However, part of its reputation owes to its usefulness for modern scholarship and its approachability, which in a circular process inspires modern imitations, and then, because it accords with those imitations, the *Bibliotheca* seems to us more natural than it is. After all, we have nothing else like it from the ancient world. If it had any direct competitors, we have little trace of them. So, while the work seems disarmingly straightforward, this veils a number of questions for which the answers remain unknown: its author's status, its date, its purpose and intended audience, its sources, and its relationship to other mythographical works. It is the same uniform and unpretentious presentation that has prompted some to regard the *Bibliotheca* as something derivative or, at least, unscholarly in its presentation. But the organization of the vast mythical system is, in and of itself, a monumental task, one that should prompt us to re-evaluate our assumptions about what such a work ought to be, its relationship to earlier supposed analogs, and whether such a text could have been conceived of and executed in the imperial period or must be a product of an earlier time. Happily, this reassessment and the more imaginative investigation of Apollodorus and his work is well underway.

## FURTHER READING

On almost any aspect of Apollodorus's work, it is profitable to consult Huys (1997) and Huys and Colomo (2004), which survey and comment on essentially all work to that point. For the text of the *Bibliotheca*, the edition of Wagner (1926) is still frequently used, but one must consult the more recent edition of Papathomopoulos (2010), which is an improvement in reporting the text in some ways but shows signs of hasty completion, and the fine multivolume edition of Cuartero (2010, 2012), which is accompanied by an excellent introduction and extensive notes but is not yet complete. Diller (1935) is still a starting place for the discussion of the manuscript tradition but must be supplemented by subsequent work, including Kenens (2013). A good overview of the discussion of the state of the text may be found in Michels (2014: 9–41), which cites earlier work scrupulously. Almost all modern translations are accurate and accessible (in English the most readily available are those by Hard (1997) and by Trzaskoma in Smith and Trzaskoma (2007), but none is based on a comprehensive knowledge of the very latest information about the text, a matter that mostly matters at the level of some individual details. A commentary is still a desideratum, but one that has been partially fulfilled by the excellent dissertations of Kenens (2011b) on 2.1–126, and Michels (2014) on 3.1–56.

On Apollodorus's sources there is a large and varied corpus of work, but it is best to start with more recent studies, which will point to earlier bibliography. Michels (2014: 72–221) aims at a complete overview, taking "source" to mean both the earlier authors potentially consulted by Apollodorus and those who lie behind information found in the *Bibliotheca*. Kenens' studies (2011a, 2012) are narrower but have important implications for both Apollodorus's use of earlier materials and how the *Bibliotheca* itself fits into later mythographical traditions, including the Byzantine. Most recently, Acerbo (2019) takes new approaches to old questions with good results.

Fletcher (2008) and Trzaskoma (2013) have picked up on earlier threads and looked more closely at Apollodorus as an individual author (and not merely as a source of mythographical data), an approach that is also reflected in many of the essays in Pàmias (2017). These explore a wide variety of issues around the *Bibliotheca*, its text, and its relationship to other mythographical works. Because it is the only volume to focus exclusively on Apollodorus, it is the best place to see how recent scholarship is approaching the mythographer from multiple perspectives, and additional bibliography can be traced backward from its individual chapters. There is yet more work to be done, and the lack of a comprehensive treatment of Apollodorus and the *Bibliotheca* remains keenly felt.

## References

Acerbo, Stefano. 2019. *Le tradizioni mitiche nella Biblioteca dello ps. Apollodoro: percorsi nella mitografia di età imperiale*. Amsterdam: Adolf M. Hakkert.

Aegius, Benedictus, ed. 1555. *Apollodori Atheniensis Bibliotheces sive de deorum origine*. Rome: Antonius Bladus.

Bethe, Erich. 1887. "Quaestiones Diodoreae Mythographae." Diss. University of Göttingen.

Bowie, Ewen. 1970. "Greeks and Their Past in the Second Sophistic." *Past & Present* 46: 3–41.

Calame, Claude. 1987. "Spartan Genealogies: The Mythological Representation of a Spatial Organisation." In *Interpretations of Greek Mythology*, edited by Jan N. Bremmer, 153–186. London: Routledge.

Cameron, Alan. 2004. *Greek Mythography in the Roman World*. Oxford: Oxford University Press.

Carrière, Jean-Claude, and Bertrand Massonie. 1991. *La Bibliothèque d'Apollodore*. Paris: Les Belles Lettres.

Croiset, Alfred, and Maurice Croiset. 1899. *Histoire de la littérature grecque*. Vol. 5. Paris: Thorin et Fils.

Cuartero, Francesc J. 2010/2012. *Pseudo-Apol·lodor. Biblioteca*. Vols. 1 and 2. Barcelona: Bernat Metge.

Cuartero, Francesc J. 2017. "The *Bibliotheca* of Pseudo-Apollodorus, *Textus Unicus*." In *Apollodoriana: Ancient Myths, New Crossroads*, edited by Jordi Pàmias, 146–157. Berlin and Boston: De Gruyter.

Delattre, Charles. 2017. "Apollodorus's Text: Experimental Layout and Edition." In *Apollodoriana*, edited by Jordi Pàmias, 176–203. Berlin and Boston: De Gruyter.

Diller, Aubrey. 1935. "The Text History of the *Bibliotheca* of Pseudo-Apollodorus." *Transactions and Proceedings of the American Philological Association* 66: 296–313.

Dräger, Paul. 2005. *Apollodor. Bibliotheke. Götter- und Heldensagen*. Düsseldorf: Sammlung Tusculum.

Edmunds, Lowell. 2017. "Helen in Pseudo-Apollodorus Book 3." In *Apollodoriana*, edited by Jordi Pàmias, 82–99. Berlin and Boston: De Gruyter.

Fletcher, Kris. 2008. "Systematic Genealogies in Apollodorus' *Bibliotheca* and the Exclusion of Rome from Greek Myth." *Classical Antiquity* 27: 59–91.

Fowler, Robert. 2013. *Early Greek Mythography*. Vol. 2: *Commentary*. Oxford: Oxford University Press.

Fowler, Robert. 2017. "Apollodorus and the Art of the Variant." In *Apollodoriana*, edited by Jordi Pàmias, 158–175. Berlin and Boston: De Gruyter.

Hard, Robin, trans. 1997. *Apollodorus: The Library of Greek Mythology*. Oxford: Oxford University Press.

Huys, Marc. 1997. "125 Years of Scholarship on Apollodorus the Mythographer: A Bibliographical Survey." *L'antiquité classique* 66: 319–351.

Huys, Marc, and Daniela Colomo. 2004. "Bibliographical Survey on Apollodorus the Mythogapher: A Supplement." *L'antiquité classique* 73: 219–237.

Kenens, Ulrike. 2011a. "The Sources of Ps.-Apollodorus's Library: A Case-Study." *Quaderni urbinati di cultura classica* 97: 129–146.

Kenens, Ulrike. 2011b. "Writing Greek Myth: A Philological Commentary on the Second Book of Ps.-Apollodorus' Bibliotheca (§§1–126)." Diss. Katholieke Universiteit Leuven.

Kenens, Ulrike. 2012. "Greek Mythography at Work: The Story of Perseus from Pherecydes to Tzetzes." *Greek, Roman, and Byzantine Studies* 52: 147–166.

Kenens, Ulrike. 2013. "Text and Transmission of Ps.-Apollodorus' *Bibliotheca*: Avenues for Future Research." In *Writing Myth: Mythography in the Ancient World*, edited by Stephen M. Trzaskoma and R. Scott Smith, 95–114. Leuven: Peeters.

Levrie, Katrien. 2018. *Jean Pédisasimos. Essai sur les douze travaux d'Héracles: Édition critique, traduction et introduction*. Leuven: Peeters.

Lo Monaco, Francesco, ed. 1991. *Angelo Poliziano. Commento inedito ai Fasti di Ovidio*. Florence: Istituto Nazionale di Studi sul Rinascimento.

Michels, Johanna. 2014. "Crouching Cow, Killing Dragon: Agenorid Myth in Pseudo-Apollodorus, *Bibliotheca*, III.1–156, a Philological Commentary." Diss. Katholieke Universiteit Leuven.

Pagès, Joan. 2017. "Apollodorus' *Bibliotheca* and the *Mythographus Homericus*." In *Apollodoriana*, edited by Jordi Pàmias, 66–81. Berlin and Boston: De Gruyter.

Pàmias, Jordi. 2017. "Preface: Apollodorus: Cutting through Mythography." In *Apollodoriana*, edited by Jordi Pàmias, 1–6. Berlin and Boston: De Gruyter.

Papathomopoulos, Manolis, ed. 2010. *Apollodori Bibliotheca post Richardum Wagnerum recognita*. Athens, Greece: Aletheia.

Robert, Carl. 1873. "De Apollodori Bibliotheca." Diss. Humboldt University of Berlin.

Scarpi, Paolo. 1999. "L'Italia di Apollodoro: Sterilità mitologica di Roma e rappresentazione dell'Italia centro-medidionale." In *Sicilia e Magna Grecia: Spazio reale e spazio immaginario nella letteratura greca e latina*, edited by Guido Avezzù and Emilio Pianezzola, 1–16. Padua: Università di Padova.

Smith, R. Scott, and Stephen M. Trzaskoma. 2007. *Apollodorus' "Library" and Hyginus' "Fabulae": Two Handbooks of Greek Mythology*. Indianapolis, IN: Hackett.

Söder, Anna. 1939. "Quellenuntersuchung zum 1. Buch der Apollodorschen Bibliothek." Diss. University of Würzburg.

Trzaskoma, Stephen M. 2013. "Citation, Organization and Authorial Presence in Ps.-Apollodorus' *Bibliotheca*." In *Writing Myth: Mythography in the Ancient World*, edited by Stephen M. Trzaskoma and R. Scott Smith, 75–94. Leuven: Peeters.

Trzaskoma, Stephen M., and R. Scott Smith. 2013. *Writing Myth: Mythography in the Ancient World*. Leuven: Peeters.

Van der Valk, Marchinus. 1958. "On Apollodori *Bibliotheca*." *Revue des Études Grecques* 71: 100–168.

van Rossum-Steenbeek, Monique. 1997. *Greek Readers' Digests?* Leiden: Brill.

Wagner, Richard, ed. 1891. *Epitoma Vaticana ex Apollodori Bibliotheca*. Leipzig: Hirzel.

Wagner, Richard, ed. 1926. *Mythographi Graeci*. Vol. 1. Leipzig: Teubner.

West, Martin L. 1985. *The Hesiodic Catalogue of Women: Its Nature, Structure and Origins*. Oxford: Oxford University Press.

Wilson, Nigel G. 1977. "Scholarly Hands of the Middle Byzantine Period." In *La paléographie grecque et byzantine. (Paris, 21–25 octobre 1974)*, 221–239. Paris: Centre National de la Recherche Scientifique.

Zuntz, Günther. 1955. *The Political Plays of Euripides*. Manchester, UK: Manchester University Press.

........................................................................................................................

# CHAPTER 10

# CONON, *NARRATIVES*

........................................................................................................................

MANUEL SANZ MORALES

OUR knowledge of Conon derives entirely from his work, a collection of fifty short mythographical tales (*Diēgēseis*, or *Narratives*) that we have in an epitome written in the 9th century by Photius. The original work, of which there is an extant papyrus (2nd century CE) that includes a few dozen lines, can be dated from 36 BCE to 17 CE. Conon's *Narratives* is unique for a lack of any unifying theme and a structure that is not the result of any clear organizational principle. Photius's epitome is generally deemed a reliable source for the varied content of the work, which includes foundation myths, local cults, mythical or historical love stories, etiological myths, incredible events, and explanations for proverbs. Among its points of interest, Conon's work provides us with information about little-known myths and rationalistic interpretations of three important myths (Midas, the earthborn Spartoi of Thebes, and Andromeda and the sea monster).

## 1. AUTHOR AND DATE

Although Conon's work has not been preserved, we have three witnesses to it. The most important one is the epitome written by Photius (*Bibliotheca* cod. 186) in the 9th century, which makes a summary of its fifty tales, one by one. The second is the extant 2nd-century papyrus (*P.Oxy.* 3648, ed. Harder 1984) that includes a part of the text (probably the original text) of tales 46 and 47. Of minor significance is the new text recently identified by Hilkens (2016) in the Syriac Chronicle of the Syrian Orthodox patriarch Michael I (1126–1199). This excerpt (Mich. Syr. *Chron.* 4.15, Syriac text with an English translation in Hilkens 2016: 614–615) relates the childhood of Romulus and Remus, and offers untraditional information that matches Conon's tale 48.

Photius himself says that the work was known as *Narratives* (*Diēgēseis*), and that it was dedicated to Archelaus Philopator. Given that this is very probably a mistake for the Cappadocian king Archelaus Philopatris, Conon should be dated to the reign of this vassal to Rome, 36 BCE to 17 CE. Perhaps Conon carried out activities in Archelaus's court as a man of letters (Archelaus himself wrote literary works: *FGrHist* 123), but this is only a hypothesis, as are the following considerations: Dio Chrysostom (*Or.* 18.12) mentions a Conon together with three other rhetors from the Augustan period. However, some scholars believe that this is a different Conon. Furthermore, the name Conon was very common (Brown 2002: 5 and n. 31, with bibliography). Moreover, three independent sources attribute to a certain Conon three works, titled *On Heracles*, *On Italy* and *On the Jews* (a fourth one, *The Islet*, is dubiously attributed to a Conon). Jacoby decided to treat all the texts as if they belonged to the same mythographer (*FGrHist* 26 test. 1 and fr. 2–4). The question of whether these are all by the same Conon is a difficult one (see Ibáñez Chacón 2007: 83–84), but this is of secondary importance in a discussion of Conon's *Diēgēseis* as mythography.

Brown (2002: 4–5) believes that "the pronounced rhetorical elements" of some tales make it possible to assume that Conon was a rhetor. It is true that there are some important differences between rhetorical narrations on mythical themes and mythographical texts given that the goals of rhetoricians and mythographers were very different (Cameron 2004: 73–75). However, the possibility that a single author might have developed both genres cannot be ruled out, considering that there was often a symbiotic relationship between mythography and rhetoric in formal education during the Imperial period, as Gibson (2013: conclusions on 304–307) has shown. Rhetoricians made use of mythographical sources in their lessons and treatises; and mythographers wrote their compilations of myths after completing at least some rhetorical training in the progymnasmata. This might mean that Conon was a rhetor, perhaps the one alluded to by Dio Chrysostom; however, the evidence permits no certainty on this point. Had Conon been a rhetor, the *Narratives* would be classified among his nonrhetorical works because of the uncommon nature of most of its myths, the inclusion of tales whose plots hardly allow for a rhetorical treatment (see section 4, "Topics," below), and, as already noted, its lack of thematic uniformity.

Concerning Conon's language, Photius states in his epilogue that Conon writes Attic Greek. However, the language itself shows both Hellenistic and Attic features. This is hardly surprising in an author who predates the emergence of Atticism by at least a century. It must, however, be taken into account that Photius had the tendency to lessen (although not methodically) the presence of Atticizing in authors he summarized (Hägg 1975: 69).

## 2. WORK AND TITLE

The term *Diēgēseis*, a title that does not occur in the extant mythographical works, has led to different hypotheses about its precise meaning. In its plural form the noun is attested in two Pseudo-Plutarchean works (*Parallela Minora* and *Amatoriae Narrationes*), in which the word *diēgēseis* means compilations of short or very short narratives. A suggestion worthy of consideration (see Cameron 2004: 71–72) is that the term might denote brief content told in a simple style, in contradistinction to a more formal narrative of a higher rhetorical level. Such language is used by the early Greek hagiographers in their lives of saints.

In addressing Conon's work, we must take into account the extent to which Photius's summary reflects its original contents. Scholars tend to think that the text of Photius's fifty summaries is very similar to the text of the fifty original tales (Treadgold 1980: 9; Cameron 2004: 72; Hawes 2014: 138; on Photius's level of fidelity to his originals, see Hägg 1975: 67–68, 204). However, although Photius himself acknowledged at the end of 3 that he was practically transcribing (*metagraphein*) Conon's text, a comparison of the length of the tales (Brown 2002: 74) shows that tales 4–22 are significantly shorter than the rest: it may be that Photius decided to be more concise after 3, only to forget or later change his mind, with the result that most of the tales after 23 are longer again. Comparisons with the text of the papyrus in 46 and 47 (Brown 2002: 37–39) show the use of different epitomization techniques on Photius's part: his tale 47 is very similar, but the text in 46 is shortened. Be that as it may, the original work would not be much longer than the epitome (32 pages in the Budé edition by Henry 1962: 8–39). Photius called it "a little book" (*biblidarion* and *ponēmation*) and declared that he had read it in a copy that contained Ps.-Apollodorus's work as well, or perhaps an epitome of it; both works make up a single codex (cod. 186) of the *Bibliotheca*.

## 3.   SOURCES

Some scholars think that Conon did not name the writers or works on which his treatise was based. But Photius affirms in his introduction that the *Diēgēseis* consist of "fifty narrations gathered from many ancient sources (or writers)," *ek pollōn archaiōn*. It is therefore possible that Conon mentioned his sources, whereas Photius considered it inappropriate or unnecessary to take them into account. Hoefer (1890) devotes himself primarily to the problem of the sources, concluding that Conon had depended on lost intermediary sources. Egan (1971: 13–14) is critical; so, too, is Brown (2002: 31–34), but he summarizes the main results. Egan (1971: 19–20) tentatively suggested that the main source could be the *Phillipica* of Theopompus of Chios (*FGrHist* 115). However, others have noted, perhaps rightly, that the whole debate is unnecessary and may not even have a solution given the overlap of second- or third-hand materials that is typical of mythographical works, as well as the difficulty of telling primary and secondary sources apart (Henrichs 1987: 246; Lightfoot 1999: 247; Hawes 2014: 144).

In any case, it may be possible to further investigate the issue, especially regarding some particular myths. For example, it is plausible that, for at least some of his tales about Thrace (see 4, 7, 10, 13, 20, 25, 32, 45, 46), Conon may have used Hegesippus of Mecyberna (directly or by intermediate sources), a local historian of Chalcidice who is the source for Parthenius's stories 6 and 16 (Hoefer 1890: 53–68; Lightfoot 1999: 227–228; Brown 2002: 33; Cameron 2004: ch. 5).

# 4. TOPICS

With some exceptions, the collection fits in well with the Hellenistic preference for unfamiliar or strange stories. For example, there are no myths about gods. When gods do appear, they take on a secondary role: recipients of cult, intervention through oracles or dreams, and the like. A rough estimate of the Greek "canonical" myths shows that they make up around 20 percent of the whole work (1, Midas; 21, Dardanus; 24, Narcissus; 27, Deucalion; 31, Tereus, Procne, and Philomela; 37, Cadmus and the Spartoi; 40, Andromeda; 45, Orpheus; tales 46, Aeneas, and 48, Romulus and Remus all tell famous Roman legends). The rest of the work consists of rare myths and even stories that cannot be classified as myths but are, rather, fables or anecdotes, which contributes to the appearance that Conon's *Narratives* is a varied work.

Scholars have tried to identify or describe topics in this varied work. The groups Brown (2002: 16–27) discerned may be taken as a starting point: foundation legends, etiological myths, erotic myths, paradoxographical myths, paroemiographical myths, fables and parables, and Trojan and Roman myths.

Conon shows a special interest (17 tales) in *ktiseis* or foundation legends, a type of story that was very popular in Hellenistic times, probably due to the influence of Alexander's foundations of new cities. Etiological myths represent the second largest group (13 tales, all of which explain cult origins) and are closely related to *ktiseis*, sometimes mixed together in the same tale (19 incorporates four etiologies, including the foundation of a city). Etiology is also present in erotic myths, which comprise four tragic love stories. Tale 16 deals with homoerotic love (22 and 24 incidentally mention lovers' gifts), whereas 2, 10, and 23 tell of tragic affairs between mythical women and men. This raises the question of the relationship between Conon and Parthenius of Nicaea (see Lightfoot 1999: 227–229), especially because the same three myths are the subject of Parthenius's tales 11, 6, and 4, respectively. There are also some minor "erotic" coincidences between both mythographers. Another common feature is the complete (or almost complete) lack of mythological motifs in some of the tales (38, the deposit of the gold; 42, Gelon of Sicily and a fable; 35, the shepherds, where Apollo is briefly involved in the plot). Each of these is an *ainos*, or "fable," rather than a myth, and that form was also used during the Imperial age in progymnasmata in rhetorical schools. It is also found in Parthenius, for instance in the story of Herippe and the Gaul (Parth. 8), which shows a complete absence of myth. Returning to the erotic myths: it is likely that Conon and Parthenius may have had some common sources. This would not be the only case of this for both mythographers, as we saw with regard to their common source Hegesippus of Mecyberna.

Narratives 5, 22, and 43 may be regarded as a group of paradoxographical myths, as they narrate incredible events and include in their plots elements that go against the laws of nature. Even though there are precedents in Greek literature, paradoxography arose as a genre in the Hellenistic times, and continued in the imperial age with such works as that of Phlegon of Tralles or the Pseudo-Plutarchean *Parallela Minora*. More questionable is the existence of groups of paroemiographical myths (tales 28 and 34) or Trojan and Roman myths (the Trojan War is incidentally present in thirteen narratives, whereas tale 48 is devoted to the myth of Rome's foundation). The organization of the tales into those specific groups is doubtful in part because of the small number of the tales, and in part because of the mixture of themes that is characteristic of these tales. For example, while tale 28 explains the proverb "Tennes' axe," the myth could also be included among the Trojan ones, given that Tennes was the son of Cycnus. And perhaps, based on even stronger arguments, it could be classed with the erotic myths, in that Tennes's stepmother falls in love with him and, after he rejects her, falsely accuses him.

That groups of myths exist does not imply that a structural or unifying principle does as well. This is the most distinctive feature of Conon's work. It has been suggested (Henrichs 1987: 245) that such a trait may have diminished the usefulness of the treatise and, ultimately, doomed it to failure. It is true that before Photius we do not have records of this work, but it should not be forgotten that the *Diēgēseis* were still read in the 2nd century, as evinced by *P.Oxy.* 3648.

In terms of his contribution to our knowledge of Greek myth, Conon may not be one of the most important mythographers, but, as Henrichs (1987: 247) has pointed out, he offers interesting variants of known myths. Crucially, he preserves at least three myths that are not found anywhere else in ancient literature: namely, the foundation of Olynthus (4), the myth of the change of control over the Didymean oracle of Apollo (33), and the origin of the cult of Apollo Gypaieus at Ephesus (35). Furthermore, the *Diēgēseis* offer other valuable details in matters of cult or history.

Conon's mythological rationalization is of particular interest. There are no traces of allegorical exegesis in his work, but explicit rationalistic exegesis appears in three myths: 1 (Midas), 37 (Cadmus), 40 (Andromeda). Some minor elements in other stories may reflect a rationalizing attitude as well (Hawes 2014: 139 n. 18 and 202 n. 88; and this volume, on rationalizing). Regarding the nature of the rationalization, we can draw two main conclusions. First of all, Conon did not propose a rationalization of his own; rather, he took from his source (or sources) myths that incorporated rationalization (Brown 2002: 30–31). Rationalization is present in just three out of the fifty myths, and these three belong to the canon of Greek myths. However, there is no rationalistic exegesis attested in the local myths, which are more characteristic of Conon and make up the majority of his work. There are also paranormal elements introduced without interpretation (for instance, in tale 43), as well as oracles and prophecies that play an important role in several etiological or foundation legends. Furthermore, tale 32 deals with Cadmus's myth without rationalization, in contrast to tale 37.

Secondly, a comparison with the most important extant works on mythological rationalization, those by Palaephatus and Heraclitus the Mythographer (see Sanz Morales 2014: 526–529; for more on these figures, see Koning, this volume, on Palaephatus; and Hawes, this volume, on Heraclitus the Mythographer), seems to indicate that Conon, while using basically the same exegetical method as Palaephatus, applied it to concrete myths in a different way; for Heraclitus, the examples are not conclusive. The interpretative methods used by Conon, such as figurative language, or people's incorrect interpretations of new and unknown facts or phenomena, are actually attested in Palaephatus. Nevertheless, the concrete solutions almost always differ. For example, the solution Conon (40) applies to the myth of Andromeda, Perseus, and the sea monster (*Kētos*) is applied by Palaephatus (37) to the myth of Hesione (Laomedon's daughter, who was saved from the monster by Heracles). And whereas the monster is interpreted by Palaephatus as a king named *Kēton*, in Conon *Kētos* is the name of the ship in which Phoenix abducts Andromeda. It may be of interest to point out that Conon offers not only a verbal solution but also a reality-based one, in that a ship can be transformed into a sea monster in the popular imagination. Although the examples are indeed few, they are certainly striking, which raises the possibility that Conon and Palaephatus may have followed different lines within the rationalistic exegesis.

## FURTHER READING

Brown (2002) offers a good critical edition, with an English translation. Because of its date it is the only edition that prints the papyrus's text (including Luppe's 1986 comments); Brown does not attempt a *constitutio textus* of stories 46 and 47 together with Photius's summary. Conon is included in Henry's (1962) Budé edition of Photius's *Bibliotheca* and, before that, in Jacoby (1957), who printed Photius's epitome as a fragment including fifty sections (*FGrHist* 26 fr. 1). There is also an edition with Italian translation and brief commentary by Otranto (2016: 233–254). On the old editions of Photius, see Egan (1971: 22–24), Brown (2002: 45–46) and the interesting remarks made by Henrichs (1987: 268).

Conon's language and style have been studied by Wahlgren (1995: 195–196) and Brown (2002: 39–44) on the basis of both the papyrus's text and, with the necessary *caveat*, Photius's summary.

There is no comprehensive study of the *Diēgēseis*, although Brown's (2002: 1–46) introduction covers its main aspects. His wide-ranging commentary makes it required reading for anyone interested in Conon. Egan's (1971) commentary, unfortunately not yet published, is useful. There are interesting observations in Henrichs (1987), especially in his rich notes; Lightfoot (1999); and Cameron (2004), although Martini (1922) remains relevant. Other contributions, not mentioned here because of space limitations, deal with particular myths.

To conclude, a possible gap in the bibliography on Conon is the dearth of studies comparing Conon with other mythographers. Such studies (see section 4, "Topics," on Conon and Parthenius) could shed further light on the nature of Conon's work.

## REFERENCES

Brown, Malcolm K. 2002. *The "Narratives" of Konon: Text, Translation and Commentary of the "Diegeseis."* Munich and Leipzig: Saur.
Cameron, Alan. 2004. *Greek Mythography in the Roman World.* Oxford: Oxford University Press.

Egan, Rory B. 1971. "The Diegeseis of Konon: A Commentary with an English Translation." Diss. University of Southern California.

Gibson, Craig A. 2013. "True or False? Greek Myth and Mythography in the Progymnasmata." In *Writing Myth: Mythography in the Ancient World*, edited by Stephen M. Trzaskoma and R. Scott Smith, 289–308. Leuven: Peeters.

Hägg, Tomas. 1975. *Photios als Vermittler antiker Literatur: Untersuchungen zur Technik des Referierens und Exzerpierens in der Bibliotheke.* Uppsala: Almquist and Wiksell International.

Harder, M. Annette, ed. 1984. "*P.Oxy.* 3648." In *The Oxyrhynchus Papyri*, vol. LII, edited by Helen M. Cockle, 5–12 and plate 2. London: Egypt Exploration Society.

Hawes, Greta. 2014 . *Rationalizing Myth in Antiquity.* Oxford: Oxford University Press.

Henrichs, Albert. 1987. "Three Approaches to Greek Mythography." In *Interpretations of Greek Mythology*, edited by Jan Bremmer, 242–277. London and Sydney: Croom Helm.

Henry, René. 1962. *Photius, Bibliothèque III ("codices" 186–222).* Paris: Les Belles Lettres.

Hilkens, Andy. 2016. "A New Fragment of the *Narratives* of Conon." *Greek, Roman, and Byzantine Studies* 56: 611–622.

Hoefer, Ulrich. 1890. *Konon: Text und Quellenuntersuchung.* Greifswald, Germany: Bamberg.

Ibáñez Chacón, Álvaro. 2007. "Un posible fragmento inédito de la *Heraclea* de Conón en la *Mitología* de Natale Conti." *Myrtia* 22: 83–93.

Jacoby, Felix. 1957. *Die Fragmente der griechischen Historiker IA. Vorrede. Text. Addenda. Konkordanz. Nr. 1–63*, 2nd ed., 190–211. Leiden: Brill (repr. 1968).

Lightfoot, Jane L., ed. 1999. *Parthenius of Nicaea: The Poetical Fragments and the Erotika Pathemata.* With Introduction and Commentaries. Oxford: Clarendon Press.

Luppe, Wolfgang. 1986. Review of *P. Oxy.* 52. Helen M. Cockle (ed.): *The Oxyrhynchus Papyri*, Vol. LII. (Graeco-Roman Memoirs, 72.) Pp. xviii+161; 8 plates. London: Egypt Exploration Society, 1984. *Classical Review* 36: 121–122.

Martini, Emidio. 1922. "Konon #9." *RE* XI: 1335–1338.

Otranto, Rosa. 2016. *Cod. 186.* In *Fozio. Biblioteca*, edited by Nunzio Bianchi and Claudio Schiano, 233–254. Pisa: Edizioni della Normale.

Sanz Morales, Manuel. 2014. "Conón y la exégesis racionalista del mito." In *Realidad, fantasía, interpretación, funciones y pervivencia del mito griego: Estudios en honor del Profesor Carlos García Gual*, edited by Aurelio Pérez Jiménez, 519–534. Zaragoza, Spain: Pórtico.

Treadgold, Warren P. 1980. *The Nature of the "Bibliotheca" of Photius.* Washington, DC: Dumbarton Oaks Center for Byzantine Studies.

Wahlgren, Staffan. 1995. *Sprachwandel im Griechisch der frühen Römischen Kaiserzeit.* Gothenburg, Sweden: Acta Universitatis Gothoburgensis.

# CHAPTER 11

..................................................................................

# CORNUTUS, *SURVEY OF THE TRADITIONS OF GREEK THEOLOGY*

..................................................................................

## ILARIA L.E. RAMELLI

RELATIVELY little is known of the life and intellectual personality of the Roman Stoic Annaeus Cornutus, philosopher and teacher of philosophy. The most famous fact about his life is that, like Musonius, he was exiled to an island by Nero. According to Cassius Dio (62.29.1–4), Nero intended to write a comprehensive history of the Romans in epic verse and consulted Cornutus, who replied that the planned four hundred books would be too long, and nobody would read them. To the objection, "But Chrysippus, whom you praise and imitate, composed many more," Cornutus answered, "But these are useful for human life!" This resulted in Cornutus's exile. Cornutus was the teacher of philosophy and a friend of the Stoic poet Persius (Euseb. *Chronicon* 7.184–185 Helm). According to the *Life of Persius*, Cornutus introduced Persius to Seneca and Lucan, the latter also a disciple of Cornutus. At his untimely death, Persius left Cornutus both riches—which Cornutus declined—and about seven hundred books. Cornutus also edited Persius's *Satires* after his death and altered a dangerous verse. In Satire 5, Persius himself calls Cornutus "beloved friend," and declares that he has "planted him deeply in the recesses" of his own heart. Cornutus took up Persius's tender years in his "Socratic bosom," straightened his morals, and molded his soul. Persius portrayed Cornutus as devoted to nightly study and the education of the young, based on Cleanthes's doctrine—in particular, Stoic ethics—which teaches "true freedom." This is not juridical freedom but moral freedom, freedom from passions—the real, inner masters (Ramelli 2016b). Only philosophy can teach moral freedom, based on the distinction between truth and appearance, Persius says; for the Stoics, who inherited Socrates's ethical intellectualism, bad moral choices depended on wrong assumptions. This is what Cornutus taught.

Cornutus wrote other philosophical, literary, rhetorical, and grammatical works, but his masterpiece deals with mythological allegoresis: it is his handbook of Greek theology,

*Survey of the Traditions of Greek Theology* (*Compendium theologiae Graecae* or *Epidromē tōn kata tēn hellēnikēn theologian paradedomenōn*)—a document from the age of Nero written in Greek by a Roman Stoic. Cornutus's handbook repeatedly addresses a boy (*pais*): this suggests an immediate pedagogic function, which is also probable given the compendious nature of the work and Cornutus's job as teacher of Stoic (philosophy). In the last chapter Cornutus refers readers to unnamed philosophical predecessors, surely Stoics, for a fuller treatment.

For each divinity, from Ouranos to Hades, Cornutus provides an allegorico-etymological interpretation of its names and epithets, its attributes, aspects of its myths and rituals, and so on (for allegoresis, see Ramelli, this volume). Section 1 of the *Survey* is devoted to Ouranos, the Sky; section 2, to Zeus; and sections 3 to Hera, 4 to Poseidon, 5 to Hades, 6 to Rhea-Atargatis, 7 to Kronos, 8 to Oceanos, and 9 again to Zeus and his multiple epithets. Section 10 deals with the Erinyes; section 11, again, with Zeus; section 12, with the Prayers; section 13, with Zeus as Fate, Necessity, and Adrasteia; section 14, with the Muses; section 15 with the Graces (to which I shall return below in connection with Seneca's probable criticism); and the long section 16, with Hermes. Section 17 is more methodological and reflects on the mythological traditions of different peoples: "Many and various myths about the gods were composed by the ancient Greeks, as others by the Magi, others by the Phrygians, and again the Egyptians and Celts and Libyans, and other races." Section 18 addresses Prometheus and Epimetheus; section 19, Athena and Hephaestus, section 20 (lengthy) again Athena; sections 21 Ares and Enyo, 22 Poseidon again, 23 Nereus, 24 Aphrodite, 25 Eros, 26 Atlas, 27 Pan as cosmos, 28 Demeter and Hestia, 29 the Hours, 30 Dionysus, 31 Heracles as universal logos, 32 Apollo and Artemis, 33 Asclepius, 34 the epithets of Artemis, and 35 again Hades, his epithets, and conclusions.

Physical allegoresis is prevalent, although there are also examples of ethical and even historical exegesis. From the viewpoint of physical allegoresis, for instance, what the ancients called Zeus is a symbol of the ether and the cosmic soul; what they named Hera is an allegory of the air; Poseidon is a symbol of the water, and so on. By way of example, I translate sections 2 and 3 (from the Ramelli 2003a edition, which has some changes vis-à-vis Lang's edition):

> Just as we are governed by a soul, so also does the cosmos possess a soul that keeps its cohesion, and this soul is called Zeus, because it lives (*zōsa*) primarily and everywhere, and it is the cause of life (*zēn*) for the living beings (*zōntes*). This is also why Zeus is said to reign over all beings, in the same way as one could say that in us, too, the soul and our nature reign. We call him *Dia*, too, because thanks to (*dia*) him all realities come to existence and are kept in existence. Some people also call him *Deus*, perhaps because he soaks (*deuein*) the earth, or has living beings participate in (*metadidonai*) life-giving humidity. The genitive of this form is *Deos*, parallel to the genitive *Dios*. He is said to dwell in heaven, because there resides the most sovereign part of the soul of the cosmos; for our souls, too, are fire. As for his wife and sister, tradition has it that she is Hera, who is the air (*aēr*). For she turns out to be immediately joined with him, rising from the earth, while he is over her. And they were born

from a flux in the same direction; indeed, by flowing toward fineness, the substance constitutes both fire and air.

The assumption that underlies Cornutus's method is that poetry and other expressions of ancient theology, such as cultic epithets, visual representations, and rituals, convey truth symbolically, and that the task of philosophical allegoresis is to decode those symbols. Such a task is philosophical and, more precisely, theological, insofar as its focus is the truth about nature and the divine. In Stoic immanentism, theology and physics are two sides of the same coin, and the application of allegoresis to traditions handed down from antiquity reveals this by showing that deities designate natural elements or forces.

Cornutus also shows traces of ethical and historical exegesis. Ethical allegoresis was already present in the Stoic allegorical tradition, while historical, rationalizing exegesis was typical of the Peripatetic tradition of Palaephatus (Ramelli 2004: ch. 4). For instance, in section 30, Cornutus provides an etiological account of the myth of Dionysus torn apart by the Titans. He explains that once farmers mixed grape clusters together and separated the parts of the grapes from each other, which the myth handed down as "the limbs of Dionysus." Likewise, in section 19 Cornutus suggests that Hephaestus is said to have been thrown to earth from heaven by Zeus because, once upon a time, the first people to use fire found it where it had been started by a thunderbolt.

Examples of ethical allegoresis are more abundant in Cornutus's handbook. For instance, in section 20, Athena, being allegorized as virtue and reason, gives rise to a number of ethical points. Her virginity indicates that virtue is pure and unstained; she is represented armed, to show that wisdom is sufficiently prepared for the greatest and most difficult deeds. Physical allegoresis, however, is predominant. This reflects a predominance in the whole of the Stoic allegorical tradition, which can be clearly explained within the framework of Stoic immanentism: physical allegoresis shows the material nature of the divine, the Stoic reduction of *theologia* to *physikē* (Ramelli 2013).

At the end of his handbook Cornutus declares (35): "The ancients were not people of no account, but they were also able to understand the nature of the cosmos and had the ability to *philosophise on it* by means of symbols and enigmata." The ancients were philosophers since they were endowed with the understanding of what exists. They expressed allegorically philosophical truths. According to Cornutus, then, the task of later philosophers, such as the Stoics, is to interpret those ancient philosophers' expressions and discover the philosophical tenets hidden under the veil of allegory. Allegorical reading performs the task of finding philosophical truths under the veil of riddles: this is why it belongs to philosophy.

Cornutus's attitude is not different from that of previous Stoic allegorists who attached to the most ancient poet, Homer, the knowledge, and veiled expression, of philosophical and scientific truths (see Ramelli 2914b and 2021). In particular, Cornutus was strongly influenced by Chrysippus, Cleanthes, Apollodorus of Athens, and Crates (see Ramelli 2004: ch. 6). Cornutus derived most of his material from, and was inspired by, them from a methodological and theoretical viewpoint, with respect to philosophical allegoresis of theological myths and its rationale and meaning. Cornutus's work is

similar to Chrysippus's and Apollodorus's *On the Gods,* as far as the evidence allows us
to judge. Cornutus was following the Stoic idea of the excellence of the first humans,
who could directly access the truth and expressed it through myths and rituals. He
joined this theory to the Stoic notion of direct, common access to truth though common
innate notions (*koinai ennoiai*). The result was support for the inclusion of mythological allegoresis in philosophy. From the perspective of Cornutus (and of Chrysippus,
who theorized it), poetry and other forms of transmission of ancient "theology," such as
rituals, cultic epithets, and visual representations, express various truths in a symbolic
way, which allegoresis must decrypt.

Etymology was abundantly employed in Stoicism in the service of philosophical
allegoresis, but the latter is far from being reduced to an etymologizing practice, as has
sometimes been suggested (Steinmetz 1986; Long 1997: 200–201). Etymology was an expression of the Stoics's theory of language, according to which names are "by nature,"
since the "first sounds" imitated the objects, and, on this basis, names were formed.
Etymology was a tool both for the understanding of the true nature of the gods—since
etymology goes back to the authentic meaning of a name—and for showing how the traditional names and epithets of deities reflect their nature, physical or ethical. This same
nature is expressed allegorically in myths. Etymology demonstrates that the allegorical
interpretation of the traditions concerning the gods is not a mere intellectual exercise;
it is "true" (*etymos*), in that etymology, according to Stoic linguistic theory, has a direct
grasp of nature. This is why it is an instrument of allegoresis.

The few exceptions to Stoic allegorical practice include Seneca, another contemporary of Cornutus. Seneca did not think that the myths invented by the ancients concealed philosophical truths; therefore, in his position a crucial condition for allegoresis
was lacking. This is why Seneca polemicized against the allegoresis of myths (Most
1989) and, perhaps, specifically against Cornutus and Musonius (as suggested by
Ramelli 2004: ch. 6.6), although Seneca sometimes applies etymology to divine names
and epithets (for example, *Ben.* 4.7.1). Seneca (*Ben.* 1.3.2–4) considers the interpretation of the mythological details concerning the Graces—such as why they are young,
virgins, and smiling—to be irrelevant to the philosophical treatment of *beneficia.* In 1.3.5
he reports the interpretation of the mythological particulars, only to reject such her-
meneutical exercises, which are in his view sterile. The names given to the Graces by
Hesiod carry no philosophical meaning (1.3.6). That the main target of Seneca's criticism is Chrysippus's exegesis of poetic myths emerges clearly from 1.3.8–9. Seneca
here disavows a tenet of Stoic etymologico-allegorical hermeneutics of the kind practiced by Chrysippus and Cornutus: namely, that the mythological names and epithets,
especially of deities, that appear in ancient poets are *etymoi,* "truth-bearing." Poets
did not aim at truth (*Ben.* 1.3.10). Cornutus himself admitted that later poets sometimes altered the original myths by their own inventions. But Seneca here suggest that
poets do not convey, as a rule, philosophical truths. Picone (2013: 70–71, referring to
Ramelli 2004: 333–334) remarks that Seneca was not really uninterested in the allegorical meaning of the Graces' myth. However, Seneca, unlike Chrysippus and Cornutus,
never uses allegoresis applied to religious myths as a *philosophical* tool. A good example

is Seneca's remark that the etymology of the name of the Graces' mother cannot be relevant to the symbolic meaning of the Graces because mothers are not named after their children, but vice versa (*Ben.* 1.3.9). This perfectly corresponds to Cornutus's opposite strategy in *Comp.* 15 of deducing the symbolic meaning of the Graces from the etymology of their mother's name. For his critique of traditional religion and myths, Seneca was appreciated by Christian authors. For Tertullian (*De Anima* 20), he "often" spoke "like a Christian." Indeed, in *Apologeticum* 12.6, Tertullian depicts Seneca as "haranguing with many bitter words about your superstition."

The allegorical work of both Cornutus and Chaeremon—another early imperial Stoic allegorist—applied to Greek and Egyptian mythography respectively, was familiar to Origen (died around 255 CE), who applied philosophical allegoresis to the Bible, especially its "myths" (Ramelli 2018b). According to Porphyry (*C. Christ.* fr. 39 Harnack), Origen inherited the allegorical method from these Stoic allegorists, but then he applied it to Jewish Scriptures. Porphyry, as a good "pagan" Neoplatonist, criticized Origen's application of allegoresis to a disqualifying book such as the Bible. In *De Antro* 4, he praises Numenius's interpretation of Genesis 1:1, but without saying that it is *biblical* allegoresis and vaguely mentioning "a prophet" instead of Moses. Porphyry holds Origen responsible for the transfer of the allegorical method from "pagan" myths, its traditional object, to the Bible; he does not mention Philo or other Jewish allegorists, let alone Clement or some "Gnostics," who preceded Origen in the application of allegoresis to Scripture. This striking, probably intentional omission had already been found in Celsus, and Origen had already responded to it (*C. Cels.* 4.51; see Ramelli 2011; in preparation).

Origen's works do indeed show reminiscences of allegoreses that are found in Cornutus and the Stoic allegorical tradition, and of Stoic etymological interpretations. In *Princ.* 2.8.2–3, for instance, *psychē*, "soul," is said to derive from *psychos, psyxis*, "cold, cooling down," according to an old Stoic etymology (*SVF* 2.222–223). In *C. Cels.* 1.24, Origen even mentions the Stoic etymological principles that are based on the Stoic notion of language "by nature" and displays allegorical interpretations of Greek mythological figures that remind readers of those of the Stoic tradition (van den Hoek 2004; Ramelli 2006; forthcoming). The Stoic exegesis of Hades as the tenebrous air that wraps the earth, as developed in Cornutus *Comp.* 35 based on earlier Stoic tradition, is also present in Origen, *Princ.* 4.3.10: the dead descend to Hades—this world—because they are judged deserving of occupying the region around the earth (for further developments in later Platonism, see Ramelli 2014a). Origen might also have drawn this interpretation from Numenius (fr. 32 Des Places), but he certainly knew Cornutus's reference too.

Cornutus and Chaeremon represent a bridge between Stoic and Christian mythological allegoresis. Confirming Porphyry's information, Jerome attests that Origen wrote ten books of *Stromateis,* where he came up with a remarkable comparative accomplishment involving Cornutus: "Origen, imitating Clement, wrote ten *Stromateis,* in which he matched the Christian ideas with those of the philosophers, and *confirmed all the truths of our faith* by means of Plato's, Aristotle's, Numenius', and *Cornutus' texts*" (*Ep.*

70.4). The very method suggested by Cornutus to discover the philosophical truth hidden in myths and rituals was taken up by Middle/Neoplatonists such as Plutarch or Porphyry, besides Origen. That method was a comparison with other peoples' mythological and cultic traditions (Boys-Stones 2003: 189–216; Ramelli 2004: ch. 9), an interest which is also evident in Chaeremon, who allegorized Egyptian mythology and was concerned with the symbolic value of hieroglyphics (Ramelli 2004: ch. 7.1; 2007: ch. 9). Here, a conflict arose between "pagan" and Christian Platonic allegorists concerning what non-Greek mythologies one should consider authoritative. Some pagan Middle/Neoplatonists, such as Celsus, Porphyry, and Julian (but not Numenius), refused to admit that philosophical truths were hidden in the Hebrew and Christian tradition. They therefore denied that the Bible hid philosophical truths to be unveiled by allegoresis. Celsus's position was refuted by Origen (*C. Cels.* 4.48; 50; 51), who intended to legitimize the transfer of the allegorical method from classical mythography to the "myths" of Scripture (Ramelli 2016a).

## FURTHER READING

Torres (2018) offers a Teubner critical edition based on that by Lang. Hays (1983) provides an English translation, with an introduction and notes, of Cornutus's handbook. Ramelli (2003a) offers the Greek edition (with improvements over Lang's (1881) Teubner edition, especially by keeping glosses and expansions which Lang had cut), full introductory and integrative essay situating Cornutus within the Stoic allegorical tradition, all testimonia and realia concerning Cornutus, a translation, a rich commentary, and a bibliography. On this work, the introduction, translation, and commentary of Nesselrath (2009) are based. A similar work in English is Boys-Stones (2018). Ramelli (2004) provides a systematic, critical study of ancient philosophical allegoresis, including the Stoic allegorical tradition; some of the most significant results are available in English in Ramelli (2011). Ramelli (2007) supplies the texts, with translations and commentaries, of all ancient philosophical allegorists (Cornutus, at 485–560). Most (1989) is a preliminary account of Cornutus's relation to the Stoic allegorical tradition, in English. Ramelli (2008b) offers critical essays, editions and translations, commentaries, apparatuses, and bibliographies regarding the Roman Stoics. Cornutus is analyzed on 945–1295, and Ramelli (2018a) situates Cornutus within the Stoic allegorical tradition and also examines Cornutus's influence. Reydams-Schils (2018) offers a very short overview, along the lines of Most's and Ramelli's research. See also Ramelli, "Allegorizing and Philosophizing" in this volume.

## REFERENCES

Boys-Stones, George. 2003. "The Stoics' Two Types of Allegory." In *Metaphor, Allegory, and the Classical Tradition*, edited by George Boys-Stones, 189–216. Oxford: Oxford University Press.

Boys-Stones, George, trans. 2018. *L. Annaeus Cornutus: "Greek Theology," Fragments, and Testimonia*. Atlanta, GA: Society of Biblical Literature Press.

Hays, Robert S. 1983. *Lucius Annaeus Cornutus' Epidrome*. Ann Arbor, MI: University Microfilms International.

Lang, Karl, ed. 1881. *Cornuti Theologiae Graecae Compendium*. Lipsiae: Teubner.

Long, Anthony A. 1997. "Allegory in Philo and Etymology in Stoicism: A Plea for Drawing Distinctions." *Studia Philonica Annual* 9: 198–210.

Most, Glenn. 1989. "Cornutus and Stoic Allegoresis: A Preliminary Report." *Aufstieg und Niedergang der römischen Welt II* 36 (3): 2014–2065.

Nesselrath, Heinz-Günther, ed. 2009. *Cornutus: Die Griechischen Götter*. Tübingen: Mohr Siebeck.

Picone, Giusto. 2013. *Le regole del beneficio: Commento tematico a Seneca, "De beneficiis."* Bk. 1. Palermo, Italy: Palumbo.

Ramelli, Ilaria L. E. 2003a. *Anneo Cornuto: Compendio di teologia greca*. Milan: Bompiani.

Ramelli, Ilaria L. E. 2003b. "Anneo Cornuto e gli Stoici Romani." *Gerión* 21: 283–303.

Ramelli, Ilaria L. E. 2004. *Allegoria, I, L'età classica*. Milan: Vita e Pensiero.

Ramelli, Ilaria L.E. 2006. "Origen and the Stoic Allegorical Tradition: Continuity and Innovation." *Invigilata Lucernis* 28: 195–226.

Ramelli, Ilaria L. E. 2007. *Allegoristi dell'età classica: Opere e frammenti*. Milan: Bompiani.

Ramelli, Ilaria L. E. 2008a. "Philosophical Allegoresis of Scripture in Philo and Its Legacy in Gregory of Nyssa." *Studia Philonica Annual* 20: 55–99.

Ramelli, Ilaria L. E. 2008b. *Stoici Romani Minori*. Milan: Bompiani.

Ramelli, Ilaria L. E. 2009. "Cornutus in Christlichem Umfeld." In Nesselrath, *Cornutus: Die Griechischen Götter*, 207–231. Tübingen: Mohr Siebeck.

Ramelli, Ilaria L. E. 2011. "The Philosophical Stance of Allegory in Stoicism and Its Reception in Platonism, 'Pagan' and Chritian." *International Journal of the Classical Tradition* 18: 335–371.

Ramelli, Ilaria L. E. 2013. "Stoic Cosmo-Theology Disguised as Zoroastrianism in Dio's *Borystheniticus*? The Philosophical Role of Allegoresis as a Mediator between *Physikē* and *Theologia*." *Jahrbuch für Religionsphilosophie* 12: 9–26.

Ramelli, Ilaria L. E. 2014a. "Macrobius: Astrological Descents, Ascents, and Restorations." *MHNH: Revista internacional de Investigación sobre Magia y Astrología Antiguas* 14: 15–32.

Ramelli, Ilaria L. E. 2014b. "Valuing Antiquity in Antiquity by Means of Allegoresis." In *Valuing the Past in the Greco-Roman World*, edited by J. Ker and C. Pieper, 485–507. Leiden: Brill.

Ramelli, Ilaria L. E. 2016a. "Origen's Allegoresis of Plato's and Scripture's Myths." In *Religious Competition in the Greco-Roman World*, edited by Nathaniel P. Desrosiers and Lily C. Vuong, 85–106. Atlanta, GA: Society of Biblical Literature.

Ramelli, Ilaria L. E. 2016b. *Social Justice and the Legitimacy of Slavery: The Role of Philosophical Asceticism from Ancient Judaism to Late Antiquity*. Oxford: Oxford University Press.

Ramelli, Ilaria L. E. 2018a. "Annaeus Cornutus and the Stoic Allegorical Tradition: Meaning, Sources, and Impact." *AITIA. Regards sur la culture hellénistique* 8: 1–16.

Ramelli, Ilaria L. E. 2018b. "Lucius Annaeus Cornutus." In *The Encyclopedia of Ancient History*, edited by Roger S. Bagnall, Kai Brodersen, Craige B. Champion, Andrew Erskine, and Sabine R. Huebner. Oxford: Wiley Blackwell (updated online version of the 2013 first edition). doi:10.1002/9781444338386.wbeah30496.

Ramelli, Ilaria L. E. 2020. Review of Boys-Stones 2018. *Classical Journal* 8.7:1–4.

Ramelli, Ilaria L. E. In preparation. *Origen of Alexandria's Philosophical Theology*.

Ramelli, Ilaria L. E. 2021. "Stoic Homeric Allegoresis." In *Brill's Companion to the Reception of Homer from the Hellenistic Age to Late Antiquity*, edited by Christina-Panagiota Manolea and Antony Makrinos, 229–258. Leiden: Brill.

Reydams-Schils, Gretchen. 2018. "L. Annaeus Cornutus." In *Philosophie der Kaiserzeit und der Spätantike*, edited by Christoph Riedweg, 141–143. Basel: Schwabe.

Steinmetz, P. 1986. "Allegorische Deutung und allegorische Dichtung in der alten Stoa." *Rheinisches Museum* 129: 18–29.

Torres, José. 2018. *Lucii Annaei Cornuti Compendium de Graecae theologiae traditionibus.* Berlin: De Gruyter.

van den Hoek, Annewies. 2004. "Etymologizing in a Christian Context." *Studia Philonica Annual* 16: 122–168.

......................................................................................................

# CHAPTER 12

# DIODORUS SICULUS, *LIBRARY*

......................................................................................................

## IRIS SULIMANI

DIODORUS was born in Sicily, as his name indicates, in Agyrium, as he himself attests. In fact, most of the details we have about the historian come from in his own writings, either directly or implicitly. He lived in the 1st century BCE, witnessing the vicissitudes of the late Roman Republic, but the precise years of his birth and death are unknown. He visited Egypt and then settled in Rome, where he probably completed the work known as *Bibliothēkē* (*Library*). Diodorus stated that he used a variety of sources and records that were available to him, especially through his knowledge of Latin, and that the entire enterprise took him thirty years (1.4.1–4). The only dates of his life that are known for certain are that he was in Egypt in 60–56 BCE, because he states that he was there during the 180th Olympiad (1.44.1, 83.8–9), and that he arrived in Rome before 45 BCE, as indicated by his remark that he saw the Rostra before the Senate house (12.26.1), which Julius Caesar removed in 45 BCE, setting up a new one in the redesigned Forum. That Diodorus was a Greek provincial who wrote in Rome during a time of significant—even tumultuous—political, social, and cultural change doubtlessly affected not only the content of his work, but also the way that he presented the mythical past itself. In other words, Diodorus's mythography is the result of a negotiation between tradition and his own innovation.

## 1. THE *BIBLIOTHĒKĒ*

...........................................................................................................................

Diodorus wrote a universal history (*koinē historia*, 1.1.1). Adopting a well-known genre, he introduced new criteria, emphasizing the chronological and geographical scope: a universal history should begin with the ancient mythologies and end in the author's own day, covering the entire inhabited world both geographically and ethnographically (Sulimani 2011). The work consists of forty books, of which only books 1–5 and 11–20 are preserved in their entirety. The rest of the books are fragmentary, and yet the *Bibliothēkē* is the most extensive history written in Greek to have survived from antiquity. Its first six books deal with "the events and the mythologies prior to the Trojan War" (1.4.6): books 1 to 3 are devoted to the non-Greeks, whereas books 4 to 6 are concerned mainly with the Greeks. Books 7 to 40 embrace universal affairs (*hai koinai praxeis*, a phrase Diodorus often used to define his type of history) from the Trojan War to the beginning of Caesar's wars in Gaul, 60/59 BCE. Thus we have most of Diodorus's mythography (1–5) and the complete history from the Persian Wars to the end of the 4th century, 480–302 BCE (11–20).

In writing his *Bibliothēkē*, Diodorus used a wide variety of sources. Scholars in the late 19th and early 20th centuries focused on these sources, attempting to reconstruct as much as possible the lost works he had employed. Although their studies had some advantages—Schwartz's article in *RE* (1903), for instance, identified Diodorus's main authorities for each book—they diminished Diodorus's personal contribution, classifying him as a mere compiler. In recent years, however, an increasing number of studies have maintained that his use of sources was considerably more complex, and that the *Bibliothēkē* also reflects his own ideas and innovations. The first five books, which contain Diodorus's mythography and were preserved in their entirety, provide a good example. It has been long argued, for instance, that Diodorus's discussion of the antiquities of Egypt in book 1 is based almost entirely on Hecataeus of Abdera's *Aegyptiaca*. More recently, however, it has been suggested that Diodorus not only used additional sources (Herodotus probably among them), but also incorporated his own thoughts, inspired by the events of his day (Sulimani 2011; Muntz 2011, 2017).

It should be noted that Diodorus employs the same working methods throughout the mythological part of his work, although it consists of two separate units, one dealing with non-Greek mythologies (books 1–3); the other (books 4–6), concentrating on the Greek myths (Muntz 2017: 28–36). Diodorus's source material for book 1, however, is somewhat distinct. Visiting Egypt, Diodorus supplemented his literary sources with information that he personally collected, either as an eyewitness (1.4.1, 44.1, 53.1) or by conversing with the Egyptian priests (1.15.2, 3.11.3) and other eyewitnesses (1.22.3–4; indicated also in 3.11.3, 38.1; see Sulimani 2011: 129–30; Muntz 2011). Moreover, despite the clear division of the mythological section into two units, one can also find stories of Greek mythical figures mingled in Diodorus's account of the non-Greek mythologies. This is not surprising. In line with the syncretism of his day, Diodorus not only identifies foreign and Greek gods with each other (for instance, the Egyptian Osiris and Dionysus: 1.11.3, 13.5, 15.6), but in his narrative of the mythologies of foreign peoples, he also integrates versions of the myths that are rhetorically attributed to local authorities. Hence, tales such as those of the Ethiopian Zeus (3.9.1–2), the Indian Dionysus (3.63.3–5), and the Egyptian Heracles (1.24.1–7, and see 1.19.1–3 in section 3 of this chapter) appear throughout the first three books.

# 2. Myths Incorporated in a Universal History

Diodorus's originality is also demonstrated in his decision to begin his universal history with the myths. As befits a "universal" history, his mythography is also "universal," embracing the myths of various peoples, such as the Egyptians, Assyrians, Libyans, and Greeks. Diodorus explains that since the mythologies include the deeds of heroes who benefited mankind, they have an important role in the general purpose of history—that is, to encourage men to act justly, to praise the good, to denounce the evil and to present the readers with a vast store of experience from which they may be able to learn. Contrasting mythology (*mythologia*) with real events (*praxeis*; 1.25.4, 98.10) and acknowledging the difficulties involved in recounting the mythical stories, Diodorus nevertheless regards them as a significant element of the antiquities of peoples, and he criticizes authors such as Ephorus for omitting them. Thus, he also makes clear that his own universal history is superior to all others (1.2.2–8, 3.2; 4.1.1–4).

Yet Diodorus does not tell the myths as he found them in his sources. Retaining the backbone of the tales, he ascribes to mythical figures (such as Heracles and Dionysus) traits and deeds of historical figures (both Greek and Roman) and incorporates real geographical data in his descriptions of the scenes in which they operated. Thus Diodorus produced a historicized version of the myths, a version that is a mixture of fact and fiction. His descriptions of the journeys of gods and heroes throughout the inhabited world, which are a conspicuous feature of the first six books, illustrate this well. For example, in his account of Heracles's itinerary westward to bring Eurystheus the cattle of Geryon, Diodorus states that Heracles founded a city in Celtica (Transalpine Gaul), naming it Alesia after the wandering (*alē*) on his campaign. Heracles settled his soldiers in the new city, intermingling many of the natives with them, and over time all the inhabitants were barbarized. Diodorus adds that from the time of Heracles onward, Alesia remained free, emphasizing that Caesar was the first to defeat it and that he brought it under Roman sway (4.19.1–2; 5.24.2). This version of the myth reveals several salient features. First, Diodorus is the only author who incorporates Alesia into the narrative of Heracles's journey with the cattle of Geryon (compare Hdt. 4.8; Apollod. *Bibl.* 2.5.10). He was obviously inspired by Alesia's conquest by Caesar, perhaps wishing to give it an ancient precedent. Second, it was common for rulers such as Alexander the Great and Caesar, whom Diodorus admired, to build new cities during their conquests. Moreover, Heracles's memorializing of his wandering through not only the foundation of a city, but also its name, closely resembles (for instance) Alexander, who founded Nicaea in India to commemorate his victory there. Third, in populating the new city with his war veterans and blending them with the local inhabitants, Heracles was, again, also operating like historical figures such as Alexander and Caesar, in whose cities there was also an assimilation of cultures, although the "barbarians" did not necessarily have the upper hand.

# 3. Methods of Depicting the Myths

In accordance with producing a historicized version of the myths, Diodorus's preferred approach to interpreting the myths is rationalization, particularly Euhemerism; yet he also uses allegoresis, though rarely (Muntz 2017: 104–117). A good example of rationalization may be found in Diodorus's version of Prometheus's tale, which he incorporated into his account of the Egyptian myths. Diodorus maintains that Prometheus was a governor of an Egyptian district who, made desperate by the damage to his district resulting from the flood of the Nile, wished to take his own life. Heracles came to his rescue, stopping the flooding of the river—also called Aetus (Eagle) because of its violent flood—and turning it back to its former course. Consequently, Diodorus adds, certain poets converted this story into a myth according to which Heracles killed the eagle that was devouring the liver of Prometheus (1.19.1–3).

Diodorus's distinctive version of the Prometheus tale, being completely different from the Greek traditional version (also given by Diodorus 4.15.2), calls for a slight digression from our discussion of the author's methods of depicting the myths. A similar story is found only in the Scholia on Apollonius Rhodius (2.1248), where it is attributed to Agroetas ("in the 13th book of the *Libyca*"). The latter's date is uncertain, but he is assumed to have lived in the 3rd or the 2nd century BCE. If indeed, Agroetas lived in the 2nd century BCE, then it is possible that Diodorus employed him directly, further indication of Diodorus's use of various sources for his narrative in book 1 (Burton 1972: 11–13; Muntz 2011: 591–592). More important, though, is the difference between Agroetas's version and that of Diodorus. While the latter makes Prometheus a governor of a specific district in Egypt that was devastated by the flooding Nile, Agroetas does not give a location for the event, simply stating that Prometheus's lands were devastated by an unlocated river called "Eagle." Some have suggested that the inspiration for Diodorus's version was Plato (*Tim.* 22d; Burton 1972: 85–86). Whether that is true, however, Diodorus is clearly adding something of his own, since he shows himself to be familiar with the division of Egypt into districts (1.54.3) and aware of the problems caused by the flood of the Nile (1.37.1–41.10).

Both allegorical and Euhemeristic interpretations are rendered by Diodorus in his discussion of the Egyptian deities. By way of syncretism, he explains that the ancient Egyptians regarded the natural elements as gods: the spirit was Zeus; the fire, Hephaestus; the earth (the dry), Demeter; the wet, Oceanus; and the air, Athena. Moreover, Diodorus uses etymology, a device typically employed in allegorical interpretation. He argues that the Egyptians call the earth "mother" because, like a vessel, it holds all growing things, and that the Greeks, similarly, named the earth Ge Meter (Earth Mother), but that the name changed into Demeter over time. Diodorus also explains that the epithets of Athena are related to air: the first, Tritogeneia (Thrice-born), was given to her because her nature changes three times a year, in the spring, summer, and winter; the second, Glaucopis (Blue-eyed), derives from the bluish appearance of the air, and not from Athena's blue eyes, a silly belief held by some Greeks (1.12.1–8). Following this, Diodorus introduces his Euhemeristic approach to the Egyptian gods. He claims that certain gods were mortals, but because of their wisdom and the benefaction they bestowed upon mankind, had gained immortality. The names of some of these gods were the same as those of the celestial gods, whereas some of them were kings in Egypt. Hephaestus, who discovered fire and invited mankind to enjoy its advantages, is given as an example (1.13.1–5).

Not surprisingly, the Euhemeristic explanation appears frequently in the mythological section of the *Bibliothēkē*, often expressed in nearly the same vocabulary. Maintaining that mythical figures performed many great deeds and believing that they could serve as role models, just as historical figures could, Diodorus includes their stories in his universal history and employs Euhemerism to make them worthy of emulation. At the beginning of his sixth book, as we learn from a fragment preserved by Eusebius, Diodorus cites Euhemerus as his source for the "terrestrial gods," mortal beings who became immortal because of their benefactions to humanity, as opposed to the "celestial gods," such as the sun and moon, who were eternal (6.1.2–3). Inspired by Euhemerus's interpretation, Diodorus ascribes the performance of good deeds and consequent deification to various figures throughout his first six books, at times, possibly of his own accord and regardless of the source he was using (as in the case of Egypt; see Muntz 2017: 116). Osiris, for instance, was granted immortality because he taught men to cultivate the vine and sow wheat and barley, thus causing them to give up their savagery and adopt a gentle lifestyle (1.17.1–2, 18.5–6, 20.5–6). Similarly, Dionysus was revered as a god because he introduced many good things that contributed to the welfare of humanity; he discovered winemaking and the storing of fruits, invented the plough, founded notable cities, taught people to honor the deity, and introduced laws and courts (2.38.5; 3.63.4, 64.1–2, 70.8). Heracles, likewise, was accorded divine honors because of the magnitude of his benefactions—notably, clearing the land of wild animals and establishing the Olympic Games (1.24.7; 4.8.5, 53.6–7; 5.64.6, 76.1).

# 4. MYTHOGRAPHY, NOT MERELY WRITING MYTHS

Now that we have treated different aspects of Diodorus's engagement with the mythical tradition, it is time to summarize. The role assigned by Diodorus to the myths and his methods of depicting them turn the mythographical part of his universal history into much more than a narrative of "the ancient mythologies." Attempting to make the mythical figures as historical as possible, he portrays them as mortals who became immortal because of their deeds; these deeds are shaped after those of historical figures, notably Alexander and Caesar, who also inspired Diodorus's description of his heroes' images and paths. Furthermore, leading these heroes to real sites along actual roads, Diodorus used the depictions of their journeys to convey some of the geographical, ethnic, and historical data he introduced into the mythological part of his work. Thus the account of the first six books is, to some extent, a geographical and ethnographic survey. Heracles's itinerary westward is, again, a good example. Setting sail from Crete, he visited Egypt, Libya, Numidia, Iberia, and Celtica (Transalpine Gaul), where he founded Alesia, and crossing the Alps, he came into Galatia (Cisalpine Gaul). He passed through the lands of the Ligurians and of the Tyrrhenians, reached Italy, arrived in Sicily and went back to Greece by way of Epirus (4.17.4–25.1). Diodorus's version of Heracles's journey with the cattle of Geryon is quite different from that of Apollodorus, for instance. According to the latter, Heracles's ports of call were Libya, Iberia, Liguria, Tyrrhenia, Italy, Sicily, the Hellespont, and the river Strymon (*Bibl.* 2.5.10). Both authors specify the places Heracles visited in the countries he traversed. Significantly, sites such as Alesia and the Alps, closely related to Roman history in Diodorus's day, and Agyrium in Sicily, Diodorus's hometown, are missing from Apollodorus's account. It seems that, in writing the myths, Diodorus was influenced by both the Greek and Roman worlds and, at the same time, incorporated into his descriptions his own thoughts, concepts and convictions. It is also possible that he intended to offer a well-established precedent for various historical events. Heracles's foundation of Alesia as a precedent for its conquest by Caesar, mentioned above, is one example; another example is the expeditions of mythical heroes, who travelled along actual routes and visited real sites, annexing lands and settling their affairs, and consequently creating an empire. These imaginary empires were used as precedents for either existing or future imperialistic expansions. Heracles's journey, as depicted by Diodorus, roughly corresponds with the boundaries of the Roman Empire and its division into provinces at the end of the republic and the beginning of the Principate. It may, therefore, provide a precedent for the Roman Empire in the historian's own day.

Despite the recent scholarly flowering, Diodorus's mythography would warrant further research. In particular, his methods of interpreting the myths—namely, rationalization and occasionally allegoresis—deserve more discussion. Additionally, Diodorus's unique versions of various mythical tales (such as Prometheus's story discussed above) need to be examined in greater detail, while comparing them with those of other authors. Finally, a study of the syncretistic features of Diodorus's narrative of the myths (for instance, identifying foreign and Greek gods with each other; employing the names of Greek deities to explain how the ancient Egyptians regarded the natural elements as gods) would be also helpful for understanding Diodorus's mythography as a reflection of its time.

## FURTHER READING

The translations of Diodorus's *Bibliothēkē* and the commentaries on the work are based on the text of Vogel, Fischer, and Dindorf (1964–1970), of which the first two volumes contain the mythological books. Notable editions (including text, translation, and explanatory notes) are those of the Loeb Classical Library (vols. 1–3) and the Budé-Les Belles Lettres edition (the volumes devoted to Diodorus's first six books are listed in the References below). The English translation of Murphy (books 1–2, 1990 and 1989, respectively) is also useful. Unfortunately, the commentaries are rarely concerned with the mythological books. The exceptions are Burton (1972); Boncquet (1987); Mariotta and Magnelli (2012); Cordiano (2012).

Although studies by Bigwood (1980) and Sartori (1983, 1984) deal with the mythical section of the *Bibliothēkē*, and although Rubincam and Sacks (who marked a turn in the treatment of Diodorus by acknowledging his original contributions) refer to the mythical books (for example, Rubincam 1987; Sacks 1990; see also Ambaglio 1995), it is only recently that considerable research into Diodorus's mythography has been conducted. See, especially, the monographs of Sulimani (2011), elaborating on books 1–5, and Muntz (2017), whose main concern is books 1–3. On the unique nature of Diodorus's mythography, see also Marincola (2019) and Sulimani (2019). On the historical and geographical elements mingled in Diodorus's mythography, see also Sulimani (2005, 2015, 2017). On Diodorus's writing techniques and his use of sources in the first six books, see Sulimani (2008, 2014) and Muntz (2011, 2012). For further discussion of the link between myth and history in Diodorus, see Muntz (2018) and Ring (2018). For various questions involving Diodorus's narration of the myths, one may also consult Rathmann (2016).

## References

Ambaglio, Delfino. 1995. *La Biblioteca storica di Diodoro Siculo: Problemi e metodo*. Como, Italy: New Press.

Bianquis, Anahita. 1997. *Diodore de Sicile: Mythologie des Grecs: Bibliothèque historique Livre IV*. Paris: Les Belles Lettres.

Bigwood, Joan M. 1980. "Diodorus and Ctesias." *Phoenix* 34: 195–207.

Bommelaer, Bibiane. 2002. *Diodore de Sicile: Bibliothèque historique Livre III*. Paris: Les Belles Lettres.

Boncquet, Jan. 1987. *Diodorus Siculus (II,1–34) over Mesopotamië: Een historische kommentaar*. Brussels: Paleis der Academiën.

Burton, Anne. 1972. *Diodorus Siculus. Book 1. A Commentary*. Leiden: Brill.

Casevitz, Michel, and Anne Jacquemin. 2015. *Diodore de Sicile: Bibliothèque historique Livre V*. Paris: Les Belles Lettres.

Chamoux, François, Pierre Bertrac, and Yvonne Vernière. 1993. *Diodore de Sicile: Bibliothèque historique Livre I*. Paris: Les Belles Lettres.

Cohen-Skalli, Aude. 2012. *Diodore de Sicile: Bibliothèque historique: Fragments, Tome 1: Livres VI–X*. Paris: Les Belles Lettres.

Cordiano, Giuseppe. 2012. *Diodoro Siculo, Biblioteca Storica, Libri VI-VII-VIII: Commento storico*. Milan: Vita e Pensiero.

Eck, Bernard. 2003. *Diodore de Sicile: Bibliothèque historique Livre II*. Paris: Les Belles Lettres.

Marincola, John. 2019. "Diodorus the Mythographer?." In *Host or Parasite?: Mythographers and Their Contemporaries in the Classical and Hellenistic Periods*, edited by Allen J. Romano and John Marincola, 75–93. Berlin and Boston: de Gruyter.

Mariotta, Giuseppe, and Adalberto Magnelli. 2012. *Diodoro Siculo, Biblioteca Storica, Libro IV: Commento storico*. Milan: Vita e Pensiero.

Muntz, Charles E. 2011. "The Sources of Diodorus Siculus, Book 1." *Classical Quarterly* 61: 574–94.

Muntz, Charles E. 2012. "Diodorus Siculus and Megasthenes: A Reappraisal." *Classical Philology* 107: 21–37.

Muntz, Charles E. 2017. *Diodorus Siculus and the World of the Late Roman Republic.* Oxford: Oxford University Press.

Muntz, Charles E. 2018. "Diodoros, Mythology, and Historiography." In *Diodoros of Sicily: Historiographical Theory and Practice in the* Bibliotheke, edited by Lisa I. Hau, Alexander Meeus, and Brian Sheridan, 365–388. Leuven: Peeters.

Murphy, Edwin. 1989. *The Antiquities of Asia: A Translation with Notes of Book II of the "Library of History" of Diodorus Siculus.* New Brunswick, NJ: Transaction.

Murphy, Edwin. 1990. *The Antiquities of Egypt: A Translation with Notes of Book I of the Library of History of Diodorus Siculus.* New Brunswick, NJ: Transaction.

Oldfather, Charles H. 1933–1939. *Diodorus of Sicily.* Vols. 1–3. Loeb Classical Library. Cambridge, MA: Harvard University Press.

Rathmann, Michael. 2016. *Diodor und seine "Bibliothēkē": Weltgeschichte aus der Provinz.* Berlin and Boston: De Gruyter.

Ring, Abram. 2018. "Diodoros and Myth as History." In *Diodoros of Sicily: Historiographical Theory and Practice in the "Bibliotheke,"* edited by Lisa I. Hau, Alexander Meeus, and Brian Sheridan, 389–406. Studia Hellenistica 58. Leuven: Peeters.

Rubincam, Catherine I. 1987. "The Organization and Composition of Diodoros' Bibliotheke." *Échos du monde classique/Classical Views* 31: 313–328.

Sacks, Kenneth. 1990. *Diodorus Siculus and the First Century.* Princeton, NJ: Princeton University Press.

Sartori, Marco. 1983. "Note sulla datazione dei primi libri della *Bibliotheca Historica* di Diodoro Siculo." *Athenaeum* 61: 545–552.

Sartori, Marco. 1984. "Storia, 'utopia' e mito nei primi libri della *Bibliotheca Historica* di Diodoro Siculo." *Athenaeum* 62: 492–536.

Schwartz, Edward. 1903. "Diodorus #38." *RE V.*1 [9]: 663–704.

Sulimani, Iris. 2005. "Myth or Reality? A Geographical Examination of Semiramis' Journey in Diodorus." *Scripta Classica Israelica* 24: 45–63.

Sulimani, Iris. 2008. "Diodorus' Source-Citations: A Turn in the Attitude of Ancient Authors towards Their Predecessors?" *Athenaeum* 96: 535–567.

Sulimani, Iris. 2011. *Diodorus' Mythistory and the Pagan Mission: Historiography and Culture-Heroes in the First Pentad of the Bibliothēkē.* Leiden and Boston: Brill.

Sulimani, Iris. 2014. "Speeches in Diodorus' First Pentad." *Ancient World* 45: 174–192.

Sulimani, Iris. 2015. "Egyptian Heroes Travelling in Hellenistic Road Networks: The Representation of the Journeys of Osiris and Sesostris in Diodorus." *ARAM Periodical* 27: 81–96.

Sulimani, Iris. 2017. "Imaginary Islands in the Hellenistic Era: Utopia on the Geographical Map." In *Myths on the Map: The Storied Landscapes of Ancient Greece*, edited by Greta Hawes, 221–242. Oxford: Oxford University Press.

Sulimani, Iris. 2019. "Diodorus' Mythography: The Distinctive Features of Mythology within Universal History." *Polymnia* 4: 1–32.

Vogel, Friedrich, Curt T. Fischer, and Ludwig Dindorf, eds. 1964–1970. *Diodori Bibliotheca Historica.* Vols. 1–6. Stuttgart: Teubner.

# CHAPTER 13

# HERACLITUS THE MYTHOGRAPHER, *ON UNBELIEVABLE STORIES*

## GRETA HAWES

HERACLITUS's *On Unbelievable Stories* (*Peri Apistōn*; in Latin: *De Incredibilibus*) is a work of interpretative mythography.[1] It can be assigned to the late 1st or 2nd century CE on linguistic grounds (Stern 2003: 53–54; Ramón García 2009: xii–xiv). As we have it, it consists of thirty-nine short entries that together take up just fifteen pages in Festa's Teubner edition. The style of the entries is quite repetitive. Typically, we get the narration of a myth, and then an explanation of the origins of the story that seeks to remove its fabulous elements. As we will see, the influence of Palaephatus's rationalistic approach is clear; but Heraclitus's interpretative tendencies range far beyond Palaephatus's, taking in Euhemeristic and allegorical speculation.

Like so much ancient mythography, the text of *On Unbelievable Stories* survived precariously. The extreme concision of the extant text suggests that we possess only an epitome, but no certainty is possible. The fullest version is in Vaticanus Graecus 305 (dated to 1254 or 1269). This is the basis for modern critical editions. Alganza Roldán (2015) discovered an excerpted version of the text in the (probably) 18th-century manuscript Iviron 1317. This manuscript contains twelve of the entries found in Vaticanus Graecus 305, with some alternate readings.

There are no ancient testimonia for *On Unbelievable Stories*. All that we know about its author and original context is speculation based on the transmitted text. The attribution to "Heraclitus" may suggest that there was at some point confusion between this text and the *Homeric Problems*. The name is not uncommon, however, and that two mythographers were named Heraclitus may simply be a coincidence. *Communis opinio*

---

[1] This chapter was produced as part of the project "Estudios sobre transmisión y recepción de Paléfato y la exégesis racionalista de los mitos," funded by Proyectos de I + D, Programa Estatal de Fomento de la Investigación Científica y Técnica de Excelencia (FFI2014-52203-P).

is against the idea that both texts are by the same author, though the possibility cannot be entirely discounted. Westermann gave this Heraclitus the label "the paradoxographer" to distinguish him from other homonymous authors. The epithet is misleading. This is no work of paradoxography but a handbook of myth interpretation. Stern's (2003: 52) suggested epithet "the mythographer" is much more appropriate.

Iviron 1317 adds some weight to the supposition that this text originated in (or at least found its way into) the context of rhetorical instruction. It gives the title as "Heraclitus' On Unbelievable Narratives and Stories" (*Herakleitou peri tōn autōn apistōn diēgēmatōn kai mythōn*). The word *diēgēma* can be used quite generally to mean "narrative" (as I translated it). More precisely, it was a technical term for a particular kind of rhetorical exercise. In the *Progymnasmata* it is the exposition of a series of events, often but not necessarily mythical (*mythikon*; on this, see Gibson 2013: 290–292; Smith and Trzaskoma, this volume, on education). Further support for this rhetorical context is apparent in Vaticanus Graecus 305, where an epigraph describes the work as "the refutation, or curing, of traditional myths which are contrary to nature" (*anaskeuē ē therapeia mythōn tōn para physin paradedomenōn*). *Anaskeuē* (refutation) is another rhetorical exercise found in the *Progymnasmata*. It taught students to reject narratives—usually mythic ones—on certain grounds: that they were unclear, implausible, impossible, inconsistent, improper, or inexpedient. The labeling of these stories as *para physin* (contrary to nature) might remind us of Servius's definition of *fabulae* as stories which are *contra naturam* ("against nature," on Verg. *Aen.* 1.235); his example there is the story of Pasiphae, which he later rationalizes (on Verg. *Aen.* 6.14; Dietz 1995). Even if these epigraphs are later additions, another piece of evidence directly connects rationalization to contemporary rhetorical training: Theon (2nd c. CE) describes examples of mythic rationalization from Herodotus, Plato, Ephorus, and Palaephatus as models for a more advanced form of *anaskeuē* (*Progymnasmata* 95.8–96.14 Patillon; see Gibson 2013; Hawes 2014: 99–103).

The title *Peri Apistōn* is conventionally used for three broadly similar mythographic works: that of Heraclitus, that of Palaephatus (4th c. BCE), and a post-antique, anonymous work (the *Excerpta Vaticana*). These three texts appear together in Iviron 1317, and the two chronologically later ones are in Vaticanus Graecus 305. They are printed together in modern editions, and in many recent translations (see "References" below). That Heraclitus's text is modeled on the example established by Palaephatus seems clear; indeed, the earliest references to Heraclitus (Eust. on *Od.* 4.450, 19.163) pair him with Palaephatus.

The influence of Palaephatus is most apparent in the format of Heraclitus's text. Even in their probably abbreviated state, Heraclitus's entries display a recognizable version of the "Palaephatean structure" (Delattre 2013: 128–130; Hawes 2014: 48–52, 95–98). This typical way of narrating rationalizing explanations begins with a straightforward "traditional" version of the myth, explains why such an event could not have occurred, and then puts forward a rationalized version of it that makes clear what kinds of misunderstandings (usually of ambivalent language) led to the traditional—but untrue—version becoming widely known. Some entries do show this full pattern (7):

> They say that [Pasiphae] fell in love with a bull; this bull was not, as many think, a creature of the herd, for it is laughable that the queen might have pursued an impossible coupling. Rather, it was a local man, named Taurus ("Bull"). She enlisted Daedalus to help her consummate her passion and, having fallen pregnant, gave birth to a son who resembled Taurus. People called him Minos' son, but he looked like Taurus, so he was called by the portmanteau, "Minotaurus."

More commonly, the brevity of treatment means not only that no single element of this structure is ever developed in full but also that elements are often omitted. Here his style differs markedly from the expansive approach of Palaephatus (Torres Guerra 2010: 148–150), though we cannot, of course, be sure that this is not entirely attributable to a later process of epitomization. Heraclitus seldom precisely analyzes why a story must be rejected (in fact, he rarely practices the rhetorical exercise of *anaskeuē* explicitly). Rather, he makes the criticism apparent by setting an innovative version against the traditional one, sometimes with the comment that this new version is "likely" (*eikos*, 13), "true" (*alēthes*, 15; 21; 23), or "more plausible" (*pithanōteron*, 26) but, more often, with just "but rather" (*de* or *alla*) signaling the opposition as he moves from one to the other. So, in his discussion of the garden of the Hesperides, Heraclitus replaces each element of the myth: the snake, by a man called "Snake"; a tree with golden apples, by a highly profitable orchard; and divine sisters, by beautiful, controlling women. The reader recognizes in these replacements an implicit critique of the plausibility of their traditional counterparts (20):

> They say that a snake guarded the golden apples of the Hesperides. But Snake was a man who made a heap of gold by tending an orchard. Beautiful women pursued him, and they entangled his soul with their lustful passions. They got him as a servant and guard of the garden for the rest of his life.

In both of the instances given, the traditional story is narrated so concisely that it amounts to little more than an allusion; in other entries, it is even omitted altogether. At least in this form, the text requires a particular kind of reader. This is not the kind of mythological text one consults to discover the details of myth: genealogies, geography, narratives, sources, and variants. The reader must already possess a broad knowledge of such data, for these bald narratives offer little aid beyond the prompting of memory. Heraclitus's stories are largely well-known ones; many had already been subject to allegorical or rationalistic analysis elsewhere. But beyond this, there is no obvious organizing principle guiding the selection or ordering; the attraction of such a text must have been its display of hermeneutic ingenuity rather than its utility as a reference guide. The reader must also recognise certain cultural assumptions about how myths can be presented and manipulated: the text assumes, but never clearly articulates, a particular perspective on the legitimacy, and the basic workings, of mythic critique. The text's logic remains implicit: Heraclitus gives practical examples of mythic critique, but—unlike Palaephatus or, indeed, the author of the *Homeric Problems*—never offers a rationale for its processes.

What is the critique of myth that this text offers? The epigraph transmitted by Vaticanus Graecus 305 describes it as treating those myths "which are contrary to nature" (*tōn para physin paradedomenōn*). Indeed, when Heraclitus does put forward an explicit rejection of a myth, he emphasizes biological possibility above all. It would be "impossible" (*adynatos*) for Atlas to hold up heaven (4), or for the Centaurs to combine human and horse body parts (5). The physical incompatibility of Pasiphae mating with a bull makes this story "laughable" (*geloion*, 7). The story of the Hydra having many heads is "without truth" (*ouch houtōs echontos talēthous*, 18). Heraclitus deems the idea that Calypso offered Odysseus immortality "irrational" (*alogon*); his argument that the story relates the offer of a pleasant and plentiful life makes clear that, once more, it is the possibility of these events that is at issue. Likewise, it is the most biologically impossible element of the story that he emphasizes when he asks, "Who could believe that, when Cadmus scattered the dragon's teeth, armed men grew up?" (19; similar is 17). These critiques of myth are reminiscent of Palaephatus's typical mode of rejection on biological grounds (Hawes 2014: 52–59).

The interpretations that Heraclitus puts forward are often broadly consistent with other prominent traditions of interpreting certain narratives. So, for example, Heraclitus emphasizes the moral virtues of Odysseus (2; 11; 16). Such a view of the hero is in keeping with his treatment elsewhere in Greek culture—particularly in philosophical contexts—as a paradigm of endurance and wisdom (Montiglio 2011). But—as has long been recognized—the most prominent interpretative habit of this text is its presentation of female characters as prostitutes. This is how he explains Medusa (1), Scylla (2), the Harpies (8), the Sirens (14), and Circe (16). Here, too, Heraclitus is "borrowing" from existing interpretative traditions. The idea that famous *hetairai* embodied a destructive allure analogous to the grasping monsters of myth appears in comedy (for instance, Ar. *Plut.* 303–315, Anaxilas, *Neottis* 22 K.-A.) and indeed in other genres too. Heraclitus has reversed this comparison; he argues not that *hetairai* are like Circe and others, but rather than Circe and others were in fact *hetairai*.

The most compelling feature of *On Unbelievable Stories*, as Jacob Stern (Stern 2003: 55) noted in his key article, is its hermeneutic eclecticism. Stern identified four main modes of interpretation in the text: rationalization (the historicist interpretation of heroic myths), Euhemerism (the historicist interpretation of myths about gods), ethical allegoresis (the revelation of philosophical principles through myth), and etymology (the exploitation of language). These modes, however, are not individuated from one another in the text. This is apparent in Heraclitus's terminology. So, although he uses the rationalistic labels "likely," "true," and "impossible" (as we have seen), he speaks, too, of the "notion" (*hypolēpsis* and cognates) behind myths, recalling the language of the allegorists (Stern 2003: 71). And yet Heraclitus is not hermeneutically consistent in applying this term: to take three examples—his Euhemeristic account of Boreas and

Orithyia (28), his allegorical explanation of the Cyclops's single eye as illustrating his lack of rationality and foresight (11), and his rationalization of the Harpies as prostitutes (8) are all described as the "underlying notions" of these myths despite their being the products of formally distinct modes of explication.

Indeed, Heraclitus can seem to combine various approaches in a single entry. Here is his account of Caeneus (3):

> It is said that he [Caeneus] was originally a woman and then was turned by Poseidon into a man who was invulnerable to bronze and iron. But in fact when he was young, he was Poseidon's boyfriend, and then as he grew into manhood, he had such strength of character that he could not be corrupted by bribes of bronze or iron (gold and silver not yet having been discovered).

Here we might assume (although it is not explicitly stated) that "Poseidon" is Euhemeristically simply a human. The whole episode is presented rationalistically as a series of events that accord with the norms of historicist reality; the idea that the episode predates the use of gold and silver for trade or currency adds a deft historicizing touch. But central to the workings of it is an allegorical observation that makes Caeneus's gift of both masculinity and invulnerability a comment on his inherent ethical properties: his manliness manifested as imperviousness to bribery, hence the connection between these ideas in the original myth.

Thus, whereas elsewhere, Euhemerism, allegoresis, and rationalization display different attitudes toward myth and are typically articulated in quite different ways and in different contexts (Hawes 2014: 23–36), in this *Peri Apistōn* they blend almost seamlessly within the quite homogeneous format of this work. There is no clear sense that the interpreter is aware that he is switching between formally distinct modes of interpretation or, indeed, that these modes might require different rhetorical strategies. The overt lack of polemic in the text in fact suggests that Heraclitus's goal is not to "save" myth—to rescue it from aspersions of impiety, recover its basic historicity, or comment on the existence and potency of the gods—but rather, to put forth a display of intellectual ingenuity that revels in the application of hermeneutic methods for their own sake. In this way, etymology—the play with language that underpins many different kinds of ancient myth criticism—seems the unifying element of the text.

## FURTHER READING

Interest in Heraclitus has increased considerably in recent years, alongside the general growth in scholarship on ancient mythography and hermeneutic traditions.

The major printed editions of this text are Gale (1671), Westermann (1843), and Festa (1902). Festa remains the standard text, although Ramón García (2009) and Alganza Roldán (2015) report alternate readings of some passages from newly discovered manuscripts (Marcianus Graecus 613 and Iviron 1317, respectively).

Translations (with commentaries) exist in Spanish (Sanz Morales 2002; Torres Guerra 2009), English (Stern 2003), German (Neiger 2007), Italian (Ramelli 2007), and Hungarian (Németh

2008). A very recent translation into English is available in the open access repository Scaife Viewer.

Several substantial studies of the text have appeared recently: Stern (2003) provides a discussion of Heraclitus's interpretative approaches along with a useful commentary; Neiger (2007) is largely concerned with the genre of the work and its ancient context; Hawes (2014, ch. 2) situates the text within the ancient rationalizing tradition. These all give bibliographic details of earlier scholarship.

## REFERENCES

Alganza Roldán, Minerva. 2015. "Un Nuevo Manuscrito de Heráclito 'Mitógrafo' y el Anónimo Περὶ Ἀπίστων (Μονή Ιβήρων 1317 = Lambros 5437)." *Emerita* 83: 63–86.

Delattre, Charles. 2013. "Pentaméron Mythographique: Les Grecs ont-ils écrit leurs mythes." *Lalies* 33: 77–170.

Dietz, David B. 1995. "*Historia* in the Commentary of Servius." *Transactions of the American Philological Association* 125: 61–97.

Festa, Nicola. 1902. *Mythographi Graeci*. Vol. 3. Pt. 2. Leipzig: Teubner.

Gale, Thomas. 1671. *Opuscula Mythologica, Ethica et Physica Graece et Latine*. Cambridge: n.p.

Gibson, Craig A. 2013. "True or False? Greek Myth and Mythography in the Progymnasmata." In *Writing Myth: Mythography in the Ancient World*, edited by Stephen M. Trzaskoma and R. Scott Smith, 289–308. Leuven: Peeters.

Hawes, Greta. 2014. *Rationalizing Myth in Antiquity*. Oxford: Oxford University Press.

Montiglio, Silvia. 2011. *From Villain to Hero: Odysseus in Ancient Thought*. Ann Arbor: University of Michigan Press.

Neiger, Giovanna. 2007. *Herakleitos: Περὶ Ἀπίστων Widerlegung oder Heilung der Widernatürlichen Mythen*. Trento, Italy: UNI Service.

Németh, György. 2008. *Földreszállt Mítoszok: Palaiphatos és Hérakleitos Mítoszmagyarázatai*. Szeged, Hungary: Lectum.

Ramelli, Ilaria. 2007. *Allegoristi dell'età Classica: Opere e Frammenti*. Milan: Bompiani.

Ramón García, Daniel. 2009. "Heraclit el Mitògraf: Edició Crítica, Traducció i Comentari." Diss. Universitat Autònoma de Barcelona.

Sanz Morales, Manuel. 2002. *Mitógrafos Griegos*. Madrid: Tres Cantos.

Stern, Jacob. 2003. "Heraclitus the Paradoxographer: Περὶ Ἀπίστων, *On Unbelievable Tales*." *Transactions of the American Philological Association* 133: 51–97.

Torres Guerra, José B. 2009. *Mitógrafos Griegos*. Madrid: Gredos.

Torres Guerra, José B. 2010. "Modelos de Narración Breve de la Antigüedad: Las Historias Increíbles de Paléfato, Heráclito y el Anónimo Vaticano." *Studia Philologica Valentina* 12: 139–157.

Westermann, Anton. 1843. *Mythographoi: Scriptores Poeticae Historiae Graeci*. Braunschweig: Westermann.

CHAPTER 14

........................................................................................

# HERACLITUS THE ALLEGORIST, *HOMERIC PROBLEMS*

........................................................................................

DAVID KONSTAN

## 1. Overview: Name, Title, and Date

THERE survives from classical antiquity an allegorical interpretation of both Homeric epics, which takes the form of a running commentary, beginning with the first book of the *Iliad* and concluding with the last book of the *Odyssey* (unfortunately, the part covering *Od.* 11–20 is missing). The author's name, as recorded in the earliest (fragmentary) surviving manuscript (M), is Heraclitus, sometimes referred to as the Allegorist or the Grammarian, to distinguish him from the pre-Socratic philosopher and also from the author (labeled the Paradoxographer) of a work entitled *Peri Apiston* (*On Incredible Tales*), a rationalizing or Euhemeristic exegesis of thirty-nine myths in the manner of Palaephatus (see Koning, this volume). The title of the work, according to the same manuscript, is *Homeric Problems: On What Homer Expressed Allegorically Concerning the Gods*. The first part of the title recalls such titles as the *Homeric Questions* or *Investigations* (*Zētēmata*) of Porphyry, pointing to a common type of philological interpretation; the second part, or subtitle, identifies the approach as specifically allegorical, perhaps with a view to situating the work in a tradition of interpretation represented by Pseudo-Plutarch *On the Life and Poetry of Homer*, Philo of Alexandria, and a host of figures whose works survive only in fragmentary form.

Nothing is known of this Heraclitus, apart from what can be inferred from his text, which is to say, from his references to predecessors, his style, and his characteristic approach to allegory. A mention of Alexander of Ephesus, a contemporary of Cicero, provides a *terminus post quem* (decisively refuting the identification of the author with Heraclides Ponticus [4th c. BCE] that was commonly assumed until the mid-19th century). The style is rhetorical, but it is not purist with respect to classical Attic, in the manner of Lucian and other writers of the Second Sophistic. Furthermore, although there are suggestions of a mystical view of Homer (Heraclitus speaks of "Homer's rites" and initiation into "his mystical wisdom," 76), Heraclitus does not have recourse to the elaborate theological exegeses of the Neoplatonic school (for instance, Porphyry's interpretation of the Cave of the Nymphs in the *Odyssey*; see Bernard 1990). It is thus plausible, though not certain, that he was active around 100 CE, which would make him a contemporary of Plutarch.

# 2. HERACLITUS AND THE ALLEGORICAL TRADITION

From the beginning, the Homeric epics were subjected to moralizing criticism concerning the behavior of gods and heroes (the pre-Socratic Heraclitus fr. 42 D.-K. and Xenophanes fr. 10–13 D.-K. are well-known examples), which was countered by defenders of Homer's wisdom and veracity and the probity of his narratives. One of the methods for rendering the poems consistent with high-minded theological views, such as those espoused by Plato and many of his philosophical successors, was allegory, a technique that reaches back to the archaic period and may even have left its mark on Homer's own verses. Much of this lively tradition is lost, which is more the pity since it represents the major current of literary hermeneutics—that is, the search for implicit meaning in texts—in classical antiquity (better known works, such as Aristotle's *Poetics* and Horace's *Art of Poetry*, look rather to formal aspects of literature). The *Homeric Problems* of Heraclitus is particularly precious as a unique example, in what survives, of a continuous allegorical commentary on both Homeric epics (as Heraclitus says, "My discussion will follow the order of the Homeric poems," 6). It may thus seem all the more surprising that the first English translation of this work appeared in 2005, and translations into other modern languages, not much earlier; but this neglect reflects the disfavor into which allegory fell in the 16th century, from which it has never entirely recovered.

Heraclitus begins his essay with a forensic flourish, as though he were writing an apology for Homer: "It is a weighty and damaging charge that heaven brings against Homer for his disrespect for the divine. If he meant nothing allegorically, he was impious through and through, and sacrilegious fables, loaded with blasphemous folly, run riot through both epics" (trans. Russell and Konstan 2005). He identifies the main detractors of Homer as Plato and Epicurus, who make an odd couple, inasmuch as Epicurus, a thoroughgoing materialist, radically rejected the immaterial entities or "ideas" posited by Plato and maintained that pleasure, rather than virtue, was the highest good. As Heraclitus writes: "Away . . . with Plato, the flatterer, Homer's dishonest accuser, who banishes him from his private Republic as an honored exile, garlanded with white wool and with his head drenched with costly perfumes! Nor need we trouble ourselves with

Epicurus, who cultivates his low pleasure in *his* private garden, and abominates all poetry indiscriminately as a lethal allurement of fable" (4). Heraclitus's criticisms are not
wholly fair, since Epicureans did employ allegory, though not specifically to defend
Homer (compare Lucretius 3.978–1023, on the torments of hell signifying the insatiable
desires of ignorant human beings), and Philodemus found in Homer's epics models for
the ideal king (*On the Good King according to Homer*). The attack on Plato, moreover,
who himself refers to allegorical interpretations of Homer (*Republic* 378D), disregards
Neoplatonic interpretations, which is consistent with a relatively early date for the work.

The authorities whom Heraclitus cites favorably, in turn, seem mainly attached, however loosely, to the Stoic tradition. Apollodorus of Athens (7), author of a treatise, *On
the Gods*, was a pupil of Diogenes of Babylon, who, in turn, was a follower of Chrysippus
and wrote a book, *On Athena*, in which he equated Apollo with the sun; Artemis with
the moon; and Zeus with Poseidon, Demeter, and Hera (the idea is that Zeus's power
extends to the sea, earth, and air, the regions with which these three deities respectively
are associated; compare Philodemus *On Piety*, ed. Obbink 1994: 19–20). Crates of Mallos
(27), whose complicated mathematical interpretation is treated with some reserve, is
identified in the *Suda* (k 2342) as a Stoic. Finally, Herodicus of Babylon (11) was a disciple
of Crates. It is worth noting that Zeno, the founder of the Stoic school, wrote a treatise
entitled *Homeric Problems* (Diogenes Laertius 7.4). Since the Stoics played a significant
role in appropriating allegory for philosophical purposes, it was natural for Heraclitus
to avail himself of their examples, and indeed, he expresses approval of them (33.1). His
own approach, however, is manifestly eclectic, and there is no basis for identifying him
as an adherent or defender of a particular philosophical school.

# 3. Allegory in Heraclitus

Appealing to the elements that form the word "allegory" (*alla* = "other,"
*agoreuein* = "say"), Heraclitus defines it as "the trope which says one thing but signifies
something other than what it says" (5). This definition accords with that of ancient
grammarians such as Trypho (lst century BCE), who in his work *On Tropes* defines allegory (3.193 Spengel) as "a word or phrase that signifies one thing in the proper sense
but provides a notion (*ennoia*) of something else, most often by way of similarity."
Whereas rhetorical theory, however, treated allegory as one among a variety of tropes
that enhance elegance or persuasiveness, Heraclitus adapts it to the specific purpose of
salvaging Homer's reputation for religious piety.

Heraclitus sensibly points to the self-conscious use of allegory by archaic poets, for
example, Alcaeus's famous image of the ship of state (Fr. Z2 Page = 326 Lobel and Page),
as evidence that the technique was not foreign to Homer (5). Such poems invite interpretation that goes beyond the surface sense. For Heraclitus, any passage in Homer
that seems to portray the gods as behaving immorally is proof that a deeper meaning
must lurk behind the plain sense of the text. Heraclitus employs several techniques for

deciphering or bringing to light the subtext. One such is etymology, which the Stoics apparently favored (for example, Cornutus). The Greek letters spelling out the name of Hera, for instance, are *eta, rho, alpha*, which are an anagram of the word for air (*alpha, eta, rho*); hence the above-mentioned equation of the goddess with the atmosphere. So, too, Ares is associated with war since his name recalls a Greek word (*arē*) meaning "harm" (31), and Ocean (Greek, *Okeanos*) is derived from *ōkeōs naiein*, "to flow quickly" (22). It follows that, where the god is named, the reference is not necessarily to the deity but rather to what he or she represents; as Heraclitus puts it, "Ares simply stands for war." Thus, if Homer calls Ares "madman, embodied evil, double-faced," it is war, not the god, that is being so described. When Homer calls Ares "brazen," the implied reference is to the warriors' armor: "for iron was scarce in those old days and they universally protected themselves with bronze." Similarly, Apollo is equated with the Sun; Poseidon ,with the sea; Athena, with wisdom or else with the rational part of the soul (an idea, Heraclitus avers, Plato cribbed from Homer in constructing his own psychological model); Aphrodite, with irrational passion (it is passion, not the goddess, that seduced Helen), and so forth. That a human being could wound a deity was a tender point, but Heraclitus is up to it: "Diomedes, with Athena (that is to say, Wisdom) as his ally, wounded Aphrodite—that is, Folly [*aphrosunē*]—not of course a goddess, but the foolishness of his barbarian adversaries" (30). We may note that the reference domain for such equivalences is quite wide, embracing astronomical entities (the sun and moon), natural phenomena (air, the sea), ethical or psychological qualities (wisdom, violence), and social activities and institutions (war, the state).

Heraclitus resorts at times to elaborate arguments in defense of substitutions, no doubt because such subtle exegeses remained controversial, but perhaps, too, to highlight his own skill by magnifying the challenge. The longest single exegesis comes at the beginning and has something of the quality of a showpiece. Hostile critics of Homer had observed that the plague Apollo sent upon the Greek host at Troy to avenge the insult to his priest afflicted the animals first and then the army, rather than Agamemnon himself, who was responsible for the offense. Heraclitus demonstrates that Apollo here must signify the sun, since the heat of the sun brings on pestilences, especially in the summer. What is more, the season must have been summer; otherwise, Hector could not have had the Trojans camp out at night without warm bedding and shelter; besides, the men on both sides sweat and are covered with dust, which would not happen in winter; and so forth (Heraclitus acknowledges that he has followed, and indeed condensed, the arguments of the 2nd-century BCE polymath Apollodorus of Athens for the equivalence of Apollo and the sun, 7—a sign of his inclination to conflate various styles of allegorical criticism). Some of Heraclitus's explications are so recondite or subtle that they almost suggest parody, at least to the modern reader. Thus, he interprets the wounding of Hera by Heracles (*Iliad* 5.392–394) as showing "precisely that Heracles was the first to use divine reason in order to bring structure to the confused mist [*aēr*] which clouds every individual's mind. . . . Homer added ingeniously, 'striking with three-pointed shaft'—the 'three-pointed' missile concisely suggests the three branches of philosophy" (34).

Heraclitus sometimes offers a historicizing version of a myth, in the rationalizing manner of Palaephatus's *On Incredible Tales*. Thus, Heraclitus explains the story in the *Iliad* about a king named Lycurgus who violently drove off Dionysus: "Lycurgus, who was the owner of an estate good for winegrowing, had gone out in the autumn, when Dionysus' crops are harvested, to the very fertile region of Nysa" (compare the interpretation of Dawn enamored of Orion, 68). If Dionysus is described as terrified, the meaning is that "fear turns the mind, just as the fruit of the grape is 'turned' as it is crushed to make wine." Heraclitus concludes: "Thus Homer understands not only how to philosophize allegorically, but also how to farm" (35), aligning himself with those who ascribed universal wisdom to the poet. Apart from allegory, Heraclitus also defends Homer by showing that his heroes are paradigms of virtue. The Stoics and Cynics, in particular, but also Plato and Philodemus, invoked Odysseus and Heracles as exemplars of wisdom and endurance (see *SVF* 3.467 = Galen, *On the Doctrines of Plato and Hippocrates* 4.7, from Chrysippus's *On the Passions*), and Heraclitus points to Achilles's integrity and Odysseus's fortitude as signs of the poet's rectitude: "In Homer, everything is full of noble virtue: Odysseus is wise, Ajax brave, Penelope chaste, Nestor invariably just, Telemachus dutiful to his father, Achilles totally loyal to his friendships" (78). Such moralizing versions of the epics were no doubt taught in the schools, as Plutarch's essay, *How a Youth Should Listen to Poems*, indicates.

Allegory was of great importance not only in pagan but also in Jewish and, especially, Christian exegesis. There are significant parallels to Heraclitus's interpretations in the Homeric scholia (especially, but not only, the D scholia), a treatise *On the Life and Poetry of Homer* attributed to Plutarch, Cornutus's *Compendium of Greek Theology*, and many other works. Philo of Alexandria, who alludes to Homer over sixty times in his works, is a rich source of allegorical interpretations of stories in the Hebrew Bible (see, for example, his *Allegories of the Laws*), and Heraclitus's debt to him (doubtless indirect) would reward further research. In turn, the relationship between allegorical interpretations of Homer, for which Heraclitus is a prime witness, and Christian allegoresis needs to be more fully explored (see Ramelli 2011, for Stoic influences, and, more generally, Pépin 1981). Taken simply on its own terms, Heraclitus's treatise is a fascinating and entertaining study of Homer's epics, frequently offering shrewd insights that are well worth the modern critic's attention.

## FURTHER READING

The best scholarly commentary on Heraclitus's work is Pontani (2005), with introduction, Greek text and facing Italian translation, and extensive notes. For an English translation with facing Greek text, a general introduction, and brief notes, see Russell and Konstan (2005). Still useful is Buffière (1962). For further textual criticism, see Neri (2010).

The fullest account of the classical background to Heraclitus is Ramelli (2004), who emphasizes the role of the Stoics in the development of the allegorical tradition; see also Goulet (2005). For a more general survey that takes account of Heraclitus's own work, see Lamberton and Keaney

(1992). Struck (2004) offers a thoughtful discussion of the entire tradition of symbolic interpretation. For a brief but lively and informative treatment, see Collobert (2009). Bernard (1990) draws a clear, but partly speculative, distinction between the later Neoplatonic style of allegory and the approach of Heraclitus and Pseudo-Plutarch.

Dawson (1992) treats pagan, Jewish, and Christian allegorists writing at different times in the intellectual hothouse of Alexandria; see also Niehoff (2011); and on Heraclitus and allegory in the Talmud, see Alexander (2016). Nieto Hernández (2014) shows that Philo's knowledge of Homer was more extensive than is commonly recognized. For the influence of classical on Christian allegory, see Pépin (1981), and, more briefly and accessibly but still rich in detail, Ramelli (2011), who emphasizes the Stoic contribution.

For Heraclitus's literary style, see Chiron (2005); see also Russell (2003).

A good survey of the entire allegorical tradition, with some excellent essays on classical and early Jewish and Christian works, is Copeland and Struck (2010).

## REFERENCES

Alexander, Philip. 2016. "Heraclitus's *Homeric Problems* and Midrash *Genesis Rabbah*: Comparisons and Contrasts." In *Sibyls, Scriptures, and Scrolls: John Collins at Seventy*, edited by Joel Baden, Hindy Najman, and Eibert Tigchelaar, 38–67. Leiden: E. J. Brill.

Bernard, Wolfgang. 1990. *Spätantike Dichtungstheorien: Untersuchungen zu Proklos, Herakleitos und Plutarch*. Stuttgart: Teubner.

Buffière, Félix. 1962. *Héraclite: Allégories d'Homère*. Paris: Budé.

Chiron, Pierre. 2005. "Aspects rhétoriques et grammaticaux de l'interprétation allégorique d'Homère." In *Allégorie des poètes, allégorie des philosophes: Études sur la poétique et l'herméneutique de l'allégorie de l'Antiquité à la Réforme*, edited by Gilbert Dahan and Richard Goulet, 35–58. Paris: J. Vrin.

Collobert, Catherine. 2009. "Philosophical Readings of Homer: Ancient and Contemporary Insights." In *Logos and Muthos: Philosophical Essays in Greek Literature*, edited by William Wians, 133–157. Albany: State University of New York Press.

Copeland, Rich, and Peter T. Struck, eds. 2010. *The Cambridge Companion to Allegory*. Cambridge, UK: Cambridge University Press.

Dawson, David. 1992. *Allegorical Readers and Cultural Revision in Ancient Alexandria*. Berkeley: University of California Press.

Goulet, Richard. 2005. "La méthode allégorique chez les Stoïciens." In *Les Stoïciens*, edited by Gilbert Romeyer Dherbey and Jean-Baptiste Gourinat, 93–119. Paris: J. Vrin.

Lamberton, Robert, and John J. Keaney, eds. 1992. *Homer's Ancient Readers: The Hermeneutics of Greek Epic's Earliest Exegetes*. Princeton, NJ: Princeton University Press.

Neri, Camillo. 2010. "Sul testo di Eraclito allegorista." *Eikasmos* 21: 249–272.

Niehoff, Maren R. 2011. *Jewish Exegesis and Homeric Scholarship in Alexandria*. Cambridge, UK: Cambridge University Press.

Nieto Hernández, María de la Purificación. 2014. "Philo of Alexandria and Greek Poetry." *Studia Philonica Annual* 26: 135–149.

Obbink, Dirk. 1994. *Philodemus on Piety: Part 1: Critical Text with Commentary*. Oxford: Clarendon Press.

Pépin, Jean. 1981. *Mythe et allégorie: Les origines grecques et les contestations judéo-chrétiennes.*3rd ed. Paris: Études Augustiniennes.

Pontani, Filippomaria. 2005. *Eraclito: Questioni omeriche sulle allegorie di Omero in merito agli dèi.* Pisa, Italy: Edizioni ETS.

Ramelli, Ilaria. 2004. *Allegoria: I, L'età classica.* Milan: Vita e Pensiero.

Ramelli, Ilaria. 2011. "The Philosophical Stance of Allegory in Stoicism and Its Reception in Platonism, Pagan and Christian: Origen in Dialogue with the Stoics and Plato." *International Journal of the Classical Tradition* 18: 335–371.

Russell, Donald A. 2003. "The Rhetoric of the Homeric Problems." In *Metaphor, Allegory, and the Classical Tradition: Ancient Thought and Modern Revisions,* edited by George R. Boys-Stones, 217–234. Oxford: Oxford University Press.

Russell, Donald A., and David Konstan, eds. and trans. 2005. *Heraclitus: Homeric Problems.* Atlanta, GA: Society of Biblical Literature.

Struck, Peter T. 2004. *The Birth of the Symbol: Ancient Readers at the Limits of Their Texts.* Princeton, NJ: Princeton University Press.

# CHAPTER 15

## HYGINUS, *FABULAE*

### K. F. B. FLETCHER

THE *Fabulae* attributed to Hyginus is one of the most useful mythographical texts from the ancient world (for *De Astronomia* linked with the same author, see Zucker, this volume; and Smith, this volume). Although its authorship and date are uncertain, it is the best and oldest example of Roman mythography and, along with Apollodorus's *Bibliotheca*, it is the most complete collection of myths, though its organization and arrangement make it easier to consult than its Greek counterpart. Comprising a table of contents listing 277 *fabulae*, a *praefatio* giving a genealogy of the gods and other divine and semi-divine beings, and 246 *fabulae*, it presents mostly Greek material in a form accessible to Roman readers of all levels.

## 1. THE TEXT

Many of the difficulties of working with the *Fabulae* derive from the way it has reached us (Soler i Nicolau 2011a: 229–231; Reeve 1983: 189–190). It survived in only one, now lost 9th- or 10th-century manuscript (Φ), edited and published by Micyllus (Jacob Möltzer or Molsheim) in 1535, and then lost. Micyllus tells us in an epistolary preface that the manuscript was so damaged and difficult to read that in many places he was simply guessing when making corrections and that he sometimes even omitted material. By contemporary standards, his edition (now referred to as F) is poor, but it forms the basis for all subsequent editions.

Although F is our only witness for the vast majority of the text, we get glimpses from two other sources. The rediscovery of some fragments of Φ shows both that Micyllus's assessment of the legibility of the manuscript was accurate and that his readings are not always correct. Our other main source is a 5th-century manuscript (N) containing some or all of *Fab.* 67–71; the versions are different enough from those in F (usually because they are shorter) that editors generally label them as separate chapters (for example, 70A).

The differences between Φ/F and N show how susceptible to alteration a text such as the *Fabulae* is, and how individual readers could have expanded or contracted these chapters. The substantial changes the work has undergone in transmission reveals one of the main characteristics—if not the defining feature—of the *Fabulae*: its adaptability. Like many ancient texts, it seems made to be altered as it spread (see Selden 2010). The constant evolution of the work, in turn, reflects one of the purposes of mythography: utility as a reference work. Unlike literary texts, the *Fabulae* is not a work with secure boundaries; its continued existence depended on adapting to the needs of new readers, who turned to it not for pleasure but as a tool.

Changes to the text are suggested also by the numerous passages in the scholia to Statius's *Thebaid* and Germanicus's *Aratea*, that are often close to passages in the *Fabulae* but rarely identical for more than a couple words at a time. The passages are similar enough, however, to show that these scholia drew on some version of the *Fabulae*, as with *Fab.* 75 and the *scholion* to Statius, *Thebaid* 2.95, which tell the story of Tiresias using very similar phrasing (see Smith 2013: 189–193). Such parallels suggest that the text had changed a great deal as it was used and adapted to new needs.

Our other source for the text of the *Fabulae* is the *Hermeneumata Leidensia* of Ps.-Dositheus, a collection of bilingual texts for learners of Greek or Latin. In this very short text, Ps.-Dositheus tells us that in 207 BCE he copied the *Genealogy* of Hyginus, "known to all." After his brief introduction, he describes the contents of the work in a way that resembles the *Fabulae* as we have it, after which there is an extraordinarily lacunose section that includes eight stories in both Greek and Latin. Only two of the stories overlap with the *Fabulae*—Philyra (*Fab.* 138) and Ulysses (compare *Fab.* 141, *Sirenes*; Cameron 2004: 317–318)—but they are relatively close (for an opposing view, see Cameron 2004: 35). This text is difficult to use, however, as the Greek seems to be a poor translation of Latin, and the Latin seems to be a poor translation of Greek, meaning the text has undergone numerous changes and multiple translations (Dickey 2012: 27). Furthermore, while the overlap between this and the *Fabulae* as transmitted by Φ is clear, there are significant differences, confirming the impression that the text changed through the ages as it found new readers and audiences. Thus, the version of the *Fabulae* transmitted by Micyllus is not the only one that ever existed, and every version might have been different.

# 2. AUTHOR, DATE, AND TITLE

Because of the paucity of our evidence, everything about the text is problematic. We do not know if *Fabulae* is the title Micyllus found in the manuscript or one he gave the text (it is fitting either way). We likewise do not know whether Micyllus found the attribution "Gaius Julius Hyginus, freedman of Augustus" in the manuscript or saw the name Hyginus and assumed it was the same famous Hyginus we know primarily from Suetonius's discussion in *On Grammarians and Rhetoricians* 20, which tells us that he was from Spain or Alexandria, in charge of the Palatine Library, and friends with Ovid.

Ancient authors attribute a variety of historical, didactic/agricultural, religious, and biographical works to this Hyginus, so the subject matter of the *Fabulae* fits his interests (Del Hoyo and García Ruiz 2009: 10–12), and there is nothing in the text that necessarily postdates his lifetime (save chapters 258–261, taken from Servius's commentary on Vergil's *Aeneid*), and it has even been argued that a possible allusion to Genesis in chapter 143 suggests an author with the librarian's background and access to the Palatine library (Inowlocki 2007). The form of the text as we have it, however, means that if Gaius Julius Hyginus was the author, the text has suffered so greatly over time that one of its most famous editors could call its author "unskilled," "semi-educated," and "foolish" (Rose 1967: xii).

Of the other known authors named Hyginus, the only one with a connection to the *Fabulae* is the author of the *De Astronomia*, a work in four books on all matters astronomical, including, in the second book, origin myths for the constellations. The subject matter of the *Fabulae* shares many similarities with this second book, which contains a tantalizing statement: "But, as Aeschylus the tragedian says in the *Phorcides*, the Graeae were guardians of the Gorgons—about which matter I wrote in the first book of the *Genealogies*" (*Astr.* 2.12). Although no extant passage of the *Fabulae* corresponds to this description, Hyginus mentions Medusa and a "Gorgo" multiple times and includes the *Phorcides* at *praefatio* 9. The reference to another book on mythological genealogies by the same author raises the possibility that the *Fabulae*—or some part of it—may originally have been called the *Genealogiae*, a claim that is also supported by Ps.-Dositheus.

Paired with the mythographical nature of the second book of the *De Astronomia*, this reference suggests that the two are by the same author. Similarly, the *Fabulae* shows a particular interest in stars; while it does not often quote sources directly, two of the three passages of poetry it contains involve constellations (14.33 quotes Cicero's *Phaenomena*; 177.2 quotes Courtney *FLP* Anon. 8). Furthermore, in several instances, the two works are among the only—if not *the* only—sources to offer a particular variant of a myth, as in *Fab.* 49 and *Astr.* 2.14, which are the only two lists of people raised from the dead by Aesculapius to include only Hippolytus and Glaucus. The closest parallel between the two works is *Fab.* 130 and *Astr.* 2.4, telling the story of Icarius and Erigone.

The work can be no earlier than the beginning of the 1st century CE because it shows the influence of Vergil's *Aeneid* and Ovid's *Metamorphoses* (below), and a *terminus ante quem* comes from Ps.-Dositheus's statement that he copied the text in 207 CE. Based on this information, we can make the following statements with some certainty: what we call the *Fabulae* was written by someone who may have been named Hyginus during the 1st or 2nd century of this era, and that it originally bore a different name, either *Genealogia* or *Genealogiae*; the text is likely by the same author as the *De Astronomia* but has undergone numerous alterations over the course of its existence. Whether the *Genealogiae* was originally the work of Gaius Julius Hyginus cannot be known, but in its current state there is no reason to connect it with that famous scholar. Regardless of the identity of its author, the work attained popularity relatively early, and its connection with a famous scholar may simply be a testament to the wealth of information it contains.

# 3. ORGANIZATION

Because *De Astronomia* 2.14 refers to the second book of the *Genealogiae*, the *Fabulae* was likely in multiple books originally, and our version of the text may bear traces of this original three-book structure, with the first book being the genealogies of the gods (similar in scope to—though much more briefly told than—Hesiod's *Theogony*); the second being the myths themselves; and the third being the lists at the end (Breen 1991: 31–33; Smith and Trzaskoma 2007: xliv–xlvi). Ps.-Dositheus's brief text may also reflect the same basic structure: he provides a table of contents that begins with a list of contents and genealogies of the Muses; he then includes a few stories about the gods before going into the bulk of the entry, which is the myths. The last item in his text is "On the Discovery of Arts" (2610/2632), a title that recalls two of the last four lists at the end of the *Fabulae*, including "Who Invented What" (274) and "Discoverers of Things" (277).

The tripartite structure is not, however, as neat as it first appears. First of all, the *praefatio* is radically shorter than the other two sections, making it unlikely that it was a separate book. Likewise, although most of the lists are at the end of the collection, some appear elsewhere—and for logical reasons. Chapters 112–115, for example, appear at the end of the section on the Trojan War and right before the section on the *Nostoi*. But since they all involve who fought and who killed whom in the Trojan War, they are in a place where they would be easy to find for someone interested in that topic.

Although some have suggested otherwise (for example, Fabre-Serris 2017), stories within the *fabulae* proper are largely grouped by saga or place (Morcillo Expósito 2003: 272; Del Hoyo and García Ruiz 2009: 15–18). The beginning of the work provides an example: it begins with a cluster of mostly Theban myths (1–11), before moving into stories involving the Argonauts (12–27); the myths involving Hercules (one of the Argonauts) come next (29–36), followed by those revolving around Theseus and the Minotaur (37–44); the focus on Theseus leads naturally to a small section on Athens (45–48). Although not all the chapters have such clear relationships to one another, subsequent clusters are apparent. The organization of the myths after the end of the Trojan section, however, is more haphazard, and it seems possible that—as is the case with Apollodorus's *Bibliotheca*—at one point the collection stopped with the death of Ulysses (127), as many of the chapters after the *Nostoi* return to events from before the Trojan War (another possibility is that the later section was added in part to include material from Vergil and Ovid). The bulk of the lists begins after *Fab.* 220, "Cura," which is the most Roman of the *Fabulae*, providing the Latin etymology of *homo* from *humus*.

This organization on the basis of saga or place makes sense from the point of view of both composition and—especially—consultation: it is easy to imagine someone picking a topic and writing all of the things that he knew about it (directly or indirectly), as well as someone using the text and finding a myth related to the one he was looking for, and then scanning the vicinity for the exact story he wanted. Such an unverifiable scenario might explain why there are occasional outlying stories, as if the author forgot about them while on a certain section, as with the "displacement" of 167 and 179, which return to Liber, who had been the subject of 129–134 (Breen 1991: 148–149).

One peculiarity of organization is the so-called doublets, two chapters that tell all or part of the same story as another *fabula*, for example, 2: *Ino* and 4: *Ino Euripidis* (Breen 1991: 74–76). While these doublets have been written off as interpolations (Dietze 1890: 6–9; Werth 1901: 15–16), the inclusion of authors' names in the title of some of these doublets suggests that they may originally have been meant to offer a different version from a specific text by a well-known author. Although none mentions him in the title, some of these doublets have a connection with Ovid's *Metamorphoses* (Breen 1991: 148–157; Fletcher 2013: 151–155). For example, both *Fab.* 180 ("Actaeon") and 181 ("Diana") tell the story of Actaeon being turned into a stag after seeing Diana bathe. The former is very brief and provides the version that Actaeon wanted to rape her; as punishment, Diana turned him into a stag, which his dogs consumed. The latter, however, is much longer, and shows multiple signs of Ovidian influence, not least the lengthy list of dogs at 181.3–4, taken from *Metamorphoses* 3.206–225, 232–233.

In addition to the doublets, there is a certain amount of repetition throughout the *Fabulae*, especially of genealogical details. Although Rose, for example, considered such repetition a sign that we do not have the *Fabulae* in its original form, we need not view it as a defect (Rose 1967: xii–xiii). Rather, such repetition increases utility, as it means that someone looking for the story of one character would not have to turn to a separate chapter just to find a key detail because it was only in a single chapter. Rather than being a sign of interpolation, this repetition likely reflects the work's purpose and may provide further confirmation that it was originally called *Genealogiae*.

# 4. Origins and Sources: Greek versus Roman

Our knowledge of the *Fabulae* is so sparse that scholars have not even been able to agree on whether the original language was Greek or Latin. While the dominant theory used to be that the *Fabulae* is nothing more than a translation of a lost Greek original, most scholars now agree that the *Fabulae* is a compilation of material from multiple sources, not all of them Greek.

The older theory rests on the fact that the work consists mostly of Greek material and that most of the Roman material is in the lists at the end, and thus easily written off as interpolations (for example, Rose 1967), as in 256, "Women who were especially chaste":

> Penelope, daughter of Icarius, wife of Ulysses. Evadne, daughter of Phylax, spouse of Capaneus. Laodamia, daughter of Acastus, spouse of Protesilaus. Hecuba, daughter of Cisseus, wife of Priam. Theonoe, daughter of Thestor < . . . Alcestis, daughter of Pelias,> wife of Admetus. Of the Romans, Lucretia, daughter of Lucretius, spouse of Collatinus.

Furthermore, there are misunderstandings of Greek, the most infamous being the reference to *Melanippen Desmontis filiam, sive Aeoli ut alii poetae dicunt* ("Melanippe, daughter of Desmontes or, as other poets say, of Aeolus," 186.1), a character who appears nowhere else and seems to have arisen from Hyginus's interpretation of the title of Euripides's play *Melanippē hē desmōtis* as "Melanippe, the daughter of Desmontes," instead of "Melanippe the captive" (see other examples in Cameron 2004: 33–35). The number and nature of such "mistakes," however, have been overestimated, as has their import (Fletcher 2013: 139–141). Furthermore, a mistake in translating a Greek word or phrase does not mean that Hyginus was translating an entire Greek work.

As is to be expected of a work of this period, however, the *Fabulae* draws on Greek literary sources, usually—if not always—at one or more removes (Cameron 2004: 33–51). For example, the two chapters with titles (4, 8) attributing a *fabula* to Euripides likely do not get their details directly from Euripides but, rather, from the so-called "Tales from Euripides," a collection of hypotheses of his plays (Cameron 2004: 45–46; for a different view, see Huys 1996 and 1997a). Traces of these hypotheses also appear in *fabulae* that do not mention Euripides, as in 96, "Achilles," which draws on a hypothesis to Euripides's *Scyrioi* (Cameron 2004: 45, with notes), leading some to suggest that most of the *fabulae* originally had tragic sources (Del Hoyo and García Ruiz 2009: 25). Similarly, many of the Greek authors Hyginus mentions by name in a chapter or title—Euripides, Hesiod (4, 154), Pherecydes (154.2)—are the ones that appear consistently throughout the mythographical tradition, making it likely that Hyginus copied these references from elsewhere (although such copying does not mean that Hyginus had not read some of these works at some point) (Cameron 2004: 42).

Many of the lists at the end are similar to those found in papyri (Cameron 2004: 238–249), proving that—despite the corruption of our text—it contains rare details found in few places, and suggests that some of its other unique details reflect a "real" mythographical tradition. *Fab.* 200, the story of Chione, provides a good example of such rare details:

> Apollo and Mercury are said to have lain in one night with Chione, or, as other poets say, Philonis, daughter of Daedalion. From Apollo she gave birth to Philammon; from Mercury, Autolycus. She later spoke arrogantly against Diana while hunting, and so was killed by her with arrows. But her father Daedalion, weeping for his only daughter, was turned by Apollo into the bird *daedalion*, that is, a hawk.

The story is familiar from Ovid (*Met.* 11.291–345), the only other source to use the name Chione. While Hyginus is likely following Ovid, he also includes the name Philonis, which appears in Pherecydes (if we can believe some scholia to Homer, *Odyssey* 19.432) and possibly even in Hesiod (fr. 64 M.-W. = *P.Oxy.* 2500). Hyginus adds a rare name to a story that is otherwise from Ovid, and includes a Latin gloss to make the Greek etymology clear.

The older theory—that the *Fabulae* is merely a translation of a lost Greek work—also depends on an overly simplistic notion of what constitutes "Greek" and "Roman." The

*Fabulae* is a collection of primarily Greek material in Latin, which in and of itself is a very Roman thing; one could describe Ovid's *Metamorphoses* the same way. But the *Fabulae* also contains more—and more deeply integrated—Roman material than previously acknowledged. In addition to the poems on constellations mentioned earlier, Hyginus quotes or cites other Latin authors (Fletcher 2013: 144–162), including Lucretius (57.3, 151.1 = *De Rerum Natura* 5.905) and Ennius (8)—although the latter may be a mistake for Pacuvius (Maeck-Desmedt 1972). Also, as mentioned above, Hyginus makes extensive use of Ovid's *Metamorphoses*, and uses the *Aeneid* on multiple occasions. The use of both Greek and Latin names for the same figure (e.g., Asclepius and Aesculapius) may also mean that Hyginus was at times using sources in Greek and at other times ones in Latin (Del Hoyo and García Ruiz 2009: 26). Finally, the "narrative voice" of the *Fabulae* is Roman; Hyginus often uses phrases such as "we (sc. Latin speakers) say" (*nos dicimus*) to gloss Greek works, or to provide an *aition*, showing his concern for his Latin-reading audience (Cameron 2004: 35).

The presence of these glosses (Werth 1901: 25–27) is an important part of the work's utility, as some of the myths do not make sense without an explanation of a Greek word. Similarly, every time he can, Hyginus translates a Greek name into Latin in the preface (Boriaud 2003: xxiv). While Hyginus does not consistently translate Greek words, and his translations are not always correct, their inclusion reflects a desire to have the myths make sense to Roman readers.

Finally, the earlier theory also depends on an anachronistic notion of translation. Roman translation was incorporative and competitive, meaning that the Romans did not translate works with a view to maintaining what we would now consider strict fidelity (Possanza 2004; McElduff 2013). Therefore, even if the *Fabulae* were based on a single lost Greek work, we would expect a Roman translator to add Roman material and make the work his own. It would not be a translation in the simple, derogatory sense of the term as used by earlier scholars.

And, while it might be tempting to write off the Roman elements scattered throughout the work as interpolations (for example, Werth 1901: 25–31), some are too integrated into the text to be simple interpolations (Fletcher 2013). Even the term "interpolation" is problematic because it implies a firm boundary between an "original" text and later impurities that, for some reason, do not belong; because the text may have never really had any set boundaries, applying such a model to the *Fabulae* is misguided.

To remove all of this material in hopes of discovering some sort of pure layer beneath it gains us nothing and would leave us with a work that is full of holes and much less useful. The dozens of Roman, Italian, and Latin elements in the text pervade the collection, from the table of contents to the chapters at the beginning to the lists at the end, and are a significant enough portion that they constitute an essential part of the work's character. The bulk of the material is Greek, but all of it is filtered through a Roman lens, made Roman by the use of Latin, the quotation of Roman authors, and the inclusion of Roman details—a situation that might serve as a working definition of Roman mythography (see also Smith, this volume).

# 5. TRENDS

Although much more work remains to be done on the nature of the *Fabulae* (for instance, on lexical details, its sources, its parallels with papyri, etc.), it is possible to say a few things about its original purpose and how modern readers should—and should not—use it. First of all, everything about the work bespeaks utility. This is a work that is not meant to be read but to be consulted. It has few literary pretensions, and instead focuses on ease of use.

Secondly, the work aims to make primarily Greek material available to a Roman audience. The audience would have been Romans with varying knowledge of Greek (including none), who wanted quick access to this Greek material. The focus on such an audience and use is also apparent in the language of the *Fabulae*: despite the occasional quotations of Roman verse, the style is mostly plain and straightforward (Del Hoyo and García Ruiz 2007; Boriaud 2003: xxx). The syntax is simple, and the sentences are generally short, with no excessive hypotaxis. While Hyginus's Latin has been criticized for not adhering to the rules of textbook Classical Latin, it is readily comprehensible by people with even a little knowledge of Latin, making it accessible to a wide range of readers with an equally wide range of purposes—possibly even students (Morcillo Expósito 2003: 271, 277; Martinho 2016). Ps.-Dositheus's remark (2617–2621) that the work has been used in paintings and pantomimes is a reminder that its appeal was not limited to those with literary interests.

The organization of the work is also straightforward. The table of contents makes it relatively easy to find a given myth, especially since many chapters begin with the same word as their title (Breen 1991: 166–168). The repetition of key details and names obviates the need to move between sections too much, and the clustering of related sagas also means that once a reader finds the right general area, it is possible to skim backward or forward a bit to find the detail for which one is looking.

At the same time, there is no attempt to provide a definitive collection of every version. With the exception of the doublets, the *Fabulae* is not very accepting of alternatives; not counting the doublets, only 32 of the 257 extant *fabulae* contain a variant (including glosses), and only seven have more than one variant. There is no attempt to catalogue numerous variants or provide an exhaustive discussion of the versions of a myth. But the inclusion of conflicting stories of, for example, the creation of humans (142, 220) suggests that there is also no effort to provide a single, canonical version. This is not a work offering a master narrative, trying to make some kind of point, or providing a continuous account of myth, but a work meant for easy consultation. It rarely presents alternative names for characters, or different endings, and it is not an analytical work of scholarship, meant to give someone a comprehensive overview of a myth; rather, it generally provides one version of a myth, in relatively straightforward fashion.

The general nature of these chapters and the lack of concern about variants suggest that the work is meant for people already familiar with the stories. The elliptical nature of the narrative presupposes an audience that is looking for a reminder of key details (for example, the names of characters and places) rather than anything deeper. Save occasional references to emotions (mostly love and the anger of the gods), there is little psychological coloring, and few details about settings. The narratives are generally reduced to their most basic elements (Breen 1991: 73; Del Hoyo and García Ruiz 2009: 19–21).

The presence of the doublets and the differences between the versions preserved in N and F suggest that this text changed a great deal as it was used, as do the later passages in the scholia to Statius and Germanicus. It is possible, too, that the lists at the end were not a part of the work in its original form. In some ways, then, the *Fabulae* has more in common with scholia than with a mythographical text such as the *Bibliotheca* in the sense that its format allows for the easy inclusion of new information (for other parallels with scholia, see Martinho 2016). The *Fabulae* is an agglutinative, living text; each new reader or copyist could add information he considered useful. Presumably this process was at work early on, too, and it seems likely that copies of the *Fabulae* would have looked significantly different from each other not long after the original time of composition. Ps.-Dositheus's claim that the work was well known is likely primarily a testament to its utility, and the same may be true of the attribution to Hyginus.

## 6. Value of the Work

Despite how little we know of its origins, the *Fabulae* is valuable for many reasons. The first is its date: it is our earliest mythographical text in Latin. Second is its scope: it is the fullest prose mythographical work in Latin from the classical period. It gives us a glimpse of the Roman mythographical tradition in a relatively early form, as Greek and Roman myth were becoming inseparable. It is perhaps no coincidence that the work is often attributed to an author contemporary with Ovid; the *Fabulae* and the *Metamorphoses* exemplify the same blending of Greek and Roman material. The *Fabulae* also offers a wide range of material, some of which is found nowhere else (Urbán 2003: 147–153; Del Hoyo and García Ruiz 2007: 51; 2009: 33), though recent discoveries continue to confirm that they are not simply Hyginus's inventions (for example, Fowler 1995). The bulk of the material is mythological, but the lists at the end show how myth could shade into other categories, and how myth became something to be collected and codified, and then consulted.

Like all works, the *Fabulae* gives indications of its intended audience, which is a thoroughly Roman one. It is the best example of Roman mythography, which is to say a work that is written in Latin, mostly about Greek material, but makes at least some connections to the Roman world. Without Greek material there is no myth, and so no mythography. A work with only Roman material would be something entirely different, more akin to the first book of Livy's *History* or parts of Valerius Maximus's *Memorable Deeds and Sayings*. To label the *Fabulae* a mere translation misses the point entirely, for the *Fabulae* is a thoroughly Roman work.

# 7. CONCLUSION

The *Fabulae* of Hyginus is, together with Apollodorus's *Bibliotheca*, the most important mythographical work to survive from classical antiquity. But like any piece of literature, it has its owns aims and should never be taken at face value, as somehow transmitting factual material without adding its own perspective and advancing its own agenda, however limited that may be. The *Fabulae* is also valuable for the view it provides of the transition of Greek myth into Greco-Roman myth, and scholarship on the *Fabulae* reflects the continued difficulties people have with such issues, as well as the long-standing impact of Romantic thinking that portrays the Greeks as creators and the Romans as copyists. The *Fabulae* is proof that the collection of myth is no less complicated than myth itself.

## FURTHER READING

The most widely available texts are Marshall and Boriaud; the former is better, though a new edition is still sorely needed. Soler i Nicolau (2011b) is the most recent edition, but it is very difficult to find and does not differ substantially from Marshall's edition save in offering the fullest critical apparatus. Huys (1997b) and Kenens (2012) provide good examples of how improvements can still be made to the text.

The *Fabulae* has now been translated into many major European languages and is thus more widely available than ever before. In the absence of a true commentary, readers must turn to the notes in these translations, of which those in Guidorizzi (2000) are the best and fullest; Del Hoyo and García Ruiz (2009) and Smith and Trzaskoma (2007) are also useful, and both provide good general introductions. Rose's (1967) edition is still useful for its notes, and for the influence it exercised on the Hyginus scholarship of the 20th century. See also Senecio (2013 German), and Takho-Godi and Torshilov (2000 Russian).

Flammini (2004) provides a text of the *Hermeneumata Leidensia*, to which Dickey (2012: 187–194) is an excellent introduction. The testimonia and fragments of C. Julius Hyginus can be found in Funaioli's *Grammaticae Romanae Fragmenta* 1.525–537, and Lasso de la Vega (1974) provides an overly optimistic biography of the librarian.

The only full-length treatment of the *Fabulae* is Breen's (1991) unpublished dissertation. It is still worth consulting but is very general and predates most of the important work on mythography. The older works by Dietze (1890), Tschiaszny (1888), and Werth (1901) are likewise still worth consulting on many points, though they tend to focus on listing and arranging material rather than analyzing; they are all quick to label as interpolations elements that do not fit their analysis. The series of articles by van Krevelen (1957, 1966, 1968, 1972) is a more sober example of the desire to correct Hyginus based on the assumption that the work is a poor translation of one or more Greek sources.

Urbán's (2003) review of Guidorizzi's translation is invaluable, and (at 147–153) catalogues over fifty places where Hyginus diverges from other sources. Cameron (2004: 33–51) has many valuable remarks on Hyginus, especially his Greek sources, but the *Fabulae* is not his main focus; Martinho (2016) focuses on Hyginus's sources and situates the *Fabulae* within larger literary and pedagogical trends. Fletcher (2013) argues for the Roman nature of the *Fabulae* in part by examining Hyginus's use of Roman poetry.

## References

Boriaud, Jean-Yves. 2003. *Hygin. Fables*. 2nd ed. Paris: Les Belles Lettres.

Breen, Anthony Bernard. 1991. "The Fabulae Hygini Reappraised: A Reconsideration of the Content and Compilation of the Work." Diss. University of Illinois at Urbana-Champaign.

Cameron, Alan. 2004. *Greek Mythography in the Roman World*. Oxford: Oxford University Press.

Del Hoyo, Javier, and José M. García Ruiz. 2007. "Peculiaridades lingüísticas en las *Fabulae* de Higino." *Revista de Estudios Latinos* 7: 39–52.

Del Hoyo, Javier, and José M. García Ruiz, eds. 2009. *Higino. Fábulas*. Biblioteca Clásica Gredos 380. Madrid: Editorial Gredos.

Dickey, Eleanor. 2012. *The Colloquia of the Hermeneumata Pseudodositheana*. Vol. 1. Cambridge, UK: Cambridge University Press.

Dietze, Johannes. 1890. "Quaestiones Hyginianae." Diss. University of Kiel.

Fabre-Serris, Jacqueline. 2017. "Un exemple de sélection, ordre et traitement mythographique chez Hygin: Les fables 1–27." *Polymnia* 3: 26–52.

Flammini, Giuseppe, ed. 2004. *Hermeneumata Pseudodositheana Leidensia*. Munich and Leipzig: K. G. Saur.

Fletcher, K. F. B. 2013. "Hyginus' *Fabulae*: Toward a Roman Mythography." In *Writing Myth: Mythography in the Ancient World*, edited by Stephen M. Trzaskoma and R. Scott Smith, 133–164. Leuven: Peeters.

Fowler, Robert. L. 1995. "Mythographic Texts. Mythological Compendium (4097)." *The Oxyrhynchus Papyri* 61: 46–54.

Guidorizzi, Giulio. 2000. *Igino. Miti*. Biblioteca Adelphi 398. Milan: Adelphi Edizioni.

Huys, Marc. 1996. "Euripides and the 'Tales from Euripides': Sources of the *Fabulae* of Ps.-Hyginus?" *Archiv für Papyrusforschung* 42: 168–178.

Huys, Marc. 1997a. "Euripides and the 'Tales from Euripides': Sources of the *Fabulae* of Ps.-Hyginus?" *Archiv für Papyrusforschung* 43: 11–30.

Huys, Marc. 1997b. "The Names of Some Kalydonian Boar-Hunters in P.Oxy. 61.4097 fr. 2, Apollodoros 1.8.2.3–6 and Hyginus, *F*. 173." *Mnemosyne* 50: 202–205.

Inowlocki, Sabrina. 2007. "Une trace de Genèse 11:1–9 dans les *Fabulae* attribuées à Hygin?" *Latomus* 66: 342–349.

Kenens, Ulrike. 2012. "Some Observations on the Catalogue of Danaids (Apollod. 2.16–20 and Hyg. *Fab*. 170)." *Mnemosyne* 65: 726–731.

Lasso de la Vega, Javier. 1974. "Cayo Julio Hyginio, Primer Bibliotecario Español." *Revista de Archivos, Bibliotecas y Museos* 77: 435–447.

Maeck-Desmedt, Claire. 1972. "Fabulae Hygini: VIII. Eadem Euripidis quam scribit Ennius." *Revue Belge de Philologie et d'Histoire* 50: 70–77.

Marshall, Peter K., ed. 2002. *Hyginus. Fabulae*. 2nd ed. Munich and Leipzig: Teubner.

Martinho, Marcos. 2016. "Os comentários de Higino aos mitos de Ceneu e de Linceu." In *Lire les mythes: Formes, usages et visées des pratiques mythographiques de l'Antiquité à la Renaissance*, edited by Arnaud Zucker, Jacqueline Fabre-Serris, Jean-Yves Tilliette, and Gisèle Besson, 85–110. Villeneuve d'Ascq, France: Presses du Septentrion.

McElduff, Siobhán. 2013. *Roman Theories of Translation: Surpassing the Source.* New York: Routledge.

Morcillo Expósito, Guadalupe. 2003. "Caius Iulius Hyginus, Mitógrafo." *Anuario de Estudios Filológicos* 26: 267–277.

Morcillo Expósito, Guadalupe, ed. 2008. *Fábulas. Astronomía.* Madrid: Akal.

Possanza, D. Mark. 2004. *Translating the Heavens: Aratus, Germanicus, and the Poetics of Latin Translation.* New York: Peter Lang.

Reeve, Michael D. 1983. "Hyginus." In *Texts and Transmission. A Survey of Latin Classics*, edited by Leighton D. Reynolds, 187–190. Oxford: Clarendon Press.

Rose, Herbert J. 1967. *Hygini Fabulae.* 3rd ed. Leiden: A. W. Sijthoff.

Selden, Daniel S. 2010. "Text Networks." *Ancient Narrative* 8: 1–23.

Senecio, Lucius. A. 2013. *Fabulae: Eine Reise durch die wundersame Welt der griechischen Mythologie.* Berlin: Autumnus Verlag.

Smith, R. Scott. 2013. "Mythographic Material and Method in the So-Called 'Statius Scholia.'" In *Writing Myth: Mythography in the Ancient World*, edited by Stephen M. Trzaskoma and R. Scott Smith, 165–200. Leuven: Peeters.

Smith, R. Scott, and Stephen M. Trzaskoma. 2007. *Apollodorus' "Library" and Hyginus' "Fabulae": Two Handbooks of Greek Mythology.* Indianapolis, IN: Hackett.

Soler i Nicolau, Antònia. 2011a. "El caso singular de las Fábulas de Higino." In *Parua Mythographica*, edited by Jordi Pàmias, 229–239. Oberhaid, Germany: Utopica.

Soler i Nicolau, Antònia. 2011b. *Higí. Faules.* 2 vols. Barcelona: Fundació Bernat Metge.

Takho-Godi, Aza A., and O. Dmitry Torshilov. 2000. *Gigin: Mify.* Saint Petersburg: Aleteiia.

Tschiaszny, Moritz. 1888. *Studia Hyginiana I.* Vienna: Verlag des K. K. Staatsgymnasiums in Hernals.

Urbán, Ángel. 2003. "Higino: Balance crítico sobre un mitógrafo traducido, desaparecido y reencontrado." *Alfinge. Revista de filología* 15: 139–164.

van Krevelen, D. A. 1957. "Bemerkungen zu Hygini Fabulae." *Philologus* 103: 151–152.

van Krevelen, D. A. 1966. "Zu Hyginus." *Philologus* 110: 315–318.

van Krevelen, D. A. 1968. "Zu Hyginus." *Philologus* 112: 269–275.

van Krevelen, D. A. 1972. "Zu Hyginus." *Philologus* 116: 313–319.

Werth, Albert. 1901. *De Hygini Fabularum Indole.* Leipzig: Teubner.

# CHAPTER 16

......................................................................................

# THE *MYTHOGRAPHUS HOMERICUS*

......................................................................................

## JOAN PAGÈS

UNDER the conventional name *Mythographus Homericus* (henceforth *MH*), we refer to a manual of mythography containing a collection of summaries of myths written in the form of comments to Homeric lemmata. As modern scholarship has reconstructed it from evidence in papyri and medieval scholia, the *MH* appears to have been originally a reasonably typical mythographical handbook of the imperial period, of the sort written in the usual summarized style comparable to Pseudo-Apollodorus: namely, mere narratives without any kind of comment, such as allegorical or rationalistic interpretation. Contrast of fully divergent versions or of varying details is rare, with most entries narrating one only version. Very well-known Panhellenic versions of myths can be found, as well as rare, forgotten stories from local curiosities. Moreover, there seems to be no conscious distinction between these two categories, to the extent that it leads us to doubt whether such a distinction made any sense for ancient compilers and readers.

As an organizational principle, the narrative myths follow the order of the Homeric text using the lemmata as they appear in the *Iliad* and the *Odyssey*. Thus, the collection could be read by itself, as a simple book about mythical plots, or as a mythographical commentary to single moments in the Homeric poems. Although it shares features with other mythographical texts, *MH* still has unique features, probably the result of a progressive conversion of an ancient commentary to Homer into a mythographical handbook, a very useful book for teachers and for any reader who wanted to learn a rich repertoire of mythical plots linked to single Homeric words and expressions.

As we will see presently, although the general characteristics of the *MH* are obvious, it proves impossible to reconstruct a single original text from the evidence available to us. We need to bear in mind that the *MH* may have started as a single coherent work, but as we can see it, it is no longer simply a work written in a specific moment of history by an anonymous author, but an "open book" persistently rewritten and modified in different periods by different hands, in order to be adapted to new social and cultural demands.

# 1. EVIDENCE FOR THE *MYTHOGRAPHUS HOMERICUS*: PAPYRI AND SCHOLIA

The most important evidence for the *MH* is found in twelve ancient documents that cover a period of five centuries. The earliest one (*P.Oxy.* 418) is found on a papyrus dating from the late 1st or early 2nd century CE, and the other seven date from the 2nd and 3rd centuries. A later fragment is found on a parchment piece dating from the 5th century. In addition to these, a small piece of text was found on an ostracon, probably a school exercise from the 1st or 2nd century, and it has been added to the list of fragments as well (*PSI* 1000; Montanari 1995a: 138–139). Therefore, it is clearly established that the *MH* was used throughout the imperial period (Cameron 2004: 27–28).

For dating the *MH* Oxyrhynchus Papyrus 418 (late 1st or early 2nd c. CE) is the *terminus ante quem*. A *terminus post quem* is more difficult to find; there is a citation of Didymus in the D-Scholia to *Il.* 22.126, who died around 10 CE. In the corresponding papyrus, there seems to have been a citation to an authority, but the name is missing. If Didymus was originally in the papyrus, that would establish the lower-end date. In that case, the first version of *MH* must have been written during the 1st century CE, in the early Roman imperial period.

Later, in the Middle Ages, the same summaries reappear in the codices of the minor scholia to Homer (the D-Scholia, though those for the *Odyssey* are also called the V-Scholia: see Dickey 2007: 18–22), copied in very similar but not identical wording. This is proof that the *MH* was merged with other exegetical material and ceased to be a self-standing work, since there are no medieval manuscripts that transmit the *MH* as a discrete work. This mixed and integrated form seems to have been found more useful and apparently made the *MH* obsolete as an individual work, which ceased to be circulated separately.

The papyri certainly preserve the original structure of the work. They are formally written in the manner of *hypomenmata*, or comments, under lemmata (Arrighetti 1968, 1977; Schironi 2012: 404–412). In contrast, in the scholia, the summaries of *MH* are interspersed between diverse exegetical material such as glosses, the so-called *quaestiones Homericae*, and material of a different nature and origin (Montanari 1995b: 69–85; 113–125). The papyri are, therefore, the oldest and most direct testimony of the *MH*. Unfortunately, the summaries that can be read in the papyrus fragments represent a tiny part of the full corpus of the presumably original *MH*, which can only be restored with the aid of the scholia.

In the manuscript tradition of the minor scholia, the Greek word *historia* (story) marks a brief mythographical summary. The term often appears in the margin or is integrated into the text to indicate the beginning of each new *historia*. Probably, the summaries from the *MH* were added to the minor scholia from the 6th century onward and began with this word, *historia*. This is not consistent in the extant codices, but the fact that many summaries are introduced by the word *historia* is proof that the writer of the scholia used a book featuring mythical stories related to Homer in the form of a commentary (Pagès 2021). Comparing the scholia and corresponding papyrus fragments shows us that the scholiast (or scholiasts) often inserted other lexicographical and exegetical comments before adding the *historia*; whereas in the papyri, the *historiae* stand alone.

By way of example, we shall analyze the *historia* that can be read under the lemma corresponding to *Iliad* 20.403–404. Let us compare the reading provided by the papyri of Oxyrhynchus 4096, fr. 3.2–11 (Luppe 1996d) and Berlin 13282.3–9 (Montanari 1984) and the corresponding D-Scholia on these lines. In the Oxyrhynchus papyrus we read, immediately following the lemma:

> Neleus, son of Codrus, following an oracle of Apollo, sent a colony from Athens and Helike in Achaea to Miletus. Then he founded there a sanctuary of Poseidon and called him "Heliconius," from the name of the Sanctuary of Helike.

The reading of the Berlin papyrus is almost identical. In both papyri the story ends here, but in the related scholion, there is material both before and after it. Considering the latter first, the scholion continues the narrative with the following comment:

> It seems that, every time they make sacrifices for the god, if the oxen low, the god accepts the victim, but if the oxen keep silence, they are distressed because they think the god is wroth against them. The story is told by Clitophon.

It is not clear whether the story in the papyri contained this final part of the text with the source reference, because both papyri are damaged at the end.

In the scholia, between the lemma and the beginning of the story we can regularly read other pieces of text featuring heterogeneous exegetical material, and the following example has exactly such material prefacing the *historia*:

> Poseidon. Either because he is revered on the mountain of Helicon in Boeotia or in Helike. Or, rather, to the god in Helike. Because Helike is not the same as Helicon, since Helicon is a mountain in Boeotia, and Helike is an island in Achaea, in which there is a shrine to Poseidon. This is the account: . . . [the *historia* follows]

This is followed by the beginning of the text from the *MH*, with an almost literal reading with regard to the two papyrus fragments just quoted. In short, we can see, based on a Homeric allusion to the oxen that low when they are driven to the altar of the sanctuary of Poseidon Heliconius, that the *MH* provides us with a summary of the founding myth of this sanctuary. Subsequently, the scholiast introduced glosses for the term *Heliconius*: it is an epithet of Poseidon, either from Mount Helicon, in Boeotia, or from the town of Helike, in Achaea, which is also mentioned in the *historia* of the *MH* as a metropolis of Miletus. The absence of all this material in the two papyri demonstrates that it did not appear in the original text of the *MH*.

We can also see how the scholiast has introduced the *historia* from the *MH* in the text of the scholia following exegetical material by means of the formula "this is the account." Given that this material does not appear in the text revealed by the papyrus, the method for restoring the text of the *MH* based on the scholia, to the extent possible, would consist of removing the glosses and comments that appear between the lemma and the *historia* (contra Montana and Montanari 2022). In cases in which we have a testimony on papyrus of the same *historia*, the two texts can be compared. This method can also be applied to the *historiae* not revealed by the papyri.

The text that has been restored from the papyri gives us a more summarized reading than that offered by the manuscripts of the scholia, leading us to deduce that the text in the scholia has been extended (van Rossum-Steenbeek 1998: 103–104). But there may also be another explanation—namely, the scholiast used a copy of the *MH* that offered readings that were far more complete than the abbreviated versions in the preserved papyri. Presumably, manuscript transmission might have gradually resulted in an excessive shortening of the stories, to the extent that some details of the stories might have been lost. Therefore, more recent copies with a more summarized text might have coexisted with the older ones featuring more complete versions. Proof of this seems to be that not all the examples from the papyri present the same degree of summarization. It is plausible that the compiler of the D-Scholia used a good exemplar of the *MH*. Undoubtedly, an early medieval philologist who was compiling material for the scholia would have chosen the best books he could find in the libraries. In some cases, other mythography has been used to rewrite *historiae* whose text had been oversummarized or damaged (Pagès 2017: 73). This is why certain passages from the *Bibliotheca* of Ps-Apollodorus or from the scholia to Euripides can also be read among the *historiae*: it was certainly easier to copy verbatim from another book than rewrite the story.

Be that as it may, these two explanations are not mutually exclusive: on the one hand, the scholiast may have chosen a good archetype of the *MH*; on the other hand, he may have extended some of the stories.

As we can see, the transmission of the text of the *MH* underwent many changes and transformations throughout Greco-Roman antiquity and the Byzantine period. A particularly relevant moment in its transmission was its incorporation into the minor scholia of the *Iliad* and the *Odyssey*. The process must have occurred sometime between the 5th century, to which the most recent papyrus fragments belong, and the 9th century, the date of the first manuscript of the minor scholia to the *Iliad* (De Marco 1932). Since there are no extant codices to the *MH* as a stand-alone work, we can presume that it ceased to circulate independently by the end of antiquity, and it has survived only amid the D-Scholia.

In short, the papyri reveal two basic facts: the first is that the *MH* remained an independent work over a long period (Montanari 1995a: 140–141), spanning, judging by the chronology, approximately five hundred years, from the end of the 1st century to the 5th century. The second is that its formal structure was typical of a *hypomnema* or commentary under lemmata. This led to its subsequent integration into the scholia, which share a formal structure with the early commentaries (Kenens 2012: 160–161).

## 2.  THE NATURE OF THE *MYTHOGRAPHUS HOMERICUS*: EXEGESIS AND MYTHOGRAPHY

All the *historiae* present the same structure: a lemma, a comment based on a myth, and a final reference to one or several authors (*subscriptio*), although the latter has not been preserved in every case. The original aim of this work seems to have been to interpret the text and mythical context of certain Homeric passages through the systematic use of summaries of myths. The *MH* can therefore be defined as an exegetical-mythographical work.

Thus, under a Homeric lemma, it provides an explanation based on a mythological plot or etiology (Pagès 2022). Let us consider an example of this. In *Iliad* 7.44 there is a reference to the fact that Helenus, son of Priam, knew the plans of the gods. The story told by the *MH* under this verse (*P.Oxy.* 3830 Luppe 1993; D-Schol. on *Il.* 7.44) explains why Helenus knew those plans: he had been granted the gift of prophecy by Apollo. But the *MH* goes on to narrate the whole myth about the origin of Helenus's and Cassandra's divinatory art, though this is not necessary to clarify the context of the passage.

We can see, then, how the *MH* interprets the words of Homer, which refer to an ancient episode in the epic tradition. In the archaic period, such a reference needed no explanation: the epic heritage was alive and well-known to the audience. Centuries later in imperial Roman times, readers were clearly not so acquainted with the Homeric contexts; nonetheless, every educated person was expected to know the Homeric poems, and so a work like the *MH* was essential, because it made up for Homer's silences.

However, the rationale for providing a *historia* that we have just seen for this particular case is not broadly applicable to the whole of the corpus. Many of the *historiae* are interested in more than explaining allusions in Homer, as we will see below in greater detail. For the moment, let us look at an example that is primarily interested in glossing a single term of the Homeric text, even when the lemma reflects a more extensive passage.

Under verse 39 of the first book of the *Iliad*, "Smintheus, if I ever built a shrine that pleased you," the Hamburg Papyrus 199, column 2, lines 27 to 30 (Kramer and Hagedorn 1984: 25–34) retains the principle of a *historia* that can be read in full in the corresponding scholion. Even though the lemma corresponds to the full quoted verse, the mythographical account only explains the origin of the Apollonian epithet "Smintheus." This *historia* recounts two different myths in order to provide an etymological explanation of the glossed term, by relating the epithet of Apollo to the pre-Hellenic term *sminthos*, "mouse." Consequently, we can say that the two myths outlined in this *historia* have nothing to do with the plot or with the mythic context of the passage mentioned. They simply would satisfy the curiosity of the reader who wondered why the priest Chryses resorts to advocating *Smintheus* to invoke Apollo, and what the origin of this advocation is.

These kinds of *historiae* are, therefore, not themselves explanations or interpretations of the Homeric passage transcribed in the lemma; rather, they are mythographical glosses—that is, summaries of myths that explain the meaning of a word. The information they provide may concern etymologies, prosopographies, etiologies, foundations and refoundations, or changes of name (*metonomasiae*) (Pagès 2022). The passage we have just quoted also serves as an example of a foundational myth and of an etiology: the two myths narrated under the aforementioned lemma also provide an account of the foundation of the shrine of Apollo Smintheus. As an example of a myth of refounding or name-changing (*metonomasia*), we will cite the *historia* about Tenes (D-Schol. on *Il.* 1.38; P. Hamb. 199 col. 1 1–18 Kramer and Hagedorn): the hero Tenes refounded the colony previously known as Leucophrys under a new name, Tenedos, derived from his own. As we can see, the recounted myth has nothing to do with the Homeric account. Certainly, Chalcas the priest is only mentioning the island of Tenedos as one of the places where Apollo is worshipped, but this has nothing to do with the founding hero called Tenes.

The interest of readers in erudite and encyclopedic information is, without doubt, the reason the text of the *MH*, and later the scholia, contain a large number of mythical accounts that, in fact, have nothing to do with the plot of the *Iliad* or the *Odyssey*, or even with specific references to other accounts that Homer refers to, such as the aforementioned myth of Tenes. We often notice that the Homeric lemma seems to be a simple pretext for a scholarly digression.

We have briefly described some significant cases. Now, from an overall perspective, we can establish a classification of the *MH*'s *historiae* depending on their content:

1. Homeric exegesis: the *historia* provides the mythical reference framework in the passages in which Homer refers to a myth without narrating it.
2. Contextual expansion: the *historia* "completes" Homer even when it is not necessary for understanding the text or its mythical context.
3. Paraphrase: in three cases, the summary of the myth is provided despite the fact that Homer narrates it *in extenso*: *historiae* of Phoenix (D-Schol. on *Il.* 9.447–448), Bellerophon (D-Schol. on *Il.* 6.155), and Thamyris (D-Schol. on *Il.* 2.595).
4. Comparison of Homer with more recent versions—that is, post-Homeric (*neoteroi*)—of the myth.
5. Mythographical excursuses suggested by a Homeric word: etymologies, prosopography, foundation myths, *aetia*.

This categorization is based on the relationship between the Homeric lemma and the story told by the *MH* on a gradual basis—namely, the first category implies a close relationship, while the fifth, being the loosest, does not. Surprisingly, the fifth one is the most common, proof that readers were interested in the plots themselves, regardless the Homeric context underlying the lemma. The five categories are complementary, not mutually exclusive.

# 3. The Problem of Sources

The relation between the *MH* and its ancient sources is very difficult to assess. Most of the citations are unspecific and provide only the bare name of an author. Furthermore, many stories lack author citation. We cannot know whether a source was cited at the end of every single story. Many citations were doubtlessly lost during the process of transmission. We do not even know whether the authors who are quoted are real sources or mere references: Is the *MH* revealing his sources or simply referring to a source to ensure the perception of the authenticity of the story told? Most of the authors are cited in the typical *subscriptio* at the end of the *historiae* (Montanari 1995a: 143–144, 154–164; van Rossum-Steenbeek 1998: 111–113; Cameron 2004: 50). The *subscriptio* usually adheres to one of the two equivalent formulae: "this author narrates it" (*historei*) or "the story is in the work of this author" (*historia para X*). The fragments on papyrus already demonstrate this.

A long list of cited authors appears in the papyri and the scholia. Hesiod is mentioned, as well as the epic cycle, under the name *kyklikoi*, "poets of the cycle" or *neoteroi*, "more recent ones"; two cyclic poets are even mentioned by name, Stasinus (Schol. on *Il.* 1.5) and Eumelus (6.130). Also, the archaic and classical lyric poets Stesichorus (Schol. on *Il.* 2.339), Alcman (Schol. on *Il.* 3.242), and Pindar (Schol. on *Il.* 3.243), and the early mythographers are often quoted, especially in the minor scholia to the *Odyssey*— namely, Acusilaus, Pherecydes, Hellanicus, Asclepiades, and so forth. We also find fragmentary historians, such as Theopompus of Chios, Philostephanus, Clitophon, and the Hellenistic poets Apollonius of Rhodes (only once, Schol. on *Il.* 1.264), Euphorion of Chalcis (D-Schol. on *Il.* 2.157; 212; 8.479; 14.295; 18.486; 24.602), Callimachus (*Aetia*, D-Schol. on *Il.* 2.145; 13.66; *Hecale*, D-Schol. on *Il.* 2.547; without title of work D-Schol. on *Il.* 2.629; 698; 17.53; 18.487), and Lycophron (D-Schol. on *Il.* 5.412; 16.36; 20.215; 24.251; V-Schol. on *Od.* 13.259; see also *PSI* 1179 fr. 7 verso 177). We also have other Hellenistic authors, such as Eratosthenes, and late-Hellenistic ones, such as Apollodorus of Athens and Didymus.

The absence of the tragic poets cited by name is surprising. Euripides is only mentioned once in a *historia* that seems to be an interpolation from the *Bibliotheca* of Ps-Apollodorus in the scholia (D-Schol. on *Il.* 14.323; Ps-Apollod. 3.4.3). There are very few collective references such as "the story is told by the tragedians" (V-Schol. on *Od.* 17.208). This absence seems to have been supplemented by consulting the work *Tragodumena* (*Tragic Plots*) by Asclepiades of Tragilus, a mythographer who is cited several times.

Some *subscriptiones* are not restricted to the aforementioned formulae. They cite not only the author but also the title of the work, including the book number. Let us examine some examples: "Philostephanus recounts it, as does Callimachus in *Aetia*" (D-Schol. on *Il.* 2.145); "Hesiod recounts it in *Catalogues* (D-Schol. on *Il.* 2.336); "the *historia* is narrated in the works of the *polemonioi* [*sic*], or cyclics, and partly in that of Alcman, the lyric poet" (D-Schol. on *Il*. 3.242); "many recall this *historia*, mainly Eumelus, author of the *Europia*" (D-Schol. on *Il*. 6.130). These citations are far more specific than the short formulae assessed above, and they might be traces of the original way of citing authors before abbreviation began to be used because of textual transmission.

Two of the examples transcribed are especially relevant because they contain a textual quotation from the work cited. Both occur at the beginning—namely, two *historiae* commenting on two passages from the first book of the *Iliad*, on verses 5 and 264. The substantial length of the quoted fragments is striking, as they comprise several verses of the work cited. These are the only two cases of a long textual quotation of the author cited in all the *MH* corpus.

The *historia* to *Iliad* 1.5 ends with the *subscriptio*, "the *historia* can be read in the work of Stasinus, author of the *Cypria*, which reads as follows: *when the innumerable tribes* etc." (Stasinus, *Cypria* fr. 1 Bernabé); on commenting on the Homeric words "Zeus' will," the *MH* narrates a story about the overcrowded Earth asking Zeus to start a war to relieve her of the weight of humanity. The *MH* ends the story with the textual citation from the *Cypria* that completes the plot.

The *historia* to *Iliad* 1.264 ends: "also recalled by Apollonius, author of *The Argonautica* (Ap. Rhod., *Argon*. 1.59–64), and says thus: *as the poets sing to Caeneus* etc." The summary from the *MH* explains the story of Caeneus, a former maiden who was turned into a man after sexual intercourse with Poseidon, and ends with Caeneus's fight against the centaurs and the way they defeated him despite his invulnerability. The passage quoted from Apollonius (1.59–64) recalls the motif of Caeneus's strength and invincibility.

Montanari (1995a: 154–164) articulated the view that in previous stages of the transmission of the text the presence of complex references and literal fragments transcribed from cited works had to be one of the original features of the *MH*. The trend toward simplifying and shortening the exegetical texts would have caused the suppression of textual fragments. The two cases assessed are probably what is left after the general suppression, unless we consider them interpolations in the D-Scholia. In view of this, the process of textual transmission tended to simplify the *subscriptiones* and the citations from sources to the extent of reducing them to the aforementioned formulae. There is, however, a major objection to Montanari's hypothesis: these two stories are not attested in the papyri. Therefore, there is no evidence of the presence of these two long quotations in the first stage of the tradition—namely, the *MH* prior to the scholia. They might have been added by the scholiast.

The question of the sources of the *MH* poses a host of problems, the main one being the reliability of the *subscriptiones*. Some scholars question the validity of these source citations and consider them to be mere learned scholarly references that come from intermediate sources, namely, prose summaries of epics and tragedy. Cameron suggests that some of them might have originated in school exercises consisting of memorizing the names of authors related to plots (Cameron 2004: 104–106). It is clear that this kind of assumption may be valid for a good number of *historiae*, but not for all of them: the *historiae* in D-Schol. on *Il*. 1.5 and 1.264 (assessed earlier) are summaries from real ancient sources since these sources are textually cited. A less radical and more cautious stance (Lünstedt 1961: 36; van der Valk 1964: 303–413; Montanari 1995a: 144) recommends analyzing each and every citation and refuses to accept that a valid general conclusion can be extracted for all of them. In most cases, the source cited is nothing more than the name of the author, as has been said. If moreover it is a fragmentary, little-documented, or even unknown writer, the analysis is impossible. Given these limitations, the question is highly complex.

The cases that allow a more thorough analysis are those in which the source cited is a preserved text. However, a simple reference to the author is of little use if we cannot identify the passage being referred to. In the cases where this is possible, it is disconcerting to discover that what the *MH* explains does not match or only partially matches the version from the cited source. This phenomenon poses a serious problem, since it is difficult to understand how the *MH* used sources. Thus, for example, in the *historia* preserved in the D-Scholion on *Iliad* 19.113 (van Thiel 2014: 535; Pagès 2011: 175–176), the *subscriptio* refers to Hesiod's *Theogony*, but the mythical version is different from that appearing in the work cited. Indeed, among other discrepancies, Styx is considered to be a daughter of Uranus, sister of the Titans, whereas in Hesiod's *Theogony* she is the daughter of Oceanus, one of the Titans. In addition, the story related here by the *MH* is not narrated in the *Theogony*. The use of an uncited intermediate source is indisputable here because the information provided is absent from the source cited, Hesiod's *Theogony*. Likely, in the uncited source, Hesiod's *Theogony* may have been quoted, even if this version differed from that of the *Theogony*. The uncited source plausibly related a divergent version and contrasted it with Hesiod's. The *MH* cites Hesiod indirectly, in an uncritical and passing way, without realizing that Hesiod's version was different. As a result, although *MH* summarizes a non-Hesiodic version of the myth, he ascribes it to Hesiod's *Theogony* because it was named by the uncited work. Probably, contrasting divergent versions and checking citations by consulting the original work cited was not part of the *MH*'s method.

In any case, citing Hesiod, although at second hand, adds legitimacy and prestige to the narrated *historia*, and makes it possible to conceal the use of a lesser or intermediary source. A similar case occurs in the *historia* at D-Schol. on *Il.* 2.336 and in Hesiod's *Catalogue* (fr. 33 M.-W.). In this *historia* the *MH* summarizes the war of Heracles against Periclymenus and the sons of Neleus in order to explain the origin of the epithet *Gerenios* in the Homeric formula *gerenios hippota Nestor* (Nestor, the Gerenian knight): at the time of that war, Nestor was too young the fight, and his father sent him to a people called the Gerenians. The story ends by citing Hesiod's *Catalogue*. The myth of Periclymenus can be read in fragment 33 of Hesiod's *Catalogue*; therefore, the *MH* seems to be referring to this passage. Nevertheless, the details match only partially, such that this *historia* can be considered another example of the way the *MH* employs citations of Hesiod.

But it is also possible some of the *subscriptiones* may refer not to the cited text but to the scholia on that text. In some cases this phenomenon can be seen because the cited text and its scholia are preserved. A very clear example is the *historia* about Aegialea (D-Schol. on *Il.* 5.412), which tells of the adultery of Aegialea, wife of Diomedes. If Lycophron (*Alex.* 610) refers cryptically to Aphrodite's punishment of Diomedes, who discovers upon returning from Troy that his wife has been unfaithful, the scholiast provides the full story. There is no doubt that the *MH* refers to the scholion that comments on this passage, and not to the text of Lycophron's poem. Ultimately, the fact of citing "Lycophron" should be understood as citing "the book of Lycophron" (which contained not only his poem but also its scholia).

We must bear in mind that, as was noted in section 2, "The Nature of the *MH*: Exegesis and Mythography," the text of the *MH* suffered multiple changes over several centuries of textual transmission during which the way of using and citing sources was also altered. As we have seen, it is possible that the oldest strata of the work provided complete references that included the name of the author, the title of the work, the book, and even the textual quotation that corroborated the direct consultation with the source. The cases of the *historiae* commented on regarding D-Schol. on *Il.* 1.5 and 1.264 may be good examples of this (unless we consider the author citation an addition of the scholiast). The fact that both *historiae* are undoubtedly exegetical in nature is highly significant in the way the two original features of the *MH* coincide: exegesis and the direct consultation of ancient sources. However, in later strata, and especially as the work gradually became more encyclopedic, with less exegetical content, the method of consulting sources gradually became less thorough. Secondary sources, more manageable and concise, began to be used: summaries (*hypotheses*) of cyclic epic poems, of tragedies, manuals and mythographical compendia, and even commentaries and scholia. Many source citations may have come from these intermediate, often unknown sources, meaning that, as we have seen, the author who is cited as an authority was in fact not directly consulted. The discrepancy in the versions seems to confirm this hypothesis (see, for instance, the case regarding the *Theogony* in the D-Schol. on *Il.* 19.113).

## 4. Mythical Versions

Based on what criteria did the *MH* choose one or another mythical version? This is also a difficult question to analyze. We might expect that the *MH* would simply opt for the version that is best-known and most coincident with well-known classical sources. However, with some frequency we encounter surprising, even odd, versions, some of which are only attested in the *MH*. Perhaps the clearest case of this is the *historia* that relates an aberrant version of the myth of Prometheus (D-Schol. on *Il.* 14.295). According to this version, Hera was raped by Eurymedon the giant and bore a son, Prometheus. It was for this reason, and not because of the theft of fire (that was a mere pretext) that Prometheus was fettered. The source cited is Euphorion of Chalcis (Pagès 2013: 253–256).

This apparent lack of consistency is surprising to the modern reader, who differentiates between the so-called canonical Panhellenic versions and local or regional ones that are absent from the classical canon and collected by antiquarian prose writers and Hellenistic poets. This categorization is perhaps just a modern distinction that would not have made sense to the mythographers. Homer, Hesiod, and the cyclic poets confer the same literary authority with their widely disseminated versions as Euphorion, Callimachus, and Lycophron do with their mythological rarities. The *MH* seems to concede equal legitimacy to all the sources it cites because it makes no distinctions. A large majority of the *historiae* contain a single version; very few examples of contrasting versions and different sources can be found (D-Schol. on *Il.* 14.319; nonetheless, it appears to be an addition by the scholiast).

Another of the problems presented by the *MH* is the contradiction arising from the fact that to explain Homer, post-Homeric myths are resorted to in some cases. This is yet another example of the loss of critical capacity as the text was expanded and modified by new hands. The aforementioned *historia* of Diomedes and Aegialea illustrates this phenomenon. In fact, the version provided is without doubt not only later than the *Iliad* but also contradicts the version told in it: Homer presents Aigialea to us as Diomedes's faithful and prudent wife, who waits for him at home while the war lasts. In contrast, the *historia* of the *MH* paints a picture of a treacherous adulteress, a figure more likely to derive from a later creation of the so-called *neoteroi*.

# 5. CONCLUSION

A thorough overall analysis of the corpus of the *historiae fabulares* makes it possible to affirm that the text of the *MH* originated as a mythographical exegesis whose aim was to provide the reader of the Homeric poems with a summary of all the myths that Homer referred to only briefly. Nonetheless, the original text did not remain intact: the work was rewritten throughout its transmission and progressively altered in accordance with the new demands of readers.

Judging by the chronology of the papyri, the *MH* circulated as a work of consultation that was independent from the editions of the text of the *Iliad* and the *Odyssey* throughout the Roman imperial era. This demonstrates the readers' interest in this kind of manual. Its use was doubtlessly based on two cultural requirements. The first and older of these was knowledge of the mythical context of the Homeric poems. The second, clearly secondary and a response to cultural demands, was the desire of the elites from the eastern part of the Roman Empire for encyclopedic erudition. A compilation of myths structured in accordance to Homeric lemmata (following the order of their appearance in Homer's poems) was interesting per se, to the extent that it made it possible to memorize brief summaries of literary motifs, something that must have been really useful, not only for schoolmasters but also for anyone wishing to display erudition at social events (Cameron 2004: 237–238).

Thus the text that we are able to restore based on the papyri and scholia is the result of a text that has evolved over several centuries. To understand this work, it is essential to bear in mind that we are not looking at a book that an author wrote and published at a given moment; rather, we are faced with two different phases in a long process of textual transmission: the papyri fragments provide evidence for the circulation of the *MH* during the imperial period, and the scholia show the reuse of the former by medieval commentators. The *MH* has therefore come down to us because it is a collective text whose authors knew how to adapt it gradually to new sociocultural contexts, so that at no time would interest in it be lost, because had that happened, it would not have survived.

## FURTHER READING

The existence of a Homeric mythographer was postulated by Panzer (1892), who was the first to use the name *Mythographus Homericus*. His thesis is based on the reading of the scholia from the perspective of studying the sources (*Quellenforschung*), a very common approach in 19th-century German criticism (Pàmias 2022). It was Pfeiffer (1937) who related Panzer's thesis to the mythographical scholia under Homeric lemmata revealed by the papyrus fragments that were discovered. Montanari (1995a) catalogued all the papyri attributable to the *MH*.

No edition of the *MH* as such has been published to date. As a result, one has to draw from recent online editions of the D-Scholia to the *Iliad* (van Thiel 2014) and to the *Odyssey* (Ernst 2006). It should be remembered that in the scholia the mythographical *historiae* are interspersed between various kinds of comments, which makes locating and reading specific passages difficult. The dissertation of Pagès (2007) may also prove useful, a *proecdosis* of the *MH* based on the manuscripts of the lesser scholia and the papyri. For editions of and studies about the papyri, see the works by Gärtner (1999); Grenfell and Hunt (1903); Haslam (1990, 1996); Kramer and Hagedorn (1984); Merkelbach (1956); Parsons (1974); Schubert (1995); and van Rossum-Steenbeek (1996; 1998: 278–311). In particular, see the several articles by Luppe (1984, 1993, 1996a–d, 1996–97, 1997a–b, 2009) on individual papyri in "References."

With regard to the nature of the *MH*, see Montanari (1995a); van Rossum-Steenbeek (1996: 85–118); Cameron (2004: 52–69); Pàmias and Villagra (2020), Pagès (2021).

Regarding the genre known as *hypomnema* (commentary), see Arrighetti (1968, 1977); Schironi (2012: 399–441, esp. 404–412).

In reference to the mythography in the D-Scholia to Homer and the so-called *historiae fabulares*, see Lünstedt (1961); van der Valk (1964); Arrighetti (1968, 1977); Montanari (1979, esp. 13–15; 1988; 1995b); Pagès (2005); Nünlist (2009: 257–264); and Montana and Montanari (2022). The majority of the studies focus basically on the *Iliad*. For the *Odyssey*, see Montanari (2002); Pontani (2005, esp. 3–7); Pontani (2022); and Villagra (2022).

As for the relationship between the *MH* and the *Library* of Pseudo-Apollodorus, see Diller (1935); van der Valk (1964); Fowler (2013: 378–384); Pagès (2017); and Michels (2022).

The recent volume by Pagès and Villagra (2022) gathers the papers delivered at the conference "The *Mythographus Homericus* 125 years after Panzer" held at Lisbon in 2017.

## REFERENCES

Arrighetti, Graziano. 1968. "Alcuni problemi di erudizione antica." *Studi Classici e Orientali* 26: 13–67.

Arrighetti, Graziano. 1977. "Hypomnemata e Scholia: Alcuni problemi." *Museum Philologicum Londinense* 2: 49–67.

Cameron, Alan. 2004. *Greek Mythography in the Roman World*. Oxford: Oxford University Press.

De Marco, Vittorio. 1932. "Sulla tradizione manoscritta degli *Scholia Minora* all'*Iliade*." *Atti della Reale Accademia Nazionale dei Lincei*. Ser. 6. 4: 373–407.

Dickey, Eleanor. 2007. *Ancient Greek Scholarship*. Oxford: Oxford University Press.

Diller, Aubrey. 1935. "The Text History of the Bibliotheca of Pseudo-Apollodorus." *Transactions and Proceedings of the American Philological Association* 66: 296–313.

Ernst, Nicola. 2006. "Die D-Scholien zur Odyssee." Diss. Universität zu Köhn. https://kups.ub.uni-koeln.de/1831/.

Fowler, Robert. 2013. *Early Greek Mythography*. Vol. 2. Oxford: Oxford University Press.

Gärtner, Thomas. 1999. "Zum Geschick der Pleiade Elektra im sogenannten *Mythographus Homericus* (*P.Oxy.* 4096) und bei Quintus von Smyrna." *Zeitschrift für Papyrologie und Epigraphik* 124: 22–24.

Grenfell, Bernard P., and Arthur S. Hunt, eds. 1903. "418. Scholia on Homer." *The Oxyrhynchus Papyri* 3: 63–65.

Haslam, Michael. 1990. "A New Papyrus of the *Mythographus Homericus*." *Bulletin of the American Society of Papyrologists* 27: 31–36.

Haslam, Michael. 1996. "On *P.Oxy.* LXI 4096, *Mythographus Homericus*." *Zeitschrift für Papyrologie und Epigraphik* 110: 115–117.

Kenens, Ulrike. 2012. "Greek Mythography at Work: The Story of Perseus from Pherecydes to Tzetzes." *Greek, Roman and Byzantine Studies* 52: 147–166.

Kramer, Bärbel, and Dieter Hagedorn, eds. 1984. *Griechische Papyri der Staats- und Universitätsbibliothek Hamburg* (P. Ham. III). Bonn: Habelt.

Lünstedt, Peter. 1961. *Untersuchungen zu den mythologischen Abschnitten der D-Scholien*. Diss. Universität zu Hamburg.

Luppe, Wolfgang. 1984. "Zum Tennes-Mythos im *Mythographus Homericus*, P. Hamb. 119." *Zeitschrift für Papyrologie und Epigraphik* 56: 31–32.

Luppe, Wolfgang. 1993. "Helenos' und Kassandras 'Berufung'." *Archiv für Papyrusforschung* 39: 9–11.

Luppe, Wolfgang. 1996a. "Die Ikarios-Sage im *Mythographus Homericus*." *Zeitschrift für Papyrologie und Epigraphik* 112: 29–33.

Luppe, Wolfgang. 1996b. "Ein neues Fragment des *Mythographus Homericus* zu Ψ 91.92." *Prometheus* 22 (2): 97–100.

Luppe, Wolfgang. 1996c. "*Mythographus Homericus P.Oxy.* 4096 fr. 10." *Zeitschrift für Papyrologie und Epigraphik* 112: 25–28.

Luppe, Wolfgang. 1996d. "Neileus' ἀποικία nach Milet: *Mythographus Homericus P.Oxy.* 4096 fr. 3." *Eikasmos* 7: 207–210.

Luppe, Wolfgang. 1996–1997. "Ein Zeugnis für die Niobe-Sage in *P.Oxy.* 4096." *Würzburger Jahrbücher fur die Altertumswissenschaft* 21: 153–159.

Luppe, Wolfgang. 1997a. "Die Psamathe- und die Plejaden-Sage im *Mythographus Homericus P.Oxy.* LXI 4096 fr. 1 und fr. 2 Kol. II." *Archiv für Papyrusforschung* 43 (1): 1–6.

Luppe, Wolfgang. 1997b. "Nachlese und Überlegungen zum *Mythographus-Homericus*-Codex P.S.I. 1173." *Zeitschrift für Papyrologie und Epigraphik* 116: 13–18.

Luppe, Wolfgang. 2009. "Zum neuen *Mythographus-Homericus*-Papyrus (PSI XV 1505)." *Prometheus* 35 (3): 219–220.

Merkelbach, Reinhold. 1956. "Literarische Texte unter Ausschluß der christlichen: P. Schubart 21." *Archiv für Papyrusforschung* 16: 117–119.

Michels, Johanna 2022. "The Varying Correspondence between the *MH* Corpus and 'Apollodorus' the Mythographer." In *Myth on the Margins of Homer. Prolegomena to the Mythographus Homericus* edited by Joan Pagès and Nereida Villagra, 133–156. Berlin and Boston: De Gruyter.

Montana, Fausto, and Franco Montanari. 2022. "The Ecdotic Problem of the *Mythographus Homericus*: Some Thoughts on the Scholiastic Side." In *Myth on the Margins of Homer. Prolegomena to the Mythographus Homericus*, edited by Joan Pagès and Nereida Villagra, 31–56. Berlin and Boston: De Gruyter.

Montanari, Franco. 1979. *Studi di filologia omerica antica I*. Biblioteca di Studi Antichi 19. Pisa: Giardini.

Montanari, Franco. 1984. "Revisione di PBerol 13282: Le *historiae fabulares* omeriche su papiro." In *Atti del XVII congresso internazionale di papirologia, Napoli 1983*, edited by Marcello Gigante, vol. 2, 229–242. Naples: Centro Internazionale per lo Studio dei Papiri Ercolanesi.

Montanari, Franco. 1988. "Filologia omerica antica nei papiri." In *Proceedings of the XVIII Congress of Papyrology, Athens 1986*, vol. 2, edited by Vasileios Mandilaras, 337–344. Athens: Greek Papyrological Society.

Montanari, Franco. 1995a. "The *Mythographus Homericus*." In *Greek Literary Theory after Aristotle: A Collection of Papers in Honour of D. M. Schenkeveld*, edited by Jelle G. J. Abbenes, Simon R. Slings, and Ineke Sluiter, 135–172. Amsterdam: VU University Press.

Montanari, Franco. 1995b. *Studi di Filologia Omerica Antica II*. Pisa, Italy: Giardini.

Montanari, Franco. 2002. "Ancora sul *Mythographus Homericus* (e l'Odissea)." In *La mythologie et l'Odyssée. Hommage à Gabriel Germain* edited by André Hurst and Françoise Létoublon, 129–144. Genève: Droz.

Nünlist, René. 2009. *The Ancient Critic at Work*. Cambridge, UK: Cambridge University Press.

Pagès, Joan. 2005. "Análisis del escolio D a Ilíada I 5: Una aproximación a la génesis del corpus." In *Actas del XI Congreso de la Sociedad Española de Estudios Clásicos*, vol. 2, edited by José F. González Castro, Antonio Alvar Ezquerra, Alberto Bernabé, Patricia Cañizares Ferriz, Gregorio Hinojo Andrés, and Celia Rueda González, 453–460. Madrid: Publicaciones de la Sociedad Española de Estudios Clásicos.

Pagès, Joan. 2007. "*Mythographus Homericus*: Estudi i edició comentada." Diss. Universitat Autònoma de Barcelona.

Pagès, Joan. 2011. "El origen del juramento estigio según el Mitógrafo Homérica." In *Parua Mythographica*, edited by Jordi Pàmias, 169–191. Oberhaid, Germany: Utopica.

Pagès, Joan. 2013. "Euphorion dans les scholies mythographiques à l'*Iliade*." In *Euphorion et les mythes: Images et fragments*, edited by Christophe Cusset, 247–264. Naples: Centre Jean Berard.

Pagès, Joan. 2017. "Apollodorus' *Bibliotheca* and the *Mythographus Homericus*: An Intertextual Approach." In *Apollodoriana: Ancient Myths, New Crossroads*, edited by Jordi Pàmias, 66–81. Berlin and Boston: De Gruyter.

Pagès, Joan. 2020. "Pélope en Lesbos: Análisis del escolio D a Ilíada 1.38 y el Papiro de Hamburgo 199 (*Mythographus Homericus*)." *Polymnia* 5: 1–19.

Pagès, Joan. 2021. "La mitografía como exégesis homérica: Estudio de algunos ejemplos del *Mythographus Homericus* y los escolios menores a Homero." *Emerita* 89: 1–26 (1).

Pagès, Joan. 2022. "Aetia and Foundation Myth in the *Mythographus Homericus*: Some Examples from the Papyri." In *Myths on the Margins of Homer. Prolegomena to the Mythographus Homericus*, edited by Joan Pagès and Nereida Villagra, 75–107. Berlin and Boston: De Gruyter.

Pagès, Joan and Villagra, Nereida. 2022. *Myths on the Margins of Homer. Prolegomena to the Mythographus Homericus.* Berlin and Boston: De Gruyter.

Pàmias, Jordi. 2022. "Panzer, the *Mythographus Homericus*, and fin de siècle German Scholarship." In *Myths on the Margins of Homer. Prolegomena to the Mythographus Homericus*, edited by Joan Pagès and Nereida Villagra, 17–27. Berlin and Boston: De Gruyter.

Pàmias, Jordi, and Nereida Villagra. 2020. "Los escolios mitográficos y el *Mythographus Homericus.*" Polymnia 5: 20–38.

Panzer, Johannes. 1892. "De Mythographo Homerico restituendo." Diss. University of Greifswald.

Parsons, Peter J. 1974. "3003. Homeric Narratives." *The Oxyrhynchus Papyri* 42: 15–19.

Pfeiffer, Rudolf. 1937. "Hesiodisches und Homerisches: Zu neuen und alten Papyri." *Philologus* 92: 1–18.

Pontani, Filippomaria. 2005. *Sguardi su Ulisse: La tradizione esegetica greca all'Odissea.* Rome: Edizioni di Storia e Letteratura.

Pontani, Filippomaria. 2022. "Notes on the Manuscript Transmission of Some Fragments of the *Mythographus Homericus* on the *Odyssey.*" In *Myths on the Margins of Homer. Prolegomena to the Mythographus Homericus*, edited by Joan Pagès and Nereida Villagra, 57–71. Berlin and Boston: De Gruyter.

Schironi, Francesca. 2012. "Greek Commentaries." *Dead Sea Discoveries* 19: 399–441.

Schubert, Paul. 1995. "4096. *Mythographus Homericus.*" *The Oxyrhynchus Papyri* 61: 15–46.

van Rossum-Steenbeek, Monique. 1996. "More on *P.Oxy.* LXI 4096, *Mythographus Homericus.*" *Zeitschrift für Papyrologie und Epigraphik* 113: 24–26.

van Rossum-Steenbeek, Monique. 1998. *Greek Reader's Digests? Studies on a Selection of Subliterary Papyri.* Leiden and New York: Brill.

van Thiel, Helmut, ed. 2014. *Scholia D in Iliadem: Proecdosis aucta et correctior secundum codices manuscriptos.* Cologne, Germany: Elektronische Schriftenreihe der Universitäts- und Stadtbibliothek. https://kups.ub.uni-koeln.de/5586/.

van der Valk, Marchinus. 1964. *Researches on the Text and Scholia of the Iliad.* Vol. 2. Leiden: Brill.

Villagra, Nereida. 2022. "Towards an Edition and Commentary of the *MH* to the Odyssey." In *Myths on the Margins of Homer. Prolegomena to the Mythographus Homericus*, edited by Joan Pagès and Nereida Villagra, 109–130. Berlin and Boston: De Gruyter.

# CHAPTER 17

# OTHER MYTHOGRAPHY
# ON PAPYRUS

## ANNETTE HARDER

MYTHOGRAPHY has been roughly defined as literature that tells, collects, and interprets myths, independently from their original literary and religious contexts, so that the mythological knowledge becomes available without the restrictions of time and place (Fornaro and Heinze 2000).[1] The corpus of this kind of material on papyrus must have been considerable: we now have a large number of papyri of mythographical works, and many of them must once have been part of a (much) longer work that is now lost, as Fowler noted in his introduction to *P.Oxy.* 61.4097 (1995: 47): "[T]hese very papyri demonstrate how much mythography has vanished without trace." Thus, the papyri offer a good indication of what must have been available in antiquity and of the importance of mythography in the world of scholarship and literary criticism and in the more popularizing traditions and education, and in society in general.

I will first give a description of the various forms of mythography and their contents (section 1, "Forms and Contents of Mythographical Papyri") and then discuss the function of these texts in society (section 2, "Mythographical Papyri in Context"). The brief compass of the chapter does not allow room for mentioning all instances of a given kind of papyrus, so I mention only representative examples; further parallels can often be found in the *editio princeps* of the papyri and in the literature cited in "References."

## 1. FORMS AND CONTENTS
## OF MYTHOGRAPHICAL PAPYRI

There are a number of larger papyri, which help us to form a picture of the various forms of mythographical papyri. Excluding the stories of the *Mythographus Homericus*, dealt with in a separate chapter (see Pagès, this volume), one may roughly distinguish two

---

[1] I wish to thank my student Anne Meijer for all her help in collecting the material for this chapter.

major groups: *narratives* (which apart from "stories" also include *aitia*, genealogies, etymologies, or other kinds of scholarly information) and all kinds of *lists and catalogues*. The specific group to which a mythographical papyrus belongs, however, cannot always be established with certainty, because many scraps are too small to form a clear judgment. Besides, we cannot be certain that these two forms were completely distinct. As we can see in the *Fabulae* of Hyginus, one and the same mythographical work might contain lists as well as narratives. In fact, we have a papyrus that has a similar format in *P.Oxy.* 53.3702, which contains lists of the heroes fighting against Troy, the suitors of Penelope, and the Argonauts, but also the story of the Danaids, possibly followed by a list (as in Ps.-Apollod. 2.15–20 (2.1.5); Hyg. *Fab.* 168 and 170). Alternatively, lists may also have been incorporated in narrative works, as in *P.Oxy.* 8.1084. Narratives, in turn, are not necessarily part of a longer narrative work (similar to, for instance, the *Bibliotheca* of Ps.-Apollodorus), but can also be part of collections of summaries of literary works (see, further, section 2.1 below, "Practical Uses") or of commentaries, which often contained stories or summaries of part of the work they were commenting on. Such narratives can be found, for instance, in the *Scholia Florentina* on Callimachus's *Aetia* (for example, the story of the Charites at Paros in fr. 7a) and in *P.Oxy.* 37.2812, probably from a commentary on a tragic text and containing a long passage about Poseidon and Apollo working for Laomedon, which may be paraphrasing Apollodorus of Athens's *Peri Theon* (see Rusten 1982: 30–53). Other examples are *P.Oxy.* 24.2390 from a commentary on Alcman, containing the story of the Dioscuri and the daughters of Leucippus, and *P.Würzb.* 1 from a commentary on Euripides *Phoenissae* with passages about Tydeus, Cadmus, and Oedipus.

Apart from the lists and narratives, there are a few other kinds of mythographical papyri, such as commentaries, scholarly monographs, and catechisms, which will be dealt with separately.

## 1.1  Narratives

The narratives on papyrus are generally short and give only the outlines of the stories without reference to a narrator, but these papyri can be embedded in the Greek literary tradition in various ways. In the first place, some papyri contain summaries of earlier literary works, like *P.Ryl.* 1.22 + *P.Yale* 2.110, which overlaps with the story of the *Ilias Parva*. In some instances, we have the remains of collections of such summaries, such as the *hypotheseis* of Euripidean plays (the *Tales from Euripides*) in *P.Oxy.* 27.2455, and the *Diegeseis* of the works of Callimachus in *P.Mil.Vogl.* 1.18 (discussed by van Rossum-Steenbeek 1997: 1–84; Cameron 2004: 52–69). In other cases, we have fragments from only one story and cannot be sure whether it is from a collection of summaries or was part of a commentary or a larger narrative work, where such summaries could be incorporated into the larger framework, as in the *Bibliotheca* of Ps.-Apollodorus; an example of this kind of ambiguity is *P.Amst.* 1.7, which tells the story of Euripides's *Peliades* (see also Sijpesteijn 1972: 108). Secondly, though the majority of the papyri are anonymous, some papyri have been attributed to or connected with specific authors (as with some of the lists, see section 2.2, "Preserving Mythical Knowledge "). Thus, *PSI* 9.1091 about the Seven against Thebes, which is written in a Doric dialect with poetic forms, has been connected with the *Argolica* of Hagias and Dercylus or works in a similar Argive tradition (see Cassio 1989). A special "non-anonymous" case is *P.Oxy.* 52.3648, which contains remains from the collection of the *Diegeseis* of Conon written in the late 1st century BCE–early 1st century CE, of which an epitome had been preserved by Photius in his *Bibliotheca* (see Henrichs 1987: 244–247; Brown 2002; Higbie 2007: 249). Conon turned the mythographical material into a small collection of stories, written with some literary pretensions, and a small portion either of his original text (or of an early variant of it) is preserved on the back of a land register from the 2nd century CE. And in the third place, in several papyri we can also observe a close connection to the later mythographical tradition in nonpapyrological sources (again, as with the lists). Thus *PSI* 14.1398 about the death of Tiresias is similar to Ps.-Apollodorus 3.84 (3.7.3) and *P.Giss.Univ.* 4.42 about Heracles, and Megara recalls, for example, Ps.-Apollodorus 2.69–70 (2.4.11).

Although all papyri are clearly part of the Greek cultural tradition, the degree of scholarly knowledge and erudition in the fragments varies. Often, we find only the basic outlines of well-attested stories, but sometimes, a fragment may contain a version that is not found elsewhere, as in *P.Vindob.Gr.* 23058 (edited by Rabbie and Sijpesteijn 1988), a narrative about the Perseids containing new information, different from Ps.-Apollodorus 2.52–53 (2.4.5–6). Also *P.Lips.* inv. 1390 with the stories of Perseus, Bellerophontes, and Hyrieus offers new material, and according to its editors, may be from a mythological handbook ordered alphabetically by the names of parts of Greece because it deals with Argolis and Boeotia (see Luppe and Scholl 2001: 18). In other instances, the text may contain quotations of sources, as in *P.Oxy.* 76.5094, which deals with the genealogy of Dymas and refers to the *Cypria* and to Demetrius of Scepsis. Thus, some papyri offer glimpses of a world of now lost material and scholarship from which the information was drawn.

## 1.2 Lists and Catalogues

Lists and catalogues are found in a relatively large number of papyri (discussed by Henrichs 1987: 248–254; van Rossum-Steenbeek 1997: 119–156; Cameron 2004: 238–249). These papyri are part of a tradition of collecting and ordering mythographical knowledge that runs through all periods of antiquity. We find it first in Homer and Hesiod, but the list of contributors to this tradition includes many later poets, as well as names like Aristotle, Apollodorus, Pliny, Hyginus, and local historiographers, who include information about the area they describe. The principles of organization are rather loose; we can sometimes detect numbers (*P.Yale* 2.108), an alphabetic arrangement (*P. Mil.Vogl.* 3.126, and perhaps *P.Oxy.* 61.4098), or perhaps the decreasing importance of the elements (*P.Oxy.* 65.4460).

As to their place in the literary and scholarly tradition, several groups of lists can be distinguished. Some lists have been (tentatively) attributed to known authors. For example, *P.Oxy.* 8.1084, with a list of the daughters of Atlas, their divine lovers, and their offspring, has been attributed to Hellanicus's *Atlantis* (= fr. 19b Fowler; see Thomas 2007). Other lists can be related to earlier literary sources, such as the Hesiodic *Catalogues* and catalogues in epic poetry, of which they seem to be brief excerpts. Thus *P.Vindob.Gr.* 26727 has been related to Hes. fr. 10(e) about the Aeolids (see Itgenshorst 1997: 192); and the list of the children of goddesses and mortal men in *P.Oxy.* 62.4308 recalls Hes. *Th.* 975–1018. Yet another group of papyri show similarities to the mythographical handbooks of later times, such as Ps.-Apollodorus's *Bibliotheca* and, particularly, Hyginus's *Fabulae* (which also clearly go back on earlier traditions; see Cameron 2004: 34). A good example is *P.Oxy.* 62.4306, which contains a series of lists on various subjects: first sacrificers, first builders of temples, epithets of goddesses, metamorphoses of women, sons of gods and mortal women, first inventors, founders of games, victors in games, murderers tried on the Areopagus, and oracles. These lists are very similar to the *indices* in Hyginus, *Fab.* 221–277, and were probably part of a similar kind of mythographical handbook. Other examples are *P.Oxy.* 61.4097, with lists of the Argonauts and hunters of the Calydonian boar, which are close to Hyginus, *Fab.* 14 and 173, Ps.-Apollodorus 1.67–68 (1.8.2), and a similar list in *P.Oxy.* 53.3702; *P.Strasb.* WG 332 (a list of Muses and their families and of victors in the funeral games for Pelias, edited by Schwartz 1957); *P.Oxy.* 62.4307 (about mothers killing their sons, like Hyg. *Fab.* 239).

The amount of knowledge displayed in the lists varies. Some lists are very simple and offer a bare minimum of information, for example, *P.Harris* 1.49 (places and festivals); *P.Yale* 2.108 (games); *P.Oxy.* 61.4098 (people killed by Heracles). Other lists give evidence of more advanced scholarship, such as *P.Corn.* 55, a list of men and their fathers and their connections with the gods, which mentions several traditions concerning the parents of Triptolemus (see Bonnechère 2006, who argues that this is a learned catalogue rather than a school text) and *P.Oxy.* 62.4306, which mentions alternative traditions in fr. 1 col. 1.17 and quotes several sources, for example, Hesiod in fr. 1 col. 2.7–11 and Homer in fr. 1 col. 2.13–17. Occasionally, the lists offer a mixture of mythological and historical information, as in *P.Oxy.* 10.1241.

## 1.3  Other Forms

Some mythographical papyri are neither lists nor narratives but may be connected with the tradition of commentaries or monographs on specific texts. Examples of this group are *P.Oxy.* 62.4309, a learned work with many quotations, which seems to be quite close to the work on the Homeric catalogue of ships by Apollodorus of Athens, and *P.Nic.* inv. 72, which contains a description of Trojan topography in relation to the *Iliad*, referring to the wall of Heracles (*Il.* 20.144–152) and the flight of Hector around the walls of Troy and may be connected with the work of scholars such as Demetrius of Scepsis, on the Trojan allies; Polemon of Ilium; or Hellanicus (Trachsel and Schubert 1999). Apart from these papyri that look like parts of monographs, there are also remains of more basic commentaries and of works in the lexicographical sphere, which give much attention to mythography. For instance, the commentary on Alcman in *P.Oxy.* 24.2389 gives information about the daughters of Leucippus and the Dioscuri and on the parents of the Muses; *P.Berol.* 1970 explains Homeric epithets in the order in which the heroes concerned appear in the *Iliad* (see Luppe and Poethke 1998: 209–213); *P.Oxy.* 15.1802 + 71.4812 is an alphabetic lexicon containing much mythographical material, but also explanations of obscure words (see Esposito 2009; Schironi 2009; West 2014); and *PSI* inv. 155 is from a list of proverbs with mythological explanations (see Salvadori Baldascino 1988; Dorandi 2006).

A few papyri have a different format altogether, such as a sequence of questions and answers. This suggests an overtly didactic aim and relates these papyri to works like Aristotle's *Problemata*, Callimachus's *Aetia* 1–2, and Plutarch's *Quaestiones Graecae* and *Quaestiones Romanae*. *P.Oxy.* 34.2688 contains a series of questions and answers on various mythological and religious subjects. It mentions, for instance, a temple of Paphian Aphrodite, Hermes and his *caduceus*, and a tomb in Argos. *P.Oxy.* 34.2689 is somewhat more carefully executed but contains a similar catechism and also includes Aphrodite at Paphos and Hermes and the *caduceus*. As Rea (1968: 26–27) argued in the introduction to the *editio princeps* of these papyri, the fact that we seem to have two versions of this catechism suggests that the work enjoyed a certain popularity in Oxyrhynchus. Another example is *PSI* 1.19, which has questions and answers about the Trojan War, where the basic level of the questions would fit a school text (see also 2.1 below).

Other works are hard to place in a certain category, such as *P.Ryl.* 1.40, which contains a learned discussion about myth and nature and mentions several mythological characters. The text is also atypical in that there is an author who refers to himself in the first person as "I" and speaks of "us Greeks" (see Luppe 1997).

# 2. Mythographical Papyri in Context

## 2.1 Practical Uses

Many lists and narratives may be considered "subliterary" in the sense that in one way or another they can be related to literary texts. In this respect, van Rossum-Steenbeek (1997: xiv–xv) quotes a few interesting and useful passages, relevant for understanding the use of mythographical narratives: an epigram from the introduction to the *Bibliotheca* of Ps.-Apollodorus, quoted by Photius (*Bibl.* 186), which tells the reader to ignore the literary works of the past and to read Ps.-Apollodorus instead, and a passage from the introduction of Parthenius's *Erotica Pathemata* (Lightfoot 1999: 308–309; also discussed by Higbie 2007: 246; and see Francese, this volume), who explains that he is offering material from the works of older poets for new poets like Gallus. These passages are particularly enlightening for the papyri with *hypotheseis* and *diegeseis* and justify van Rossum-Steenbeek's use of the term "readers' digests" (another relevant passage is a request for prose summaries in a papyrus letter in *P.Oxy.* 18.2192, discussed by Cameron 2004: 59). Apparently these works could be used to replace the reading of the originals, either to give later poets quick access to their material for further use or to give readers a shortcut to the literary works of earlier generations and hence to Greek culture of the archaic, classical, and Hellenistic period. A possible example of material used by a poet is *P.Turner* 11, about the spring-nymph Cyane changed into a fountain, which recalls Ovid, *Met.* 5.409–437. However, the fragment is somewhat atypical, as it has direct speech at the beginning and the end, which suggests a longer narrative than is usual in mythographical texts, and Luppe 2001 suggests that the fragment is from a novel. In Callimachus, *Aetia* fr. 75.54–77 we have an example of a poet describing his use of mythographical material and turning the prose text into an elegiac summary.

Lists, too, probably had a practical use. The evidence shows how, through these lists and the handbooks that incorporated them, the earlier tradition became widely available and was then used by later authors for their own purposes. On the one hand, the lists may be directly related to earlier, more elaborate texts of authors like Hesiod and serve as a shortcut to these works; on the other hand, they can serve as lists of *exempla* to be used by prose authors whose work was not primarily mythographical or by poets. A good example is *P.Oxy.* 62.4308 with a list of the children of goddesses and mortal men. This list can be related to earlier sources (Hes. *Th.* 975–1018) but was apparently part of a widespread tradition as it can also be related to later handbooks (Hyg. *Fab.* 233) and other lists in papyri (for example, *P.Mil.Vogl.* 3.126; *P.Strasb.* WG 332). A similar list of goddesses and mortal men in *P.Oxy.* 62.4308 may be the kind of material used in Clement of Alexandria, *Protr.* 2.33.8–9, and the list of games in *P.Yale* 2.108 recalls Clement, *Protr.* 2.34; Pliny, *NH* 7.205; Hyginus, *Fab.* 273 (for similar observations on *P.Mil.Vogl.* 3.126, see Parsons 1966: 673–674). An example of a list related to the work of poets may be found, for example, in *P.Med.* inv. 123, with a list of the dogs of Actaeon, which is similar to Hyginus, *Fab.* 181 and may provide the kind of text used as a source by poets such as Ovid in *Met.* 3.10–214 (see Daris 1970). The catalogue of Apollo, Dionysus, and Heracles and their young lovers in the elegiac poem in *P.Oxy.* 54.3723 may go back on a similar source.

At another level a number of mythographical papyri, written in so-called schoolhands, can be related to schools and education (for a full treatment of this subject, see Cribiore 1996), and they may have played an important role in helping pupils "to acquire . . . the mythological knowledge that was necessary to participate in the prerogatives of the Graeco-Roman elite" (Huys 2013: 131). At a basic level, these papyri may contain mythical names that were written a few times as part of a writing exercise, as in *P.Vindob. Gr.* 26011k (see Harrauer and Sijpesteijn 1985: 42–43). On a more advanced level, these papyri can contain narratives of mythical stories or lists and recall the task of teachers of literature described by Tertullian (*De idol.* 10.1): "They have to preach the gods of the gentiles, and tell their names, genealogies, stories and every one of their trappings and honors." An example of lists in a school context is *P.Oxy.* 65.4460 with lists of *Iliadic* heroes and gods and some genealogical information, discussed and compared to similar lists in school contexts by T. Schmidt in the introduction to the *editio princeps*. Also *P.Oxy.* 61.4099, containing a mixture of lists and *sententiae*, seems to belong to this category, as argued by Huys (1996: 211): "Perhaps the manual was destined from the beginning for use in schools, and contained also some non-mythological texts to be memorized by the pupils, or else was quickly interpolated with these elements . . . At any rate our papyrus may have been one particular excerpt of a manual in the vein of the *Fabulae* adapted to classroom practice" (1996: 211, see note 11 for further examples of school papyri containing a combination of mythological and genealogical material and *sententiae*). Narrative papyri from a school context are *P.Strasb.*G 1352 (*BIFAO* 61 [1962] 174), a narrative about the Trojan War, where the hand suggests a school text, and *P.Mich.* inv. 1319. The Michigan papyrus shows that the first stage of education, when writing and spelling were taught, could make use of mythographical material and that, interestingly, in this case the material was also part of the *Tales from Euripides* (see Harder 1979; Huys 2013: 122). An example of a school text at a more advanced level is found in a papyrus from the Fayum, which seems to have contained a paraphrase of a poem, offering an example of a well-known exercise in literary education (edited by Barns 1949: 1–3, without inventory number). Also *P.Mil.Vogl.* 3.123 with remains of encomia of mythological characters like Minos, Rhadamanthys and Tydeus may be related to educational practice and for the papyri with questions and answers Epictetus, *Diss.* 2.19.6–7, about a series of questions about the Trojans as part of the job of a *grammaticus*, suggests a school context (for further evidence and discussion see Smith and Trzaskoma, this volume, on education).

Although strictly speaking, the description above applies to Egypt, where the papyri were found, there are links to Roman culture in several of the examples discussed and it may be relevant to compare the results with Cameron's (2004: 217–252, 253–303) conclusions about the importance of mythological knowledge in Roman society, for instance, for poets and orators, for understanding visual art, and in political contacts. *Mutatis mutandis* much of what is said there would help to explain the use and importance of the papyri.

## 2.2 Preserving Mythical Knowledge

Most mythographical papyri refer to myths that are well known from earlier Greek literature, and taken together, the papyri offer a good picture of the wide range of mythographical knowledge still available in later centuries. By means of their contents, which are thus embedded in the Greek cultural tradition, these works helped to keep this tradition alive at various levels. Even so, there are hints of a certain selection, as a majority of the papyri concern Homer and the Trojan War (fitting in with the observations about the scholarly attention on Homer in mythography in Higbie 2007: 250–251). These "Homeric" papyri may refer to basic facts about the stories, but also contain links with the scholarly discourse on Homeric geography and topography, as well as vocabulary. We find, for example, a history of the Trojan War in *P.Vindob.* Gr. 29790 (*MPER* NS 1.18 (1932) 132–133), a description of the geography of the travels of Odysseus in *P.Mich.*

18.760 and of Trojan topography in *P.Nic.* inv. 72, and explanations of Homeric epithets in *P.Berol.* 1970. These papyri show how Homer and the Trojan War were at a relatively late date still an important part of the mythographical tradition.

This becomes particularly clear when we compare the evidence on Homer with what the papyri offer about other important groups of myths, also prominent in earlier literature but not partaking in the authority of Homer, such as Theban and Argive myths, Argonaut myths, and the story of Heracles. Here the results are limited to simple narratives and lists, and the number of papyri dealing with these myths is considerably smaller. For Theban myth, one may, for example, compare *PSI* 9.1091 about the Seven against Thebes, *P.Oxy.* 61.4099 with a list of the Epigoni, and *PSI* 14.1398 about the death of Tiresias; for Argive myth, *P.Oxy.* 53.3702 and *P.Hibeh* 2.221 about the Danaids, *P.Köln* 7.285 about the daughters of Proetus, and *P.Vindob. Gr.* 23058 about the Perseids and Heracles; for the Argonauts, *P.Hibeh* 2.186 about Jason and Heracles in Colchis, *P.Oxy.* 53.3702 and 61.4097 containing some lists of Argonauts, and *P.Amst.* 1.7 about the daughters of Pelias (?); for Heracles, *P.Petrie* 2.49 about Heracles in Arcadia, *ChLA* 5.304 about Heracles and Eurystheus (a Latin papyrus), *P.Giss.* 4.42 about Heracles and Megara, and *P.Oxy.* 61.4098 about people killed by Heracles.

There is still, however, evidence of wide and varied mythical knowledge in several of the papyri with lists, for example, *P.Oxy.* 62.4306 with its rich variety of lists (see 1.2), and in papyri dealing with more obscure aspects of myths, such as *P.Berol.* 13426 (Schubart in Gercke and Norden 1924: 42–43) about a version of the story of Orpheus not attested elsewhere. Here much earlier material, also from local traditions, seems to have been digested. Apart from the various groups of myths, other texts deal particularly with gods in lists, treatises, or narratives. Thus *P.Oxy.* 8.1084 offers a list of the sons born of the daughters of Atlas who mated with gods; *P.Mil.Vogl.* 2.43 discusses the relative power of Zeus, Poseidon, and Hades; and *P.Vindob. Gr.* 29381 (*MPER* N.S. 3.44, 1939, 71–72) offers an allegorical discussion of Dionysus. In *P.Oxy.* 37.2812 (perhaps part of a commentary), the story of Apollo, Poseidon, and Laomedon is told.

## 2.3  Style, Handwriting, and Format

The prose style in these papyri is sober and the information is generally restricted to the bare facts in lists or the outlines of narrative plots. This suggests that the texts were meant for practical use rather than esthetic pleasure (see also Cameron 2004: 217, who observes that the people who used these texts "needed to know the basic facts. It was the modest task of the mythographer to supply those facts"; Higbie 2007: 239). The texts generally show no signs of a narrator, but there is an exception in *P.Oxy.* 53.3702, where we find a first-person announcement directed to a reader in fr. 1 col. 2.37–38, and in *P.Mich.* 18.762, where the author refers to himself. There may also be an instance of direct speech in *P.Turner* 11 (if this is mythography; see section 2.1, "Practical Uses," above) and of indirect speech in a Fayum papyrus which may be part of a paraphrase of a poem (col. 2.5 and 2.15; see also 2.1).

A small number of mythographical papyri are in formal and careful literary hands, but these are exceptional. Only occasionally do we get glimpses of somewhat more ambitious mythographical works in a careful literary handwritten along the fibers, such as *P.Oxy.* 8.865 or *P.Nic.* inv. 72, on which Trachsel and Schubert (1999: 236–237) remark that the latter was a more scholarly work intended for educated readers of the *Iliad*. Most papyri are described by their editors as being in informal hands, which may show the characteristics of a proficient scribe, but often also contain cursive elements. The texts are sometimes written along the fibers with no text on the back, such as *P.Oxy.* 62.4307 and *P.Mil.Vogl.* 3.126, but quite a few of the papyri, including some in more formal hands, are written on the backs of documents, such as *P.Corn.* 55 and *PSI* 14.1398. A smaller number of papyri are in school hands, which are sometimes clearly unskilled or clumsy, for example *P.Strasb.* G 1352, and sometimes a little more experienced, such as *P.Vindob. Gr.* 29790. Occasionally papyri give the impression of a kind of "collective volumes," serving as a personal notebook, with mixed contents, such as *P.Heid.* 4.289, which contains some (possibly) mythographical prose and the beginning of the *Iliad* (see Papathomas 2009), and *P.Berol.* inv. 9571 (see Schubart 1941; Del Corno 1974), which contains a (learned) text about Dionysus and dithyramb on the back of a document and a discussion of the days of the *Odyssey* on the front (written below and between the columns of the document). Some other papyri with miscellaneous contents are *P.Oslo* 2.12 and *PSI* 1.18 and 19.

This small survey shows that, generally speaking, the mythographical texts were not the kind of texts of which one made prestigious editions. The papyri suggest, on the one hand, that they were used in schools, and on the other hand, that they could be used for immediate intellectual or other purposes, without the need to preserve them in a well-made edition, as one would more readily do with literary texts. The general format and layout of many of these papyri fits in with the informality of the hands and unpretentious editions, as Fowler (1995: 46) in the *editio princeps* of *P.Oxy.* 61.4097 remarks about the papyri with lists: "[T]ypically these books move abruptly from topic to topic, providing the reader at most with a heading at the start of a new section; they may not be greatly concerned with such niceties of production as the alignment of columns."

## 2.4 Time and Place

Only a few mythographical papyri are from the pre-Christian area, but among these the 3rd century BCE is relatively well represented, with at least four papyri (*P.Hibeh* 2.221; *P.Hibeh* 2.186; *P.Petrie* 2.49; *P.Mil.Vogl.* 3.123). Then there are many papyri from the 1st to the 3rd centuries CE and only a few papyri attributed to the 4th and 5th centuries CE. Even allowing for the fact that there are considerably fewer papyri from the Ptolemaic period than from the first few centuries CE, this state of affairs is striking, as is the abrupt decline after the 3rd century CE, which is not quite the end of papyrus finds as such (but fits in with the end of the flourishing of mythography; see Higbie 2007: 238). One may wonder whether mythography flourished particularly under the cultural conditions of the early Hellenistic period and of first three centuries CE, when the Second Sophistic revived the interest in the ancient Greek tradition. However, this is only a tentative suggestion; the evidence for the Ptolemaic period seems too scant to draw firm conclusions, and concerning the Christian area, further research on the papyri in their cultural context would be required.

As would be expected most mythographical papyri are from Oxyrhynchus, but we also have papyri from other places, including Philadelphia, Tebtynis, Hermoupolis, and Karanis. Apparently, the interest in this kind of material in Roman Egypt was fairly widespread.

# 3. CONCLUSION

Altogether, one can say that the variety of the mythographical material on papyri and the glimpses we are able to get of their use and context confirm the idea of Trzaskoma and Smith (2013: xxii), who speak about "creative mythography" as an active response to specific needs of later periods rather than a passive or degenerate collection of earlier material. This brief survey has shown that there are several forms of mythographical papyri: mainly narratives and lists or catalogues, but also other forms such as catechisms and learned monographs. The texts are generally well embedded in the Greek literary and scholarly tradition, because they may summarize the work of earlier authors or show similarity to later mythographical and scholarly work (or both). It has also become clear that these texts had several practical uses: for readers who needed a shortcut to earlier literature; for authors of prose and poetry, who used the mythographical material in their own works; and in schools, where mythography could be used at various levels in the educational system. As to the contents, there is a certain focus on stories and information related to Homer and the Trojan War, whereas other groups of myths are also represented, but to a lesser extent. On the other hand, there are also glimpses of knowledge that is otherwise lost. Not surprisingly, given the practical purpose of the papyri, the style of the texts is generally sober, and so is the layout of the papyri, which are often in informal hands and written on the back of documents. A striking fact is the distribution of the papyri in time, particularly the abrupt decline after the 3rd century CE.

Several of the these conclusions could benefit from refinement by means of further research. Particularly, the practical use that was made of the mythographical information and the way in which these texts are embedded in the Greek tradition, and helping to keep it alive across the generations would be worth exploring more systematically, to help us refine our views of the transmission and ongoing relevance of Greek culture in Hellenistic and Roman Egypt, both as intellectual capital for its own sake and as a means to establish a Greek identity and acquire social status in the new Graeco-Roman world. A careful analysis of grammar, style, contents, and connections with other texts should form the basis for this research, but the physical aspects of the papyri should also be taken into consideration, including the distribution of the papyrus finds across time and small-scale, but intriguing issues such as the use and nature of the "collective volumes" discussed in section 2.3, "Style, Handwriting, and Format."

## FURTHER READING

For mythography in the papyri a few works are particularly relevant. A general and very useful background for these texts is provided by Cameron (2004), in which the chapter "Myth and Society" (217–252), in particular, helps to sketch a context in which the various mythographical texts played their part. Less elaborate but also very useful is the survey of Hellenistic mythography by Higbie (2007), which includes interesting sections on Parthenius, Conon, and the mythography related to the Homeric epics.

Other works focus on specific aspects of mythographical papyri and are listed here in chronological order. The article by Henrichs (1987) is an important early study of mythographical texts and addresses three issues, two of which are relevant for the study of mythographical papyri: the *Diegeseis* of Conon and catalogues with mythical names. Cribiore (1996) offers a discussion of school papyri, among which quite a number have mythographical content. The monograph by van Rossum-Steenbeek (1997) offers an extensive survey (including the texts) of the various kinds of summaries and catalogues in papyri and studies them as "subliterary" works, possibly intended to replace the reading of the actual literary works on which they are based. Huys (2013) focuses on the mixture of simplification and erudition in the papyri, aimed at enabling people to answer the cultural demands of their time, and may be read against the background of Cameron's (2004) monograph, with its emphasis on the role of mythography in ancient society.

Apart from these general studies, the editions of the individual papyri often contain much relevant information and further references, which may also shed light on larger issues.

## REFERENCES

Barns, John W. B. 1949. "Literary Texts from the Fayum." *Classical Quarterly* 43: 1–8.

Bonnechère, P. 2006. "Notes Trophoniaques, I: Triptolème, Rhadamanthe, Musée, Eumolpos et Trophonios (P.Corn. 55)." *Zeitschrift für Papyrologie und Epigraphik* 158: 83–87.

Brown, Malcolm K. 2002. *The Narratives of Konon.* Munich and Leipzig: Saur.

Cameron, Alan. 2004. *Greek Mythography in the Roman World.* Oxford: Oxford University Press.

Cassio, Albio C. 1989. "Storiografia locale di Argo e dorico letterario: Agia, Dercillo ed il Pap. Soc. Ital. 1091." *Rivista di Filologia e Istruzione Classica* 117: 257–275.

Cribiore, Rafaella. 1996. *Writings, Teachers and Students in Graeco-Roman Egypt.* Atlanta, GA: Scholars Press.

Daris, Sergio. 1970. "P.Med.Inv. 123." In *Proceedings of the Twelfth International Congress of Papyrology*, edited by Deborah H. Samuel, 97–102. Toronto: A. M. Hakkert.

Del Corno, Dario. 1974. "P.Berol. 9571 verso über den Dithyrambos: Pindar und die Poetik des Aristoteles." In *Akten des XIII: Internatiolnalen Papyrologenkongresses*, edited by Emil Kiessling and Hans-Albert Rupprecht, 99–110. Munich: Beck.

Dorandi, Tiziano. 2006. "Il *peri paroimion* di Clearco di Soli." *Eikasmos* 17: 157–170.

Esposito, Elena. 2009. "Fragments of Greek Lexicography in the Papyri." *Trends in Classics* 1: 255–286.

Fowler, Robert L. 1995. "4097. Mythographic Texts. Mythological Compendium." *The Oxyrhynchus Papyri* 61: 46–54.

Fowler, Robert L. 2000. *Early Greek Mythography*. Vol. 1. Oxford: Oxford University Press.

Gercke, Alfred, and Eduard Norden. 1924. *Einleitung in die Altertumswissenschaft* Vol. 1.9. Leipzig: Teubner.

Harder, M. Annette. 1979. "A New Identification in *P.Oxy.* 2455?" *Zeitschrift für Papyrologie und Epigraphik* 35: 7–14.

Harrauer, Hermann, and Pieter J. Sijpesteijn. 1985. *Neue Texte aus dem antiken Unterricht*. Vienna: Brüder Hollinek.

Heinze, Theodor, and Sotera Fornaro. 2000. "Mythographie." *Der Neue Pauly* 8: 627–632.

Henrichs, Albert. 1987. "Three Approaches to Greek Mythography." In *Interpretations of Greek Mythology*, edited by Jan N. Bremmer, 242–277. London and Sydney: Croon Helm.

Higbie, Carolyn. 2007. "Hellenistic Mythographers." In *The Cambridge Companion to Greek Mythology*, edited by Roger D. Woodard, 237–254. Cambridge, UK: Cambridge University Press.

Huys, Marc. 1996. "P.Oxy. 61.4099: A Combination of Mythographic Lists with Sentences of the Seven Wise Men." *Zeitschrift für Papyrologie und Epigraphik* 113: 205–212.

Huys, Marc. 2013. "Traces of Scholarship and Erudition in Greek Mythographic Papyri from the Roman Period." In *Writing Myth: Mythography in the Ancient World*, edited by Stephen M. Trzaskoma and R. Scott Smith, 115–131. Leuven: Peeters.

Itgenshorst, Tanja. 1997. "Das mythologische Fragment P.Vindob. Gr. 26727: Eine neue Lesung." *Zeitschrift für Papyrologie und Epigraphik* 119: 189–192.

Lightfoot, Jane L. 1999. *Parthenius of Nicaea*. Oxford: Clarendon Press.

Luppe, Wolfgang. 1997. "Der mythologische Text P.Mich. Koenen 762." *Archiv für Papyrusforschung* 99: 233–237.

Luppe, Wolfgang. 2001. "P.Berol. inv. 11 056: Ein Roman-Fragment?" *Archiv für Papyrusforschung* 47: 20–25.

Luppe, Wolfgang, and Günter Poethke. 1998. "Homerika der Berliner Papyrus-Sammlung." *Archiv für Papyrusforschung* 44: 209–218.

Luppe, Wolfgang, and Reinhold Scholl. 2001. "Ein Leipziger Mythologie-Papyrus (P.Lips. inv. 1390)." *Archiv für Papyrusforschung* 47: 4–18.

Papathomas, Amphilochios. 2009. "Zum Prosatext des homerischen Fragments P.Heid. IV 289." *Archiv für Papyrusforschung* 55: 32–35.

Parsons, Peter J. 1966. "Papiri della Università degli Studi di Milano (P.Mil. Vogliano). Vol. 3." *Gnomon* 38: 672–675.

Rabbie, Edwin, and Pieter J. Sijpesteijn. 1988. "Eine neue Perseiden-Genealogie in P.Vindob. G 23058." *Wiener Studien* 101: 85–95.

Rea, John R. 1968. "2688, 2689. Greek Questions." *The Oxyrhynchus Papyri* 34: 000–000.

Rusten, Jeffrey S. 1982. *Dionysius Scytobrachion*. Opladen, Germany: Westdeutscher Verlag.

Salvadori Baldascino, L. 1988. "Una raccolta di proverbi in PSI inv. 155." *Studi Classici e Orientali* 38: 263–270.

Schironi, Francesca. 2009. *From Alexandria to Babylon: Near Eastern Languages and Hellenistic Erudition in the Oxyrhynchus Glossary (P.Oxy. 1802 + 4812)*. Berlin and New York: De Gruyter.

Schubart, Wilhelm. 1941. "Über den Dithyrambus." *Archiv für Papyrusforschung* 14: 24–29.

Schwartz, Jacques. 1957. "Une source papyrologique d'Hygin le mythographe." In *Studi in onore di Aristide Calderini e Roberto Paribeni*, vol. 2, 151–156. Milan: Ceschina.

Sijpesteijn, Pieter J. 1972. "The Rejuvenation Cure of Pelias." *Zeitschrift für Papyrologie und Epigraphik* 9: 104–110.

Thomas, Oliver R. H. 2007. "Charting the Atlantic with Hesiod and Hellanicus." *Zeitschrift für Papyrologie und Epigraphik* 160: 15–23.

Trachsel, Alexandra, and P. Schubert. 1999. "Une description de la topographie de Troie dans un papyrus de Genève Pack² 1204): Réédition." *Museum Helveticum* 56: 222–237.

Trzaskoma, Stephen M., and R. Scott Smith. 2013. *Writing Myth: Mythography in the Ancient World*. Leuven: Peeters.

van Rossum-Steenbeek, Monique. 1997. *Greek Readers' Digests?* Leiden and New York: Brill.

West, Stephanie. 2014. "Notes on *P.Oxy.* 1802 + 4812 (The Oxyrhynchus Glossary)." *Zeitschrift für Papyrologie und Epigraphik* 191: 39–45.

# CHAPTER 18

························································

# GREEK MYTHOGRAPHY
# AND SCHOLIA

························································

## NEREIDA VILLAGRA

SCHOLIA are comments preserved in the manuscripts of a literary work, most typically placed in the margins alongside the text, which is commented on and usually organized by lemmata. The *lemma* is the word, or group of words, from the main text that is copied to introduce the scholion. Its function is to highlight the word or phrase being commented on and to guide readers to the location of the passage being discussed. Scholia can refer to different aspects of the literary text: style, textual criticism, vocabulary, metrics, interpretation, historical context, or mythical traditions. They derive from different commentaries and often cite authorities from different periods. Indeed, they are the result of both a selection and an accumulation of previous scholarly works. The term *scholia* has traditionally designated the commentaries in medieval manuscripts, but it can also be applied to the marginal and interlinear notes found in papyri, which are considered the antecedents of the exegetical *apparatus* of medieval codices (Henrichs 1971: 97–149; McNamee 1977; Lundon 1999: 25–52; Gonis and Lundon 2001: 111–115). In this chapter, *scholia* will only refer to the scholarly notes found in medieval manuscripts of ancient Greek literature, as traditionally used. The commentaries preserved in papyri will not be discussed (see Harder, this volume).

Even though not every manuscript contains scholia, the scope of scholia is almost as vast as the manuscript tradition of ancient Greek and Latin literature itself. Furthermore, not all the corpora of scholia are equally relevant for the study of mythography. I therefore limit the discussion here to the scholia to Homer, Pindar, Euripides, and Apollonius Rhodius because of the amount and the type of mythographical texts or the varying approaches that are preserved in them. This selection does not exhaust the mythographical material preserved by scholia. Other corpora with a substantial amount of mythography are the scholia to Lycophron, Aratus, Hesiod, Theocritus, Sophocles, and Aeschylus, from which the richest in mythographical notes are the scholia to Lycophron. Scholarly works preserved as independent commentaries, such as those of Eustathius, or of lexicographers such as Stephanus Byzantinus, also contain an important amount of mythographical material, sometimes paralleled in the scholia.

In the past two decades, scholars of mythography have focused on fragmentary early mythographers (Fowler 2000, 2013; Dolcetti 2004; Pàmias 2008; Andolfi 2019; *BNJ*) and on Hellenistic and imperial texts, some of which are partially or totally transmitted by scholiastic corpora, such as the *Catasterisms*, the *Mythographus Homericus* (henceforth, MH), or the narrative hypothesis to Euripides (Pagès 2007; Pàmias and Zucker 2013; Meccariello 2014). There has been no corresponding survey of the types of mythographical texts one can find in scholia, for scholia have traditionally been seen as mere containers of previous scholarship. However, there is an ongoing reassessment of these corpora, which are now no longer seen as neutral conveyers of fragments. As Montana (2011: 107) puts it, any example of medieval scholia is an "exegetic *editio variorum* designed to be made up in an orderly way alongside or around the text commented upon . . . , which is in turn the result of a carefully planned and systematic editorial process of compiling and stratifying different sources." Focusing on the medieval scholia contributes in three ways: In the first place, when studying fragmentary mythography, we tend to select the words that might go back to the author in question, losing sight of their context. Assessing the mythography in the scholiastic corpus can give some counterbalance to this bias. Second, the ways in which scholiasts use both mythographical materials and the authority of mythographers informs us about the reception of the genre in Byzantine times. Indeed, when discussing possible new approaches to the question of the birth of scholiography, Antonietta Porro (2014: 202–203) considers an approach that studies the needs of exegesis—why did a text need elucidation at that specific point, and how is it explained?—useful to better understand the changes from antiquity to the medieval period. In the third place, scholia preserve mythographical material that is not attributed to any authority and is, therefore, underassessed as part of the mythographical tradition.

In the first part of the chapter, I will refer to the origin and formation of scholia and their relationship to mythography. The parts that follow are devoted to the each of the abovementioned corpora, providing a description of the main types of mythographical material or methods found in them. This description of mythography is based on formal criteria. I will establish a typology of texts and address their relationship to the poem they are commenting on from a synchronic perspective. However, one must bear in mind that the scholia in each manuscript tradition are the result of the diachronic reception of the scholarship on the poetical text. At the same time, scholia as we find them in modern editions are an abstraction of different manuscript traditions. An in-depth study of the mythography on a specific corpus of scholia—which is not the purpose of this chapter—should, therefore, also include a study of the history of the manuscripts themselves.

# 1. The Origins of Scholiastic Corpora

It is difficult to place the birth of scholiastic corpora as a whole in a specific period because each corpus has a different history. Montana rightly warns of the dangers of generalization and of inference from one corpus to all scholiastic corpora (Montana 2014: 5, 8). In general terms, the traditional debate revolves around the material conditions that are necessary for scholia to appear, the type of handwriting, and what it was written on (for a survey of the historical debate, see Montana 2014: 1–14). One view is that they were an invention of the 9th-century Byzantine Renaissance, a period in which a new type of script was introduced: the minuscule (Zuntz 1975; 1965: 272–275). According to Zuntz's hypothesis, this prompted the copying of all existing literature in the new format, and at this point, Byzantine scholars, who had access to imperial and Hellenistic exegetical materials, selected information, combined different materials, and compressed them into the margins of the new minuscule manuscripts. Others have contested Zuntz's thesis, arguing that the scholia originated in a much earlier period (Wilson 1967: 244–256). More recent studies of papyrological documentation have shown the existence of papyri with marginal notes. This is adduced as proof that the minuscule was not essential for the birth of this commentary forma (McNamee 1995: 399–414; 1998: 269–288). However, other scholars consider the nature of medieval scholia to be substantially different from the marginal notes in papyri (Montana 2011: 106–107).

There is agreement that the Byzantine scholars had access to previous independent commentaries on the poets and to late-antique codices with marginalia. But there were previous steps in the process of reconfiguring the exegetical and scholarly literature: the substitution of the papyrus scroll with the new format of the codex, which started around the turn of the era, and the foundation of the Museum of Alexandria and its library by Ptolemaeus Euergetes in the 3rd century BCE, which entailed the birth of philology and textual criticism. In this erudite environment, editions and new commentaries on the great poems were produced for the first time. Indeed, independently from the debate about whether papyri scrolls and codices with marginalia should be considered scholia, is the important fact that fragmentary papyri show that the practice of conflating different materials into a single commentary (*hypomnēma* or *syngramma*) and of writing interlinear notes or short comments in the margins of literary texts already existed, before the introduction of codex format. Thus, Byzantine scholia represent a point of arrival of different scholarly processes which had begun long before. In each moment, the previous literary and paraliterary materials were manipulated to fit the new context. At the same time, scholia have open and fluid transmission and therefore cannot be studied with "evolutionary categories," as several scholars have pointed out (Montana 2011: 110; Porro 2014: 202; Montana 2019: 99–106).

# 2. Greek Mythography in Scholia

The activity of early Greek mythographers seems to have involved reconfiguring mythical data from epic and lyric poems and from other oral or local traditions (Trzaskoma 2013: xv–xvii). Fowler (2006: 35–46) stresses, among other characteristics, the summary style of the mythography genre and relates it precisely to the activity of abridging and reorganizing previous mythical information. If we take into account the cultural panorama of the Library of the Museum in Alexandrian times (Montana 2015: 82–145), it seems plausible that scholars would have rearranged the early mythographers' works, among others, to make consultation easier (Pàmias 2020). New mythographical works also appeared in the Hellenistic period, such as Asclepiades's *Tragodoumena* (4th c. BCE), Palaephatus's *Peri Apiston* (also 4th c. BCE), and Eratosthenes's *Catatsterisms* (3rd c. BCE). In the imperial period other mythographical works were composed as well (for instance, Ps.-Apollodorus's *Library*, maybe 1st c. CE), and also new commentaries to the poetic works, such as those of Didymus (Schironi 2015; 2018: 18–22). When writing his commentaries Didymus must have had earlier mythographical works at his disposal—some possibly already abridged and rearranged—and adapted them to the new needs of his readers. Thus, this scholarly activity preserved a good amount of mythographical material but also reshaped it. Some Hellenistic and imperial mythography had an independent manuscript transmission (for instance, Palaephatus's *Peri Apiston* or Apollodorus's *Library*), but much of it was integrated into commentaries and subsequently into scholia, such as the *Catasterisms*. The MH had probably an exegetical nature already in its original form (Pagès, this volume, and 2021; Pagès and Villagra 2022). Hence, it is hard to trace a clear-cut line between mythography and scholarship, for both activities often converge and overlap (Trzaskoma 2013: xix–xx).

Cameron (2004) describes the cultural panorama of imperial times as a moment in which mythographical companions to and summaries of earlier Greek works, now considered to be difficult texts, were frequently produced and popular. Companions, such as the MH, and summaries, such as the tragic narrative *hypotheses*, must have been elaborated with the aid of mythographical works, which were available to imperial scholars and teachers.

Our corpus of surviving scholiastic texts—the manuscripts with scholia—is mainly to be placed in a later period and a different cultural context, the Byzantine world (Pontani 2015: 297–455). When the monks in the monasteries copied the works of Homer and added marginal scholia, selecting, abridging and adapting the existing commentaries at their disposal, they also preserved part of the earlier mythographical material while refashioning it (Pontani 2015: 327–331). This is an unavoidable consequence of the repeated action of extracting a passage from its original context and adapting it to a new context and to new needs (Darbo-Peschanski 2004b: 9–21; 2004a: 291–300).

As a result, one should not diminish the importance of scholia by reducing their role to that of container of lost mythographers. What we find in scholia is a mélange of fragments of earlier sources, anonymous mythographical narratives, paraphrases of the main poetic text, and pieces of mythography that were probably composed ad hoc during the process of commenting on the poems. In fact, when we navigate through scholiastic corpora, we find a range of what Henrichs (1987: 243) termed "mythographical information" dealing with traditions, figures, places, or details, and providing "*relevant myths* as background material for the explanation of major authors," as well as the use of different mythographical procedures, such as comparing different versions or variants of a myth, citing a mythographer's authority, or listing mythological information.

If we leave aside *Quellenforschung*, the source-oriented scrutiny of scholia, we can describe two sets of typologies, one that characterizes the kinds of mythographical texts that play an important role in the commentaries, and a second that describes the motivation for inserting mythographical material. Of course, a formal classification is always a simplification of a complex textual reality, and these two typologies often converge, but not always in a predictable way. Likewise, there is often inconsistency even within a single set of typologies. For instance, many scholia combine different types of structures or modes and do not fall into only one category. However, the typologies are useful to organize and describe the role of mythography in these corpora. First, in terms of structure, the mythographical material can be classified into the following categories:

1. Narrative texts, often presented as *historiae*. They can cite an authority, several, or none.
2. *Zitatennester*, groups of references of authorities contrasting mythical details, such as names or different versions.
3. Lists, often containing genealogies, but sometimes consisting of catalogues of mythical figures or other elements.

Regarding the relationship to the poetic text, mythographical material can be aimed at:

1. Addition, supplying material that is not found in the poetic text (e.g., *historiae*)
2. Elucidation, explaining the sense of the poetic text
3. Comparison, placing the poetic text within the broader tradition (*Zitatennester* tend to be of this sort.)

# 3. SCHOLIA TO HOMER

The scholia to Homer are the richest collection of scholia on poetry, which is to be expected, for the Homeric poems were the most commonly referred to texts throughout antiquity. They have been traditionally divided into two big groups: scholia *maiora*, grammatical commentaries, and scholia *minora*, related to elementary education (Schironi 2020: 155–156). The whole set of Homeric scholia can, in turn, be classified into four different groups, which correspond to different manuscript traditions and broadly reflect different scholarly approaches to the poems. In the scholia to *Iliad*, we can distinguish between the D scholia, which contain mainly lexicographical comments, *historiae*, *zetemata* (questions of interpretation), and summaries; the bT scholia, of an interpretative or exegetical nature; the A family of scholia, composed from grammatical scholia also called VMK (*Viermännerkommentar*); and the h-scholia, a mixture of scholia of the D, bT, and VMK or A types (Montanari et al. 2017: 1–21). In the case of the *Odyssey*, approximately the same groups can be identified, though it is not possible to isolate an equivalent to the Iliadic A family. The D scholia of the *Odyssey* are often referred to as V scholia, and the bT scholia are referred to as "exegetical" scholia. There is no clear parallel in the *Odyssey* to the Iliadic h-scholia (Pontani 2005: 145–152, 181–182).

For both the *Iliad* and the *Odyssey*, the D and V scholia are the most important corpus for the study of mythography. The main type of mythographical text in this corpus are narratives, often explicitly named *historiae* by a subscription citing the narrative's source (for an alternative interpretation of the subscriptions, see Delattre 2016). Many of them have parallels in papyri from the imperial period and are assumed to derive from the *MH* (see Pagès, this volume). There remains some controversy about using mechanical approaches to assign mythographical material in the D/V scholia without parallels in papyri to the *MH* (Pagès and Villagra, 2022), particularly because the entries are not homogenous and use multiple procedures. Take, for instance, the following example:

> Sch. (EHPQV) *Od.* 7.324b (Ernst). "Tityus, earthly (*gaieion*) son": Tityus, son of the earth, a form of the possessive. Zeus joined with Elara, the daughter of Orchomenos, or according to others of Minyas and, because of Hera's jealousy, he hid her under the earth. She gave birth to an outstanding son, who was called Tityus (he felt passion for Leto and was shot with arrows by Apollo). Rhadamanthys had gone to see Tityus (being also the son of Zeus, he chastened him). Indeed, it appears that the Phaeacians dwell close to the Isles of the Blessed.

After translating the adjective *gaieion* that is applied to Tityus and explaining its grammatical nature, the scholion uses a mythographical narrative to explain why Tityus is called son of the earth and how he died. But it also reformulates the immediate context of the verse, in which Alcinoous tells Odysseus that the Phaeacians once sailed with Rhadamanthys to Euboea to fetch Tityus. It thus helps to elucidate the reason Rhadamanthys joined the Phaeacians to visit him—Tityus was his brother. At the end, it is pointed out that the Isles of the Blessed were close to Phaeacia, information the scholiast possibly inferred from the poem itself. This is not the typical procedure of the MH, and it is quite probable that the mythographical narrative in this commentary has a different origin.

The bT or exegetical scholia sometimes preserve *historiae* that are similar or even parallel to the ones in the D scholia. In most cases, the texts in the exegetical scholia offer differences from the version in the D scholia. They are generally presented in a much more abridged form, and at other times they cannot go back to a common source. In those cases, it is hard to explain what their relationship was, if any, to the MH. A few of the bT scholia preserve narratives that left no trace in the D scholia. There are two possible stances in these cases: some scholars consider that these narratives must be representative of a different stage of the MH tradition (Pagès Cebrián 2007: 16–18). Other scholars defend the interpretation that only the *historiae* of the D/V scholia should be seen as deriving from the MH (Montanari 1995: 136–172; 2002: 129–144), and they envisage the *historiae* in the exegetical or grammatical scholia as part of other scholarly activity.

The D/V and bT or exegetical scholia are also a rich source of other types of mythographical texts: short narratives that are often introduced as literal quotations from mythographers, *Zitatennester*, and texts in a question-and-answer format that cite the authority of a mythographer. The most quoted mythographers are Pherecydes and Hellanicus. The scholia in the bT corpus usually explain the main text using the mythical narratives and cite the names of mythographers to provide authority. The following example can be considered a *Zitatennest* because two mythographers are cited together as authorities along with what seems to be their *ipsa verba*:

> Sch. (T) *Il.* 23.296c (Erbse): "The Anchisiad Echepolus": Acusilaus, in the third book of the *Genealogies*, understands "Echepolus" as a proper name, saying as follows: "Of Cleonymus was born Anchises, and from him Echepolus." And Pherecydes says in book three: "Cleonymus, son of Pelops, was living in Cleonae after Atreus established him there; his son was Anchises, of whom was born Echepolus."

Acusilaus and Pherecydes are quoted to explain the term "Echepolus" used in the poetical text, which could either be a proper name or an epithet meaning "owner of horses." The quotation of Pherecydes is a short narrative giving the genealogy of this mythical figure, thus proving that Echepolus was the name of the hero.

There is much less mythographical material in the scholia A or VMK to the *Iliad*, edited by Erbse. In few cases a mythographer is quoted in order to discuss grammatical matters, for instance, sch. [A] *Il.* 23.296c, where Acusilaus is cited for the interpretation of Echepolus as name and not as epithet. But most times the authority of mythographers is invoked only to complete or contrast a detail, mainly names of mythical figures. For instance, in sch. [A] *Il.* 19.116a, the scholiast cites Didymus, who, in turn, quotes Pherecydes and Hesiod in order to give the name of Sthenelus's wife: Amphibia, according to Pherecydes (fr. 68), or Nicipe or Antibia according to Hesiod (fr. 319 M-W). It is unclear whether the reference to Hesiod goes back to Didymus or to the scholiast. Pherecydes is used here through a *Mittelquelle*, Didymus, in order to complete the information of the poem, which did not give the name of Sthenelus's wife. At the same time, his version is compared to Hesiod's.

The summaries of each book of the poems—or of smaller sections—are another type of mythographical text found in the medieval manuscript tradition of Homer. They are introduced with the title "hypothesis" and appear at the beginning of each book in the manuscripts that belong to the D scholia. There is usually more than one hypothesis for the same book in the same manuscript. Homeric hypotheses are also preserved in papyri. The situation is similar to what happens with the narrative hypotheses to

Euripides (see Meccariello, this volume). However, the Homeric hypotheses show no uniform characteristics, and the hypotheses in papyri, which are considered to be school exercises, rarely preserve texts related to the *hypotheses* in the medieval manuscripts.

# 4. SCHOLIA TO PINDAR

The exegetical scholia to Pindar form a large corpus of commentaries on the four books of epinicia, which can be divided into *vetera* and *recentia*. Here we treat the old scholia, which preserve material going back to Alexandrian scholarship and are considered to have almost no interpolations by Byzantine scholars (Deas 1931: 55). Deas believed that the basis of the corpus of old scholia is a summary of Didymus's first comprehensive commentary to the complete works of Pindar, which would, in turn, have relied on even earlier scholarship (1931: 27–29; on Didymus's work see Braswell 2011, 2013). Some papyri from the period between the 1st and the 6th centuries CE preserve fragments of commentaries on Pindar that show connections to the material preserved in the scholia (McNamee 1977, 2007; Lefkowitz 1975: 269–282).

Even in antiquity, Pindar was recognized as a difficult author, and this is reflected in the scholia, which mainly focus on explaining the poems. The presence and function of mythography is also determined by this need for clarification. In general, the distribution of the mythographical information is uneven, and sometimes we find mythographical narratives associated with odes that contain only allusions rather than a mythical narrative.

One can find a number of mythographical narratives that are explicitly presented by the scholiast as *historiae*. Most of them are comments to the *Pythian* 4—probably the most narrative of Pindar's poems—and deal with the Argonautic tradition. But they occur elsewhere as well; an *historia* explaining an allusion in *Olympian* 4 provides an illustrative example of the main role of mythography in the corpus. It is prompted by an allusion to the mythical figure Erginus, the son of Clymenus (20). The passage of the ode (17–27) and the *historia* run as follows:

> I will not steep my speech
> in lies; the **test** (*diapeira*) of any man lies in **action** (*ergon*).
> So the son of Klymenos
> was set free of **dishonor** (*atimias*)
> at the hands of Lemnian women.
> As he won the race in bronze armor
> and came to Hypsipyle for his garland, he spoke:
> "Here am I in my speed.
> My hands are as good as my heart.
> Many a time even on young men gray hairs
> appear, against the likelihood of their youth."
>
> (Trans. Lattimore)

The *historia* is the following:

> Sch. Pind. (BCDEQ) *Ol.* 4.32c (Drachmann). When Hypsipyle was celebrating funerary games for her father Thoas, the king of the Lemnians, the Argonauts, who were on their way back from fetching the Golden Fleece, happened to arrive there. They were persuaded to join the games and so they competed. Indeed, there was one of them, Erginus, who was younger in age but prematurely grey-haired. He was laughed at and mocked by the women, as if he was not able to compete because of his grey appearance. But, through his **actions** (*ergon*) it was proved that he surpassed the other competitors. The sons of Boreas, Zetes and Calais, were there. The mockery against him ended and, contrarily, admiration was aroused. *This is why* [Pindar] says that the **action** (*peiran*) made the Lemnian women stop the **insolence** (*hybreos*) against him.

The scholion uses the mythographical narrative to provide more complete information about an episode that Pindar only alluded to, and it also explains the meaning of the obscure term *diapeira* (see a full discussion in Delattre 2016). There is no explicit effort in the commentary to attribute the narrative to a specific authority. The concern of the commentator is to make clear the sense of *diapeira*, and therefore, he provides a narrative of the myth that mirrors Pindar's text, as can be noted in the boldface terms. At the end of the narration he refers explicitly to the sense of Pindar's words (in italics). However, the mythical narrative cannot depend only on the Pindaric text because it includes details that do not appear in the poem. We find, in sum, great fluidity in passing from mythographical to exegetical procedures.

Besides the narratives explicitly presented as *historiae*, we can also find accounts of marginal myths, such as the scholion on the theft by Pandarus of the dog that guarded Zeus's shrine in Crete, for which Tantalus was punished (sch. Pind. *Ol.* 1.91a). The narrative comes at the beginning of a long *Zitatennest* that provides contrasting versions of Tantalus's punishment, quoting different poetic elaborations, and also gives an interpretation of the myth. Another example is the story on the origin of the *iunx*, a kind of spell using a wyrneck: there was a girl who cured Zeus of his longing for Io and was turned by Hera into the bird (sch. Pind. *Nem.* 4.56a). The term *iunx* is used by Pindar metaphorically to refer to his passion for singing poetry. The scholion identifies the metaphor ("*iunx* means passion [*epithymia*]") and expands on its origin, a mythographical procedure.

The term *historia* is also used to refer to the vulgate version of a myth, which is compared to the Pindaric one. Other times, scholia point to "further reading," as in a scholion to colon 43 of *Nemean* 11, where Hellanicus is cited in the following terms: "About the foundation of a colony in the Aeolid, Hellanicus has an account in the first book of the *Aeolica*." It is difficult to determine whether the scholiast expected his readers to follow up such reference or, more likely, the reference was copied from earlier materials at a time when direct access to the *Aeolica* was no longer possible.

Besides commenting on the position of Pindar's version in relation to the common tradition, scholia also contrast the names of mythical figures and genealogical variants. Different types of authorities are quoted to provide the *comparanda*, such as Homer, the tragedians, Apollonius, and mythographers. The most quoted mythographer is Pherecydes (twenty times), followed by Hellanicus and Herodorus (five times each). The name Asclepiades is mentioned fifteen times, and it is not always clear to which Asclepiades the scholia refer. On three occasions it must be the mythographer, because the title of his work, *Tragodoumena*, is given. In other cases, the Asclepiades mentioned can be a grammarian, identified by Deas (1931: 15–16) with Asclepiades of Myrlea (1st c. BCE), who wrote commentaries on several poets.

Some of the citations of mythographers occur together in texts that have a *Zitatennest* format. Mythographers may be quoted next to other mythographers but also next to poets, historians, or philosophers. Sometimes *Zitatennest*-scholia introduce narratives, as we see in the following example, where after several variants on the name of Phrixus's stepmother are given, Pherecydes's version is briefly summarized to contrast it to the version of the ode:

> Sch. Pind. (BDEGQ) *Pyth.* 4.288a. "Of the *godless arrows* of the stepmother": He was wronged because his stepmother felt passion for him and plotted against him, for which reason he had to escape. She is called Demodice by Pindar in the *Hymns*, or Gorgopis according to Hippias. Sophocles calls her Nephele in the *Athamas*, and Pherecydes calls her Themisto. **Pherecydes says that when the crop was ruined, he spontaneously and voluntarily offered himself for sacrifice.** The "*godless arrows*" are allegorically the purposes, words or acts. For, since he did not give into the demands of the stepmother, he was plotted against, according to the common tradition.

The paraphrases of Pindar's odes occupy a halfway position between mythography and exegesis. They are intended as a sort of translation into easier language. The paraphrases of the mythical exempla of the odes form texts with formal features that are close to mythography. They preserve some of the poetical flavor of the Pindaric verses but use more prosaic vocabulary and a simplified syntactical structure. Sometimes they add elements that are not present in the poem. Another example will illustrate the difficulty of establishing a clear-cut line between paraphrase and mythographical narrative. In *Pyth.* 4.90–95 Pindar compares Jason to different gods and to Otus and Ephialtes, who are compared, in turn, to Tityus in the way they died—shot by Artemis. A scholion to these verses starts paraphrasing the poem, as the inclusion of the vocative "O daring Ephialtes" shows:

> Sch. Pind. (BDEGQ) *Pyth.* 4.156a.1. "It is said that in Naxos he died": They say that in blessed Naxos died Otus, the son of Iphimedia, and you, O most daring Ephialtes. Of Iphimedeia and Aloeus were born Otus and Ephialtes. They behaved in an ungodly way with Artemis and, therefore, the goddess transformed herself into a deer and appeared between them when they were hunting in Naxos. Assuming they were shooting the deer, they unknowingly wounded each other. Indeed, (Pindar) uses them as a point of comparison with the exceptionality of Jason's body.

As we can see, after the paraphrasis the scholiast, with no transition, tells the myth of Otus and Ephialtes to explain the allusion to their death in the second comparison.

Although it is not necessary to understand the poem, the scholiast includes information on the birth of the Aloads. At the end, an explanation is given for why Pindar uses Otus and Ephialtes as comparison. Thus, the scholion combines the rephrasing with a narrative to provide clarification as well as contextual and extratextual information.

Finally, accounts on the mythical foundation of the Olympian, Pythian, Nemean and the Isthmian games are included as introductory material to each book of odes. The foundation myths of the Pythian and Nemean games are labeled in the manuscripts as *hypotheseis*, whereas the account on the foundation of the Olimpic games is introduced by the expression "let us now speak of" (*lekteon*), and the accounts on the Isthmian games with the expression "this is the story (*historia*)."

## 5. SCHOLIA TO EURIPIDES

The scholia to Euripides have had an uneven transmission. Not all the plays have been transmitted with scholia. There is a large quantity of material for the Byzantine triad, *Orestes, Hecuba*, and *Phoenissae*, and we also have scholia to *Medea, Hippolytus, Alcestis, Andromache, Rhesus*, and *Troades*. In general, it is accepted that the old scholia go back to Aristophanes of Byzantium and to other Alexandrian scholars but are channelled through the comprehensive commentary of Didymus in the 1st century (Mastronarde 2017: 1–26). The mythological information, together with the lexicographical notes and the paraphrases, is considered to belong to the early Roman period. There are also later Byzantine scholia by Manuel Moschopolus and Thomas Magister and the metrical scholia of Demetrius Triclinius (Zuntz 1965: 272–275; Dickey 2007: 31–34).

An important type of mythographical text preserved in the Byzantine manuscript tradition—and in several imperial papyri—are the narrative hypotheses, which can be described as narrative summaries of the plays, often with additional background material, which circulated as an independent book that is sometimes called "Tales from Euripides" (see Meccariello, this volume). Besides the hypotheses, a large amount of mythographical material is inserted in the scholia to the tragedies. I will focus on the old scholia to the *Phoenissae* as case study.

A handful of scholia use the verb *historei*, "tells," and give the name of an authority. In this way, both narratives and genealogical data are introduced. Besides the genealogical variants attributed to an authority, several scholia transmit anonymous genealogical lists. The narratives are often presented as verbatim quotations and usually have an additive function. An example is the scholion to verse 53. The mention of Oedipus's marriage to his mother in the prologue is commented on by the scholiast with a narrative on the three different marriages and the various children of the hero. It is attributed to Pherecydes as *ipsissima verba*.

The famous Pisander scholion (sch. *Phoen.* 1760; see Edmunds 2006: 16; Lloyd-Jones 2002: 1–14; Mastronarde 1994: 31–38) is perhaps the most remarkable *historia*. Here is the passage it is commenting on:

O citizens of a famous country, look at me; I am Oedipus, who solved the famous riddle, and was the greatest of men, I, who alone controlled the murderous Sphinx's power, am now myself driven from the land in dishonor and misery. (*Phoen.* 1758–1761, trans. Coleridge 1938)

The purpose of the scholion is to add information to the allusion made by Oedipus about his life at the end of the tragedy. The *historia* contains an extensive narrative on why the Sphinx was sent to Thebes, those she killed, how Laius tried to eliminate it, how Laius was killed by Oedipus, Oedipus's marriage to his mother, how everything was discovered and what happened to Oedipus afterward. Thus, it seems, if the preserved text reflects the original form of Peisander's story (an author about whom we know little), Peisander had recourse to many traditions and combined them to compose it. The *historia* gives antecedents and details on the killing of Laius that do not appear in the prologue of the piece. At the same time, it offers a version of the events after the discovery of Oedipus's identity that is different from the version followed by Euripides. Also, the children of Oedipus are identified not as Jocasta's but as Euryganias's. Therefore, it provides alternative variants to the tragic version. However, the scholiast does not explicitly compare both versions. Nor is the *historia* related to a lemma that highlights the variation. The purpose of the story is probably only to flesh out the allusion, without concern about aligning completely with the text of the play. The fact that it provides a contrasting version seems secondary and not relevant for the scholiast.

Mythographical narratives are also referred to in an anonymous way, with a simple "they say" (*phasi*), as we can see in a scholion that explains the etiology of the fountain Dirce (sch. *Phoen.* 102), which has an additive purpose similar to many *historiae* of the MH. Other cases are self-contained narratives.

In *Zitatennest*-type scholia, mythographers can appear next to other mythographers, historians, poets or grammarians. The most cited mythographers in the scholia to this tragedy are Pherecydes (six times), Asclepiades (two times) and Pisander (two times).

In general, the main purpose of the mythographical scholia to this tragedy is to add information, providing a great deal of erudition. When several authorities are quoted, the scholia also contrast Euripides's version to other treatments. Indeed, the accumulation of materials can result in an accumulation of functions too. The large number of alternative mythical versions and details fits well with the idea that the scholia to Euripides go back to an imperial commentary, for an imperial scholar would have had better access to a big number of Hellenistic sources than a scholiast.

# 6. SCHOLIA TO APOLLONIUS RHODIUS

The scholia to the *Argonautica* derive from a commentary partially preserved also in other scholarly works, especially the 9th-century *Etymologicum Genuinum*. According to a subscription at the end of book 4, the scholia come from the commentaries by

Sophoclius, Theon, and Lucillus of Tarrha, about whom very little is known. In the 5th century CE, these three commentaries would have been combined into one that would have been used by the Byzantine scholars (Wendel 1932; Fränkel 1964; Herter 1955: 239–246).

A large part of the scholia deal with comparing Apollonius's poem to Homer's, and other authors at different levels, including the mythological. Indeed, they are an extremely rich source of mythography, which is not unexpected, given the nature of the *Argonautica*, a highly allusive and erudite poem about a journey of many heroes. The scholia provide hundreds of *Zitatennester* offering alternative versions that quote a variety of authorities: poets, historians, mythographers, philosophers, and grammarians. The information that is compared to Apollonius's version can deal with genealogical variants and details but also with different versions of the myths. Many of the cited authorities were Apollonius's own sources. Cameron (2004: 63) proposes that much of this material must go back to the work *On the Stories of Apollonius* by Chares, an obscure scholar who, according to the scholia, was a pupil of Apollonius.

Regarding the ways to present the mythographical information, the verb *historein* is frequently used to introduce a mythographer's narrative or variant. The passive form is also used to refer to anonymous traditions. As in other corpora, the term *historia* often means "myth." For instance, a scholion to the first book (sch. 1.760–762a) contrasts Apollonius's version of the origin of Tityus, son of Elara, to Homer's version, who calls him "the son of Gea." The scholiast quotes Pherecydes to explain the contradiction between the two poets: Elara was his mother, but then Tityus was buried alive and is therefore called "born from the earth (*gēgenēs*)." The scholiast then adds "the *historia* looks unreliable and untrustworthy, because Gea gave Tityus a second birth," explaining the sense of the Apollonian verses and dismissing Pherecydes's *historia*.

On a few occasions, we find a subscription. For instance, two scholia to the first book quote Hecataeus with a subscription similar to the MH's: "The *historia* is in Hecataeus" (sch. 1.118–121a; 1.256–259). Another scholion says, "The *historia* [is told] clearly in the *Shield* of Hesiod" (sch. 1.747–751a). Anonymous variants and narratives often depend upon the expression "they say" (*phasi*), but sometimes anonymous stories are directly narrated. A representative example of this corpus is the first mythographical scholion to book 1, a comment on the name of the ship *Argo* that contrasts Apollonius's explanation of the origin of the name of the ship to that of Pherecydes. The scholion then adds information about the ship:

> Sch. 1–4e (Wendel): "They drove the Argo." Apollonius calls the ship *Argo* from Argus, its builder, but Pherecydes makes it come from Argus, the son of Phrixus. It is said that it was the first ship. But others say that Danaus built the first ship when he was pursued by Aegyptus, and because of that it was called *Danais*.

To the first book of the *Argonautica* alone there are around eighty scholia that can be considered mythographical. The catalogue of the heroes naturally has the most mythographical comments, since so many mythological figures are briefly alluded to in it: it occupies around two hundred verses (24–229) and around thirty scholia to this passage are mythographical. Many of these scholia provide genealogical information about the heroes participating in the expedition or their relatives, or about toponyms and other geographical information. Other sections of book 1 to which many scholia provide mythographical information are the stop of the Argonauts at Lemnos (609–909) and the stop at the land of the Doliones (934–1154).

A scholion to 1.57 illustrates the type of comments in the catalogue of heroes. It starts with the geographical location of Gyrtona, Coronus's city. Then it adds two accounts about Caeneus, his father. The narratives are related to verses 58–64 of the poem, where Apollonius explains Caeneus's combat with the Centaurs that led to his death:

> Sch. A.R. 1.57–64a (Wendel). "Gyrtona Coronus (left)": Homer says, "they inhabited Gyrtona" (2.738). It is a city in Thessaly or Perrhaebia, as Suidas says. It received its name from Gyrtona, the daughter of Phlegyas. Coronus is the son of Caeneus. It is told that Caeneus was originally a woman. After Poseidon had intercourse with her, she was transformed into a man, because she asked for this and also asked to be invulnerable. He contended with Apollo and was beaten. He ordered the peoples who passed by to make an oath on his spear. From this comes the proverb "the spear of Caeneus." Some say that it was Caeneus who sailed with the Argonauts and not Coronus. Apollonius took this from Pindar, who says "Caeneus, beaten by the green silver firs, left, cleaving the earth with his right foot." This happened to him because he didn't sacrifice to the gods or pray to them, but to his spear. Because of that Zeus sent the Centaurs to attack him, and they thrust him into the earth.

The opening narrative adds information on the figure of Caeneus. After that, the scholion compares Apollonius's version to other anonymous traditions in which the Argonaut was Caeneus and not Coronus. It cites Pindar as Apollonius's source for verses 1.58–64. The closing narrative explains the reason for Caeneus's death, also alluded to by Apollonius. Both in this case and in the former example on the ship *Argo*, the mythographical information appears fully integrated into the activity of commenting on the poem with a comparative method.

Summaries to the four books have been also transmitted at the beginning of each book. Two of the summaries for the first book are introduced with the term *hypothesis*. The summaries to the other books are introduced by the expression *ta kephalia*, "the main contents."

## 7.  CONCLUSIONS

Every formal type and function of scholia are present, in different degrees, in every corpus. The D scholia to Homer contain more *historiae* than the other corpora, but we also find *historiae* in the scholia to Pindar, Euripides, and Apollonius Rhodius. There is a greater tendency to explain the poems in the scholia to Pindar. The scholia to Apollonius

Rhodius tend more to comparison, containing more *Zitatennester* than other scholia, whereas in Euripides we find a large amount of extratextual amplification; and the three procedures are well represented in the scholia to Homer.

The largest part of the mythographical material in these four corpora is embedded in the commentary on the poems. As we have seen, mythography can be fully integrated in the interpretative comments in a very fluid way, and in some cases it is even integrated in grammatical matters. Indeed, the way to argue for an interpretation of the poem, to contrast the procedure of the poet, or provide context is to deploy a mythographical narrative or a genealogy or to quote mythographers as authorities. The fact that mythographers are quoted next to poets, historians, grammarians, and philosophers also speaks of this embeddedness. Indeed, we often see poets or grammarians being used as sources of myths. As a result, the original genre of the cited authors is made irrelevant; all the earlier writers are equally sources of material for the commentary. It is also significant that the authority of figures such as Pherecydes or Hellanicus is in many cases equated to the authority of poets. This suggests that these mythographers were not considered to be authors who simply put in prose the poetic mythical traditions, but as the source of information worth preserving.

The described picture suggests that mythical traditions were a cultural element basic to understanding the literary heritage. Mythography was therefore seen as part of scholarship. The opposition between mythography and erudition, on one hand, and philology and critical interpretation, on the other, is often not so clear-cut. In fact, mythography in the scholia can be described as a methodology to understand the poems and assess their place inside tradition. In this sense, it can be seen a type of scholarship (Meliadò 2015). Therefore, scholia cannot be considered just a neutral source of mythographical fragments. Of course, it is legitimate to use the texts preserved in scholia to reconstruct the mythography of earlier periods, but at the same time, one should take into account the stance towards mythography adopted by the creators of such corpora, for it reflects the specific mindset of the Byzantine Renaissance and its reception of the former scholarly traditions. This is an ample avenue for further research.

## FURTHER READING

A useful introduction to scholia and scholarship is Dickey (2007), which gives a comprehensive description of scholia and other scholarly works. A basic manual on the history of scholarship is still Reynolds and Wilson (1968). The recent monumental Montanari, Matthaios, and Rengakos (2015) devotes four chapters to the history of scholarship, from its beginnings to the Byzantine period. A description of exegetical and philological concepts in scholia can be found in Nünlist (2009, with a chapter on mythography at 257–264). Radová (2011) gives a typological classification of the scholia to Apollonius Rhodius, Sophocles, Pindar, Aeschines, and Thucydides, as well as a description of scholia as a genre.

On the formation of scholia, see Montana (2011). A useful survey of the historical debate can be found in Montana (2014). The classic papers on the origin of scholia are White (1914),

Zuntz (1975), a reprint from his 1938 and 1939 papers, Wilson (1967, 1996, rev. ed.). Porro (2014) provides a panoramic survey of the state of the art and presents new avenues of research in the field of scholiography.

On the reassessment of the formation of the scholiastic corpora, especially its chronology, in the light of papyrology, see McNamee (1997, 1995, 1998, 2007). On commentaries to the *Iliad* in papyri, see Pagani (2020). For scholia minora on papyri, see Henrichs (1971), Lundon (1999), and Gonis and Lundon (2001). On the relationship of a scholion to the poetic text it comments on, see Trachsel (2019), Villagra–Pàmias (2020), and Pagès (2021).

About the types of commentaries, see Schironi (2012) and Dubishar (2015). Regarding the quotations in antiquity, see Darbo-Peschanski (2004a, 2004b). A description of mythography as a scientific discipline can be read in Meliadò (2015).

A general and clear presentation of the different types of Homeric scholia is found in Schironi (2020). There is an increasing interest for ancient homeric scholarship and in the last years several papers on the iliadic scholia have appeared, Montana (2019, 2020, 2021), Pagani (2020) and also a collective volume: Beck, Kelly and Phillips (2021).

Regarding the text of the scholia to Homer, the reference edition of the A (or VMK) and the bT scholia to the *Iliad* is still Erbse (1969–1988). A team composed by A. Kelly, B. Beck, T. Phillips and O. Thomas is translating Erbse's edition. The first volume is expected for 2023. The D scholia to the *Iliad* can be read in Van Thiel (2014). A new edition of all scholia to the *Iliad*—A, bT, D and h—is being prepared by a team lead by Montanari (Montanari et al. 2017). See Montana 2020a for a methodological discussion. On the Aristarchean tradition of commentaries on Homer, see Schironi (2015, 2018, 2021) and Montana 2020b.

An edition of the V scholia to the *Odyssey* is Ernst (2004). A new comprehensive edition of all the scholia to the *Odyssey*—V and exegetical—is being prepared by Pontani. Three volumes covering books 1 to 8 have already been published (Pontani 2007–2020). In Pontani (2005) one can read a thorough description of the exegetical tradition of the *Odyssey*. For a discussion on the selection of the scholia that would go back to the MH see Pagès (this volume; 2007), Montanari (1995, 2002), and Pagès and Villagra (2022). On the hypotheses to the books of the Homeric poems, see van Rossum-Steenbeek (1998: 53–74).

The reference edition of the scholia to Pindar is Drachmann (1903–1927) (reprint 1964). On the history of the corpus, see Deas (1931). Lehrs (1873) is a detailed study of the scholia still worth consulting. A translation of the scholia to O. 1 and 2 is Daude et al. 2014 and 2020. On Didymus's commentary on Pindar, see Braswell (2011), who comments on one scholion that preserves Didymus's explanation of the importance of the myth in the ode. For a study on pindaric scholarship see Braswell (2012) and Österdahl (2021), a dissertation on the same topic. A commented translation of Didymus's fragmentary commentary is Braswell (2013). Schneider (2009) compares the scholia to the fourth *Pythian* to the Homeric scholia and concludes that there was no separate, specifically mythographical commentary on Pindar. This paper is in the first of two volumes dedicated to the Pindaric scholia, David and Calame (2009) and David et al. (2015). Of special interest is the survey of the term *historia* by Vassilaki (2015). As already mentioned, Radová (2011) provides a typological classification of the scholia. There are several works on Pindaric scholarship: Lefkowitz (1985), Pontani (2013), and Fera (2019) are case studies of the exegetical activity of scholiasts. Philips (2013) studies the use of Callimachus as an authoritative source. Lefkowitz (1985) analyzes the interpretative ways of Pindaric scholiasts. On the scholarship on Pindar preserved in papyri, see McNamee (1977, 2007), Ucciardello (2012), and Merro (2019).

The reference edition of the scholia to Euripides is Schwartz (1887–1891). Zuntz (1965) is a classical study on the transmission of the plays of Euripides. A new electronic edition of the scholia is in preparation by Mastronarde in www.euripidesscholia.org, with the purpose to offer "an open-ended repository of the ancient and medieval annotations in Greek found in the papyri and medieval manuscripts" (Mastronarde 2020: 1). Mastronarde (2017) provides a comprehensive study on the scholia to Euripides. The scholia to *Orestes* 1–500 have been published as book in Mastronarde (2020). The book is based on the electronic edition of the site, which will offer always a more updated edition of the scholia, since Mastronarde is still working on the scholia. Merro (2008) offers an edition of the scholia to the *Rhesus* and Cavarezan (2016) an edition of the scholia to the *Hippolytus*. On the history of the scholia to Euripides's *Phoenissae* see Mastronarde and Bremer (1982). On the narrative *hypotheses*, see Meccariello (2014).

The reference edition of the scholia to Apollonius Rhodius is Wendel (1935; 1999, repr.). Surveys of the history of the corpus are Wendel (1932), Fränkel (1964), Herter (1955). In the introduction of his commentary to Apollonius's *Argonautica*, Mooney (1912) gives a useful survey of the scholia. Lachenaud (2010) provides a translation and an introduction that deals with some aspects of mythography. On the use of myth in the scholia to Apollonius see Radová (2009) and for a typological classification see Radová (2011). More bibliography on the use of an earlier version of the preserved scholia to Apollonius by later poets in Dickey (2007).

## REFERENCES

*Sigla*

BNJ: *Brill's New Jacoby*. Edited by Ian Worthington et al. Brill Scholarly Editions online. http://referenceworks.brillonline.com/browse/brill-s-new-jacoby.

*Studies and Texts*

Andolfi, Ilaria. 2019. *Acusilaus of Argos' Rhapsody in Prose*. Berlin and Boston: De Gruyter.

Beck, Bill, Adrian Kelly, and Tom Phillips. 2021. *The Ancient Scholia to Homer's Iliad: Exegesis and Interpretation, Bulletin of the Institute of Classical Studies* 64.1. Oxford: Oxford University Press.

Braswell, Bruce K. 2011. "Didymus on Pindar." In *Ancient Scholarship and Grammar: Archetypes, Concepts and Contexts*, edited by Stephanos Matthaios, Franco Montanari, and Antonios Rengakos, 181–197. Trends in Classics Supplementary Volumes 8. Berlin and New York: De Gruyter.

Braswell, Bruce K. 2012. "Reading Pindar in Antiquity." *Museum Helveticum*, 69.1: 12–28.

Braswell, Bruce K. 2013, ed and trans. *Didymos of Alexandria: Commentary on Pindar*. . Basel: Schwabe Verlag.

Cameron, Alan. 2004. *Greek Mythography in the Roman World*. Oxford: Oxford University Press.

Cavarzeran, Jacopo. 2016. *Scholia in Euripidis "Hippolytum."* Berlin and Boston: De Gruyter.

Celoria, Francis. 1992. *The Metamorphoses of Antoninus Liberalis: A Translation with a Commentary*. London and New York: Routledge.

Coleridge, Edward P. 1938. "The *Phoenissae*." In *The Complete Greek Drama*, 2 volumes, edited by Whitney J. Oates and Eugene O'Neill. New York: Random House.

Darbo-Peschanski, Catherine. 2004a. "La citation et les fragments: Les Fragmente der griechischen Historiker de Felix Jacoby." In *La citation dans l'Antiquité*, edited by Catherine Darbo-Peschanski, 291–300. Grenoble, France: Jérôme Millon.

Darbo-Peschanski, Catherine. 2004b. "Les citations grecques et romaines." In *La citation dans l'Antiquité*, edited by Catherine Darbo-Peschanski, 9–21. Grenoble, France: Jérôme Millon.

Daude, Cécile, Sylvie David, Michel Fartzoff, and Claire Muckensturm-Poulle. 2014. *Scholies à Pindare: Traduction commentée*. Vol. 1: *Vies de Pindare et scholies à la première Olympique. "Un chemin de paroles" (O. I, 110)*. Besançon, France: Presses universitaires de Franche-Comté.

Daude, Cécile, Sylvie David, Michel Fartzoff, and Claire Muckensturm-Poulle. 2020. *Scholies à Pindare*. Vol. 2: *Scholies à la deuxième Olympique*. Besançon, France: Presses universitaires de Franche-Comté.

David, Sylvie, and Claude Calame. 2009. *Traduire les scholies de Pindare: Problèmes de méthode*. Dialogues d'histoire ancienne. Supplément 2. Besançon, France: Presses universitaires de Franche-Comté.

David, Sylvie, Cécile Daude, Evelyne Geny, and Claire Poulle-Muckenstrum. 2015. *Traduire les scholies de Pindare II. Interprétation, histoire, spectacle*. Dialogues d'histoire ancienne. Supplément 13. Besançon, France: Presses universitaires de Franche-Comté.

Deas, Henry T. 1931. "The Scholia Vetera to Pindar." *Harvard Studies in Classical Philology* 42 :1–78.

Delattre, Charles. 2016. "Référence et corpus dans les pratiques de commentaire: Les emplois de historia." *Revue de Philologie, de Littérature et d'Histoire Anciennes* 90: 89–110.

Dickey, Eleanor. 2007. *Ancient Greek Scholarship*. Oxford: Oxford University Press.

Dolcetti, Paola. 2004. *Ferecide di Atene, Testimonianze e frammenti*. Alessandria, Italy: Edizioni dell'Orso.

Dubischar, Markus. 2015. "Typology of Philological Writings." In *Brill's Companion to Ancient Greek Scholarship*, edited by Franco Montanari, Stephanos Matthaios, and Antonios Rengakos, 545–599. Leiden: Brill.

Drachmann, Anders B. 1903–1927. *Scholia uetera in Pindari carmina*. 3 vols. Leipzig: Teubner. Reprint 1964.

Edmunds, Lowell. 2006. *Oedipus*. London: Routledge.

Erbse, Hartmut. 1969–1988. *Scholia graeca in Homeri Iliadem*. 7 vols. Berlin: De Gruyter.

Ernst, Nicola. 2006. "Die D-Scholien zur Odyssee: Kritische Ausgabe." PhD thesis. Universität zu Köln. http://kups.ub.uni-koeln.de/id/eprint/1831.

Fera, Maria C. 2019. "Criticism of Pindar's Poetry in the Scholia Vetera." In *Approaches to Greek Poetry*, edited by Marco Ercoles, Lara Pagani, Filippomaria Pontani, and Giuseppe Ucciardello, 233–260. Berlin: De Gruyter.

Fowler, Robert L. 2000. *Early Greek Mythography*. Vol. 1. *Texts*. Oxford: Oxford University Press.

Fowler, Robert L. 2006. "How to Tell a Myth: Genealogy, Mythology, Mythography." *Kernos* 19: 35–46.

Fowler, Robert L. 2013. *Early Greek Mythography*. Vol. 2. *Commentary*. Oxford: Oxford University Press.

Fränkel, Hermann. 1964. *Einleitung zur kritischen Ausgabe der Argonautika des Apollonios*. Göttingen: Vandenhoeck and Ruprecht.

Herter, Hans. 1955. "Bericht über die Literatur zur hellenistischen Dichtung seit dem Jahre 1921: II. Teil: Apollonios von Rhodos." *Jahresbericht über die Fortschritte der Klassischen Altertumswissenschaft* 285: 213–410.

Henrichs, Albert. 1971. "Scholia Minora zu Homer. I." *Zeitschrift für Papyrologie und Epigraphik* 7: 97–149.

Henrichs, Albert. 1987. "Three Approaches to Greek Mythography." In *Interpretations of Greek Mythology*, edited by Jan Bremmer, 242–277. London: Routledge.

Lachenaud, Guy. 2010. *Scholies à Apollonios de Rhodes*. Fragments 9. Paris: Les Belles Lettres.

Lefkowitz, Mary R. 1985. "The Pindar Scholia." *American Journal of Philology* 106: 269–282.

Lehrs, Karl. 1873. *Die Pindarscholien: Eine kritische Untersuchung zur philologischen Quellenkunde; Nebst einem Anhange über den falschen Hesychius Milesius und den falschen Philemon.* Leipzig: S. Hirzel.

Lloyd-Jones, Hugh. 2002. "Curses and Divine Anger in Early Greek Epic: The Pisander Scholion." *Classical Quarterly* 52: 1–14.

Lundon, John. 1999. "Lexeis from the Scholia Minora in Homerum." *Zeitschrift für Papyrologie und Epigraphik* 124: 25–52.

Gonis, Nikolaos, and John Lundon. 2001. "Scholia Minora to *Iliad* I 595–604, II 4–10." *Zeitschrift für Papyrologie und Epigraphik* 136: 111–115.

Mastronarde, Donald J. 1994. *Euripides: Phoenissae.* Cambridge, UK: Cambridge University Press.

Mastronarde, Donald J. 2017. *Preliminary Studies on the Scholia to Euripides.* Berkeley: California Classical Studies.

Mastronarde, Donald J. 2020. *Euripides Scholia: Scholia on Orestes 1–500.* California Classical Studies. Berkeley: University of Berkeley Pressbooks. https://escholarship.org/uc/item/7xp733bb.

Mastronarde, Donald. J., and Jan M. Bremer. 1982. *The Textual Tradition of Euripides' Phoinissai.* Cambridge, UK: Cambridge University Press.

McNamee, Kathleen. 1977. "Marginalia and Commentaries in Greek Literary Papyri." Diss. Duke University.

McNamee, Kathleen. 1995. "Missing Links in the Development of Scholia." *Greek Roman and Byzantine Studies* 36: 399–414.

McNamee, Kathleen. 1998. "Another Chapter in the History of Scholia." *Classical Quarterly* 48: 269–288.

McNamee, Kathleen. 2007. *Annotations in Greek and Latin Texts from Egypt.* American Studies in Papyrology 45. New Haven, CT: American Society of Papyrologists.

Meccariello, Chiara. 2014. *Le Hypotheses narrative dei drammi euripidei: Testo, contesto, fortuna.* Rome: Storia e Letteratura.

Meliadò, Claudio. 2015. "Mythography." In *Brill's Companion to Ancient Greek Scholarship*, edited by Franco Montanari, Stephanos Matthaios, and Antonios Rengakos, 1057–1089. Leiden: Brill.

Merro, Grazia. 2008. *Gli scoli al Reso euripideo: Introduzione, testo critico e commento.* Messina: Dipartimento di Scienze dell'Antichità Università di Messina.

Merro, Grazia. 2019. "Theon's Pindaric Exegesis: New Materials from Marginalia on Papyri." In *Approaches to Greek Poetry*, edited by Marco Ercoles, Lara Pagani, Filippomaria Pontani and Giuseppe Ucciardello, 213–232. Berlin: De Gruyter.

Montana, Fausto. 2011. "The Making of Greek Scholiastic *Corpora*." In *From Scholars to Scholia: Chapters in the History of Ancient Greek Scholarship*, edited by Franco Montanari and Lara Pagani, 105–162. Trends in Classics Supplement 9. Berlin: De Gruyter.

Montana, Fausto. 2014. "Introduction: From Types to Texts". In *The Birth of Scholiography: From Types to Texts*, edited by Fausto Montana and Antonietta Porro, 1–14. Berlin: De Gruyter.

Montana, Fausto. 2015. "Hellenistic Scholarship." In *Brill's Companion to Ancient Scholarship*, edited by Franco Montanari, Stephanos Matthaios, and Antonios Rengakos, 60–183. Leiden: Brill.

Montana, Fausto. 2020a. "Editing Anonymous Voices: The Scholia Vetera to the *Iliad*." In *Sicut dicit: Editing Ancient and Medieval Commentaries on Authoritative Texts*, edited by Shari Boodts, Pieter De Leemans, and Stefan Schorn, 97–125. Turnhout: Brepols.

Montana, Fausto. 2020b. "Poetry and philology. Some thoughts on the theoretical grounds of Aristarchus' Homeric scholarship." In *More than Homer Knew. Studies on Homer and His Ancient Commentators*, edited by Antonios Rengakos, Patrick J. Finglass, and Bernhard Zimmermann, 161–171. Berlin and Boston: DeGruyter.

Montana, Fausto. 2021. "Exegetical dialogue through compilation. Examples from the h-family of the *Iliad* scholia." In *The Ancient Scholia to Homer's Iliad: Exegesis and Interpretation, Bulletin of the Institute of Classical Studies* 64.1, edited by Bill Beck, Adrian Kelly, and Tom Phillips. Oxford: Oxford University Press, 6–16.

Montanari, Franco. 1995. "The *Mythographus Homericus*." In *Greek Literary Theory after Aristotle: A Collection of Papers in Honour of D. M. Schenkeveld*, edited by Jelle G. J. Abbenes, Simon R. Slings, and Ineke Sluiter, 136–172. Amsterdam: VU University Press.

Montanari, Franco. 2002. "Ancora sul *Mythographus Homericus* (e *l'Odissea*)." In *La mythologie et l'Odyssée*, edited by André Hurst, Françoise Létoublon, and Gabriel Germain, 129–144. Geneva: Librairie Droz.

Montanari, Franco, Stephanos Matthaios, and Antonios Rengakos. 2015. *Brill's Companion to Ancient Greek Scholarship*. Leiden and Boston: Brill.

Montanari, Franco, Fausto Montana, Davide Muratore, and Lara Pagani. 2017. "Towards a New Critical Edition of the Scholia to the *Iliad*: A Specimen." *Trends in Classics* 9: 1–21.

Mooney, George W. 1912. *The Argonautica of Apollonius Rhodius*. Dublin: Dublin University Press.

Nünlist, René. 2009. *The Ancient Critic at Work: Terms and Concepts of Literary Criticism in Greek Scholia*. Cambridge, UK: Cambridge University Press.

Österdahl, Pontus. 2021. *Pindaric Scholarship between Aristarchus and Didymus. An Edition of the Fragments with Explanatory Notes and a Discussion of Early Pindaric Scholarship*, Diss. University of Stockholm.

Pagani, Lara 2020, "Papyrus Commentaries on the *Iliad*." In *Sicut dicit. Editing Ancient and Medieval Commentaries on Authoritative Texts*, edited by Shari Boodts, Pieter De Leemans, Stefan Schorn, 331–362. Turnhout: Brepols.

Pagès, Joan. 2007. "*Mythographus Homericus*: Estudi i edició comentada." Diss. Universitat Autònoma de Barcelona.

Pagès, Joan. 2021. "La mitografía como exégesis homérica: Estudio de algunos ejemplos del *Mythographus Homericus* y los escolios menores a Homero." *Emerita* 89.1: 1–26.

Pagès, Joan and Nereida Villagra. 2022. *Myths on the Margins of Homer. Prolegomena to the Mythographus Homericus*, Berlin: De Gruyter.

Pàmias, Jordi. 2008. *Ferecides d'Atenes, Històries*. Vol. 1. *Introducció, edició crítica, traducció i notes*. Barcelona: Fundació Bernat Metge.

Pàmias, Jordi. 2014. "The Reception of Myth." In *Approaches to Greek Myth*, 2nd ed., edited by Lowell Edmunds, 44–83. Baltimore, MD: Johns Hopkins University Press.

Pàmias, Jordi. 2020. "Pherekydes von Athen: Struktur der Historiai (oder: Der längere Weg von Athen bis Alexandria)." *Classica & Mediaevalia* 68: 1–13.

Pàmias, Jordi, and Arnaud Zucker. 2013. *Ératosthène de Cyrène: Catastérismes*. Paris: Les Belles Lettres.

Philips, Thomas. 2013. "Callimachus in the Pindar Scholia." *Cambridge Classical Journal* 59: 152–177.

Pontani, Filippomaria. 2005. *Sguardi su Ulisse: La tradizione esegetica greca all'Odissea*. Rome: Storia e letteratura.

Pontani, Filippomaria. 2007–2020. *Scholia Graeca in Odysseam*. Vols. 1–4. Rome: Storia e letteratura.

Pontani, Filippomaria. 2013. "Noblest Charis: Pindar and the Scholiasts." *Phoenix* 67: 23–42.

Pontani, Filippomaria. 2015. "Scholarship in the Byzantine Empire (529–1453)." In *Brill's Companion to Ancient Scholarship*, edited by Franco Montanari, Stephanos Matthaios, and Antonios Rengakos, 297–455. Berlin: De Gruyter.

Porro, Antonietta. 2014. "The Birth of Scholiography: Some Conclusions and Perspectives." In *The Birth of Scholiography: From Types to Texts*, edited by Fausto Montana and Antonietta Porro, 192–205. Berlin: De Gruyter.

Radová, Irena. 2009. "Mythology in the Scholia on Apollonius Rhodius." In *Greek Research in Australia: Proceedings of the Eighth Biennial International Conference of Greek Studies, Flinders University June 2009*, edited by Marietta Rossetto, Michael Tsianikas, George Couvalis, and Maria Palaktsoglou, 85–92. Adelaide, AUS: Department of Languages, Modern Greek, Flinders University.

Radová, Irena. 2011. *Altgriechische Scholien: Ein typologischer Versuch*. Prague: Koniasch Latin Press.

Reynolds, Leighton. D., and Nigel G. Wilson. 1968. *Scribes and Scholars: A Guide to the Transmission of Greek and Latin Literature*. Oxford: Oxford University Press.

Schironi, Francesca. 2012. "Greek Commentaries." *Dead Sea Discoveries* 19: 399–441.

Schironi, Francesca. 2015. "Aristarchus' Work in Progress: What Did Aristonicus and Didymus Read of Aristarchus?" *Classical Quarterly* 65: 609–627.

Schironi, Francesca. 2018. *The Best of the Grammarians: Aristarchus of Samothrace on the "Iliad."* Ann Arbor: University of Michigan Press.

Schironi, Francesca. 2020. "Homeric Scholia." In *The Cambridge Guide to Homer*, edited by Corinne O. Pache, Casey Dué, Susan Lupack, and Robert Lamberton, 609–622. Cambridge, UK: Cambridge University Press.

Schironi, Francesca. 2021. "Aristarchus in his own words? What can the 'most secure' Aristarchean fragments tell us about Aristarchus' commentaries, and their transmission.'" In *The Ancient Scholia to Homer's Iliad, Bulletin of the Institute of Classical Studies* 64.1, edited by Bill Beck, Adrian Kelly, and Tom Phillips, 17–34. Oxford: Oxford University Press.

Schneider, Jean. 2009. "Scholies de la IVe Pythique et scholies homériques." In *Traduire les scholies de Pindare I. De la traduction au commentaire: Problèmes de méthode*, edited by Sylvie David and Claude Calame, 147–173. Dialogues d'histoire ancienne Supplément 2. Besançon, France: Presses universitaires de Franche-Comté.

Schwartz, Eduard. 1887–1891. *Scholia in Euripidem*. 2 vols. Berlin: Georg Reimer.

Trachsel, Alexandra. 2019. "Mythographie: commenter Homère ou collectionner des récits mythologiques? L'exemple d'Apollon Sminthée", *Polymnia* 4: 33–63.

Trzaskoma, Stephen M. 2013. Introduction to *Writing Myth: Mythography in the Ancient World*, edited by Stephen M. Trzaskoma and R. Scott Smith, xv–xxiv. Leuven: Peeters.

Ucciardello, Giuseppe. 2012. "Ancient Readers of Pindar's Epinicians in Egypt: Evidence from Papyri." In *Receiving the Komos: Ancient and Modern Receptions of the Victory Ode*, edited by

Peter Agócs, Chris Carey, and Richard Rawles, 105–140. Bulletin of the Institute of Classical Studies, Supplement 112. London: University of London.

Van Rossum-Steenbeek, Monique. 1998. *Greek Readers' Digests? Studies on a Selection of Subliterary Papyri*. Leiden, New York, and Köln: Brill.

Van Thiel, Herman. 2014. *Scholia D in Iliadem: Proecdosis aucta et correctior; Secundum codices manu scriptos*. Cologne. http://kups.ub.uni-koeln.de/id/eprint/5586.

Vassilaki Ekaterini. 2015. "Entre histoire et légende: Recherche sur les emplois des mots ἱστορία, ἱστορεῖν, ἱστοριογράφος et ἱστορικός dans les scholies aux Olympiques de Pindare." In *Traduire les scholies de Pindare*, vol. 2: *Interprétation, histoire, spectacle*, edited by Sylvie David, Cécile Daude, Evelyne Geny, and Claire Poulle-Muckenstrum, 93–117. Dialogues d'histoire Ancienne Supplément 13. Besançon, France: Presses universitaires de Franche-Comté.

Villagra, Nereida, and Jordi Pàmias. 2020. "Los escolios mitográficos y el *Mythographus Homericus*." *Polymnia* 5: 20–38.

Wendel, Carl. 1932. *Die Ueberlieferung der Scholien zu Apollonios von Rhodos*. Berlin: Weidmann.

Wendel, Carl. 1935. *Scholia in Apollonium Rhodium vetera*. Berlin: Weidmann. Reprint, 1999.

White, John W. 1914. *The Scholia of the Aves of Aristophanes*. Boston and London: Ginn and Company.

Wilson, Nigel G. 1967. "A Chapter in the History of Scholia." *Classical Quarterly* 17: 244–256.

Wilson, Nigel G. 1996. *Scholars of Byzantium*. London: Duckworth.

Zuntz, Günther. 1965. *An Inquiry into the Transmission of the Plays of Euripides*. Cambridge, UK: Cambridge University Press.

Zuntz, Günther. 1975. *Die Aristophanes-Scholien der Papyri*. Berlin: Seitz.

..................................................................................................

# CHAPTER 19

# OVID AND MYTHOGRAPHY

..................................................................................................

## JOSEPH FARRELL

OVER the longue durée, there is probably no one whose influence on the reception of classical mythology has been more imposing than that of Ovid. It may also be that no other poet who is as widely read as Ovid survived primarily because of his engagement with mythography. The *Metamorphoses* is crucial in this regard, but Ovid's entire oeuvre reflects this engagement, either by anticipating aspects of the *Metamorphoses* or by taking a pointedly different approach from that of the magnum opus.

Ovidian mythography involves two traditions that are mutually informing but readily distinguishable. The first I will call the literary tradition, in which most poets share. As a *doctus poeta*, Ovid knows and reacts in sophisticated ways to earlier treatments of specific myths, whether they are famous or relatively obscure. This aspect has a lot to do with establishing the poet's relation to, and, if possible, his place within, the "canon" of Greek and Roman writers who were essential reading for any educated, cultivated person.

Such intertextual self-fashioning includes a scholarly approach to earlier writers; but one must also consider Ovid's engagement with the second tradition, that of actual scholarship. From at least the Hellenistic period onward, poets drew on prose works of an antiquarian, historical, scientific, philosophical, or otherwise scholarly sort, not only as sources, but to some extent also as models. This engagement extended to frankly derivative or utilitarian texts—commentaries, catalogues, and the like—that modern scholarship has traditionally classified as "subliterary" or "paraliterary." For example, the structure of the *Metamorphoses* looks as if it were based on that of a more straightforward mythological encyclopedia. It may be that this structure derives ultimately from an earlier poem, such as Hesiod's *Catalogue of Women* (Ludwig 1965; Ziogas 2013). But very similar structures inform such works as the "libraries" of universal history by Diodorus Siculus and of Greek mythology mistakenly ascribed to Apollodorus of Athens (Bethe 1887; Laudien 1905, 1914, 1915; Dietze 1905; discussed by Cole 2004, 2008). It seems likely that Ovid meant his debt to both traditions to be apparent and that making a hard and fast distinction between them would be misguided. But some distinction remains useful and also valid as an expression of ancient attitudes in general. If this were not the case, then the energy generated through hybridiziation—by crossing "elevated" poetic genres with more "utilitarian" prose ones—would be much less impressive than, in Ovid especially, it obviously is.

Ovid's predecessors in drawing on scholarly mythography are the poets of the Hellenistic world, especially those who created mythographical surveys that focused on particular motifs. These include Callimachus in his *Aetia*, Eratosthenes in his *Katasterismoi*, Phanocles in his *Erotes* or *Kaloi*, and Parthenius in his *Erotika Pathemata*. But where these works do not pretend to comprehensive treatment, Ovid claims precisely that; and this puts the *Metamorphoses* into a different category from any other ancient poem. While its stated theme of mythic transformation is virtually identical with that of Nicander's *Heteroioumena* (a significant source of individual stories: see Plaehn 1882), Nicander apparently chose transformation as a mythological motif around which a poem, otherwise heterogeneous and by no means comprehensive, could be organized. Ovid instead made transformation the main theme of a comprehensive poetic survey that would include even myths in which transformation played only a minimal role, if any.

In this sense, the *Metamorphoses* exists in a liminal area between mythological catalogue poems having no pretense to be comprehensive treatments of anything, and prose works that aimed to present a virtually complete, well-organized survey of Greek (and in some cases Roman) mythology (and, sometimes, history) from beginning to end. It would be a mistake to regard the poem as "really" belonging to one tradition or the other, or entirely to both. Just as with Ovid's other generic experiments, it is important to maintain a sense of the conceptual distinctness between the traditions involved and of the seriousness with which Ovid participates in them.

The second main point is in some ways orthogonal to the first. The *Metamorphoses* has been influential not only as a poem but also as a substantial and widely read collection of mythological material. It is not the only such collection, but it would be impossible to name any other single work that played such a commanding role in determining what constituted classical mythology.

An important aspect of Ovid's seriousness about mythography as a theme consists in his deployment of mythographical motifs, topoi, and procedures. These include both the larger organizing structures and the microstructures or topoi of earlier mythographical works. Let us examine the chief characteristics of these features in that order.

# 1. UNIVERSALIZING MACROSTRUCTURES

There are many theories of how to understand the structure of the *Metamorphoses*. Among these, it has been observed that the "song of Silenus," another freewheeling composition that makes up the bulk of Vergil's Sixth *Eclogue*, follows a broadly similar sequence of topics (Skutsch 1901: 31; Due 1974: 27–28; Knox 1986: 10–14; 1990: 183–193; Barchiesi 2005: 148–150; Ziogas 2013: 54–57). Had Vergil been the later writer, one could believe his poem to be a kind of précis of the *Metamorphoses* as a whole; but could Ovid have conceived the fifteen-book *Metamorphoses* as an enormous elaboration of some fifty or so lines of Vergil? More likely, both poems are drawing on some familiar general structure that had previously been used to encompass and organize the Greek myths in their entirety. What might this have been?

The genre of which this structure is most characteristic is that of universal history (Wheeler 2002); and the most imposing work of universal history that survives from antiquity is Diodorus Siculus's *Bibliotheca Historica*, which was mentioned above. About a century ago, it was perceived that there are strong similarities between the macrostructure of this work and that of the *Metamorphoses* (Bethe 1887). In his preface, Diodorus states that "if a man should begin with the most ancient times and record to the best of his ability the affairs of the entire world down to his own day, so far as they have been handed down to memory, as though they were the affairs of some single city, he would obviously have to undertake an immense labour, yet he would have composed a treatise of the utmost value to those who are studiously inclined" (1.3.6, trans. Oldfather 1933). This plan, which Diodorus himself followed, anticipates that of Ovid in two important respects. The first is the chronological scope of the work, "from the most ancient times down to his own day," a phrase the is closely paralleled in the proem of the *Metamorphoses* (*primaque ab origine mundi/ad mea . . . tempora*, 1.3–4). The second is the cosmopolitan *urbs/orbis* motif. Not much later, in summarizing his research methods, Diodorus emphasizes "the abundant supply which Rome affords of the materials pertaining to the proposed study. For the supremacy of this city, a supremacy so powerful that it extends to the bounds of the inhabited world, has provided us in the course of our long residence there with copious resources in the most accessible form" (1.4.2–3). It seems clear that Diodorus is presenting Rome as something more than a convenient center of scholarship. By the same token, Ovid represents the universe as immanently Roman from the beginning and as becoming ever more so over time. Our fragmentary knowledge of Diodorus's text (only books 1–5 and 11–20 of what were 40 books are extant) and of his sources prevents us from deciding whether Ovid was following Diodorus specifically or simply drawing on attitudes and procedures that were widely shared among universal historians. But that he does allude to these structures and motifs seems clear enough.

A second, related frame of reference is that of universal chronography. Before a work like that of Diodorus could be written, more basic work had to be done. Above all, it was necessary to work out the chronological relationships between events that had been previously recorded discretely within the various local traditions of the Greeks and other peoples, such as the Egyptians and the Persians. The classic form of such works was the king list, a record of who ruled, when, and for how long in a specific place. Such a list might be extended as new forms of government came into being. Thus, the Athenian archon lists are presented in ancient chronicles simply as an extension of the list of the earlier tyrants and kings, all the way back to Cecrops. Similarly, in the case of Rome, consular *fasti* continued the list of kings from Romulus to the Tarquins and, before that, those of Alba Longa and Troy. Of course, within each tradition the chronographer had to make decisions in the face of conflicting information about the order of rulers, the length of their respective rules, and so forth. To coordinate two or more different traditions, at a time when different cities used different calendars and other methods of reckoning time, was even more difficult. The first Greek scholar who managed to do it was Castor of Rhodes, whose *Chronologica* or *Chronica* appeared in about 60 BC. It was quickly followed by other, probably derivative works in Latin, including the *Chronica* of Cornelius Nepos, Atticus's *Liber Annalis*, and Varro's *De Gente Populi Romani*. All of these works should have been available for Ovid to use (Cole 2004, 2008).

For chronographers like Castor and historians like Diodorus, mythic time—that is, the period from Deucalion's flood to the Trojan War—includes only a minority of the material with which they are concerned. For Ovid, it comprises almost the entire *Metamorphoses*. Scholars have taken different positions on whether the poem presents mythic time as more-or-less coherent or as flagrantly incoherent. As is often the case, the answer is that Ovid does both, and it may be that one can interpret this procedure as a way of exploiting the different perspectives of chronography and history. As Thomas Cole (2004, 2008) has argued in painstaking detail, there is good reason to believe that Ovid worked to preserve chronological decorum throughout the *Metamorphoses*, but no detailed argument is required to prove that Ovid's narrative style does almost every-thing possible to conceal that fact. Understanding this, one confronts a number of inter-pretive possibilities. One might conclude that the appearance of chaos is the point, and that Ovid is satirizing the universalizing pretensions of writers like Castor and, implic-itly, of those in power who justified their rule with reference to similarly universalizing concepts. Conversely, one could emphasize that there is, after all, a solid structure un-derneath the chaotic surface, and that this structure supports the entire edifice of the Roman *oecumene*. One might even see this Roman substrate as immanent in the struc-ture of the universe but manifesting itself more and more clearly over time, as was noted above; and one could go on from there, with increasing subtlety, toward either a more parodic or a more panegyric reading of the poem. The point is not to solve that problem, or even to suggest that it is soluble, but to make it clear that Ovid generates these inter-pretive issues by engaging specifically with the major tropes and protocols of compre-hensive mythography in both its historical and its chronographic form.

## 2. FLEXIBLE MICROSTRUCTURES

On a smaller scale, Ovid draws on all available traditions, and especially on elements that are common to most of them, to lend a mythographical color to his work. He never employs these straightforwardly, but instead adapts them to his particular literary aims in each given case. The number of tropes and commonplaces involved is great; those of etiology, allegory, deceit, divination and prophecy, divine *phthonos* (envy, spite), human transgression, ritual antagonism, and sex and sexuality have long been staples of Ovidian criticism, even if not always in relation to mythography as such. Conversely, the seemingly forced coincidences that so bothered Quintilian when Ovid used them to effect transitions from one story to another have just lately been shown to derive from "synchronisms," an important element used by chronographers to coordinate different mythic traditions (Cole 2004, 2008) and by historians for more tendentious purposes (Feeney 2007). In the space that remains I will focus on three other motifs: the use of catalogues, citation of mythological variants, and reference to research methods.

## 3. CATALOGUES

Ovid is fond of lists and catalogues, which are important in mythography as well. His fascination with the form probably goes back to Hesiod, the *fons et origo* of the mythographical tradition. Both *Theogony* and *Catalogue of Women* are essentially lists of divine and heroic genealogy. Ovid clearly reflects this poetic and mythographical tradition, but he does so in curious ways, staying almost entirely away from genealogy and often substituting other kinds of catalogues for the expected family trees. In these respects, he both follows and extends a tendency of earlier Greek poetry (Asquith 2005). The result is that any focus on genealogy as such is surprisingly absent from his work, with the important exception of one family, as we shall see.

Possible interest in Hesiod's *Catalogue* is evident already in Ovid's amatory works. In *Amores* 1.7 and 1.10, Ovid follows the lead of Propertius by citing famous women of myth in series and using language that points to the recurring *ē hoiēi* formula that gave Hesiod's catalogue its unofficial title. In *Amores* 2.4, Ovid simply lists the different kinds of women (all, in effect) who appeal to him (Hardie 2005: 296). The *Ars Amatoria* is a catalogue of women in a different sense: Rome, Ovid declares, contains every kind of woman in the world (1.55–56). Further, just as in the war of love, every modern woman is an Amazon (2.742, 3.1), so different kinds of women may be represented by a specific mythical prototype—statuesque women, for instance, by Andromache (2.645, 709, 3.778). The transition to book 3, in which women are addressed, may even imitate the one from *Theogony* to *Catalogue* in that it is very quickly followed by a catalogue of mythical heroines (Gibson 2003: 86). In the same book, women are "catalogued" by various characteristics (for instance, hair, 3.135–168; physical defects, 251–290; character flaws, 501–524). The *Heroides* is more literally a catalogue of heroic women (Barchiesi 1996), but Ovid treats these heroines quite differently from Hesiod. Instead of being mortal women who are raped or seduced by gods and become the mothers of heroic families, they find themselves in variously difficult relationships with mortal men, procreation being generally beside the point. Occasionally, however, the *Heroides* uses the "loves of the gods" motif in a way that probably bespeaks Ovid's interest in not just its poetic pedigree but specifically its mythographical one. In *Heroides* 19, Hero begs Neptune to let Leander swim the Hellespont, reminding the god that he himself had known the pangs of love by naming five of his paramours. These who include Amymone, Tyro, Alcyone, Calyce, and Medusa (*Her.* 19.129–138). Curiously, the *Metamorphoses* (6.115–122) also contains a list of Neptune's dalliances, six this time, as images on Arachne's tapestry. The two lists share only one name, that of Medusa, but it has been shown that they both derive from a single list, Hesiodic at its core, but augmented by (probably) Apollodorus of Athens and (possibly) Philodemus of Gadara (Obbink 2004; see also Farrell 2013). It seems likely, as well, that Hero adopts the allegorical perspective of Apollodorus, whose interest is to disclose the true nature of the divinities he discusses (here reflected in Hero's contention that Neptune is a lover himself), while Arachne adopts one similar to that of Philodemus, in that both find the extremes of erotic passion that are involved in these myths to be either incompatible with the concept of divinity or else a reproach to the god.

The structure of the *Metamorphoses* itself may derive, directly or indirectly, from that of *Theogony* and *Catalogue of Women*, which during the classical period traveled as, effectively, a single work (West 1966: 48–52). As has been noted, this structure may well have influenced writers before Ovid; at any rate, Ovid appears to treat it as something he could expect readers to recognize in spite of his many departures from it. He begins with the creation of the world and moves quickly to the origin of the most important heroic families. In book 1, Ovid tells the stories of Lycaon (206–243), Deucalion (313–415), and Io (583–750). Lycaon is the grandfather of Arcas (see *Met.* 2.496–497), the eponymous hero of the Arcadians, traditionally the oldest of all peoples (a point made implicitly in the *Metamorphoses* because Lycaon is the first individual mortal whose story is told). Deucalion is known from other sources as progenitor (through his son Hellen) of the Hellenes. Io is daughter of the river Inachus and is known from other sources as the sister of Phoroneus, the patriarch of the Argives. Thus, Ovid begins as if his purpose, in accordance with a standardized genealogical structure, were to account for the major heroic genealogies of the Greeks. But he shows no interest in heroic genealogy as such. In fact, in his treatment of Deucalion, he comes close to stating this as a policy. The myth of a primeval flood entered the mythographical tradition at a fairly early date, and Deucalion is widely known as its hero; but as it happens, the earliest complete version that we have is Ovid's (Smith 2015). He places the episode at an appropriately inaugural point in book 1 of the *Metamorphoses*, but he treats it in a way that, from a mythographical point of view, is almost paradoxical. Consulting the version in Ps.-Apollodorus (*Bibl.* 1.46–48), which is later than Ovid's but obviously derives from an earlier Greek source, one finds that he treats the miracle of the stones, which Pyrrha and Deucalion threw over their shoulders to create a new race of earth-born humans, in very cursory fashion, almost as if it were a rather embarrassing parlor trick. The focus of his account is instead a lengthy list of Pyrrha and Deucalion's own offspring, who were presumably conceived in the conventional way. Ovid's approach is exactly the opposite: he narrates the miracle elaborately and says nothing at all about Hellene and his sons Aeolus, Dorus, and Xuthus, or about Xuthus's son Ion, all of whom together are the eponymous heroic ancestors of the largest and most important Greek ethnic groups.

On occasion, instead of the genealogical catalogues one might have expected, Ovid provides *Metamorphoses* with substitute catalogues of things like the names of Actaeon's hunting dogs (3.206–225). All of this is in keeping with Ovid's general predilection for catalogues, and, indeed, with the fact that some critics, in seeking to explain the generic identity of the *Met*, have been content to call it a *Kataloggedicht* (Martini 1970: 105–134), a category that can be applied to his *Ibis*, as well (Krasne 2013). It is for this reason all the more strange that the *Metamorphoses*, as a poem that alludes to the general structure of systematic mythography, virtually excludes such a basic element of that genre from its repertoire of devices. The only actual genealogical catalogue in the poem that takes the ultratraditional form of a king-list is the list of Alban kings, which appears in the *Fasti*, as well, but in a slightly, and gratuitously, different form (Farrell 2013: 232–239). This (quite fictitious) list was, after all, crucially important in linking Augustus and his adoptive Julian ancestors back to Iulus, Aeneas, and Troy. Nor is it surprising that the two lists are almost, but not quite, identical. The list was indispensable, but Ovid evidently found it equally important to establish that even this ideologically canonical king list contained its variants.

# 4. Mythic Variants

Prose mythography abounds in variant versions of particular myths, and Ovid exploits this feature in different ways. Implicitly, his famous doublets of stories like those of Persephone (*Met.* 5.341–661, *F.* 4.417–620), Daedalus (*Ars* 2.21–98, *Met.* 8.183–285), Cephalus and Procris (*Ars* 3.685–746, *Met.* 7.490–8.5), and a few others, differ in their details, as do his two versions of the Alban king list cited above. In a more limited way, in different passages he acknowledges variants that make Theseus the son of Aegeus (*Met.* 8.174, 405, 560) or of Neptune (9.1), Alcyone the daughter of Aeolus (*Met.* 11.410–748) or of Sciron (7.401), and so on. In a poem as expansive as the *Metamorphoses*, these widely separated variants might not have been immediately noticeable; but the poem's main theme calls attention to competing metamorphic *aetia*. O'Hara (2007: 124–125) cites the multiple origin stories of the dove (the Assyrian queen Semiramis, 4.47, and the daughters of Anius, 13.644–174), the swan (Cycnus, son of Sthenelus and a cousin of Phaethon, 2.377–380; son of Apollo, 7.371–380; and son of Neptune, 12.64–145), the hyacinth (Apollo's *eromenos* Hyacinthus, 10.214–219, and the hero Ajax, 13.394–398). In the cases of the swan and the hyacinth, Ovid himself cross-references the variants. But it is, again, the *Fasti* that most explicitly and regularly flags variants. Mythography is not Ovid's only inspiration for this motif. Green (2004: 153 ad *F.* 1.319–332) cites the use of multiple explanations in Callimachus's *Aetia*, an important model for the *Fasti*, and in didactic poetry more generally, as sources. But he also shows that the motif is particularly common in the *Fasti*. Competing etymologies are probably the most common source of variants, but these are frequently rooted in myth or ritual. In book 4, the poet explains that April is so called either from Venus's Greek name, Aphrodite, or because she was born of the sea (*aphros*), or because it is the month when nature "opens up" (from the Latin *aperio*) after being "closed" during the winter (4.61–132). Both etymologies are attested by Varro and Verrius Flaccus (Fantham 1998: 101–102 ad *F.* 61–84), who follow the usual procedure by giving one explanation and then noting that *alii* have a different one. Ovid injects an element of animus by alleging that Envy (*Livor* 85) is behind the second explanation, but he then resolves the matter by explaining that Venus is responsible for the opening of the year. This slightly discordant note is absent from his earlier variants, but it becomes increasingly evident in the proems of book 5 (1–110), when three separate factions among the Muses disagree about the etymology of May (named either for Maiestas, for the *maiores*, or for Maia, the mother of Mercury), and book 6 (1–100), where Juno, Juventas (representing the *iuniores*), and Concordia (because she "joined" the Romans and the Sabines together under Romulus and Titus Tatius) quarrel about which of them is responsible for the name of June. In these latter cases, the poet expresses aporia (5.108–110) and declines to adjudicate the matter (6.97–100), which represents a retreat from the confidence he showed earlier in the poem (Barchiesi 1991).

# 5. Modes of Research

In her letter to Leander, discussed in section 3, Hero writes that she knows about Neptune's love affairs from her reading (*Her.* 19.136). Ovid refers often enough to tradition via the "Alexandrian footnote" (Norden 1903: 122–124; Ross 1975: 78; Hinds 1998: 1–3), but only once (I believe) does he refer directly to archival research, when in the proem to the *Fasti* he tells Germanicus that he will recognize sacral lore excavated from ancient records (*sacra recognosces annalibus eruta priscis*, 1.7, paraphrased 4.11; see also Miller 1991: 10).

On the other hand, Ovid not infrequently represents himself as conducting fieldwork in which myth and ritual play important roles. This is a trope that originates, as far as the extant literature is concerned, with Herodotus, and in Ovid's day it was probably more commonly found in travel literature than in mythography more narrowly defined (Jones 2001). An important early example is *Amores* 3.13, in which he tells the story of an excursion to Faliscan territory in south Etruria, where he witnesses a festival in honor of Juno (Farrell 2014). The poem relays Ovid's experience with a wealth of ethnographic and antiquarian detail, including a highly allusive summary of the festival's founding myth, which cannot be supplemented from any other source. This poem is recognized as an important precursor of the *Fasti* (Miller 1991: 50–57), which employs the motif of field research more frequently (Wilkinson 1955: 244–250; Miller 1991: 108–139). Sometimes, this involves the motif of a chance encounter with some informant who, for one reason or another, has access to information that is useful to the poet. While attending the *ludi scaenici* on April 6, the third day of the Megalensia, Ovid is reminded that it is also the anniversary of the Battle of Thapsus of 46, Julius Caesar's final victory in the civil war, by one of Caesar's veterans, whom he just happens to meet (4.377–386). On the twenty-fifth of the same month, the date of the Robigalia, as Ovid is returning to Rome from Nomentum, he encounters a ritual procession and takes the opportunity to get information from the priest in charge (4.905–942). There is some reason to suspect that a few of his informants are not as reliable as these (Newlands 1995: 67). Relegation to Tomi gave Ovid the chance to continue exploring these motifs, as well as access to "new information" about very familiar myths. For instance, *Tristia* 3.9 comments on Ovid's "discovery" that Tomi is where Medea murdered her brother Absyrtus (from whose "slaughter" [*caede*, 6—which is *tomê* in Greek] the place got its name). Similarly, in *Pont.* 3.2, the poet writes about meeting an old Scythian who recounted the story of Iphigeneia among the Taurians from a native's point of view (compare *Trist.* 4.4), repeating the motif of the "local informant" that is also found in several passages of the *Fasti* (compare Rutledge 1980).

These are just a few examples, but they may serve to illustrate that Ovid drew on a number of mythographical traditions. Some of these had already been assimilated to poetry, to various extents, and Ovid certainly explored the poetic potential that was latent in more straightforward applications of these motifs. At the same time, he exploits that potential to an unusual degree, and does so with increasing frequency and imagination over the course of his career.

## 6. Mythography after Ovid

So far as we can tell, Ovid never officially received canonical status. If we can believe his testimony, his poetry was not to be found in imperial libraries, and Quintilian makes it clear that he did not regard Ovid as a poet worth teaching, imitating, or, perhaps, even reading. But even if we have no indication that "official" literary culture took much interest in Ovid, he was certainly read and imitated by other creative writers of the classical period, including Phaedrus, Persius, Seneca, Petronius, Martial, the Flavian epicists, and Apuleius. His influence obviously takes many forms that are not confined to mythography as such. Authors of the 4th-century Renaissance, such as Claudian, and of the Merovingian period, such as Venantius Fortunatus, knew Ovid well and used him as both a source and a stylistic model.

Ovid's influence on classical and late-antique scholarship is a somewhat different matter. In keeping with the poet's noncanonical status, there is little evidence of an ancient commentary tradition on his works (Ronconi 1984; Hollis 1996; Dewar 2002; Cameron 2004: 3–32; Wheeler 2004–2005). He is cited by Servius and other commentators on canonical authors, but these citations reinforce the impression that Ovid remained outside the canon. Servius, for instance, cites the *Amores* and the *Fasti* just once each, and though he cites the *Metamorphoses* some eighteen times, the accuracy of his citations is so poor that he must not have known the poem at first hand (Haynes 2014). Not surprisingly, citations seldom, if ever, involve matters of Latinity; instead, the focus is squarely on the usefulness of the *Metamorphoses* as a mythological handbook.

In addition to commentators on other authors, ancient mythographers, too, mined the *Metamorphoses*. A work entitled *Narrationes*, which belongs to the 3rd century and is attributed to a probably fictitious individual named Lactantius Placidus, summarizes tales from Ovid in very simple terms but adds information not found in Ovid himself (see also Smith, this volume). *Narrationes* would appear to have influenced the anonymous author of a commentary on Germanicus, produced by about 300, as well as Vibius Sequester, perhaps a half-century later, and the author of a commentary on Statius perhaps a century after that. Quite a bit later, they were used by two of the three authors known as the "Vatican Mythographers." The first of these, who worked sometime between 875 and 1075, appears to have used the *Narrationes*, and his work was used in turn by the second, although the most important source of both these works is the commentary of Servius (Kulcsár 1987; Herren 1998–1999). Other early Medieval scholarship devoted to or deriving from Ovid that was produced through the 11th century appears to arise from independent traditions (Hexter 1987; Knox 2009: 329–333). With the *aetas Ovidiana* of the 12th and 13th centuries, however, the process of establishing Ovid among the most important mythographical sources of classical antiquity, and of finally granting him a place in the canon of classical authors, though not yet complete, was set on an irreversible course.

## FURTHER READING

The literature on Ovid's engagement with previous literature is vast. The Greek tragedians, especially Euripides, have long been recognized as influential on Ovid's treatment of particular myths (Currie 1981; D'Anna 1959; Davis 1995; Auhagen 1999; Dangel 2009; Curley 2013), but until fairly recently his deployments of stories from tragedy were seldom regarded as components of a coherent mythic or mythographical structure. More recently, critics have detected evidence of such a design, especially in of Ovid's large-scale works, including chronography and universal history in the *Metamorphoses* (Cole 2004 and 2008, reviving ideas put forth by Bethe 1887; Dietze 1905; and Laudien 1905, 1914, 1915; Wheeler 2002) and the Roman calendar in the *Fasti* (Feeney 2007). In the process, Hesiod has come to be seen as an important conceptual and formal model (Ziogas 2013). At the same time, Ovid's use of not only tragedy but also Hellenistic "catalogue poetry" of various kinds (pioneered by Plaehn 1882) has begun to be reassessed (Martini 1970; Barchiesi 1996; Obbink 2004; Asquith 2005; Hardie 2005; Krasne 2013; Farrell 2013, 2014) along with his relationship to Roman predecessors such as Vergil (again following in the wake of an early pioneer, Skutsch 1901: 31; see Due 1974: 27–28; Knox 1986: 10–14; 1990: 183–193; Barchiesi 2005: 148–150; Ziogas 2013: 54–57) and Propertius (Miller 1991). Ovid's reception by later mythographers has been studied by Kulcsár (1987); Herren (1998–1999); Hexter (1987); Hollis (1996); (Herren 1998–1999); Cameron (2004); Wheeler (2004–2005); Knox (2009: 329–333); Haynes (2014); and Smith (2015).

## REFERENCES

Asquith, Helen. 2005. "From Genealogy to *Catalogue:* The Hellenistic Adaptation of the Hesiodic Catalogue Form." In *The Hesiodic "Catalogue of Women": Constructions and Reconstructions*, edited by Richard L. Hunter, 266–286. Cambridge, UK: Cambridge University Press.

Auhagen, Ulrike. 1999. *Der Monolog bei Ovid*. Tübingen: Gunter Narr Verlag.

Barchiesi, Alessandro. 1991. "Discordant Muses." *Proceeding of the Cambridge Philological Society* 37: 1–21.

Barchiesi, Alessandro. 1996. Review of *Ovid, Heroides XVI–XXI*, by E. J. Kenney. *Bryn Mawr Classical Review* 1996.12.01. https://bmcr.brynmawr.edu/1996/1996.12.01/.

Barchiesi, Alessandro. 2005. *Ovidio: Metamorfosi 1 (Libri I–II)*. Milan: Fondazione Lorenzo Valla.

Bethe, Erich. 1887. "Quaestiones diodoreae mythographae." Diss. University of Göttingen.

Cameron, Alan. 2004. *Greek Mythography in the Roman World*. Oxford: Oxford University Press.

Cole, Thomas. 2004. "Ovid, Varro, and Castor of Rhodes: The Chronological Architecture of the *Metamorphoses*." *Harvard Studies in Classical Philology* 102: 335–422.

Cole, Thomas. 2008. *Ovidius Mythistoricus: Legendary Time in the "Metamorphoses."* Studien zur klassischen Philologie 160. Frankfurt: Peter Lang.

Curley, Dan. 2013. *Tragedy in Ovid: Theater, Metatheater, and the Transformation of a Genre*. Cambridge, UK: Cambridge University Press.

Currie, Harry M. 1981. "Ovid and the Roman Stage." *Aufstieg und Niedergang der römischen Welt* II 31 (4): 2701–2742.

D'Anna, Giovanni. 1959. "La tragedia latina arcaica nelle *Metamorfosi*." *Atti del convegno international ovidiano, Sulmona, Maggio 1958*. 2.217–234. Rome: Istituto di studi Romani.

Dangel, Jacqueline. 2009. "Tragédie et élégie en interface dans l'oeuvre ovidienne: Essai sur les frontières génériques." In *La théâtralité de l'oeuvre ovidienne*, edited by Isabelle Jouteur, 21–39. Paris: Nancy: Association pour la diffusion de la recherche sur l'antiquité.

Davis, Peter J. 1995. "Rewriting Euripides: Ovid, *Heroides 4*." *Scholia* n.s. 4: 41–55.

Dewar, Michael. 2002. "*Siquid habent veri vatum praesagia*: Ovid in the 1st–5th Centuries A.D." In *Brill's Companion to Ovid*, edited by Barbara Weiden Boyd, 383–412. Leiden: Brill.

Dietze, Johannes. 1905. *Komposition und Quellenbenutzung in Ovids "Metamorphosen."* Hamburg.

Due, Otto S. 1974. *Changing Forms: Studies in the Metamorphoses of Ovid*. Copenhagen: Gyldendal.

Fantham, Elaine, ed. 1998. *Ovid: Fasti Book IV*. Cambridge, UK: Cambridge University Press.

Farrell, Joseph. 2013. "Complementarity and Contradiction in Ovidian Mythography." In *Writing Myth: Mythography in the Ancient World*, edited by Stephen M. Trzaskoma and R. Scott Smith, 223–252. Leuven: Peeters.

Farrell, Joseph. 2014. "The Poet in an Artificial Landscape: Ovid at *Falerii (Amores, 3.13)*." In *Lire la Ville: Fragments d'une archéologie littéraire de Rome antique*, edited by Damien Nelis and Manuel Royo, 215–236. Bordeaux, France: Ausonius Éditions.

Feeney, Denis. 2007. *Caesar's Calendar: Ancient Time and the Beginnings of History*. Sather Classical Lectures 65. Berkeley: University of California Press.

Gibson, Roy K., ed. 2003. *Ovid: Ars Amatoria Book 3*. Cambridge, UK: Cambridge University Press.

Green, Steven J. 2004. *Ovid, Fasti 1: A Commentary*. Leiden and Boston: Brill.

Hardie, Philip. 2005. "The Hesiodic *Catalogue of Women* and Latin Poetry." In *The Hesiodic "Catalogue of Women": Constructions and Reconstructions*, edited by Richard L. Hunter, 287–298. Cambridge, UK: Cambridge University Press.

Haynes, Justin. 2014. "Citations of Ovid in Virgil's Ancient Commentators." In *Classical Commentaries: Explorations in a Scholarly Genre*, edited by Christina S. Kraus and Christopher Stray, 216–232. Oxford: Oxford University Press.

Herren, Michael. 1998–1999. "The Earliest European Study of Graeco-Roman Mythology (A.D. 600–900)." *Acta Classica Universitatis Scientium Debreceniensis* 34–35: 25–49.

Hexter, Ralph. 1987. "Medieval Articulations of Ovid's *Metamorphoses*: From Lactantian Segmentation to Arnulfian Allegory." *Medievalia* 13: 63–82.

Hinds, Stephen E. 1998. *Allusion and Intertext: Dynamics of Appropriation in Roman Poetry*. Cambridge, UK: Cambridge University Press.

Hollis, Adrian. 1996. "Traces of Ancient Commentaries on Ovid's *Metamorphoses*." *Papers of the Leeds International Latin Seminar* 9: 159–174.

Jones, Christopher P. 2001. "Pausanias and His Guides." In *Pausanias: Travel and Memory in Roman Greece*, edited by Susan E. Alcock, John F. Cherry, and Jaś Elsner, 33–39. Oxford: Oxford University Press.

Jouteur, Isabelle, ed. 2009. *La théâtralité de l'oeuvre ovidienne*. Paris: Nancy: Association pour la diffusion de la recherche sur l'antiquité.

Knox, Peter E. 1986. *Ovid's* Metamorphoses *and the Traditions of Augustan Poetry*. Cambridge, UK: Cambridge Philological Society.

Knox, Peter E. 1990. "In Pursuit of Daphne." *Transactions of the American Philological Association* 120: 183–202.

Knox, Peter E. 2009. "Commenting." In *A Companion to Ovid*, edited by Peter E. Knox, 327–340. Chichester, UK: Wiley-Blackwell.

Krasne, Darcy. 2013. "Starving the Slender Muse: Identity, Mythography, and Intertextuality in Ovid's *Ibis*." In *Writing Down the Myths*, edited by Joseph Falaky Nagy, 67–85. Turnhout: Brepols.

Kulcsár, Péter. 1987. *Mythographi Vaticani I et II*. Corpus Christianorum Series Latina 91c. Turnhout: Brepols.

Laudien, Arthur. 1905. "Studia ovidiana." Diss. Griefswald.

Laudien, Arthur. 1914. "Der römische Sagenkreis in Ovids *Metamorphosen*." *Jahresbericht des Philologischen Vereins 40, Sokrates* 2: 281–287.

Laudien, Arthur. 1915. "Zur mythographischen Quellen der *Metamorphosen*." *Jahresbericht des Philologischen Vereins 41, Sokrates* 3: 129–132.

Ludwig, Walther. 1965. *Struktur und Einheit der Metamorphosen Ovids*. Berlin: De Gruyter.

Martini, Edgar. 1970. *Einleitung zu Ovid*. Darmstadt: Wissenschaftliche Buchgesellschaft.

Miller, John F. 1991. *Ovid's Elegiac Festivals*. Studien zur klassischen Philologie 55. Frankfurt: Peter Lang.

Newlands, Carole E. 1995. *Playing with Time: Ovid and the* Fasti. Ithaca, NY: Cornell University Press.

Norden, Eduard. 1903. *P. Vergilius Maro, Aeneis Buch VI*. Leipzig: B. G. Teubner.

O'Hara, James. 2007. *Inconsistency in Roman Epic: Studies in Catullus, Lucretius, Vergil, Ovid and Lucan*. Cambridge, UK: Cambridge University Press.

Obbink, Dirk. 2004. "Vergil's *De pietate*: From *Ehoiae* to Allegory in Vergil, Philodemus, and Ovid." In *Vergil, Philodemus and the Augustans*, edited by David Armstrong, Jeffrey Fish, Patricia A. Johnston, and Marilyn B. Skinner, 175–209. Austin: University of Texas Press.

Oldfather, Charles H., trans. 1933. *Diodorus of Sicily: Library of History*. Vol. 1: Bks. 1–2.34. Loeb Classical Library 279. Cambridge, MA: Harvard University Press.

Plaehn, Gustav. 1882. "De Nicandro aliisque poetis Graecis ab Ovidio in Metamorphosibus conscribendis adhibitis." Diss. Halle.

Ross, David O., Jr. 1975. *Backgrounds to Augustan Poetry: Gallus, Elegy, and Rome*. Cambridge, UK: Cambridge University Press.

Ronconi, Alessandro. 1984. "Fortuna di Ovidio." *Atene e Roma* 29: 1–16.

Rutledge, Eleanor S. 1980. "Ovid's Informants in the *Fasti*." In *Studies in Latin Literature and Roman History II*, edited by Carl Leroux, 322–331. Collection Latomus 168. Brussels: Latomus.

Smith, R. Scott. 2015. "Bundling Myth, Bungling Myth: The Flood Myth in Ancient and Modern Handbooks of Myth." *Archiv für Religionsgeschichte* 16 (1): 243–262.

Skutsch, Franz. 1901. *Aus Vergils Frühzeit*. Leipzig: B. G. Teubner.

West, Martin L., ed. 1966. *Hesiod. "Theogony."* Oxford: Clarendon Press.

Wheeler, Stephen M. 2002. "Ovid's *Metamorphoses* and Universal History." In *Clio and the Poets: Augustan Poetry and the Traditions of Ancient Historiography*, edited by David S. Levene and Damien P. Nelis, 163–190. Leiden: Brill.

Wheeler, Stephen M. 2004–2005. "Before the *Aetas Ovidiana*: Mapping the Early Reception of Ovid." In *Aetas Ovidiana?*, edited by Damien Nelis = *Hermathena* 177–178: 5–26.

Wilkinson, Lancelot P. 1955. *Ovid Recalled*. Cambridge, UK: Cambridge University Press.

Ziogas, Ioannis. 2013. *Ovid and Hesiod: The Metamorphoses of the "Catalogue of Women."* Cambridge, UK: Cambridge University Press.

........................................................................................

# CHAPTER 20

# PALAEPHATUS,
# *UNBELIEVABLE TALES*

........................................................................................

## HUGO H. KONING

## 1. AUTHOR AND CONTENT

........................................................................................

IT is rather difficult to pin down the rationalizing mythographer known as Palaephatus. Scholars generally believe that he was a Peripatetic working in Athens around 330 BCE, but this broad consensus is one of convenience. Evidence for his life and intellectual context are slim. Our main source is the *Suda*, which contains four entries for Palaephatus, three of which in all likelihood refer to the mythographer (the multiplication presumably owing to some mix-up of biographical details). The few other sources we have confirm—at least, do not contradict—this briefest outline of Palaephatus's date and place. Neither stylistic analysis nor *Quellenforschung* can bring us much further: his language is simple and common, and the myths he presents are generally standard, unremarkable versions. The association with the Lyceum is generally assumed but hardly obvious from his work (see esp. Zucker 2016). It is likely that his name, meaning "teller of old tales," is a pseudonym.

The *Suda* credits this elusive character with several books on history and mythology; all that we have left, however, is a rather short compendium discussing fifty-two separate myths and their explanations (the last seven of which are spurious), preceded by a brief introduction. This text is transmitted under the title *Unbelievable Tales* (*Peri Apistōn*).

The exact relationship between our text and the original work by Palaephatus is impossible to determine. According to one of the entries in the *Suda*, there were originally five books; and there are other sources that refer to Palaephatus's treatment of myths that are absent from our version of *Unbelievable Tales* (see Stern 1996: 4–5; unfortunately, no collection of Palaephatus's testimonia exists). Our text is therefore presumably an epitome, perhaps created sometime before the 10th century. Whether the compiler only used authentic, Palaephatean material or also included that of other authors is debated. To my mind, the strongest arguments favor the first view, and it seems safe to say that what we have was written by Palaephatus, with the obvious exception of the last seven entries (46–52); these are late Byzantine additions that deviate from the preceding material because they offer only summaries of myths but no rationalizing explanations.

The selection criteria used by the epitomizer are largely unclear to us. Hence, we do not know why he included the myths we have and excluded others; nor do we know whether he took his myths from all five of the original books—if there were five in the first place. The order of the myths seems rather random as well; little attention was paid to geographical or genealogical sequence, which are otherwise common organizational structures in mythography. We do recognize certain thematic clusters, perhaps taken wholesale from the original—some entries focus on Heracles (7, 18, 24, 32, 36–40, 44, 45), some on Thebes (3–6, 41), some on different persons with the same name (Glaucus, 25–27)—but nothing indicates that this is purposeful on the part of the author (see further Stern 1996: 22–24). We are thus left all the more in the dark regarding the structure of the original work.

## 2. Rationalizing Aims and Methods

In the proem the author sets out the aims and methods of his rationalizing approach (on rationalizing generally, see Hawes, this volume), claiming first of all that traditional myths, said to be believed only by overcredulous people, are the products of extravagant fantasy by eager-to-please poets and *logographoi* (early historians). Furthermore, only "research"— that is, on-site autopsy and interviews with locals—can bring out the truth behind those tales. Both claims should be regarded as commonplaces well-known from historiography since they are not followed up in the book. There is no reason to assume that Palaephatus engaged in extensive traveling, and there is no mention of him cross-examining local experts. Similarly, the poets and logographers do not return as significant factors in the supposed process of mythopoesis.

Palaephatus bolsters his position in the proem with two philosophical notions, one attributed (probably wrongly) to Melissus and (the otherwise unknown) Lamiscus: "what came into being still exists and will exist hereafter." This slogan entails the Aristotelian concept of the fixity of species, the main text-internal piece of evidence for Palaephatus's alleged Peripatetic affiliation. Armed with this notion, the author is able to reject anything that is impossible by the standards of contemporary reality. For instance: there could never have been a Minotaur, because there are not any today, either (*Palaeph.* 2).

The other philosophical doctrine adhered to concerns the relationship between words and things, a familiar sophistic topic that is treated in several Platonic dialogues. Palaephatus's idea is often summarized as being based on a dichotomy between "deeds" (here taking the place of the more common "things"), which were there first, and the "words" for them, which came later. This view is expressed by Plato's characters Gorgias and Hermogenes (see Santoni 1998: 13–14; 2000: 23–24), the logic obviously being that if it were the other way around (that is, first words, then things or deeds), the words would have no referent and would make little sense. Palaephatus's position, however, seems slightly more complicated in that he further subdivides "words" into *onomata* (names) and *logoi* (words or stories), the first subcategory being earlier than the second. It seems likely that such a distinction should be understood as a polemic against the view expressed in Plato's *Critias*, where mythology is described as an attempt to explain the "names" of the first people, their "deeds" being utterly lost (see Van den Berg 2017). In contrast to this view, Palaephatus argues that *both* "names" and "deeds" can still be known, despite the nefarious influence of mythification and forgetfulness. This claim allows him to contend that the strange and impossible myths the Greeks tell each other must have some kernel of truth. It is Palaephatus's task to reconstruct the actual event, and, at the same time, demonstrate how historical truth became a tale of wonder.

Palaephatus's proem does not adhere to the strictest demands of theoretical preciseness and coherence. And his basically historicizing approach is not unique, either; before him, Hecataeus, Herodotus, and Hellanicus had already voiced the opinion that certain mythical tales were nothing more than the warped renderings of some misunderstood historical reality (see Stern 1996: 10–16; Smith and Trzaskoma 2007: xx–xxiii). Euhemerus, slightly later than Palaephatus, in fact, reduced all myth and religion to this process of mythification. What *is* undeniably original, however, is Palaephatus's completely systematic, consistent, and univocal treatment of the myths under investigation. It is obviously from "exemplary practice rather than theoretical axioms" (Hawes 2014b: 142) that the treatise derives its strength. When we see the mythographer at work, we understand the technique—and the ideological gap between him and Euhemerus, the other historicizing rationalist from this period. Whereas Euhemerus traces back the gods to historical individuals and thus casts doubt on faith and religious practice as a whole, Palaephatus stays clear of myths that feature divinities and hardly even mentions the gods. He applies his method exclusively to tales of heroes and monsters, creating belief instead of disbelief (paraphrasing Stern 1996: 8): his reconstruction of ancient history, devoid of hybrid creatures and impossible superhumans, is indeed quite realistic.

# 3. Palaephatus's Explanations: Structure

Nowhere is Palaephatus's methodical rigor more visible than in the Procrustean structure of his entries. First, he presents us with a summary of the myth in question (sometimes obviously narrated in such a way as to facilitate the explanation that comes later), which he then proceeds to criticize briefly as illogical, inconsistent, or physically impossible. Next comes the reconstruction of true events, comprising of historical and realistic elements that replace the mythical ones. Concluding remarks often close off the entry. An example is *Palaeph.* 7, on the horses of Diomedes (the translations here and elsewhere are taken from Stern 1996):

> They say that Diomedes's horses ate men. Ridiculous! Horses enjoy barley and oats rather than human flesh. Here is the truth: men of long ago made their living with their own hands, and it was by tilling the ground that they acquired food and abundant resources. But a certain Diomedes became preoccupied with the breeding of horses. His delight in them reached the point that he lost his property: he sold everything he had and squandered it on the raising of his horses. So his friends called the horses "man-eaters"—and that is how the myth began.

The items in the *Peri Apistōn* vary considerably in length, but not much in structure. The (near) omnipresence of the schema (mostly analyzed as bipartite; see, for example, Santoni 2000: 13–14; Hawes 2014a: 48; or tripartite, for example, Stern 1996: 17; Gibson 2012: 87) may find its origins in a Peripatetic penchant for systematization. The rigidity may also have been inspired by more practical concerns, since the strictly uniform treatment of myths made Palaephatean exegesis instantly recognizable and comprehensible to any reader (Santoni 2000: 12; Hawes 2014b: 135–136; Delattre 2013: 149). This suggests that the original work was meant as a catalogue-like reference book (however it was organized), fragmenting the whole of Greek mythology into separate, self-contained episodes. The myths are cut loose from any social context, an effect that is further enhanced by the colorless, unadorned summaries (so typical in mythography) that start off every item.

## 4. Rationalizing Strategies

Scholars usually pay a great deal of attention to the hermeneutic strategies adopted by Palaephatus, discerning several types for the sake of convenience (Osmun 1956: 133–135; Stern 1996: 18–21). The obvious usefulness of such categories, however, should not divert us from what they have in common. All of Palaephatus's explanations point at the historical truth by showing us how the actual facts were transformed into mythical tales. Palaephatus thus argues from the myths, and despite his promises of empirical research, he does not employ arguments or proofs that are independent from the texts he is analyzing. He offers us plausibility and narrative logic, nothing more. Modern categories may obscure the fact that in his work, there is but one cause for mythopoesis: misunderstanding. It thus seems wise to keep categories to a minimum, allowing for misunderstood (1) appellations, (2) situations, and (3) expressions, or, to use Palaephatus's terms, misunderstood "names," "deeds," and "words."

The first type of explanation is put to use quite frequently. We encounter human individuals with the name of an animal, who are mistaken for the animal itself: the mythical dragon guarding Thebes was really a king called Dracon (item 3); similarly, the Ram who saved Helle and Phrixos (30) and the Bull who slept with the Cretan queen Pasiphae (2) were, in fact, men called Ram and Bull, respectively. By extension, the names Scylla (20) and Pegasus (28) actually belonged to ships, not mythical creatures. Occasionally, Palaephatus invents transparent place names: the Hundredhanders were denizens of a place called "Hundredhand" (19), just as the three-headed giant Geryon lived in "Tricranium" (24). To solve the myth of the Sphinx, Palaephatus even goes so far as to claim that the word *ainigma* (riddle) means "ambush" in the Theban dialect, allowing for a reconstructed reality in which Sphinx (in reality, an Amazonian queen) regularly killed off Thebans by setting "ambushes" (4).

The second category is that of misunderstood situations. For instance: it is far more likely, when hunters saw Atalanta and Melanion entering a cave and lions leaving it, that the lovers were devoured by the beasts instead of turning into them (13; the same goes for Callisto and the bear, 14). Amazons were not war-like women, but simply men wearing women's clothing (32). The hero known as Glaucus "of the Sea" (27) was not a man miraculously turned into an aquatic immortal, but an excellent fisherman and diver who eventually died at sea and thus was never seen again. Palaephatus does not argue these cases: he relies on the reader's common sense.

Scholars often single out a specific type in this category, that of the so-called first inventor (*prōtos heuretēs*): a technological innovation is misunderstood by others and an incredible tale is fabricated to account for it. The best-known example of this explanatory device is found in item 1, on Centaurs—these fantastical beasts were, in fact, the first horseback riders, taken as impossible hybrid creatures by surrounding peoples. Other examples include Lynceus, whose mythical ability to see under the earth is explained by his invention of a lamp that could be used in mines (9); Pandora, we are told, was not really made up of clay, but regularly applied an earthen cosmetic to her face (34); and Medea, whose awful reputation of boiling old men can be derived from her invention of the sauna (43).

The third type, "misunderstood expression," hinging on the literal interpretation of a metaphor, is a very productive tool. It is employed when Palaephatus rounds off his reconstruction of the "actual" event by presenting some unknown observer(s) who comment(s) on it. This small bit of direct speech is understood literally and causes mythification. Actaeon, for instance, spent all his money on his hunting dogs and thus, in the end, was said to be "devoured" by them (6; just like Diomedes was by his horses, 7); similarly, the musicians Zethus and Amphion asked the members of their audiences to pay them for performances with stones for the wall of Thebes—hence, word got around that "the wall was built with a lyre" (41).

Direct speech is mostly absent from mythography because of its tendency "to tell its story as economically as possible" (Fowler 2006: 40). Palaephatus uses it sparingly as well, except for these anonymous comments—they occur in more than half of the items, often as part of rationalizations that in fact hinge on explanations of the first or second type. For instance: after explaining the Winged Horses of Pelops as the name of a ship (29), Palaephatus still finishes off the entry with direct speech: "The people said: 'Pelops carried off Oenomaus's daughter on his Winged Horses and took to flight.' Thus the myth was fashioned." Another example is the item on Daedalus (21), that rationalizes the myth of his supposedly "walking" statues by crediting the renowned sculptor with inventing statues that whose feet are apart instead of together; Palaephatus then still imagines people saying, "Daedalus made his statue walking, not standing." The prominence of misunderstood expressions is presumably not merely a case of "overlap" (Stern 1996: 19), but illustrates Palaephatus's belief, voiced in the proem, that the people's "words" are crucial to the process of the creation of myths.

# 5. OUTLOOK AND INFLUENCE

Myths, then, come to be by mistake, not intention. The influence of poets and logographers is at best secondary, enhancing the mythical element to create fascinating and astonishing tales that because of their appeal have become canonical. There is, apparently, no function for myths other than simple entertainment; Palaephatus cannot credit the human imagination with more than the capacity to twist empirical reality. This is surely a limited and overly simplistic view, for which Palaephatus has been severely criticized by modern scholars—and the same goes for his rationalizations, some of which are considered more fanciful than the myths they are meant to explain.

The absurdity of some of the explanations, coupled with the obvious falsity of his promise of empirical research, may suggest that Palaephatus's rationalizations are not made in earnest, an impression that is strengthened by the similarity between his work and rhetorical exercises (Gibson 2012). I believe, however, that the methodical rigor, the size of the original book, and the absence of any obvious attempts at humor amply demonstrate that the Palaephatean project was meant quite seriously. Palaephatus's direct influence on two other short collections called *Peri Apistōn*—one by Heraclitus the Mythographer (1st or 2nd c. CE; see Hawes, this volume) and one by an anonymous, undatable mythographer—further demonstrate that it was, in fact, taken seriously. Palaephatus's *Unbelievable Tales* may at times strike us as rather unbelievable; but it is the first systematic and consistent, "scientific" attempt at a historicist-rationalist reading of Greek mythology.

## FURTHER READING

### Text, Translations, and Commentaries

The standard critical edition of Palaephatus is that of Festa (1902), a volume containing similar material written by Heraclitus Mythographus and an anonymous author. The most accessible translation-cum-commentary is that in Stern (1996); he offers a relevant introduction, literal translation, thorough commentary, and many cross-references. The translation of Santoni (2000) comes with a detailed introduction and commentary. There are also recent annotated translations: Jarkho (1988a, 1988b), Russian; Sanz Morales (2002) and Torres Guerra (2009), Spanish; Ramelli (2007), Italian; Brodersen (2002), German; and Koning (2016), Dutch.

## Studies

For questions of date and authorship, see von Blumenthal (1942); Fornaro (2000); and Santoni (2012). The most reasonable and complete treatment of the subject can be found in appendix I of Hawes's monograph (2014a: 227–238); Zucker (2016: 15–17) neatly sums up the question.

Hawes's monograph also offers the best discussion of Palaephatus's place in Greek rationalizing mythography; one should also consult her (2014b) article. Still useful on Palaephatus's intellectual context is Wipprecht (1902: 11–20). Gibson (2012) focuses on the use of Palaephatus in rhetorical exercises in (late) antiquity; see on the 'genre' of Palaephatus's project Bouvier (2015), and on his reconstruction of history Koning (2022).

Santoni (1998) discusses the theoretical assumptions in Palaephatus's proem; see on the proem also Hunter (2016). Trachsel (2005) makes an attempt to track down Peripatetic traces in both Palaephatean theory and practice; Zucker (2016, esp. 17–22) rightfully casts doubt on oft-assumed Aristotelian influences. Van den Berg (2017) relates the tricky relationship between "deeds," "names," and "words" in the proem to older speculations on the origin of myths, already present in Plato's *Critias*.

Osmun (1956) offers a convenient discussion of Palaephatus's exegetic tools, and so does Stern (1999).

## References

Blumenthal, Albrecht von. 1942. "Palaiphatos." RE 18: 2451–2455.

Bouvier, David. 2015. "Palaiphatos ou le mythe du mythographe." *Polymnia* 1: 25–60.

Brodersen, Karl. 2002. *Die Wahrheit über die griechischen Mythen*. Stuttgart: Reclam.

Delattre, Charles. 2013. "Pentaméron Mythographique: Les Grecs ont-ils écrit leurs mythes?" *Lalies* 33: 77–170.

Festa, Nicolaus. 1902. *Mythographi Graeci III.2*. Leipzig: Teubner.

Fornaro, Sotera. 2000. "Palaiphatos." *Neue Pauly* 9: 163–164.

Fowler, Robert L. 2006. "How to Tell a Myth: Genealogy, Mythology, Mythography." *Kernos* 19: 35–46.

Gibson, Craig A. 2012. "Palaephatus and the Progymnasmata." *Byzantinische Zeitschrift* 105: 85–91.

Hawes, Greta. 2014a. *Rationalizing Myth in Antiquity*. Oxford: Oxford University Press.

Hawes, Greta. 2014b. "Story Time at the Library: Palaephatus and the Emergence of Highly Literate Mythology." In *Between Orality and Literacy: Communication and Adaptation in Antiquity*, edited by Ruth Scodel, 125–147. Leiden: Brill.

Hunter, R. 2016. "'Palaephatus', Strabo and the Boundaries of Myth." *Classical Philology* 111: 245–261.

Jarkho, Viktor N. 1988a. "Palaephatus: Des choses incroyables: Traduction et commentaire de V. N. Jarkho," Part 1. *Vestnik Drevnej Istorii* 186: 216–237.

Jarkho, Viktor N. 1988b. "Palaephatus: Des choses incroyables: Traduction et commentaire de V. N. Jarkho," Part 2. *Vestnik Drevnej Istorii* 187: 219–233.

Koning, H. 2016. *Mythen moet je niet geloven! Mytheverklaringen uit de Oudheid*. Budel: DAMON.

Koning, H. 2022. "The Aetiology of Myth." In *Inventing Origins? Aetiological Thinking in Greek and Roman Antiquity*, edited by Antje Wessels and Jacqueline Klooster, 164–182. Leiden: Brill.

Osmun, George F. 1956. "Palaephatus: Pragmatic Mythographer." *Classical Journal* 52: 131–137.

Ramelli, Ilaria L. E. 2007. *Allegoristi dell'età classica: Opere e frammenti*. Milan: Bompiani.

Santoni, Anna. 1998. "Sulla prefazione del Περὶ Ἀπίστων di Palefato." *Kleos* 2–3: 9–18.

Santoni, Anna. 2000. *Palefato: Le storie incredibili*. Pisa, Italy: ETS.

Santoni, Anna. 2012. "Palaiphatos." In *Dictionnaire des philosophes antiques V*, edited by Richard Goulet, 85–89. Paris: CNRS Éditions.

Sanz Morales, Manuel. 2002. *Mitografos griegos*. Madrid: Ediciones Akal.

Smith, R. Scott, and Stephen M. Trzaskoma. 2007. *Apollodorus' "Library" and Hyginus' "Fabulae": Two Handbooks of Greek Mythology*. Indianapolis, IN: Hackett.

Stern, Jacob, trans. 1996. *Palaephatus. On Unbelievable Tales*. Wauconda, IL: Bolchazy-Carducci.

Stern, Jacob. 1999. "Rationalizing Myth: Methods and Motives in Palaephatus." In *From Myth to Reason? Studies in the Development of Greek Thought*, edited by Richard Buxton, 215–222. Oxford: Oxford University Press.

Trachsel, Alexandra. 2005. "L'explication mythologique de Palaïphatos: Une stratégie particulière." *Maia* 57: 543–556.

Torres Guerra, José B. 2009. *Mitógrafos griegos: Traducción, introducción y notas*. Madrid: Gredos.

van den Berg, Robert M. 2017. "Palaephatus on ὀνόματα, λόγοι and ἔργα." *Mnemosyne* 70: 308–315.

Wipprecht, Friedrich. 1902. *Zur Entwicklung der rationalen Mythendeutung bei den Griechen*. Vol. 1. Tübingen: Laupp.

Zucker, Arnaud. 2016. "Palaiphatos ou la clinique du mythe." In *Lire les mythes: Formes, usages et visées des pratiques mythographiques de l'Antiquité à la Renaissance*, edited by Arnaud Zucker, Jacqueline Fabre-Serris, Jean-Yves Tilliette, and Gisèle Besson, 43–66. Villeneuve d'Ascq, France: Presses du Septentrion.

.....................................................................................................................................

# CHAPTER 21

# PARTHENIUS, *EROTIKA PATHEMATA*

.....................................................................................................................................

## CHRISTOPHER FRANCESE

## 1. WORK, DATE, AND AUTHORSHIP

.....................................................................................................................................

PARTHENIUS of Nicaea's collection *Erotika Pathemata* ("Disastrous Love Stories") is exceptional in preserved Greek mythography in that it includes a preface. Addressed to the Roman public official and poet C. Cornelius Gallus (1st c. BCE), this short paragraph is the only good evidence we have of a Greek mythographer's intentions, apart from Palaephatus's protestations of his own reliability in the preface to *On Unbelievable Tales*. Parthenius, who was also a poet, says with un-Palaephatean modesty that he has compiled the little collection for his own use and is sending it on to Gallus as being particularly appropriate for him. Parthenius hopes that the work will aid Gallus in both reading and writing poetry. This is mythography for a creative purpose, and it provides a rare glimpse into a Greek scholar-poet's workshop.

The most striking thing about the thirty-six tales is their rarity and novelty. Nothing hackneyed here. The stories run the gamut from mythological to semihistorical to historical time. We find lesser-known episodes from Trojan mythology (Odysseus and Polymele, 2; Paris and Oenone, 4; Peisidice and Achilles, 21), tales from the foundation stories and chronicles of Greek islands and cities (Lyrcus, from Caunus, 1; Leucippus, from Magnesia-on-the-Maeander, 5; Polycrite, from Naxos, 19), and stories of Greek tyrants (the mother of Periander, 17; Phayllus, 25). There is a virtually unattested love affair between Heracles and the ancestor of the Celts (Celtine, 30; elsewhere only at *Etym. Mag.*, s.v. Keltoi), a love story set against the capture of Sardis by Cyrus the Great (Nanis, 22), and even an extended narrative about an Ionian woman captured by a Celt and taken back to Gaul (Herippe, 8). Almost all of Parthenius's poetry is lost, and we do not have his versified versions of any of the stories in the collection, apart from a brief self-quotation dealing with Byblis (11).

The preface dates the work to the later 40s or the 30s BCE when Gallus was active as a poet—at any rate, before Gallus's death in 27 or 26. By that time Parthenius would have been old. He had been captured as an adult by the Romans during the Third Mithridatic War, in 72 BCE, and brought to Italy. Another thing that makes Parthenius unusual among mythographers is that we actually know a bit about his life and intellectual milieu. He lived amid a sizable community of Greek intellectuals in Italy, many of whom made substantial contributions to Roman intellectual life in the late Republic. Some scholars have argued that Parthenius helped to shape the stylistic development of Latin poetry by popularizing the style of Callimachus—Parthenius was a scholar-poet very much in the Callimachean mold. But this view is controversial.

We have the *Erotika Pathemata* (the conventional title, derived from the words of the preface) thanks to a single manuscript: Palatinus Heidelbergensis graecus 398. That treasure trove of rare mythography is also the unique source for Antoninus Liberalis's *Metamorphoses*, which immediately follows. The larger collection was put together for a scholar in Constantinople in the 9th century. In both Parthenius and Antoninus, notations written on the left or right margins in the same hand give the names of the principal character in each story, and a sequential numbering. These serve as titles in modern editions. There are also short notes or scholia: at the top or foot of the page are twenty-six notes that refer to various lost Hellenistic works (poetry and prose) that tell Parthenius's stories ("Philetas tells the story in his *Hermes*," 174v). A few notes point out etiologies or make some other short comment ("this is said to be the origin of the Celtic race," 187r). These scholia are very consistent between Parthenius and Antoninus but do not appear in the preceding work in Pal. graec. 398, the pseudo-Plutarchean *On Rivers*. In the body of *Erotika Pathemata* itself are five substantial quotations from now largely lost Greek poems of Hellenistic date, including one by Parthenius himself. This unusual feature points to Parthenius's lofty literary milieu and has added to literary historians' fascination with the collection.

## 2. CONTENT

The frequency of incest, cannibalism, and even necrophilia (31) shows a taste for the sensational, even shocking. Parthenius is fond of stories of young women who fall in love with invading enemies, the so-called Tarpeia motif. Roman poets treat the story of Scylla, who betrayed her city Megara for the love of the invader Minos, as trite: "Why should I bother mentioning Scylla, daughter of Nisus?" asks Vergil rhetorically (*Ecl.* 6.74, see Tibull. 1.4.63–64, Ov. *Am.* 3.12.21–22). Parthenius provides three rarer legends with the same pattern (9, 22, 21). Another notable group comprises stories of incestuous desire (2, 5, 13, 17, 28, 31, 33). These are both themes we know Parthenius treated in his own poetry as well (fr. 24, 28, 29 Lightfoot = *Suppl. Hell.* 637b, 640, 641). Among earlier poets, such pathological love stories are favored not so much by Callimachus as by another scholar-poet, Euphorion of Calchis (3rd c. BCE).

Structurally, the hallmarks of the collection are the stories' disastrous endings, and the generally forbidden, pathological, or doomed nature of the erotic passions themselves. A substantial number of the stories involve maidens and adult women who act boldly on their forbidden desires. Eros, both masculine and feminine, is directed at a virgin outside marriage or other improper love object, such as a family member, a visiting foreigner, or an armed enemy. The ensuing disaster is usually a death (especially the death of a family member), suicide, exile, the fall of a regime, or some other political upheaval. The word *pathēmata* is ambiguous: it could mean "misfortunes, disasters" or "passions, strong emotions," or, more neutrally, "incidents, happenings." The actual content of the book gestures more toward the first of these meanings: usually *illicit* love destined to lead to *catastrophe*.

Some of the most venerable Greek myths, from Phaedra and Medea to Tereus and Procne or Pyramus and Thisbe, have this same, roughly binary, tragic structure of love and death. Note the strong contrast here with the happy endings, idealized characters, and episodic plots of love stories in the Greek novels, a genre of erotic fiction that flourished in the centuries after Parthenius's death. Older scholars have nonetheless looked for the roots of the Greek novel in Parthenius and his sources (see, for example, Rohde 1914).

Parthenius includes little in the way of explicit comment, but there are certainly hints about how he imagined the material being treated in verse. A pathetic rather than a moralistic viewpoint is evident in Parthenius's collection in the repeated reference to lamentation (for example, 10.4, 26.4, 28.2, 36.5); the resort to the grotesque, such as focusing on the corpse of the dead lover (31.2, 35.4); and the Euripidean conception of love as a disease (for example, 5.2, 17.2), which the protagonists try to resist but to which they succumb (for example, 13.1, 16.1, 36.3). It is no coincidence that the *epicedium*, or poetic lament, was a favorite poetic form of Parthenius (fr. 6, 8–9, and 27 Lightfoot). Parthenius chose to include in *Erotika Pathemata* his own verses describing the lament of Byblis, her suicide, and the lament of the Milesian women after her death (11.4)—presumably for Gallus's benefit, as a poetic model.

Not that the tone of *Erotika Pathemata* is entirely gloomy. There are some happy endings (see stories 2 and 6), and frequent hints of playful urbanity and wit, such as in the tale of Leucippus, who dresses as a girl to get closer to Daphne (15), or Circe from the *Odyssey*, who resorts to magic only when pestered beyond endurance by an unwanted suitor (12). The pleasure of the collection lies in the discovery of little-known variations on familiar types and amusing sidelights on well-known mythological figures.

Olympian gods are conspicuous by their absence. A brief appearance by Apollo in the Daphne story is the lone exception (15). There is a general avoidance of the fantastic. Orion appears in Ps.-Apollodorus as a giant who, after being blinded, walks into the sunrise and is healed by the sun's rays. In Parthenius, Orion is simply a rather uncouth man (20; compare Apollod. 1.25–27). Parthenius admits a few metamorphoses, on the authority of others (11.4, 13.4, 15.4). Elsewhere he omits metamorphoses prescribed by tradition: Niobe leaping from a cliff rather than becoming one (33.3); Circe, instead of turning men into animals, making them merely *think* they are animals (12.2). This humanization of the mythical world perhaps derives from a Callimachean urge toward mythographic verisimilitude (see Call. *Hymn* 1.59–64). It is certainly a less obtrusive and subtler form of rationalism than, say, that of Palaephatus (Lightfoot 1999: 230–231).

Geographically, the focus is on the Aegean, especially the areas around Miletus and Troy. But there are also some tales from the Greek mainland, Sicily, and southern Italy. The mythical map is roughly similar to that of Callimachus's *Aetia*, with the addition of the Celtic-themed stories. The Roman world, of course, came in much closer contact with Celtic peoples in Parthenius's lifetime, thanks to Caesar's conquests in Gaul (for a comparative example, see Sulimani, this volume).

In its prose style the work is elegant, though not rhetorical, and there are enough repetitions to show it is not highly polished. The dialect is a literary *koine* that is generally, but inconsistently, Ionic. Although the syntax can be informal, the vocabulary is often elevated, with a considerable number of poeticisms, even Homeric unique words (Lightfoot 1999: 294–297; Mayer-G'Schrey 1898).

## 3. Sources

A careful reading of the preface suggests that the stories in *Erotika Pathemata* were not summaries of Hellenistic poetic texts, as editors of the fragments of Hellenistic poets have sometimes assumed or implied. Rather, they are fuller versions of stories the poets told elliptically: "For those stories, as they are found in some of the poets, are not told in a self-standing manner (*mē autotelōs*): you will understand most of them from these."

The scholia point to specific earlier authors and works. These footnotes may or may not derive from Parthenius himself (by Parthenius: Cameron 2004: 105–110; not by him: Lightfoot 1999: 246–256, the majority opinion). They cite poets sixteen times, historians fifteen times, philosophers four times, and a grammarian once. The notes all refer to authors earlier than Parthenius and are accurate insofar as they can be checked. Beneath the story of Harpalyce, for instance, is a note, "told by Euphorion in *Thrax*, and by Dectadas" (fol. 180v). We know from a papyrus fragment that Euphorion did in fact tell the story of Apriate, though in an allusive way that rules out the idea that Parthenius was simply summarizing this passage of Euphorion (*Suppl. Hell.* 415 i 12–21 with Lightfoot 1999: 516–518). Poetry per se does not seem to have been a significant source, despite the verse quotations and generally poetic perspective of the work as a whole.

Two important sources of material must have been local historians of the Greek cities (Hellanicus of Lesbos, Neanthes of Cyzicus, and Aristodemus of Nysa are cited in the scholia), and the works of Peripatetic philosophers (Aristotle himself and his followers Theophrastus and Phanias of Eresus are cited in the scholia). The Peripatetics used disastrous love stories to illustrate the powerful, warping effects of Eros on human behavior. Many Peripatetic works, such as those cited in the scholia, were newly available in Italy in Parthenius's day, edited by his fellow Mithridatic war captive Tyrannio of Amisus (Marshall 1976: 259–260).

While these works are mostly lost, later historians and essayists used them as well. Consider the story of Polycrite (Parth. 19), the savior of the island of Naxos in a war with nearby Miletus. Plutarch (*Mor.* 254) records at length both the local Naxian version, which emphasizes topographical and military detail, and the Aristotelian version, which is much more novelistic. Parthenius combines elements of both, adding a typically macabre twist (not in either of the others) in which Polycrite is buried alive under the garlands and girdles of her admirers. Parthenius's vocabulary is characteristically rich in poeticisms, suggesting that he rewrote freely.

Lightfoot's (1999) exhaustive commentary collects this parallel material and shows us each story in its original context as a local, dynastic, or etiological myth; as an erotic novelette; and as part of a wider story type within Greek myth and culture. Several general trends emerge. Like Ovid, Parthenius depoliticizes the local myths he tells. He introduces the tyrant Phayllus (25), forgetting even to tell us what state he is a tyrant of (Phocis). Erotic psychology dominates, and while the accounts can be quite full, the material is bleached of patriotic, religious, or philosophical significance. Parthenius edits out divine intervention and obviously fantastic elements, and gravitates toward the grotesque and the violent, and to extreme violations of human custom such as parricide, incest, and cannibalism. There is pathos, yet he treats these events in a distanced way, and not without dry humor and paradox.

# 4. Intellectual Milieu

Parthenius grew up in the kingdom of Nicomedes IV Philopator of Bithynia, in the cities of Nicaea and Myrlea. According to the Suda (π 664), Parthenius "was taken as war spoils by Cinna when the Romans defeated Mithridates but was subsequently freed because of his learning." His capture and enslavement probably occurred in the spring of 72 BCE, when the proconsul Lucullus and his legates methodically pillaged the cities of Bithynia and Pontus, which had remained loyal to Mithridates VI Eupator (Sherwin-White 1994: 235–236). After the Mithridatic war, Parthenius came to Italy and was active there as a poet and a scholar. Many such learned Greeks could be found staying at the villas and busy among the book collections of Roman nobles, for example, in the famous library of Lucullus himself. This environment is idealistically depicted by Plutarch as a bustling "residence of the Muses" (*Luc.* 42).

The preface to *Erotika Pathemata* reflects the close collaboration of Roman authors with learned Greeks and freedmen, a phenomenon that is familiar from the letters of Cicero of the same period (for example, *Att.* 4.11.12). Here is the preface in full:

> To you in particular, Cornelius Gallus, I thought it most appropriate to send the collection of disastrous love stories which I have assembled in as very brief a compass as possible. For these stories, as they are found in some of the poets, are not told in a self-standing manner: you will understand most of them from these. It remains

for you yourself to put the most appropriate ones into hexameters or elegies. Please do not think less of them because they lack that stylistic refinement (*to peritton*) in which you so excel. I have compiled them simply as a little ancilla (*hypomnēmation*), and now perhaps they will serve the same purpose for you as well.

The word *hypomnēma* covers any kind of informal written work or set of notes, sometimes notes explicitly intended for later reworking as a formal piece of *belles lettres* (Lightfoot 1999: 218). Cicero wrote a *hypomnēma* about his own consulate and sent it to Posidonius so that he could write about the same matters in a more polished way (*Att.* 2.1). A closer analogy to *Erotika Pathemata* lies in the informal compendia of scholars known as *grammatici*, who assisted practicing authors. The presence of such scholars is, in fact, an important precondition for the learned and polished styles that we associate with the Golden age of Latin poetry. *Grammatici* produced summaries of long or difficult works and offered advice on the proper forms of geographical names, stylistic critique, and help in resolving disagreements in the Greek sources; they also served as reading companions. We have documentation of an extensive circle of scholars around Vergil, for example (Horsfall 1991: 32–43). Macrobius, in fact, refers to Parthenius as Vergil's *grammaticus in Graecis*, "scholar in things Greek" (*Sat.* 5.17.18), which places Parthenius squarely in that class of literary collaborators, even though Parthenius is not known to have written "grammatical" works per se.

The informal tone of the preface forms a contrast to the flowery prefaces usually written by Greeks for Roman patrons (Graefenhain 1892; Zimmermann 1934) and suggests actual friendship and collaboration. This does not mean that the work was not also intended for wider distribution. Parthenius made it first for his own use ("assembled" and "compiled" are in the middle voice), but he probably imagined it circulating more widely in his circle of like-minded *amici*. The word for stylistic refinement that Parthenius disclaims for the work itself (*to peritton*) connotes extravagance, refined elaboration, detail, and all the sophisticated erudition of Alexandrian poetry (Lightfoot 1999: 370). It is a hint at their shared Callimachean literary values.

Cameron (2004) has made a strong case that Roman poets did, in fact, routinely use prose mythographical handbooks as source material, as did their counterparts in the Renaissance. But extant Latin poetry uses almost none of the stories Parthenius tells in *Erotika Pathemata*. Even Vergil's catalogue of unhappy lovers in the underworld (*Aeneid* 6.455 ff.) passes them over, no doubt because the names would have been completely unfamiliar to the Roman audience. As with that crucial Greek model, Callimachus's *Aetia*, neoteric and Augustan Latin poets were more interested in the aesthetic, the manner of treatment, than in recondite mythology for its own sake.

The best Latin examples of Parthenius's characteristic combination of mythographic novelty, historical subject matter, and sympathetic treatment of illicit passion is probably Propertius's elegy about Tarpeia (4.4), a traitorous lover who would have been right at home in *Erotika Pathemata*. The neoteric poet C. Helvius Cinna wrote a miniature epic (*Zmyrna*, frr. 6–8 Courtney) on the incestuous love of Cinyras's daughter, which, if it survived, would help us assess Parthenius's influence in the 50s BCE. Ovid's narratives of incestuous love in the stories of Canace and Macareus (*Heroides* 11), Byblis (*Met.* 9.450 ff., see Parth. 11), and Myrrha (*Met.* 10.298–502; see Parth. fr. 29 Lightfoot = *Suppl. Hell.* 641) suggest the kinds of fuller treatments of the incest theme that Parthenius had in mind. The pseudo-Vergilian *Ciris* also likely owes something to Parthenius's example (Lyne 1978: 25–47). But overall, Parthenius's peculiar, antiheroic approach to erotic mythology represents a road not taken in extant Latin literature.

## FURTHER READING

Lightfoot (1999) is the essential commentary and has a rich chapter devoted to Parthenius's mythography (215–302). Her text of *Erotika Pathemata* differs from Martini's (1902) Teubner edition in some seventy places and prints many good suggestions in the apparatus. Some relatively small errors and needless divergences from the manuscript were corrected in her Loeb edition (2009), which is now the best Greek text. Fuller information on textual criticism can be found in Calderón-Dorda (1988: xlix–li). Cameron (2004: 106–116) effectively reverses Lightfoot's view on the scholia and makes a strong case that they are by Parthenius.

Lightfoot tends to neglect literary aspects and the contemporary social and intellectual context. On learned Greeks and other scholars in the late Republic, see Rawson (1985); and Griffin (1994). The sources are helpfully collected by Hillscher (1892). On *grammatici* in particular, see Della Corte (1981); Funaioli (1907); and Kaster (1995). On Parthenius as a *grammaticus*, see Francese (1999). Pfeiffer (1943) showed that in Parthenius's poetry, narrative and exquisite scholarship are fully integrated with passionate personal statements, and he saw this as an important precedent for Latin elegy. Clausen (1964) and Crowther (1976), see Parthenius as a kind of literary father figure for Callimachean and neoteric poets in Rome, a view strongly challenged by Lightfoot (1999: 72). Francese (2001) looks at literary aspects of *Erotika Pathemata* and compares it with Greek erotic fiction more generally, including Euripides and the Greek novel, and with specific Latin passages. The collection edited by Zucker (2008), based on a conference, covers various literary aspects.

## REFERENCES

Calderón Dorda, Esteban. 1988. *Partenio de Nicea: Sufrimientos de amor y fragmentos.* Madrid: Consejo superior de investigaciones cientificas.

Cameron, Alan. 2004. *Greek Mythography in the Roman World.* Oxford: Oxford University Press.

Clausen, Wendel. 1964. "Callimachus and Latin Poetry." *Greek, Roman and Byzantine Studies* 5: 181–196.

Clausen, Wendel. 1987. *Virgil's "Aeneid" and the Tradition of Hellenistic Poetry.* Berkeley: University of California Press.

Crowther, Nigel B. 1976. "Parthenius and Roman Poetry." *Mnemosyne* 29: 65–71.

Della Corte, Francesco. 1981. *La filologia Latina dalle origini a Varrone.* 2nd ed. Florence: La nuova Italia.

Francese, Christopher. 1999. "Parthenius Grammaticus." *Mnemosyne* 52: 63–71.

Francese, Christopher. 2001. *Parthenius of Nicaea and Roman Poetry.* Frankfurt: Peter Lang.

Funaioli, Gino. 1907. *Grammaticae Romanae Fragmenta*. Leipzig: Teubner.

Graefenhain, Rudolf. 1892. "De more libros dedicandi apud scriptores Graecos et Romanos obvio." Diss. Marburg.

Griffin, Miriam. 1994. "The Intellectual Developments of the Ciceronian Age." In *The Cambridge Ancient History*, vol. 9, 2nd ed., edited by J. A. Crook, Andrew Lintott, and Elizabeth Rawson. 698–728. Cambridge, UK: Cambridge University Press.

Hillscher, Alfred. 1892. "Hominum litteratorum Graecorum ante Tiberii mortem in urbe Roma commoratorum historia critica." *Jahrbücher für classische Philologie, Supplementband* 18: 353–444.

Horsfall, Nicholas. 1991. *Virgilio: l'epopea in alambicco*. Napoli: Liguori.

Kaster, Robert A. 1995. *C. Suetonius Tranquillus: De grammaticis et rhetoribus*. Oxford: Oxford University Press.

Lightfoot, Jane L. 1999. *Parthenius of Nicaea: The Poetical Fragments and Ἐρωτικὰ Παθήματα*. Oxford: Clarendon Press.

Lightfoot, Jane L. 2009. *Hellenistic Collection: Philitas, Alexander of Aetolia, Hermesianax, Euphorion, Parthenius*. Loeb Classical Library. Cambridge, MA: Harvard University Press.

Lyne, Richard O. A. M. 1978. *Ciris: A Poem Attributed to Vergil*. Cambridge, UK: Cambridge University Press.

Marshall, Anthony J. 1976. "Library Resources and Creative Writing at Rome." *Phoenix* 30: 252–264.

Martini, Edgar. 1902. *Parthenii Nicaeni quae supersunt. Mythographici Graeci*. Vol. 2, fasc. 1, Suppl. Leipzig: Teubner.

Mayer-G'Schrey, Richard. 1898. "Parthenius Nicaeensis quale in fabularum amatoriarum breveiario dicendi genus secutus sit." Diss. Heidelberg.

Pfeiffer, Rudolf. 1943. "A Fragment of Parthenios' *Arete*." *Classical Quarterly* 37: 23–32.

Rawson, Elizabeth. 1985. *Intellectual Life in the Late Roman Republic*. Baltimore, MD: Johns Hopkins University Press.

Rohde, Erwin. 1914. *Der griechische Roman und seine Vorläufer*. 3rd ed. Leipzig: Breitkopf und Härtel.

Rostagni, Augusto. 1933. "Partenio di Nicea, Elvio Cinna ed i 'poeti novi.'" *Atti della Accademia delle Scienze di Torino* 68: 497–545.

Sherwin-White, Adrian N. 1994. "Lucullus, Pompey, and the East." In *Cambridge Ancient History*, vol. 9, 2nd ed., edited by J. A. Crook, Andrew Lintott, and Elizabeth Rawson, 229–273. Cambridge, UK: Cambridge University Press.

Universitätsbibliothek Heidelberg. *Cod. Pal. graec. 398. Sammelhandschrift*. Permalink: http://digi.ub.uni-heidelberg.de/diglit/cpgraec398.

Zimmermann, Franz. 1934. "Parthenios' Brief an Gallus." *Hermes* 69: 179–189.

Zucker, Arnaud, ed. 2008. *Littérature et érotisme dans les "Passions d'amour" de Parthénios de Nicée*. Grenoble, France: Jérôme Millon.

CHAPTER 22

# PAUSANIAS, *DESCRIPTION OF GREECE*

WILLIAM HUTTON

## 1. PAUSANIAS AS MYTHOGRAPHER

By any reckoning, Pausanias's *Periegesis Hellados* (*Description of Greece*) is one of the richest sources for Greek myth. As a rough but revealing index of the text's value, William Smith's venerable *Dictionary of Greek and Roman Biography and Mythology* (1849) cites Pausanias over 1,700 times, considerably more often than any other author. A massive ten volumes in length, the *Periegesis* takes the reader on a virtual tour of the southern and central mainland of Greece, recording what was worth seeing in the author's day (mid-2nd c. CE), and imparting the mythical and historical backstories of the places and monuments he visits. Nothing is known of Pausanias aside from scattered self-referential comments in the text, but researching and composing the *Periegesis* seems to have occupied at least a decade or two of his mature years (Pretzler 2007: 16–25; Bowie 2001). Pausanias frequently claims to be writing from the perspective of a visitor to the places he is describing, and modern archaeological research has demonstrated that his claims to eyewitness knowledge are generally legitimate (Habicht 1998: 28–63).

To evaluate Pausanias's mythographical testimony, it is important to keep in mind certain characteristics of his work. Most obviously, the *Periegesis* never pretends to be a comprehensive compendium of Greek myth. Nearly all of the mythical material Pausanias includes in his text serves the primary purpose of adding information about one of the sites or monuments on his itineraries. As such, we do not usually get complete stories of gods and heroes but how gods and heroes left their mark on the cultural and monumental landscapes of particular places. Apart from Pausanias's historical and biographical narratives, which often verge into the realm of myth-history (as does his lengthy narration of the Messenian Wars in book 4 [see Luraghi 2008: 94–100] and his accounts of the fabulous deeds of famous athletes like Euthymus of Locri [see Currie 2002]), among the longest unitary mythical accounts are the three stories of star-crossed passion that he gathers in book 7: Agdistis and Attis (7.17.10–11); Comaitho and Melanippus (7.19.2); and Coresus and Callirhoe (7.21.4–5). Even these stories, however, serve to give color to his account of the places and monuments that are pertinent to the narratives. Because Pausanias's mythical material helps to illustrate the distinctive character of the various places he visits, he is not consistently concerned with reconciling discrepant traditions (Hawes 2017: 7–8). It has been plausibly suggested that imparting a sense of the diversity of Greek traditions was one of his chief goals (Jost 2006).

An important consideration in the interpretation of Pausanias's mythographical testimony is the literary nature of his text. Pausanias's career played out during the heyday of the Second Sophistic, and while he is hardly a typical author of the period, he does partake of some of its major trends, including a reverence for the early history and traditions of Greece, an intense consciousness of issues of authorial self-presentation, and a tendency to echo and pay homage to revered literary models (Bowie 1996; Akujärvi 2005: 25–130; Hutton 2017). These characteristics are important to keep in mind in evaluating all of Pausanias's testimony, not least on mythographical issues. Among his literary predecessors, Pausanias models himself most closely on Herodotus (Hutton 2005: 190–233). Echoes of Herodotus, both obvious and subtle, pepper the text and often turn up in the way Pausanias presents and comments on myth. Approaching Pausanias as though he were a guileless collector of data is a path to misunderstanding.

# 2. Interpretative Methods: Allegory and Rationalizing

Certain cognitive dispositions seem to underlie much of Pausanias's treatment of myth. He presents himself as a pious individual whose concept of divinity holds little room for gods behaving in unjust or all-too-human ways (Pirenne-Delforge 2008: 64–72). At the Argive Heraion he tells the story of Zeus changing himself into a cuckoo to woo Hera, and appends to it the Herodotean comment, "I record this story and similar ones told about the gods without accepting them, but I record them nevertheless" (2.17.4; compare Hdt. 7.152). Since Pausanias does not express such sentiments toward all of the myths he records, many readers are surprised when much later in the work, after recounting a local Arcadian variant of the myth of Cronus devouring his children, he says (8.8.3):

> When I began my account I tended to attribute these stories the Greeks tell to foolishness, but when I came to deal with Arcadian matters I started adopting a more circumspect attitude toward them: I began to suppose that those of the Greeks who were considered wise in olden days did not speak directly but cryptically.

This is one of the most thoroughly discussed passages in the *Periegesis* (Veyne 1988: 95–102; Pirenne-Delforge 2008: 6–72; Hawes 2014: 178–185), and in addition to expressing skepticism, it seems to show an openness to allegorical interpretation. Yet Pausanias is far from a systematic allegorizer in the mold of Cornutus. While there are occasional references to allegorical interpretations in the text (for example, 3.15.11, 7.23.7–8, 7.26.8), Pausanias exhibits no consistent allegorical doctrine (Pirenne-Delforge 2008: 108–112; Hawes 2014: 191–194).

In line with his views on divine myth, Pausanias shows a consistent trend toward rationalization, frequently advocating versions of myths that are stripped of their fantastic and supernatural aspects: the hound of Hades was, as Hecataeus suggested, just a venomous snake (3.25.5), and the Hydra did not have multiple heads (2.37.4). In her study of rationalization in Greek mythography, Greta Hawes (2014: 175–222) demonstrates that while Pausanias does not rationalize every myth he encounters, he is certainly an heir to the rationalizing mythographical tradition. Hawes (2014: 206–207) makes the plausible suggestion that Pausanias's tendency toward rationalization may arise partly from his experience as a visitor to the places where the myths are set. Sitting in one's library far from Greece, it is easier to accept that there might be a passage to the underworld at Cape Tainaron than it is if one actually goes to Tainaron, as Pausanias did, and finds no evidence of such a passage (3.25.5).

The most noteworthy exception to this rationalizing tendency comes late in the work, in Pausanias's discussion of the early traditions of Arcadia. After relating the traditional story of Lycaon's metamorphosis into a wolf, Pausanias says that he finds it persuasive, because the story has been told by the Arcadians from time immemorial and because, in those olden days, mortals consorted directly with gods. Pious mortals felt the favor of the gods more immediately, and wicked ones, like Lycaon, felt their wrath more swiftly and decisively (8.1.4–5): "Thus someone might well believe that Lycaon became an animal and Niobe daughter of Tantalus became a stone." Someone might also believe, according to Pausanias, that in those days, humans like Heracles and Britomartis (who were worshipped as gods in Pausanias's time) actually did join the ranks of the immortals.

The contrast between what Pausanias says in this passage and his general skepticism toward divine myth and fabulous transformations probably arises from the context in which the passage occurs. Arcadia was a numinous place for Pausanias, home to an aboriginal population that had unparalleled access to the primordial mythical and religious traditions of the Greeks (Pirenne-Delforge 2008: 67–72, 333–341; Baleriaux 2017: 141–145, 156–158). Like his aforementioned acceptance of the potential allegorical wisdom contained in the "foolish" myths of the Greeks, which comes slightly later in his Arcadian account, his acceptance here of the early tales of the Arcadians allows Pausanias to portray himself, late in his work and late in life, as having gained wisdom from his travels and research. It also gives him a platform for one of his frequent moralizing pronouncements, which in this case takes aim at the contemporary practice of emperor worship: "But in my time—since evil has increased to such an extent and spread across every land and every city—not one single god ever arises from humankind, except in name alone and in flattery addressed to the powerful." In sum, one should not read this passage out of its many contexts. As Hawes (2014: 201–205) points out, despite the openness to some cases of metamorphosis that Pausanias shows here, he is consistently skeptical when he treats examples of the motif elsewhere: Actaeon did not really become a stag (9.2.3–4), for instance, and Callisto was not necessarily transformed into a constellation (8.3.7).

Pausanias's rationalizing predilections play an important role in his accounts of the early histories of the places he visits, where he generally makes no discernible distinction between the historical and the legendary (Bowie 1996; Pirenne-Delforge 2008: 43–54). In his recounting of the earliest history of the city of Argos (2.15.4–16.3), for instance, Inachus is not a river god but a mortal king; Io is not the daughter of the river but of mortal parentage; and Io's metamorphosis into a cow is omitted. No mention is made of the divine lineage of Perseus, and of his career rich in superhuman deeds, the only things narrated are his accidental killing of his grandfather and his foundation of Mycenae. The effect of these mythographical choices on Pausanias's part is to allow the stories of these legendary figures to be woven seamlessly together with the stories of later, more historical figures. This weaving is even accomplished on the level of language. As he does in most mythical stories, in the early phases of his account, he presents the stories of Inachus and his descendants as reported speech: "They say that Inachus was king." As the story goes on, reported speech transforms unobtrusively into direct statements: "Argos son of Phoroneus named the land after himself." This slippage into direct speech in a long passage of reported speech is not uncommon in Greek and other languages, but given the overall tendency of such passages in Pausanias, an argument can be made that we are dealing with a case of "artful slipping" (Richman 1986), the effect of which is to anchor the real-world history of Argive identity in the most distant past.

# 3. Pausanias's Sources

Pausanias cites over fifty authors and anonymous texts as sources and exhibits a strong preference for older works. He names Arriphon of Lycia as a contemporary source (2.37.3) and cites a few others, otherwise unknown to us, who might be contemporary as well, such as Procles of Carthage (2.21.5–6; 4.35.4; see Sánchez Hernández 2010). But aside from such rare exceptions, his datable sources are from no later than the Hellenistic period, and in fact, the sources he cites the most frequently, which include Asius, Pamphus, Homer, Hesiod, the poems of the Epic Cycle, Stesichorus, and Pindar, date to the earliest days of Greek literature. Among these authorities Homer is clearly his favorite; there are well over a hundred citations and direct quotations of the poet.

Pausanias obviously knew his Homer thoroughly, but a legitimate question to ask is whether he read the other sources he cites in their original form or through compilations. At one point, he adduces information from the archaic Corinthian poet Eumelus (2.1.1), and the term he uses for the text (*syngraphē*) suggests that what he is citing is a prose epitome. To his credit, Pausanias acknowledges that Eumelus might not have written it himself. On another occasion he states that he is consulting a compilatory source, Callippus of Corinth, for quotations of poems that he admits to not having read in the original (9.29.2; 38.10). Pausanias's honesty in these instances may tempt us to surmise that it was his normal practice to consult original texts, but it would be reckless to assume that the rest of his work is free of the influence of compendia and epitomes. Cameron (2004: 236–237) is probably right when he suggests that earlier mythographical collections may have pointed Pausanias to fruitful sources on various topics, and that he may, at least in some cases, have followed those leads back to the original texts.

Whether he is working from original texts or compilations, Pausanias takes pains to present himself not as a passive consumer of information but as an energetic and critical evaluator of his sources. He frequently asserts that he is has read (*epilegesthai*) the texts he is discussing (for example, 1.22.7; 2.4.2; 4.2.1; 8.37.12; 9.27.2; 10.12.11), and he describes himself as conducting his research energetically (*polypragmonōn*: 1.28.7; 8.6.1; 8.16.3; 9.30.3). He claims that to determine a detail concerning the genealogy of the heroic royalty in Messenia, he read the *Great Eoiai*, the *Naupaktia*, and works of Cinaethon and Asius without finding anything of use (4.2.1; but see Cameron 2004: 236 on this passage). While it is prudent to treat such claims with caution, there is no reason to doubt that a great amount of bibliographical spadework lies behind his text. Seeing a figure labeled "Xenodike" among the captive Trojan women in Polygnotus's paintings in Delphi (10.26.1), he declares that none of the poets or prose writers who deal with that episode mentions her. This is the statement of someone who is confident in his command of the existing literature, and as far as we can tell, it is accurate.

Pausanias often delves into problems of pseudepigraphy (for example, 4.33.7; 8.18.2; 10.5.6). He notes that the people in the region of Mount Helicon accept only the *Works and Days* as a legitimate product of their countryman Hesiod (9.31.4–5), and he seems, in general, to respect their verdict. Only early in his work (1.3.1; 1.28.6; 1.43.1) does he name Hesiod unequivocally as the author of other poems (specifically, the *Theogony* and the *Catalogue of Women*). Pausanias shows frequent interest in the absolute and relative chronology of his sources (for example, 5.7.8; 7.21.9; 8.21.3; 9.29.8; 10.5.12). On the relative ages of Homer and Hesiod, he says that he investigated the question exhaustively (9.30.3) but refrains from staking out his own position in the contemporary debate, which he describes as "captious" (*philaition*). He similarly refuses to take a position on the debate over Homer's place of origin (10.24.3). As Akujärvi (2005: 90–129) has amply demonstrated, one of Pausanias's primary authorial gambits was to foreground his authority as a diligent researcher.

In addition to his written sources, perhaps the most distinctive feature separating Pausanias's work from other mythographical texts is the large amount of information he claims to have obtained on-site (Lacroix 1994; Pretzler 2005), often in personal communication with the local inhabitants. As Palaephatus shows in his preface, claims of gathering rare and recondite information from local sources could be as much a trope in mythographical writing as it is in historiography (Hawes 2014: 45–48), but in contrast to Palaephatus, there is evidence that Pausanias actually did the extensive traveling that such research would entail. On numerous occasions Pausanias refers to his encounters with local notables who serve as *exēgētai* (guides) for visitors to their communities (Jones 2001). In most places Pausanias does not mention particular individuals as informants, but instead refers to what "the Corinthians say," or what "the Athenians say." This complicates our evaluation of the information, not only because such formulations are obviously generalizations, but also because in many cases they may refer to written compilations of local lore.

Recently, Gaertner (2006) argued that written sources lie behind the majority of Pausanias's citations of local information. Gaertner focused on one type of information—explanations for the origins of cult practices and cult names for the gods—and found in nearly every case that there was comparable material in other mythographical texts. Yet if some of the parallels Gaertner points to are striking (for instance, Pausanias 3.13.3–5 in comparison to the scholia to Theocritus 5.83 on the origin of the cult of Apollo Carneus), his conclusions concerning Pausanias's dependence on written texts go far beyond the evidence. When written information can be found that parallels an alleged oral source, it does not follow that the oral source is a fiction. Most of Pausanias's local informants were probably highly literate, and the phenomenon of "feedback," whereby oral traditions can be influenced by input from written sources, is well attested in the field of folklore studies (Henige 1974). Pausanias himself provides evidence of that process in the Greece of his day on the frequent occasions when his local informants adduce passages from Homer and other authors to support their assertions (for example, 3.21.5; 4.3.2; 5.19.7; 6.25.3; 8.25.8; 9.18.2). Moreover, in many of the cases Gaertner cites, Pausanias adds unique information of the very kind one would expect local sources to emphasize. For instance, other sources say that Saron of Troezen drowned in a hunting accident and gave his name to the Saronic Gulf, but Pausanias alone adds that Saron was the king of Troezen, had founded the shrine of Saronian Artemis, and was buried in the precinct of the shrine (2.30.7). In sum, there is no reason to doubt that Pausanias provides us with a valid window into local mythology, yet Gaertner's analysis serves to remind us that local traditions of Pausanias's Greece were not hermetically isolated from the literary vulgate circulating in his day.

When Pausanias has to deal with incompatible versions of a story, his usual practice is to present the differing accounts without choosing sides. For instance, at a remote city in Laconia called Pyrrhichus (3.25.2), Pausanias reports that "they" (presumably the locals) say that the place was named after Pyrrhus son of Achilles. Others, however, say that Pyrrhichus was one of the divinities known as Curetes, and a third group says that a Silenus named Pyrrhichus settled there. Pausanias supplies a quotation from Pindar that indirectly supports the third option, but he refrains from pronouncing a final judgment on the issue. Sometimes such passages go on at great length, as with his discussion of the Graces in his account of Boeotia (9.35.1–7): commenting on the number, names, cult, and iconography of the goddesses, he catalogs the testimony of five literary sources, along with five separate artistic portrayals. Pausanias does not announce a preference for any particular version; in fact, in discussing the different names given to the goddesses by the Lacedaimonians and Athenians, he declares both sets of names to be "fitting" (*eoikota*), showing once more that he felt no compulsion to harmonize competing local

accounts. There are numerous such doxographical catalogs in the *Periegesis*, for example, 2.3.8–9 (Medea's children), 8.53.5 (Rhadamanthys), and 9.27.2–3 (Eros).

Occasionally, Pausanias does express a preference for one version of a story over another, and in Herodotean fashion, he often walks us through the reasoning that leads to
his conclusions. For instance, at the small city of Las in southern Laconia, he is told that
the local eponymous hero, Las, was killed by Achilles when the latter was on his way
to Sparta to join in the courtship of Helen (3.24.10–11). Pausanias rejects this idea and
opines that Patroclus must have killed Las instead. While he observes that Achilles is not
listed among Helen's suitors in the *Catalogue of Women,* he does not consider this evidence conclusive. What clinches the argument for him is that in Homer's telling, Achilles
was not bound by the Oath of Tyndareus, and he also cites Homeric evidence that
Achilles was younger than the generation that courted Helen. In weighing competing
accounts, Pausanias exhibits some definite tendencies in the choices he makes. When
the local information conflicts with his standard written sources, he deems the local version more believable in some cases (for example, 4.2.3; 2.16.4; 8.3.7). More often, however, the written sources are granted authority over local claims, as in the case of Las (see
1.41.1; 2.12.6; 9.38.7). In general, Pausanias takes pains to signal his critical independence
from his local informants. At one point in Argos he charges that "the Argive guides are
aware that not all they say is true, but they say it nonetheless" (2.23.6). This is only one of
several cases where what he hears in Argos strikes him as questionable (see 2.19.8; 2.21.1,
4, 10; 2.23.3).

Where written sources conflict, Pausanias likewise exhibits some marked preferences.
Homer, once again, is king (Duffy 2013); in the hundred-plus citations of Homer, never
once does Pausanias accuse the poet of error. As a rule, the most ancient verses (*epē*),
encompassing not only the works of Homer but also Cyclic poetry, catalogue poetry,
hymns, and didactic works, hold the most authority for him. He often grants later poets
and writers credibility as well—for example, Apollonius of Rhodes (2.12.6); Hermesianax
(7.17.9)—but most of them eventually come in for some criticism: Stesichorus's account
of Actaeon's metamorphosis is discounted in favor of a fully rationalizing explanation
of his demise (9.2.3); Pindar's description of Lynceus's superhuman eyesight is deemed
implausible (4.2.7).

Like Thucydides (who on occasion also serves as Pausanias's model), Pausanias
laments the embellishments on tradition that "the poets" (*hoi poiētai*) and others are
prone to introduce: choral poets and tragedians have propagated misinformation about
Theseus (1.3.3); Archilochus assigns new punishments to Tantalus in the underworld
(10.31.12; see also 3.25.6, 7.21.5, 10.6.6). Particular targets of Pausanias's disapproval in
this regard are the three canonical Athenian tragedians, who are almost never cited as
authoritative sources of information (the only exceptions, both from Aeschylus, are
2.24.4 and 8.6.6). Aeschylus is charged with spreading the misinformation that the
Eumenides had serpents in their hair (1.28.6), and that only seven Argive heroes led
the expedition against Thebes (2.20.5). On the authority of Homer and the *Thebaid*,
Pausanias discounts Sophocles's claim that Oedipus died in Attica (1.28.7; 1.30.4), and
that his four famous children were the result of his union with Jocasta (9.5.10). As for

Euripides, it scarcely seems likely that Pausanias was ignorant of the plays, but his text is free of any unequivocal evidence to the contrary. A plausible inference is that the three tragedians epitomized Pausanias's misgivings about the testimony of "the poets:" they were willing to modify the inherited traditions, and, unlike most other post-Homeric authors, their versions had gained enough currency to supplant more genuine versions. Hence Pausanias's apparent dismay at what must have seemed to him an egregious example of literary feedback when he learns that the Argives themselves, who should know better, venerate a monument to the seven heroes who went to Thebes: "even the Argives have come to follow the poetry of Aeschylus" (2.20.5).

One final, slightly contrarian observation: while there is no cause to doubt that Pausanias conducted much laborious mythographical research in both the library and the field, his literary aims must also be kept in mind when evaluating his efforts. At one point (8.37.6), Pausanias states that "Aeschylus son of Euphorion was the one who taught the Greeks the tale, an Egyptian one, that Artemis was the daughter of Demeter and not of Leto." This statement gives the impression that Pausanias found this assertion about Artemis's parentage in Aeschylus and then researched the subsequent tradition to conclude that it had some impact on later writers. What it is, in fact, is an uncredited paraphrase of Herodotus (2.156.6). Likewise, his statement that most of the poems attributed to Musaeus were actually written by Onomacritus (1.22.7) is another nod to Herodotus (7.6). On occasion what looks like earnest, painstaking research on Pausanias's part may instead be the sort of literary role-playing in which authors of the Second Sophistic frequently engage.

In sum, despite such caveats, the value of Pausanias as a mythographical source is hard to overstate. He preserves a vast amount of information found in no other source, and there is good reason to think that much of it derives from his own research into local traditions that no one else bothered to record and into texts that few of his contemporaries bothered to read. Evaluation of any element of his testimony, however, must remain constantly attentive to the overarching contexts provided by Pausanias's intellectual and literary predilections.

## FURTHER READING

The best general introductions to Pausanias and the *Periegesis* in English are those of Habicht (1998) and Pretzler (2007), while Pirenne-Delforge (2008) offers the most comprehensive study on Pausanias's treatment of myth and religion to date, although Hawes (2021), which appeared after this survey was written, is sure to become a crucial resource on the topic. Myth in the *Periegesis* is also the topic of substantial chapters by Patterson (2010), on kinship myth, and by Hawes (2014), on rationalizing. Pausanias also figures prominently in Paul Veyne's thought-provoking study *Did the Greeks Believe in Their Myths* (1988), which should now be read alongside Hawes's (2014: 178–185) critique. Frateantonio (2009) studies the way Pausanias responds to the contemporary competition between Greek communities, which often plays out on the field of myth, and Akujärvi (2005) presents a meticulous analysis of the ways in which Pausanias constructs his stance as an authority on many topics, including myth.

Gaertner (2006) investigates the ties between the *Periegesis* and other written compilations of mythographical material, although, as noted, his conclusions do not follow from the evidence presented. It would go beyond the scope of this survey to catalogue the numerous studies of particular myths and the mythic traditions of particular communities that draw heavily from Pausanias's testimony. A number appear in a collection of essays edited by Pirenne-Delforge (1998). Brief studies of individual myths encountered in the text can be found in commentaries to the *Periegesis*. Unfortunately, the latest complete commentary in English is that of Frazer (1898). Although Frazer's discussions of myths are outdated archaeologically and in other respects, they still useful on occasion, particularly for the comparative material he adduces from other cultures. Commentary projects have been undertaken in recent decades by scholars writing in Italian (Musti et al. 1982–2017) and French (Casevitz et al. 1992–2005). The Italian series has recently been completed, while in the French series only six of the ten books have been covered so far (although publication of a seventh, Book III, is expected soon).

## References

Akujärvi, Johanna. 2005. *Researcher, Traveller, Narrator: Studies in Pausanias' "Periegesis."* Stockholm: Almqvist and Wicksell.

Alcock, Susan E., John F. Cherry, and Jaś Elsner, eds. 2001. *Pausanias: Travel and Memory in Roman Greece*. Oxford: Oxford University Press.

Baleriaux, Julie. 2017. "Pausanias' Arcadia between Conservatism and Innovation." In *Myths on the Map: The Storied Landscapes of Ancient Greece*, edited by Greta Hawes, 141–158. Oxford: Oxford University Press.

Bingen, Jean, ed. 1996. *Pausanias Historien*. Entretiens sur l'Antiquité Classique 41. Geneva: Fondation Hardt.

Bowie, Ewen L. 1996. "Past and Present in Pausanias." In *Pausanias Historien*, edited by J. Bingen, 207–230. Geneva: Fondation Hardt.

Bowie, Ewen L. 2001. "Inspiration and Aspiration: Date, Genre, and Readership." In *Pausanias: Travel and Memory in Roman Greece*, edited by Susan E. Alcock, John F. Cherry, and Jaś Elsner, 21–32. Oxford: Oxford University Press.

Cameron, Alan. 2004. *Greek Mythography in the Roman World*. Oxford: Oxford University Press.

Casevitz, Michel, Janick Auberger, François Chamoux, Anne Jacquemin, Madeleine Jost, Yves Lafond, et al., eds. 1992–2005. *Pausanias: Description de la Grèce*. 6 vols. Paris: Les Belles Lettres.

Currie, Bruno. 2002. "Euthymos of Locri: A Case-Study in Heroization in the Classical Period." *Journal of Hellenic Studies* 122: 24–44.

Duffy, William S. 2013. "The Necklace of Eriphyle and Pausanias' Approach to the Homeric Epics." *Classical World* 107: 35–47.

Frazer, J. G. 1898. *Pausanias's Description of Greece*. London: Macmillan.

Frateantonio, Christa. 2009. *Religion und Städtekonkurrenz: Zum politischen und kulturellen Kontext von Pausanias' "Periegese."* Berlin: De Gruyter.

Gaertner, Jan F. 2006. "Die Kultepiklesen und Kultaitia in Pausanias Periegesis." *Hermes* 134: 471–487.

Habicht, Christian. 1998. *Pausanias' Guide to Ancient Greece*. 2nd ed. Berkeley: University of California Press.

Hawes, Greta. 2014. *Rationalizing Myth in Antiquity*. Oxford: Oxford University Press.

Hawes, Greta. 2017. "Of Myths and Maps." In *Myths on the Map: The Storied Landscapes of Ancient Greece*, edited by Greta Hawes, 1-13. Oxford: Oxford University Press.

Hawes, Greta. 2021. *Pausanias in the World of Greek Myth*. Oxford: Oxford University Press.

Henige, David P. 1974. "The Problem of Feedback in Oral Tradition: Four Examples from the Fante Coastlands." *Journal of African History* 14: 223–235.

Hutton, William. 2005. *Describing Greece: Landscape and Literature in the "Periegesis" of Pausanias*. Cambridge, UK: Cambridge University Press.

Hutton, William. 2017. "Pausanias." In *The Oxford Handbook of the Second Sophistic*, edited by Daniel S. Richter and William A. Johnson, 357-369. Oxford: Oxford University Press.

Jones, Christopher P. 2001. "Pausanias and His Guides." In *Pausanias: Travel and Memory in Roman Greece*, edited by Susan E. Alcock, John F. Cherry, and Jaś Elsner, 33-39. Oxford: Oxford University Press.

Jost, Madeleine. 2006. "Unité et diversité: La Grèce de Pausanias." *Revue des Études Grecques* 119: 568–587.

Lacroix, Léon. 1994. "Traditions locales et légendes étiologiques dans la *Périègèse* de Pausanias." *Journal des Savants* 1: 75–99. https://doi.org/10.3406/jds.1994.1575.

Luraghi, Nino. 2008. *The Ancient Messenians: Constructions of Ethnicity and Memory*. Cambridge, UK: Cambridge University Press.

Musti, Domenico, and Luigi Beschi, Umberto Bultrighini, Gianfranco Maddoli, Mauro Moggi, Massimo Nafissi, et al., eds. 1982–2017. *Pausania: Guida della Grecia*. 10 vols. Milan: Fondazione Lorenzo Valla and Mondadori.

Patterson, Lee. 2010. *Kinship Myth in Ancient Greece*. Austin: University of Texas Press.

Pirenne-Delforge, Vinciane, ed. 1998. *Les Panthéons des cités: Des origines à la "Périégèse" de Pausanias* (*Kernos* suppl. 8). Liège, Belgium: Centre international d'Étude de la Religion grecque antique.

Pirenne-Delforge, Vinciane. 2008. *Retour à la source: Pausanias et la religion grecque* (*Kernos* suppl. 20). Liège, Belgium: Centre international d'Étude de la Religion grecque antique.

Pretzler, Maria. 2005. "Pausanias and the Oral Tradition." *Classical Quarterly* 55: 235–249.

Pretzler, Maria. 2007. *Pausanias: Travel Writing in Ancient Greece*. London: Duckworth.

Richman, Gerald. 1986. "Artful Slipping in Old English." *Neophilologus* 70: 279–291.

Sánchez Hernández, Juan P. 2010. "Procles the Carthaginian: A North African Sophist in Pausanias' *Periegesis*." *Greek, Roman, and Byzantine Studies* 50: 119–132.

Smith, William. 1849. *A Dictionary of Greek and Roman Biography and Mythology*. 3 vols. London: Taylor and Walton.

Veyne, Paul. 1988. *Did the Greeks Believe in Their Myths? An Essay on the Constitutive Imagination*. Translated by Paula Wissing. Chicago: University of Chicago Press.

# CHAPTER 23

····································································································

# TRAGIC MYTHOGRAPHY

····································································································

## CHIARA MECCARIELLO

As a theatrical genre consisting—in most cases—in the enactment of myths, ancient Greek tragedy was an obvious source for mythographers in their activities of collecting and organizing mythical stories. Although mythography was not yet perceived as a self-standing genre in the first half of the 5th century BCE, what we think of as mythography was already being produced and consumed during Aeschylus's lifetime. This also entails the reverse possibility that early mythography influenced the tragedians in their creative employment of mythical stories on the Athenian stage. Thus, contributions in both directions might have already started in the 5th century, and the potential for cross-fertilization continued to exist uninterruptedly in the broader Graeco-Roman world as tragedy became part of the cultural curriculum of any cultivated Greek, and mythography, in turn, provided easy access to the totality of myth that constituted a substantial part of the Greek literary heritage.

This chapter explores different kinds of attested or reconstructable interactions between the two genres. The first part focuses on the mythographical impulse of tragedy and discusses passages and aspects of extant plays that betray the influence of mythographical practices. The second section surveys the production and use of mythography in the ancient study of tragedy, taking into account specialized works, remains of introductory and interpretive material, and plot summaries. Finally, the third section turns to how tragedians became sources of myths and examines, in particular, their presence in the extant mythographical production.

As we will see, the available evidence suggests that the last two decades of the 5th century BCE were a crucial period in what we may call "coevolution" of tragedy and mythography. On the one hand, mythographical patterns can be detected especially in late plays of Euripides (approximately 415–406 BCE); on the other hand, myth-related research on tragedy starts to surface in our documentation between the 5th and 4th centuries, the earliest known example probably being Glaucus's *On the Myths of Aeschylus*. Significantly, the 4th century will see the rise of a new concept of mythography as a "self-conscious," specialized activity (Fowler 2013: xiv–xv) in the wake of the "invention of mythology," which can be ascribed to the middle of the 5th century at the earliest

(Fowler 2011). The dialogue between tragedy and mythography may thus reflect a new position of myth and myth-writing in the literary landscape, which Euripides would wink at in the last decade of his production.

# 1. The Mythographical Impulse of Tragedy

Although the prehistory of Greek tragedy is shrouded in obscurity and the extant sources on the topic are less likely to draw on historical records than to employ conjectural reconstruction, an ancient tradition espouses the view that the enactment of mythical stories was an innovation introduced by tragedians of the second or third generation. In an entry of the Byzantine *Suda* lexicon referencing the Peripatetic Chamaeleon's work *On Thespis* (*Suda* s.v. omicron 806 = Chamael. fr. 41 Martano), tragedians are said to have "turned gradually to mythical plots" (*mythoi* and *historiai*); and in Zenobius's collection of proverbs (*CPG* I 5.40, 2nd c. CE), this evolution is characterized as a departure from choruses originally singing dithyrambs for Dionysus to the writing of "*Ajaxes* and *Centaurs*." Plutarch (*Quaest. Conv.* 615 A) also identifies tragedy's enactment of "myths and sufferings" as an innovation of Phrynichus and Aeschylus.

In any case, the notion that tragedy typically draws its contents from mythology is an unproblematic assumption in 4th-century authors. Aristotle's discussion of the structure of the tragic plot presupposes tragedians' regularly resorting to mythical subjects (*Poet.* 13–14, 1452b28–1454a15); and the mythical subject matter of tragedy, which allows an author to easily select a plot from a well-known set of stories needing no invention or preliminary explanation, is one of the main advantages of tragedy over comedy according to the humorous characterization of the two genres offered by the 4th-century comedy writer Antiphanes (fr. 189 KA). Accordingly, in the surviving corpus of Greek literature, tragedians are often said to tell, choose, use, manipulate, and even make myths (see, for example, Lycurg. *Leoc.* 100, Diod. Sic. 20.14.6, Ael. *VH* 5.21, Strabo 4.1.7, sch. AB Eur. *Alc.* 1).

If such myth-centrism is an evident aspect of tragedy (notwithstanding the existence of rarer, nonmythically themed plays; see Kotlińska-Toma 2015: 23–28), the influence of specialized myth-writing on tragedy-writing is far from obvious. It is, in fact, hard to detect specific mythographical hypotexts in our extant tragedies because of the fragmentary survival of early mythography. We are, however, in a better position when it comes to identifying structural and formal elements of the plays that show a resemblance to specific traits of myth-writing as encoded in extant Greek mythography.

In fact, as prose narratives of collected remote stories, early mythographical works already show a well-defined, imitable style and register, the same as that found in later mythographical handbooks (Fowler 2006). A study by de Jong (2010) has demonstrated that many of the traits of these mythographical works can also be found in a specific subset of tragic narratives—namely, the Euripidean prologues. In particular, as summaries—in narratological terms: "they cover a long time span within a short compass" (de Jong 2010: 31)—and in their strong genealogical character, several Euripidean prologues show similarities with extant fragments of early mythographers both in type of content and structure. The tendency becomes particularly evident in passages of the late plays, such as *Iphigenia in Tauris* 1–5, *Phoenissae* 7–13, *Helen* 4–22, *Ion* 1–13, *Archelaus TrGF* F 228 and 228a, which can be fruitfully compared to scraps of early mythography, such as (all references to Fowler) Hellanicus fr. 4, Antiochus of Syracuse fr. 6, Acusilaus fr. 1, Pherecydes fr. 95, Andron of Halicarnassus fr. 7. These all include genealogies and geographical references, and mention marriages, colonizations, foundations, or denominations; significantly, they summarize past events one after the other as in a chain, normally using a simple, unembellished, almost chronicle-like style. Take, for instance, the opening of *Iphigenia among the Taurians*:

> Pelops the son of Tantalus went to Pisa and with his swift horses won as a bride the daughter of Oenomaus. She gave birth to Atreus, whose sons in turn were Menelaus and Agamemnon. It is from this last that I was begotten, I, Iphigenia, daughter of Tyndareus' daughter Clytemestra. (*IT* 1–5, trans. Kovacs 1999)

Furthermore, several Euripidean prologues show a unique "anti-illusionistic nature," in that they lack either an onstage addressee or emotional justification, which, crucially, differentiates them from other monological prologues found in Greek tragedy, such as those of Aeschylus's *Agamemnon* and *Eumenides* and Sophocles's *Trachiniae* (de Jong 2010: 23; see also the prologue of Euripides' *Medea*).

In de Jong's view, these Euripidean prologues should be considered in combination with the speeches that are often spoken by gods *ex machina* at the ends of the plays, which display the same genealogical and summary structure but with an opening to the dramatic future (for example, *IT* 1435–1474, *Hel.* 1642–1679, *Ion* 1553–1605). Thus, prologues and exodus speeches would provide tragedies with a sort of mythographical frame and betray the playwright's intentional dialogue with contemporary mythography.

The thesis that Euripides experimented with the use of mythographical "conventions," especially in his late tragedies, is further supported by the ancient characterization of the playwright. Ancient critics already pointed out the originality of his prologues, identifying his propensity to indulge in long genealogies and generous use of straightforward narratives lacking dramatic justification and poetical quality as peculiar, typical, and reprehensible features of his production (for instance, Ar. *Ran.* 945–947, *Ach.* 47–51 with sch. *ad* 47, Anon. Seg. *Ars Rhetorica* 64–65, *Vit. Eurip. TrGF* T A 1 IA 2 and A 4 9–11, sch. Aesch. *Eum.* 1a, sch. T *Il.* 15.64c). Even the idea that Euripides was actually reading and using mythography can be found in a scholion on his *Phoenissae* (71). In identifying a contradiction in his treatment of the predramatic events that brought Polynices to Argos, the scholion refers to the tragedian's adoption of two different versions, one from Hellanicus and one from Pherecydes. The bookish Euripides may well have used mythographical handbooks (Fowler 2006: 44, quoting Ar. *Ran.* 943), deriving from them both contents for his plots and structural traits. It is also tempting to see his engagement with mythography behind the mythical comprehensiveness of a play like the *Phoenissae*, which has been characterized as "a Theban mythical megatext that incorporates most of the versions of the Theban saga" (Lamari 2010: 195): a trait characteristic of the mythographical handbook.

If Euripides chose to adopt elements of contemporary mythography, what was his purpose in doing so? According to de Jong (2010: 33), writing about myth in the same way as professional myth-writers would stress the status of myth as myth—in other words, as fiction—and that of tragedy as art rather than reality. However, it is by no means certain that any concept of myth as fiction was widespread in Euripides's time. It might be more relevant to note that mythography, as an intellectual activity aimed at private reading, entails a detachment of myth from ritual and performative contexts. Thus, in embracing an occasion-free genre, Euripides might have meant to wink at myth's private accessibility and thereby enlarge the intellectual range of tragedy.

## 2. Mythography and the Study and Reading of Tragedy

Significantly, when tragedy itself became widely accessible for individual reading and study, and different types of paraphernalia were produced to meet readers' and students' needs, tragic myths became the focus of lively and varied intellectual activity.

### 2.1. Studying Tragic Myths in Antiquity

The treatises *On the Myths of Aeschylus* (Aesch. *TrGF* T 86) and *On the Myths of Sophocles* (Soph. *TrGF* T 149, *BNJ* 328 T 1) are known respectively as works by Glaucus (plausibly of Rhegium, 5th–4th c. BCE) and Philochorus (4th–3rd c. BCE). Heraclides of Pontus (4th c. BCE) is also credited with a work *Peri tōn par' Euripidēi kai Sophoklei*, perhaps, *On Issues in Euripides and Sophocles*, which might have included discussions of myths; but Jacoby's hesitant addition of *mythōn* after *tōn*, restoring the title *On the Myths in Euripides and Sophocles*, has been widely rejected (*FGrHist* 328 no. 21 [comm. with n. 5]; Heracl. T 1 and fr. 180 Wehrli = no. 17.31 Schütrumpf; Eur. *TrGF* T 209). Too little survives of these works to allow an assessment of their relationship with mythography. Interestingly the only fragment that can be ascribed with certainty to Glaucus's work concerns the debt of Aeschylus's *Persians* to Phrynicus's *Phoenissae* (*hyp.* Aesch. *Pers.* 1–7 West = Glauc. fr. 7 Lanata). The quotation of the first line of Phrynicus's play, very similar to Aesch. *Pers.* 1, and the discussion of the different dramatic arrangement of the first scene suggest that Glaucus was here concerned with imitation or even plagiarism (hence his use of the verb *parapoiein*), and that the word *mythos* in the title does not have the connotation of the modern "myth," but rather the Aristotelian meaning of "composition of events," "plot" (Arist. *Poet.* 1450 a). However, a Glaucus, likely the same author, is also credited with a more strictly mythological discussion on the death and burial of Polyxena (sch. Eur. *Hec.* 41), which may well come from the same or a similar work.

As for Philochorus's *On the Myths of Sophocles*, no fragments survive, but the fact that a *Letter to Asclepiades* is ascribed to him and credited with a treatment of Hecuba's story (sch. Eur. *Hec.* 1) might indicate that the Atthidographer was engaged in "scholarly polemic" within the study of tragic myths (Cameron 2004: 58).

A better-documented example of interplay between tragedy and mythography is Asclepiades of Tragilus's six-book *Tragodoumena* (*FGrHist* 12 T 1 = Steph. Byz. *Ethn.* s.v. tau 162 Billerbeck). This 4th-century BCE work, now lost, was widely used in ancient scholarship on myth-based poetical works (for example, on Pindar, Apollonius Rhodius, and Euripides) and by later mythographers (Apollod. *Bibl.* 2.6, 3.7, Hyg. *Astr.* 2.21), and thanks to these reuses a fair number of fragments have been handed down to us. From them we may infer that Asclepiades's project, though based on tragedy, was not an exposition or simple survey of tragedy's mythical data; rather, it was a scholarly work resulting from research on tragic myths. The *Tragodoumena* probably included comparisons with other accounts and extra information, such as names and genealogies, meant to complement and elaborate on tragic mythological references. For example, Asclepiades is our ultimate source for the text of the riddle of the Sphinx and for further details of the story that surrounds it. This information is potentially useful for a reader of, say, Euripides's *Phoenissae*, whose prologue only mentions the riddle, without reporting its text (Ath. 10.456b = Asclep. *FGrHist* 12 fr. 7a; *sch.* Eur. *Phoen.* 45 = Asclep. *FGrHist* 12 fr. 7b): the riddle is indeed found in the play's prefatory material (hyp. (e) Diggle), where its heading carries the name of Asclepiades in some manuscripts.

A further example of both Asclepiades's method and the later uses of the *Tragodoumena* is his research on the offspring of Calliope and Apollo (*FGrHist* 12 fr. 6a-c), preserved verbatim in a scholion on the *Rhesus* (sch. Eur. *Rh.* 895) and heavily excerpted in the scholia on Pindar and Apollonius Rhodius (sch. Pind. *P.* 4.313a and sch. Ap. Rhod. 1.23–25a). In the fuller verbatim version, four sons of the Muse are listed in order of their births, and the outstanding musical talent of Orpheus, the youngest, is singled out. When this passage is reused in the scholia on Pindar, it is heavily cut so as to include only the sons' names (with one omission); more drastically, in the scholion on Apollonius Rhodius, Asclepiades is quickly referenced regarding Orpheus's birth from Calliope and Apollo.

Finally, it might be relevant to note that a didascalic record referring to a Lenaean contest of the mid-fourth century BCE mentions a tragedian named Asclepiades (*TrGF* vol. 1 DID A 3b, 54, see Pressler 1997): if not a namesake, the possibility that the author of the *Tragodoumena* was occasionally a playwright himself could shed new light on the rationale behind his prose work, and suggest that individual authors could occasionally be versed in both tragedy and mythography.

## 2.2  Paraliterary Works: Scholia and Hypotheses

As ancillary materials meeting the various needs of the readers of tragedy, the prefatory and exegetical apparatuses that were transmitted alongside the plays in the medieval manuscripts or independently by papyrus fragments reserve substantial space to myth-related aspects. The surviving corpora of tragic scholia are quantitatively the most prominent example of this phenomenon. A varied and stratified body of marginal notes compiled in the Byzantine period on the grounds of earlier commentaries, they include heterogeneous material ranging from simple scholastic paraphrases and vocabulary elucidations to erudite notes reflecting scholarly activity of the Hellenistic and imperial periods.

In their internal variety, scholia are cluttered with mythical information of different type. The scholiasts, acting as compilers of variants themselves or excerpting previous reference works, provided readers with paraliterary aids, such as short mythological narratives that expanded on potentially obscure references in the dramatic text. Thus, for example, when we encounter a cryptic reference to Odysseus as "the abject line of Sisyphus" in the parodos of Sophocles's *Ajax*, a scholiast promptly explains it by referring to the alleged encounter between Anticlea and Sisyphus that took place when she was on the way to Ithaca for her marriage to Laertes; and another note further elaborates on Sisyphus's bad name (sch. *Aj.* 190 b Christodoulos).

But sometimes mythological expansions do not elucidate the text, and the text instead appears to be a pretext for lavishing on readers source names and erudite details. The scholion on the first line of Euripides's *Alcestis* is an instructive example. The play's prologue presents Apollo's servitude at the palace of Admetus, a crucial antecedent of the plot, as a punishment sent by Zeus for the murder of the Cyclopes, which Apollo had committed to avenge the killing of his son Asclepius by the Cyclopean-forged lightning of Zeus (*Alc.* 1–7). The first part of the scholion, an exposition of several attested reasons for Apollo's servitude, can help elucidate the specific angle of the Euripidean treatment. By contrast, the second part of the note, an erudite list of different attested reasons for the killing of Asclepius, based on a catalogue of his healings (Cameron 2004: 99–103), is less clearly related to interpretive purposes, because Euripides does not go that far in his chain of motives.

In this and other contexts, scholiasts' debt to mythographers is well documented. Hellanicus, for example, is mentioned twelve times in the extant scholia on Euripides, Pherecydes as many as twenty. However, mythographers do not enjoy a special status, and their names can appear side by side with poetical sources. A scholion on Euripides's *Phoenissae*, for example, cites both Hellanicus and the epic poet Antimachus as sources for two different genealogies of Parthenopaeus, without alluding at any point to the different nature of their respective works (sch. MTA Eur. *Phoen.* 150).

Another instance of a paraliterary work with a strong focus on mythology is a 6th-century papyrus preserving select commentary notes on Euripides's *Phoenissae* (P. Würzb. 1). Probably a school text, the papyrus shows a trait that is typical of earlier commentaries (*hypomnemata*) in that it consists of self-standing notes, not marginal additions to a manuscript of the play, and refers to each commented passage by reporting the relevant lemma. Among the extant notes, we can observe a high density of short mythographical passages elaborating on less-detailed references found in the tragic text: the latest editors observe that as many as fifteen of the thirty preserved notes concern myths (see, for example, the notes to lines 417 on Tydeus, 638 on Cadmus, 1043 on Oedipus, 1108 on Atalante), and nine more are about the gods (Essler, Mastronarde, and McNamee 2013: 87–88). As a school text, the papyrus clearly documents the need of early Byzantine students for simple explanations of mythological references.

Mythology also plays an important role among the heterogeneous short introductions to single plays known since antiquity as "hypotheses." This label is applied to different typologies of introductory texts, from simple plot summaries to more erudite overviews on several aspects of a given play. Prefixed to the text of the relevant drama in the medieval manuscripts, or transmitted by papyrus fragments, the extant hypotheses are often anonymous and incorporate material that cannot always be traced to a specific cultural environment. In some instances, however, the name of an ancient scholar is attached to them.

This is, for example, the case with the hypotheses ascribed to the Hellenistic grammarian Aristophanes of Byzantium (around 265/257–190/180 BCE), a well-defined set with a recurring structure devoted to the Aeschylean, Sophoclean, and Euripidean production. These erudite pieces include, among others, a brief section on each play's mythical subject (*mythopoiia*), in which the grammarian identifies parallel treatments of the same myth within the tragic canon and sometimes indicates essential differences between them. Comparisons of mythical versions also appear in anonymous hypotheses of an erudite or miscellaneous nature, such as the one prefixed to Sophocles's *Ajax* (lines 54–60 Christodoulos), where different accounts of the eponymous character's death are considered, or the one attached to Euripides's *Medea* (hyp. (a) Diggle), in which Pherecydes, Simonides, Aeschylus, and Staphylus are referenced on aspects of the Medea myth that are only vaguely pertinent to the play plot. Similar but longer and more verbose surveys of tragedy-related myths are found in the manuscripts of plays that were particularly appreciated in the Byzantine period, such as Aeschylus's *Seven against Thebes* and Euripides's *Phoenissae*, reflecting late readers' near-obsession with mythological and genealogical details (Essler, Mastronarde, and McNamee 2013: 87).

Finally, the so-called narrative hypotheses—a nomenclature proposed by van Rossum-Steenbeek (1998: 1–2) for the same collection of tragic plot summaries that Zuntz (1955: 135) labeled "Tales from Euripides"—are a special case of the intersection of tragedy and mythography. Mere expositions of the plays' mythical events, they are found not only in the tragic manuscripts, but also in papyri from the 1st to the 3rd or 4th centuries CE. The papyri preserve them in the form of a seemingly self-standing alphabetical collection, detached from the tragic texts and covering the entire Euripidean and Sophoclean production. Accordingly, several scholars see the collection in its entirety as a sort of mythographical compendium, addressed to readers interested in mythology rather than drama (for example, Zuntz 1955: 135).

However, what the narrative hypotheses offer is an account of the tragic *mythoi*, with *mythos* understood as "composition of events," according to the Aristotelian meaning: in other words, these texts can be seen as *mythographia* inasmuch as they are written accounts of plots (*mythoi* in the Aristotelian sense), and those plots happen to be myths (in the modern sense). Their being at the crossroad of tragedy and mythography is due to the specific contents of tragedy and the narrative character of the hypotheses; but certainly, despite the occasional addition of onomastic details, they do not share the comprehensive and multisource nature of mythographical compilations, nor do they elaborate on tragic myths as does Asclepiades's *Tragodoumena*. The alphabetical arrangement is also a clear indication that the user was supposed to browse them by play, not by mythical segment: nothing about Euripides's treatment of Polyxena's sacrifice can be found under the letter *pi*, nor is *Phoenissae* a transparent title for the contents of the Theban myth. It is also important to keep in mind that in most papyri each hypothesis is preceded by a heading including the title and first line of the play, which allows the identification of the dramatic text and documents a strong connection between each hypothesis and the respective play, before the summaries were included in the tragic manuscripts as prefatory material. This practice suggests that the narrative hypotheses were meant to be used in the reading and study of tragedy, either as introductions to the reading of the actual play–the function they perform in the medieval manuscripts–or as concise reminders of the play's contents, a particularly desirable tool, for example, in the context of anthological readings.

Because of their wide circulation in the Graeco-Roman world, these easy-to-access plot summaries were likely available to Imperial and Byzantine mythographers. But, as we will see in the next section, this does not necessarily imply that mythographers did not or could not access the tragic texts as well.

## 3. TRAGEDY AS A SOURCE FOR MYTHOGRAPHERS

The movement of mythological information from tragedy to mythography is a basic assumption for scholars of Greek tragedy. Numerous passages from mythographical works have been used to reconstruct the plots of lost plays and feature as *testimonia* to lost plays in modern fragment collections. Ps.-Apollodorus's *Library* and Hyginus's *Fabulae*, for example, are among the most quoted sources in Kannicht's (2004) edition of Euripidean fragments—twenty-eight and twenty passages respectively. However, in only a very few cases do these passages explicitly mention a tragic source, and their importance often lies in providing a general account of the relevant myth rather than one that is certainly or overtly related to a tragic plot.

The extant text of the *Library* contains three mentions of "the tragic poets" in general (Apollod. *Bibl.* 2.5, 2.23, 2.25), and four of Euripides (2.11, 3.74–75, 3.94–95, 3.109).

Euripides, the only tragedian named in that text, is overall the most represented in mythography, being, for example, the only explicit tragic source in the extant versions of Ps.-Plutarch's *Parallela Minora* and Hyginus's *Fabulae*, as well as the most quoted in the catasterism tradition (on catasterisms, see Zucker, this volume). However, our texts of Ps.-Eratosthenes *Catasterisms* and Hyginus's *Astronomica* still mention Aeschylus, Sophocles, and even a minor tragedian like Sositheus (Erat. Cat. 16, 22, 24, 36; Hyg. *Astron.* 2.6, 2.10, 2.12, 2.15, 2.27, 2.37).

There is no homogeneity in the ways tragedians are cited, apart from the regular absence of verse quotations. Play titles are sometimes indicated alongside the author name, but there is no reference to the dramatic structure or the refraction of voices typical of the genre. Variety can also be observed when it comes to the typology of information drawn from tragedy. The four references to Euripides in Ps.-Apollodorus's *Library* are a good example: they consist of three brief genealogical variants or mythical details (2.11, 3.74–75, 3.109) and a single longer passage tacitly summarizing the plot of the *Alcmaeon in Corinth* (3.94–95). In the same handbook, generic references to "the tragic poets" occur twice in the context of an opposition with epic authors, as if to underline a genre-based agreement (Apollod. *Bibl.* 2.23 and 2.25, against the author of the *Nostoi* and Homer, respectively); but in the remaining case, "many of the tragedians" are grouped together with Castor, author of *Chronica*, against Hesiod and Acusilaus (*Bibl.* 2.5).

As Huys showed in his analysis of Hyginus's *Fabulae* 4 and 8—whose headings contain the name of Euripides—and of Ps.-Apollodorus's section on Alcmaeon (Huys 1996: 172–173; 1997b: 312–313), a notable recurring feature of the mythographical passages plausibly containing tragic plot summaries is the profusion of information on the play's antecedents, as is normally found in prologues, while the dramatized events are more or less severely abridged; the denouement of the plot, including details of the mythical future, also receives proportionally large attention. Prologues are thus likely to be the main source, followed at distance by the exodus scenes.

This characteristic, which is paralleled, to a lesser extent, in the narrative hypotheses (Meccariello 2014: 58–61), is clearly a function of the density in the tragic prologues of summary-like information on the predramatic time, especially since the verifiable cases are Euripidean; but it is also indicative of the obvious fact that mythographers are only instrumentally interested in tragedy. Behind this method seems to lie an implicit separation between myth and its theatrical embodiment, a preference for the bare story and its factual details over the peculiarities of tragic invention in terms of plot organization, characters' motivation, and broader issues. Thus, the difference between the extant narrative hypothesis of the *Hecuba* and the summary of its myth preserved by Ps.-Plutarch, expressly drawing on Euripides (*Par. min.* 311 D), appears to be not only quantitative (Ps.-Plutarch refers just to Polydorus's murder and not to the story of Polyxena, both at the core of the play and consequently of the hypothesis) but also qualitative (Ps.-Plutarch omits most details specific to the dramatized plot, such as the finding of Polydorus's corpse and the judgment against his murderer Polymestor). In other words, the mythographer shows interest in the key points of the story, not in how the playwright connects them on the stage.

Were the tragedians direct or indirect sources for mythographers? In certain cases firsthand knowledge can be safely ruled out. One patent example is Hyginus's mention of "Melanippe daughter of Desmontes" (*Melanippen Desmontis filiam, Fab.* 186), which clearly stems from a misunderstanding of the title *Melanippe in Chains* (*Melanippe he Desmotis*), a mistake that a reader of the play would hardly have made. In many cases, it is hard to tell whether a mythographer used a tragic text directly: the Ps.-Plutarchean passage on Hecuba mentioned earlier does name Euripides as its source but shows no signs of dependence on the actual play, nor does it follow Euripides when calling Polymestor Priam's son-in-law.

On the other hand, there are sufficient grounds to maintain that Ps.-Apollodorus had direct access to Euripides's *Phoenissae.* Two of the shorter passages in which he mentions the tragedian clearly show knowledge of a specific *rhesis* of the play, the messenger speech that narrates a crucial phase of the conflict between Argives and Thebans (1090–1199). This passage is recalled both in *Bibl.* 3.75, where Euripides is the explicit source on Parthenopaeus's death at the hands of Periclymenus (compare *Phoen.* 1153–1157; Huys 1997b: 311–312), and in *Bibl.* 3.109, regarding the genealogy of Atalante (compare *Phoen.* 1162; Huys 1997b: 313–314). Moreover, the entire Apollodorean account of the battle between Thebans and Argives, starting from 3.73, draws on the Euripidean version, including echoes of *Phoen.* 1172–1188 in the description of Capaneus's death and the subsequent reference to the Argives's turning to flee. A textual contact with the extant narrative hypothesis of the play is a possibility, and Krenn (1971: 94–95) has shown resemblances between this summary and various points of Ps.-Apollodorus's sections 3.57–79. However, the hypothesis cannot be Ps.-Apollodorus's only source on the play, since it does not refer to Parthenopaeus's and Capaneus's deaths, or to the genealogy of Atalante. This fact and the above-mentioned textual parallels between the mythographer's account and the play itself rather suggest firsthand knowledge of the *Phoenissae.* This is not at all surprising, as this tragedy was widely used in schools in the Graeco-Roman world and was plausibly part of the literary knowledge of any cultivated Greek (Cribiore 2001); Ps.-Apollodorus was certainly among them.

Further, Ps.-Apollodorus's interspersing of the *Phoenissae* references with non-Euripidean details such as the *aristeia* of Astacus's sons in *Bibl.* 3.74–75 exemplifies a common characteristic of the mythographical method—namely, the combining of multiple sources. This aspect is often indicated explicitly either in the presentation of mythographical works offered by ancient readers or in mythographers' programmatic introductions (see, for instance, the characterization of Dionysius Scytobrachion in Diod. Sic. 3.66.5–6, or the epigram prefixed to Ps.-Apollodorus's *Library* in the copy that was available to the patriarch Photius in 9th-century Constantinople [Phot. *Bibl.* 186]). The phenomenon is particularly evident in Ps.-Apollodorus's treatment of the Alcestis myth, which includes two mutually exclusive versions of her return on earth, only one of which is somewhat compatible with the Euripidean treatment (*Bibl.* 1.104–6, see Huys 1997b: 325, Villagra 2017: 49–50).

# Conclusions

The examination of different types of contact between tragedy and mythography has shown that an influence of myth-writing on tragedy-writing is ascertainable for the 5th century BCE, but as far as we can tell, it was probably limited to Euripides, and is particularly evident in the last decade of his production. In this chronological span we see three different but likely related phenomena which suggest a coevolution of tragedy and mythography: while mythography starts to be perceived and presented as a self-standing intellectual activity, tragedy starts to be the object of specific myth-centered studies and even to substantially incorporate mythographical elements and structures in its own texture.

Because of the too-fragmentary survival of post-Euripidean tragedy, we cannot follow the influence of mythography on tragedy in the Hellenistic and Roman periods; an influence of Hellanicus and Pherecydes on Lycophron's non-fragmentary *Alexandra* is likely but elusive (Hornblower 2015: 18–19). However, we do have rich evidence of the opposite phenomenon—namely, the use of tragedy in mythographical compilations as an immediate or remote source for various types of mythical information. Finally, tragedy and the mythographical method uninterruptedly intersected in several works surrounding the study of tragedy: comparison of parallel treatments or other types of mythological research are documented both in a 4th-century BCE work like Asclepiades's *Tragodoumena* and in the remains of the prose apparatuses produced in the Hellenistic, Roman, and Byzantine periods as aids for readers, students, and scholars working on Greek tragedy.

The prominence of Euripides that has consistently emerged is not surprising: his works were more popular in antiquity than those of any other tragedian, as shown by tragedy's survival dynamics reflected in both papyri and medieval manuscripts. Furthermore, Euripides was used more extensively than Aeschylus and Sophocles in school, which entails a more substantial production or at least circulation and survival of paraliterary works on his plays. More specifically to mythography, one may argue that Euripides's prominence as an explicit source of myths is also related to the inner characteristics of his production, which were already identified by ancient critics and made specific sections of his plays ideal for incorporation in mythographical works. It is also worth noticing that the most prominent use of tragedians other than Euripides appears in relatively early specialized studies of tragic plots, such as those by Glaucus, Philochorus, Asclepiades, and Aristophanes of Byzantium, and in the catasterism tradition, which is likely to be rooted into Eratosthenes's work and the Alexandrian scholarly environment.

## Further Reading

A discussion of ancient passages on the original Dionysiac content of tragedy can be found in Pickard-Cambridge (1964: 124–126); Easterling (1997); and Mirhady (2012). Scullion (2002, 2005) reconsiders the problem on the grounds of a radically skeptic approach to ancient sources. An overview of the general topic of myth and drama is offered by Sommerstein (2005).

On Euripides's mythographical attitude, see de Jong (2010); on his *Phoenissae* as a mythological megatext, see Lamari (2010).

A survey of the intersections between mythography and scholarship in antiquity is offered by Huys (2013). For a recent discussion of Glaucus, Philochorus, and Heraclides of Pontus in this connection, see Fowler (2019: 45–46). The most recent and thorough study of the Würzburg papyrus, including a new edition, translation, and commentary, is by Essler, Mastronarde, and McNamee (2013). Meccariello (2019) discusses its mythographical passages as evidence for mythographical activities in late antique schools. The formation of Greek scholia has been recently discussed afresh by Montana (2011). Nünlist (2009: 257–264) offers a good synthesis of ancient critics' approaches to mythological aspects as attested in the scholia to several literary genres and an overview of the relevant technical terminology. For tragic hypotheses, Zuntz (1955: 135–146) is a ground-breaking study, and van Rossum-Steenbeek (1998) offers a further classification and overall analysis. On the narrative hypotheses specifically, see Meccariello (2014), which collects and discusses all the relevant texts and includes an updated bibliography. The debate over the attribution of these texts to Dicearchus of Messana and over the nature of the "hypotheses of the *mythoi* of Euripides and Sophocles" ascribed to him by Sextus Empiricus, has been recently summarized by Verhasselt (2015).

Three articles by Huys (1996, 1997a, 1997b) survey the verbal correspondences between the narrative hypotheses, on the one hand, and Ps.-Apollodorus's *Library* and Hyginus's *Fabulae*, on the other. These studies also refer to the earlier debate on the relationship between these mythographical works and tragedy. The topic has also been addressed by Luppe (1984), who overconfidently attempts a reconstruction of the Greek hypotheses he believes to be behind Hyginus's *Fabulae* 4 and 8. Ps.-Apollodorus's possible use of tragic hypotheses and of Asclepiades's *Tragodoumena* is also discussed in Villagra (2017).

## References

Cameron, Alan. 2004. *Greek Mythography in the Roman World*. Oxford: Oxford University Press.

Cribiore, Rafaella. 2001. "The Grammarian's Choice: The Popularity of Euripides' *Phoenissae* in Hellenistic and Roman Education." In *Education in Greek and Roman Antiquity*, edited by Yun Lee Too, 241–260. Leiden: Brill.

de Jong, Irene. 2010. "Euripides and His Prologues: A Reappraisal." *Pharos* 17: 21–34.

Easterling, Patricia E. 1997. "A Show for Dionysos." In *The Cambridge Companion to Greek Tragedy*, edited by Patricia E. Easterling, 36–53. Cambridge, UK: Cambridge University Press.

Essler, Holger, Donald J. Mastronarde, and Kathleen McNamee. 2013. "The Würzburg Scholia on Euripides' *Phoenissae*: A New Edition of P.Würzb. 1 with Translation and Commentary." *Würzburger Jahrbücher für die Altertumswissenschaft* 37: 31–97.

Fowler, Robert L. 2000. *Early Greek Mythography*. Vol. 1: *Text and Introduction*. Oxford: Oxford University Press.

Fowler, Robert L. 2006. "How to Tell a Myth." *Kernos* 19: 35–46.

Fowler, Robert L. 2011. "*Mythos* and *Logos*." *Journal of Hellenic Studies* 131: 45–66.

Fowler, Robert L. 2013. *Early Greek Mythography*. Vol. 2: *Commentary*. Oxford: Oxford University Press.

Fowler, Robert L. 2019. "Myth(ography), History and the Peripatos." In *Host or Parasite? Mythographers and Their Contemporaries in the Classical and Hellenistic Periods*, edited by Allen J. Romano and John Marincola, 29–52. Berlin and Boston: De Gruyter.

Hornblower, Simon. 2015. *Lykophron: Alexandra. Greek text, Translation, Commentary, and Introduction.* Oxford and New York: Oxford University Press.

Huys, Marc. 1996. "Euripides and the 'Tales from Euripides': Sources of the *Fabulae* of Ps.-Hyginus? Part 1." *Archiv für Papyrusforschung* 42: 168–178.

Huys, Marc. 1997a. "Euripides and the 'Tales from Euripides': Sources of the *Fabulae* of Ps.-Hyginus? Part 2." *Archiv für Papyrusforschung* 43: 11–30.

Huys, Marc. 1997b. "Euripides and the 'Tales from Euripides': Sources of Apollodoros' *Bibliotheca*?" *Rheinisches Museum für Philologie* 140: 308–327.

Huys, Marc. 2013. "Traces of Scholarship and Erudition in Greek Mythographic Papyri from the Roman Period." In *Writing Myth: Mythography in the Ancient World*, edited by Stephen M. Trzaskoma and R. Scott Smith, 115–132. Leuven: Peeters.

Kannicht, Richard. 2004. *Tragicorum Graecorum Fragmenta.* Vol. 5: *Euripides.* Göttingen: Vandenhoeck and Ruprecht.

Kotlińska-Toma, Agnieszka. 2015. *Hellenistic Tragedy: Texts, Translations and a Critical Survey.* London: Bloomsbury.

Kovacs, David. 1999. *Euripides. Trojan Women. Iphigenia among the Taurians. Ion.* Loeb Classical Library. Cambridge, MA: Harvard University Press.

Krenn, Johann. 1971. "Interpretationen zu den Hypothesen in den Euripideshandschriften." Diss. University of Graz.

Lamari, Anna A. 2010. *Narrative, Intertext, and Space in Euripides' "Phoenissae."* Berlin and New York: De Gruyter.

Luppe, Wolfgang. 1984. "Euripides-Hypotheseis in den Hygin-Fabeln *Antiope* und *Ino*?" *Philologus* 128: 41–59.

Meccariello, Chiara. 2014. *Le hypotheseis narrative dei drammi euripidei: Testo, contesto, fortuna.* Roma: Edizioni di Storia e Letteratura.

Meccariello, Chiara. 2019. "Impulso mitografico e mitografia nelle pratiche educative greche antiche." *Polymnia* 4: 147–75.

Mirhady, David C. 2012. "Something to Do with Dionysus: Chamaeleon on the Origins of Tragedy." In *Praxiphanes of Mytilene and Chamaeleon of Heraclea: Text, Translation, and Discussion*, edited by Andrea Martano, Elisabetta Matelli and David C. Mirhady: 49–71. New Brunswick: Transaction Publishers.

Montana, Fausto. 2011. "The Making of Greek Scholiastic Corpora." In *From Scholars to Scholia: Chapters in the History of Ancient Greek Scholarship*, edited by Franco Montanari and Lara Pagani, 105–161. Berlin and New York: De Gruyter.

Nünlist, René. 2009. *The Ancient Critic at Work. Terms and Concepts of Literary Criticism in Greek Scholia.* Cambridge: Cambridge University Press.

Pickard-Cambridge, Arthur W. 1964. *Dithyramb, Tragedy, and Comedy.* 2nd ed. Revised by Thomas B. L. Webster. Oxford: Oxford University Press.

Pressler, Frank. 1997. "Asklepiades #4." *Der Neue Pauly* 2: 89.

Scullion, Scott. 2002. "'Nothing to Do with Dionysus': Tragedy Misconceived as Ritual." *Classical Quarterly* 52: 102–137.

Scullion, Scott. 2005. "Tragedy and Religion: The Problem of Origins." In *A Companion to Greek Tragedy*, edited by Justina Gregory, 23–37. Malden, MA: Blackwell.

Sommerstein, Alan H. 2005. "Tragedy and Myth." In *A Companion to Tragedy*, edited by Rebecca Bushnell, 163–180. Malden, MA: Blackwell.

van Rossum-Steenbeek, Monique. 1998. *Greek Readers' Digests? Studies on a Selection of Subliterary Papyri.* Leiden: Brill.

Verhasselt, Gertjan. 2015. "The Hypotheses of Euripides and Sophocles by 'Dicaearchus.'" *Greek, Roman, and Byzantine Studies* 55: 608–636.

Villagra, Nereida. 2017. "Lost in Tradition: Apollodorus and Tragedy-Related Texts." In *Apollodoriana: Ancient Myths, New Crossroads*, edited by Jordi Pàmias, 38–65. Berlin and Boston: De Gruyter.

Zuntz, Günther. 1955. *The Political Plays of Euripides*. Manchester, UK: Manchester University Press.

# PART III

## INTERPRETATIONS AND INTERSECTIONS

# CHAPTER 24

··················································································

# RATIONALIZING AND
# HISTORICIZING

··················································································

## GRETA HAWES

GREEK myths ostensibly narrate the deep past of the Mediterranean; in this very basic way, they were intrinsically historical.[1] Moreover, myths communicated etiologies for why the world had become as it was; the deeds of ancestors were part and parcel of the political visions of the present. We might say, then, that historicization was an inherent aspect of the social functions of many of these stories. Nonetheless, one ancient form of critique of these myths targeted their ahistorical nature: that is, that what was said to happen in these stories could not have happened in real life. Monsters, superhuman feats, divine interventions, and metamorphoses belong to a narrative realm that is beyond sober historiography. This chapter is given over to one solution to the need to historicize myth in this way: rationalistic interpretation. Rationalization turned the fabulous stories that were circulating in the present into corrupted accounts of prosaic events in the past. By identifying a misunderstood turn-of-phrase or an ambiguous situation, the interpreter could champion a new version of the story, one that accorded with the biological and historical standards of the present. To take some examples from Palaephatus, the tradition's most prominent ancient exponent, Actaeon was not devoured by his dogs but financially destroyed through the keeping of them (6), Callisto did not turn into a bear; rather, her friends saw her enter a cave, from which a bear then appeared, and spread the story about her (14). And Scylla was no monster; this was the name of a trireme used in piratical raids (20).

These seemingly simplistic manipulations of traditional material in fact illuminate important currents at work in ancient myth more generally. Rationalizations appear in Greco-Roman literature from the late archaic period onward, and the sheer range of contexts and genres in which they are found show the flexible utility of this way of

[1] This chapter was produced as part of the project "Estudios sobre transmisión y recepción de Paléfato y la exégesis racionalista de los mitos," funded by Proyectos de I + D, Programa Estatal de Fomento de la Investigación Científica y Técnica de Excelencia (FFI2014-52203-P).

thinking about myth. Most obviously, the application of historicist ideals to traditional stories can be said to project a seemingly dogmatic distinction between what we might roughly term "myth" and "history." Rationalizations emphasize the gulf between the fabulous stories of the distant past and the observable norms of historical reality; moreover, they ostensibly paper over this gap by producing historiographically appropriate explanations for the traditional material. In defining traditional myths as ahistorical and then producing historicized versions of them, rationalizers project one of the most explicit ancient conceptions of myth as a recognizable body of stories.

The question of what exactly constitutes an emic category of "Greek myth" was one of the key debates in the field in the decades following the publication of Detienne's (1981) book *L'invention de la mythologie*. "Myth" has been defined and delineated differently in different contexts and periods of antiquity. One of the most important insights to have emerged from recent interest in ancient mythography is the recognition that the modes of organization and narration that are characteristic of (though not homogeneous within) mythography create and shore up a particular conception of myth as a cultural phenomenon. The mythographical impulse may be native to ancient myth, but it is not coterminous with the full experience of myth in antiquity. The rationalistic attitudes that are apparent in the works of mythographical authors and elsewhere are similarly distinctive. Indeed, rationalization is of heightened value to us in part because it often projects an unusually dogmatic response to myth. The process of rationalization points out the nonhistorical nature of Greek myth. Its traditional incompatibility with biological and historical norms thus becomes a defining feature. More than this, the most prominent rationalizations targeted very well-known stories. Indeed, they required that the stories be well-known because manipulating stories into new forms assumes that there is some conventional agreement on their "traditional" forms. In this way, the processes of rationalization required a particular—albeit implicit—definition of mythic phenomena.

Beyond this, rationalization also illustrates the flexibility and creativity of the mythic tradition. The mid-20th-century model, which had Greek culture progressing "from *mythos* to *logos*," would make rationalization one weapon in the arsenal that should have put an end to the irrational explanations provided by myth. In fact, the opposite is true. Rationalization did not spell the end of storytelling; rationalistic manipulations created new variants that made it possible to tell the stories in new ways. Rationalization, then, is another engine in the striking proliferation of myth through antiquity, one further aspect of the agonistic culture which spurred on innovation in the realm of stories, as elsewhere. Indeed, like mythography more generally, rationalization became a key conduit for the transmission of myth beyond antiquity.

This chapter looks at the ancient rationalizing tradition from two different viewpoints. I will first survey in a broadly chronological sweep the most notable mythographical texts that include rationalistic material. I then offer a study of rationalizations of the stories of Minos, Pasiphae, the Minotaur, and Theseus's expedition to Crete, which illustrate the various dynamics of rationalization.

# 1. Chronological Survey: From Early Prose Writing to Medieval Europe

Rationalistic interpretations of myths are not the exclusive preserve of mythography; instances from tragedy, philosophy, and comedy suggest the existence of a diffused and recognizable tradition from at least the classical period (see Dowden 1992: 42–47; Stern 1996: 10–11; Hawes 2014a: 13–17; Sumler 2014). Nonetheless, the prominence of rationalistic attitudes in some mythographical texts makes rationalization an important constitutive feature of the genre. The critique of myth is in any case intricately bound up in its origins. Hecataeus began his *Genealogies* by labeling the "stories of the Greeks" "laughable" (fr. 1 Fowler). Fragments of *Genealogies* suggest a concern with cutting stories down to size: Hecataeus makes Aegyptus the father of not even twenty sons instead of the traditional fifty (fr. 19), portrays Geryon as just a king (fr. 26), and argues that Cerberus was no "hound of Hades" but a snake with a fatal bite (fr. 27). Similar gambits are found among the fragments of other authors in the early mythographical corpus: Acusilaus has a real bull, not Zeus in disguise, abduct Europa (fr. 29); Hellanicus replaces the story of Achilles's fight against the Scamander with the story of a river dangerously in flood (fr. 28); Herodorus says that Poseidon and Apollo did not build the walls of Troy; rather, Laomedon paid for their construction using money dedicated to these gods (fr. 28).

The second half of the 4th century gives us two authors who develop this tradition in radical ways: Palaephatus and Euhemerus. Palaephatus worked in the ambit of the early Peripatetics; he was probably writing in Athens in the 340s or 330s. The preface to his *On Unbelievable Stories* (*Peri Apiston*) provides a rationale for rationalization, couched in the methodological language of philosophy and historiography. The text itself goes on to narrate forty-five myths one after another, explain why each could not have happened, and then offer a rationalized replacement for it. The hermeneutic homogeneity of this text is its most distinctive feature: Arnaud Zucker describes its author as inventing "a machine for metamorphosing myths" ("une machine à métamorphoser le mythe," Zucker 2016: 43). Lévi-Strauss's notion of myth as bricolage gave rise to the image of myth as a piecemeal patchwork with "rough stitches" and "faulty joins" (Finley 1975: 16). But Palaephatus presents the fabric of myth as if always being of equal weight and composition, and he stitches it together with an eye for complementary colors and regular patterning. His systematic treatment of myth as a series of isolated narratives and the consistent application of rationalistic methodologies makes this an important document in the development of ancient mythography: here is the first extant text that seeks to both collect and systematize myths, on the one hand, and to interpret them, on the other (Trzaskoma 2013: xvii; Hawes 2014b).

The *Sacred History* of Euhemerus of Messene (active around 300 BCE) survives largely in Diodorus and in Ennius's fragmentary Latin translation. Where Palaephatus largely avoided discussing myths of the gods, Euhemerus used rationalistic interpretations in the service of a broader argument about the origins of divine worship. The *Sacred History* tells of how Zeus, an early king, established cults to himself and to his predecessors, Ouranus and Cronus; these gods thus take on the cast of Hellenistic dynasts. Whereas their aims and approaches might differ, Palaephatus and Euhemerus rely on the same underlying assumption: the fantastic stories now told are the result of exaggeration and misunderstanding in the past. When Euhemerus explains Ouranus's name as a nickname, "heavenly," which referenced his innovations as an astronomer (test. 49 Winiarczyk), his hermeneutic methodology bears comparison with that of Palaephatus, as, indeed, does his general concern with "first inventers," a common rationalistic trope throughout antiquity.

Also preserved largely by Diodorus are the fragments of two works by Dionysius Scytobrachion (mid-3rd c. BCE). His *Argonauts* tells the famous story without its fabulous elements: Aietes's fire-breathing bulls (*tauroi*) become guards from a tribe named "Tauroi;" the ram that supplied the golden fleece is a man named "Ram" killed by these Taurians (his skin was gilded by Aeetes after an oracle connected his survival to the possession of this "golden skin"); and Medea has no magical powers, merely a skill with herbs. His *Libyan Stories* was, seemingly, Euhemerist in tone: it narrated the dynastic affairs and conquests of the Amazons and the Atalantoi, who share the names of the Titans and Olympian gods, and ended with an account of the travels of Dionysus. Rusten (1980: 112) describes both works as "meant purely as entertainment," and it is difficult to argue with this assessment. Although both works draw on ethnographic and philosophical material, their main interest is the way they use this material to present a new way of telling these stories. This innovative approach to narrative plays with—and plays up—the gulf that separates the mythical adventures of epic from the conventions of prose writing.

This concern with narrative variety and mythographical self-awareness is also apparent in two texts from the Augustan period. Conon's *Diegeseis* includes three rationalized myths: Midas was said to have the ears of a donkey because he had many informants (1); Cadmus's arrival in Thebes was a straightforward military expedition (37); and Perseus saved Andromeda as she was being abducted in a ship called Ketos, "sea monster" (40). Notably, these are relatively well-known stories in a collection in which obscure tales otherwise dominate; their appearance in rationalized form thus adds a striking kind of narrative interest (Brown 2002: 27–31; see Sanz Morales in this volume). Conon's contemporary Ovid does something similar, albeit with more subtlety. His *Metamorphoses* includes a number of understated gestures in the direction of existing rationalized alternatives while purportedly giving a "traditional" account. Thus, whereas Conon explicitly replaced Andromeda's sea monster with an eponymous sailing vessel, Ovid retains the monster, but compares its movement through the water to that of a ship (4.706–709). Likewise, in describing Icarus as "lacking an oar" (8.228) as he falls through the air dragging his molten wings, he nods toward the prominent rationalizing tradition that had Icarus die in a shipwreck as he was trying to escape Crete (for example, Cleidemus *BNJ* 323 F17, Palaephatus 12, Diod. Sic. 4.77.5–6).

The Imperial period gives us particularly rich material for rationalization. Notable is Heraclitus's *On Unbelievable Stories*, which is obviously modeled on Palaephatus's work of the same name, although broader in its hermeneutic range and much less expansive in its narrative style. Its diffuse relationship to the Palaephatean model points to the existence of a more substantial tradition of such texts (Hawes 2014a: 115–118; see also Hawes, "Heraclitus the Mythographer, *On Unbelievable Stories*," in this volume), a tradition perhaps also attested by our third rationalizing treatise, the late, anonymous *Excerpta Vaticana*. The probable rhetorical context of Heraclitus's work suggests that rationalistic interpretations were a familiar element of schoolroom teaching, and indeed, allegorical commentaries from the same period do include examples of rationalistic interpretation. When another Heraclitus, the author of the *Homeric Problems*, in the middle of a detailed allegory, explains that Lycurgus was said to have pursued Dionysus violently because he, a prominent landowner, had left his estate at the time of the grape harvest (35), we see how easily rationalizations may fit alongside other kinds of explanations. Ancient myth interpretation was an eclectic practice; few ancient examples of it display exact hermeneutic consistency.

Pausanias's *Description of Greece* is another key source for rationalistic material from this period. It displays not merely the variety of mythic phenomena, but also the different responses that myths provoked. Rationalization is just one attitude toward myth of many that Pausanias displays (Veyne 1988: 95–102; Hawes 2014a: 175–222; Hutton in this volume). His various rationalistic comments are part of a general tendency to favor unusual variants and to record disputed traditions. The geographical perspective of his work illuminates the utility of historicized myth in the discussion of local landscapes from a touristic point of view. Oftentimes, a rationalistic version is introduced in service to a larger argument. To take a famous example, when Pausanias records Hecataeus's explanation of Cerberus as a big snake after confirming that no passage leads underground from the cave at Taenarum where Heracles is supposed to have retrieved the "hound of Hades" (3.25.5), he has quite obviously chosen a story to fit the place. Likewise, when he encounters at Argos the place where Medusa's head was supposed to be buried, he suggests that the story should rather be told that Perseus killed "Medusa," the leader of a Libyan tribe, and brought back her head to prove the beauty of the woman (2.21.5).

It is not simply that certain authors and certain genres found rationalized variants more attractive. Some mythical figures attracted disproportionate rationalistic attention: Cadmus is one such example (Edwards 1979: 39–42), Heracles another (for example, in Dionysius of Halicarnassus; see Garstad 2014: 233–237). Likewise, historicized biographies of Romulus are prominent in the narration of Rome's early history. Thus, against the traditional suckling of Romulus by a she-wolf, there was, from at least the time of Cato, the alternative explanation that *lupa* here meant a prostitute, and thus a woman saved the infant founder of Rome, not a wild beast. This way of telling the story is found in both Greek and Latin writers (for example, Cato, *Origines* 1 fr. 16; Valerius Antias, *Annales*, fr. 2; Licinius Macer fr. 1; Livy 1.4; Dion. Hal. *Ant. Rom.* 1.84.1; Plut. *Rom.* 4.3). Here, then, we see not merely the phenomenon by which Greek authors present us with some of the most detailed accounts of Roman traditions but the way that a distinctly Greek hermeneutic mode could be equally at home explaining the central tenets of Roman myth.

Rationalizations proliferate in late-antique and post-antique sources. The efficiency with which this hermeneutic mode could both produce a seemingly historical vision of the past and downgrade the pagan heroes and gods to mere mortals made it particularly useful to Christian writers. Yet this later material often complicates our picture of ancient rationalization. For example, John Malalas features rationalizations prominently in his *Chronicle*, a "universal" account of events from the creation of Adam to the reign of Justinian. When he reports that Semele had gone into early labor after being terrified by a thunderstorm, and thus the child, Dionysus, was said to have been "sheltered by Zeus" because of his premature birth (2.24), Malalas attributes the material to Palaephatus although this explanation is not found in his *On Unbelievable Stories* as it survives. More work is still needed on the Byzantine fragments of Palaephatus. It is, in any case, too simplistic to assume that post-antique writers are merely compiling earlier material, although the third, anonymous treatise (*Excerpta Vaticana*) does provide some evidence of this. As we will see in an example below (section 2, "Thematic Discussion: The Minotaur as Case Study"), the tradition of rationalization maintained its inherent creativity and adaptability. Byzantine writers are not merely responding to a set of existing material but reshaping it and adding to it (Alganza Roldán, Barr, and Hawes 2017; Alganza Roldán 2017).

The Latin commentary tradition provided another conduit that secured rationalization's longevity. Servius offers numerous rationalizations in his commentary on the *Aeneid* (Jones 1961, 221–222; Dietz 1995, 73–75). When he attributes to Varro an explanation of Aeolus's power over the winds as relating to a man whose knowledge of atmospheric conditions was such that he seemed to control them, he is in fact promoting a rationalization found in similar form in Palaephatus (17) and Diodorus (5.7.5); see also Pliny, *NH* 3.92–94. When Fulgentius, who frequently mixes rationalizations with allegories in his *Mitologiae*, explains the story of Actaeon as relating to a man financially destroyed by his maintenance of a pack of hounds for hunting (3.3), he secures the place of Palaephatus's original explanation (6)—via the Second and Third Vatican Mythographers—in the medieval tradition of allegorizing Ovid. Similar interpretations are found in Arnulf of Orleans (3.2); Giovanni del Virgilio (3.2), the *Ovide Moralisé* (3.571–566), and Pierre Bersuire's *Ovidius Moralizatus* (3.5–6). That Actaeon could become so intricately associated with wastefulness is clear from Dante's poetic punishment of spendthrifts in the *Inferno* 13.109–129: they are chased down and ripped apart by hounds.

## 2. THEMATIC DISCUSSION: THE MINOTAUR AS CASE STUDY

The stories of Minos, Pasiphae, and the Minotaur are found in a great many different contexts in ancient literature. As such, they highlight the broad utility of myth, not

merely as a body of stories or a kind of prehistoric history, but also as a common repertoire of well-known images and themes that could be used to illustrate various ideas
and arguments. Cretan stories attracted unusually strong interest from rationalizers in
part because, as we will see, the stories of Minos seemed to stand on the cusp of the period accessible to historical knowledge. In this section, I discuss the various rationalistic
explanations that developed, and the different dynamics of ancient rationalization that
these illustrate. I look first at the historiographical utility of rationalization, then at its
relationship to biological debates, and, finally, at the way in which rationalization can
serve as a new kind of storytelling, producing mythical narratives that sit alongside the
already rich corpus of variants and versions.

It is too simplistic to say that the Greek past may be divided between a *spatium
mythicum* and a *spatium historicum*. Certainly, the Greeks had various ways of
categorizing the stories of the past, but strict distinctions rarely hold sway. Herodotus
seems to be invoking a qualitative layering of the past when he deems that Polycrates
was the first thalassocrat because Minos should not count as he did not belong to
"the so-called human epoch" (3.122). Elsewhere, however, he makes the famous
king of Crete a key figure in the story of the development of naval power in the
Mediterranean (1.171). Thucydides's comment that "Minos was the first whom we
know through report to have obtained a fleet" (1.4) couches the problem differently
(see Irwin 2007) but produces a similarly disjunctive sensibility. Here is a figure
about whom our knowledge is problematic, but whose historical relevance cannot
be denied: in Thucydides it is Minos's naval innovations that prompt further human
progress: safety and wealth, the expansion of empires, and the fortification of cities
(Thuc. 1.4–8).

Minos illustrates the deep paradox of mythic history. Traditional myth assumes a
past made up of qualitatively different epochs; in historical terms, the truth status of
these stories is suspect. And yet there must also be a sense in which the past is a timeline leading to the present, since accounts from the distant past often explain present
circumstances. Whereas Minos's reputed naval prowess gives him a place in the history
of the Mediterranean, other stories prove less conducive to historical logic: how can one
reconcile this proto-thalassocrat with the king who kept his bull-headed stepson locked
up in the Labyrinth? The utility of rationalization is that it can make all stories from the
past seem to conform to a single qualitative measure: that of plausibility based on the
everyday experience of what is possible in the present.

This sense of reconciling the stories of the past to the norms of the present is apparent in some fragments of Atthidography. The *Atthides*—classical and Hellenistic
chronicles—seemingly organized Athens's traditions into a chronological framework.
Athens's early history was bound up with Crete's through stories of various hostilities
between Minos and the mainlanders, culminating in the tribute of Athenian youths, and
Theseus's slaying of the Minotaur. Our best source for the Atthidographers' accounts
of these events is Plutarch's *Life of Theseus*, where they provide notably historicized
versions that contrast with more conventional tragic ones (Hawes 2014a: 153–155, 161–
163). We cannot, of course, evaluate how typical Plutarch's selection of Atthidography

was, and in any case, we are dealing with a quite heterogeneous tradition (Rhodes 1990). Nonetheless, the very fact that rationalized accounts appear in them seems notable in works that traced the story of Athens in a linear manner from the distant past to the present, and which thus would have had to confront the formal incompatibility of the different kinds of stories about Athens' past.

Plutarch's Atthidographical fragments recast the story of Theseus's defeat of the Minotaur and escape from Crete in historiographically plausible terms. Cleidemus (first half of the 4th c. BCE) set the whole episode in the context of a Panhellenic "decree" (*dogma koinon*) concerning the number of sailors allowed on a vessel. Minos's death while pursuing Daedalus in contravention of this decree precipitates an escalated conflict between Crete and Athens. Theseus responds by building a fleet, sailing to Crete, and defeating Minos's son Deucalion at Knossos (*BNJ* 323 F17 = Plut. *Thes.* 19.8). The whole description is shot through with precise details: the fleet is assembled at Thymoetadae, "away from the public road," and at Troezen (where Pittheus was in charge); those who had once been Minos's hostages serve as guides for the voyage; Theseus gets control of the harbor after the Cretans mistake him for an ally; and the battle itself is fought "at the gates of the Labyrinth," with no hint that this is anything more than a normal local landmark.

Cleidemus's story narrates shifts in international relations. It begins with the enmity of Minos against Daedalus and ends with Ariadne, now ruling in Crete, making a peace treaty with the Athenians. More subtly, it maps the way that the amassing of a fleet allowed the Athenians to defeat the formerly dominant power of Crete; here, then, is the backstory of Athens's naval supremacy. These details of the law of the sea and of naval tactics take the story out of the traditional heroic world that it should inhabit. And yet, the basic outline of the story remains: Daedalus pursued by Minos, the Athenian hostages, Theseus's expedition, and the benevolence of Ariadne. The creation of history out of myth retains much of what is recognizable of the traditional material but rejects its most salient feature: its accommodation of the fabulous.

The existence of one rationalization need not preclude the creation of another. Philochorus (before around 260 BCE) treated the episode differently. He puts into the mouths of supposed epichoric informants the—by now well-established—claim that Taurus ("Bull") was in fact a man, specifically, a cruel general of Minos's (*BNJ* 328 F17a = Plut. *Thes.* 15.2–16.1, compare Demon 327 F5). His Labyrinth is just a prison, where the Athenian youths are kept, to be awarded as prizes in games held to commemorate Minos's son Androgeos. Minos lets Theseus, one of the hostages, compete in these games. Theseus's appearance provokes desire in Ariadne, and his performance so impresses Minos that he sets all the hostages free. Philochorus sticks more closely to the famous traditional elements of the story—the existence of a "bull," the love of Ariadne, incarceration in a Labyrinth—but these are all explained pragmatically as ordinary occurrences. The episode is predicated on a set of interpersonal relationships: Taurus mistreats the Athenian hostages and is rumored to be having an affair with Pasiphae; all this motivates Minos's decision to have Theseus fight Taurus and his generosity when Theseus defeats him.

By converting the traditional story of Theseus into these new forms, Cleidemus and Philochorus push the limits of Athens' history back further into the chronologically marginal territory identified by Herodotus and Thucydides. But the "histories" that these two writers create are formally incompatible. Cleidemus has Theseus fight a battle with Minos's son after the death of his father and after the episode of the Athenian tribute; Philochorus makes the central combat that of Theseus and Taurus, with Minos still alive and ruling in Crete. As is typical of myth, rationalized versions proliferate, and they do not cohere into a single agreed and unchanging account of the past. More than this, while both versions might be said to manipulate the mythic material into something more historiographically appropriate, each holds to a different model of historical causation. Cleidemus takes the distanced view of international diplomacy, regulation, and military campaigns. Philochorus, by contrast, reduces the story to a set of personal relationships: Theseus "wins" because he gives Minos the upper hand over a love rival. These different ways of understanding Crete's place in the past in fact accord with the existing habits of thinking about Minos. We have already seen that Greek historians had to account for the dominance of Minos in the early history of Aegean sea power. But Minos's "history" could just as well be told on a human scale as a series of family dramas: his sexual dysfunction cured by Procris, his wife's dalliance with a bull, and his incarceration of the resulting offspring. However strikingly innovative these rationalizations may seem as versions of the story of Theseus, they are entrenched in established conventions.

The classification of stories is no objective practice; it is typically a preliminary stage in their rejection or transformation. What is called "myth" shifts with the context. We have already seen two ways of identifying the "mythic" (for want of a better word). For Herodotus, the line is to be drawn chronologically: Minos is beyond "the human epoch." Plutarch, likewise, suggests a diachronic distinction (the events of the distant past are like the farthest regions on a map—*Thes.* 1.1); but he appends to this a distinction based on genre: when he contrasts Philochorus's rationalized account with "the most tragic myth" (*ho tragikōtatos muthos*, 15.2), he is observing that the "same" story might be told quite differently in different narrative contexts: here, as what is typical of tragedy is often held to be inappropriate to historiography. A third distinguishing feature, (im)plausibility, is of course implicit in both of these categorizations. What, indeed, constitutes plausibility is a subjective judgment. Articulation of this ideal is most apparent when biological possibility is the issue. And this is the most obvious criticism to be leveled against a creature with the form of the Minotaur.

Diodorus illustrates one way of signaling the "mythic" quality of the conception of the Minotaur: when he narrates the story, he employs distinctive distancing terminology: "according to the myth handed down'" (*kata de ton paradedomenon muthon*, 4.77.1); "they say" (*muthologousi*, 4.77.2); "it is said" (*legetai*, 4.77.4). Servius is more overt. When he describes the story of Pasiphae as a *fabula* but that of her sister Phaedra as a *historia,* he sets up these terms—which are often contrasted in the Latin grammatical tradition—not according to whether the event narrated happened or not (*sive facta sive non facta*) but rather according to its biological possibility. The story of Phaedra is a *historia* presumably because her illicit desire for her stepson accords with nature (*secundum naturam*); the *fabula* of her sister Pasiphae, however, is "against nature" (*contra naturam, ad* Verg. *Aen.* 1.235), presumably because this famous story of bestiality produces a famously hybrid creature, the Minotaur. (For the terminology, see Dietz 1995; Servius' rationalization is given later in this section) The idea of a creature who was both two discrete creatures yet fully neither raised practical questions that could be played for laughs. In Euripides's *Cretans*, Minos, confronted with the news of his new-born grandson, asks whether it walks on two legs or four, and then, who should suckle it, a human or bovine wet nurse? (fr. 472b).

The existence of such a creature could also be denied outright, and this is what Palaephatus does (2):

> Firstly, it is impossible for one kind of animal to have sex with another kind if their genitals are not compatible: it's not possible for a dog and an ape to mate, nor a wolf and a hyena, nor an antelope with a deer, for they come from different species.

Palaephatus's sense of plausibility here assumes that conditions in the past were identical to those of the present, and if interspecies hybrids are (with a few notable exceptions) impossible in the present, creatures like the Minotaur cannot have been produced by such interspecies mating in the past, either. The basic idea that species are individually distinct and cannot interbreed is an Aristotelian one (Li Causi 2005: 97–98), although here Palaephatus puts it to striking use.

Palaephatus's subsequent account of why people came to speak of a violent creature called "Minotaurus" presents a rationalization of the myth. At Minos's court was a handsome man called "Taurus" with whom Pasiphae had an affair. Minos sent the resulting child away, and, as he grew up, became ever more disobedient. In the end, he retreated to an underground chamber, and Minos would send men to him to be killed. The biological "problem" of the Minotaur's parentage is solved here with a typical rationalizing gambit: what seemed to be an animal is, in fact, a man with an unusual name. Beyond this, we are led to understand that the Minotaur's fierce reputation was not a product of his bestial nature, but rather the rebelliousness of a teenager who had been abandoned by his putative father to live with shepherds in the hills.

The prominence of rationalizations of the Minotaur in the ancient tradition is a direct result of the overtly "mythical" reputation of this story and the ease with which such a creature can be disproved on scientific grounds. Whereas (to return to Servius's formulation) the story of Phaedra, if we ignore the issue of divine motivation, contains little that could not happen given the right circumstances, that of Pasiphae contains obvious impossibilities. It is not, as Servius notes, a question of whether something happened or did not happen—what would count as narrative proof of that?—but of recognizing that certain *fabulae* simply contravene the laws of nature. This is a particular kind of classification, one that leaves no room for the divine or the supernatural. Because rationalization removes the patently implausible elements of myth, it makes of these stories quite banal accounts. And it has most potency when used in relation to stories like that of the Minotaur, against which obvious objections can be raised.

With the examples of John Malalas's *Chronicle* and perhaps some of the *Atthides*, we have seen that rationalizations could be put to the service of producing a linear account of early Greek history. And yet, this is not the typical function of rationalization in ancient mythography. The format of the three *On Unbelievable Stories* treatises, in which each myth is atomized and explained in isolation, gives primacy to the explanation of peculiarities of mythic language. This approach is less an attempt to explain the past than it is a way of explaining away myth's apparent fabulousness. Rationalizing mythographers are not interested in fitting myths together into a single, comprehensive system; indeed, Plutarch's *Theseus* illustrates the difficulty of creating coherency by combining different explanations. Nor do such rationalizers typically use external data—the evidence of tombs and other physical monuments, for example—in support (though this can be done, as Pausanias shows). Rather, they seek to make sense of stories in a piecemeal fashion. Rationalization can be as much a display of hermeneutic ingenuity as anything else.

To return to our example of the Minotaur, if the existence of a human-bovine hybrid must a priori be discounted, then one must be able to explain why stories of the "Minotaur" are still told. Pausanias, indeed, takes to calling him the "so-called Bull of Minos" (*ho Minō kaloumenos tauros*, 1.22.5, 1.27.10, 3.18.1), as if to signal a disconnect between what something might be called and what it actually was. His solution, nonetheless, does attempt to "save" appearances: "women give birth to monsters more amazing by far in our own day" (1.24.1). In other words, a congenital defect might account for this famous monster too; the connection between the form of the Minotaur and observable "monstrous" birth had already been made—albeit implicitly—by Plutarch (*De Curiositate* 10). Elsewhere, however, it is the Minotaur's *name* that becomes the target of rationalistic attention. We have already seen that Palaephatus maintained the idea that the Minotaur was the offspring of Pasiphae and a bull, but he made this "Bull" a man. Philochorus also makes Taurus human, though there his rumored affair with Pasiphae does not produce offspring. Indeed, one might say that the violent Taurus of Philochorus's account takes the roles of both the bull and the Minotaur of the traditional one. Heraclitus the mythographer adopts Palaephatus's idea of an affair that produces an awkward result, and adds what is left unsaid in Palaephatus, the reason why this child was given such a strange name. He says that uninformed people (*hoi polloi*) recognised that while he was Minos's son in name, he resembled Taurus, and so they invented the portmanteau "Minotaurus" (7).

Such rationalizations give of a sense of novel ingenuity in part because they make very familiar statements suddenly mean something else. The mytheme "Pasiphae conceived a desire for a bull, and the result was the Minotaur" seemingly communicates a tale of divinely inspired bestiality and a monstrous birth. But given the right explanation, it can just as well narrate an illicit affair. The skill of the rationalizer resides in his ability to find these potential ambiguities and to exploit them to make unexpected sense of familiar stories.

This technique of rationalization is, in any case, endlessly adjustable. The basic idea that the father of the Minotaur was a man named Taurus could be taken in various directions. We have already seen that Palaephatus makes it the basis of a relatively detailed account of the Minotaur's abandonment and troubled adolescence. Heraclitus's more compact account, by contrast, makes the key idea the joke of a nickname which references the two "fathers" of this child. The anonymous author of the third *On Unbelievable Stories* (*Excerpta Vaticana*) concentrates on another facet of the story: he explains the traditional role of Daedalus as Pasiphae's accomplice by saying that Pasiphae used to watch the artist at work and that she used the excuse of his creation of a particularly life-like cow to cover her visits there to meet with Taurus (7).

The same mythic elements can, thus, be combined in various ways. Rationalization allows any number of different explanations for its stories about the past to flourish. The mark of a successful rationalization is not its ability to create a definitive account of the past, but its ability to make sense of—by transforming—the data of myth. While we find rationalizations of the same myth often cohering around certain broad ideas, there is freedom within this, too. We might also identify a certain competitiveness: "flyting," the agonistic aspect of storytelling, marks mythography from the beginning; in this respect it shares in the combatant tone of epic storytelling (Martin 2013). Rationalizers typify this dynamic, rarely settling on a single explanation. Late-antique and post-antique writers continue to value innovation. So, Servius gives us a rationalization whose outline should now be familiar to us, but whose details are quite new (*ad* Verg. *Aen.* 6.14):

> Taurus was Minos's secretary. Pasiphae fell in love with him and would sleep with him at the house of Daedalus. Because she bore twins, one the son of Minos and the other the son of Taurus, she was said to have given birth to the "Minotaur," since after a little while the pair revealed their mixed paternity.

Here the name references a different kind of hybridity: the double paternity of twins. And likewise the 12th-century Byzantine scholar John Tzetzes agrees that Pasiphae used the house of Daedalus to meet with Taurus (the general of Minos), and explains that because they shut themselves up in there, they were said to be shut up in Daedalus's "wooden cow" (*Chil.* 1.528–529).

These manipulations of mythic language make of the mythic tradition a set of riddles requiring ingenious solutions. It is, in its own way, a playfully imaginative approach to myth, even while it ostensibly denies the imaginative force of Greek storytelling in its traditional forms: myths can only be accounts of real events. As Charles Delattre puts it, the discourse of rationality may be set up in opposition to mythic thinking, and yet, in truth, "rationalistic storytelling is not beyond myth; it is merely one version among others" ("le récit rationalisé ne sort pas du mythe, il n'en est qu'une version parmi d'autres," Delattre 2013: 355). As a constituent part of the experience of myth in antiquity, it shapes the tradition in its own way. Most notably, the rationalistic attitude projects onto its chosen myths a particular way of thinking about myth. It is the meaning of mythic language which is at stake; the broader resonances of this language—in cult, in local politics, and in mimetic performance—are seldom of consequence in the rationalistic mythographers. Rationalizers frequently seem to manipulate the forms of traditional stories without regard for the broader implications that such changes might have for the use of these stories as expressions of communal identity, or cult. In this way, they seem to take the mythographical impulse to its furthest expression: they treat myths as merely narrative entities, without obvious significance for broader cultural dynamics.

## FURTHER READING

Ancient mythic rationalization has seldom received sustained interest, although this situation has changed in recent years thanks in part to renewed interest in mythographical authors. The most comprehensive discussion of the ancient rationalizing tradition, and particularly of its relationship to ancient mythography, appears in Hawes (2014a). This supersedes the two-volume study by Wipprecht (1902, 1908), which is itself a product of a flurry of scholarly activity on the hermeneutic mode in the late 19th and early 20th centuries.

More specific surveys of the material surveyed in this chapter can be found in relation to individual rationalizing authors. For bibliographic information on the early mythographers, Palaephatus, Heraclitus the mythographer, Conon, Ovid, and Pausanias, see the relevant chapters in this volume. On Euhemerus, see Winiarczyk (2013); on Dionysius Scytobrachion, see Rusten (1980). Translations of the three *On Unbelievable Stories* treatises are available in the open access repository Scaife Viewer.

## REFERENCES

Alganza Roldán, Minerva. 2017. "Juan Tzetzes, exégeta de Paléfato." In *La mitología griega en la tradición literaria: De la Antigüedad a la Grecia contemporánea*, edited by Minerva Alganza Roldán and Panagiota Papadopoulou, 181–203. Granada: Centro de Estudios Bizantinos, Neogriegos y Chipriotas.

Alganza Roldán, Minerva, Julian Barr, and Greta Hawes. 2017. "The Reception History of Palaephatus 1 (On the Centaurs) in Ancient and Byzantine Texts." *Polymnia* 3: 186–235.

Brown, Malcolm K. 2002. *The Narratives of Konon*. Leipzig: De Gruyter.

Delattre, Charles. 2013. "Pentaméron mythographique: Les Grecs ont-ils écrit leurs mythes." *Lalies* 33: 77–170.

Detienne, Marcel. 1981. *L'invention de la mythologie*. Paris: Gallimard.

Dietz, David B. 1995. "*Historia* in the Commentary of Servius." *Transactions of the American Philological Association* 125: 61–97.

Dowden, Ken. 1992. *The Uses of Greek Mythology*. London and New York: Routledge.

Edwards, Ruth B. 1979. *Kadmos the Phoenician: A Study in Greek Legends and the Mycenaean Age*. Amsterdam: Adolf M. Hakkert.

Finley, Moses I. 1975. *The Use and Abuse of History*. London: Chatto and Windus.

Garstad, Benjamin. 2014. "Hero into General: Reading Myth in Dionysius of Halicarnassus, Nonnus of Panopolis, and John Malalas." *Preternature* 3: 227–260.

Hawes, Greta. 2014a. *Rationalizing Myth in Antiquity*. Oxford: Oxford University Press.

Hawes, Greta. 2014b. "Story Time at the Library: Palaephatus and the Emergence of a Hyper-Literate Mythology." In *Between Orality and Literacy: Communication and Adaptation in Antiquity*, edited by Ruth Scodel, 125–147. Leiden: Brill.

Irwin, Elizabeth. 2007. "The Politics of Precedence: First 'Historian' on First 'Thalassocrats.'" In *Debating the Athenian Cultural Revolution: Art, Literature, Philosophy, and Politics 430–380 BC*, edited by Robin Osborne, 188–223. Cambridge, UK: Cambridge University Press.

Jones, Julian W. 1961. "Allegorical Interpretation in Servius." *Classical Journal* 56: 217–226.

Li Causi, Pietro. 2005. "Generazione di ibridi, generazione di donne: Costuzioni dell'umano in Aristotele e Galeno (e Palefato)." *Storia Delle Donne* 1: 89–114.

Martin, Richard. 2013. "The 'Myth before the Myth Began.'" In *Writing Down the Myths*, edited by Joseph F. Nagy, 45–66. Turnhout: Brepols.

Rhodes, Peter J. 1990. "The Atthidographers." In *Purposes of History: Studies in Greek Historiography from the 4th to the 2nd Centuries BC*, edited by Herman Verdin, Guido Schepens, and Els De Keyser, 73–81. Leuven: Orientaliste.

Rusten, Jeffrey S. 1980. *Dionysius Scytobrachion*. Opladen, Germany: Westdeutscher Verlag.

Stern, Jacob, trans. 1996. *Palaephatus. Περὶ ἀπίστων. On Unbelievable Tales.* Wauconda, IL: Bolchazy-Carducci.

Sumler, Alan. 2014. "Myth Rationalization in Ancient Greek Comedy: A Short Survey." *Quaderni Urbinati di Cultura Classica* 136: 81–98.

Trzaskoma, Stephen M. 2013. Introduction to *Writing Myth: Mythography in the Ancient World*, edited by Stephen M. Trzaskoma and R. Scott Smith, xv–xxiv. Leuven: Peeters.

Veyne, Paul. 1988. *Did the Greeks Believe in Their Myths? An Essay on the Constitutive Imagination.* Chicago: University of Chicago Press.

Winiarczyk, Marek. 2013. *The "Sacred History" of Euhemerus of Messene.* Berlin: De Gruyter.

Wipprecht, Friedrich. 1902, 1908. *Zur Entwicklung der rationalistischen Mythendeutung bei den Griechen.* 2 Vols. Tübingen: H. Laupp.

Zucker, Arnaud. 2016. "Palaiphatos ou la clinique du mythe." In *Lire les mythes: Formes, usages et visées des pratiques mythographiques de l'Antiquité à la Renaissance*, edited by Arnaud Zucker, Jacqueline Fabre-Serris, Jean-Yves Tilliette, and Gisèle Besson, 43–66. Lille: Presses du Septentrion.

# CHAPTER 25

# ALLEGORIZING AND PHILOSOPHIZING

ILARIA L.E. RAMELLI

## 1. Philosophical Allegoresis: Definition and Centrality of the Defense of Myths from Impiety Charges

THIS chapter focuses on ancient philosophical allegoresis of myths. Allegoresis (from "allegorical" + "exegesis") is the allegorical interpretation of texts, rituals, traditions, iconography, epithets, and the like. Allegory is both a manner of composing—writing an allegorical text in which the literal level differs from its symbolic meaning(s)—and a hermeneutic method, also called "allegoresis." *Allēgoria* means saying (*agoreuein*) some things but meaning others (*alla*). This is the definition that was given in the early imperial age by Heraclitus the Allegorist in his *Homeric Allegories* (5), an allegorical interpretation of Homer. The term *allēgoria* is far more recent than the use of allegory or allegoresis and entered rhetorical terminology relatively late. I suspect this is because theoretical reflection on allegory first arose, not in rhetoric, but in philosophy.

Indeed, in antiquity allegoresis was especially applied to mythography and religiously authoritative texts, both by "pagan" philosophers, such as Stoics, and by Middle and Neoplatonists, who allegorized myths concerning divinities, rituals, deities' cultic epithets, and the like, and by philosophically minded Hellenistic Jewish and Christian exegetes, who read the Bible allegorically. The work of all these allegorizers was aimed at finding deeper meanings and philosophical truths in the traditional accounts, thereby defending myths against accusations of superficiality or impiety. The goal was to find in Homeric and other myths, as well as in Scripture, meanings "worthy of the divine" (Ramelli 2018b).

Allegoresis of myths began as early as the 6th century BCE with Theagenes of Rhegium, who first allegorized Homer and practiced Homeric philology. He identified Homeric deities with physical qualities such as hot and cold, dry and moist, and ethical notions, according to a note by Porphyry on *Iliad* 20.67 (8A2 D.-K.; Biondi 2015; Domaradzki 2017). Such allegoresis, physical and ethical, will appear again in Stoicism. It seems to have been dictated by the desire to avoid the embarrassment raised by myths such as the theomachy: this was therefore allegorized as the opposition between physical qualities, dry versus moist, hot versus cold, and so forth. Apollo, Helios, and Hephaestus represent fire; Poseidon and Scamander, water; Hera, air; Athena, wisdom; Ares, folly, and the like. The strategy of defending of Homer from charges of impiety by allegorizing his myths was still being adopted in the 1st–2nd century CE by Heraclitus the Allegorist and Dio of Prusa, *On Homer*, Oration 53.3. Dio claims that Homer's myths are not impious, but "hide rational accounts about nature" (*physikoi logoi*) that must be detected through philosophical allegoresis. Dio offers here a small treatise of exegesis of Homeric myths including Plato, Aristotle, Zeno, Perseus, and Crates, a Stoic allegorizer on whom see below.

After Theagenes, the Derveni papyrus (4th c. BCE) allegorizes a more ancient Orphic poem. Ramelli (2007: 897–944) pointed out here exegetical parallels with later Stoic allegoresis. The latter may have been prompted also by Plato's ban on Homer, and by the purpose of finding worthy meanings in Homer's myths. This was also the aim of Theagenes and later Heraclitus.

Heraclitus's *Homeric Problems concerning What Homer Expressed Allegorically about the Gods* (see Konstan in this volume) opens with a defense of allegoresis (1–5) and concludes with a polemic against Plato, who had attacked Homer (76–79). The principle of what is worthy of the divinity inspires the use of allegoresis for Heraclitus just as, later, for the Christian philosophical allegorist Origen. As Heraclitus states at the beginning, "If Homer meant nothing allegorically, he was impious through and through, and sacrilegious fables, loaded with blasphemous folly, run riot through both epics" (trans. Russell and Konstan 2005). Heraclitus sets out to rescue Homer from that charge by demonstrating that what Homer says about the gods is allegorical, and therefore worthy of the divinity, as the Stoic allegorists also maintained about Homer and other myths. Thus, Heraclitus spells out the principle of philosophical allegoresis applied to Homer: "Anyone who is prepared to delve deeper into Homer's rites and be initiated in his mystical wisdom will recognize that what is believed to be impiety is in fact charged with deep philosophy" (53). Homer expressed philosophical truths allegorically.

Ps.-Plutarch's *Life and Poetry of Homer*, also from the early imperial age, ferreted many philosophical concepts out of Homer's text. These works, just as the scholia to Homer, drew on the tradition of Stoic allegoresis, on which more below in section 2. Middle and Neoplatonists, too, abundantly cultivated philosophical allegoresis, as we shall see. Porphyry in the 3rd century CE interpreted the Cave of the Nymphs in Homer, *Od.* 13.102–112, as an allegory of the universe (Akçay 2019). In the 4th century the Neoplatonist Sal(l)ustius voiced the position of Platonic allegorists, that myths never happened historically, but are allegories of eternal truths (*On the Gods and the Cosmos*

4.9). His friend, the emperor Julian, similarly asserted that mythological events never happened but are to be interpreted allegorically (*To the Mother of the Gods* 170–171). The late Neoplatonist Proclus in the 5th century will write that the inventors of myths "fashion likenesses of the indivisible by way of division, of the eternal by what moves in time, and of the noetic by the perceptible" (*Commentary on Plato's Republic* 1.17).

Allegoresis was one form of the rationalization of mythography, along with other approaches such as the historicizing one adopted by Palaephatus (4th c. BCE) and Euhemerus (3rd c. BCE), but also by Herodorus (5th–4th c. BCE) and Dionysius Scytobrachion (3rd c. BCE; Ramelli 2004a: 205–231). Other examples come from Heraclitus *On Incredible Things*, the anonymous *On Incredible Things*, and Conon from the Augustan age. For the allegorists, myths originated from physical or ethical truths expressed symbolically; for the historical rationalizers of myths, they originated from historical facts that were later misunderstood and reframed fantastically. The Sophists, as reported by Plato (*Phaedrus* 299c–e), historicized the myth of Boreas and Orithyia, and Herodotus (1.1–2) the myths of Io, Europa, and Medea and the story of Cyrus's nurse. Hellanicus rationalized Achilles's battle with the river Scamander. Herodorus, the author of a *Discourse on Heracles*, rationalized Prometheus's myth, and Dionysius Scytobrachion in his *Lybica* rationalized the Argonautic myth and identified deities with human benefactors, later divinized, like Euhemerus (possibly linked with the Cyrenaic school) in his *Sacred Inscription*. Palaephatus authored *On Incredible Things* and *Cyprian, Delian, Attic*, and *Trojan Stories*. He systematically expounded each myth and remarked that it was incredible (*apiston*), ridiculous, and absurd and then rationalized it, for instance, denying the existence of mythological monsters such as the Centaurs or the Minotaur.

Palaephatus's line was close to Peripatetic circles (he claims to have been a disciple of Aristotle), whereas philosophical allegoresis became prominent in the Stoic and Platonic traditions. Allegoresis, as demonstrated by Ramelli (2004a: 458–478; 2011c), was part and parcel of *philosophy* in Stoicism from the Old Stoa to Roman Stoicism—although not all Stoics were allegorists—and then in "Middle" and Neoplatonism, when a debate arose about which myths were eligible to be allegorized philosophically, and thereby valued as bearers of truth.

## 2. STOIC ALLEGORESIS OF MYTHOGRAPHY

For the Stoics, allegory was part of philosophy, not only a rhetorical device or an etymologizing exercise, although etymologies were often used in Stoic allegoresis. Already Zeno allegorized Homer and Hesiod, thus revealing hidden philosophical truths in their works (Ramelli 2004a: 81–85; 2007). With this intention he composed a commentary on both Homeric poems (*Homeric Questions*) and one on Hesiod's *Theogony*. He also established the principle, which was followed by his disciple Perseus, that in Homer some things are written "according to opinion" and others "according to truth" (*SVF* 1.274). The philosopher's task is to distinguish the latter from the former and interpret them allegorically to find the truth that is hiding there. So, Zeno could defend Homer by interpreting him allegorically in philosophical terms, at the same time enhancing the value of his own philosophy by showing that it was already taught by Homer. Zeno applied physical allegoresis to ancient myths (*SVF* 1.166–167): deities were identified with physical principles. For example, Hera symbolized air; Zeus, ether, Poseidon, the sea; Hephaestus, fire, and so on (*SVF* 1.169). Physical hermeneutics dominated Stoic allegoresis. But Zeno also initiated Stoic ethical allegoresis. For instance, he interpreted the Dioscuri as representing "right arguments and morally good dispositions" (*SVF* 1.170). Zeno sometimes used etymology. For instance, in his exegesis of the beginning of Hesiod's *Theogony*, he has the name Chaos derive from *kheomai*, "I am poured, I flow" (*SVF* 1.103). This etymology will appear again in Cornutus and other allegorical exegetes.

Cleanthes, too, allegorized archaic poetry, even proposing textual emendations to support his own exegeses (Ramelli 2004a: 86–95; 2007). For him, poetry is the most suitable means of expressing the sublimity of the divine (*SVF* 1.486; 1.538). In *SVF* 1.482, he divides philosophy not simply into logic, physics, and ethics, the standard Stoic division, but into three couples: dialectic and rhetoric, ethics and politics, and physics and theology. Thus, physics and theology are distinguished from each other but also reciprocally related. Indeed, in Stoic immanentism, physics coincides with theology; Cleanthes considers the objects of physics and theology to be coextensive, and consistently allegorizes deities as physical elements. For instance, the allegorical interpretation that Zeus is the ether, which was taken over by Chrysippus (*SVF* 2.1061), is one of the most stable in the whole Stoic tradition. In Cleanthes's *Hymn to Zeus* (*SVF* 1.537), Zeus represents the universal *logos* and *nomos* (law, both physical and ethical). He is also, traditionally, the father of all humans, to whom it is right for them to pray (lines 3–4). Cleanthes distinguishes theology from physics from the disciplinary viewpoint: theology explains the universe, conceived as a mystery; deities are regarded as mystical figures, and myths as endowed with a peculiar epistemological status. For myths are expressed in a more sublime form than the discursive *logos*—that is, the symbolic form, which calls for allegoresis. This is why theology is founded on allegoresis and allegoresis is part and parcel of philosophy. Cleanthes paid much attention to the allegoresis of the god of poetry, Apollo, his name, epithets, and attributes in ancient myths, having frequent recourse to etymology (*SVF* 1.540–543; 1.502). In his Homeric exegesis, Cleanthes used both textual emendations (*SVF* 1.535) and etymologies (e.g., *SVF* 1.549; 1.526) in support of his allegorico-philosophical interpretation.

Chrysippus, especially in *On Deities* 2, also employed allegoresis to interpret myths, for instance in Orpheus, Musaeus, Homer, and Hesiod. Moreover, he provided the first theory of Stoic allegoresis in *On Deities* 1 (Ramelli 2004a: 96–139; 2007). Here, he illustrated the relationship of allegory to theology conveyed in poetry, rituals, iconography, and myths in general. Chrysippus declares that the Logos is expressed differently by philosophers, poets, and institutors of laws and customs in various cities, including rituals: theology is handed down in the physical form, taught by philosophers; in the mythical form, taught by poets; and in the form attested by laws and customs, established by individual cities (*SVF* 2.1009). Thus, poetry, which narrates religious myths, and cultic traditions need to be interpreted allegorically to reveal the Logos they contain under a veil, that is, the Stoic philosophical truths. Chrysippus's theory implies that allegory is an essential feature of theology and, consequently, of philosophy. It supplies the crucial connection between theology and physics, which is the gist of the Stoic system, which lacks a real metaphysical level. For Chrysippus, allegory is the main tool to study theology, in its traditional forms, and to relate it to physics and ethics. Therefore, allegory is a core instrument of cultural unity, the need for which was paramount for Chrysippus, with his vast cultural interests. Like Chrysippus, another Stoic leader, Antipater of Tarsus, regularly brought in quotations from ancient poets, from Homer to Sophocles and Euripides, while discussing philosophical arguments.

In Nero's age, the Stoic Cornutus (Ramelli, this volume) composed a manual of philosophical allegoresis of mythography. He declared the ancients to be nothing less than philosophers since they were endowed with the understanding of the cosmos. What they expressed allegorically are philosophical truths to be deciphered by allegoresis. Cornutus's attitude is similar to that of previous Stoic allegorists who attached to the ancient Homer the knowledge and veiled expression of philosophical and scientific truths. This position was upheld, for instance, by Crates of Mallus, who held Homer in high esteem for being extremely competent in various disciplines (Ramelli 2004: 171–203; 2021a). Crates coined for himself the designation "critic," as an expert in philology, linguistics, and literature, whose competences were framed by the Stoic philosophical system. Crates was probably, and Apollodorus of Athens was certainly, a disciple of Diogenes of Babylon, in turn a disciple of Chrysippus. All of them allegorized religious traditions to find philosophical truths therein.

Diogenes devoted his treatise *Athena* to the allegoresis of myths, names, and attributes of this goddess. His physical interpretation of the divinities is in line with Zeno's and Chrysippus's: Zeus represents the cosmos and is its soul (as Logos and hegemonic); the part of Zeus that spreads into the sea is Poseidon, that which spreads into the air is Hera, and that which spreads into the ether, the highest element, is Athena; this is why the myth represents her as born from Zeus's head (*SVF* 3.2.33). Apollodorus of Athens (2nd c. BCE) composed a treatise *On the Gods* in twenty-four books, which, like that by Chrysippus, was devoted, at least in part, to the allegoresis of ancient poetic, iconographical, and cultic traditions concerning deities, heroes, and Hades (Henrichs 2014). He used the works of his Stoic predecessors, especially Cleanthes, Chrysippus, and Diogenes, and commentaries on Homer and Hesiod. Apollodorus, too, made extensive use of etymology in his allegoresis—for instance, Zeus is "Dodonaeus" as giver (*didonai*) of goods (F88), as Cleanthes had suggested (*SVF* 1.535.1). In *On the Gods* (*BNJ* 244 fr. 95a–96), Apollodorus interpreted many of the epithets for Apollo etymologically, in reference to his physical identification with the sun. I have argued for the presence of common material in Apollodorus, Cornutus, Macrobius, and some scholia to Aeschylus; Apollodorus's interest in Athena, who symbolizes intelligence and contemplation, and his etymologico-allegorical interpretation of her myths and epithets was likely due to Diogenes's *On Athena*: for both Athena and Poseidon, I have demonstrated a continuity between Chrysippus's, Diogenes's, and Apollodorus's interpretations (Ramelli 2004a: 140–169, esp. 159–161).

Like Chrysippus, Apollodorus also allegorized iconographic representations of divinities: for example, Hermes is tetragonal because the inventions of the Logos, symbolized by him, number four (fr. 129, taken over by Cornutus, 16). Cultic ceremonies and things sacred to each deity or hero were also allegorized by Apollodorus, as later by Cornutus. For instance, the serpent is sacred to Asclepius because it takes off old age just as medicine liberates people from illness. This explanation appears again in Cornutus (34). Some historico-etiological rationalization of myths are also found in Apollodorus, as then in Cornutus. For example, the Athenian custom of sacrificing an apple to Heracles is explained by an anecdote: once, the ox for the sacrifice fled, so they took an apple, placed four sticks in it as legs, to represent the ox, and thus celebrated the sacrifice (fr. 115). Apollodorus also showed interest in non-Hellenic—especially Egyptian—myths, traditions, and allegoreses (fr. 104), as did Cornutus and Chaeremon later. Apollodorus often quoted poets (Homer, Sophocles, and others) in support of his exegeses, as did Chrysippus and then Cornutus. His material on Hades and its rivers went straight into Cornutus. Even the distribution of the contents was similar in Apollodorus's and Cornutus's works (Ramelli 2004: 162–166).

Cornutus, indeed, was influenced by Apollodorus and probably collected most of his materials from him, besides Chrysippus, Crates, and other Stoic allegorizers. Cornutus shared the assumption of the excellence of the most ancient humans, who could directly access the truth and expressed it in myths, rituals, and traditions. Therefore, he supported the subsuming of allegoresis under philosophy, as a way of detecting the philosophical truths that the ancients hid in poetry, myths, and ritual traditions. In his handbook Cornutus offered an allegorico-etymological interpretation of each divinity's names and epithets, attributes, aspects of myths and rituals, and other features. Physical allegory is prevalent (see the examples in my chapter on Cornutus, this volume). Theological traditions express truth symbolically, and the task of philosophical allegoresis is to decode the symbols. Such a task is *philosophical*, insofar as its focus is the truth about nature and the divine. In Stoic immanentism, theology and physics are two sides of the same coin, and the application of allegoresis to ancient myths reveals the dovetailing of theology and physics.

The Stoics used etymology in the service of philosophical allegoresis, but Stoic philosophical allegoresis cannot be reduced to etymologies or a linguistic disambiguation exercise, any more than Philo's scriptural allegoresis can be reduced to an etymological exercise, although etymology is consistently deployed in both Philo's and Stoic allegoresis. Etymology was a constituent of the Stoic theory of language, according to which names are "by nature" (a view that could be traced back to Plato's *Cratylus*: see Ramelli 2004a: 464–470; see Pellizer, this volume). For the "first sounds" were imitations of the objects that the ancients experienced around them. The ancients are responsible for the constitution of names, and Stoic philosophical etymology is responsible for their interpretation, by detecting in words their first constituents and meanings. Etymology was deemed a tool both for grasping the nature of things, since etymology goes back to the authentic (*etymos*) meaning of a word, and for showing how the traditional names and epithets of deities reflect their nature, thus revealing physical or ethical truths. This nature is expressed allegorically in myths. This shows that the allegoresis of myths can catch the truth, because, according to Stoic linguistics, etymology has a direct grasp on nature, that is, truth. This is why it is used as a tool within Stoic philosophical allegoresis.

By applying allegoresis, the Stoics did not merely aim at supporting their own philosophical system (Ramelli 2004a: 447–478). This might have been the case at the beginning of their school, but it was already less so in Chrysippus's day, and much less so in imperial Stoicism. Of course, the Stoics' interpretation of myths was *Stoic*, as is clear from Chrysippus's *On Deities* 2, in which materials from Hesiod, Homer, and other poets were adapted to Stoic theology as expounded in *On Deities* 1. But a sheer "apologetic" interpretation of Stoic allegoresis is unsatisfying since interest in allegoresis among Stoics increased over time instead of diminishing. If Stoic allegoresis had simply been intended to prove the truth of Stoicism, one should expect that over time, as the Stoic system became consolidated, Stoic interest in allegoresis of myths would decline. In such a unified and structured system, at a certain point the support of allegoresis, applied as it was to Homer, poetry, and other mythological and cultic traditions, would have become too unsystematic to be helpful. Therefore, Stoic allegoresis did not merely serve an apologetic agenda.

I rather suspect that Stoicism, with its philosophical instrument, allegoresis, aimed at integrating into its philosophical system the ancient treasury of tradition: myths, cults, and their iconographic representations. Its goal was the creation of a comprehensive cultural synthesis that embraced the whole traditional heritage. This, having been undermined by rationalism, needed to be legitimated philosophically. Stoicism could thereby value the legacy of myth as a bearer of encrypted truth, in all its traditional expressions: poetry, epithets, rituals, iconography, and so on. The Stoics engaged in poetry, literature, linguistics, etymology, and the like; thus, they valued the legacy of antiquity in terms of poetry and other forms of mythology, by means of allegoresis, in accord with their own philosophical system. Their use of allegoresis was likely intended to build a vast cultural unity, systematic and based on the Logos. For the whole Stoic allegorical theory focuses on the Logos. Different divinities are allegorized as partial manifestations of the same Logos-Pneuma, which extends to different places in various modalities; the Logos also inspired ancient poets, the inventors of myths and rituals, and the ancients who created the "natural" language that etymology recovers.

From Zeno to the early imperial age, the time of Heraclitus's *Homeric Allegories* and pseudo-Plutarch's *Life and Poetry of Homer*, Stoics continued to represent Homer as well steeped in a variety of disciplines (see Ramelli 2004: 377–446; 2007; 2021a; Russell and Konstan 2005). This was intended to project onto antiquity, at the origin of culture, the above-mentioned Stoic ideal of a unity based on the Logos. In Cicero's *De Natura Deorum*, among the speeches (the Epicurean in book 1, the Stoic in book 2, and the Academic in books 1 and 3), the Stoic is by far the most extensive, representing the broadest range of disciplines (Ramelli 2004: 233–258; 2007). Thus, it reflects the Stoic ideal of a wide-ranging cultural unity revolving around theology and physics and, additionally, embracing logic, mathematics, physiology, cosmology, astronomy, ritual, legends, customs, traditions, poetry, rhetoric, linguistics, etymology, and more. The Stoics valued ancient myths, not to the detriment of philosophy, but because tradition, if opportunely decoded, was for them a source of philosophy and the proof of its naturalness. Inspired as they were by the Logos, myths expressed philosophical truths under symbolic veils.

The cultivation of cultural unity—the probable primary aim of Stoic philosophical allegoresis—has great philosophical value because it refers to the unity of the Logos. The Stoic system is monistic and unitary and revolves around the Logos-Pneuma-Zeus that extends to all nature and all reasoning. The Stoics conceived the cosmos itself as a whole. For Chrysippus, nothing in the universe happens independently of the rest, because the whole cosmos is directed by the same Logos and all causes are interconnected (*SVF* 2.945; see also *SVF* 2.528–533; 2.576; 2.620; 2.945; 2.1013). If allegoresis reveals the identity of theology and cosmology, this means that it covers all, since there is nothing beyond the cosmos and the divine, which, moreover, coincide. Philosophy reflects the unity of all. Thus, Chrysippus and Posidonius emphasized that though philosophy has three parts, it is a unity (*SVF* 2.35; 2.38), like the universe. For Posidonius, "the parts of philosophy are inseparable from one another" (*SVF* 2.38). There is "one and the same virtue" for all of philosophy (*SVF* 2.35). The Stoics' multifarious cultural interests (Chrysippus, Posidonius, Apollodorus and Crates, the speech of Balbus in Cicero's *De natura deorum*, Cornutus) needed the ideal of cultural unity.

# 3. Philosophical Allegoresis in Platonism, "Pagan" and Christian

The philosophical value of allegoresis passed on from Stoicism to Platonism. Philo and Plutarch, both related to "Middle Platonism," renounced Plato's criticism of Homer and considered the work of the ancient poet to be useful for philosophy. They seem to have been the first thinkers in the Platonic tradition to value Homer; this attitude continued in Neoplatonism. Plutarch adopted Stoic allegoresis of myths and rituals, especially in *De Daedalis Plataeensibus* (in Eusebius *PE* 3.1–2). In section 1 Plutarch programmatically declares:

> Among the ancients, Greeks and barbarians, the study of nature (*physiologia*) was a theory of nature (*logos physikos*) wrapped up and covered in myths, often as a mysterious theology, hidden in enigmata and implied meanings (*hyponoiai*), in which what is said overtly is mostly clearer than what is hidden; yet, what is hidden is more significant than what is said explicitly. This is manifest in the Orphic poems and the Egyptians and Phrygian myths, but what expresses the ancients' thought is above all initiation ceremonies and the symbolic rituals in sacred ceremonies.

Plutarch's interest in non-Greek myths and rituals, evident also in *Isis and Osiris*, is similar to that of the Stoics Chaeremon, who allegorized Egyptian hieroglyphics, and Cornutus, who in *Handbook* 17 declared: "Many and various mythological accounts have arisen among the ancient Greeks; some appeared among the Magi, others among the Phrygians, and, again, the Egyptians, the Celts, the Libyans, and the other peoples." Plutarch is interested in the most archaic statues—in accord with the principle, shared by Cornutus, that originally humankind had access to truth—and all iconographic expressions of original wisdom. Plutarch refers (fr. 190.6–9 Sandbach) to an original wisdom shared by Greeks and barbarians as an evaluative parameter of both myths and iconographic representations: "Plutarch, criticising the Ionics on the basis of the ancient philosophy approved among the Greeks and barbarian nations, declared that some of them introduced a wrong use of statues." In *Daed.* 3, allegorizing a myth about Zeus and Hera, Plutarch, like Cornutus, has continual recourse to the etymologico-allegorical explanation of the epithets of the deities. He allegorizes the legend of the friendship between Hera and Leto in a physical sense, by identifying Hera with the earth and Leto with the night, the earth's shadow (*Daed.* 4). He inherited from the Stoic allegorical tradition the para-etymology of Leto from "forgetfulness" (*Leto-Letho*), which has a parallel in Heraclitus, *Homeric Allegories* 55. Plutarch in this connection cites Homer and interprets his verses allegorically (see Ramelli 2004: 391–402)

However, Plutarch criticizes the philosophical allegoresis of Homer and other poets. In *De Audiendis Poetis* he implicitly agrees with Plato's attack on allegoresis (Dawson 1992: 59–66). In *De Pythiae Oraculis* 30.409c–d, Plutarch attacks those who loved "enigmata, allegories, and metaphors." *Isis and Osiris* 57, though, is devoted to the allegoresis of the Egyptian myth: its characters are identified with Hesiod's primeval substances. Plutarch draws comparisons between the Egyptian, Persian, Chaldaean, and Greek mythologies, to support the theory of cosmic dualism expressed by the Isis myth (369b–371c). Isis is identified with the earth, Osiris with Eros, and Typho with Tartarus; but Osiris and Isis are also identified with Plato's Porus and Penia, and their child Horus with Eros. The Earth (Isis, Penia) is matter, and Eros (Osiris, Porus) the first principle; the cosmos originated from their union. However, Plutarch warns that *mythos* is not *logos*; it cannot be treated as a scientific theory but always needs hermeneutics (*Is.* 58). Like Cornutus (17), Plutarch also distinguishes between the ancient mythography that contained philosophical truths and mere poetic fictions (*Is.* 358–359). Like Cornutus, in *Is.* 363d Plutarch applies comparative mythology and physical allegoresis: "Just as the Greeks allegorize Cronus (*Kronos*) as time (*khronos*), Hera as air, and the birth of Hephaestus as the transformation of air into fire, likewise among the Egyptians, Osiris is the Nile that joins Isis, who is the earth." Plutarch takes over Stoic physical allegoresis by declaring that the Isis myth "is connected with a physical truth."

Plutarch claims in *De Audiendis Poetis* that Homer conceals a "silent teaching" and declares his preference for the moral exegesis of certain myths over the physical one (4.19–20b); he criticizes the excesses of etymological allegoresis, such as those of Cleanthes, who in *Iliad* 16.223, instead of *ana Dōdōnaie*, "Lord of Dodona," read *anadōdōnaie* "Zeus who gives" (*didōsi*) in reference to the vapors that from earth tend "upwards" (*anō*). He disapproves of certain writers who force the text

> with what used to be called implied meanings [*hyponoiai*] but are now called allegories. These people say that Helius reveals the adultery of Aphrodite with Ares, because when Ares' star joins that of Aphrodite it predicts adulterous births, but they do not remain concealed when the Sun is ascendant and descendant. In turn, Hera's beautification for Zeus and her trick with Aphrodite's girdle signify, they say, the purification of the air as it nears the fiery element—as though the poet himself did not provide the solutions.

Plutarch's own exegesis of such Homeric episodes is, instead, ethical (19e–20b).

But in *Roman Questions* 12.266e–f, Plutarch, like Cornutus, expresses the conviction that the knowledge of the truth must be sought in the remotest antiquity: "Why do they deem Saturn the father of truth? Perhaps . . . because the age of Cronus, as described by the myth, likely participated in truth to the utmost extent." That traces of this original wisdom remained also in the most ancient cultic traditions is an assumption that underlies the argument used by Plutarch in the same work (364–365b). Here the identification of Osiris with Dionysus is supported on the grounds that the traditional rituals of both deities are alike. Here, too, the influence of Stoic allegoresis is clear. Likewise, in *Convivial Questions* 3.10.658f–659a, Plutarch identifies the gods of Greek mythology with stars, in accord with a primarily Stoic allegorical tradition. But in *On Common Notions* 34.1076f, he ridicules the conception of the stars as gods who are citizens of the cosmos, which also rested on Chrysippus's allegoresis of Zeus as the cosmos, the residence of all rational beings (*SVF* 2.645). The Platonist Plutarch could not adhere to the immanentism of the Stoic allegorical tradition and the identification of the divinity with physical realities or the immanent Logos. There remains an ultimate polarity, reflected in the twofold exegetical level theorized in *De Audiendis Poetis* 23: "When the poets use the names of the deities, sometimes in their concept (*ennoia*) they comprehend the deities themselves, sometimes by the same names they designate certain powers and faculties of which the deities are givers and causes." Thus, Plutarch left the door open for divine transcendence.

Middle and Neoplatonists valued the most ancient traditions, not only the Greek, but of various peoples, which were to be allegorized to discern an original wisdom therein. But the choice of these ancient traditions was paramount. While Herodotus and Plato had stressed the intellectual debt of Greek thinkers to the Egyptian tradition, Plutarch, in a context in which the superiority of the Greek cultural heritage, assumed by the Second Sophistic, was contested by the claims of rival cultures, such as Egypt, Judea, and India, recognized the wisdom of the Egyptians but always reminded his readers that philosophy was the gift of the Greeks (Richter 2011: 198). Diogenes Laertius, too, acknowledged that there were wisdom traditions among other peoples, such as the Magi, Chaldeans, and Druids (1.1), but underlined that philosophy was the great invention of the Greeks (see my introduction to Reale and Ramelli 2005). Plutarch significantly rewrote travel stories, in which itinerant Greeks were bearers, not receivers, of wisdom. Likewise, in Philostratus's *Life of Apollonius*, the traveling Apollonius of Tyana instructed other cultures before engaging with Indian Gymnosophists.

Deciding which myths were to be allegorized was relevant to the debate between "pagan" and Christian Platonists. Numenius seems to have been the only non-Christian and non-Jew to allegorize biblical episodes (besides Amelius, who interpreted the Johannine Prologue, though from Eusebius's report in *PE* 11.19.1, it is unclear that it was an allegorical exegesis). This cultural operation implied that philosophical truths were embedded in the Bible which, consequently, was regarded as authoritative. The defenders of the presence of philosophical truths in Scripture, both in Hellenistic Judaism and among Christian apologists, also claimed that Moses, as author of the Torah, was anterior to Plato and had inspired him more or less directly, or that both were inspired by the same Logos. On this assumption, Greek philosophy derived from the more ancient and authentic Hebrew philosophy. But "pagan" Platonists, such as Celsus, Porphyry, and later thinkers, at least in anti-Christian works, denied that the Bible contained a philosophical gist.

The question here was: Which traditions are to be deemed authoritative and susceptible of allegoresis? Greek myths or "barbarian" myths—that is, Egyptian, Babylonian, Persian, Indian, and similar traditions? The Bible, conceived as "Hebrew myths"? Allegorizing these myths meant recognizing them as endowed with a nugget of philosophical truth coming from remote times, to be decoded by allegoresis. The same attitude toward "the ancients" as knowers of truths expressed symbolically, as found in the Stoic Cornutus, also underlies the Neoplatonist Porphyry's exegesis of Homer's cave of the Nymphs: "Very properly, the ancients consecrated caves and grottoes to the cosmos, taking it as a whole and in its parts, presenting the earth as a symbol of matter, from which the cosmos derives . . . By means of caves they represented the cosmos, which derives from matter" (*The Cave of the Nymphs* 5). Porphyry calls Homer "theologian" (*De Antr. Nymph.* 31–32). Homer is for him, as for the Stoic allegorists, a source of philosophical truth, and that truth for Porphyry is the same as Plato's—just as for the Stoics it was the Stoic truth. As Porphyry explains, Homer's intelligence and perfection in every virtue allowed him to "express allegorically, in the fiction of a despicable myth, images of more divine truths" (*De Antr. Nymph.* 36). This is why in his *Homeric Questions* Porphyry aimed at demonstrating that Homer never erred. His attitude is the same as that of Origen or other Christian exegetes toward the Bible: to value one's own ancient authoritative text, often denying authoritative status to other traditions. Thus, Porphyry and other "pagan" Platonists, in their anti-Christian writings, denied authority to the Bible, while Christians denied authority to "pagan" myths.

The *Suda* attributes to both Proclus and his teacher Syrianus a lost work, *On the Agreement between Orpheus, Pythagoras, Plato, and the Chaldean Oracles*. This reflects well the ideal of the School of Athens, which contemplated the construction of a scientific theology embracing all traditional divinities interpreted in the light of Plato's philosophy. This interpretation was conducted by means of philosophical allegoresis, whose structural role was the same as in Stoic theology. From Proclus's and Syrianus's viewpoints, truth is one—that is, Plato's—truth; but first, truth was expressed symbolically by Homer and Hesiod, and then in images by the Pythagoreans, dialectically by Plato, and, finally, theosophically by the *Chaldean Oracles* (Proclus, *Platonic Theology* 1.4). Proclus observes: "All of Greek theology is the child of Orphic mystagogy: Pythagoras was the first who received initiation from Aglaophamus, and Plato in turn received from the Pythagorean and Orphic doctrines perfect knowledge concerning the gods" (*Platonic Theology* 1.5). Sara Rappe, noting that the same direct line of transmission from Orpheus to Pythagoras to Plato had already been drawn by Iamblichus, who inspired Proclus, comments: "The theory behind Proclus's synthesis of various philosophical dialects into a single theological language is the unity of primordial tradition," a concern that seems to me to be at work already in Stoic allegorists (see above, section 2). Rappe continues: "By reading Plato in Pythagorean terms and Pythagoras in Platonic terms, by insisting upon the equivalence of *mythos* and *logos*, by substituting mythic names for metaphysical terms, and by authorising his interpretations through reference to the *Chaldean Oracles*, Proclus creates a totalising speech that sweeps up the entire history of philosophy" (Rappe 2000: 169). In his *Commentary on Plato's Republic*, at the beginning of the sixth essay, Proclus prepares his project of reconciling Plato with Homer through an account of archaic myth as containing philosophical truths, to be interpreted allegorically. This endeavor, like that of the Stoic allegorists, probably also aimed at preserving the cultural and literary heritage of a "classic" for future generations (on Proclus's reconciliation of Homer with Plato, see Chlup 2012: 185–200).

Middle and Neoplatonism, both "pagan" and Christian, absorbed several features of Stoic thought, among which was allegoresis as part and parcel of philosophy (Ramelli 2009, 2011c). This is why the Middle/Neoplatonist Origen included his theorization of biblical allegoresis, not in any exegetical work, but in his *philosophico-theological* masterpiece, *On First Principles*. This is because Origen, like the Stoics, regarded allegory as a constitutive part of *philosophy*.

Likewise, the aim of Origen's philosophical allegoresis structurally parallels that of Stoic philosophical allegoresis. I have argued that the Stoics availed themselves of the allegoresis of myths not simply to support their own philosophical system (a merely "apologetic" function of allegoresis), but also and primarily with the intention of defending and preserving ancient mythical traditions by integrating them into a unitary philosophical system centered in the Logos. Correspondingly, it is not simply the case that Origen deployed the Bible to defend his own metaphysical system; he also and especially put metaphysics, and his whole (Christian Platonic) philosophy, in the service of the interpretation of Scripture, which, in his view, was the privileged repository of truth—and, at the same time, taught much the same truths as Plato (Ramelli 2021b, forthcoming a, c, d). Origen's aim was to provide the Bible, and Christianity, with a philosophical foundation, making it the core of a unitary philosophical system focused on the Logos, just as the Stoic system was. To Origen's mind, the Logos is Christ-Logos (Ramelli 2015).

Indeed, Origen was familiar with imperial Stoic allegorists, such as Cornutus and Chaeremon (Porphyry, *c. Chr.* fr. 39 Harnack: see Ramelli, this volume, on Cornutus, and 2006b). The source, the "pagan" Neoplatonist Porphyry, is hostile, not to Origen *tout court*, whom he admires as a philosopher, but to his adhesion to Christianity—an illegal religion in the Empire, as Porphyry himself stressed (Ramelli 2019, 2021c)—and to his application of allegoresis to such a disqualifying book as the Bible. Porphyry blames Origen for the transfer of the allegorical method from "pagan" myths, its traditional and legitimate object, to the Jewish-Christian myth. He does not take into account Philo, Aristobulus, or other Jewish allegorical exegetes, let alone Clement or various "Gnostics," who preceded Origen in allegorizing Scripture: this striking omission was probably intentional, and was already found in Celsus (Orig. *C. Cels.* 4.51: see Ramelli 2011b, and [on Clement] 2016a).

In his works Origen shows traces of Stoic etymological allegoresis and uses allegorical exegeses of Greek mythical figures that remind readers of Stoic, and specifically Cornutus's, interpretations (see my chapter on Cornutus, this volume). Origen was also familiar with Middle Platonic and Neopythagorean philosophical allegorists, such as Numenius and Philo. Philo allegorized the Greek version of the Hebrew Bible in light of Platonism; his cosmological and allegorical exegesis was "imported" into Christianity by Clement of Alexandria (for example, Ramelli 2008a, 2012, 2018a). Numenius allegorized, not only the Septuagint, but also what later became the New Testament. Origen esteemed Numenius, whom he quotes four times in *Contra Celsum*, 1.5 (fr. 1b desPlaces); 4.51 (fr. 10a); 5.38 (fr. 53); 5.57 (fr. 29). For Numenius, "in his desire for learning, wanted to examine our Scriptures, too, and was interested in them *as susceptible of allegorical interpretation*, and not full of odd ideas" (*C. Cels.* 4.51).

This was crucial in Origen's debate with "pagan" Middle and Neoplatonists who claimed that the application of allegoresis to the Jewish-Christian Scriptures was illegitimate since no philosophical truth could be expected to be expressed allegorically there. Again, Origen informs us that Numenius, who interpreted Plato better than Celsus did and studied the Pythagorean doctrines in depth, quoted Moses and the prophets in many passages of his works and offered what were very likely allegorical interpretations of them—for instance, in his *Hoopoe*, *On Numbers*, and *On Place*. In *On the Good* 3 Numenius interpreted allegorically a story about Jesus, without mentioning his name. Numenius inspired Origen exegetically and theologically. His allegoresis of the Jewish-Christian Bible parallels his exegesis of Plato. Later, Amelius, Plotinus's disciple, likewise interpreted not only Plato but also the "myth" of the Johannine Prologue—and likely did so with Origen's exegesis in mind (as argued by Ramelli 2021d).

Because of Numenius's biblical philosophical allegoresis, Origen esteemed him much more than Celsus, who, like Porphyry, admitted of no biblical allegoresis. Numenius's definition of Plato as "a Greek-speaking Moses" (Eusebius *PE* 11.10.14 = fr. 8 desPlaces) is owed to the persuasion that Plato and the Bible conveyed the same teachings. Numenius, like Clement, probably influenced Origen's view of the relationship between Platonism and what already Philo called the Mosaic philosophy. In his Commentary on the Song of Songs, prologue 3.2–4, Origen, after speaking of the division of philosophy into ethics, physics, "epoptics," and logic, posits *epoptica* as the crowning of philosophy. He thus considers theology (epoptics deals with "divine and heavenly things") to be part and parcel of philosophy; it cannot be studied without a philosophical background. Then Origen claims that Greek philosophers drew inspiration from Solomon's wisdom—hence, the obvious priority of the Bible, but also the inescapable affinity between its teaching and Plato's.

Origen was also conversant with "Gnostic" allegorists, chiefly Valentinians, such as Heracleon. Origen criticized their allegoresis of the New Testament (which was often paired with their refusal to allegorize the Old Testament with deleterious consequences with respect to the principle of finding in Scripture meanings "worthy of God"). "Gnostic" allegorists refused to acknowledge in the New Testament the presence of both a literal and a spiritual meaning; they eliminated the historical level, reducing the New Testament to myth (*mythos*, as opposite to *logos* and history). Notably, this is also the main difference between the use of allegoresis by Christians and by "pagan" Platonists (Ramelli 2011c). Christian Platonists, such as Origen, Eusebius, and Gregory of Nyssa, also kept the historical level of Scripture, while "pagan" Platonists maintained that what myths narrate never happened historically. Thus, they exclusively stuck to the allegorical/symbolic sense. Origen clearly exalted Philo by referring to those Jews who interpreted the Law not only literally, but also allegorically (*C. Cels.* 7.20), yet not exclusively so. For Philo retained the literal, historical level of the Bible along with its spiritual meanings. He refused to consider Scripture fictional. Philo and Origen deemed Scripture a historical record in the first instance (Ramelli 2018a). Neoplatonic exegetes of myths did the opposite. For example, Sal(l)ustius, deeply influenced by Iamblichus, in *On the Deities and the World* 4.9, declared squarely that the facts narrated in myths never happened, but are symbols of eternal truths.

Origen thought that the *defectus litterae* occurs only rarely in Scripture. Few passages are actually deprived of a literal meaning and only have "bare spiritual meanings," unwrapped in literal/historical clothes, to supply readers with pointers to more sublime meanings. Apart from these cases and from the Biblical accounts of the creation and the end of the world, and the Song of Songs, in all other cases the literal level must be retained along with the spiritual (Ramelli 2014). The Bible almost always narrates historical events, not mere allegories of eternal truths. In this respect, Origen's Biblical allegoresis, which retained the historical level, like Philo's and Clement's, differed from both Stoic and Middle-Neoplatonic allegoresis of myths. Origen employed *allēgoria* and related terms sparingly because they belonged to "pagan" allegoresis of myths; therefore, their application to Scripture would have entailed the assimilation of the whole Bible to mythography and the denial of its historicity. However, Origen's allegoresis shared more with Platonic than with Stoic allegoresis: the division between immanent and transcendent, as opposite to Stoic immanentism, and the need for unity and coherence in allegoresis (Ramelli 2006a).

Middle Platonic allegoresis, in turn, was influenced by Stoic allegoresis. For instance, as I briefly mentioned, Cornutus indicated a comparative method between two or more peoples' mythological and ritual traditions (Ramelli 2004a: 346–358; 447–479) to find the philosophical truth hidden in myths and rituals. Middle–Neoplatonists such as Plutarch, Numenius, and Porphyry seem to have taken it up. This interest in different peoples' religious traditions also appears in the imperial Stoic Chaeremon, who interpreted Egyptian mythology allegorically and was concerned with the symbolic value of hieroglyphics. His work attracted the attention of Clement of Alexandria (Ramelli 2004a: 349–358; 2007).

Around the time of Clement, Diogenes Laertius, like Tatian and some imperial Platonists, was involved in a discussion concerning the value of various peoples' mythological traditions (see my introductory essay in Reale and Ramelli 2005; forthcoming d). As a result, a debate arose between "pagan" and Christian Platonic allegorists about which traditions to deem authoritative and therefore endowed with philosophical meanings. "Pagan" Middle/Neoplatonists such as Celsus, Porphyry, and Julian, but not Numenius, refused to lend Biblical myths any philosophical value: Scripture concealed no philosophical truths to be detected by allegoresis. Christian allegorists such as Clement and Origen, as already Philo and his predecessors in Hellenistic Judaism, instead, claimed for the Bible the status of a text that contained philosophical truths in a symbolic form. But the "pagan" Middle Platonist Celsus asserted that in the Bible

> there is no deeper doctrine beyond the literal sense of the words . . . The more reasonable among Jews and Christians try to allegorise in some way the Biblical stories; yet, these are not susceptible of any allegorical interpretation, but, on the contrary, are *bare myths, and of the most stupid kind.* . . . However, the allegories that appear to be written on these myths are far more disgraceful and unlikely than the myths themselves. (in Origen, *C. Cels.* 7.18; 4.50–51)

In his response, Origen turned these charges back against "pagan" mythology. The question at stake was which among the ancient traditions (for example, Greek, Egyptian, Persian, Indian, Hebrew) deserved to be deemed authoritative, in that it expressed philosophical truths under the veil of symbols. Indeed, allegorizing myths meant to acknowledge that they concealed philosophical truths that required decipherment through philosophical allegoresis.

## FURTHER READING

Calame (2015) offers a good introduction to Greek mythology and mythography; Copeland and Struck (2010) and Rolet (2012) follow the development of allegory, including allegoresis applied to mythography. In Martin (2016) see especially ch. 1, the sections on rejecting myth, rationalizing myth, and allegorizing myth. Ramelli (2004) and (2007) offer a complete critical appraisal of ancient allegoresis with a commentary on the relevant texts. Ramelli (2011c, forthcoming a, b) delves into the debates between "pagan'" and Christian Platonists about philosophical allegoresis of mythography (Greek or biblical).

## References

Akçay, Nilüfer. 2019. *Porphyry's On the Cave of the Nymphs in its Intellectual Context.* Leiden: Brill.

Biondi, Francesca. 2015. *Teagene di Reggio rapsodo e interprete di Omero.* Pisa, Italy: Serra.

Blönnigen, Christoph. 1992. *Die griechische Ursprung der jüdisch-hellenistischen Allegorese und ihre Rezeption in der alexandrinischen Patristik.* Frankfurt: Lang.

Boys-Stones, George R. 2001. *Post-Hellenistic Philosophy.* Oxford: Oxford University Press.

Boys-Stones, George R. 2003. "The Stoics' Two Types of Allegory." In *Metaphor, Allegory, and the Classical Tradition*, edited by George R. Boys-Stones, 189–216. Oxford: Oxford University Press.

Calame, Claude. 2015. *Qu'est-ce que la mythologie grecque?* Paris: Gallimard.

Chlup, Radek. 2012. *Proclus: An Introduction.* Cambridge, UK: Cambridge University Press.

Copeland, Rita, and Peter Struck, eds. 2010. *The Cambridge Companion to Allegory.* Cambridge, UK: Cambridge University Press.

Dawson, David. 1992. *Allegorical Readers and Cultural Revision in Ancient Alexandria.* Berkeley: University of California Press.

Domaradzki, Mikolaj. 2017. "The Beginnings of Greek Allegoresis." *Classical World* 110: 299–321.

Griffin, Svetla S., and Ilaria L.E. Ramelli, eds. 2022. *Lovers of the Soul, Lovers of the Body: Philosophical and Religious Perspectives in Late Antiquity.* Hellenic Studies 88. Cambridge, MA: Harvard University Press.

Henrichs, Albert. 2014. "Three Approaches to Greek Mythography." In *Interpretations of Greek Mythology*, 2nd ed., edited by Jan Bremmer, 242–277. Oxford: Routledge.

Lamberton, Robert. 1989. *Homer the Theologian.* Berkeley: University of California Press.

Lamberton, Robert. 2012. *Proclus the Successor on Poetics and the Homeric Poems.* Atlanta, GA: Society of Biblical Literature.

Long, Anthony A. 1997. "Allegory in Philo and Etymology in Stoicism." *Studia Philonica Annual* 9: 198–210.

Martin, Richard. 2016. *Classical Mythology: The Basics.* London: Routledge.

Ramelli, Ilaria L. E. 2004a. *Allegoria, I, L'età classica.* Milan: Vita e Pensiero.

Ramelli, Ilaria L. E. 2004b. Review of Boys-Stones 2001. *Aevum* 78: 196–200.

Ramelli, Ilaria L. E. 2006a. *Il βασιλεύς come νόμος ἔμψυχος tra diritto naturale e diritto divino: spunti platonici del concetto e sviluppi di età imperiale e tardoantica.* Naples: Bibliopolis.

Ramelli, Ilaria L. E. 2006b. "Origen and the Stoic Allegorical Tradition." *Invigilata Lucernis* 28: 195–226.

Ramelli, Ilaria L. E. 2007. *Allegoristi dell'età classica.* Milan: Bompiani–Catholic University.

Ramelli, Ilaria L. E. 2008a. "Philosophical Allegoresis of Scripture in Philo and Its Legacy in Gregory of Nyssa." *Studia Philonica Annual* 20: 55–99.

Ramelli, Ilaria L. E. 2008b. *Stoici romani minori.* Milan: Bompiani.

Ramelli, Ilaria L. E. 2009. "Origen, Patristic Philosophy, and Christian Platonism." *Vigiliae Christianae* 63: 217–263.

Ramelli, Ilaria L. E. 2011a. "Ancient Allegory and its Reception throughout the Ages." Review article of Copeland and Struck 2010. *International Journal of the Classical Tradition* 18: 569–578.

Ramelli, Ilaria L. E. 2011b. "Origen the Christian Middle/Neoplatonist." *Journal of Early Christian History* 1: 98–130.

Ramelli, Ilaria L. E. 2011c. "The Philosophical Stance of Allegory in Stoicism and Its Reception in Platonism." *International Journal of the Classical Tradition* 18: 335–371.

Ramelli, Ilaria L. E. 2012. "Philo and Origen: Allegorical Exegesis of Scripture." *Studies in Christian-Jewish Relations* 7: 1–17.

Ramelli, Ilaria L. E. 2014. "Valuing Antiquity in Antiquity by Means of Allegoresis." In *Valuing the Past in the Greco-Roman World*, edited by James Ker and Christoph Pieper, 485–507. Leiden: Brill,

Ramelli, Ilaria L. E. 2015. "*Ethos* and *Logos*: A Second-Century Apologetical Debate between 'Pagan' and Christian Philosophers." *Vigiliae Christianae* 69: 123–156.

Ramelli, Ilaria L. E. 2016a. "The Mysteries of Scripture: Allegorical Exegesis and the Heritage of Stoicism, Philo, and Pantaenus." In *Clement's Biblical Exegesis*, edited by Veronica Černuskova, Judith Kovacs, and Jana Platova, 80–110. Leiden: Brill.

Ramelli, Ilaria L. E. 2016b. "Origen's Allegoresis of Plato's and Scripture's Myths." In *Religious Competition in the Greco-Roman World*, edited by Nathaniel P. Desrosiers and Lily C. Vuong, 85–106. Atlanta, GA: Society of Biblical Literature.

Ramelli, Ilaria L. E. 2018a. "Philo as One of the Main Inspirers of Early Christian Hermeneutics and Theology." *Adamantius* 24: 276–292.

Ramelli, Ilaria L. E. 2018b. "The Role of Allegory, Allegoresis, and Metaphor in Paul and Origen." *Journal of Greco-Roman Christianity and Judaism* 14: 130–157.

Ramelli, Ilaria L.E. 2019. "Porphyry and the Motif of Christianity as παράνομος." In *Platonism and its Legacy*, edited by John F. Finamore and Tomáš Nejeschleba, 173–198. Lydney, UK: Prometheus Trust.

Ramelli, Ilaria L. E. 2021a. "Stoic Homeric Allegoresis." In *Brill's Companion to the Reception of Homer from the Hellenistic Age to Late Antiquity*, edited by Christina-Panagiota Manolea and Antony Makrinos, 229–258. Leiden: Brill.

Ramelli, Ilaria L. E. 2021b. "Origen's Philosophical Exegesis of the Bible against the Backdrop of Ancient Philosophy (Stoicism, Platonism) and Hellenistic and Rabbinic Judaism." *Studia Patristica* 103: 13–58.

Ramelli, Ilaria L.E. 2021c. "Origen and Porphyry: Continuity and Polemics between Psychology and Eschatology." In *Philosophos – Philotheos – Philoponos*, edited by Mikonja Knežević, 187–211. Belgrade: Gnomon Centre for the Humanities.

Ramelli, Ilaria L.E. 2021d. "The Logos/Nous One-Many between 'Pagan' and Christian Platonism: Bardaisan, Clement, Origen, Plotinus, and Gregory of Nyssa." *Studia Patristica* 102: 11–44.

Ramelli, Ilaria L. E. Forthcoming a. "The Relevance of Greco-Roman Literary Themes to New Testament Interpretation: The theme of slavery and freedom - Gal 3:28 and relations to Gal 4." In *The Cambridge Handbook of Historical Biblical Exegesis*, edited by Stanley E. Porter and David J. Fuller. Cambridge: Cambridge University Press.

Ramelli, Ilaria L. E. Forthcoming b. "Allegory." In *Brill Encyclopedia of Early Christianity*, edited by Paul Van Geest et al. Leiden: Brill. Online from 2018. https://referenceworks.brillonl ine.com/entries/brill-encyclopedia-of-early-christianity-online/allegory-SIM_00000113.

Ramelli, Ilaria L. E. Forthcoming c. "Stoicism and the Fathers." In *Brill Encyclopedia of Early Christianity*, edited by Paul Van Geest *et alii*. Leiden: Brill. https://referenceworks.brillonl ine.com/entries/brill-encyclopedia-of-early-christianity-online/stoicism-and-the-fathers-SIM_036681.

Ramelli, Ilaria L. E. Forthcoming d. "'Revelation' for Christians and Pagans and their Philosophical Allegoresis: Intersections within Imperial Platonism." In *An Open Crossroad: Divination in Later Antiquity*, edited by Elsa Simonetti. Cambridge: Cambridge University Press.

Rappe, Sara. 2000. *Reading Neoplatonism*. Cambridge, UK: Cambridge University Press.

Reale, Giovanni, and Ilaria Ramelli. 2005. *Diogene Laerzio. Vite e dottrine dei più celebri filosofi*. Milan: Bompiani.

Richter, Daniel S. 2011. *Cosmopolis: Imagining Community in Late Classical Athens and the Early Roman Empire*. Oxford: Oxford University Press.

Rolet, Anne, ed. 2012. *Allégorie et symbole: Voies de dissidence? De l'antiquité à la renaissance*. Rennes: Presses Universitaires de Rennes.

Russell, Donald, and David Konstan. 2005. *Heraclitus. Homeric Problems*. Atlanta, GA: Society of Biblical Literature.

Saffrey, Henry. 1992. "Accorder entre elles les traditions théologiques: Une caractéristique du néoplatonisme athénien." In *On Proclus and His Influence on Mediaeval Philosophy*, edited by Abraham Bos and Paul Meijer, 35–50. Leiden: Brill.

# CHAPTER 26

........................................................................................................

# ETYMOLOGIZING

........................................................................................................

## EZIO PELLIZER[†]

## 1. CATALOGUES, GENEALOGIES, AND ETYMOLOGIES

........................................................................................................

IF we consider the rhapsodic performance of the "catalogue" as one particularly old form of organizing mythological material and—after the introduction of writing—as one of the earliest forms of "mythography," we will be able to see that, in its earliest application, we are not dealing with mere lists of names but with the systematization of genealogies (that is, with lists of ancestors) that may go back in time three or four generations.[1] In the famous *Catalogue of Ships* (Hom. *Il.* 2.494–877), we find names and places of origin, but in the case of the twins Ascalaphus and Ialmenus (*Il.* 2.511–515), for example, the poet identifies both of their parents and notes the circumstances of their union (they were born of a divine marriage between Astyoche and the god Ares). What we have, then, is a true and proper *eoea* (*eoia*), a genealogy that records the circumstances of the two heroes' birth (secret, in an upstairs room, virgin mother), the place (in the house of Actor, in Boeotia, in Orchomenos or Aspledon), and the full lineage, reaching back to their grandfather and great-grandfather. Thus, names of four generations are listed: (a) the twins Ascalaphus and Ialmenus; (b) Ares and Astyoche; (c) Actor; and (d) finally, in the form of a patronymic, Azeus father of Actor.

The first works written in prose that we today call "mythographical" could, therefore, have easily been called *Genealogiae* in the 5th century BCE—a title that appears frequently in references to the works of the logographer Hecataeus of Miletus (eight times) or those of Acusilaus of Argos (nine times), and many others (also *Historiae*, see Fowler

---

[1] I thank Franco Montanari, Lara Pagani, and Davide Muratore (University of Genoa), Sotera Fornaro, and Anna Maria Piredda (University of Sassari) for their useful bibliographic suggestions and for having generously helped me find some important texts online. I am also grateful to the editors for translating this chapter from my Italian to English.

2000: esp. 3, 123; 2006; 2013; Sluiter 2015: 896–922). This title returns as a possible title of Hyginus's *Fabulae* and, again, in the work of Boccaccio (14th c. CE). In some cases, we encounter prose versions of poetic catalogues of the type we find amply attested in Hesiod's *Theogony* and, in other cases, in Homer or in the rhapsodic tradition more broadly. As a result, these works, whether in prose or in poetry, could also be called *Theogony, Theology,* or *Heroology.* In the fragments of Acusilaus (first half of 5th c. BCE) we already find an attempt to narrate a foundation myth with eponymous figures that seem to be primarily autoschediastic—that is, invented for the purpose of explaining a text in some way (for example, see Acusil. fr. 43 Fowler = Schol. Hom. *Od.* 17.207). At other times, ancient catalogs with long lists of names can convey, through the examination of etymologies, a kind of generalized description, for example, of the sea (the list of Nereids) or of artistic activity (names of the Muses, daughters of Mnemosyne).

The most basic process involves personification, whereby a physical reality (*līmos,* "Hunger") or a moral or psychological condition (*aidōs,* "Shame," or *atē,* "Blind Folly") is simply taken up as a personal name and usually represented as being anthropomorphic, born of a father and mother and inserted into a genealogical system. In other words, some psychological, moral, or behavioral states are endowed with qualities that strictly belong to human subjects, rendering them capable of fulfilling various "authorial" functions within narrative structures (see Stafford and Herrin 2005). Another productive mechanism that develops primarily at the beginning of the Hellenistic age is found in stories involving metamorphosis. An account, usually emotional or passionate, is constructed to explain an existing botanical, zoological, or geographical object. Here, we have a kind of narrative reversal in which a human character gives his own name to the object into which he has been transformed.

Thus begins, already in the most ancient written texts that we possess, a sort of speculation or reflection on the names and on their "true (*etymo-*) significance (*-logia*)," that is, their etymology. This onomastic investigation, in the most ancient poetic texts, focuses, above all, on personal names, and the earliest explorations concern the names of gods, or more generally, of prodigious beings (Giants, Orph. fr. 63 Kern; Cyclopes, Hes. *Th.* 144–145; Titans, Orph. fr. 57 Kern; Hes. *Th.* 207–210; Kraus 1987: 31). From the very beginnings of rhapsodic mythography, it was inevitable that they would look for some element in the "true" names of characters that was related to the events in their lives. Let us therefore try to highlight the forms and functions these onomastic speculations, explanations, and interpretations may have taken in not only the creation of mythical accounts but also their validation.

## 2. RHAPSODIC ETYMOLOGIES

Hesiod offers some unique explanations of Aphrodite's names and epithets. For instance, he connects the name to *aphros* (sea foam) and *duō* (plunge), a folk etymology that, according to Risch (1947: 76), gave rise to the myth of the goddess's birth. He also interprets etymologically a well-known formulaic expression from the rhapsodic tradition—namely, the adjective *philommeidēs*. The epithet is interpreted, in a completely contextual and erroneous way, not by explaining it as a compound of *meidiaō* (lover of smiles), but by having it derive from *mēdea* (testicles) because Aphrodite emerged from the sexual organs of Uranus, which were cut off by Cronus (Hes. *Th.* 195–200). It should be noted that a few verses later, the epithet *philomeidēs* is used in its traditional sense, which is clearly the correct one, for the Nereid Glauconome, who was certainly not described as "lover of sexual organs" (*Th.* 256). Also, some seven hundred verses away (*Th.* 989) the name/epithet combination used (following Homeric practice) must be meant in this sense for Aphrodite herself (see also fr. 176 M-W; for additional discussion of this and other etymologies discussed here, see Nieto Hernández, this volume).

The derivation from *aphros*, "foam," even if it is based on a vague acrophonic analogy, was destined to cross generations and different languages. See Ovid, *Met.* 4.537–538 (Michalopoulos 2001: 32):

> If it is true indeed that I arose
> from sea foam in the depths, on that occasion
> commemorated by my name (*nomen*) in Greek (*Graium*). (trans. Martin)

Even more famous are some Homeric etymologies, for example, the numerous ones concerning Odysseus's name that are already found in the *Odyssey*. The most explicit is formulated by his maternal grandfather, who chose for the newborn the name Odysseus because he himself, Autolycus son of Hermes, came to Ithaca "because he was hated (*odyssamenos*) by many" (see Hom. *Od.* 19.406–408; Sulzberger 1926; Kanavou 2015: 90–101). At *Odyssey* 1.62, in turn, the gods of Olympus take to semantic wordplay on the hero's name. Athena asks, "Why do you hate (*ōdysao*) him so much, Zeus?" (see Mirto 2007: 222–225; and Hainsworth's commentary to Hom. *Od.* 5.340 in Heubeck, West, and Hainsworth 1988: Ino daughter of Cadmus pities Odysseus because Poseidon is angry at him, *ōdysato*). Odysseus recognizes that Poseidon, especially, hates him, *odōdystai* (5.423). Zeus and Helios are later also said to hate him, *odysanto* (19.275–276).

We will limit ourselves here to the observation that the first and best-known of these etymological denominations follows a process that is uncommon in Homeric onomastics. Here, the naming does not concern the newborn child but the situation in which the maternal grandfather finds himself. Further, it does not celebrate the grandfather's qualities or deeds, but the hostility he faced from many. The newborn was presented to Autolycus by the nurse Eurycleia when he arrives on the island of Ithaca to celebrate his daughter's giving birth to his grandson. Eurycleia expressly asks him to choose a name to give to the baby in the presence of his mother, Anticleia, and father, Laertes (*Od.* 19.399–412). When naming a son, it is far more common that the name evokes the deeds, positive qualities, or even misfortunes of the *father* (for instance, Neoptolemos, Megapenthes, and a great many more). As we saw above, there is also an attempt in the poem to explain the meaning of Odysseus's name by associating it with the misfortunes of its bearer rather than with those of his maternal grandfather.

Another interesting etymology *ex eventu* is expressed by Aphrodite in the *Homeric Hymn to Aphrodite* when the goddess, as a mother, chooses the name that Anchises is to give to Aeneas. The son she has just conceived should be called *Aineias* for the dreadful (*ainon*) sorrow that came over the goddess because she had slept with a mortal (*Hom. Hymn Aphr.* 198–199). At any rate, the newborn will be handed over to the father, who is to keep the name of his divine mother a secret by saying that he was born of a Nymph. Examples of this type abound in Hellenistic narratives.

# 3. ETYMOLOGIES ON THE STAGE

In a well-known scene from Aeschylus's *Prometheus*, one of the foundational figures of traditional Greek identity, Io, the daughter of Inachus the river god of Argos, appears on stage. Loved by Zeus, transformed into a heifer, and guarded by the hundred eyes of Argos, the young girl eventually flees because of the torment caused by the gadfly sent by Hera (Risch 1947; for Aeschylus, Jouan 1978; Reinberg 1981). In this early traditional tale, Io's journey traces a vast geographic map, from the Ionian Sea to the Bosporus, and ends not in Greece but in Phoenicia and Egypt.

During the gripping prophecy delivered by the chained Titan, the poet of the *Prometheus* lingers briefly on the concept of eponymy: a place will be named after an eponymous person or an event in that character's life. For us, of course, the toponym is prior, and the etymologizer invents an ex post facto etymology by exploiting linguistic elements found in the name or event. Here are the cases to which Prometheus refers: the sea is called *Io*-nian because Io passed through it, and the strait is called *Bosporus* (Bosphorus) after her crossing as a heifer (*bous*); both names are still in use today. Even Io's son will bear a name taken from events that preceded his birth; he will be called Epaphus after the "touch" (*epaphōn*) with which Zeus will free the girl-heifer from her torment, allowing her to give birth to her son in the form of a woman. In the Hesiodic tradition, we find a fragment that attributes the naming of Euboea to Io's travels: *Eu-boia* ("Good-Cow" Island) was first called Abantis, but the name was changed by the will of Zeus because of the fugitive cow (fr. 296 M-W = Steph. Byz. s.v., I 12–13 Billerbeck).

Aeschylus is also well-known for his free interpretations of Helen's portentous name, which are all based on deliberate etymological (*etētymōs*) wordplay at the beginning of the second stasimon of the *Agamemnon* (see Jouan 1978: 69–87), where it is claimed that it contains an omen of her future destiny (683–684, *pronoiaisi tou peprōmenou*). Here, it is supposedly tied to the root *hel-* from *haireō*, "hand over for destruction, destroy," because Helen will be the cause of the destruction of ships, heroes, and cities (*hele-naus*, *hel-andros*, *hele-ptolis*, Aesch. *Ag.* 681–690). Needless to say, the name of Eteocles's adversarial brother, Polyneices, will be interpreted as destined to indicate a hero "of much discord" (Aesch. *Sept.* 658; Loraux 1988). Sophocles does not fail to mention Ajax (*Aias*), defining the hero as "ill-named" (*dysōnymon, Aj.* 914), and the same hero effectively produces the connection of the eponymy of the proper name with the *aiai*, a Greek word of lament (*Aj.* 430–433), when it is reported that he had fallen prey to folly. The idea that the petals of the flower that grows from Ajax's blood were inscribed with the lament *AI AI*, an allusion to the unfortunate name of Aias (Euphor. fr. 40 Powell) is found in Ovid, *Met.* 13.394–398 (Michalopoulos 2001: 22). Yet a few years earlier, around 480 BCE, Pindar (*Isth.* 6.49–54) had represented Heracles in the act of making an auspicious toast in which he prophesied that the unborn child would be a brave warrior. During the toast, Heracles virtually "commanded" the parents, Telamon and Eriboea, to give the child the name suggested by an eagle (*aietos > Aias*) that had appeared in the sky to confirm the truth of the prediction (etymology reoccurs at Ps.-Apd., *Bibl.* 3.162).

Euripides presents numerous other examples of "etymological interpretations" in the *Ion*, where Xuthos connects the revelation of the identity of his son, named Ion, with the casual encounter of the first person who will "come" (*ionti*) toward him (661–662). Even better known, with emotional effect, is the ominously prophetic "interpretation" of the name of Pentheus (a *nomen agentis*), connected with the common noun *penthos* ("sorrow"; Eur. *Bacch.* 367–368), which also occurs in an Aristotelian example drawn from the less well-known tragedian Chaeremon (*Rhet.* 1400b). Aristotle also mentions a variant Euripidean "etymology" of the name Aphrodite, interpreted in connection with *aphrosynē*, "folly" (see Eur. *Tro.* 990; and Calame 1985: 32 n. 10). One of the best-known etymologies, without doubt, is that of Oedipus, which is explained as a bimembral passive verbal compound of the verb *oideō*, "swell," and *pous*, "foot," because he had been found abandoned with his feet pierced and swollen, "Swollen-Feet" (Soph. *OT* 1034–1036).

# 4. FREE ETYMOLOGIES

In Plato's *Cratylus*, one finds a light-hearted discussion about Hector's infant son, who has two names (*Il.* 6.402–403): Hector called him Scamandrius after the name of the famous Trojan river Scamander; the Trojans called him Astyanax, "because his father alone protected Ilium." In a passage of this famous dialogue, which appears particularly ironic and playful, Socrates declares:

> And Homer, as you know, says that the Trojan men called him Astyanax (*king of the city*); but if the men called him Astyanax, the other name of Scamandrius could only have been given to him by the women. (trans. Jowett)

The reasoning of Socrates—who tries to get Hermogenes to admit that because the Trojan women are less wise than their male counterparts, the name that the men have chosen is more "correct" than the one derived from the river—goes beyond the limits of the ridiculous (or beyond irony), and certainly does not offer a "scientific" explanation of the two names. Both are completely straightforward and easy to interpret, consistent with two common but different denominative processes: one being the creation of an adjective from the name of a river (or of a people or of another geographical feature), and the other, as we have seen, being the naming of a character using a compound that describes qualities of the father.

Elsewhere one finds completely plausible etymologies, for instance, that of Agamemnon, from *agastos kata tēn epimonēn* (*Crat.* 395a), "remarkable for his streadfastness," which is not too far removed from modern etymological explanations. One may also note that already in Plato there is a plurality of *etyma* of the same name based on the presence of certain letters (for instance, Atreus in *Crat.* 395b–c), contradicting the very idea of etymology, which requires a single explanation if it is to be "true." If a lexeme has one "true" meaning, it ought to be univocal, not pluralistic. We will see that this principle is found in later authors (for example, in Cornutus), and it is still operative even in modern times. At any rate, Plato's *Cratylus* has provoked centuries of various interpretations in the illusory search for a "real" correspondence between the formal aspect of names and their "meaning"—that is, between words and reality (see Genette 1976: 11–40; Eco 1993: 16–19, on the "Adamic language"). It should be noted that Plato had already observed the curious presence of a double linguistic register in the Homeric poems, namely, the duplication of lexemes to indicate the same referent (Clay 1972; Lazzeroni 1997; Mirto 2007).

In Xenophon's *Symposium*, we find an interpretation of Ganymedes's name that explains how Zeus loved and was pleased with (*ganymai*, "I am happy, pleased") not the boy's body but his mind and wise thoughts (*mēdea* 8.30). Socrates's himself calls the interpretative method used here *mythologein*, not *etymologein*. For us, this terminology is interesting because it highlights the function that binds the account (*mythos*) to the very essence of the personal name.

Other authors devote themselves to a kind of investigation that was, for them, theological. Around 100 BCE, Apollodorus of Athens wrote an extensive work called *Peri Theon* in which etymologies seem, from the surviving fragments, to have been rather numerous, and he also appears to have composed an *Etymologiae*. A treatise called *Peri Heroōn kai Daimonōn* (*On Heroes and Divinities*) is attributed to the historian and philosopher Posidonius. Needless to say, for the ancient Greeks, the gods, *daemones*, and heroes were not only a mythical but a religious reality, as well. It is only later, in a Neoplatonic context, that one finds examples in which it is recognized that some of the more or less fantastic accounts told about the gods could be seen as philosophically "inspired" to allow weaker souls to gain access to the perception of the divine (Sallustius, 4th c. CE, defends the importance of *mythoi*).

We should also acknowledge authors such as Strabo (1st c. BCE–1st c. CE), Plutarch (1st–2nd c. CE), and Pausanias (2nd c. CE). Although they are not considered to be "mythographers," their vast corpora contains numerous accounts that are of great interest in terms of mythography—for example, stories of local folklore, deeds of traditional heroes, and so on—and etymologies often play a part. Plutarch, a man of extensive Greek learning and an intellectual of the first order, offers some relevant examples, reporting differing variants about heroes belonging to "myth," for example, Romulus and Theseus. As far as etymology goes, Plutarch shows an extensive understanding of its use, even in the form of eponyms. It is sufficient to mention the numerous explanations of the prophetic name of Rome (Pellizer 1997: 83–85). For Strabo (Patterson 2013) and Pausanias (Pellizer 1993: 297–299), etymologies often play a significant role in the naming of places (for example, Paus. 8.10.1: the mountain Alesion in Arcadia is named after the wandering (*alē*) of Rhea).

Under the name Apollodorus (not the aforementioned Apollodorus of Athens but the so-called Ps.-Apollodorus), we have extant the most important handbook of Greek mythology, the *Bibliotheca*, in which the instances of "etymology" or of eponymy are not numerous. I will take as an example Apis, who gave his name to the land Apia, the Peloponnesus, and afterward became Sar-apis and was identified directly with the late and syncretic Egyptian god, whereas Argos, son of Zeus, named the region Argolis, and Pelasgus gave his name to the Pelasgians (2.2). The eponyms continue into book 2, with Aegyptus and Danaus giving their names to the people of Egypt and the Argive Danaans (2.10–13).

As might be predicted, many etymologies are found in the extensive ethnographic or geographic work of Stephanus of Byzantium, the *Ethnika* (6th c. CE), which offers, among other things, numerous accounts to justify the mythical naming (eponyms) of numerous places (see the new edition of Billerbeck 2006–2017).

# 5. Etymological Interpretation and Theology

When we subject material that we call mythical to systematic etymological interpretation, it is impossible to avoid a brief examination of the criteria by which the Stoic Annaeus Cornutus (1st c. CE) composed his unique treatise, the so-called *Theologia* (see Ramelli 2003; and this volume, on Cornutus). This short treatise appeared only a few decades after the work of Varro, whose *De Lingua Latina* dealt extensively with etymology in a now-lost section that seems to have concentrated on the linguistic mechanics of derivation rather than deeper meaning (Blank 2008). Cornutus, by contrast, has a clear didactic and pedagogical goal, providing important proof that etymological research had developed in a Stoic context and could be applied to names from both Greek and Latin accounts. In comparison with the *Cratylus*, which was popular throughout antiquity and beyond because of its attempts to investigate words in relation to "reality," it does not seem possible to speak of progress (Genette 1976: 11–40). Stoic interpretations run decisively in the direction of explaining names (above all, of gods and heroes) as allegorical transformations of natural forces, celestial bodies, or atmospheric phenomena. But there recurs the idea of the "multiplicity of *etyma*," which seems to us intolerable and contradictory (see the introduction to Ramelli 2003). An analogous approach is found in the imperial treatise *Homeric Allegories*, attributed to a certain Heraclitus and dated around the 1st century or the beginning of the 2nd century CE (see Konstan, this volume; Pontani 2005). The author undertakes an extensive defense of the "unseemly issues" in Homer, justifying them according to a systematic application of allegoresis, but he also attempts etymological explanations, for example, Apollo's epithets (*Phoibos, Hekaergos, Lykaios*; Heracl. *Quaest. Hom.* 7.5–11), examining many different possible hypotheses. It is worth noting that in these actual interpretations of Greek mythology (and religion)—as can be gleaned from the important Apollodorus of Athens—the verb *theo-logeō* is used (22.1; 40.2), which should probably be compared to *mytho-logeō*, of which we spoke earlier.

To turn to the Homeric commentators, numerous etymologies (and *paretymologies*, a term already used by the scholiasts themselves) are found in the complex and extremely knotty tradition of the Homeric scholia (compare the so-called D-Scholia, attributed to the ancient scholar Didymus, or the Pergamene and Aristarchean scholia; see Irigoin 1991; Broggiato 2003). Modern scholarship continually strives to clarify the relationship between the activity of the commentators on Homer and the so-called *Mythographus Homericus* (Pagès Cebrian 2007; and Pagès, this volume). Let us consider an interesting example of "multiple etymologies" regarding the Homeric epithet *Pallas* (schol. D Hom. *Il.* 1.200, and other scholia), which would derive (a) from the verb *pallein*, "to brandish"; (b) from her killing of the giant Pallas; (c) from the fact that during her birth she "leapt out" (*anapalthēnai*) of Zeus's head; (d) from having carried the heart of Dionysus while it was still beating, *pallomenēn*; and (e) from a young companion of hers named Pallas, a daughter of Triton, whom she unintentionally killed (Apd. 3.144), where, strictly speaking, there is no etymology. The same can be said for the epithet "Tritogeneia," explained in multiple ways at schol. D Hom. *Il.* 8.39, where an interpretation of Democritus (fr. 68 B2 D-K) is cited, falsely, as an example of *etymologein*, when instead, it is clearly an *allegorical* interpretation: "because she is intelligence (*phronēsis*), from which three things emerge (*aph' hēs tria symbainei*), reasoning well, being able to speak eloquently, and acting as one should." Other etymologies listed in the Homeric scholia are "raised by the river god Triton" and also "born on the third of the month's last ten days" (see the *Suda*, s.v. Tritogeneia). We should therefore recall that even in this kind of scholarship, multiple and accumulated sets of etymologies accompanied the Homeric poems from the Alexandrian period to Eustathius of Thessaloniki (3rd c. BCE–12th c. CE; see Sluiter 2015).

# 6. ETYMOLOGIES AND ETIOLOGIES IN THE GREEK AND LATIN WORLD

A fundamental mechanism, which generated new narratives starting in the Hellenistic period in Alexandria, is the one tied to the creation of new entities named after characters whose stories are frequently of a tragic, emotional, or unbelievable nature. The basic principle that guides the syntax of these narratives is causality—that is, the investigation into causes (*aitia*). As demonstrated in the extensive work of Callimachus's *Aitia* or in the large number of works concerning metamorphoses (for example, *Heteroioumena, Alloiōseis, Metabolai*), the universe can be seen as the result of a succession of events that affect the very naming of reality itself. In this vast network of ideas reappear different but analogous approaches, such as the investigation, at the most basic level, into "original entities" and their "first discoverers" (*prōtoi heuretai*) of customs, objects, human institutions, and narrative techniques that are undertaken to account for the existence of a fountain, river, mountain, city, flower, plant, insect, bird, or other animal. In some cases, the narrated myth aims to account for a "name-change" (*metonomasia*) of some of these natural features, which have been personified and validated by a myth.

Strange as it seems, the production of one or more (mythical) accounts also occurs in the naming of constellations (catasterism), where the adventures of some humans (heroes), animals (zodiac), or monsters function as a narrative explanation for the placement of their images in the starry sky. In Latin, for instance, we have Hyginus's *Astronomia* (see Zucker, this volume, on catasterism; Smith, this volume, on mythography in Latin), which includes quotations from Greek (for instance, 2.1.1 *arktoi*, "the Bears"; 2.4.5 the *Aletides*), which in turn brings up the wider problem of the translation of concepts and interpretations of myth from one language into another. Less surprising is the creation of accounts whose protagonists are human characters as "first discoverers." For example, we find the satyr Crotus inventing applause (*krotos*), and so, too, though preserved only in Latin sources, the figure Cerasus, inventor of the mixing (*kerasai*) of wine and water (for Crotus, see Ps.-Eratosth. *Cat.* 28; Hyg. *De Astr.* 2.27; *Fab.* 224; his name is found written on Greek vases, among Satyrs and Sileni in a Dionysiac *thiasos*. For Cerasus, see Hyg. *Fab.* 274).

Astronomical figures and their narrative validation presuppose mental mechanisms of great complexity, which go back in time to epochs and cultures that exceed the scope of this analysis. At any rate, one can say that, starting as early as the learned Eratosthenes of Cyrene (3rd c. BCE), there arose a rather extensive mythographical tradition that collected hundreds of accounts of gods, heroes, objects, or the animals associated with them that are placed in the starry sky, with the concomitant naming of the constellation related to the account.

A phenomenon worth noting is the inventive capacity that is found in a poetic work like Ovid's *Metamorphoses*, where one can reasonably suppose that the poet invented or created new accounts or modified existing ones as he wished—in particular, regarding the names of the protagonists—in relative freedom from any possible sources he may have had. In some cases, we can compare stories in which the poet confines himself to changing the names, maintaining their spatial (geographic) locations and preserving their essential narrative structures. For example, the story of Iphis and Anaxarete, set in Salamis on the island of Cyprus, and the Cretan story of another Iphis who changes sex are present in the Hellenistic tradition (perhaps in Nicander or Hermesianax, as can be seen in the versions of Antoninus Liberalis, *Met.* 17 and 39; see Ovid, *Met.* 9.666–797, Iphis and Ianthe; 14.698–761, Iphis and Anaxarete). In Ovid, the geographic placement is the same, but the names of the characters have been changed completely. An instructive case of the inverse process, where the place changes but the names remain the same, is the famous Ovidian version of the legend of Pyramus and Thisbe, which the Latin poet sets in Mesopotamia (4.51–166), whereas the Greek sources place it in Cilicia. The story also serves to explain (as an *aition*) the color of mulberries, while it could have been the story of the eponym of the river Pyramus and of the spring Thisbe in the area of Mallos (southwest Turkey).

Later, Latin collections (see Smith, this volume) will feature hundreds of Greek stories from the enormous but mostly lost output of earlier scholars, poets, and compilers. A valuable text is the *Fabulae* of Hyginus (see Fletcher, this volume) of which one redaction has come down to us, probably epitomized. In it there appears some attempt to explain the names of Greek heroes on the basis of a *Greek* etymology. For instance, in *Fab.* 7, the explanation of names of the Theban heroes Amphion and Zethus is "because [their mother] had given birth along the road" (*amphi hodon . . . eteken*) after having "searched" for a suitable place (*apo tou zētein topon*). A straightforward case is Pyrrha, the "secret" name Achilles had in Scyros, which is explained with "because 'red' is *pyrrhon* in Greek" (*Fab.* 96). More elaborate is the name change (*metonomasia*) of the young Podarces, who was called Priam based on "the fact that he was ransomed" (*apo tou priasthai*) by his sister Hesione (*Fab.* 89).

A few centuries later, another mythographer writing in Latin, Fulgentius (see Nimmo Smith, this volume; Garstad, "On Mythography in the Latin West," this volume), will make ample use of Greek etymologies in his *Mitologiae*, employing a limited knowledge of Greek in a completely free fashion (Wolff and Dain 2013: 194–198, collect more than a hundred, mostly Greek, though some are truly bizarre, such as that for Admetus [1.22, where it is derived from Latin *adire metus*]). A few more examples will suffice (for further discussion, see Hays 2013: 309–333): Hercules is derived from *heroon kleos*, "the glory of heroes" (2.2, *virorum fortium fama*). The example of Odysseus, to which we will return, is derived "as if from *holōn xenos*, or 'a foreign guest of everyone'" (2.8, *quasi olon xenos, id est omnium peregrinus*). Rarer are Latin etymologies, such as Iuno, which is derived from *iuvare* (2.1).

At the end of the western Roman Empire, an extensive summa of ancient wisdom in the Latin language will explicitly carry the title of *Etymologiae sive Origines*, the work of Isidore, a scholar from Seville (6th–7th c. CE; Amsler 1989: 133–165). The wide-ranging principle of etymology, which runs into the fundamental problem of conceptually translating Greek (and even Hebrew) into Latin, is generalized here. Again, one example must suffice: the name of the Umbrians (the local people of modern Umbria) is explained etymologically as deriving from the Greek *ombros*, "rain" (9.2.87, drawn in all likelihood from Pliny, *NH* 3.112). Even the principle of eponomy, which is the discovery (at all costs) of a "founding hero" of a certain geographical or institutional reality, is in this type of study conducted in a systematic manner.

# 7. GENERAL FEATURES
# OF ANCIENT ETYMOLOGIZING

The problem of etymological "science" and the use that ancient mythographers made of it is certainly a considerable one. There can be no doubt that names had significant influence on attempts to give reality some meaning. In particular, personal names (theonyms and anthroponyms, names of gods, heroes, and monsters) stimulated the investigation of analogies (or polarities) that somehow explained or interpreted their significance in relation to the individual, their qualities, or the events of their life. Thus, the practice of *mythologein* could turn to elements contained in the name to illustrate, describe, or narrate the characteristics of the person in question.

The complexity of the relationship between the signifier and the signified, which even today explains the tendency—or temptation—among interpreters to look for allusions to the character's qualities and experiences in the name. The basic idea is that a micro-enunciation can be hidden in the name (Calame 1986: 27–30)—sometimes descriptive, sometimes narrative, or sometimes ominous or prophetic, but always related to the history or the qualities of the bearer. This principle, even if justifiable in the naming of infants or children in accordance with the events surrounding their birth (Moses, Oedipus, Theseus), is not justifiable for the names of adults, unless in the case of *cognomina ex virtute*, such as when Paris received the new name Alexandros because he had defended (*alex-*) the shepherds (*andr-* "man") from their enemies (thus "he received an additional name," *prosōnomasthē*, Apd. 3.150). Otherwise, short of granting personal names a prophetic value (of the *nomen-omen* variety), those that reflect a hero's misfortunes could be considered implicit proof of the bearer's fictional nature. If a young woman is called at birth "she who pays the penalty for the crime," and then as a teenager commits the crime of betraying her father and her city by handing the city over to the enemy, it is logical to suppose that her personal name was invented *for the purpose* of the narrative. Such is the case with the name Pisidice if we understand it as "she who pays the penalty for her crime." But it remains to be explained why the same name was also attributed, even in earlier times, to other heroines who were completely innocent of crime. It is clear that "Pisidice" could be interpreted simply as "she who persuades (*peisi-* from *peithō*) for justice." In the same way, the well-known Polyneices poses problems if the prevailing etymology is correct, since he, like his brother Eteocles, would have an "invented" name.

In some works, the invented element features prominently, motivated by an interest in paradoxography. At times, particularly creative etymologies are engendered through systematic invention. One example will suffice, again concerning the name Odysseus (Ptol. Chennos, *Nova Hist.* 1.9):

> Because Odysseus had big ears (*ōta*), he was initially named *Outis*; but it is also said that on a rainy (*hysai*) day his pregnant mother, since she was no longer able to hold

off, gave birth to him along the side of the road (*odos*), and for this reason he was at the time named *Odys*seus.

In some cases, we are able to find the (intentional) formation of a series of names, the creation of which seems obviously ad hoc; that is, they were invented for the purpose of literary display. I refer, for example, to the names of the twelve Amazons we find in the *Posthomerica*, a late epic poem by Quintus Smyrnaeus (perhaps 4th c. CE). They accompanied Penthesileia on her expedition to help the Trojans after Hector's death, and were all slaughtered by the Achaeans (Meriones, Diomedes, and Achilles himself) together with their queen Penthesileia, herself killed by Achilles. An etymological examination of their names, almost all of which are found only in this poem, reveals an artificial mythopoetic process. In other words, the poet constructs a series of female personal names (one thinks of the nine Muses or of the fifty-one Nereids of Hesiod) based on the simple semantic principle that describes their qualities, in this case, their warlike qualities (Polemousa, Bremousa, Clonie, Derimachia, Derinoe) or the "masculine" gender (Alcibia, Antandra, Evandra, Antibrote, Armotoe, Hippotoe, *Posthom.* 1.42–47) of these warrior-women, and these are added to the traditional names (Hippolyte, Penthesileia, Myrine, and many others) in the context of a rather typical involvement of the Amazons in the Trojan War, of which we find no trace in Homer. The Amazons are mentioned in the *Iliad* only twice (*Il.* 3.189, 6.186), and one reference is connected to a hill in the proximity of the Troad (*Il.* 2.813–814), but the Amazons turn out not to be present in Troy during the war. In the 12th century Tzetzes will explicitly invent the names of twenty Amazons (*Carm. Il.* 3.179–182 and Tz. Schol. on the passage).

In the *Ethnica* of Stephanus of Byzantium (6th c. CE) the principle of *eponymy* of cities and places, the names of which lead back to a personal name or, more precisely, to the founder (who is sometimes suspect, probably invented ad hoc, that is, autoschediastic) is applied systematically. The process is operative even for "historical" foundations, such as the numerous cities named Heraclea and Alexandria (or Washington), but in many cases it is a "mythopoetic" device, where it is obvious that it is the name of the cities that "generate" the name of an "eponymous" hero or heroine (for example, Mycenae, Rome; see Pellizer 1991: 116–117; 1997: 83–84), and not vice versa.

An analogous phenomenon, but completely unique in ancient works, arises with a text falsely attributed to Plutarch, *De Fluviis et Montibus*, where we witness a systematic mythopoesis that accounts for the vast number of real geographic places (rivers and mountains), as well as botanical and mineral items, by fabricating a series of mini-accounts—all of which function as eponyms and produce the renaming (*metonomasia*) of existing rivers and mountains, in addition to validating the origins of a complex reality of magical plants and stones. In extreme cases such as this, the eponym becomes a productive criterion and in a certain sense "produces" new myths, new accounts that do not have a tradition and so fabricate, so to speak, their own etymologies. One example must suffice: a plant is called "Araxa," which means "virgin-hater" in the language of the locals, and this foreign word will become the eponym of the Araxes river (Ps.-Plut. *De*

*Fluv.* 23.2). This name first appears because of a macabre tale of four murdered virgins. As a result, legend holds that the plant, if it is picked by a virgin, bleeds and wilts.

# 8. BRIEF CONCLUSIONS

The process of "investigating etymologies" thus proves to be an extensive and productive mechanism used to form traditional accounts (myths), starting from the first written documentation of poetic texts relating the world of gods and heroes. These begin with "catalogues" (for example, the Nereids), in which personal names are listed that somehow "signify" etymologically the qualities or the affairs of the bearers. Generally, we frequently find etymology being used to explain real, existing entities ("nommer le monde," Delattre 2011), whether geographic (cities, races, peoples, mountains, rivers), or more generally "cultural," seeking the causes (*aitia*) of their names and explaining through narratives—frequently emotional, tragic, or extraordinary—their "truth." Sometimes, this line of investigation can itself generate new myths and create, through invention, personal names that serve only to explain the existence of a place name (e.g., Mycenae, Thebes, Rome).

The "scientific" aspect of these etymologies is certainly not very lofty, and this explains why sometimes the same etymological "science" has been subjected to irony (Socrates himself, Voltaire) or derision, or why from Augustine to Luís Borges (Jurado 2002; Eco 1993: 90–95, speaks of a "furore etimologico"), there has been expressed justifiable uncertainty about the utility of this line of research into the "true meanings" of words, especially of the proper names of gods, heroes and heroines, and cities—if for no other reason than that the very word "etymology," if analyzed "etymologically," proves to be not much more than a tautology ("true speech" means almost nothing). Furthermore, etymologies are often reduced to a mere translation of a simple lexeme, or of a compound of multiple lexemes, in a different "original" language. By examining the methods of this practice in Greek and Roman mythographical works, we have tried to highlight the complex mechanisms that lie at the heart of this extensive search to give names to the world. Rather than limit ourselves to making fun of the results (sometimes superficial, at times ridiculous, and often completely outlandish) of these secular attempts to make sense of the ancient stories of the past, we have preferred to analyze the functions of etymologies as generative structures that are present and widespread in a great number of accounts the Greek and Latin tradition has passed down to western culture over the centuries.

At present, we lack a complete inventory of all the etymologies produced in antiquity—especially in late antiquity—that somehow "explain" the origin and meaning of the names of gods, heroes, humans, and monsters, male and female, in the vast legacy of stories that have been passed down to us, whether in mythographical texts or in numerous other works. These include not only lexicographical and etymological works, but also geographical, historical, and scholarly ventures as well. Would research of such a kind be useful? Certainly, it would be rather intriguing, if we were to attempt to catalogue all the oddities that the quest for "truth" in names has suggested to learned Greeks and Romans—and which today could suggest to modern scholars, who sometimes seem to compete with the ancients in devising bizarre and sometimes unbelievable interpretations. One example will suffice for all: Anchises, etymologically, should be interpreted as "he who stands nearby, *ankhi-*, to *Isis*"! (*Room's Class. Dict.* 1982: 48).

## FURTHER READING

As mentioned earlier, there is no complete inventory of etymologies from antiquity, and the same goes for etymologies of mythical names and figures. Similarly, there is no comprehensive study of how etymologies function throughout the mythical storyworld. A good starting point now is Sluiter (2015), which embraces the multiplicity of etymological interpretations by taking several myths as case studies for how etymologies are "tools for thinking." Kanavou (2015) is a comprehensive study of Homeric names and includes a number of ancient etymologies of figures tied to the Trojan Cycle. Other studies of etymology in early Greek literature include Sulzberger (1926); Risch (1947); and Salvadore (1987); the latter also considers Plato's *Cratylus*. On that seminal text, see Silverman (1992) and, especially, Sedley (2003). Some early Greek mythographers employed etymology, especially Hellanicus (see Fowler 2013: esp. 687–688).

Discussion of etymologies in Hellenistic scholarship on Homer, some dealing with myth, may be found Schironi (2018: 340–376) on Aristarchus; and see Lallot (1991a, 1991b); Apollodorus of Athens, who may have written a separate work called *Etymologies*, explored etymologies as revealing the true nature and powers of divinity in his fragmentary *On the Gods*, for which see the brief remarks at Pfeiffer (1968: 260–263). On etymology in the context of Stoic allegoresis (including Cornutus) see the two chapters by Ramelli in this volume. Turning to the Roman world, a fundamental study is O'Hara (1996), which comprehensively treats Vergil but offers an excellent overview of etymological wordplay from Homer onward, with further bibliography (7–41). A useful guide to Ovid's etymological explorations, with some attention to myth, is Michalopoulos (2001). Amsler (1989) treats etymology in late antiquity and into the medieval period.

## REFERENCES

Amsler, Mark E. 1989. *Etymology and Grammatical Discourse in Late Antiquity and the Early Middle Ages*. Amsterdam: J. Benjamins.

Billerbeck, Margarethe, ed. and trans. 2006–2017. *Stephani Byzantii Ethnika*. Berlin and Boston: De Gruyter.

Blank, David. 2008. "Varro and the Epistemological Status of Etymology." *Histoire Épistémologie Langage* 30: 49–73.

Broggiato, Maria. 2003. "The Use of Etymology as an Exegetical Tool in Alexandria and Pergamum: Some Examples from Homeric Scholia." In *Etymologia: Studies in Ancient Etymology*, edited by Christos Nifadopoulos, 65–70. Munich: Nodus.

Calame, Claude. 1985. "L'antroponimo greco come enunciato narrativo; appunti linguistici e semiotici." In *Mondo classico: Percorsi possibili*, edited by Franco Baratta and Franca Mariani, 27–37. Ravenna, Italy: Longo.

Calame, Claude. 1986. "Le nom d'Œdipe." In *Edipo: Il teatro greco e la cultura europea*, edited by Bruno Gentili and Roberto Pretagostini, 395–403. Rome: Edizioni dell'Ateneo.

Clay, Jenny. 1972. "The Planktai and Moly: Divine Naming and Knowing in Homer." *Hermes* 100: 127–131.

Delattre, Charles. 2011. *Pseudo-Plutarque: Nommer le monde*. Villeneuve d'Ascq, France: Presses du Septentrion.

Eco, Umberto. 1993. *La ricerca della lingua perfetta nella cultura europea*. Rome: Laterza = *The Search for the Perfect Language*. Translated by James Fentress. Oxford: Blackwell, 1995.

Fowler, Robert L. 2000. *Early Greek Mythography*. Vol. 1: *Text and Introduction*. Oxford: Oxford University Press.

Fowler, Robert L. 2006. "How to Tell a Myth: Genealogy, Mythology, Mythography." *Kernos* 19: 35–46.

Fowler, Robert L. 2013. *Early Greek Mythography*. Vol. 2: *Commentary*. Oxford: Oxford University Press.

Genette, Gérard. 1976. *Mimologiques: Voyages en Cratylie*. Paris: Seuil.

Gibson, Craig A. 2013. "True or False? Greek Myth and Mythography in the Progymnasmata." In Trzaskoma and Smith, *Writing Myth*, 289–308.

Hays, Gregory. 2013. "Fulgentius the Mythographer?" In Trzaskoma and Smith, *Writing Myth*, 309–333.

Heubeck, Alfred, Stephanie West, and J. B. Hainsworth, eds. 1988. *A Commentary on Homer's Odyssey*. Vol. 1. Oxford: Oxford University Press.

Irigoin, Jean. 1991. "Du jeu verbal à la recherche étymologique: Homère et les scholies homériques." *Revue de Philologie* 65: 127–134.

Jouan, François. 1978. "Nomen-Omen chez Eschyle." In *Problèmes du mythe et de son interprétation (Actes du Coll. de Chantilly, 24–25 avril 1976)*, edited by Jean Hani, 69–87. Paris: Les Belles Lettres.

Jowett, Benjamin. 1892. *The Dialogues of Plato*. Vol. 1. Oxford: Oxford University Press.

Jurado, Francisco García. 2002. "Lengua perfecta e inutilidad etimológica: Entre San Augustín y Jorge Luis Borges." *Variaciones Borges* 14: 23–38.

Kanavou, Nikoletta. 2015. *The Names of Homeric Heroes: Problems and Interpretations*. Berlin: De Gruyter.

Kraus, Manfred. 1987. *Name und Sache: Ein Problem im frühgriechischen Denken*. Amsterdam: B. R. Grüner.

Lallot, Jean. 1991a. "Ἐτυμολογία: L'étimologie en Grèce ancienne d'Homère aux Alexandrins." In *Discours étymologiques: Actes du Colloque International organisé à l'occasion du centenaire de la naissance de W. von Wartburg*, edited by Jean-Pierre Chambon and Georges Lüdi, 135–148. Tübingen: Niemeyer.

Lallot, Jean. 1991b. "L'étymologie chez les grammairiens grecs: Principes et pratique." *Revue de Philologie* 65: 135–148.

Lazzeroni, Romano. 1997. "Lingua degli dei e lingua degli uomini." In *Scritti scelti di Romano Lazzeroni*, edited by Tristano Bolelli and Saverio Sani, 209–235. Pisa, Italy: Pacini Editore.

Loraux, Nicole. 1988. "Poluneikes eponumos: Le nom des fils d'Oedipe, entre épopée et tragédie." In *Métamorphoses du mythe en Grèce antique*, edited by Claude Calame, 151–166. Geneva: Labor et Fides.

Martin, Charles. 2004. *Ovid*, Metamorphoses. New York: W. W. Norton.

Michalopoulos, Andreas. 2001. *Ancient Etymologies in Ovid's Metamorphoses*. Leeds, UK: Francis Cairns.

Mirto, Maria S. 2007. "Etimologia del nome e identità eroica: Interpretazioni umane e divine." *Il Nome nel testo* 9: 221–229.

O'Hara, James J. 1996. *True Names: Vergil and Alexandrian Tradition of Etymological Wordplay*. Ann Arbor: Michigan University Press.

Pagès Cebrian, Joan. 2007. "*Mythographus Homericus*: Estudi i Edició Comentada." Diss. Universitate Autònoma de Barcelona.

Patterson, Lee E. 2013. "Geographers as Mythographers: the Case of Strabo." In Trzaskoma and Smith, *Writing Myth*, 201–221.

Pellizer, Ezio. 1991. *La peripezia dell'eletto: Racconti eroici della Grecia antica*. Palermo, Sellerio.

Pellizer, Ezio. 1993. "La mitografia." In *Lo spazio letterario della Grecia antica*, vol. 1.2, edited by Giuseppe Cambiano, Luciano Canfora, and Diego Lanza, 283–303. Rome: Salerno.

Pellizer, Ezio. 1997. "Miti di fondazione e infanti abbandonati." In *Filosofia, storia, immaginario mitologico*, edited by Marcella Guglielmo and Gian Franco Gianotti, 81–93. Alessandria: Dell'Orso.

Pfeiffer, Rudolf. 1968. *History of Classical Scholarship from the Beginnings to the End of the Hellenistic Age*. Oxford: Clarendon Press.

Pontani, Filippomaria. 2005. *Questioni omeriche sulle allegorie di Omero in merito agli dei*. Pisa, Italy: ETS.

Ramelli, Ilaria. 2003. *Anneo Cornuto. Compendio di teologia greca*. Milan: Bompiani.

Reinberg, Consuelo. 1981. "Etimologia in Eschilo: Modalità e significato della riflessione linguistica in un testo poetico." *Sandalion* 4: 31–57.

Risch, Ernst. 1947. "Namendeutungen und Worterklärung bei den ältesten griechischen Dichtern." In *Eumusia: Festgabe für Ernst Howald zum sechzigsten Geburtstag am 20. April 1947*, 72–91. Erlenbach-Zürich: Rentsch.

Salvadore, Marcello. 1987. *Il nome, la persona: Saggio sull'etimologia antica*. Geneva: Università di Genova.

Schironi, Francesca. 2018. *The Best of the Grammarians: Aristarchus of Samothrace on the Iliad*. Ann Arbor: University of Michigan Press.

Sedley, David. 2003. *Plato's* Cratylus. Cambridge: Cambridge University Press.

Silverman, Allan. 1992. "Plato's *Cratylus*: The Naming of Nature and the Nature of Naming." In *Oxford Studies in Ancient Philosophy*. Vol. 10, edited by Julia Annas, 25–71. Oxford: Clarendon Press.

Sluiter, Ineke. 2015. "Ancient Etymology: A Tool for Thinking." In *Brill's Companion to Ancient Greek Scholarship*, edited by Franco Montanari, Stefanos Matthaios, and Antonios Rengakos, 896–921. Leiden: Brill.

Stafford, Emma, and Judith Herrin, eds. 2005. *Personification in the Greek World: From Antiquity to Byzantium*. Aldershot, UK: Ashgate.

Sulzberger, Max. 1926. "ΟΝΟΜΑ ΕΠΩΝΥΜΟΝ. Les noms propres chez Homère et dans la mythologie grecque." *Revue des Études Grecques* 39: 381–447.

Trzaskoma, Stephen M., and R. Scott Smith, eds. 2013. *Writing Myth: Mythography in the Ancient Word*. Leuven: Peeters.

Wolff, Étienne, and Philippe Dain, eds. 2013. *Fulgence: Mythologies*. Villeneuve d'Ascq: Presses du Septentrion.

# CHAPTER 27

..........................................................................................

# CATASTERISMS

..........................................................................................

## ARNAUD ZUCKER

AMONG the learned practices and the elaborate products of the Hellenistic mythography taken up in Latin culture, the traditions classified under the name of "catasterisms" enjoy a special status. This term actually covers three distinct notions, defining at the same time a form of divine intervention, a type of narrative, and a delimited corpus. Indeed, it refers to (a) the result of a divine process of transposition into heaven of heroes, animals, or objects; (b) the mythological account of such a transposition; (c) the astromythological reference book attributed to Eratosthenes (3rd c. BCE) that provides the description of all the constellations with the history of their origin and the related tradition. These three levels combine different aspects of mythology (mythology, mythography, and literature), making up an original discourse that accompanies the development of astronomical knowledge and imagination significantly stimulated by the popular and learned work of Aratus (4th–3rd c. BCE), the *Phaenomena*.

The complexity of this cultural formula is inscribed in the very history of the Greek term "catasterism," which has ambiguous origins (Santini 1998): even though the cultural reception links it to *kat-asterizein* (arrange in constellation), it is probable that the root is actually *kata-stērizein* (fix). In fact, the title given to the collection of Eratosthenes (in the Suda) is *katastērigmos*, normally associated with the verb *stērizein*, and referring precisely in the first literary occurrence to the celestial context: Zeus "fixed the rainbow in a cloud" (*Il.* 11.28 and 4.443). The fundamental operation appears to be natural or cosmic and to take part in the formation of the world, whose stars are original elements. This opportunistic shift or confusion can be seen as a form of etymological motivation that has conflated the two meanings of "fixing permanently" and "placing among the stars." The often periphrastic formulas used to signal the constitution of constellations, both in Greek and Latin (Bartalucci 1989), bear witness to these two options. But this pivot term between divine gesture and cultural construction is also used to refer to *the drawing of constellations* by astronomers on spheres, which artistically reproduced the founding act of the gods. This ambivalence is characteristic of Greek "poetic" thought, which considers divine activity and the human narrative of this activity as analogous or even cooperative processes. Catasterization is therefore not a single operation, but a series of heterogeneous interventions, carried out by gods, astronomers, and poets (Zucker 2011a).

## 1. THE CATASTERISMOGRAPHIC TRADITION

The collection of Eratosthenes's *Catasterisms*, which has come down to us in epitomized form, in two distinct but very close recensions—known as *Epitome* and *Fragmenta Vaticana* (Robert 1878; Olivieri 1897a, b; Rehm 1899)—clearly and durably organizes the three meanings and the three levels mentioned. It presents itself as an astronomical catalogue of the traditional constellations, which most probably accompanied a series of illustrations, since the initial sentence of each chapter always contains a deictic reference to a picture (Pàmias 2014: 196; Zucker 2016a). This illustrated mythographical companion deals with a well-defined and necessarily limited corpus. The collection of Eratosthenes, as the Latin version of this work composed by Hyginus (1st c. BCE) and the further texts derived from it show, offers forty-two chapters devoted to a constellation, to which are added a chapter on the planets and another one on the Milky Way. Some chapters include minor asterisms (either independent of the main figure like the donkeys in Cancer or Crater and the raven in Hydra, or part of it, such as the head of Medusa in the hand of Perseus or the serpent held by Ophiuchus). The work has a threefold dimension—iconographic, mythographical, and astronomical—because following the images it proposes (1) an identification of the character, sometimes pointing out postural details or attributes of the figure; (2) a mythological episode related to it and leading to its catasterization; and (3) a precise description of all its stars and where they are situated in the figure. The astronomical significance of this text is indisputable, and the number of stars listed by Eratosthenes (732) is close to that of the catalogue of Ptolemy four centuries later (1025), and the general depiction is quite similar (Zucker 2016b: 1065–1157). The corpus of celestial figures is imposed by previous astronomical tradition and does not result from free selection: the canonical list contains twenty animals (with five minor asterisms), fifteen heroic characters, six objects (with two minor asterisms), and one river.

Relying on an abundant literary documentation, Eratosthenes aims to systematically identify the members of this motley cluster, offering mythological narratives for each figure and accounting for its stellar genesis. Unlike other mythological narratives, catasterismic tales, as *ekphraseis* of the constellations, link a heroic figure with an ever-present reality of the physical world, and not only a trace—like the fountain of Hippocrene or a footprint of Heracles—but the very hero (or a famous object), pinned in the sky and perpetually in motion. Thus, in the opening chapter of Eratosthenes's *Catasterisms*, the text briefly relates the myth of Callisto, up until the moment Zeus raises her to heaven and names the constellation "Bear:" it is Callisto who still dominates the heavenly vault, and whose disposition and stars are described in the last paragraph. The sequence is therefore a peculiar and distinct mythographical procedure; it does not develop the story of a hero (heroic biography) but argues for the identification of a figure who is already present in the sky but generally anonymous—or, rather, of a traditional *picture*, intending to explain why (s)he or it has been brought to heaven and eternally exhibited before our eyes. The narrative order does not follow a heroic chronology, but a rhetorical program that seeks to uncover the identity of the image by finding a name for the image and a motivation for its presence in the heavens. Eratosthenes's text was progressively aggregated to the Aratean tradition of the *Phaenomena* (Martin 1956: 51–53) and passed on to Latin (Le Bourdelès 1985). Indeed, Hyginus (1st c. BCE) proposes a Latin version in books 2 and 3 of his *Astronomy*, very close to the unabridged original (Cameron 2004: 33–34, 42). The later catasterismic literature, comprising adaptations, scholia (in Scholia to Aratus and Scholia to Germanicus) or commentaries (in Aratus Latinus) more or less derives from Eratosthenes's opus (Pàmias and Zucker 2013: lxxxii–lxxvii).

## 2. A Divine Promotion of What?

What kind of mythological process is catasterization? Apparently, the word refers to a god's *transfer* to heaven of a hero (such as Orion or Perseus) or an object (like the Crown or the Lyre). If many deities in the classical pantheon (Artemis, Athena, Hera, Apollo, Dionysus) are endowed with this power, two gods are distinguished by their major roles in animating heaven: Zeus, who is responsible for three-quarters of the catasterizations, and Hermes, who stages the entire night sky and "who organized the arrangement of the constellations between them" (Erat., *Cat.* 20), signing his work with the initial of his father's name (Zeus, or Dia), by placing a Delta in the sky.

This does not yet constitute "a well-represented category of metamorphosis" (Cameron 2004: 22) since cosmic beings preserve their terrestrial appearance, such as Perseus or Callisto, who had already been changed into a Bear, before his celestial promotion. They are subtracted from the sublunary world and, at the same time, immortalized in the sky. Unlike metamorphosis, which preserves the human mind while introducing a displacement of form and continuity of function and temperament, catasterization specifically aims at illustrating the character in its recognizable and everlasting state. Far from blurring the traces, it thus serves memory, both of the hero and of men. Whereas metamorphosis is often the solution to a dead end (Dupont 1972), catasterization is the benevolent epilogue of a drama. Its function, often emphasized in the texts, is to protect from oblivion or reward a character's virtue, or to compensate for his or her misfortune by honorary reparation, as Ovid points out: "The gods see righteous deeds" (*di pia facta vident, Fast.* 2.117). The reasons given for such divine action are almost always positive: divine intervention is justified by the intent of honoring the memory of a hero (*mnēmē/memoria*) and of rewarding him or her (*timē/beneficium, honos, praemium*) for the courage shown. However, it is also sometimes stressed as punishment, as for Cassiopeia, whose *impietas* (Hyg., *Astr.* 2.10) leads her to appear in heaven upside down, or for the criminal Triopas, identified with Ophiuchus, who is consequently exposed to the Serpent (Hyg., *Astr.* 2.14.3). The catalogue of "constellar" heroes is not, indeed, a selection of the *crème* of the heroes since the figures, the contexts, and some names are already established and pertain to tradition. The motivation given for the presence of heroes in the celestial museum has therefore to be flexible.

This process cannot be regarded as an *apotheosis* either. Admittedly, Hyginus's list of "mortal heroes who have been made immortal" (*Fab.* 224) largely corresponds to the list of constellations: Hercules, Dionysus, Castor and Pollux, Perseus (*in stellas receptus*), Ariadne, Callisto (*in Septentrionem relata*), Cynosoura (*in Septentrionem relata*), Crotos (*in stellam Sagittarium* [*sic*]), Icarus and Erigone (*in stellas, Icarus in Arcturi, Erigone in Virginis signum*), Ganymedes (*in Aquario duodecim signorum*), Myrtilus (as Charioteer), Asclepius, Pan, Ino, Melicertes. But in some cases, the celestial ascent is achieved without divine intervention, and the text indicates that the character "is received in heaven" (Ovid, *Fasti* 2.202 and *Met.* 2.529) or even that he spontaneously "ascended to heaven" (Erat., *Cat.* 18, 19; Ovid, *Fasti* 3.808 and *Met.* 5.617). Nor can this interpretation of a divinization process be valid for Procyon, Argo, or other celestial objects. Whatever its identity (Nile, Eridanus, or Phasis) the River cannot physically be the terrestrial river, nor the Triangle be the Nile delta.

As a matter of fact, catasterization is not even a *concrete transfer* as the celestial characters are often considered and sometimes explicitly described as a simulacrum. According to the frequently used terminology, they are only drawings, in the celestial background, structuring a cluster of stars: an image (*eidōlon, figura, effigies*), an imitation (*mimēma*), a copy (*typos, formatio*), a pattern (*skhēma, species*), or a picture (*eikōn, diatypōsis*) of a mythological character or object (Santoni 1989; Pàmias and Zucker 2013: lxxiii–lxxiv). The different options for describing this process already appear in Aratus's *Phaenomena*, whose purpose is to describe constellations and meteorological phenomena: Zeus fixed (*estērixen*) the signs in the sky and distinguished the constellations (lines 10–11); Dionysus placed the crown (lines 71–72), but the Virgin entered heaven on her own (line 134), and only the name (*onoma*) of Cepheus rose in the sky (line 181), where the image (*agalma*) of Andromeda is to be found (line 197).

Behind the actions of the gods loom the hands of men who have designated and formed the constellations over time (Arat. 370–378): the ancient astronomers are to be credited for the picture of the Dolphin in heaven (Hyg., *Astr.* 2.17.3), and the mathematician Conon "found" a hair loop near the Lion (namely, Berenice's Hair: Hyg., *Astr.* 2.24). This ambivalence, though logically strange, is a form of complementarity or cooperation: "Indeed, since the hero had been suitably represented as a hunter, people also wanted to express (*significare*) an element of context. This is why they represented (*finxerunt*) the hare fleeing before his feet. Some say it was established there (*constitutum*) by Mercury" (Hyg., *Astr.* 2.33.1). The ambiguous or "shared" character of this operation is also to be found in the fact that, oftentimes (for instance, Hyg., *Astr.* 2.9, 23, 36, 38), it is expressed through the verb *numerare* (*inter astra*) referring to the integration in a series, and not a concrete transfer.

In this equivocal construction, the physical status of the constellation is not stabilized, and the process is not always reduced, as Martin (2002a) thinks, to "the representation in the sky of a character by a cluster of stars." From the lack of standardization and regular "procedure," one might conclude that the precise link between the terrestrial and the heavenly reality matters less than the statement of a *sort of* identity and a narrative continuity between the two conditions. Eratosthenes even dares to justify the presence of a second bear in the heaven (the little Bear, *Cat.* 2) by explicitly mentioning Artemis's wish to "duplicate the tribute" paid to Callisto. One can wonder about this scandal (ontological duplication) or simply recognize that the notion of identity is rather flexible in this context, and probably in other mythographical accounts as well. The shift that led the planets "belonging to divinities" to be assimilated into them reflects a similar looseness. Heracles can be tripled (on Olympus, in Hades, as the constellation of the "Kneeler"); or Zeus represented under several avatars (Eagle, Taurus, Swan)—as he has his tomb in Crete (Callim. *Hymn* 1, 8–9)! Although they are mobile by virtue of their nocturnal and annual movement, the celestial figures are also frozen and part of the so-called fixed stars. The heroic figure thus appears to be rather a narrative label or a reminder for the cluster of stars, and its connection is chiefly an opportunity to fashion new stories or to bring back old ones.

The sky or, rather, pictures that can be projected thereon, offers an exceptional showcase for an ideological promotion. Although this use seems to have been limited in the case of Eratosthenes to some Ptolemaic references (Pàmias 2004), the advertising potential provided by this celestial display has been exploited since the introduction of Berenice's Hair by the astronomer Conon and the imperial apotheoses throughout the later history of the representation and revision of the constellations in heaven invaded by Christian imaginary (with the *Coelum Stellatum Christianum* by Julius Schiller, published in 1627) and by scientific instruments populating the southern hemisphere in the 17th and 18th centuries (Ridpath 1988; Zucker 2016b: 280–296).

## 3. The Astromythic Program

Each catasterism ensues from a separate intervention, and one can doubt that this apparent tinkering results in a unity and expresses a consistent conception. Yet, despite the disconnected nature of the divine operations of catasterization, the general picture has a certain logic, reinforced in the course of the astronomical and iconographic tradition, since identities are simplified and standardized, as seen in the Scholia to Germanicus, which provide fewer identifications than Hyginus's *Astronomy*. Two networks stand out in heaven, one divine, the other heroic. The first relates three main territories occupied by characters (or symbols) linked to Zeus, Artemis, and Athena. Zeus is, indeed, particularly prevalent in heaven through avatars (Taurus, Swan) or characters involved in his history and linked, in particular, to his advent, from his birth (the Goat) to his reign (Eagle, Capricorn, Altar, Aquarius, Delta). In Eratosthenes's *Catasterisms*, more than half of the constellations (22 of 42) belong to the "cycle" of the king of the gods. Alongside the cycle of Zeus, there are two main divine cycles. The one of Artemis mainly stages two great myths, that of Callisto (Great Bear, Little Bear, Boötes) and that of Orion (Orion, Scorpio, Dog, Procyon, Hare, Pleiades), in which the goddess plays a major role and to which one can add the myth of Hippe, sometimes identified with the constellation of the Horse. This cycle seems to be connected to the idea of punishment for excessive conduct, which in all three cases involves rape. The second focuses on the character of Perseus, whose protector is Athena, but it also includes two other constellations: Argo and the Charioteer. By contrast, it is made up of positive figures that embody a civilizing mission, and are rewards for some legitimate boldness or ambition. The divine network seems to underline a balance between two complementary virgins (Athena and Artemis), on the one hand, and the male fertility principle (Zeus), on the other, as an oscillation between two types of power that share the inheritance of Ouranos. Besides, owing to the primitive character of "starry" Ouranos (*Il.* 4.44), all celestial figures belong to heroic times and predate the Trojan War.

In terms of mythographical potential, the constellations naturally fall into two categories: "closed" figures, which have a proper name that precisely identifies them (like Perseus or Orion), and "open" figures, which have a generic name (like the Boötes or the Centaur). The latter are far more numerous, since there are only six onomastically identified figures (Cepheus, Cassiopeia, Andromeda, Perseus, Orion, Argo). Even when they seem clearly determined, for example, the Bears or Aquarius, anonymous figures are never univocally fixed. The constraints are therefore reduced, and catasterismic narratives, in accordance with the general mythographical practice, which aims at compiling rather than normalizing, integrate, on several levels, the variants of the tradition: in the identification and in the unfolding of the tale. Far from seeking to establish a single identity, the texts take advantage of the generic entry to collect all the candidates that tradition has associated with the figure. Even in the undoubtedly reduced form of the *Epitome* of Eratosthenes, this savvy choice of multiplicity is perceptible, since in seven chapters we find various identifications (Little Bear, Taurus, Horse, Eagle, Sagittarius, Dog, River), and up to three for the "Horse" (ch. 8: horse of the Helicon, Pegasus, Hippe). In Hyginus's *Astronomy*, only seven of the thirty-six "open" constellations are related to a single heroic character (Cygnus, Cancer, Scorpion, Sea Monster, Altar, Hydra, Southern Fish).

All the other chapters afford an opportunity for a competition between multiple candidates introduced by the tradition that are surely prior to Eratosthenes and Aratus: three candidates for the Twins and the Charioteer, five for the Virgin and Ophiuchus, and so on. The "Kneeler" (Hercules) testifies well to this intense activity of erudite deciphering of image and mythographical variation. For this constellation, about which Aratus says that "the image (*eidōlon*) is like a man who suffers," and that "no one can clearly designate or say which is the person bent on which task" (lines 64–65), Hyginus introduces no fewer than seven heroes and nine scenes of effort or suffering, often specifying the warrant of the identification (*Astr.* 2.6): Hercules killing the dragon (Eratosthenes), Ceteus lamenting (Araethus), Theseus and the rock of Troezen

(Hegesianax), Thamyris imploring (anon.), Orpheus murdered (anon.), Hercules fighting against the Ligures (Aeschylus), Ixion (anon.), Prometheus (anon.). This compilation, which testifies to the role of the Alexandrian mythographer-astronomer in the selection (the dominant tradition is ascribed to him), shows that the exegesis of the constellation album constitutes a real playground and mythographical emulation for poets and historians. The number of identities of the Kneeler is indeed much greater; it can be increased to fifteen nominees, if we take into account the rest of the known literature and the heroes not listed by Hyginus: Talas (or Talos), Salmoneus, Sisyphus, Perseus, Atlas, Marsyas, Chiron, Tantalus, and "Uranoscopus" (Boll 1903: 108, 260–263, 268, 278). But in later literature directly derived from this tradition (Scholia to Aratus and Aratus Latinus), this abundance tends to be reduced, as for Ophiuchus, for which only the identification with Asclepius is preserved among the five proposed by Hyginus (Carnabon, Hercules, Triopas, Phorbas, Asclepius). In general, Latin terminology tends to specify certain Greek figures and to reduce their identities, preferring "Swan" to Bird, "Eridanus" to River, "Pegasus" to Horse, and "Heracles" to Kneeler (Le Boeuffle 1973; Bishop 2016). This evolution characterizes both astronomical literature and mythographical tradition.

The mythographical narrative itself develops a particular type of etiology: it does not care to rationalize the myth but to justify the exceptional character of the figure and the reason for this celestial honor, mentioning famous rituals (for the Charioteer and the Altar) or practices of worship (Dolphin) to motivate the selection. It does not seek to systematically develop the hero's biography, but chiefly develops the episode suggested by the picture through its posture (for instance, Andromeda attached to the rock, the Cygnus taking flight, the Taurus charging, the Aries deprived of its skin), which is not always the ultimate instant of his career. The visible presence of the stars in heaven perhaps adds to the authority of the history associated with them. It is noteworthy that never does Hyginus—and Ovid only once (in *Fast.* 5.604)—designate these narratives by the term of *fabula*, always using the word *historia* (Bartalucci 1989: 363–364). But the catasterismic narrative does not always limit itself to the mere justification of the name, and the nature, structure and content vary greatly, as does the length of the chapters, ranging from 27 words for Procyon to 834 for Boötes in the *Astronomy*. Hyginus is very elliptical (196 words in all) in the chapters concerning the episodes of Andromeda (Cepheus, Cassiopeia, Andromeda, Cetus) and Medusa (Perseus), and of the history of Perseus described as a *notissima historia* (*Astr.* 2.9); and the main part of Hyginus's chapter on the Lion (*Astr.* 2.24) is devoted to Berenice, sister and wife of Ptolemy II, and to her "Lock of hair" (*Coma Berenices*) located in the tail of the Lion.

The unfolding of the narrative can be interspersed with variations, or it may comprise scholarly details that are irrelevant to the identification issue (or the astronomical perspective), revealing its strong interdependence with the rest of the mythographical tradition, as in Hyginus's chapter on Argo (*Astr.* 2.37):

> According to some, it was called in Greek Argo because of its rapidity; according to others, because Argos invented it. It was the first ship on the sea, according

to many accounts, and it was above all for this reason that it was represented in stars. According to Pindar, this ship was built in a city of Magnesia called Demetrias. According to Callimachus, it was on the same territory, near the temple of Apollo Actius . . . Homer explains that this place is indeed on the territory of Thessaly.

The mythographical use of the traditional data in the catasterismic literature, as it appears in the *Astronomy*, is closer to the practice of selection and the miscellany of scholarly notations than to heroic mythography, such as the Pseudo-Apollodorus's *Library* or Hyginus's *Fabulae*. The narratives incorporate a large number of cultic (on Panathenaea, Dionysia, sacrifices, fertility rites, abstinence from fish, the rod of doctors or athletic games), technical (2.2.1, 2.4, 2.12.1, 2.37), or iconographic etiologies (2.17.3, 2.41), already widely present in Eratosthenes.

# 4. The Use of Sources

Such compilations are based on considerable documentation in their archiving work. The sources of Eratosthenes preserved in the *Catasterisms* (21, of which 6 are absent from Hyginus) or represented in the version of Hyginus (40) comprise poets, historians, philosophers, and include rare texts such as the *Naxica* of Aglaosthenes, *Heracles* of Antisthenes the Socratic, *Elegies on Love* of Artemidorus, and *On Justice* of Heraclides Ponticus. These sources are generally shared by the two authors and referenced in the same chapters (see Zucker 2015: 104–119): Euripides (6/6), Hesiod (4/4), Aratus (4/4), Pherecydes (3/3), Aeschylus (3/4), Aglaosthenes (2/3), and so forth. The catasterismic sections of the *Aratus Latinus* retain most of these references, adding Latin ones such as Ovid and, above all, Nigidius Figulus (for his *Sphaera*) quoted nine times in the *Scholia to Germanicus*. The crucial pair of texts (Eratosthenes/Hyginus) sometimes preserves otherwise unknown variants, such as, in *Cat.* 1 (and *Astr.* 2.1), a version of the myth of Callisto by the comic poet Amphis (Henrichs 1987). But most parts of this mythographical patchwork are anonymous and introduced by frequent and vague discourse markers (*legetai, phasi/fertur, dicitur, existimatur*). Despite some syntactic or stylistic clues (Pàmias 2014), it is difficult to determine both the limits of the borrowings attributable to the cited sources and the precise content of the original texts. Hyginus seems to be a faithful witness to the mythographical practice of Eratosthenes, and his work mentions many authors who are actually "involved" in the Eratosthenian legacy, the order of appearance of the common authors being always the same in both texts (Zucker 2015). Hyginus conceives his catalogue of astronomical myths as a whole and distributes matter and information, as is proved by the numerous internal references (33) referring either below (*quo posterius [plura] dicemus*, 2.1.2, 2.2.2, 2.4.4, 2.5.3, 2.30) or above (*ut supra diximus*, 2.1.1, 2.21.2, 2.25.2). Yet it does not aim at any standardizing of myths or at constructing a module that would make it possible to produce a coherent and unified narrative from divergent traditions, putting the polyphony of tradition before the readability of the plot. This is all the more astonishing because the author is probably the same as that of the *Fabulae*, to whom the text of *Astronomy* apparently refers when dealing with Perseus and Phrixus. The two mythographers, even though they are responsible for the choice of the transmitted identifications and variants, do not adopt a critical position on them, unlike classical authors, who often use mythological narrative as an opportunity for competition and exegetical quarreling. At most, one notes the criticism reported by Eratosthenes of the identification of the Horse as Pegasus "insofar as the figure does not bear wings" (*Cat*.18), and the debate on the anatomy of Sagittarius (*Cat*. 28), where he bears witness to a traditional dispute but does not take a personal position. The only two objections formulated by Hyginus, and likely to have been in the Eratosthenian original, are philological and concern the origin of the name Phoenice (*Astr.* 2.2.1) and the etymology of *aidōs*, related by "uneducated persons" to the name of Hades (2.12).

# 5. THE RELATIONSHIP BETWEEN CATASTERISMIC MYTHS AND ASTRONOMICAL DATA

Is there any astronomical relevancy in the myths selected by the catasterismic literature? The astrothetic part of all the chapters, delineating the number and position of the stars, proves the astronomical and scientific nature of this literature, which is undisputable in the case of the learned Eratosthenes. Beyond generic motivation (the enhancement of a character), we must therefore consider the hypothesis that, at least in some cases, the identification and the myth attached to a celestial figure may have been motivated by the situation or the astrophysical context of the constellation. Astronomers are indeed supposed to be responsible, even without any common and systematic program, for identifying or progressively "inventing" the constellations (*Astr.* 2.14.5). The mythographer has no hold on the repertory of the figures, most of which are inherited from Mesopotamian astronomy, and already defined in the literature, but it is possible that in the choice of specific heroes (for example, Andromeda or Orion) or in the selection of candidates (open figures) or episodes, physical reality did play a role. The investigation of the coherence between image, physical situation, and narrative is complex, because of the nonsystematic formation of the celestial representation and the obscure and transcultural origin of the constellations, the Babylonian substratum being itself composite and largely devoid, in its choices and arrangements, of any clear logic. The Great Bear illustrates this complexity well: it is a duplicated constellation, a figure absurdly endowed with a long tail and which "spies on Orion" in epic (*Il.* 18.488; *Od.* 5.274), although no relation between the two figures is ever reported in astronomical literature (Zucker 2011b).

It is clear, however, that the stellar context often determines the identification and the narrative proposed. The grouping in the same boreal sector of the Andromeda family (Cassiopeia, Cepheus, Andromeda) and Perseus is not the result of mere chance, nor is the remoteness of the Cetus (the sea monster) in the southern part, or the identification of the horse that shares a common star with Andromeda as Pegasus (Hyg., *Astr.* 3.10.1). The position of the Dragon under the foot of the Kneeler (or Heracles), the proximity of the Bears and Boötes (or Arctophylax), of the Dog and Orion, of the Southern Fish and the Water Stream, or of the Altar and the Centaur most probably oriented the identification of the figures through the possibility of making up a mythical narrative that could join them in the sky. These relationships are usually explicitly stated in the texts. Hyginus (*Astr.* 2.1.5) testifies to the search for a connection between the mythological identity and the astral destiny of the constellations concerning the Great Bear, which is "alone deprived of the baths of the Ocean" (*Il.* 18.489):

> This constellation, according to general opinion, does not set; and those who seek an explanation of the fact say that Tethys, the wife of the Ocean, does not receive it at the moment when the rest of the stars reaches the west, because Tethys is the nurse of Juno, who triumphed over her rival Callisto.

The mythographical narrative thus integrates or introduces many details or variants that astronomically influence the myth. The original detail reported by Eratosthenes, and without any parallel to the loss of a horn by the ram of Phrixos (*Cat.* 29), could be thus explained by the fact that only one horn of the ram is illustrated with stars (according to the Ptolemaic tradition). Astronomical iconography also influences the narrative, as with the presence of a boat at the feet of Sagittarius (*Cat.* 28), borrowed from the Egyptian zodiacs and whose presence is symbolically motivated.

The traditional iconography is, indeed, the starting point of mythographical expansion, which essentially consists in a literary description and exegesis of the pictures (Santoni 2009: 33). Kimpton (2014) discusses "the presentation of the night sky as art, in which the constellations represent man-made, visual epitomes of the stellar myths that explain them." This dependence concerns almost all figures, including the six "closed" constellations. But the iconographic tradition also displays significant fluctuation, and the texts confirm that some attributes, or even the postures of the figures, are variable: Does the horse have wings? Is the virgin headless? What does the Centaur hold in his hands? Is there any Crown or a Boat near the feet of the Sagittarius? These hesitations give the mythographer or the astronomer the possibility of new candidates. In this complex tradition, where poets, draughtsmen, astronomers, and philologists interact, sometimes in conflicting ways, discrepancies favor imagination and exegesis, and the mythographer finds material for inspiration and commentary. Eratosthenes comments on the figuration and identification of Sagittarius (ch. 28) as a quadruped centaur:

> This is the Archer whom the majority of people consider a Centaur, which others dispute, arguing that we do not see him on all four legs, but that he is standing and

shooting at the bow; yet no Centaur has ever used a bow. He is indeed a man, but with horse-legs, and a tail like that of the Satyrs. This is why it seems implausible to the aforesaid people that it is a Centaur, and more likely that it is Crotos, the son of Eupheme ("Renown").

Incidentally, it is worth noting that Crotos, unknown before Eratosthenes, is in fact almost exclusively confined to catasterismic literature (Pàmias and Zucker 2013: 265, 417).

But it can be assumed that celestial iconography could also produce original myths to account for astronomical data and motivate them narratively, even if this hypothesis cannot be extended to the whole of heaven. Orion ("the summer") is a glaring example (Renaud 2004). It is mentioned six times in the Homeric epic, the first three times as a constellation and (only in the *Odyssey*) three times as a hero. In ancient times, this "homonymy" may well have generated a mythological narrative combining in a single lifeline the heroic saga and the celestial promotion of Orion. Many philologists have endeavored to show the relations between the mythical episodes of the hero's career and certain astronomical phenomena: the gigantic size, the pursuit of the Pleiades, the ability to walk on water, the abduction by Aurora, the journey to the Sun, movement from the west to the east and back, explicit connection with the Scorpion, as well as the eve of the Bears on Orion. The complex it forms and the richness of Orionian folklore led some to think that the myth of Orion was derived from the characteristics of the constellation (Renaud 2003a; 2003b: 165; 2004: 225), and that astronomical register would have priority over the mythical register. The common myth that accounts for the triple constellation Hydra-Crater-Crow and closely links the three figures also seems to have been tailor-made. It appears for the first time in the *Catasterisms* and is exceptionally reported elsewhere (Ovid, *Fast.* 2.240–266; Aelian, *NA* 1.47).

However, special catasterismic mythography remains an occasional tinkering, and authors rarely show the need to physically or systematically motivate celestial figures, especially when they include several asterisms. Thus, the presence of the Kids in Auriga or the Donkeys on the carapace of Cancer, like the Hyades on the Bull's forehead, does not give rise to a justification or a common myth.

# 6. THE FIRST CATASTERISMS

Even though catasterismic literature, based on Eratosthenes, claims many sources, sometimes archaic, it is not possible to determine with any certainty the author of the first "catasterism" (for the first known evidence of catasterisms in the Greek iconographic tradition, see Barnes 2019). Homer cites a handful of constellations or stars (Ursa Major, Boötes, Orion, Hyades and Pleiades, Sirius and Arcturus), but the identification of the constellations does not mean mythological continuity and the passage of heroic to cosmic space. All the sources cited by Eratosthenes are used to validate elements of the selected mythological narrative, but there are few authors, no doubt, who have narrated or commented on the catasterization of a figure. The name of the constellation, the account(s) associated to the figure, and the transfer operation that introduces continuity between the hero and the heavenly outline are independent components, assembled only in catasterismic discourse. When, for example, Eratosthenes says about the Big Dipper (*Cat.* 1, Ursa Maior) that Hesiod "says she is the daughter of Lycaon," this simply means that the archaic poet mentioned the genealogy and myth of Callisto with which Eratosthenes identifies the constellation, but the catasterismic narrative itself cannot be attributed to Hesiod. Witness this other reference to Hesiod about the Virgin (*Cat.* 9; Hyg., *Astr.* 2.25.1.), who "tells in the *Theogony* she is the daughter of Zeus and Themis and is called Dike." The original text (*Th.* 900–901) simply names the daughter of Themis, and Aratus is the first author to identify the constellation and say that "she flew to heaven and settled in the region where it still appears at night to humans in the form of the Virgin" (lines 134–136).

It is likely that the constitution of an "album" of the constellations and the systematization of the process of catasterization are contemporary phenomena, and that the latter was induced by the former. This formula requires a stable catalogue of constellations. But the traditional and complete nomenclature of constellations was probably not stabilized before the classical period and the time of Euctemon (fl. 432 BCE), author of a *Parapegma* whose numerous mentions provided by Geminus (*Introduction to the Phaenomena*) contain a large number of constellation names. The systematic application to the constellations of a catasterismic perspective and process cannot therefore be anterior to it, and it is likely Alexandrian. The catasterismic conception, as a modality of mythography, corresponds entirely to the erudite and refined speculation of Alexandrian Hellenism, to its taste for catalogues and etiological collections. Nevertheless, the identification of the names of constellations with heroes, as for the family of Andromeda attested by Eudoxus (active around 365 BCE), cannot be considered a coincidence or a simple case of homonymy. When Hesiod described the Pleiades as virgins in heaven fleeing Orion (*Op.* 619–620), or when Simonides names these "celestial Pleiades" (fr. 555 PMG) it seems that the constellation is personified, and fully integrated, at least implicitly, into a mythographical network.

The numerous studies devoted to the Great Bear, which regularly opens up the catalogues of stars and receives an almost univocal identification (Callisto), have not made it possible to ascertain whether Hesiod already explicitly mentioned the nymph's catasterism. But even if he identified the constellation with Callisto, it is probable that he considered the first as an extension or avatar of the Arcadian heroine. Despite Henrichs's (1987: 261) view, assimilation of the two figures named Callisto, or even continuity from one form to the other, is hardly doubtful, although, again, the nature of this identity (transfer, image, double?) is unclear. The vagueness of the "ontological" status of the constellation and of its relationship with its heroic referent, which is blatant and persists throughout the catasterismic tradition, is perhaps precisely the symptom and the trace of this ancient emergence in various texts of a relationship differently expressed between hero(es) and constellation(s).

However, the first cases of explicit articulation between a hero and his transfer or his celestial representation probably date from the 5th century BCE. It is believed that Sophocles and Euripides clearly linked the group of constellations of the Andromeda family (Cepheus, Cassiopeia, Perseus, Andromeda, Cetus) with their mythical counterparts (Robert 1878: 244). But the preserved verses, which evoke the immortality of Helen in the confines of the ether alongside her brothers Castor and Pollux (E., *Or.* 1635–1637) or the assimilation to stars of the Dioscuri (E., *Hel.* 140), do not describe a *transformation* into a constellation. Hyginus's formulation about the Kneeler (*Astr.* 2.6.3) suggests that Aeschylus discussed the question of its identity: "Aeschylus, in his tragedy *Prometheus Delivered*, says that it is Hercules in a fight, but specifically against the Ligurians and not against the Dragon." Yet as for Panyassis (5th c. BCE), who "recognized" this figure (Avienus *Ph.* 175), the issue was perhaps only to give a name to an anonymous figure. Pherecydes of Athens (5th c. BCE) is probably the first to widely extend this perspective and to identify generic constellations with mythological figures (Pàmias 2005: 30–33) before Aratus. He seems to have explicitly included in his mythographical narratives catasterismic developments which Eratosthenes echoes for Draco (*Cat.* 3), the Northern Crown (*Cat.* 5), the Bull (*Cat.* 14), the Ram (*Cat.* 19), and probably the Charioteer (*Cat.* 13), Perseus (*Cat.* 22), the River (*Cat.* 37) and Orion (*Cat.* 32).

It seems that the Eratosthenian step consisted essentially in (1) a systematic treatment of the complete corpus of constellations and of their mythological "genesis"; (2) the creation of a mythographical module linking an image, a narrative and an astrothetic description; (3) and the inscription of catasterization (transfer or image) as the epilogue of the mythological narrative of the heroic figure.

# 7. The Place of Catasterisms in the Mythographical Tradition

Even though the catasterismic tradition begins partly before Eratosthenes and is not strictly limited to his posterity (Pàmias 2017), it is closely connected to it, and his work probably enjoyed great diffusion. The narratives of catasterisms are present in various editorial contexts, especially in compilations (such as the *Catasterisms*, or the second book of Hyginus's *Astronomy*) and exegetical literature (mainly the additions to Aratus's *Phaenomena* in the Latin adaptations, and collections of scholia). But this literature, which arose at the junction of astronomy and mythography and was closely dependent on thee two genres, had very little impact on the former, and its procedure barely pervades the latter. Neither Hipparchus in his *Commentary to the Phaenomena* nor Ptolemy in his *Almagest* alludes to the heroic identity of the constellations, whose names are always used in a purely conventional manner. In the *Tetrabiblos*, these identities do not influence the characteristics and power of the stars nor their relation to the planets

(1.9) at all. In mythographical collections, constellation myths appear, at best, as an additional and isolated section, for example, as in the Second Vatican Mythographer (Supplements M and E), and are otherwise the subject of passing references. The *Library* of Apollodorus only briefly refers to two catasterisms (Santoni 2017) using the word *katasterisas*: that of the Hyades (3.29) and Callisto (3.101). Hyginus's *Fabulae* report ten cases of catasterism, most often by a rather abstract formula which indicates their inclusion in a list (*in astrorum numerum referre*, forms of which are found at 14.33, 130.5, 133.1, 177.1, 188.2, 192.2, 194.8, 195.3 and 197.1). In only two cases, this mention is accompanied by a list of stars (Argo: 14.33, Callisto: 177.3) in chapters that structurally present themselves as real catasterismic units, although the description of the stars does not coincide with the tradition, nor even with the version of Hyginus's *Astronomy*. In the *Metamorphoses*, Ovid only mentions two catasterisms (Robinson 2013: 468), that of Callisto and Arcas (2.507), and of the Ariadne's Crown (8.177–182); he also briefly alludes to the catasterization of Hippe (that is, The Horse, 2.647), of the Twins (8.252), and of Icarus (scil. Boötes) and Erigone (scil. Virgo, 10.450–451). But these rare references differ little from those of the apotheosis of Romulus (14.812–828), Augustus (15.449) or Caesar (15.843–851).

In the six preserved books of the *Fasti* (half of the original) devoted to the Roman calendar and thus to constellations and their mythical origin (*causa signi*), as seasonal indicators, Ovid reports 21 myths of constellations (Robinson 2013: 475–480), mainly relying on Eratosthenes (Robinson 2000: 43–45; Robinson 2007), which are astronomically accurate (Lewis 2014). For the most part he simply proposes an identification of the figure, and specifies how it enters the sky only in 9 cases where the transfer appears to be concrete: Callisto and Arcas (2.188), Ampelos (that is, Vindemiator) in the Virgin (3.460), Orion (5.543), Taurus (5.617), and the Twins (715–720). But the poet, who hardly ever (4 cases only) gives the number of stars (Robinson 2013: 462), is little concerned with astronomy, and the reference to the constellation is mainly a pretext for the development of a mythical narrative. Ovid deals very casually indeed with the mythological relationship between the two realities (heroic and celestial) as appears in the conclusion of the story about the Centaur: "The ninth day was come when thou, most righteous Chiron, didst gird thy body with twice seven stars" (5.414, trans. Frazer).

# 8. CONCLUSION

The Eratosthenes collection belongs to these thematic "companions" with specialized purposes, long considered by critics as subliterary texts (Cameron 2004: ix), but which were widely circulated and used by prominent poets, such as Virgil (Cameron 2004: 255–256) or Ovid (Robinson 2013). Like the collections of genealogies, metamorphoses, and love stories, this catalogue of catasterisms expresses and illustrates some common issues of ancient mythography: transmitting authoritative narratives and multiple (often divergent) traditions on heroes; actualizing myths by giving them a repercussion in history or space; explaining aspects of the physical world through an etiological process; and expressing the pivotal function of the myths (especially moral). But it is characterized by two distinctive features: (a) the primary object of the narrative is not a heroic name or substrate, but an image: discourse is centered on a figure, often anonymous, and motivated by the need to identify it—though it is also a pretext for a mythological narration; (b) it stands as an exegesis of the physical heavens and the cultural tradition attached to them, connecting myth and celestial reality and combining astronomical knowledge and mythographical compilation. The characteristic narrative shifter (the catasterization), which ensures the link between the hero and his cosmic expression, is neither theorized nor fully justified by the search for regular correspondences or analogies between the mythological version and the celestial characteristics, and the chapters resulting from this hybridisation often give the impression of a collage. This process, roughly joining the physical world and the mythological imaginary, is supposed to organize a mythology of constellations which almost always is astral in name only. Relying on scarce anterior catasterismic allusions, this systematic compendium, typical of Alexandrian productions, is very permeable to the poetic tradition but indeed generates few original myths in return.

## FURTHER READING

There is still no general discussion on catasterismic mythography as a genre. This literature was "discovered" by German scholars in the 19th century (Rehm, Robert, Breysig) but long received little attention except by editors of Eratosthenes, Hyginus, and Aratus (such as Martin 1956, 2002a; and Pàmias and Zucker 2013). The best introduction to ancient astral lore is Boll and Gundel (1924). Unlike metamorphosis, catasterization as divine process has not been studied, nor has the specific contribution of astromyth to general mythography (for a first limited attempt, see Renaud 2004). A systematic study on references to catasterisms in Latin poetry is also still a *desideratum* (for a case study, see Castelletti 2012). Most studies focus on the relation between catasterism and imperial apotheosis (Calzascia 2014), the connection with astrology (Green 2004; Domenicucci 1996), or the astronomical relevancy in Latin poetry (Kimpton 2014; Lewis 2014; Loos 2008; O'Hara 1992).

## REFERENCES

Barnes, John T. 2014. "*Asteras Eipein*: An Archaic View of the Constellations from Halai." *Hesperia* 83: 257–276.

Bartalucci, Aldo. 1989. "Il lessico dei Catasterismi nel De astronomia di Igino e nei testi omologhi." *Studi classici e orientali* 38: 353–372.

Bishop, Caroline. 2016. "Naming the Roman Stars: Constellation Etymologies in Cicero's *Aratea* and *De Natura Deorum*." *Classical Quarterly* 66: 155–171.

Boll, Franz. 1903. *Sphaera. Neue griechische Texte und Untersuchungen zur Geschichte der Sternbilder*. Leipzig: Teubner.

Boll, Franz, and Wilhelm Gundel. 1924. "Sternbilder, Sternglaube und Sternsymbolik bei Griechen und Römern." In *Ausführliches Lexikon der Griechischen und Römischen Mythologie*, vol. 6, edited by Wilhelm H. Roscher, 867–1072. Leipzig and Berlin: Teubner.

Breysig, Alfred August B. 1867. *Germanici Caesaris Aratea cum scholiis*. Hildesheim: G. Olms.

Calzascia, Sonja C. 2014. "Deifications and Catasterisms in Ovid's *Fasti*." *Giornale Italiano di Filologia* 66: 139–162.

Cameron, Alan. 2004. *Greek Mythography in the Roman World*. Oxford: Oxford University Press.

Castelletti, Cristiano. 2012. "Why Is Jason Climbing the Dragon? A Hidden Catasterism in Valerius Flaccus' *Argonautica* 8." *Illinois Classical Studies* 37: 141–165.

Domenicucci, Patrizio. 1996. *Astra Caesarum: Astronomia, astrologia e catasterismo da Cesare a Domiziano*. Pisa: ETS.

Dupont, Florence. 1972. "Se reproduire ou se métamorphoser." *Topique* 9–10: 139–160.

Green, Peter. 2004. "Getting to Be a Star: The Politics of Catasterism." In *From Ikaria to the Stars: Classical Mythification, Ancient and Modern*, 234–249. Austin: University of Texas Press.

Henrichs, Albert. 1987. "Three Approaches to Greek Mythography." In *Interpretations of Greek Mythology*, edited by Jan N. Bremmer, 242–277. London: Croom Helm.

Kimpton, Frederick. 2014. "The *Fasti's* Celestial World and the Limitations of Astronomical Knowledge." *Classical Philology* 109: 26–47.

Le Boeuffle, André. 1973. "Le vocabulaire latin de l'astronomie." Diss. Lille.

Le Bourdellès, Hubert. 1985. *L'Aratus Latinus: Étude sur la culture et la langue latines dans le nord de la France au viiie siècle*. Lille: Presses du Septentrion.

Lewis, Anne-Marie. 2014. "In Further Defense of Ovid's Astronomical Accuracy in the *Fasti*." *American Journal of Philology* 135: 411–449.

Loos, Jaap. 2008. "How Ovid Remythologizes Greek Astronomy in *Metamorphoses* 1.747–2.400." *Mnemosyne* 61: 257–289.

Martin, Jean. 1956. *Histoire du texte des Phénomenes d'Aratos*. Paris: C. Klincksieck.

Martin, Jean. 2002a. "Sur le sens réel des mots catastérisme et catastériser (Καταστερισμός, Καταστερίζειν)." *Pallas* 59: 17–26.

Martin, Jean. 2002b. *Aratus. Phénomènes*. Paris: Les Belles Lettres.

O'Hara, James J. 1992. "Naming the Stars at *Georgics* 1.137–38 and *Fasti* 5.163–82." *American Journal of Philology* 113: 47–61.

Olivieri, Alessandro. 1897a. "I Catasterismi di Eratostene." *Studi Italiani di Filologia Classica* 5: 1–25.

Olivieri, Alessandro. 1897b. *Mythographi Graeci: Pseudo Eratosthenis, Catasterismi*. Leipzig: Teubner.

Pàmias, Jordi. 2004. "Dionysus and Donkeys on the Streets of Alexandria: Eratosthenes' Criticism of Ptolemaic Ideology." *Harvard Studies in Classical Philology* 102: 191–198.

Pàmias, Jordi. 2005. "Ferecides de Siros y Ferecides de Atenas. Una nueva aproximación." *Cuadernos de Filología Clásica* 15: 27–34.

Pàmias, Jordi. 2014. "Les *Catastérismes* d'Ératosthène. Choix mythographiques et production du savoir." *Revue des Études Grecques* 127: 195–206.

Pàmias, Jordi. 2017. "Non-Eratosthenic Astral Myths in the *Catasterisms*." In *Certissima Signa*, edited by Filippomaria Pontani, 45–54. Venice: Edizioni Ca' Foscari (Digital Publishing).

Pàmias, Jordi, and Arnaud Zucker. 2013. *Ératosthène de Cyrène: Catastérismes*. Paris: Les Belles Lettres.

Rehm, Albert. 1899. *Eratosthenis Catasterismorum Fragmenta Vaticana*. Ansbach, Germany: von C. Brügel.

Renaud, Jean-Michel. 2003a. "Le Catastérisme chez Homère: Le cas d'Orion." *Gaia* 1: 205–214.

Renaud, Jean-Michel. 2003b. "Orion: De la météorologie à la mythologie." In *La météorologie dans l'antiquité*, edited by Christophe Cusset, 159–168. Saint-Étienne: Publications de l'Université de Saint-Étienne.

Renaud, Jean-Michel. 2004. *Le Mythe d'Orion: Sa signification, sa place parmi les autres mythes grecs et son apport à la connaissance de la mentalité antique.* Liège: C.I.P.L.

Ridpath, Ian. 1988. *Star Tales.* New York: Universe Books.

Robert, Carl. 1878. *Eratosthenis Catasterismorum Reliquiae.* Berlin: Weidmann.

Robinson, Matthew. 2000. "Prolegomena to the Study of Ovid's *Fasti* with Commentary on Book 2.1–532." Diss. University of Oxford.

Robinson, Matthew. 2007. "Ovid, the *Fasti* and the Stars." *Bulletin of the Institute of Classical Studies* 50: 129–159.

Robinson, Matthew. 2013. "Ovid and the *Catasterismi* of Eratosthenes." *American Journal of Philology* 3: 445–480.

Santini, Carlo. 1998. "Sulle tracce dei *Catasterismi* di Eratostene a Roma." In *Sciences exactes et sciences appliquées à Alexandrie*, edited by Gilbert Argoud and Jean-Yves Guillaumin, 359–366. Saint-Étienne: Publications de l'Université de Saint-Étienne.

Santoni, Anna. 2009. *Eratostene. Epitome Dei Catasterismi.* Pisa, Italy: ETS.

Santoni, Anna. 2017. "Myths of Star and Constellation Origins in the Bibliotheca." In *Apollodoriana. Ancient Myths, New Crossroads*, edited by Jordi Pàmias, 126–145. Berlin and Boston: De Gruyter.

Zucker, Arnaud. 2011a. "Les Catastérismes." In *Lieux de Savoir II. Les gestes de l'intelligence, L'intelligence des gestes*, edited by Christian Jacob, 603–622. Paris: Albin Michel.

Zucker, Arnaud. 2011b. "Pourquoi l'ourse tourne-t-elle au pôle?" In *Ta Zôia: L'espai a Grècia II*, edited by Montserrat Reig and Montserrat Jufresa, 63–72. Tarragona: ICAC.

Zucker, Arnaud. 2015. "Hygin et Ératosthène: Variation mythographique ou restitution d'un original perdu." *Polymnia* 1: 83–125.

Zucker, Arnaud. 2016a. "Le 'livret' lacunaire d'Eratosthène: De l'image au texte." In *Eratosthenes' Catasterisms Receptions and Translations*, edited by Jordi Pàmias, 69–78. Mering: Utopica.

Zucker, Arnaud. 2016b. *L'encyclopédie du ciel. Mythologie, astronomie, astrologie.* Paris: Bernard Laffont.

# CHAPTER 28

....................................................................................................

# LOCAL MYTHOGRAPHY

....................................................................................................

DANIEL W. BERMAN

## 1. LOCAL MYTH, LOCAL MYTHOGRAPHY: DEFINITIONS AND PROBLEMS

CRITICAL approaches to myths, ancient or modern, rely on various strategies of categorization. One distinction we use for Greek myths, as well as for the prose compilations of them that we call "mythography," is that of "Panhellenic" or "local." In a sense, these two terms are clear enough: "Panhellenic" myth, the subject of "Panhellenic" mythography, treats stories that span the breadth of the Greek-speaking world, having value and interest across many communities or locales. "Local" myth, treated by "local" mythographers, by contrast, is strongly tied to the particulars of a specific community and its territory. Here, we find variants of stories that seemingly appear nowhere else, and we understand those versions to be particular to a specific location, perhaps to its cult practices or the idiosyncrasies of its topography.

The two poles are easily identified: on one side we place the Homeric epics (or at least large portions of them); Hesiod; or the internationally oriented works of mythographers, such as Hellanicus, perhaps, or Ps.-Apollodorus, certainly. At the other extremity might be something like the Lindian Chronicle, an inscribed chronicle of mythical and historical events related specifically and exclusively to the sanctuary of Athena Lindia on Rhodes: it is purely locally oriented, and physically exists in a single place, meant for local inhabitants or travelers to see and associate with that place (see Higbie 2003).

These categories, however, are, in fact, rather slippery, and at least in the context of mythography, they require additional investigation and clarification. Gregory Nagy has probably done the most to popularize the use of the term "Panhellenic" by classicists; he has promoted the concept of a Panhellenic oral poetics in books such as *The Best of the*

*Achaeans* and, especially, *Pindar's Homer*. Nagy (1990: 54) defines the term, specifically in reference to poetry, in this way:

> By Panhellenic poetry . . . I mean those kinds of poetry and song that operated not simply on the basis of local traditions suited for local audiences. Rather, Panhellenic poetry would have been the product of an evolutionary synthesis of traditions, so that the tradition that it represents concentrates on traditions that tend to be common to most locales and peculiar to none.

The utility of the concept is clear enough, and we might easily extend it beyond ancient poetry per se to its content, at least when that content is mythic. Not all myth, or the mythography that catalogues it, can be called Panhellenic, and teasing out strands of stories that clearly have import beyond a particular *polis* or even a sanctuary within a *polis* and its *chora* is often productive. The rise of Panhellenic myth, especially in the archaic period and beyond, can be seen as a significant factor—perhaps *the* significant factor—in the growth of a "Hellenic" identity that culminates, one might say, with the events of the Persian wars or, perhaps, ultimately in the Hellenistic world post-Alexander. Still, as a category standing in opposition to another we wish to call "local," it has drawbacks. For example, should we also be able to speak of "regional" myth (and thus mythography), such as the regionally colored myths in the verses of Corinna? And, more critically, the relationships between a Panhellenic mythology and the specifics of local cult and myth can be complicated and reciprocal—a matter I shall treat below.

The "local" side of the equation has been even less easy to define. Clearly, some strands of myth can be associated with particular places, at particular times. Though the term was already in use, Jacoby, in his monumental work collecting and editing fragments of the Greek historians (*FGrHist* 297–607; see the discussion in Marincola 2007: xx-xxii), influentially categorized some *logopoioi*—that is, writers who transcribed stories, to define that term as broadly as possible—as "local." He based this judgment on structure as much as content, collecting some texts he saw as "chronicles" (*horographiai*) and categorizing them as late-to-develop variants of historiography. Some of these writings eventually appear to enter into a broader framework of myth, and others do not. Many present what seem to be odd outliers to our mainstream ideas of what constitutes the particulars of known myths. We often hear about these "local" versions secondhand, for instance, from Pausanias or, even more frequently, when they are cited by scholars from the Hellenistic period and later.

The interactions of universally relevant myth with more local traditions can be quite instructive. Jeremy McInerney has recently explored this relationship, examining some of the ways myths with local content—his work centers on sanctuaries of Athena Alea, Apollo Maleatas, and Athena Aphaia—can enter into a more Panhellenic discourse (McInerney 2013). Clearly, through the 7th to 5th centuries BCE, some myths that we might categorize as local grew to a Panhellenic scale and reach. But this model—development from local, little-known versions of stories, often related to local instantiations of deities and cult practices associated with them, into a more main-stream, generally known body of mythic material—is not always as easy to trace as we might like. In particular, the "local" side of this model as witnessed by the surviving lit-erary tradition is often evasive. Although Pausanias, a later writer with an unparalleled interest in local versions of stories, and epigraphically based texts, such as the Lindian chronicle, represent two types of witnesses to local versions and variants of myths, an-cient "citations" are devilishly problematic, as Cameron has disconcertingly shown (2004: 124–163). And what about the earliest mythographers, many of whom are associ-ated with particular places but for whom direct textual evidence is distressingly scarce?

The relationship can also work in the reverse: "local" myths chronicled in mythographical texts are at times clearly accessing the stream of broader, more Panhellenic, stories to define relationships between a locale and the greater Greek world. This is most easily traced on the periphery, in colonies or other settlements that are more recent than the *metropoleis* of Greece proper, and is a common strategy, especially in the Hellenistic and later periods. A good example is the so-called *Pride of Halicarnassus* examined by Jan Bremmer in a recent study (2013), an inscription that asserts details of local character while interspersing those details into broader "Panhellenic" myths from the epic tradition.

Then what of the category "local mythography"? Mythography, especially in its early stages in Greece, is far from a uniform genre—if we can call it a genre at all. The mythographical texts we can reconstruct, and feel confident knowing something about on the level of structure, are organized in different ways: geography and genealogy are the two most consistent modes of organization, but these are often combined or sometimes employed in parallel, and there is lively scholarly debate about even our most promi-nent early mythographers concerning the nature and structure of their works (see, for instance, Trzaskoma and Smith 2013, especially the editors' useful introduction). Some early mythographers clearly wrote works that had Panhellenic pretensions. Hecataeus wrote a collection, and, it seems, an evaluative synthesis, of the stories of "the Greeks" (fr. 1 Fowler), which began with the assertion that they were, more or less, "all absurd" (*geloioi*), at least those before his own work; this statement alone, with its expressed sub-ject "the Greeks," implies a Panhellenic perspective. And it seems that the genealogies of Pherecydes of Athens and some works of Hellanicus of Lesbos were organized in ways that extended their reach to the breadth of the Greek world (on Pherecydes see *BNJ* 3 and Fowler 2013: 706–727; on Hellanicus, Fowler 2013: 682–695). But some early my-thography seems quite local as well, for example the very same Hellanicus's *Atthis*, the first of its kind most likely, and perhaps the earliest example of "local" historiography/mythography (more on that below). Later, in the Hellenistic period and beyond, much of the mythography that survives in any proportion seems to fall toward the nonlocal side of the spectrum, but there are exceptions, some already mentioned.

Some long-standing mythographical traditions do seem to be significantly rooted in the locales of their production. In Athens, there are the Atthidographers, who produced local histories that took the form of yearly chronicles but, certainly in their accounts of the earliest years of their city's tradition, treated mythic material together with what we would understand as more historical information. But a look even at the Atthidographic tradition raises some immediate questions of categorization: Phillip Harding's recent collection and edition of the fragments of the Atthidographers begins with Hellanicus, *of Lesbos*, whom Harding, as have others before him, credits with founding the genre in Athens (Harding 2008: 5–6). Harding remarks that it is seemingly "contradictory" (6) that a non-Athenian should establish the genre, but rightly notes that there is no compelling reason for this not to be so. Hellanicus was prolific, and his work wide-ranging, especially from a geographical standpoint: of his geographically oriented works, we hear of a *Troica, Aeolica* or *Lesbica, Argolica, De Arcadia, Boeotiaca, Thessalica, Cypriaca,* and *De Chio Condita,* in addition to the *Atthis.* So, is Hellanicus a "local" mythographer? If we measure by the content of his work, at least on Athens and Attica, he appears local indeed. But by other measures—say, his language, a version of the Attic-Ionic prose that was typical of the period, with literary origins primarily in Ionia (see Fowler 2013: 689–692); the fact that he is from Lesbos; or that he may qualify as a "local" mythographer of more than one *locale*—by these measures, he may not be.

There are, of course, mythographers who are local in the sense that they are *locals* and in the sense that their *subject* is local; the Athenian Atthidographers who took over the genre after Hellanicus, for example, would fit this category—at least if we are concerned with the mythical portions of their works. Many others might, as well, from around the Greek world. If we define "local mythography" as mythography that is necessarily centered on a specifically defined place, we have a certain set of surviving texts; if we define it further as mythography practiced by indigenous people about their own specific place, we have another, smaller set. And chronology is important, as I have noted. Especially in the Hellenistic period and later, a "local" variant can access the broader current of myth via a type of back-formation, whereas our earliest "local" mythography is more likely to be operating solely within its (geographically) local environment.

There is, finally, also the problem of "myth" itself, and the related one of "ethnography." If "local historians" are sometimes "local mythographers," it is because a distinction is being made between "myth" and "history." This chapter is not the place to interrogate these categories, but it should be noted that the boundary between those two prose subjects, and thus between "mythography" and "historiography," is fluid. It is much easier to identify the poles of the spectrum defined by the two concepts than it is to mark the boundary between them. And what about those who compose what is traditionally categorized as "ethnography," a portion of which might be defined intrinsically as a local or regional type of mythology? When do tales of far-away peoples, whose customs are curious, become the local myths of a particular (noncentral) place?

"Local mythography" is thus an exceedingly complex, even problematic, concept, delineated by boundaries of chronology (on an axis of "chronological verifiability," we might say), defined by the slippery question of when a subject ceases to be mythical and becomes instead historical, as well as by geography (an axis of "geographical verifiability"), defined by the question of what degree of geographical proximity (and, crucially, from what perspective?) do events or other material require to be considered "local." Put simply, we can define "local mythography" *if* we can define what it means to be "local" and to be a "myth." But that is a big *if*.

## 2. A MYTHOGRAPHER, BUT LOCAL? ARMENIDAS OF THEBES

A look at evidence for the writings of one early mythographer, Armenidas (*BNJ* 378), offers focus and potential insight. He is an apt first example because he is early and has an apparently circumscribed, or "local," interest. Our witnesses to Armenidas's work come solely in the form of citations by later authors, which can be collected into seven or eight fragments (most likely seven, since one fragment is probably misidentified as his work). As for his date, linguistic indications point to the late 5th or early 4th century BCE. He uses two Ionic verb forms in one passage and possibly an Ionic dative (*Hermaisin*, which is an emendation, though generally considered a good one; both are in fr. 6), which together point to a date around the end of the 5th century (see Schachter in *BNJ* 378, and the commentary in Fowler 2013). If we accept these—and the verb forms, especially, seem convincing—this makes him one of our earlier mythographers, in the same general milieu chronologically as Hellanicus or Pherecydes, or perhaps a generation younger.

Where did Armenidas write, or from where did he hail? Those are more difficult questions. We might look for answers in two ways: through linguistic clues and through the content of the fragments and our testimonia about them from the writers who transmitted them. Linguistically, there is his name and one other tantalizing clue. The name Armenidas is quite rare, its only independent attestation coming in a heavily restored inscription from Orchomenos, in Boeotia. This points, if anywhere, toward Boeotian origin, but we would like more support than a single rather untrustworthy inscription to make this claim. The other linguistic clue makes his Boeotian pedigree more plausible, however: in one fragment (fr. 7), he is said to have used the name "Ariartos" in place of "Haliartos" for the Boeotian town; with the *rho* and lack of aspirate this name is seen on local coins as early as the 4th century and is definitively epichoric. That Armenidas uses local Boeotian dialect to name one of the more prominent cities in the region is certainly significant, though how to interpret this is less than clear; the use of a particular dialect or dialect forms can be an indicator of either the author's or his audience's affiliations, or both. More generally, the fact that Armenidas writes in Ionic, the standard dialect for prose works of this period, shows that there is also, in the linguistic sense at least, "a bid . . . made for a place on the international stage" (as Fowler 2013: 639 puts it).

Still, *Ariartos* does indicate some type of a Boeotian connection. This is confirmed by the scholiast to Apollonius of Rhodes, who tells us that Armenidas wrote a *Thebaica* (fr. 1). It may be his only work; it is the only named work we hear of. It appears to have consisted of more than one book, since the second fragment, also drawn from the comments of the scholiast to Apollonius of Rhodes, mentions that he is using as his source the "first book" of Armenidas. This fragment treats features of the topography of Thebes, and no title is given for the work from which it comes. The two comments of the scholiast taken together seem to imply that a multivolume *Thebaica* was Armenidas's only work (thus Fowler and Schachter, though both admit that it must be provisional).

We thus have an author who wrote in prose, probably at the end of the 5th century or in the very early 4th, who probably wrote a *Thebaica*, and who uses a Boeotian dialect to name a Boeotian town. Local? Perhaps. I have already mentioned that one fragment, fragment 2, treats some features of Theban topography, but what about content more generally? Only three of the fragments we have are clearly connected to Thebes: fragment 2 concerns Amphion and the walls of Thebes; 5 treats the Theban acropolis (usually called the Cadmeia); and fragment 6 mentions the well-known "seven pyres" of Thebes. In all three cases, topography seems important, and the connections between the physical landscape of Thebes and the city's mythic past are underscored.

According to the scholiast on Apollonius of Rhodes's *Argonautica* (on 1.740), Armenidas reports that the stones of the walls of Thebes followed Amphion's lyre of their own accord, and that Amphion's lyre was given to him by the Muses (this second phrase is not included in Fowler's text, fr. 2). The scholiast goes on to state that this last detail is in agreement with Pherecydes but at odds with Dioscorides, who says Apollo gave Amphion the lyre. The story of the building of the walls of Thebes by the twins Amphion and Zethus reaches back to the *Odyssey* (11.260–265), but the famous detail of Amphion's magical lyre (balanced by Zethus's brawn) is not in Homer and seems to originate with the epic poet Eumelus (in his *Europeia*; Schachter in *BNJ* cites West [2002] on Eumelus). A good source for the story that is contemporary with the probable date of Armenidas is Euripides's fragmentary *Antiope* (see the commentary in *BNJ*). We can make two quick conclusions: here Armenidas is clearly treating a Theban subject, one connected to the city's topography. But the details he is credited with transmitting are not unexpected, unique, or really that surprising; even the indication that the lyre came from the Muses—which is perhaps why Armenidas's authority is invoked at all—seems not to be particularly idiosyncratic, since the scholiast says that Pherecydes transmitted the same detail. A preliminary conclusion based only on this fragment might be that while Armenidas is indeed treating a local subject, his treatment tends more to the mainstream, with parallels in Pherecydes and even Euripides, as well as in earlier epic.

Another fragment (fr. 6) shows some similarities, and in this case, opens some interesting avenues of understanding depending on how we interpret its language. The scholiast to Pindar's *Olympian* 6 offers a comment with a critical perspective when Pindar mentions the seven pyres on the plain of Thebes: how can there really be seven, since Amphiaraus was swallowed up with his horse at Oropos; Polynices wasn't buried at all; and Adrastus went back to Argos? After listing a few ways out of this conundrum, our commentator cites Armenidas, who he says writes, " . . . making seven pyres at the Hermai at a place called the 'seven pyres.' " The comment continues, " . . . either after the Seven against Thebes, or after the seven children of Niobe, who were cremated there."

There is topography here, but not of a particularly specific nature. The mention of a place called the Hermai seems promising, and Schachter (in *BNJ*) understands this to indicate a location near the classical agora. But because this seems to be based primarily on the fact that herms are often set up in agoras, it can only be speculative. Also enigmatic is the final set of clauses, beginning with *ē apo* in Greek, "either after." Schachter, following Jacoby, accepts what follows as the words of Armenidas, making him something of a Herodotean writer, presenting the reader with choices for the identities of the people the pyres commemorate: either the Seven or the Niobids. Fowler, however, rejects this interpretation and takes the clause as the scholiast's: Armenidas locates the pyres at the "Hermae," but says no more; then the scholiast adds they might be the pyres of the Seven or of the Niobids. If we understand the fragment this way, perhaps here we do see some particularly epichoric material from Armenidas, since he is cited solely to locate the pyres on the landscape (even if not very helpfully). On the other hand, if we were to attribute the explanatory either-or statement to the mythographer, we would be tempted to see, again, a more "international," or "Panhellenic" outlook.

Armenidas the Theban writer with particularly Theban information might be glimpsed in another fragment (fr. 5) as well. It comes from the Hesychius lexicon and can be found in Photius and the *Suda*. Under the heading *Makarōn nēsos*, "Island of the Blest," the lexica read "the acropolis of Boeotian Thebes of old, according to Armen<i>das." This fragment as well treats topography, in a sense. But the detail it transmits is unique in our record, and somewhat puzzling. As Fowler notes in his commentary, "Toponyms denoting places in the beyond, when they finally get pinpointed on the map, do so on the edges of the known world, not in the middle of an ancient mainland city" (Fowler 2013: 500). It is odd to see the Cadmeia, the Theban acropolis, associated with the Island of the Blest, and the oddity has provoked divergent responses from critics. Schachter suggests that it indeed represents an old Boeotian tradition, perhaps stemming from stories about the location of a monument to or the remains of Alcmene; Pherecydes apparently related a story that her body was spirited away by Hermes, to be wedded to Rhadamanthys at the Isles of the Blest, and a stone coffin was left in her stead in Thebes (see Schachter in *BNJ*; the attribution to Pherecydes is transmitted by a marginal note in a manuscript of Antoninus Liberalis 33). Jacoby had suggested a version of this, as well as a few other possible explanations, including that Zeus was occasionally said to have been born at Thebes or that Hector's bones were supposedly deposited there (a curious detail transmitted by Pausanias 9.18.5).

Interpretations based on misunderstandings, either of terminology or context, are also possible and, potentially, more persuasive. Burkert suggested a misinterpretation of the word *enēlysios*, a place struck by lightning, and quite relevant to the Cadmeia as the location of Semele's demise at the hands of Zeus and his thunderbolt (Burkert 1961, cited in Fowler 2013: 500). The Cadmeia could be described somewhere, perhaps by Armenidas even, as *enēlysios*, and then a connection between Elysium and the Island of the Blest, based on the easy misunderstanding of that word as *en Ēlysiōi* ("in Elysium") might explain the entries in the lexica. This is clever and may be right. In fact, one of the few uses of this rare word is by Aeschylus in the *Argeioi* in reference to Capaneus's incineration by a thunderbolt on the plain of Thebes (Mette fr. 263a). And further speculation is possible: Latte, editor of the Hesychius lexicon, suggested that the origin of the lexica entries was a joke on the comic stage; his idea has earned the phrase a place in modern collections of comic fragments (Kassel-Austin adesp. 386; see the notes in Fowler 2013: 500). This does not exclude Burkert's reading—the misinterpretation could even be a deliberate pun—but does potentially rob Armenidas of the fragment entirely.

If it is Armenidas, and he is here transmitting an alternative name, or a kind of nickname, for the Cadmeia, this is potentially solid local information and promotes his local status. However, a misunderstanding, or even a pun, seems most probable, and suggests a more Panhellenic scope. We can imagine Armenidas, possibly correctly attributed but with the content of the citation corrupted at some point, describing the Cadmeia as "thunderstruck," *enēlysios*, naturally enough, and this detail finding a reflection in our tradition, via the lemma in the lexica. Of the other four fragments (not including here fr. 4, which should probably be attributed to Andromenides, not Armenidas), there is the one attesting to Armenidas's use of epichoric "Ariartos" for Haliartos, which I briefly mentioned earlier, transmitted by the grammarian Stephanus of Byzantium, while three others (1, 3, and 8) do not treat Boeotia or Thebes directly, though one (fr. 8) does mention Aktaion, whose story is set in Boeotia. Thus, Armenidas would be, on the whole, fairly mainstream, international, Panhellenic, paralleled in some significant instances even by Athenian tragedy.

If this has been a rather lengthy exposition of a single mythographer, I hope to have given some perspective on what an early example of "local" mythography can look like. Armenidas may not be representative of all writers from his period, but his output, and its transmission to us, is relatively typical. I wish to suggest here that what we can discern of the explicitly Theban material in Armenidas is really rather bland: he appears as an author who shows some—some, not many—distinctively local characteristics but has pretentions that reach beyond the local. On the conceptual axes I have sketched, Armenidas appears to be solidly in the "mythical" quarter but less clearly "local;" his "localness," if it exists, stems more from primarily superficial points of Theban or Boeotian character, especially topography, than from any particularly obscure epichoric content.

# 3. A Local Tradition, but Mythography? Athens and Atthidography

Examining an early mythographer's writing that falls, in some ways at least, under the rubric of "local" has led us to question the utility of the category. But what of a local *tradition* such as Atthidography, to which I shall turn very briefly here as a second example?

Chronicling the history of Athens, beginning with the mythic origins of the Athenian people, seems to have originated with Hellanicus, who is in a sense the converse of Armenidas: the *Atthis* he purportedly wrote is clearly local in its content, and it begat a long tradition of chronicling Athenian myth and history, but Hellanicus himself is not Athenian, as I have noted. He was followed in the genre by the Athenians Cleidemus, Androtion, Phanodemos, Melanthius, Demon, and Philochorus; we have fragments of all these authors, but by far the most survive from Philochoros (Harding 2008: 1 and throughout; Melanthius and Demon are probably but not verifiably Athenian, as Harding notes). These works were written in clear, unadorned prose and mined as source material by later writers and intellectuals, including Harpocration, Strabo, and Dionysius of Halicarnassus, among many others.

Atthidography has often been cited as a paradigm of the category "local history" or "local historiography." Jacoby identified it as such, and the recent work of Harding does so as well, though Harding is critical of Jacoby's categorization of "local history" as a late development in the genealogy of Greek historiography (see Harding 2008: 4–5; and Marincola 2007: xx-xxii). Whether or not that is the case, every "local history" of the sort that Hellanicus's *Atthis* surely was should accurately be characterized as a hybrid of local history and local mythography. Hellanicus and other Atthidographers began their works with tales of autochthony and the earliest Athenian kings, bringing their narratives down through what we would inarguably call the genealogies and chronologies of myth, eventually reaching the first recorded eponymous archon (Creon) in 683/682 BCE. From that point, there may be some discussion about whether what they transmitted is "myth" or "history" (many would suggest that much of it is a mixture of these), but there will be little doubt that Atthidography that treats the period before the first historical archon is better defined as mythography than historiography.

For the Atthidographers, however, the distinction is inconsequential; their subject matter is treated uniformly and without adornment. A few examples will suffice. The earliest Athenian myth was treated in a matter-of-fact way: we hear, for example, of the early Athenian king Cecrops and his lineage in a fragment of Androtion transmitted by the *Lexicon Rhetoricum Cantabrigiense* (*BNJ* 324 fr. 1): "Androtion in the first book of his *Atthis* says there were three daughters of Cecrops: Agraulus, Herse, and Pandrosus; from Pandrosus Keryx was born by Hermes." This matter-of-fact style of relating "myth" moves from that category toward "history": the archonship of Creon, first on the historical archon lists and a natural boundary between these modern categories, was almost certainly mentioned by Hellanicus and used as a chronological reference point by him and subsequent Atthidographers (see Harding 2008: 86), and after Creon's archonship the genealogical structure continues to hold, for example, when Philochoros, cited by Harpocration s.v. "Propylaia" (*BNJ* 328 fr. 36), cites the archon Euthymenes (437/436) to fix a date when construction of the acropolis Propylaia was begun. The Atthidographic works move from genealogy to chronology fixed to archonships, marching through the generations and years to the present in similar style and format, no formal distinction made between what we would call "myth" or "history."

Thus the problem of definition becomes that very matter of chronology: at the point in time when we are willing to accept that the content the Atthidographers treat is historical, that is verifiable in some way or another, or perhaps based on a type of "documentation" or "documentary evidence"—in this case, the archon list beginning with Creon—we can say that Atthidography is "local history"; before that, it is "local mythography" (see again Harding 2008: 3–4; and more generally, 2007: 185–187). If Armenidas's work was decidedly mythical if not so clearly local (other than being written, most probably, by a native), Hellanicus, the first Atthidographer, is decidedly local (except that he is not Athenian) but not entirely mythical, and the Athenians who followed him wrote material that similarly ranges from "mythical" to "historical." Local mythography and local history are two sides of the same coin.

# 4. Local Mythography: Categories and Conclusions

This discussion has focused on definitions: how do we delineate what is "local," let alone what is "myth," the subject of "mythography"? Other contributions to this handbook will go some way toward answering the second question, especially as it concerns "mythography," though the status of "myth" as a concept will surely continue to be debated, refined, and contested (see "Further Reading" below). I have attempted to understand local mythography by resorting to axes, a mytho-historical axis and a center-peripheral or center-universal axis (defined as axes of "chronological verifiability" and "geographical verifiability"). Most prose texts that compile and recount myths can be represented as lines drawn along or parallel to the chronological axis, at some point moving from the world of myth to that of documented "history," however we wish to define it. (This is not the place to open a theoretical discussion of this continuum or how we wish, specifically, to define these poles. I hope it is sufficient to acknowledge that on each far end of this spectrum the categories are distinct enough.) If we drew the two axes perpendicularly to form a matrix, other texts might be points upon it; the *Library* of Ps.-Apollodoros, for example, would be situated squarely in the "universal" and "mythical" quadrant.

The result of this attempt is to see "local mythography" as a category with soft edges on all sides, with both terms allowing a degree of slippage: both rely on a type of proximity, chronological or geographical, to the "here and now:" proximity to "here" defines what is "local" and to "now" at least contributes to what is "myth" (though extent of geographical distance from a defined center can also serve to delineate a narrative as "mythic").

A taxonomy of local mythography might thus look like this:

A. **Works of mythographers with a particularly local interest**. These would include Armenidas, as discussed in some detail here, and many others—essentially, as many of those Jacoby categorized as "local historians" (*FGrHist* 297–607) as treat some "myth" in addition to more contemporary historical events of their respective states, sanctuaries, or locales. The local interest might be expressed in multiple ways, and connections to larger trends in or bodies of mythology might occur through a variety of strategies. Earlier mythography of this type, such as of Armenidas or others (for example, Timaeus of Tauromenion, *BNJ* 566, who wrote an *Italica* and *Sicelica* according to the *Suda*) tends to focus on local ritual or topographical material, with varying degrees of idiosyncrasy, while later examples, of which there are very many, may be more occupied with connecting newer traditions to Panhellenic or universal narratives.

B. **Robust local traditions**. The Atthidographers, or perhaps the annalistic tradition in Rome, would fall into this category. These represent attempts to create a linear narrative, often through an annalistic format, from earliest myth to the present, in which individual authors engage in creating and then mostly modifying an existing tradition. The revision and competition a continuous tradition creates gives traditions such as this a specific and particularly local character.

C. **Publicly displayed mythographical texts**. The local connection here is obvious since the text is physically ensconced in a local center. I have mentioned the Lindian chronicle and the *Pride of Halicarnassus* above; the *Marmor Parium* is another well-known example, though it is less focused on a particularly circumscribed geographical location than the former two (*BNJ* 239; see Higbie 2003: 271–273). They can be categorized as subgroups of either of the above categories and can employ strategies of later local mythography.

D. **"Secondary" local mythography**. This includes descriptions of myths and rituals transmitted by prose writers with interest primarily in geography or ethnography (for example, Pausanias, Strabo, but also historiographers such as Herodotus and Thucydides). This category has not been explored in detail here. Clearly, however, the historians engage in a type of local mythography when they recount the local traditions of their subjects. Obvious examples would be the Egyptian material in Herodotus (for which the boundary between local mythography and ethnography is indistinct) or material from the *archaeologies* (of either Athens or Sicily) in Thucydides.

This taxonomy is by necessity incomplete. Prose authors can connect to traditions of myths that are strongly tied to place in multiple ways. They can be local themselves, recounting traditions that are relevant to their own lived experience in a place, or, on the far other end of the spectrum, they can attempt to insert Panhellenic or otherwise nonlocal traditions into a local context. And there is quite a bit of room between these two poles for diverse strategies. Mythography, as prose writing in general, is a form of knowledge dispersion that by its nature is meant to reach a public—a readership or perhaps an oral audience. Texts can travel, can even be performed. Thus a writer like Armenidas is in some sense like a Pindar (though clearly he did not attain the broad success of Pindar): he is local insofar as we can see something of where he is from in his work, and even a reflection of this in his name, but his pretensions go beyond the walls of Thebes, or the Boeotian plain, to a Greek world that is increasingly, by the late 5th and early 4th centuries, becoming interconnected and even cosmopolitan.

We can say something similar about Atthidography. In a sense, as a tradition, it may be more locally oriented than a single author such as Armenidas' work because each successive Atthidographer is looking to his predecessors and editing and rewriting interpretations of Athenian myth and history. But the first appearance of an *Atthis*, by Hellanicus in the 5th century, must be understood as the appearance of a document that was not meant solely for Athenians. In this sense, it is similar to the *Thebaica* of Armenidas; it is in conversation with a wider stream of myth and seeks to situate itself within, or at the borders of, that stream.

Perhaps in the end, it is most useful to define "local mythography" by defining what it is not: though no contribution in this handbook is specifically dedicated to "universal mythography," which could, we might say, be exemplified by the *Library* of Ps.-Apollodorus, local mythography is easily distinguished from something as universal as the *Library* is. We wish to find in something "local" a connection to a particular place, to a center. Thus, the concept of local mythography has at its core a geographical ideal, of place-in-space (on the terms, see Tuan 1977: 3–7 and throughout). The extent to which a text is connected to place and its particulars can vary widely. And of course, the extent to which a text transmits "myth" is equally variable. Within those porous boundaries, however, lies a prose tradition of expressing stories that connect to the particulars of a city, sanctuary, or region, often in distinction to more universal or universally accepted ("Panhellenic") norms of myth or ritual. Here is where "local mythography" resides. It is directly in the crosshairs of a traveler and writer such as Pausanias. And the concept has survived to the present day: summer-camp stories told around the campfire about summers long ago, or the "historical" markers that dot a city like Philadelphia, where I live—at least those that tell stories that would be difficult or impossible to verify—are our modern local mythographies. They are stories about the past of a place, defining what that place is and what it means for those who inhabit it in the present.

## FURTHER READING

The monumental and still standard collection and reference for texts that fall under the rubric of mythography is Jacoby's *Die Fragmente der griechischen Historiker* (*FGrHist*); the texts that Jacoby categorizes as "local histories" comprise numbers 297–607 of *FGrHist* and include many texts that we ought to define as "local mythography." Jacoby also devoted a special supplement (text and commentary) to the Atthidographers, numbers 323a–534. Many scholars, however, have begun to rethink Jacoby's categorizations, and more recent collections organize texts somewhat differently. Works of "local" mythographers are included in *Brill's New Jacoby* (*BNJ*), which is an ongoing project to update Jacoby's work and make it digitally available, with translations and updated commentary. The early mythographers (6th to 4th centuries BCE) are collected by Fowler (2000), text, and (2013), commentary, and these include many we would call "local."

There are a few studies either devoted to local versions of mythography or to "local myth" that intersect with prose retellings of those myths: Bremmer (2013) treats a Hellenistic example, the so-called *Pride of Halicarnassus*, and Graf in Dowden and Livingstone (2011) instructively discusses the "local character" of myth. McInerney (2013) also productively counterpoises local and Panhellenic myth in a way that intersects with the discussion presented here.

On defining key terms of "myth" and "local" in the context of historiography and mythography, see the helpful discussions of Harding (2007, 2008) and Marincola (2007). More generally on the problems of defining and theorizing myth in the Greco-Roman world, see (among many instructive discussions) Graf (1996), Dowden and Livingstone (2011: 3–23), and Edmunds (2014, especially the "General Introduction," 1–41).

## References

*BNJ* = *Brill's New Jacoby* online . General editor: Ian Worthington.

Bremmer, Jan. 2013. "Local Mythography: The Pride of Halicarnassus." In *Writing Myth: Mythography in the Ancient World*, edited by Stephen M. Trzaskoma and R. Scott Smith, 55–74. Leuven: Peeters.

Burkert, Walter. 1961. "Elysion." *Glotta* 39: 208–213.

Cameron, Alan. 2004. *Greek Mythography in the Roman World*. New York: Oxford University Press.

Dowden, Ken, and Niall Livingstone. 2011. *A Companion to Greek Mythology*. Chichester, UK: Wiley-Blackwell.

Edmunds, Lowell, ed. 2014. *Approaches to Greek Myth*. 2nd ed. Baltimore, MD: Johns Hopkins University Press.

Fowler, Robert L. 2000. *Early Greek Mythography*. Vol. 1. Oxford: Oxford University Press.

Fowler, Robert L. 2013. *Early Greek Mythography*. Vol. 2. Oxford: Oxford University Press.

Graf, Fritz. 1996. *Greek Mythology: An Introduction*. Baltimore, MD: Johns Hopkins University Press.

Graf, Fritz. 2011. "Myth and Hellenic Identities." In *A Companion to Greek Mythology*, edited by Ken Dowden and Niall Livingstone, 211–226. Chichester, UK: Wiley-Blackwell.

Harding, Phillip. 2007. "Local History and Atthidography." In *A Companion to Greek and Roman Historiography*, edited by John Marincola, 180–188. Oxford: Blackwell.

Harding, Phillip. 2008. *The Story of Athens: The Fragments of the Local Chronicles of Attika*. London: Routledge.

Higbie, Carolyn. 2003. *The Lindian Chronicle and the Greek Creation of Their Past*. Oxford: Oxford University Press.

Jacoby, Felix. 1876–1959. *Die Fragmente der griechischen Historiker (FGrHist)*. Leiden: Brill.

Marincola, John, ed. 2007. *A Companion to Greek and Roman Historiography*. Oxford: Blackwell.

McInerney, Jeremy. 2013. "The Gods of (Con)fusion: Athena Alea, Apollo Maleatas and Athena Aphaia." *Classica et Mediaevalia* 64: 49–80.

Nagy, Gregory. 1990. *Pindar's Homer: The Lyric Possession of an Epic Past*. Baltimore, MD: Johns Hopkins University Press.

Schachter, Albert. "Armenidas." In *Brill's New Jacoby*, no. 378.

Trzaskoma, Stephen M., and R. Scott Smith, eds. 2013. *Writing Myth: Mythography in the Ancient World*. Leuven: Peeters.

Tuan, Yi-Fu. 1977. *Space and Place: The Perspective of Experience*. Minneapolis: University of Minnesota Press.

West, Martin L. 2002. "'Eumelos': A Corinthian Epic Cycle?" *Journal of Hellenic Studies* 122: 109–133.

# CHAPTER 29

## MYTHOGRAPHY AND PARADOXOGRAPHY

### IRENE PAJÓN LEYRA

THE aim of this chapter is to offer readers a panoramic view of the mythographical content appearing in extant paradoxographical collections, its relationship to other kinds of material included in them, and a review of the role of paradoxographers as transmitters of mythical tales. So-called paradoxographical literature consists of catalogues or lists of rarities that concern two main thematic areas: on the one hand, the natural world— mainly zoology and hydrology—and on the other, ethnographic information. It is a specific branch of historiographical literature, directly linked to the influence of the school of Aristotle, and more concretely, to the interest among the philosophers of the Lyceum in natural science and ethnography (on Peripatetic influence, see Sassi 1993: 456–458).

The beginning of the Hellenistic age brought to Greek culture, among other things, the birth of new literary genres and cultural manifestations in connection with new political circumstances and especially new centers of intellectual activity, notably Alexandria and Pergamum. One of these new cultural manifestations was paradoxography, which arose out of the concentration of books and other written materials in the great Hellenistic libraries (see Fraser 1972: 454). Using their personal taste as the sole criterion of selection, paradoxographers created their catalogues of curiosities by extracting the anecdotes they found particularly astonishing from works written by earlier authors, mainly historians and scientists, whom they took as reliable authorities capable of providing them with objective, unquestionably verified information.

Given the connection of paradoxography to historiography—that is, to the description of facts from direct experience rather than the sphere of legendary tales of the heroic past—we should not expect anecdotes relative to myth to appear very frequently in the paradoxographical catalogues. Indeed, they only represent a minority among the items in the lists of rarities. This notwithstanding, even though they are the exception and not the rule, mythographical stories do have a place and do play a role in paradoxographical literature and therefore deserve specific study. The function and import of references to myths in paradoxographical catalogues, however, have not yet been systematically dealt with by scholars. Hence, the main aim of this study is to contribute to filling this gap by analysing the specific function of myths within these ancient collections of marvels.

# 1. The Paradoxographer and His Sources: Christian Jacob

Although the compilers of paradoxographical lists took their *paradoxa* from the written sources they excerpted (see Schepens 1996: 389–390, who calls it "derivative literature"), it is hardly a matter of simply copying word for word. Rather, paradoxographers modified the original content in both subtle and substantial ways. In an important work, still the most thorough study of the paradoxographers' methods, Jacob (1983) analyzed Antigonus's (3rd c. BCE) use of Aristotle in his *Mirabilia* and articulated how the original materials underwent modification to fit the new context. Some of these are minor, for instance, modifications of word order, transformation into an indirect style, and so forth. Other changes, however, are more substantial and are almost always aimed at increasing the capacity of the *paradoxa* to astonish. He identifies three main ways they accomplish this goal:

1. Paradoxographers remove every expression of doubt or hesitation in the original text, presenting the anecdote as an objective description of a curiosity. Since it comes from an authorized source, it should be taken by readers as an extraordinary phenomenon proven to be true (Jacob 1983: 132, with examples).
2. Paradoxographers also carefully eliminate every attempt to clarify the causes of the described curiosity which may have existed in the original text. Thus, phenomena that were not regarded as particularly mysterious or abnormal in the original text often appear in paradoxographical collections as unexplained mysteries that defy logic and common sense (133).
3. Finally, any mention of parallel examples is omitted in order to present the anecdote as something unique and unusual, attributing an exceptional nature to facts that, in their original context, were often not regarded as particularly rare or outstanding (133).

Although there are few other examples where we can compare the paradoxographical collections to the source texts, analysis of these cases reveals a similar methodology. Thus, as a working hypothesis, we can assume that the method Jacob described was in all probability widely accepted by other paradoxographers and generally implemented in their works.

When it comes to the inclusion of mythographical items in paradoxographical texts, however, we will see that Jacob's analysis is in need of some refinement. This, in part, owes to the extraordinary nature of myths, where there is less need to eliminate the causes of *paradoxa* and any parallel examples because myth in and of itself is able to promote perplexity and act as a support for the marvellous character of a story or phenomenon.

# 2. MYTHS IN PARADOXOGRAPHICAL CATALOGUES

Let us now focus on how paradoxographers deal with the mythographical material included in their lists of rarities, with particular attention to the catalogues that have reached us in relatively complete condition and are attested directly and not through indirect references of later authors, who might have altered the contents and intentions of the original texts. In this context, the core of our analysis will be the works of Antigonus, Apollonius (despite his showing little interest in mythography), and Phlegon of Tralles. These are the three paradoxographical collections transmitted in the famous codex *Palatinus Graecus* 398 (Heidelberg). We will also consider the pseudo-Aristotelian *Mirabiles Auscultationes*. Where appropriate, we will also consider later works that depend on earlier lists of rarities, such as the anonymous *Paradoxographus Florentinus*, the *Paradoxographus Vaticanus*, and the *Paradoxographus Palatinus*, as well as the paradoxographers we know only indirectly and other fragmentary pieces.

Starting from the oldest extant paradoxographical catalogues—Antigonus and Ps.-Aristotle's chapters 1–151 (chs. 152 to 178 are more than likely a later addition), both dated to the 3rd century BCE—some differences in the respective treatments of mythographical material may be observed. As to authorial preferences, for instance, Ps.-Aristotle, with few exceptions, perceptibly pays specific attention to stories of traveling heroes (Heracles and his Twelve Labours, Jason and the Voyage of the Argonauts, the Nostoi of the Trojan War or the flight of Daedalus from Crete to the Adriatic, among others), so that a significant number of his *paradoxa* link the peculiarities of a certain place or its inhabitants to the visit of a figure from the Greek heroic past. Antigonus, by contrast, is less interested in geography but focuses on other aspects of mythical figures (Hephaestus and his lameness, the male offspring of Heracles) or deals with local traditions concerning relevant Greek cities or regions (such as Athens, Delos, Lesbos, Lemnos, or Olympia). This difference, of course, is not rigid: occasionally, references to the legendary journeys of heroic figures are also represented in Antigonus's catalogue (for instance, Heracles's labors in *Mir.* 2, and Diomedes's journey back from the Trojan War in 172), while local traditions not connected to heroic travel also appear in the Ps.-Aristotelian text (see *Mir. Ausc.* 82, which places the rape of Persephone in Sicily, and 83, on Crete as Zeus's birthplace). Still, despite the isolated cases, the different tendencies of both paradoxographers are clear.

Because of the predominance of legendary travel traditions relating to the heroes, the geographical sphere of Ps.-Aristotle's mythographical content is much wider than that of Antigonus, reaching westward to the Adriatic Sea, Magna Graecia, Sicily, Sardinia, and Iberia and eastward to the Bosporus and the Black Sea. In contrast, Antigonus's mythography, with few exceptions, focuses more on stories restricted to the area of Greece and the Greek islands. Such a limitation in Antigonus's mythography is surprising, given that he dedicated an ample section of his list (*Mir.* 129–173) to the summary of the paradoxographical work of Callimachus, which was organized according to geographical criteria and covered regions extending as far as Iberia, the Black Sea, Egypt, Ethiopia, Arabia, and India. In the entire section on Callimachus, however, only the myths mentioned in items 131 (on the presence of Heracles in Demonesus, at the entry of the Black Sea) and 172 (on the birds of the island of Diomedes in the Adriatic) go beyond the limits of Greece and the Greek islands.

Ps.-Aristotle, furthermore, shows special interest in the material vestiges of the visits of diverse heroes and heroic expeditions, which is rare in other paradoxographers. The author mentions (*Mir. Ausc.* 58), for example, an inscription engraved on the so-called orichalcs of Pheneus stating that "Heracles, son of Amphitryon, dedicated them when he took Elis," to explain afterward that Heracles conquered Elis in accordance with the oracle pronounced by Augeas's daughter after her father's death. Similar cases abound: chapter 98 calls attention to a great rock in the Iapygian promontory: it was said that the hero could lift and move it using just one finger; chapter 100 describes the beautiful and impressive constructions built by Iolaus when he conquered Sardinia following the instructions of Heracles (probably referring to the cyclopean constructions found on the island, sometimes connected by modern scholars to an early Greek influence; see Vanotti 2007: 180–181, with bibliography); and chapter 108 points to Lagaria, in southern Italy (compare Str. 6.1.14), as the place where the instruments used to build the Trojan horse were still exhibited in the sanctuary of Athena Hilenia. Further information about sanctuaries allegedly founded by the heroes or statues and stelae made by them or dedicated to them as memorials of their presence are the topic of many other anecdotes in this author. Take, for example, *Mir. Ausc.* 109, on Diomedes's axes exhibited in the sanctuary of the Achaean Athena; 110, on a necklace dedicated to Artemis by Diomedes; and 131, on a stela dedicated to Deiope, found when the Athenians were building the sanctuary of Demeter in Eleusis.

In the other extant paradoxographical collections, myths only appear sporadically, but they reflect the same range of options: they can either refer to local traditions not connected to the geographical movements of a mythical character (for example, *Par. Flor.* 24, or *Par. Vat.* 19), or to heroic travel (*Par. Vat.* 18), and in the second case, on some rare occasions they also refer to the material traces of the traveling divinities (*Par. Vat.* 14).

The paradoxographers offer different kinds of mythographical material. However, such variety is hard to interpret as the product of particular choices on the part of the compilers, insofar as these mythographical stories were more than likely already present in their sources. The presence or absence of myths in a paradoxographical catalogue or section is, therefore, a consequence of the interest of the authors excerpted in such contents rather than a manifestation of the paradoxographer's attitude. It must be noted, for instance, that the section Antigonus dedicates to the summary of Aristotle's *History of Animals* (chs. 60–115) only offers mythographical content in one case: item 111, where examples of men and women who only beget male or female offspring are compared to Heracles, who had seventy-one sons and only one daughter. In Antigonus's section dedicated to book 9 of the *History of Animals* (*Mir.* 26–60), which may not be by Aristotle but is certainly Peripatetic, mythographical material is also extremely rare: only items 45, on the lameness of the linnet compared to that of Hephaestus, and 56 (see next section), on the parturition of she-wolves in relationship to Leto, make reference to myths or mythical characters. The lack of mythographical material in these sections clearly reflects the scarce interest of Peripatetic zoology in myths. The greater part of the mythographical material Antigonus transmits, however, is concentrated in the fourth section of the catalogue (chs. 115–128, a miscellaneous collection of materials of diverse origins) and in the section dedicated to the summary of Callimachus's work (chs. 129–173), a fact that might be expected considering this author's interest in myths as a poet and the likely relationship of his paradoxographical work to his poetic activity (see Schepens 1996: 403–404).

Similarly, the predominance of local myths or stories of mythical journeys also indicates the diverse interests of the original authors. Ps.-Aristotle includes mythographical stories only in its central section (chs. 78–136). Myths go practically unmentioned in chapters 1–77 and 137–151, once again closely related to Peripatetic science, and totally missing from the final section (items 152–178). This lack of mythographical information in the case of the chapters excerpting the Ps.-Plutarchean *De Fluviis*, where myths associated to rivers and mountains play a crucial role, requires an attempt at explanation. The reason for the absence of myths in the paradoxographical catalogue could perhaps be that in the original source, myths are not presented as direct explanations of the natural curiosities the paradoxographer selects (see next section).

The interest in tracking traveling heroes must be attributed to the sources the author uses in this central section, which have been the subject of some discussion among scholars. In the case of the chapters on Magna Graecia and the lands west of the Mediterranean, scholars attribute the information to Lycus of Rhegium or Timaeus of Tauromenium, while in the east they point to Theopompus (see Vanotti 2007: 39–46, with bibliography). However, the loss of the original texts of the excerpted authors leaves the attitudes and approaches with which they included these myths in their works unclear to us, and, above all, impedes us from evaluating the extent of credibility they were granted. Perhaps these historians were interested in reflecting traditions regarding ancient Greek influence in these areas or their connections with the Greek legendary past, or perhaps they were trying to detect the deep and venerable roots of the Greek colonies in these regions. They may also perhaps have received the traditions of the Greek colonies about their own origin with scepticism. And the same doubts affect the interpretation of the meaning of myths amongst the sources of Antigonus and Callimachus (on the role of myth in historiography, the study by Veyne 1988, especially 5–15, is a reference point; see also Henrichs 1999: especially 225–229; Stadter 2004; Candau Morón, González Ponce, and Cruz Andreotti 2004; Delattre 2010; and the recent general surveys by Saïd 2010 and Griffiths 2011).

All these aspects of the role of myths in the historians who were excerpted remain a mystery, but it is clear that these myths passed through the filter of the summarizing process the paradoxographers executed. Leaving aside the analysis of the role of mythographical material in the original texts then, the meaning of these myths in the final product—after the paradoxographical rewriting of the sources—deserves specific attention.

# 3. Myths as Explanations of Extraordinary Phenomena

Despite their differences, the paradoxographers coincide in significant aspects when dealing with myths. For instance, they usually preserve rare versions of well-known mythical stories or, rather, marginal details that are frequently not transmitted by other sources. Vanotti (2007: 37) considers this aspect particularly relevant in Ps.-Aristotle, which frequently transmits unique variants of myths not attested in other sources (see *Mir. Ausc.* 51, 57, 58). This feature, however, is by no means exclusive to Ps.-Aristotle; it can also be found in Antigonus and other paradoxographers (see, for example, Antig. *Mir.* 2, 4, 56, 117, 131, 163, all including information that is missing or extremely rare outside paradoxographical works).

However, apart from a predilection for infrequently attested versions and rare details of myths, perhaps the most significant feature all paradoxographers share is that the greater part of the mythological traditions they mention are not at the core of the *paradoxa*. Rather, they appear as collateral explanations for the natural or ethnographic curiosities they deal with, accounting for the origin of certain natural phenomena or strange customs along the same line as Antigonus's chapter 56. To take one example:

> Regarding the parturition of wolves, he [Aristotle] mentions something totally mythical, of which he also seems conscious. For he states that they all give birth during twelve days of the year. He says the reason for this, according to the story, is that Leto, in the shape of a she-wolf, was brought within twelve days from the Hyperboreans to Delos.

The detail of Leto's metamorphosis, apart from Aristotle and his commenters, is only attested in the sphere of paradoxographical literature (see *sch.* Ap. Rhod. 2.124, quoting Philostephanus, fr. 32 Müller). The core of the *paradoxon*, as may be appreciated, is not the mythical tale—that is, the story about Leto and her journey to Delos from the country of the Hyperboreans transformed into a she-wolf—but the fact that all wolves give birth during the same twelve-day period of the year. This specific detail in the myth of Leto acts as the explanation for the curious fact but is not the curious fact itself.

Comparison with the original version in Aristotle's *History of Animals* once again reveals the method of rewriting as Jacob explained it:

> There is an account given of the parturition of the she-wolf that borders on the fabulous, to the effect that she confines her lying-in to within twelve particular days of the year. And they give the reason for this in the form of a myth, viz. that when they transported Leto in so many days from the land of the Hyperboreans to the island of Delos, she assumed the form of a she-wolf to escape the anger of Hera. Whether this is the time of the parturition or not has not yet been verified; I give it merely as it is currently told. (Arist. *Hist. An.* VI 35, 580a 15–21; translation by D'Arcy Thompson 1910)

As expected, according to Jacob's analysis, the doubts Aristotle expressed about verification of the information regarding the time of parturition of wolves are diligently eliminated in the paradoxographical version. However, the paradoxographer maintains the mythical reason the source gave, even if he does not eliminate, but he rather seems to insist on Aristotle's consciousness about the mythical nature of the explanation.

Similar cases abound. For instance, the incapability of cicadas in Rhegium to sing (Antig. *Mir.* 1 and 2) is presented to the reader as the result of Heracles's prayers, because their song bothered him when he slept. A similar muteness affects the frogs in Seriphos (*Mir.* 4), even if its "mythical" origin—so the paradoxographer explains—is sometimes attributed to Heracles, sometimes to Perseus (apart from paradoxographical authors, only Ael. *NA* 3.37 attributes the loss of the frogs' voice in Seriphos to Perseus). Ps.-Aristotle (*Mir. Ausc.* 51) explains the particular morphology of the leaves of the olive tree called *kallistephanos* because of its divine origin in the land of the Hyperboreans, from where it was brought to Olympia by Heracles. Antigonus *Mir.* 163 describes a river in Crete which, during rainy days, protects those sitting in it from getting wet. According to the paradoxographer, the traditional explanation states that Europa washed herself in that river after having had intercourse with Zeus. The strange behaviour of the birds in the island of Diomedes, dealt with by Antigonus (*Mir.* 172) and Ps.-Aristotle (*Mir. Ausc.* 79), is explained through a myth: these birds are the companions of the hero after their metamorphosis (on these birds and their identification, see D'Arcy Thompson 1895: 59; 1918; Keller 1963: 206; Pollard 1977: 73, 101). Further items of Ps.-Aristotle present similar cases: we have already mentioned chapters 82 and 83, which respectively explain the peculiarities of a cave in Sicily and those of Cretan fauna through the myths of the rape of Persephone and the birth of Zeus. Apart from these items, chapter 81 explains the pestilential water of a lake near the Electrides Islands, in the Adriatic Sea, saying that Phaethon fell into that water when he was struck down by Zeus. Again, the pestilence of the water is explained through a myth in chapter 97: Heracles fought the Giants close to the Iapygian Promontory, so that their spilled blood accounts for the bad smell. Many other anecdotes offer similar examples. Myths as explanations do not just appear in the context of *paradoxa* regarding natural phenomena; they are also present in anecdotes concerning ethnography: Ps.-Aristotle's chapter 88, on the Iberian custom of not using money, links such practice to Heracles's visit, since the hero conducted a military campaign against them precisely because he was attracted by their wealth.

In the works of later paradoxographers the role of myths remains the same. For instance, *Par. Flor.* 24 describes a fountain in Arcadian Cleitor: everyone who drinks its water comes to hate wine. An inscription on it, so the paradoxographer says, links the phenomenon to Melampus, the mythological seer and healer who cured the daughters of Proetus from the madness Hera inflicted upon them. The poisonous water of the river Perinthus in Thrace is attributed to the drops of Gorgon blood that fell in it as Perseus carried Medusa's head in his hands (*Par. Vat.* 18), and the strange changes in sound produced by the river Marsyas in Phrygia, according to the compiler (*Par. Vat.* 19), are a consequence of Marsyas the flutist's drowning in that river. Again, the paradoxographer attests a unique version of the story, whereas, according to the *vulgata*, Marsyas died skinned by Apollo, and it was his blood that gave rise to the river (see, for example, Lib. *Narr.* 20, Ps.-Plu. *Fluv.* 10.1, Palaeph. 47; compare also Xen. *An.* 1.2.8).

As noted, the mythographical material in these works does not seem to have an origin different from that of the other contents of the *paradoxa* but were presumably already present in the sources the compilers used, together with parallel examples, expressions of doubt or disbelief, and the rational explanations and accounts of the scientific mechanisms governing the phenomena.

The elimination of every explanation that could account for strange phenomena was given in Jacob's article as one of the main elements of the rewriting method the paradoxographers used. Nevertheless, when these explanations are connected to a myth, they are apparently not subjected to the same rigor; rather, they pass the filter of rewriting and are able to remain in the final text. In these cases, the extraordinary and unexplained go beyond the limits of the exotic and the curious to enter the field of the supernatural and religious. The mythical ingredient turns merely curious anecdotes into real miracles, understood as facts that break with natural rules because of supernatural intervention. Again, the loss of the original texts impedes our knowing to what extent the excerpted sources kept a distance with respect to these mythical explanations. Cases such as that of Antigonus *Mir.* 56 and its comparison with the Aristotelian original leave the door open to the possibility that stories reflected by their sources as mere traditional tales or legends without clear factual value appear transformed into proven miracles in the works of the paradoxographers, thus blurring the—never completely clear—boundary between myth and history.

# 4. MYTHS AS PARALLEL EXAMPLES OF PARADOXA

Myths as explanations of extraordinary phenomena cause miracles to enter paradoxography and turn the exotic and unusual into supernatural. However, in some cases, the contrary process may be observed, such that paradoxographical anecdotes help bring mythical traditions back within the bounds of nature.

Examples of *paradoxa* that consist of a mythical story—that is, where myth is at the center of the *paradoxon* and does not act as a subordinate explanation for the real curiosity—are scarce in most of the paradoxographers. Antigonus *Mir.* 118 and *Par. Vat.* 31 and 32 show interest in mythical tales per se, but apart from these isolated examples, only in one of the extant collections—that of Phlegon of Tralles—is a particular interest in pure mythographical *paradoxa* observed.

Phlegon's collection of marvels dedicates its first three entries to long stories about dead people who come back to life: the famous tale of Philinnion and her hidden trysts with the young guest of her parents as a *revenant* (Phlegon, *Mir.* 1); the story of Polycritus, who comes back after his death when his hermaphrodite son is about to be sacrificed (Phlegon, *Mir.* 2); and that of the Syrian Buplagus, who gets up on the battle-field where he died and pronounces oracles against Rome (Phlegon, *Mir.* 3). However, apart from this first section, other thematic series in the catalogue combine curious stories that happened in historical times, recorded and transmitted by reliable sources, with the mythical parallels of such stories. For instance, the series of cases of androgyny and spontaneous transsexuality collected in items 6 to 10 is preceded by the stories of Teiresias and his famous transformation into woman and back to man (Phlegon, *Mir.* 4; compare *Par. Vat.* 31), and the story of Caenis, turned into a man, Caeneus, through the power of Poseidon (Phlegon, *Mir.* 5).

Astonishing and aberrant cases that happened shortly before Phlegon's own time and that were included in the records of the Roman religious administration—the sources Phlegon used to obtain such information—appear in Phlegon's paradoxographical collection together with similar examples provided by mythical tradition. Again, items 28 and 29 give accounts of extraordinary cases of multiple births: a woman in Alexandria who delivered twenty children in four pregnancies (the source of Phlegon is Antigonus *Mir.* 110) and another Egyptian woman who, in just one delivery, gave birth to five babies. Given the extraordinary and exceptional character of the case, they were raised at the expense of the Emperor Trajan (other sources link the same story to the Emperor Hadrian; Stramaglia 2011, 57). After such anecdotes, both of them verified in principle and guaranteed historically trustworthy (on the value of references to a king or kingly figure as guarantee of trustworthiness in ancient literature, see Gómez Espelosín 1994, 152–153), the paradoxographer includes two references to mythical cases that corroborate the extraordinary fertility of Egyptian women. First, Phlegon in *Mir.* 30 refers to Euryrrhoe, daughter of the Nile, who gave her husband Aegyptus, the eponymous hero of the country, fifty children. *Mir.* 31, for its part, mentions the fifty daughters of Danaus, born from Europa, who is also a daughter of the Nile.

As we have seen, during the process of excerpting and rewriting, mythical explanations did not follow the same rules as for the more scientific clarifications that we find for other astonishing phenomena. The case of Phlegon proves that mythical stories offering parallel examples of collected nonmythical anecdotes also have a place in the catalogues of rarities: instead of being avoided, as was the normal practice of the paradoxographers according to Jacob, mythical parallels are respected.

Moreover, sometimes the intention to give rationalistic explanation for myths, making them fit the laws of nature, may be observed. Items 34 and 35 of Phlegon, for instance, link the existence of centaurs to the area of the mountains of Arabia, transforming a mythical creature into an exotic being that lives at the limits of the known world but still belongs to the sphere of the physical world, not to that of the supernatural in a legendary tradition (see Shannon-Henderson 2019). Furthermore, the paradoxographer challenges readers to check the trustworthiness of the information about the existence of centaurs by visiting the storage rooms at the emperor's palace in Rome and "seeing for themselves" (*historēsai*) the mummified specimen of this creature, which was brought alive to Egypt from Arabia as a present for Claudius and then embalmed and transported to Rome after its death (see Mayor 2001: 239–240 for an interpretation of the nature of its body; for further testimonies about centaurs see Stramaglia 2011: 59).

Moreover, Phlegon describes the finding, inside a large wine jar, of a head thrice the human size, identified by an inscription as belonging to Idas, the foremost hero of Messenia (Phlegon, *Mir.* 11). This item starts off a series of reported findings of what apparently are the bones and complete skeletons of giants (on the interpretation of these bones, which probably belonged to extinct prehistoric animals, see Mayor 2001: 104–156). At the end of this series (ch. 15), Phlegon wonders if in the past nature (*physis*) produced beings of a particularly large size, once again recasting myths and mythical creatures within the bounds of natural processes. In other cases, the intention of explaining myths as deriving from the bizarre fancy of nature is not explicit; nevertheless, the intention to erase the border between myth and history by pointing out similarities between abnormal facts of the present and their parallels in a mythical past is clear in Phlegon, and perhaps in other paradoxographers as well: an Oxyrhynchus papyrus (*P.Oxy.* 2.218), transmitting the remains of a paradoxographical collection, shows a very similar mix of historiography (and ethnography) and mythography, where the connection between mythical and nonmythical anecdotes is merely a matter of thematic similarity (see Pajón Leyra 2014, 2017).

Two of the main rules for the rewriting process in paradoxographical literature—that is, elimination of causes and elimination of parallel examples—do not apply where these causes and parallel examples consist of myths. The process of re-elaboration intended to "build the marvellous" (*construction du merveilleux*) considers myth as able to promote perplexity and act as a support for the marvellous character of a story or phenomenon. We began this chapter by defining paradoxography as a branch of historiography. However, in light of the explanation of the role of myths given here, this definition should perhaps be refined. Paradoxographical literature should be described as a crossroads, a meeting point between the natural and the supernatural in a space where, through the authority of sources, miracle and science can appear side by side and talk to each other.

## Further Reading

The earliest study dedicated to paradoxography (Christ, Schmid, and Stählin 1920) is defined by a negative vision of this kind of literature, regarded as a degenerated branch (*Parasitengewächs*) of Peripatetic science. However, later works show more neutral and objective approaches considering paradoxography as a literary genre which, even if it is not the product of elevated intellectual activity, deserves consideration. Ziegler (1949) and the articles by Giannini (1963, 1964) are the earliest instances of a new attitude, followed by the studies of Schepens (1996) and Delcroix (1996), dealing with paradoxography in the context of *letteratura di consumo* (consumer literature) in antiquity, by Sassi's study of "Mirabilia" (1993), and by Pajón Leyra (2011), a monograph on paradoxographical literature.

The earliest extant edition of the works of the paradoxographers is that of Xylander (1568), including the catalogues of rarities by Phlegon, Apollonius and Antigonus (the authors transmitted by the *Codex Palatinus Graecus* 398). Further editions of diverse corpora of paradoxographical literature are that of Westermann (1839; adding Ps.-Aristotle, Michael Psellos's *Peri Paradoxōn Akousmatōn* and the anonymous treatise *On Women*, as well as fragmentary authors), Keller (1877; including the three paradoxographers of the *Pal. Gr.* 398 and the *Paradoxogaphus Vaticanus*), and Giannini (1965; for the moment, the most complete edition of the extant corpus of paradoxographical catalogues).

Individual paradoxographers have also been the subject of critical studies and commentaries, among which the works by Flashar (1990); Brodersen (2002); Vanotti (2007); and Stramaglia (2011) deserve special attention.

At this moment, new critical editions and in-depth commentaries of the works of the paradoxographers, including philological, literary and historical aspects, are being published under the direction of Stefan Schorn, as part of volume 4 of *Die Fragmente der Griechischen Historiker*, dedicated to antiquarian literature and including a substantial section on paradoxography. A renewed vision of these texts, as well as a fresh perspective on this kind of literature, is expected to emerge from this wide-ranging project.

## References

Brodersen, Kai. 2002. *Phlegon von Tralleis: Das Buch der Wunder und Zeugnisse seiner Wirkungsgeschichte*. Darmstadt: Die wissenschaftliche Buchgesellschaft.

Buxton, Richard, ed. 1999. *From Myth to Reason? Studies in the Development of Greek Thought*. Oxford: Oxford University Press.

Christ, Wilhelm von, Wilhelm Schmid, and Otto Stählin. 1974. *Geschichte der griechischen Literatur. Zweiter Teil: Die nachklassische Periode der griechischen Literatur. Erster Band: von 320 vor Christus bis 100 nach Christus*. Munich: Beck (= 1920).

Candau Morón, José M., Francisco J. González Ponce, and Gonzalo Cruz Andreotti, eds. 2004. *Historia y mito: El pasado legendario como fuente de autoridad: (actas del simposio internacional celebrado en Sevilla, Valverde del Camino y Huelva entre el 22 y el 25 de abril de 2003)*. Málaga: Centro de Ediciones de la Diputación de Málaga.

D'Arcy Thompson, Wentworth. 1895. *A Glossary of Greek Birds*. Oxford: Clarendon Press.

D'Arcy Thompson, Wentworth. 1910. *The Works of Aristotle Translated into English*. Vol. 4: *Historia Animalium*. Oxford: Clarendon Press.

D'Arcy Thompson, Wentworth. 1918. "The Birds of Diomede." *Classical Review* 32: 92–96.

Delattre, Charles. 2010. Introduction to *Mythe et fiction*, edited by Danièle Auger and Charles Delattre, 11–19. Paris: Presses Universitaires de Paris Nanterre.

Delattre, Charles, trans. 2011. *Pseudo-Plutarche. Nommer le monde: Origine des noms de fleuves, de montagnes et de ce qui s'y trouve*. Villeneuve d'Ascq, France: Presses du Septentrion.

Delcroix, Kris. 1996. "Ancient Paradoxography: Origin, Evolution, Production and Reception. Part II: The Roman Period." In *La letteratura di consumo nel mondo greco-latino. Atti del Convegno Internazionale. Cassino, 14–17 settembre 1994*, edited by Oronzo Pecere and Antonio Stramaglia, 410–460. Conference publication. Cassino: Università degli Studi di Casino.

Flashar, Hellmut. 1990. *Aristoteles. Mirabilia. Aristoteles Werke in Deutscher Übersetzung, Band 18: Opuscula, Teil II*, 6–154. Berlin: De Gruyter.

Fraser, Peter M. 1972. *Ptolemaic Alexandria*. 3 vols. Oxford: Oxford University Press.

Giannini, Alessandro. 1963. "Studi sulla paradossografia greca I. Da Omero a Callimaco: Motivi e forme del meraviglioso." *Rendiconti del Instituto Lombardo* 97: 247–266.

Giannini, Alessandro. 1964. "Studi sulla paradossografia greca II. Da Callimaco all'età imperiale: La letteratura paradoxográfica." *Acme* 17: 99–140.

Giannini, Alessandro. 1965. *Paradoxographorum Graecorum Reliquiae*. Milano: Istitutoo Editoriale Italiano.

Gómez Espelosín, Francisco J. 1994. "Estrategias de veracidad en Ctesias de Cnido." *Polis* 6: 143–168.

Griffiths, Alan. 2011. "Myth in History." In *A Companion to Greek Mythology*, edited by Ken Dowden and Niall Livingstone, 195–207. Oxford: Blackwell.

Henrichs, Albert. 1999. "Demythologizing the Past, Mythicizing the Present: Myth, History, and the Supernatural at the Dawn of the Hellenistic Period." In *From Myth to Reason? Studies in the Development of Greek Thought*, edited by Richard Buxton, 223–248. Oxford: Oxford University Press.

Jacob, Christian. 1983. "De l'art de compiler à la fabrication du merveilleux: Sur la paradoxographie grecque." *Lalies* 2: 121–140.

Keller, Otto. 1877. *Rerum Naturalium Scriptores Graeci Minores*. Leipzig: Teubner.

Keller, Otto. 1963. *Die antike Tierwelt II*. Hildesheim: Georg Olms (= 1913).

Mayor, Adrienne. 2001. *The First Fossil Hunters: Paleontology in Greek and Roman Times*. Princeton, NJ: Princeton University Press.

Pajón Leyra, Irene. 2011. *Entre ciencia y maravilla: El género literario de la paradoxografía griega*. Zaragoza, Spain: Prensas Universitarias de Zaragoza.

Pajón Leyra, Irene. 2014. "Little Horror Stories in an Oxyrhynchus Papyrus: A Re-edition and Commentary of P.Oxy. II 218." *Archiv für Papyrusforschung* 60: 304–330.

Pajón Leyra, Irene. 2017. "Anonymous, Collection of Horror Stories Including Ethnography and Mythography (P. Oxy. II 218) (1683)." In *Die Fragmente der Griechischen Historiker Part IV*, edited by Stefan Schorn. Leiden: Brill.

Pigon, Jakub, ed. 2008. *The Children of Herodotus. Greek and Roman Historiography and Related Genres*. Cambridge, UK: Cambridge Scholars.

Pollard, John. 1977. *Birds in Greek Life and Myth*. London: Thames and Hudson.

Saïd, Suzanne. 2010. "Muthos et historia dans l'historiographie grecque des origines au début de l'Empire." In *Mythe et fiction*, edited by Danièle Auger and Charles Delattre, 69–96. Paris: Presses Universitaires de Paris Nanterre.

Sassi, Maria M. 1993. "Mirabilia." In *Lo spazio letterario della Grecia Antica*, vol. 1: *La produzione e la circolazione del testo*, tomo 2: *L'Ellenismo*, edited by Giuseppe Cambiano, Luciano Canfora, and Diego Lanza, 449–468. Rome: Salerno Editrice.

Schepens, Guido. 1996. "Ancient Paradoxography: Origin, Evolution, Production and Reception. Part I: The Hellenistic Period." In *La letteratura di consumo nel mondo greco-latino, Atti del Convegno Internazionale. Cassino, 14–17 settembre 1994*, edited by Oronzo Pecere and Antonio Stramaglia, 375–409. Conference publication. Cassino: Università degli Studi di Cassino.

Shannon-Henderson, Kelly E. 2019. "Phlegon's Paradoxical Physiology. Centaurs in the Peri Thaumasion." In *Medicine and Paradoxography*, edited by George Kazantzidis, 141–162. Berlin: De Gruyter

Stadter, Philip A. 2004. "From the Mythical to the Historical Paradigm the Transformation of Myth in Herodotus." In *Historia y mito: El pasado legendario como fuente de autoridad: (actas del simposio internacional celebrado en Sevilla, Valverde del Camino y Huelva entre el 22 y el 25 de abril de 2003)*, edited by José M. Candau Morón, Francisco J. González Ponce, and Gonzalo Cruz Andreotti, 31–46. Málaga: Centro de Ediciones de la Diputación de Málaga.

Stramaglia, Antonio. 2011. *Phlegon Trallianus. Opuscula de Rebus Mirabilibus et De Longaevis*. Berlin and New York: Teubner.

Vanotti, Gabriella. 2007. *Aristotele. Racconti meravigliosi*. Milan: Bompiani.

Veyne, Paul. 1988. *Did the Greeks Believe in their Myths? An Essay on the Constitutive Imagination*. Translated by Paula Wissing. Chicago: University of Chicago Press.

Westermann, Anton. 1839. *Paradoxographoi. Scriptores Rerum Mirabilium Graeci*. Brunswick and London: G. Westermann; Black and Armstrong.

Ziegler, Konrad. 1949. "Paradoxographoi." *RE* 18.3: 1137–1166.

# CHAPTER 30

## MYTHOGRAPHY AND EDUCATION

### R. SCOTT SMITH AND STEPHEN M. TRZASKOMA

CHILDREN in ancient Greece and Hellenized Rome would have been exposed to stories about the mythical past from nearly every quarter. This familiarity began early in life, but it would have formed part of a continuum of experience with mythical narrative and information that would—at least for elite male children—have been capped by increasingly complex and demanding training through formal education. As youngsters, such children would have heard their first stories about gods, heroes, and monsters from their caregivers, whether parents, slaves, or freed individuals. Plato's insistence that nurses should take care to choose morally appropriate stories (*Resp.* 377e; see also Ps.-Plut. *De Lib. Educ.* 5) indicates that storytelling was an expected part of childrearing, but it also demonstrates a societal division of experience: the store of common mythical stories would have been shared by all levels of society, but elites' relationship to myth would have been dramatically different once formal schooling began. An enslaved nurse could tell a boy a mythical tale, hopefully a morally improving one, but that nurse would not have access to the intellectual apparatus of myth criticism that proliferated in the ancient world from the classical period onward. The educated elite, however, would go through a multistage process of increasing sophistication, and the mythical content and methods of that education would likewise show an amplified complexity as students progressed.

It may seem dramatic to frame it this way, but one aim of that pedagogical program was to inculcate mythographical habits of mind in every single student, and these intellectual habits, in turn, intersected with and informed almost all of the rest of their educational experience and what they did with it when they entered adult life. Putting the myth-related aspects of education into an explicitly mythographical framework has only recently become part of the scholarly discourse on the topic (in, for instance, Gangloff 2002; Gibson 2013; and Trzaskoma 2017), but the basic hypothesis we will be working from in this chapter is an extension of this new turn. Our view, simply put, is that all ancient students were taught—not exclusively, of course—through mythographically derived materials, coached to "have a worldview shaped by mythographical texts" (Trzaskoma 2017: 473), and trained to a greater or lesser extent, depending on what age a student stopped his schooling, *to be practitioners of mythographical methods*.

This strong formulation, to be sure, must remain merely a hypothesis, but it is worth exploring here and investigating further in the future how knowledge of mythology, acquired continually through a variety of avenues, was augmented through formal education and shaped into mythographical habits and practices. Of course, we are not arguing that the (or even a) point of ancient education was to produce writers of mythographical treatises, but that the general intellectual atmosphere of the ancient world consisted of mythographical elements, and that this formed an epistemological cycle: as students emerged from their education with systematic mythographical habits of mind and participated in civic, literary, scholarly, and artistic aspects of life, those habits shaped these aspects, making it crucial for students in the future to be trained similarly so that they, too, could participate effectively in these domains.

As we mentioned above, mythological information—narratives and what we might term mythological data (names, relationships, connections)—would have been acquired continuously by almost all members of ancient society. This would have been fundamentally the same for elite children, but with differences of detail, primarily because of the resources wealth could bring to the process. While walking through town with their *paedagogi*, for instance, well-off children would pass by sanctuaries of the gods and hear stories about them, some of which might have resembled the local myths reported by Pausanias. Visual and plastic arts, too, could introduce or reinforce already known stories. From an early period, temples were richly decorated with scenes from all sorts of mythical cycles. The descriptions of the mostly mythical paintings in the elder Philostratus's *Imagines* (for a related discussion, see the final section of Leach's chapter in this volume), which are explicitly addressed to a child (1.1., *ō pai*), shows that art collections like the Delphic Lesche (Paus. 10.25.1–31.12) could be used for learning about myths, but also how a viewer's knowledge of myth contributed to the interpretation of the art and to his view of the artist's aims and "truth" in a multidirectional process. Vases, reliefs, and sarcophagi (on vases and sarcophagi, see Topper and Newby, respectively, in this volume) also presented scenes from the rich storehouse of Greek myth. The houses and villas of the wealthy in and around Pompeii and Herculaneum were richly decorated with wall paintings of mythical figures, exposing the young to representations of heroic and divine stories (see Leach, this volume). And, of course, from an early period, rhapsodic, choral, and tragic performances featuring mythical characters such as Theseus, Heracles, Meleager, and Tantalus were part of civic life and a clear avenue for transmission of myth. As time went on, other performance genres such as mime and pantomime, joined these. It is impossible to give a complete account of how this informal education in mythical narrative and data interacted with more formal instructional activities, but it should not be forgotten that any individual's education in myth would have been tangled and composite.

# 1. The Educational System and Myth

By contrast, the exposure to mythical accounts in their written form was for the most part limited to a relatively small elite with access to literate education. Over time, the role of written texts in the education of young, mostly male, elites increased during the Hellenistic period. The transition from a *paideia* linked to the *polis* and focused on athletics, music, and training for war to one based more on literature had its roots already in the classical period, owing much to the sophists, Isocrates, and Plato (Marrou 1982, pt. 1, chs. 1–7; summary overview: Morgan 1998: 9–25). But it was only in the Hellenistic period that we find crystalized the general institution of formal education based on the written text—an institution that, despite some variation, endured with surprising consistency into and through the Roman period. Since mythography—literally "writing myths"—is intimately tied to literacy, it is no surprise that mythographical texts burgeoned precisely at the moment when the education of the elite became more and more focused on literacy and the reading of written texts.

Evidence from the ancient authors who wrote on Greco-Roman education (especially Quintilian, Plutarch, and Libanius), as well as from documentary papyri, reveals a rather homogenous educational praxis across time and space despite the lack of any centralized authority. Broadly speaking, it was based on a progression of steps. First, at age six or seven, a child would learn the basics of writing and reading under an elementary teacher. Following this, at around eleven years of age, a student would move on to instruction by a *grammaticus* (Greek, *grammatikos;* we use the Latin term throughout for consistency), whose main responsibilities focused on the reading of poets and the correctness of speech. Finally, at around 15, the few students who were to attain the highest level of education would begin study under a *rhetor*, or specialist in composition, argumentation, and public speaking. Of course, not all students went through the stages at the same ages, and allowances must be made for local variations, but in the broadest terms, the structure of Hellenistic and post-Hellenistic education seems to have been consistent throughout the Mediterranean and to have persisted during later time periods.

As will become clear, myth—and in our view, mythography, as well—was deeply embedded at all three levels. Students were exposed to the mythical poetry of Homer, Euripides, and others from a surprisingly early point in the curriculum. And throughout, they were asked to copy, read, memorize, categorize, summarize, and criticize Greek myths in a variety of exercises. As Huys (2013: 117) notes, "[M]ythology is omnipresent in school papyri, not so much as a separate subject, but as an element interwoven into all kinds of exercise" (see Bonner 1977: 239). To be precise, however, when one is "categorizing," "summarizing," or "criticizing" myth, activities that happened primarily at the advanced stages of ancient education, these tasks are very different from a basic one such as copying a passage from a mythical text, and we have moved from students' merely learning myth to their *manipulating* myth. That is, advanced students are performing the basic activities of both systematic and interpretive mythography, and any texts produced during this process are examples of mythography, no matter how simplistic, short, or crude they may be in comparison to our more scholarly mythographical texts. And, despite the strangeness of speaking of oral mythography, we must assume that invisible to us was a huge amount of in-person instruction and practice in the methods of mythography that were never recorded in writing for preservation.

So, how was mythography embedded into the exercises that students were given? We wish to focus on the occasions in the educational cursus when students were asked to write down myths or to compose texts interpreting them, as well as the ways in which these exercises intersected, in both form and function, with mythographical texts proper: lists, narrative stories, and summaries (systematic mythography), as well as rationalizing and allegorizing criticism of myth (interpretative mythography). As will become apparent, these exercises not only use and frequently replicate mythographical texts, they also perpetuate the forms we have come to know from mythographical collections. In other words, any students involved in formal education for any length of time were not only exposed to existing formal mythography, but were required to become active practitioners of its methods, even if they were not being trained strictly in the production of large-scale mythographical texts.

Two caveats are perhaps necessary. First, it is impossible to do justice to all the evidence from school exercises, which come from the 4th century BCE to the eighth century CE in both Greek and Latin. Second, some "school exercises" may not in fact belong to the classroom—just as some mythographical compendia may in fact be pedagogical. As a shortcut, we generally rely on the judgment of Cribiore (1996) to identify proper school texts.

# 2. Basic Literacy: Writing Down Names and Domains of Knowledge

After learning how to write the alphabet, a student moved on to writing and pronouncing syllables (*ban, ben, bēn, bin,* and so on), followed by whole words. A number of word lists have been preserved in schoolbooks from late antiquity (for instance, in the *Hermeneumata Leidensia*), but papyri from Egypt give us the clearest glimpse into the kinds of lists that were most common: birds, gods, rivers, names of months, and, above all, mythological figures (for a temporal and geographical table: Morgan 1998, table 5). The well-known *livre d'écolier* (Guéraud and Jouguet 1938), a Greek notebook from the 3rd century BCE, shows a progression of exercises: after a list of syllables and numbers, there are lists of gods and rivers, followed by lists of words, mostly names, grouped by number of syllables. Although none of the monosyllables are mythological in nature, the rest are predominantly so. Some are quite familiar, others rather obscure. For instance, the following are tetrasyllabic names:

> Menelaus, Amphimachus, Ascalaphus, Elepenor, Antimachus, Polynices, Eteocles, Hippomedon, Antilochus

This notebook, written in a "teacher's or a professional scribe's hand" (Cribiore 1996: no. 379), would have likely served as a model for students to copy. Model word lists could also have been written on other materials, such as the one on an *ostrakon* containing syllabified mythological names found at a military outpost in Egypt (*O. Claud.* 2.415, Cribiore 2001: 136–137; Cribiore 1996: no. 113, with pp. 42–43): Paris, Peleus, Perseus, Pentheus, Procne, and so on. Other word lists were clearly student copies. An example is a disyllabic list from the 1st century CE (*P.Genova* 2.53), written in a hand that shows control over letter formation but still lacks fluency (Cribiore 1996: no. 100). This list, broken down alphabetically into twenty-four groups of four words each, includes mostly mythological figures, especially from Homer's *Iliad*; and this is true of many other lists, even though a wide variety of non-Homeric figures are also represented (see the word lists at Cribiore 1996: no. 390; and Milne 1908: 122). What is important here is that such practice could theoretically be done with completely randomized lists of words, but instead, the dominant method is to use lists that already reflect knowledge categories. To put it another way, although these are basic handwriting and reading exercises, they are, simultaneously, ways of controlling knowledge by dividing it into analytical domains beginning from an early point in a student's intellectual formation (just as learning to arrange things in alphabetical order is another preparatory form of mental organization). The most prominent of these domains is myth, which is thus segregated into a category of material of its own in the intellectual formation of the very young. Although it would be facile to call this mythography, it was evidently deemed a worthwhile preparatory activity, and the assemblage of mythical data—though merely at the level of names that belong together precisely because they are those of figures from myth—is a necessary precursor to mythography and to a mythographical mindset.

The most elaborate list of names comes from the justly famous *P.Bour.* 1, a papyrus notebook dating from the 4th century CE (probably in a Christian context; see Cribiore 1996: no. 393; Baplu and Huys 2009). It includes some two hundred names, nearly all mythological, organized first by number of syllables, and then alphabetically. It is elementary in nature, and according to the most recent editors (Baplu, Huys, and Schmidt 2010: 61), "one of the important functions of copying this notebook must have been learning to write as a preparation to read texts . . . Most listed words were propaedeutic to correctly reading—and thus pronouncing, since in ancient practice reading implied reading aloud—classical Greek literature, especially but not exclusively the Homeric poems." Indeed, Homeric names are found consistently throughout this word list, but they form only a fraction of the list, and what we have here is really a broad collection of mythological names: some are major figures (such as Theseus, Perseus, and Heracles), while others are more obscure (such as Bienor, Thestor, and Neleus).

The inclusion of obscure figures from Boeotian legend such as Hyrieus and Hyperes, two sons of Poseidon and Alcyone, seems at first glance ambitious, but, as Huys notes (2013: 121), the word lists tended to include unusual names. The propensity toward the unusual or difficult is symptomatic of the way ancient educators viewed early education. As Quintilian explains it (*Inst.* 1.1.34–35), it was important not to spend time on common material but to practice with the obscure so that students could simultaneously acquire basic skills and, alongside them, some recherché knowledge. This helps to explain the appearance of difficult names on other lists, such as that of the *livre d'écolier* mentioned earlier, where we find Pityocamptes (Pine-Bender), an epithet for Sinis not found in extant Greek poetry but exclusively in mythographical works (Huys 2013: 120)—and in this list. One can easily imagine a classroom setting in which a student, after writing out and pronouncing either Hyrieus or Pityocamptes, asks the teacher who this figure was. The teacher's response would naturally have involved some comment, perhaps a brief story, to satisfy a student's curiosity. But, just as the student is acquiring practical knowledge of reading and writing, even in the absence of such additional lessons from the teacher, so, too, is he acquiring a sense of the scope of myth, of what belongs to its domain—and therefore less directly, what does *not* belong to it. The implicit lesson is that *these* people and *these* places go together, not because they appear in a single work that tells a myth, but because they belong to myth, and both teachers and students are thus engaging in a heuristic technique of organizing the world and their knowledge of it.

## 3. THE GRAMMATICUS AND MYTHOGRAPHY

After achieving a level of literacy, and absorbing a great deal of implicit knowledge, the student would move to the next level of education under a *grammaticus*. In the opening of Dionysios Thrax's *Ars Grammatica*, the subject (*grammatikē*) is defined as the "knowledge of what is in essence said by poets and prose writers." He breaks the subject into six areas of study, the third of which is most pertinent for our purposes: ready exposition of unfamiliar words and subject matter (*historiai*). The term *historiai*, translated here as "subject matter," covers real persons and places, but it particularly implies mythological references (Sext. Emp. *Math.* 1.43, 91–94, 252–253; Cicero *De Or.* 1.187; Quintilian 1.8.18; Marrou 1982: 281). Not only were *grammatici* expected to know the poems themselves, but they had to be experts in the broader mythical tradition and able to explain the oblique references found in the works of poets. Juvenal (7.231–260) provides an insightful anecdote about what parents expected their children's teacher to know about the text of Vergil: What were the names of Anchises's nurse and Anchemolus's stepmother? How old did Acestes live to be, and how many jars of Sicilian wine did he give to the Trojans? We might suspect that Juvenal is exaggerating here, until we realize that Servius (*ad Aen.* 10.388) actually provides the full story (*historia*) of Anchemolus's lineage, identifying his stepmother as one Casperia. In a wonderful reversal of roles, we find Tiberius asking his retinue of *grammatici*—here perhaps "myth experts" (see Francese 1999 on this term)—such obscure questions as "Who is the mother of Hecuba?" "What was Achilles's name among the maidens?" and "What song did the Sirens sing?" (Suetonius, *Tib.* 70; compare Tiberius's *philologoi* at Plut. *De Def. Or.* 419d). These vignettes assure us that teachers were expected to have a firm command of mythical lore.

Doubtlessly, the knowledge of the *grammatici* was grounded in mythographical texts that provided this kind of information, both while they themselves were students and after they had entered professional life, when they would have passed it on, in turn, to their pupils when they were reading the foundational poetic works. No canonical list of poets survives from antiquity, although Quintilian's list of Greek poets seems to follow that sanctioned by the Hellenistic critics Aristarchus and Aristophanes (*Inst. Or.* 10.1.46–54). Other lists are headed by expected authors such as Homer, Hesiod, Pindar, and Euripides, paralleled by high numbers of papyri (Sex. Emp. *Math.* 1.58.2; Libanius *Ep.* 1036), but we find other more ambitious school texts listed as well (Stat. *Silv.* 5.3.152–158). Of course, in a Roman context, where Greek and Roman authors were read side by side, one must include Vergil and (to a lesser degree) Horace, Lucretius, and Ovid.

The allusive nature of this poetry, however, makes it less than ideal for *learning* myths in the form of complete narrations, and school commentaries and other works of criticism, including mythographical criticism, prove that help was needed for the basic understanding of myths, for contextualizing mythical individuals and places within the larger body of myths, and for interpreting the works for intellectual and moral purposes. As a consequence, when a student moved on to study with a *grammaticus*, he also entered a new phase of mythical and mythographical learning. He was expected to learn more and more detailed information but also to do new things with that information. Students just embarking on the *Iliad* then, as now, could be confused by the bulk of characters or by patronymics such as *Peleiades* and *Atreides* (Hom. *Il.* 1.1, 1.7), and they probably had some difficulty remembering which gods sided with the Greeks, and which with the Trojans, confusion that probably resonates with every teacher of myth today. There are also unexplained references to the wider mythical tradition. Take, for example, the famous fifth line of the *Iliad*, "for the will of Zeus came to pass," which alludes to an unexplained reason for the mass destruction in the Trojan War. Or consider the allusion to Aristaeus at Vergil, *Georgics* 1.14–15, "O forester, whose three hundred white bullocks graze on the fertile thickets of Ceos." It stretches credulity to think that the usual way a reader would have learned about Aristaeus's migration to Ceos was from an allusive poetic reference such as this; more likely, it would have to have come from a mythographical text consulted during the course of reading, whether on the student's or the teacher's part.

Of all the poets, Homer was king and the first one read in the educational cursus, in both Greece and Rome (at least by Quintilian's day). A student preparing to read the *Iliad* might have been asked to write out preliminary material such as basic lists of gods and heroes and their genealogies. A papyrus, likely from the early 3rd century CE (*P.Oxy.* 65.4460, originally edited by Schmidt), shows just such a list, which includes the most important Achaean heroes from the *Iliad*, followed by the Olympian gods, all with basic genealogies (father and mother) and the occasional other tidbit (Hermes's mother Maia is noted as "daughter of Atlas," and he is "a herald"). Although the original editor regards the list of heroes as part of a "mythological compendium," it is likely that both lists are from a school context (Bagnall 2011: 330). Whichever is true, the potential for easy confusion between a circulating mythographical work and a school text is instructive, although such lists, in our view, would have been less necessary for an advanced student or an already literate reader, who would have encountered this basic material earlier in his or her education. For a more elementary learner, the rote reading and copying of such lists would have given them practice in basic skills, just as copying word lists had in the first phase of study. But just as that repetitive and unimaginative work was thought to have additional benefits (recall Quintilian's advice to challenge students), so, too, the grouping together here of exclusively Iliadic heroes and similar activities would presumably extend this sort of learning. No ancient educational source explicitly describes or theorizes this process for this stage of learning, but it is reasonable to suppose it must have instilled mythographical mental habits. Leaving aside the obvious fact that students were imbibing massive amounts of mythical data, they were being asked to further organize the mythical domain, tying parts of it to individual authors and beginning to draw increasingly sophisticated lessons through the act of making more complex associations.

The simultaneous acquisition of mythical information and its organization are thus deeply embedded in the curriculum and inextricably linked. We can also see this when we look at other writing exercises designed to prepare learners to read Homer, such as the series of exercises found in a papyrus from the 2nd century CE (*P.Oxy.* 56.3829). After a catechism that is also found on three other papyri (see Cameron 2004: 118; see Cribiore 2001: 209; Bonner 1977: 238), there is an introduction (*hypothesis*) to the *Iliad* that gives the mythical background, followed by a summary of the first book (also termed a *hypothesis*). Since the damaged papyrus includes only the end of the catechism, the following example includes material, set in square brackets, drawn from another papyrus (*PSI* 1.19 = Cribiore 1996: no. 405) to give us a sense of what the whole would have looked like:

> [What gods support the Trojans (*barbaroi*)? Ares, Aphrodite, Apollo, Artemis, Leto, Scamander. Who is the king of the Trojans? Priam. Who is the Trojan general?] Hector. His advisors? Polydamas and Agenor. Who are the heralds? Idaios and Eumedes, Dolon's father . . . Who are the seers? Helenus and Cassandra, Priam's children.
>
> The introduction (*hypothesis*) to Homer's *Iliad* from the beginning. Condemning the heroic age of godlessness, Zeus along with Themis schemed to obliterate it entirely. Celebrating the marriage of Thetis and Peleus on Mt. Pelion at the home of the centaur Chiron, he invited all the other gods to his house, but on Zeus' orders Hermes kept Eris from entering. Angered, she threw a golden apple into the banquet, over which conflict arose among Hera, Athena and Aphrodite. Zeus made it a prize for the most beautiful . . .

Only the barest traces of the rest of the story remain, but one can make out the names Alexandros, Asia, Hera, and the beginning letters of the word "war." Obviously, we have a complete account of pre-Iliadic events. Then comes the summary of the first book, starting with a quotation of the first line ("Rage..."):

> Agamemnon had as his concubine a prisoner of war, Chryseis, the daughter of Chryses, the priest of Apollo. But he did not give her back to her father when he begged. Therefore...

The papyrus breaks off at this point, but in its original form, it would have likely looked like other *hypotheses* (here, "summaries") of Homer's books, which were not meant to obviate the need to read the epic, but to prepare learners to read the poetry itself, which was hard enough for those familiar with the outline of the story (Cribiore 2001: 205; van Rossum-Steenbeek 1998: 157–163).

Here we encounter not only propaedeutic exercises in preparation for reading, but also various ways of relating a piece of literature to the wider mythical world, and in forms that we would call mythographical. The catechism, which probably reflects the oral nature of a classroom setting, continues the organizational methods found in the elementary lists mentioned earlier. Another catechism (*Disc.* 2.19.6–7), as Epictetus dramatizes it, also asks students to tie this material to authorities whom we would call mythographers, such as Hellanicus. This practice of source citation is a feature of mythographical texts (Cameron 2004: 116–119). The *hypothesis*, in turn, used here in the meaning of "introduction," not "summary," not only gives students the necessary background to understand the *Iliad*, but also illustrates for them the relationship between text and the wider mythical tradition. If this narrative were not found in a school context but on its own, one would be hard-pressed to decide whether it was part of a mythographical manual such as Ps.-Apollodorus's *Library*, a summary of the *Cypria*, a scholion, or, as here, a school exercise.

The papyrus then moves to the fragmentarily preserved summary (we would also call this, confusingly, a *hypothesis*) of the first book of the *Iliad*. Several *hypotheses* of Homeric books from a school context have survived (van Rossum-Steenbeek 1998: 73; compare Huys 2013: 122). We also find student copies of *hypotheses* of Euripides's plays (usually a mixture of background and summary), for instance, a twice-copied version of Euripides's *Temenidae* that shows "remarkable overlap with the alphabetic collection known as the 'Tales of Euripides'" (Huys 2013: 122–123 on *P.Mich.* inv. 1319 = van Rossum-Steenbeek no. 13). We are accustomed to think of examples of the former as "mythography" and of the latter as "school exercises," but they are fundamentally one and the same. Students, in other words, were being made to produce mythographical works, not for wider circulation, of course, but for their own benefit and intellectual training. The very structures and principles of mythography, then, were being written into their minds and reinforced continually, both at a specific moment such as the one we are contemplating (preparing to read the first book of the *Iliad*) and subsequently through the actual reading of it and when moving on to other texts.

As noted above, Homer's poem—like all ancient mythological poems—includes a number of unexplained references and the names of people and places that are connected in one way or another to myth, even if Homer himself does not elaborate on most of these links. This is the "subject matter" (*historiai*) that a *grammaticus* was supposed to explain. If the narrative stories found in the D-Scholia to Homer and separately in the papyri (both deriving from the *Mythographus Homericus*; see Pagès, this volume), most frequently introduced as *historiai*, are representative of the kinds of material students would encounter in class, then reading Homer would have been slow going because references had to be, and were, fully explained. In the first ten lines there are six substantial *historiai*, and thirteen in the first hundred lines. These narratives abound in names and genealogies. Take, for instance the *historia* for the reference to Tenedos at Schol. (D) *Il.* 1.38 (Our translation):

> Tenedos is an island lying in view of Troy. It did not yet have this name, since Tennes and Leucothea had not yet been born to Cycnus son of Poseidon. The people in the past called it Leucophrys. When, however, Tennes and Leucothea were born to Cycnus, their mother did not survive, and Cycnus remarried Phylonome or (as some say) Polybia. Now, Phylonome fell in love with Tennes, now a grown man, and sent him messages about getting together. When he rightfully made sure the bonds of nature were not broken, she went to his father and accused him of trying to rape her. Cycnus believed the accusation, arrested his son, put him in a chest and threw it into the nearby sea. Poseidon saved him because of his modesty and because he was his grandson. He made the chest land on the island Leucophrys. The people there saw the chest, took off the cover, and learned what had happened. They not only made him their king, they also named the island Tenedos after him.

This sort of example, which could be multiplied many times, both in the *MH* and elsewhere, reveals that underlying the attempt to read an individual line or understand an individual reference in a poem is the larger goal of having students acquire and create for themselves mental maps of myth, a process that is an obvious analog to systematic mythography. In looking at the passage above, we may note that most of the information after the first brief sentence is entirely unnecessary for understanding the line of Homer to which it is attached, which simply refers to Tenedos as a cult center for Apollo. Instead, we are given an etiological explanation for the name change of the island and learn about Tennes, a lesser-known light in the mythological galaxy. The poem, in addition to being read for its own sake, provides an opportunity to expand and organize a student's knowledge of myth, as well as geography, which, it should be noted, is here learned *through* references to myth. It wasn't just access to this information that came from the *grammaticus* and written mythographical resources but also access to a blueprint for the construction of a mythographical understanding of myth, a mythographical mentality.

As we saw with the lists of Homeric characters, students studying with a *grammaticus* continued doing what seems the most elementary of exercises, the writing out of lists. But unlike the lists associated with the earliest stage of education, those produced at this level begin to show greater organizational principles. Consider *P.Oxy.* 61.4099, which probably is from a school context (Huys 1996: 205). In the surviving text, we find lists of mythical groupings: the names and basic genealogies of the Epigoni, and the individual names of the Moerae, Horae, Charites, Sirens, Gorgons, Titanesses, Eumenides, and Harpies. So, again we see that students are not just passively learning mythical data, they are being asked to actively organize and systemize it as a mythographer does (see, for example, the list of Epigoni at Hyg. *Fab.* 71). Such lists—again, in both school exercises and mythographical works—could also be organized thematically according to other principles, such as the affairs Zeus had with mortal women at *P.Mil. Vogl.* 3.126 (= van Rossum-Steenbeek no. 64), with which we can compare Hyginus's list (*Fab.* 226, titled *Mortal Women Who Slept with Jupiter*). Given the predilection of poets (especially those like Ovid), novelists, and orators to accumulate mythological exempla that are related by theme, the reading and production of these lists needed to be part of the curriculum of the *grammaticus.* But the aim of this was not to help students understand the basic meaning of a nest of exempla, which are generally obvious on the surface, so much as to train those who might go on to produce and manipulate groups of exempla in future literary works or in speeches. When they appear, then, they are part of the mental framework of both their authors and their readers in a self-reinforcing fashion: readers expect them, and authors produce them because of their orientation as readers themselves. We noted earlier that the goal of the average *grammaticus* was not to produce mythographers qua mythographers, and so we must suppose that instilling a mythographical frame of mind had a more general purpose, one that was useful for any educated individual.

As students progressed, they would be asked not only to copy mythical subject matter, but also to start producing it themselves—again, in a sort of feedback loop that shows the interchange between the use and production of mythographical material. We have numerous examples of student copies of narratives, for instance, on a tablet dated April 24, 327 CE, where the story of Agamemnon and Iphigenia is written out three times (Cribiore 1996: no. 146). Another example, once thought to be an original composition, contains the beginning of the story of Adrastos and his daughters (*P.Oxy.* 124, 3rd c. CE; see Cribiore 1996: no. 284; see also p. 32):

> Adrastos, the king of Argos, married a woman of the same station and had two daughters, Deipyle and Aigialia, who, though not unattractive, were unlucky in terms of marriage, for no one wooed them. So Adrastos sent an embassy to Delphi to find out the reason ... [papyrus breaks off]

Even if the story is not an original composition, the very act of writing it down would have introduced students to both the content and manner of producing a basic narrative. In it, we find a style typical of mythographical summaries, a simplicity of form, an efficient narrative form that is heavily reliant on participles (particularly genitives absolute), and we also see a focus on genealogy, another feature of mythography.

By contrast, a papyrus now in the Ashmolean Museum (Barns 1949), dated to the 2nd century BCE and written in a "rapid" student hand but clumsily executed, was clearly an attempt on the part of the student to paraphrase or summarize an unidentified epic or lyric poem about Heracles. We find a mythographical parallel for this student-driven attempt to summarize a literary text in the *Erotica Pathemata*, which contains prose summaries of literary myths and was composed, perhaps not coincidentally, by the well-known *grammaticus* Parthenius. But at a certain point, it is clear that students move from copying and summarizing to a more active role in organizing mythical material for themselves.

## 4. MYTHOGRAPHY UNDER THE RHETOR

The turn to original composition, no matter how basic it seems to us, was valuable both for students who ended their education at this point and for those going on to study with a rhetor. If Quintilian's extensive reading list (10.1.42–72) is any indication, students at this stage were expected to continue to read poets and prose writers on their own, mainly to study models of varying styles, but the emphasis increasingly shifted to learning to speak and compose clearly and persuasively. Thus, the exercises continued to evolve from passive reception of knowledge to active composition, and mythical subject matter and mythographical principles were even more important than they had been in earlier stages.

As preparation for composing complete speeches (*melētai* or, in Latin, *declamationes*), students would go through a series of fourteen or so graded exercises known as *progymnasmata* (see Kennedy 2003; Gibson 2008; in Egyptian papyri Cribiore 2001: 220–230). The order and number of the *progymnasmata* varied slightly, but these were increasingly challenging exercises aimed at improving clarity in writing and speaking, as well as a student's ability to make their own argument or refute that of an opponent. *Rhetores* clearly expected their pupils to be able to select and deploy mythical subject matter, and it is obvious from actual examples of ancient rhetoric and writing that this was as an expectation in schools because orators and writers in the real world did so regularly. Moreover, we continue to see developments analogous with mythographical writings in these exercises. Students had to select and narrate appropriate examples but also interpret and *use* them, a twin necessity that reflects systematic and interpretive mythography. Of the different *progymnasmata*, this mythographical work is most obviously important in the following types: narration, refutation, confirmation, comparison and speech in character.

### 4.1 Narration (*Diēgēma*)

Craig Gibson's (2013) recent study, on which we rely heavily here, has clarified the role of mythography in the *progymnasmata* for the exercises of narration (*diēgēma*), refutation (*anaskeuē*), and confirmation (*kataskeuē*). Narration, defined by Aphthonius as the "exposition of an action that has happened or as if it has happened," was supposed to explain the "who, what, when, where, and why of a story, and should do so clearly, briefly, persuasively and with good Greek" (trans. Gibson). While these narrations could be of historical, mythical/dramatic, or political types, almost all of the preserved examples in our Greek handbooks involve myth. The mythical stories as presented resemble the stories (*historiai*) that students would have encountered and copied under the *grammaticus*. Although slightly more elegant, with carefully balanced phrases, these retained the simplicity and efficiency of the narration, along with the heavy emphasis on participles. Take, for example, this sample narrative from Ps.-Libanius:

> The river Ladon fathered (*egennēse men*) the beautiful Daphne, but Apollo (*ethaumase de*) admired her. Being in love with her (*pathōn*), when he was unable to persuade her, he began to chase her. But she prayed to earth not to be caught and, obtaining (*tychousa*) the object of her prayer, disappeared. And her body (*men*) became a tree, and the tree (*de*) was the laurel. But the god did not stop longing for her, but rather changed some parts of the girl into limbs and became a lover of her leaves. (8.2.17, trans. Gibson 2008, Greek added)

As Gibson (2013: 293) notes, there is no literary version with the same details as that of Ps.-Libanius. Although meant to represent an original composition, this summary is written in the style of systematic mythography, familiar from the earlier exercises that included copying *historiai* and other mythical narratives. Whether a specific rhetor supplemented his students' knowledge of a myth by drawing directly upon mythographical texts as direct models at the time of composing a narrative is unclear. We do know that Theon read Asclepiades's *Tragodoumena* as well as Palaephatus's *On Unbelievable Tales* (Gibson 2013: 294), so it is not inconceivable that a rhetor would reach for a readily available potted summary from a mythographical work. In either the case, the advanced exercises to some degree are always students' own work, and that means that they regularly created materials that we in other contexts would unhesitatingly call mythography.

The examples in our rhetorical handbooks, like the one above, are rather polished. Examples from papyri can be less so. Take the summary of the Philoctetes myth published by Milne (1908: 128 = Cribiore 1996: no. 351), which shows a shaky command of grammar and some spelling corrections, as if the student was not completely comfortable with composition:

> After the end and death of Achilles, the seer Calchas ordered the Achaeans to go get Philoctetes from Lemnos because he had Heracles' bow. For he [subject unexpressed] had abandoned him after he had been bitten by a snake and he was not at all treated. But Odysseus and Diomedes bring [present tense] him back, and Machaon son of Asclepios cured him...and extremely . . . Philoctetes.

If this were merely a copying exercise, we might find mistakes, but not the clumsiness of the language, which here gives strong indication that this is an original composition. Presumably, a student would be asked to write tens, perhaps hundreds, of such narratives before moving onto the next exercise in the *progymnasmata*.

## 4.2 Refutation (*Anaskeuē*) and Confirmation (*Kataskeuē*)

Narration, as seen above, was preliminary to more advanced exercises, specifically refutation and confirmation, which trained orators in critical argumentation. Although they do not follow directly on narration in the list of progymnasmata given above in section 4.1, the exercises, as we shall see, depend on narrative as the basis for criticism. Refutation was aimed at dismantling weaknesses in a narrative, and mythical stories were often the first to be subjected to this form of criticism because they were the easiest (Gibson 2013: 296, citing John Geometres; see also p. 304). Again, nearly all of the examples provided by our ancient theorists are mythical in nature. Before embarking on refuting the narrative elements of a story, students would consult a pre-existing narration, whether from a mythographical handbook or from a teacher's composition, or write out their own. In the latter case, a student was expected to include precisely those elements that were going to be subjected to refutation. As for models of refutation, in addition to literary examples, for instance Plato's criticism of the myth of Oreithyia and Boreas in the *Phaedrus*, Theon also specifically names the work of the rationalizing mythographer Palaephatus (see Koning in this volume for Palaephatus's method) and gives four examples from his work.

In this exercise students were asked to refute elements in the narrative under six headings, whether something was unclear, unbelieveable, impossible, illogical, inappropriate, or inexpedient. For example, Medea's murder of her children is incredible because that sort of thing rarely happens. Heracles could not have killed Busiris because he had lived eleven generations earlier; as Gibson notes (2013: 298), "[S]urely a mythographical source establishing a chronology for Heracles's life lies behind this interesting claim." Sexual couplings between gods and mortals are inappropriate. One could go on, but this gives a sense of the procedure. Although the primary aims of rationalizing mythographers (making the story plausible) and rhetors (dismantling implausible elements) are different in emphasis, they are two sides of the same coin, or, perhaps better, they are two different stages in the same mental process, and Palaephatus almost always begins his construction of plausibility with a very brief gesture toward identifying first the implausible elements of just the sort that the rhetors employ.

After this comparatively simple exercise comes the more challenging exercise of confirmation, in which students were expected to defend narrative elements under the opposite headings: clear, credibile, possible, logical, appropriate, and expedient. Although again mythical subjects form the majority of examples, not all mythical subjects are suitable for this kind of exercise; a narrative that serves as the basis for a confirmation, we are told, should not contain elements that are "contrary to nature," such as Perseus's ability to fly and the three-headed man Geryon (John of Sardis 84.19–85.3). Such supernatural ideas are difficult to defend.

Not that the examples in the handbooks do not try. The confirmation of the story of Pasiphae in Ps.-Nicolaus shows the allegorical tendencies at work in defending the myth. Her divine parentage is explained by the fact that the Sun "gives everything life."

That her affliction continued into adulthood, when she was queen and had the wealth to indulge her sexual peccadilloes, merely shows that luxury and desire are the natural consequences of excessive wealth. Her calling on Daedalus to satify her passion makes sense because "arts love to help sick natures." Despite the obvious problem with the hybrid offspring, it would have been strange to have the offspring reflect only one of the parents; the only reasonable outcome of Pasiphae's mating with a bull was the Minotaur (Gibson 2013: 301). Here, the story's *narrative* coherence is praised despite the unbelievable status of the story itself, and allegory—an approach perfectly at home in freestanding mythography—is the tool.

Not all confirmation is allegorical in nature. For instance, in the confirmation of the story of Aphrodite and Adonis, Doxapatres emphasizes that the story is clear because the timing makes sense: Aphrodite fell in love with Adonis when he was a man. (Aphthonius, on the other hand, criticizes the clarity because it was *unclear* when this affair took place, before or after her marriage to Hephaestus.) But allegory was a common feature of confirmation. Some ancient theorists refer to the philosophical truths and "divine mysteries" put forward by the poets, who are to be praised. The story of Admetus, for instance, is simply a way to advocate for piety toward the gods. If Admetus can put off death through his piety, then should we all not be devoted to the gods (Ps.-Nicolaus 314.12–15)?

## 4.3 More Advanced Composition

Later exercises in the *progymnasmata* (encomium, comparison, and speech in character) also heavily featured myth, but in a more inventive way. In these exercizes students interact creatively within a preexising framework of myth to practice certain kinds of argumentation that could be used in actual speeches. These exercises, which did not require much originality (Cribiore 2001: 229), nonetheless demanded ingenuity to select and organize sometimes very specific mythical details. For encomium (speech of praise) the lengthy example from Ps.-Libanius concerning Diomedes both draws from Homer's text and includes several details that must come from elsewhere (Gibson 2008: 197–207). For instance, Diomedes's homeland is praised (1.2); Homer is the source that Argos is beautiful and cherished by Hera (*Il.* 4.51–52), but we also learn that it was the "first place to produce men from earth and the Argives were the oldest of all peoples," a detail that seems to originate with Acusilaus (fr. 23 Fowler; see Paus. 1.14.2). His lineage is also worth praising since he is descended from the gods (Ares his great-great-grandfather through Oeneus), and his father Tydeus was famous for his march on Thebes (ch. 3). In contrast with Odysseus and Achilles, Diomedes willingly went to war and was instrumental in exposing the latter's disguise (chs. 5–6). After a long list of his exploits in the *Iliad*, arranged mostly chronologically, he alone is credited with the theft of the Palladion (ch. 17).

The approach to the tenth exercise, comparison, is much the same. At Aphthonius 43 Achilles is compared with Hector, the latter of whom is judged "nearly equal to" the former (Kennedy 2003: 114–115). In this example, the writer compares the lands from which each hailed (Thessaly and Troy), noting that "both founders were descendants of the gods." Both Achilles and Hector themselves were also descended from Zeus, and their genealogies are given in full, which is typical of mythographical texts. The great acts of their forefathers are also compared: Aeacus put an end to drought and Peleus was given a goddess in marriage, while Dardanus "dined with the gods" and Priam's walls were built by gods. Both were killed by gods, Hector at Athena's hands, Achilles at Apollo's. Here, the student must be drawing to some degree on materials learned earlier, whether from a *grammaticus*, rhetor, or mythographical handbook for the occasion. The art is in the deployment of the mythological details in a meaningful comparison.

In the eleventh exercise, speech in character (*ethopoiia*; Latin *prosopopoeia*), an exercise which is well attested in papyri, we encounter speeches put in the mouths of mythical characters during specific moments: what would Cheiron say when he learned Achilles was hiding among Lycomedes's daughters (Ps.-Libanius 14)? What would Niobe say when confronted with her dead children (Aphthonius 42–44)? How would Clytemnestra defend herself to Orestes just before he kills her (*P. Vindob. G* 29789; see Cribiore 2001: 229 with n. 37)? For such dramatic speeches—called by Quintilian "by far the most difficult" type of exercise (*Inst.* 3.8.49)—a student must not only have control of a vast store of mythological material, garnered from literary and non-literary sources, but must also be concerned with maintaining character with consistency. In other words, these exercises are the culmination of the series of earlier educational steps that provided students with not only the details of but also the organizational principles that could be brought to bear on the mythical storyworld.

# 5. Conclusion

In all three stages of their education, students consistently wrote down myths, but this fact alone does not justify our saying that they were thereby "doing mythography." Rather, it is the formation of a mythographical frame of mind that took place through this writing and the growing familiarity with the organizational and interpretive methods of mythography that lead us to this conclusion. This process was not aimed at producing mythographers but evolved because it was deemed necessary by surprisingly durable aesthetic and intellectual standards of the day for all educated people to have recourse to mythographical frameworks—especially those who would themselves produce texts of almost any literary or oratorical genre. These abilities were formed through a process that began with reproducing lists and summaries, moving on to creating one's own, and still later, applying interpretive criticism to mythical narratives and organizing mythical details in more complicated exercises that approached real-life situations, ones that demanded the ability to recall, associate, organize, and deploy facts in compelling ways.

Viewed broadly, there is a symbiotic relationship between educational practices and mythography (Gibson 2013: 305). On the one hand, students were asked to copy names, lists, summaries, and *historiae* to obtain a working knowledge of the broad mythical tradition. Many of these were doubtlessly drawn from mythographical sources, whether directly or at some remove. On the other hand, the very act of copying and composing lists and summaries went a long way to reinforce and perpetuate mythographical forms. This is even true of the creative organization of mythical details found in the later rhetorical exercises. As Trzaskoma (2017: 469–470) puts it, students of rhetoric "not only would have benefitted from the organizational work of mythography, they would also have been to a large degree practicing it."

Thus, it should not be surprising that mythographical forms occur not only in systematic or interpretive mythographical texts such as those of Antoninus Liberalis, Cornutus, Parthenius, and Hyginus, but also in more rhetorically motivated works. Consider the list of "handsome young men" to whom Chaereas is compared in the novelist Chariton (1.1.3): Achilles, Nireus, Hippolytus and Alcibiades, which we may set side by side with Hyginus *Fab.* 270 ("The Most Beautiful Men," including Nireus and Achilles) and 271 ("The Most Beautiful Teenagers"). One could also call attention to the catalog of tragic women or of Zeus's disguises in Achilles Tatius (1.8 and 2.35–38), the latter of which finds analogs in several documents (see Trzaskoma 2017: 470–471): *P.Mil. Vogl.* 3.126 and Hyginus, *Fabulae* 226, noted above, and Philodemus's *De Pietate*. Similarly, one might consider the ways in which mythographical forms rehearsed under the *grammaticus* and rhetor found their ways into the works of other authors of the so-called Second Sophistic such as Aelius Aristides or Dio Chrysostom (Saïd 2008; Gangloff 2006; Trzaskoma 2017). Limitations of space demand that we leave a fuller examination of that issue for another time.

## FURTHER READING

For comprehensive overviews of ancient educational practices, see Marrou (1982) and Bloomer (2015); for Rome specifically, Bonner (1977); Bloomer (2011); and Wolff (2015). Recent studies that include studies of papyri have proliferated. In particular, Cribiore's study of the handwriting on papyrus (1996) has categorized different school hands, while Cribiore (2001) comprehensively analyzes the evidence from Egypt against what we know from other literary sources, including Libanius' orations and letters (see Norman 1964). Morgan (1998) is also useful. Trzaskoma (2017) draws the connection between elite education, mythography, and literary production in the Second Sophistic.

The study of subliterary papyri by van Rossum-Steenbeek (1998) helpfully collects far-flung material in one place and offers a synthetic study of Homeric and other hypotheses, Callimachean *diegeseis*, the Mythographicus Homericus, and catalogic papyri. The online *Catalogue of Paraliterary Papyri*, once an invaluable resource, is no longer available; it is hoped that the University of Leuven might see fit to reinstate it in the near future.

For overviews of the *progymnasmata* and mythography see Gangloff (2002) and especially Gibson (2013), while Kennedy (2003) offers studies and translations of several ancient handbooks, with numerous examples. A good translation of Ps.-Libanius's *progymnasmata* can be found in Gibson (2008), which also helpfully has the facing Greek. Rhetorical exercises in Egyptian papyrus can be found in Cribiore (1996: nos. 344–357; see Cribiore 2001: 228 n. 31 for more bibliography). Clark's study of rhetoric in Greco-Roman education is outdated but still offers useful information.

# References

Bagnall, Roger S., ed. 2011. *The Oxford Handbook of Papyrology*. Oxford: Oxford University Press.

Baplu, Nele, and Marc Huys. 2009. "P.Bouriant 1, fol. I–V: Re-edition and Commentary of the Syllabic Word-Lists." *Zeitschrift für Papryologie und Epigraphik* 169: 29–57.

Baplu, Nele, Marc Huys, and Thomas Schmidt. 2010. "The Syllabic Word-Lists in P. Bouriant 1 Reconsidered." In *Proceedings of the Twenty-Fifth International Congress of Papyrology*, edited by Traianos Gagos and Adam Hyatt, 53–68. Ann Arbor: University of Michigan Library.

Barns, John W. B. 1949. "Literary Texts from the Fayûm." *Classical Quarterly* 43: 1–3.

Bloomer, W. Martin. 2011. *The School of Rome: Latin Studies and the Origins of Liberal Education*. Berkeley: University of California Press.

Bloomer, W. Martin, ed. 2015. *A Companion to Ancient Education*. Chichester, UK: Wiley Blackwell.

Bonner, Stanley F. 1977. *Education in Ancient Rome: From the Elder Cato to the Younger Pliny*. Berkeley: University of California Press.

Cameron, Alan. 2004. *Greek Mythography in the Roman World*. Oxford: Oxford University Press.

Clark, Donald L. 1977. *Rhetoric in Greco-Roman Education*. Westport, CT: Praeger.

Cribiore, Raffaella. 1996. *Writing, Teachers, and Students in Graeco-Roman Egypt*. Atlanta, GA: Scholars Press.

Cribiore, Raffaella. 2001. *Gymnastics of the Mind: Greek Education in Hellenistic and Roman Egypt*. Princeton, NJ: Princeton University Press.

Francese, Christopher. 1999. "Parthenius Grammaticus." *Mnemosyne* 52: 63–71.

Gangloff, Anne. 2002. "Mythes, fables et rhétorique à l'époque impériale." *Rhetorica* 20: 22–56.

Gangloff, Anne. 2006. *Dion Chrysostome et les mythes: Hellénisme, communication et philosophie politique*. Paris: Jerôme Millon.

Gibson, Craig A. 2008. *Libanius's "Progymnasmata": Model Exercises in Greek Prose Composition and Rhetoric, Translated with an Introduction and Notes*. Atlanta, GA: Society of Biblical Literature.

Gibson, Craig A. 2013. "True or False? Myth and Mythography in the Progymnasmata." In *Writing Myth: Myth and Mythography in Greek and Roman Worlds*, edited by Stephen M. Trzaskoma and R. Scott Smith, 289–308. Leuven: Peeters.

Guéraud, Octave, and Pierre Jouguet. 1938. *Un Livre d'écolier du IIIe siècle avant J.-C.* Cairo: Imprimerie de l'Institut français d'archéologie orientale.

Hawes, Greta. 2014. *Rationalizing Myth in Antiquity*. Oxford: Oxford University Press.

Huys, Marc. 1996. "P. Oxy. 61.4099: A Combination of Mythographic Texts with Sentences of the Seven Wise Men." *Zeitschrift für Papyrologie und Epigraphik* 113: 205–212.

Huys, Marc. 2013. "Traces of Scholarship and Erudition in Greek Mythographical Papyri from the Roman Period." In *Writing Myth: Mythography in the Ancient World*, edited by Stephen M. Trzaskoma and R. Scott Smith, 115–131. Leuven: Peeters.

Kennedy, George A. 2003. *Progymnasmata: Greek Textbooks of Prose Composition and Rhetoric*. Atlanta, GA: Society of Biblical Literature.

Marrou, Henri I. 1982. *A History of Education in Antiquity*. Translated by George Lamb. Madison: University of Wisconsin Press.

Milne, J. Grafton. 1908. "Relics of Graeco-Egyptian Schools." *Journal of Hellenic Studies* 28: 121–132.

Morgan, Teresa. 1998. *Literate Education in the Hellenistic and Roman Worlds*. Cambridge, UK: Cambridge University Press.

Norman, Albert F. 1964. "The Library of Libanius." *Rheinisches Museum für Philologie* 107: 159–175.

Saïd, Suzanne. 2008. "Aristides' Uses of Myth." In *Aelius Aristides between Greece, Rome, and the Gods*, edited by William V. Harris and Brooke Holmes, 51–67. Leiden: Brill.

Trzaskoma, Stephen M. 2017. "Mythography." In *The Oxford Handbook of the Second Sophistic*, edited by Daniel S. Richter and William A. Johnson, 463–475. Oxford: Oxford University Press.

van Rossum-Steenbeek, Monique. 1998. *Greek Readers' Digests? Studies on a Selection of Subliterary Papyri*. Leiden: Brill.

# CHAPTER 31

····················································································

# MYTHOGRAPHY AND POLITICS

····················································································

## LEE E. PATTERSON

## 1. POLITICAL MYTHS

····················································································

AMONG its myriad uses in Greek society, myth had many political applications.[1] It could, for instance, be a means of expressing a community's political, social, or cultural identity or a prominent family's claim to noble origins, for example, through a heroic ancestor. Myths with political implications can be found in many walks of life, responding to various needs. The primary concern of this chapter is the role mythography played in the process of political mythopoesis (mythmaking), for indeed, to understand such political outcomes, one often has to turn to the source recording the myth. One of the challenges scholars face is deciding whether a myth recorded in, for example, a historical narrative served a political purpose for the players in that narrative or for the historian who had his own agenda, or both. Before discussing mythography, therefore, it is may be better to begin with a brief consideration of how political myths worked in ancient Greece (for some recent studies, see the "Further Reading" section at the end of the chapter).

Myth provided a powerful tool for the political machinations of communities, families, and prominent individuals. This was only possible because of the basic reality the Greeks ascribed to myths, especially heroic myths. In general, the world of the heroes was perceived as real; their time on earth was, essentially, an earlier era, the equivalent of ancient history (Calame 2003: 12–27). The Trojan War, as told by Homeric and later tradition, actually happened, as did the Argonautic expedition and the adventures of Heracles, Theseus, Perseus, and other heroes. The Thebes ruled by Oedipus and sacked by the Seven was the Thebes of Epaminondas; the Athens that

[1] I am grateful to the editors, Scott Smith and Stephen Trzaskoma, for their guidance, insight, and expertise, which most definitely elevated the quality of this work. For any errors that may remain I am solely responsible.

warred against the Amazons and supported the Heraclidae was the Athens of Pericles (Patterson 2010: 22–25; Brillante 1990: 94). But belief in the reality of myths was complicated. A smaller number of Greeks accepted the underlying historicity, but did not necessarily accept all the stories at face value (Patterson 2010: 4–6, 25–27; Veyne 1988: 11–14). Some of the more fantastical elements were often rejected, sifted out, as it were, while the basic reality might be retained, as in the case of Theseus, who was thought to have contributed to the Athenian constitution but whose slaying of a bull-headed man generated significant incredulity (Arist. [*Ath. Pol.*] 41.2; Thuc. 2.15; Paus. 1.3.3; compare Plut. *Thes.* 16.2). Generally speaking, the authors in the present study who included myth in their discussions are among the more skeptical. But the fact that Theseus and the other heroes were real meant that their actions had consequences, political, cultural, ethnographical, and so on, that continued to be felt in the "modern" era of Hecataeus, Aristotle, and Pausanias—that is, they accounted for some of the political realities of the present era.

This mindset explains the efforts of noble and royal families in the Archaic period to assert their preeminence by articulating heroic origins, especially important for those who guided the policies of the oligarchical *poleis* throughout Greece and, in some cases, attempted to broaden their influence beyond their own *polis*. The most famous example is the Return of the Heraclidae. By the mid-seventh century, this story had become entrenched in the collective memory of the Greeks, or at least of the Peloponnesians. This lengthy tale, preserved for us in many sources (for instance, Apollod. *Bibl.* 2.8-1–5; Diod. Sic. 4.57–58; see also Tigerstedt 1965: 28–34; Vanschoonwinkel 1995: 127–131; Hall 1997: 56–57), recounts how the descendants of Heracles "returned" to the Peloponnesus to claim the territories that had originally belonged to the hero. It is essentially a justification for the movement of Dorian peoples into the Peloponnesus from the north and their subsequent hegemony there (Tigerstedt 1965: 34–36; Dowden 1992: 70–73; Hall 1997: 60–62). The generation that saw success (after some earlier misfires) was led by Temenus, who ultimately acquired Argos, while his brother Cresphontes took Messenia, and Sparta went to the sons of a third brother, Aristodemus, who became the ancestors of the two royal houses. The argument that the original story was invented in the 8th century by the ruling dynasty of Argos, the Temenids, is sound for a number of reasons, including the leadership role of Temenus, putative founder of the Temenids and the only Heraclid to be an eponym for a Dorian dynasty, and the deeper cultic associations of Heracles with the Argolid (Tigerstedt 1965: 34; Hall 1997: 61). The purpose of this myth was to explain and justify the hegemony of Argos, which seems to have been the top power in the Peloponnesus in the eighth century. In the centuries that followed, that dynamic began to change as Sparta eventually overtook Argos as the hegemon in a process that remains difficult for us to reconstruct. But one of the means by which the Spartans articulated the new reality as they saw it in the seventh century was their appropriation of the original Argive myth, to which they now gave a new spin, essentially connecting their dual monarchy, founded by Agis and Eurypon, with the family of Temenus, specifically, his brother Aristodemus (Patterson 2010: 32–34, 2021: 420-423). As we will see, this development may have happened in the context of the Spartans' renewed efforts to subdue Messenia to the west, as suggested in the surviving fragments of the lyric poet Tyrtaeus.

One of the most common types of political myth was the charter myth, a story that explained the origins of a community. Such myths were necessary if the *polis* was especially old, as we might say of the cities of Ionia. Historically, we would say that they were originally colonies established on the western littoral of Anatolia, primarily during the Dark Age period. During the following Archaic period, the threads of a tradition developed that linked these cities to Athens, whose founding heroes were sons of the Athenian king Codrus, including Androclus, founder of Ephesus; Neleus of Miletus; Cydrelus of Myus; Nauclus of Teos, and Cnopus of Erythrae (Strabo 14.1.3 C632–633; Paus. 7.2). Perhaps the most fertile source for charter myths was the Trojan War; many communities asserted a link to that most Panhellenic of traditions as a way to not only enhance their antiquity but also ennoble themselves, even in dubious contexts, as in the case of Phygela, or Pygela. This was a city in Ionia that chose not to emphasize any links to the Ionian Migration but, instead, according to Strabo, claimed to be descended from soldiers left behind by Agamemnon, who had suffered from a disease of the buttocks (*pugalgias*), from which the city's name derived (Strabo 14.1.20 C639).

Individuals could also take advantage of the political benefits myth afforded. Alexander the Great immediately comes to mind, and we will touch on his efforts later. Another example is Cimon, son of Miltiades, of Athens. Although he lived in a democracy, Cimon retained the archaic aristocratic call for political self-promotion, and he took advantage of a communal myth that served similar purposes for Athens. In 476/475 Cimon claimed to have found the bones of Theseus on the island of Scyros, which he dutifully brought back to Athens (Plut. *Thes.* 36.1–2; Paus. 3.3.7). For the Athenians possession of the bones meant that Theseus had returned home. Through him Athens' power would be as it had been in his day and, further, its greatness would justify Athenian supremacy in the Delian League. As for Cimon, Plutarch suggests that his prestige at home was greatly enhanced (*Cim.* 8.6). Cimon improved the political fortunes of his family in part by associating it with Theseus, as attested by a new Theseion built in Athens (Walker 1995: 55–61; McCauley 1999).

## 2. POLITICAL MYTHOGRAPHY

A fundamental feature of mythography is appropriation. When one writes down myths, whether as a historian, a geographer, an epic poet, a tragedian, or any other kind of "mythographer," one renders an authoritative version. Whether that means reaffirming a commonly held tradition or applying a corrective depends on the author's agenda. Because of our reliance on texts, in matters of politics the question of authorial intent is vital, for we can read a text as merely the record of a myth or as itself a contribution to the mythopoesis by which a constructed identity or political claim originally took form, or as something in between.

Authors often contributed to this mythopoesis with some degree of self-awareness. For instance, as he embarks on Book 4 of his universal history, Diodorus acknowledges the difficulties of including mythological material in a historical account, including problems of verification, the complexity of details, and variants among sources. But he nonetheless fills Book 4 with stories of Heracles, Theseus, the Argonauts, and so on because the heroes of old continued to be important to the contemporary culture of the Greeks (4.1.1–4). Even so, while he may be more accommodating of myth than, say, Ephorus, who began his history with the Return of the Heraclidae, a tradition easier to subject to verification, Diodorus still applies a critical eye to myth as needed, often distancing himself from a mythological narrative with such phrases as "it is said" and "the myth writers say" (Marincola 1997: 119–121).

The nature of surviving texts and their relationship to political myths as first formulated present us with significant challenges. This relationship is often quite distant, with the written document far removed from the original circumstances in which the political myth first developed. This is especially true when we consider that most political myths, particularly in the Greek world, were originally oral in nature, not surprising given the high degree to which orality prevailed among the general populace of ancient Greece. The traditions that arose to legitimize archaic noble houses or situate a *polis'* foundation in the complex mosaic of Hellenic identity responded to specific circumstances, often centuries before their earliest written transmission, as one suspects of the individual charter myths in Ionia. Our access to these traditions only begins when someone writes them down, or at least a version of them. At the hands of the writers recording these myths, of whatever genre, these traditions continued along wider avenues of Greek public memory.

Sometimes the original political purpose of the myths had fallen by the wayside altogether by the time they got written down. Oral transmission generally created the conditions for a story to have more variants as it responded to fluctuant circumstances. Greta Hawes has argued that texts fix the form of a story and thus remove it from its original context (2014b: 129). I agree that many texts have that power. Where political uses of myth are concerned, a writer can carry a myth beyond its original context and neutralize the political agenda that gave rise to it (though we might add that in the fullness of time some myths might have already lost that power before they were first written down). In such writings the myth in question loses its authority to support any political or cultural claims made by those who had originally invented it (or promoted it), as one sees in Strabo when he rejects a local myth in Messenian Pylos, namely its claim to be Nestor's Pylos. He does not reject the existence of Nestor or the name of his city, but he gives a Pylos in Triphylia (southern Elis) that distinction based on an analysis of Homer (8.3.7 C339–340; Patterson 2013: 218). However, an additional nuance is called for here: such decontextualization need not involve an outright rejection of a political myth. A good deal of mythography in the writings of historians and the like involves the perpetuation of a canon, as we might say of Herodotus when he preserves a detail about Argead history without promoting Argead propaganda (see below). Indeed, part of Herodotus's motivation is given in the preface of his work when he refers to his objective of preserving the memory of past deeds. Propagation, as of the Argeads' heroic lineage, is one example of the impulse of memory that drives historiography.

But other texts have the power to go in the opposite direction. In fact, a written myth can even provide a continuation of a political agenda, by which the author shares in, to one extent or another, the promotion of the myth for political purposes. It can be a wholesale investment of the agenda, as when Tyrtaeus encourages his fellow Spartans to honorable combat on the front lines by promoting their Heraclid origins (frr. 2, 11, 19 West). Interestingly, from both sides of contextualization, however close to the original myths a writer may be, these authors must make choices. They control the shape of their narrative, including what myths (or version of myths) to include and why. What motivates that shape may differ: an active employment of a living myth for an immediate political purpose (Tyrtaeus) or the promotion of a particular myth on more academic grounds (Herodotus), which sometimes involves a rejection of all other versions (Strabo). What follows is a sketch of these matters, beginning with an example of "active" mythography, so to speak, the investment of Tyrtaeus in the Heraclidae story. Afterwards we will see myths whose original political claims have at least remained in the canon, whatever the author's attitude toward them, followed by political myths rejected by analytical writers on various grounds.

## 3. ACTIVE MYTHS

Hecataeus is a good example of someone who made choices that both established the correct lines of mythological narrative, as he saw it, as when he sought to unravel myriad and suspect mythological traditions and claims (*FGrHist* 1 fr. 1), and actively employed a myth from which he derived immediate benefit by asserting the divine origins of his own family (fr. 21, compare Hdt. 2.143). Though not political as such, his claim of descent from Zeus in the sixteenth generation is an active myth; it lives for him in a way that it cannot for others reading it unless they somehow attach themselves to the narrative by claiming kinship with Hecataeus and thus join him in claiming descent from Zeus through his line. In a way that is what Tyrtaeus seems to have done with the Heraclidae story, as suggested by the surviving fragments, and this myth is most certainly a political one. In both cases we see a writer who has a stake in the mythopoesis to which he contributes. The political dimension lies in how the mythographer's narrative casts his community in the proper light. As a member of the culture that benefits, as he sees it, from the promotion of this narrative, he contributes to the positive reshaping of his culture in some way (like Gehrke's "intentional history": for example, 2010: 16–17). This is, of course, an example of epichoric myth, which can manifest as a local history that, for instance, refashions a community's origin in the context of the Trojan War, thus elevating and ennobling that community. This is the sense by which I mean "active," but of course political myths, for instance the Heraclid origins of the Macedonian Argeads, that have achieved canonical status in the pages of, say, Arrian's account of Alexander, are also active expressions of Greek culture, only in a context very removed from that of their creation. As we shall see, Arrian's relationship to the Heraclid story is quite different from the story of Tyrtaeus.

When I speak of "active" myths in the sense of the invested mythopoesis described above, I think especially of Acusilaus when he writes of the Argolid, Pherecydes writing of Athens, and Tyrtaeus of Sparta. Evidence for the two prose writers can be seen in their efforts to rework traditional genealogies and stories as they relate to the origins and traditions of the Argolid and of Attica (Fowler 2013: 626–627, on Acusilaus, and 708–709, 714, on Pherecydes). The same can be said of any local historian, whether a writer of prose or verse, relating epichoric myth, as with the epic poet Asius of Samos. His version of the origins of his *polis* predates the Ionian migration and has elements of autochthony and a stronger link to divinity (the father of the eponymous Samos was a son of Poseidon while his mother was the daughter of the river god Maeander) as compared to a different source Pausanias read for the Ionian association (Paus. 7.4.1–2). In each case the myths in question are active in that their very publication is part of the mythopoesis that allows the myth to serve its intended political function. The myth is alive for them and for their communities.

Putting them aside, I wish to focus here on Tyrtaeus. With this poet we find ourselves in Sparta in the mid-seventh century BCE, as it works to solidify its control of Messenia. The so-called Second Messenian War forms the backdrop of Tyrtaeus's military poetry, in which he rouses Spartan soldiery to victory in battle, despite the terrors of hoplite warfare. His is patriotic verse, often with a mythological layer intended to cast the Lacedaemonian venture in the proper political light. As we saw above, the Return of the Heraclidae story became part of the canon of Hellenic collective memory by the mid-seventh century. It provides the context in which we see Tyrtaeus operating, giving us glimpses of how the Spartans appropriated the myth for their own purposes. While it may seem odd for Argos' rival to adopt an Argive myth, in fact, it was typical for a myth, once it had entered the collective memory of enough Greeks, to change hands and become transformed to suit new political purposes (Patterson 2010: 36–37). Tyrtaeus's modification revolved in part around the implications of the Spartans' Heraclid origins for the soldiers fighting in Messenia. Much of his encouragement takes the form of reminders of their heroic lineage, whence the soldiers will derive their superiority in combat (frr. 11, 19). Fragment 11 is particularly pointed in ascribing this noble ancestry to the soldiers themselves, not just the kings: "for you are of the race of unconquered Heracles" (*Hēraklēos gar anikētou genos este*), Tyrt. fr. 11, line 1).

The scholarship on Tyrtaeus, however, has made clear that this is more than a literary convention in the manner of Homeric poetry. There is a deep political dimension to Tyrtaeus's exhortations. Tarkow has shown that the celebration of Heracles benefits the entire community (compare the self-promotion of a typical Homeric hero). Fuqua, meanwhile, has suggested a cultic aspect to this promotion in that the well-being of the community depended on the goodwill of the hero. Tyrtaeus, then, not only ennobles the entire citizenry by making Heracles the ancestor of all Spartans but also exclaims the hero's importance to the collective enterprises of the community, in this case the conquest of Messenia (Tarkow 1983: 49–60; Fuqua 1981: 223; Patterson 2010: 37–38). More recently, in her reading of fr. 2, which connects the Spartan duarchy with the Heracleidae, Romney has suggested Tyrtaeus's purpose, at least in this poem, was to promote obedience to the kings in a matrix of shared Heraclid-Dorian continuity (2017: 10–14).

# 4. CANONIZATION OF POLITICAL MYTHS

The type of mythography described in the previous section represents a small percentage of the literary treatment of political myths. Nonetheless, there are many accounts that seem to accept political claims based on mythological arguments. This is hardly surprising since most myths that survive in our sources had entered the collective memory of the Greeks, their preservation made possible by the momentum of tradition. Much of this was done in the arena of oral storytelling, but authors working in various genres also contributed to this preservation, usually by passing along what they found in their sources. Along the way there might be varying degrees of editorializing, and thus we face the challenge of understanding the extent a writer was intervening in the transmission of a political myth, as when, for instance, he put a new spin on a detail to win a scholarly argument (or conversely reject the invention to win the argument while retaining the basic myth itself).

The Return story itself has mostly survived because of its preservation in such writers. From Herodotus and Pindar to Ephorus to Diodorus and beyond, the original purpose of the Return, to justify the original hegemonies of Argos and then Sparta in the Archaic period, no longer mattered, at least to the mythographers (the Return, of course, remained a point of pride for such players as Cleomenes I: see Hdt. 5.72). But the myth itself was deeply enshrined in panhellenic tradition. In fact, it played an essential role in Strabo's ancient chronology by providing a basic reference point against which the timing of other events was measured (Clarke 2008: 143–150). Though losing its political punch centuries after the Spartan endeavor to conquer Messenia, the claim of the Spartan kings to be descendants of Aristodemus's sons, whose sons were Agis and Eurypon, the eponyms of the dual monarchy, was readily acknowledged in the later sources, even to the point of differentiating Heraclid royalty and the common Dorian populace (Hdt. 1.56, 6.53, 7.204, 8.131; Thuc. 1.12.3; Paus. 5.3.5).

The volume of political myths in the extant corpus of Greek texts, whether they retained their original political intent, is staggering. Such myths are represented in virtually all genres. In some, such as Greek tragedy or lyric poetry, we generally give less regard to whether the myth was considered historical, though of course there are exceptions. We have noted Tyrtaeus. We might also mention Sophocles's *Tereus*. The origins of Tereus, a man of demonstrated cruelty, seem to predate Sophocles, with the earliest extant references in Aeschylus (Gantz 1996: 240–241; Zacharia 2001: 91). The playwright's innovation may have come in identifying Tereus's homeland as Thrace.

Thematically, this may have served Sophocles's plan of ascribing Tereus's loathsome treatment of Procne and Philomela to his foreign origins (Burnett 1998: 54), but we must also acknowledge that the play was written in the aftermath of a treaty between Athens and Thrace in 431. As we shall discuss further in the next section, Thucydides implies that there was a popular version in Athens concerning a putative link of kinship by way of Tereus, suggesting a common belief in his historicity (Thuc. 2.29). Sophocles very likely wrote his play under the influence of the environment in which this topic was circulating. Unfortunately, the fragmentary nature of the play makes it impossible to say how "active" his mythography was, that is, the extent to which Sophocles's literary effort was a contribution to the public discussion in 420s Athens to which Thucydides seems to be reacting.

Otherwise, when analyzing political mythography, we tend to direct more attention to prose works, especially history, geography, biography, oratory, and philosophy, where we see allusions to myths in a political context more often than in poetic works. The examples are many. Aeschines's *On the Embassy*, a famous judicial oration concerning Athenian diplomatic overtures to Philip of Macedon, alleged that Amphipolis belonged to Athens because it had been founded by Acamas, son of Theseus (2.31). In his biography of Solon, Plutarch makes his own contribution to the legend of the famous lawgiver by ascribing to him the promotion of Salamis's Athenian identity by way of Ajax's sons Philaeus and Eurysaces (*Sol.* 10), even though it is far more likely that Peisistratus was responsible for this particular mythopoeic effort (Patterson 2010: 70–71). The hero Oxylus features in the geographic works of Strabo and Pausanias, where he is described as a guide for his distant Heraclid cousins under Temenus; in return, they allowed him to reclaim his ancestral land in the northwest Peloponnesus. Oxylus led an Aetolian army against Elis and eventually became its king (Ephorus *FGrH* 70 frr. 115, 122; Strabo 8.1.2 C332, 8.3.33 C358; Paus. 5.3.5–4.4; Apollod. *Bibl.* 2.8.3). This Heraclid origin was a point of pride for the Eleans, who erected in the agora a statue of Oxylus on which Ephorus read an inscription identifying him as the founder (Strabo 10.3.2 C463). Strabo and Pausanias, of course, rely more broadly on myth to achieve the goals of their respective enterprises: Strabo's geographic survey of the *oikoumene* and Pausanias's *periegesis* of Greece. In both cases, we often see charter myths and other narratives that add an important layer to the locations they describe, supplementing topographical, cultural, historical, and other information. Such accounts play an important role in the articulation of identity, as expressed by the locals or as applied by writers, or both. Though both authors certainly apply correctives as needed—and we will discuss the example of Strabo in the next section—by and large they embrace the mythological traditions promoted locally or in literary accounts of these places (for example, see Patterson 2013, 2017, for Strabo; and Hawes 2021; Patterson 2004, 2010: 124–153, for Pausanias).

I have mentioned the acknowledgment of the Argead royal house's Heraclid origins in Herodotus, and I argued that Herodotus had no stake in the promotion of Argead propaganda. But being the great storyteller that he was, Herodotus did include a pedigree of the Argeads to clarify part of his account of someone who most certainly did make political use of it: Alexander I. We are told that Alexander, who took part in the Olympic

Games, in which only Greeks were allowed to participate, convinced the judges of his Hellenicity by offering proof of his descent from Perdiccas, a Temenid (descendant of Temenus), who had fled Argos and eventually settled in Macedonia (5.22). Presumably, the proof was the pedigree that Herodotus relates at 8.139. Earlier, he tells the story of how Perdiccas and his brothers founded the country of Macedonia (8.137–138). We have no way of knowing what Herodotus's source is for the story or the geneaology, but Alexander himself, who died in 454, would not be a bad guess. Herodotus spends much time discussing Alexander's negotiation of his precarious position as vassal of the Persians while secretly favoring the Greeks (7.173, 8.140, 9.44–45), and this charter myth fits in well with that narrative.

In any case, the propagation of the Argead charter myth not only continues in Thucydides, who extends the Heraclid inheritance to Perdiccas II (2.99.2, compare 5.80.2), but is taken to a higher level in response to the politics of the fourth century. In a letter to Philip II the Athenian rhetorician Isocrates appeals to the Macedonian king to bring an end to the internecine strife afflicting the Greek world for decades and unify it by launching an expedition against the Persian Empire. He cites Philip's Heraclid origins to ennoble the king, making him worthy of the Greeks' loyalty and offering hope that Philip has the greatness in him to bring about this desired outcome (Isoc. 5.76–115). Finally, of course, the Argeads' Temenid heritage is acknowledged throughout the corpus of Alexander historiography, especially in sections where Alexander stresses his Heraclid origins (for example, Arr. *Anab.* 2.5.9, Diod. Sic. 17.4.1). In general, the Alexander historians accept the tradition itself, but in the next section we shall see quibbles with some of Alexander's more outlandish claims based on it.

# 5. THE ANALYTICAL SCALPEL

We come now to the extreme wing of intellectual mythopoesis, the expression of incredulity on rational or other grounds. Even here, it must be stressed, I do not mean a rejection of myth *qua* myth (as opposed to what we would consider history), but rather an application of correctives based on individual perceptions of canon, authenticity, and plausibility (see also the detailed analysis of this mindset at Calame 2003: 12–27). Every time an author applies his analytical scalpel in service to this goal, he is establishing rules to which he expects the story to conform. To be sure, he operates in the same mode as mythographers invested in "active" myths or propagating canonical traditions: he makes choices as they do, but the choices of this brand of mythography have somewhat different aims. We are reminded of Hawes's (2014b: 129) thesis that mythographers establish new contexts when they determine a version of a story that no longer responds to the changing conditions of an oral environment. Rosalind Thomas's (1989: 183–184) important study of the transition from orality to writing (in many sectors) makes the point that inconsistences are part and parcel of oral transmission, which lacks the controls that mythographers want because it involves more organic responses to changing circumstances.

Our starting point in illuminating the analytical mindset is, naturally, Hecataeus. From the first fragment of Jacoby's collection, we see his plan clearly: "Hecataeus of Miletus says the following: I write about those things as seem true to me, for in my view the stories of the Greeks are many and ridiculous" (*FGrHist* 1 fr. 1). Standing as he does at a very early stage of prose writing, Hecataeus is responding primarily to oral traditions that were circulating in the Greek world. But his stance, as Fowler has pointed out, is "insolent." Hecataeus presumes to replace the Muses with himself, rendering mythological narratives "as seem true to *me*" (*hōs emoi phainontai*). He is asserting the authority to establish the *correct* version of the story (Fowler 2013: 668; Martin 2013: 57–58; Bertelli 2001: 80–84; see Pàmias, this volume, especially section 6). This mindset seems to account for the incredulity in play in the following examples.

Let us now return to Tereus. We have considered Sophocles's possible perspective, as suggested by the surviving fragments of his play, but Thucydides's treatment comes from entirely different motivations. This section (Thuc. 2.29) falls amid his discussion of the treaty in 431 between Athens and the Odrysian dynasty of Thrace, led by King Teres, a potentially useful ally in the newly launched Peloponnesian War. While discussing this diplomacy Thucydides inserts a remark about Tereus (essentially, an aside to the main narrative about the diplomacy), as if he had been a topic of the conversation during the negotiations. The historian is in any case responding to something, for he feels compelled to correct mistaken notions about Athenian-Thracian kinship through Tereus. His objections are based on a healthy application of reason and common sense: that Tereus was not from Thrace, but from Phocian Daulis, that he was not connected to Teres's dynasty, and that his marriage to the daughter of Athens' king Pandion would make less strategic sense if he were from faraway Thrace. This position seems to put him at odds with stories circulating in Athens, reminding us of the same dynamic attending Hecataeus's complaints almost a century earlier.

Despite my listing Strabo in this section, the myths he rejects form a tiny portion of the ones that animate his *Geography*. While he usually includes myth, epichoric or otherwise, as one of the facets of a location worth recording, he occasionally does find fault with his sources or the locals. We saw the example of Messenian Pylos above. There, and in other cases, the basis of the rejection is how the story matches up with Homer. Strabo took his predecessors to task when sorting out the ancient identity of the island of Cephallenia (10.2.14 C456). We know what the Cephallenians themselves believed about their origins. In the Hellenistic period, they depicted their founder, Cephalus, on coins and listed him as a part of the genealogical link to Magnesia-on-the-Maeander during a diplomatic venture (*I.v. Magnesia* 35; Rigsby 1996: 212; Patterson 2010: 114–117). But Strabo begs to differ. Despite the tradition linking Cephallenia with Taphos, where Cephalus set up his kingdom (unnamed sources), and the one linking Cephallenia with Dulichium (Hellanicus, Andron), Strabo insists that Cephallenia had been ruled by Odysseus (based on Homer *Il.* 2.631) and Dulichium (and the other Echinades) by Meges (*Il.* 2.625–630). Strabo similarly rejects Nauplius as the founder of Nauplia, a port in the Argolid, preferring an etymological explanation (the city to where *ships* may *sail*) because the traditions of Nauplius and his son Palamedes are more recent than Homer and thus cannot be affixed to the location of Nauplia. As Strabo continues in this mode, his analysis goes astray with a second argument based on a mistake. He says that Nauplius could not have founded Nauplia around the time of the Trojan War because, as the son of Poseidon and Danaus's daughter Amymone, he is far too early. In fact, Strabo has confused him with Nauplius son of Clytoneus and father of Palamedes (8.6.2 C368). The analytical scalpel in this case has cut in the wrong place.

It is perhaps fitting to end with the historiography of Alexander the Great. Even in his own lifetime, the Macedonian king who conquered the Persian Empire in the 330s BCE was, by all accounts, an enigma, a king whose mental stability was often questioned. Matters are made worse by the fact that our main surviving sources are centuries removed from Alexander, preserving earlier material and likely filtering it as well. Nonetheless, by and large, the traditions of Alexander's Heraclid origins on his father's side and of his Aeacid descent on his mother's were not rejected by his chroniclers, especially as these traditions predated Alexander himself, as we saw earlier in the case of his ancestor Alexander I. But during his Asian campaign, some of Alexander's mythopoeic practices proved too much for the historians. Putting aside the thorny issue of Alexander's alleged pretensions to divinity, even his heroic associations provided occasions for abuse. For instance, as Alexander progressed through the Indus river valley basin in the 320s, suddenly new stories of Heracles and Dionysus seemed to come out of nowhere, and Alexander took full political advantage of them. One episode involved diplomatic overtures to an Indian village called (by the Macedonians) Nysa, immediately evoking the name of Dionysus's birthplace. Moreover, as soon as Alexander saw ivy growing on nearby Mt. Merus (Greek, "Thigh Mountain"), his mind was made up. As he was approaching the edge of the world, he was now about to pass the farthest point reached by Dionysus (Arr. *Anab.* 5.1.2–2.7, *Ind.* 1.5; Curt. 8.10.7–18; Just. *Epit.* 12.7.6–8). Arrian, though he wrangled with his own uncertainties and ultimately decided to take a neutral stand (5.3.1–4), refers to the more extreme skepticism of Eratosthenes, who had no reservations about accusing the Macedonians of fabricating such details to flatter Alexander (likewise, at Strabo 15.1.7 C687). Elsewhere Arrian expresses more doubt and, in response to the evidence of Dionysus and Heracles in India presented by Megasthenes, an envoy of Seleucus I who traveled to the court of Chandragupta, more readily raises suspicions about Macedonian flattery (*Ind.* 6.1).

This applies even more in the case of Heracles, for whom the evidence, says Arrian, is even more tenuous than it is for Dionysus (*Ind.* 5.8–10). One famous episode involved the assault on the mountain fortress of Aornus, associated in local legend with Krishna, an Indian deity with certain similarities to Heracles (Bosworth 1988: 123). So Alexander made the necessary association and, as the sources stress, was motivated to capture Aornus because Heracles was said to have failed in his attempt (Arr. *Anab.* 4.28.4; Diod. Sic. 17.85.2; Curt. 8.11.2; Just. *Epit.* 12.7.12). But Arrian uses the word *kompos* to explain the inclusion of Heracles in the story; that is, it was a Macedonian "boast" (4.28.2). Similar doubt is expressed about the claims of an Indian tribe called the Sibi (or Sibae), supposed descendants of Heracles's followers. On this basis Alexander, who otherwise slaughtered thousands of Indians as he made his way down the Indus, spared the Sibi this gruesome fate (Diod. Sic. 17.96.1–3; Curt. 9.4.1–3; Just. *Epit.* 12.9.2). Arrian and Strabo also highlight the dubious example of the Caucasus Mountains, which Alexander's flatterers moved into central Asia where they claimed to have found the cave in which Heracles had released Prometheus, again giving the Macedonian king the chance to surpass in geographic scope the achievements of his heroic forebears (Arr. *Anab.* 5.3.2–3; Strabo 15.1.8 C688). Taken together, these episodes suggest that in the minds of Eratosthenes, Strabo, and Arrian some suspicious mythopoesis was happening.

# 6. Conclusions

As discussed at the outset, to a very high degree myth served to promote political interests in the Greek world, whether consciously or organically. As in any other culture, the Greeks relied heavily on myth to explain origins and present realities, but the myriad etiological traditions that were employed to account for the foundation of cities, origins of certain communal features, beginnings of dynasties and other prominent families, kinship among different communities, ethnic and other identities, and other political conditions are simply staggering. Our impression of this state of affairs, of course, comes mainly from the mythographers, with hints in epigraphical, archaeological, and other mediums. Their endeavors were part of the greater mythopoesis that, we can surmise, more often took place orally from the Dark Age period (and probably Mycenaean) to the Roman. Writers reacted to this grander mosaic and to each other, sometimes enhancing old traditions by writing them down for the first time, whatever their distance from and level of investment in the myths in question.

Authorial intent explains the diverse forms mythography took. Attitudes toward myth and its political uses varied, and the genres represented are many. The majority of recorded myths that could have political implications tended to animate poetry and prose narratives that did not require an evaluation of their veracity or plausibility. These stories were part of the traditions given sanction by the collective memory of the Greeks (or some segment of them), and they provided the necessary reference points for the audience to appreciate and enjoy the latest version of the myth, as in the case of so many Greek tragedies. On the other hand, the reactions of Hecataeus and Thucydides often reveal a frustration with the looser standards of authority they encounter in the wider circles beyond their intellectual milieu. Strabo and Pausanias as well, and any other author confronting local myths that were part of the lived experience of communities throughout the *oikoumene*, made decisions about how far to accept the political claims made based on mythical precedents. The most extreme application of their analytical scalpels stands in contrast to an investment of "active" myths, but even here, it bears repeating, we are often dealing with the rejection of alternatives in which the mythographer was not invested. Wherever each writer fell in this mosaic of authorial intent, collectively, they played an essential role in the creation, promotion, appropriation, and negotiation of political myths in ancient Greece.

## FURTHER READING

The bibliography on political myths has grown tremendously in recent years, and of course mythography plays a key role in these studies since our access to such mythmaking depends in large part on texts. Much of the scholarship has specifically concerned itself with constructed identities. For instance, Gehrke refers to it as "intentional history" (*intentionale Geschichte*), a subjective self-categorization by which the identity of a group is constructed (2001, 2010). Clarke (2008) takes on how time (including mythical time) was constructed and negotiated in the creation of local identity. Other studies have investigated how identity emerges in the interplay of myth and geography (Hawes 2017; Patterson 2017). Myth plays an important role in Skinner's (2012) challenge to the orthodoxy that an ethnography of otherness had not developed earlier than the period of the first interactions of the Greeks with the Persians. My own approach to these issues considers constructed identity in the context of kinship diplomacy, in which such identities were employed to create connections that supported or enabled a diplomatic venture, for instance, a treaty, alliance, *asylia*, material assistance, or foreign domination (Patterson 2010). Other recent items include Graf (2011), Fowler (2015), Mac Sweeney (2013, 2015), Hawes (2021), and Patterson (2021). Other studies focus on the analytical treatment of ancient mythopoeic phenomena. Hawes (2014a) considers the response to mythological traditions by analytical writers who employed what they considered more rational tools for discovery. The essays in Marincola, Llewellyn-Jones, and Maciver (2012) consider invocations of the past (including mythic past) astride the constructs we have come to expect in historiography. Another collection, Grethein and Krebs (2012), examines the "plupast," an arena of earlier experience (including mythical) embedded in a historical narrative that allows the author to situate an immediate event in deeper layers of context to cast the current event in a particular light. Also important is an essay by Martin (2013), building on his earlier observations, which describes a transformative mythopoesis, a written engagement of mythological variants that service political jockeying—in other words, a continuation in new genres of a practice commonly found in Homeric poetry.

## REFERENCES

Bertelli, Lucio. 2001. "Hecataeus: From Genealogy to Historiography." In *The Historian's Craft in the Age of Herodotus*, edited by Nino Luraghi, 67–94. Oxford: Oxford University Press.

Bosworth, A. Brian. 1988. *Conquest and Empire: The Reign of Alexander the Great*. Cambridge, UK: Cambridge University Press.

Brillante, Carlo. 1990. "History and the Historical Interpretation of Myth." In *Approaches to Greek Myth*, edited by Lowell Edmunds, 93–138. Baltimore, MD: Johns Hopkins University Press.

Burnett, Anne P. 1998. *Revenge in Attic and Later Tragedy*. Berkeley and Los Angeles: University of California Press.

Calame, Claude. 2003. *Myth and History in Ancient Greece: The Symbolic Creation of a Colony*. Princeton, NJ: Princeton University Press.

Clarke, Katherine. 2008. *Making Time for the Past: Local History and the Polis*. Oxford: Oxford University Press.

Dowden, Ken. 1992. *The Uses of Greek Mythology*. London: Routledge.

Fowler, Robert L. 2013. *Early Greek Mythography*. Vol. 2: *Commentary*. Oxford: Oxford University Press.

Fowler, Robert L. 2015. "History." In *The Oxford Handbook of Ancient Greek Religion*, edited by Esther Eidinow and Julia Kindt, 195–209. Oxford: Oxford University Press.

Foxhall, Lin, Hans-Joachim Gehrke, and Nino Luraghi, eds. 2010. *Intentional History: Spinning Time in Ancient Greece*. Stuttgart: F. Steiner.

Fuqua, Charles. 1981. "Tyrtaeus and the Cult of Heroes." *Greek, Roman, and Byzantine Studies* 22: 215–226.

Gantz, Timothy. 1996. *Early Greek Myth: A Guide to Literary and Artistic Sources*. 2 vols. Baltimore, MD: Johns Hopkins University Press.

Gehrke, Hans-Joachim. 2001. "Myth, History, and Collective Identity: Uses of the Past in Ancient Greece and Beyond." In *The Historian's Craft in the Age of Herodotus*, edited by Nino Luraghi, 286–313. Oxford: Oxford University Press.

Gehrke, Hans-Joachim. 2010. "Representations of the Past in Greek Culture." In *Intentional History: Spinning Time in Ancient Greece*, edited by Lin Foxhall, Hans-Joachim Gehrke, and Nino Luraghi, 15–33. Stuttgart: F. Steiner.

Graf, Fritz. 2011. "Myth and Hellenic Identities." *A Companion to Greek Mythology*, edited by Ken Dowden and Niall Livingstone, 211–226. Chichester, UK: Wiley-Blackwell.

Grethlein, Jonas, and Christopher B. Krebs, eds. 2012. *Time and Narrative in Ancient Historiography: The "Plupast" from Herodotus to Appian*. Cambridge, UK: Cambridge University Press.

Hall, Jonathan M. 1997. *Ethnic Identity in Greek Antiquity*. Cambridge, UK: Cambridge University Press.

Hawes, Greta. 2014a. *Rationalizing Myth in Antiquity*. Oxford: Oxford University Press.

Hawes, Greta. 2014b. "Story Time at the Library: Palaephatus and the Emergence of Highly Literate Mythology." In *Between Orality and Literacy: Communication and Adaptation in Antiquity*, edited by Ruth Scodel, 125–147. Leiden: Brill.

Hawes, Greta. 2017. *Myths on the Map: The Storied Landscapes of Ancient Greece*. Oxford: Oxford University Press.

Hawes, Greta. 2021. *Pausanias in the World of Greek Myth*. Oxford: Oxford University Press.

Mac Sweeney, Naoíse. 2013. *Foundation Myths and Politics in Ancient Ionia*. Cambridge, UK: Cambridge University Press.

Mac Sweeney, Naoíse, ed. 2015. *Foundation Myths in Ancient Societies: Dialogues and Discourses*. Philadelphia: University of Pennsylvania Press.

McCauley, Barbara. 1999. "Heroes and Power: The Politics of Bone Transferal." In *Ancient Greek Hero Cult: Proceedings of the Fifth International Seminar on Ancient Greek Cult, 21–23 April 1995*, edited by Robin Hägg, 85–98. Stockholm: Svenska Institutet i Athen.

Marincola, John. 1997. *Authority and Tradition in Ancient Historiography*. Cambridge, UK: Cambridge University Press.

Marincola, John, Lloyd Llewellyn-Jones, and Calum Maciver, eds. 2012. *Greek Notions of the Past in the Archaic and Classical Eras: History Without Historians*. Edinburgh: Edinburgh University Press.

Martin, Richard. 2013. "The 'Myth before the Myth Began.'" In *Writing Down the* Myths, edited by Joseph Falaky Nagy, 45–66. Turnhout: Brepols.

Patterson, Lee E. 2004. "An Aetolian Local Myth in Pausanias?" *Mnemosyne* 57: 346–352.

Patterson, Lee E. 2010. *Kinship Myth in Ancient Greece*. Austin: University of Texas Press.

Patterson, Lee E. 2013. "Geographers as Mythographers: The Case of Strabo." In *Writing Myth: Mythography in the Ancient World*, edited by Stephen M. Trzaskoma and R. Scott Smith, 201–221. Leuven: Peeters.

Patterson, Lee E. 2017. "Myth as Evidence in Strabo." In *The Routledge Companion to Strabo*, edited by Daniela Dueck, 276–293. London and New York: Routledge.

Patterson, Lee E. 2021. "Heracles as Ancestor." In *The Oxford Handbook of Heracles*, edited by Daniel Ogden, 418–431. Oxford: Oxford University Press.

Rigsby, Kent J. 1996. *Asylia: Territorial Inviolability in the Hellenistic World*. Berkeley: University of California Press.

Romney, Jessica M. 2017. "Let Us Obey: The Rhetoric of Spartan Identity in Tyrtaeus 2W." *Mnemosyne* 71: 1–19.

Skinner, Joseph E. 2012. *The Invention of Greek Ethnography: From Homer to Herodotus*. Oxford: Oxford University Press.

Tarkow, Theodore A. 1983. "Tyrtaeus 9D: The Role of Poetry in the New Sparta." *L'Antiquité Classique* 42: 48–69.

Thomas, Rosalind. 1989. *Oral Tradition and Written Record in Classical Athens*. Cambridge, UK: Cambridge University Press.

Tigerstedt, Eugène N. 1965. *The Legend of Sparta in Classical Antiquity*. Vol. 1. Stockholm: Almqvist and Wiksell.

Vanschoonwinkel, Jacques. 1995. "Des Heraclides du mythe aux Doriens de l'archeologie." *Revue belge de philologie et d'histoire* 73: 127–148.

Veyne, Paul. 1988. *Did the Greeks Believe in Their Myths?* Translated by Paula Wissing. Chicago: University of Chicago Press.

Walker, Henry. 1995. *Theseus and Athens*. Oxford: Oxford University Press.

Zacharia, Katerina. 2001. "'The Rock of the Nightingale': Kinship Diplomacy and Sophocles' *Tereus*." In *Homer, Tragedy and Beyond: Essays in Honor of P. E. Easterling*, edited by Felix Budelmann and Pantelis Michelakis, 91–112. London: Society for the Promotion of Hellenic Studies.

CHAPTER 32

..................................................................................................

# MYTHOGRAPHY AND GEOGRAPHY

..................................................................................................

## MARIA PRETZLER

FROM the earliest days, the Greeks used myth to define different places and peoples, and when geography became a special branch of scholarship, most experts considered mythical traditions as an unavoidable aspect of their enquiries. This chapter has a big task, since mythology and geography were closely related from the very beginning of Greek literature. I am not going to provide a historical survey of geography in the ancient world: the aim is to show the role mythical material played in geographical writing, and how geographical writers engaged with earlier mythographical traditions and other forms of scholarship. I start with the big concepts involved in geography, particularly where the mythical tradition influenced complex questions concerning the overall shape of the inhabited world. The main part of the chapter is concerned with geography focused on specific places and regions: here, geographers drew on a long tradition of local and supraregional myths which had become a common means of explaining the identity and connections of communities all around the Mediterranean. A number of geographical works are discussed, but the second part of the chapter is focused on Strabo's *Geography*. This is not only the largest geographical work to survive from antiquity, but it is also our main source for fragments of earlier geographical works. This part of the chapter therefore covers geography and its preoccupations in the Hellenistic period, with a particular focus on geographical commentary on the Homeric epics.

## 1. DESCRIBING THE WORLD: THE MYTHICAL EDGES OF THE OECUMENE

..................................................................................................

What is geography? In the purest sense, ancient geography was concerned with describing the shape of the earth and the distribution and location of its landmasses.

This involved speculating about the edges of the earth and the farthest regions of the continents, with the increasing awareness that the actual world was bigger than the areas ancient geographers could speak about with any certainty (Arnaud 2014). From the beginning, such inquiries were therefore bound up with the ancient mythical traditions, which speak of Earth surrounded by Ocean. Myths are usually thought to be set in the distant past, but they were also placed in unknown, distant regions, at the edges of the world: this is where ancient accounts located fabulous animals, monstrous peoples that were not quite human, and utopian communities such as the Hyperboreans. As knowledge of distant regions increased, especially after Alexander's campaign and then with the Roman conquests around the western Mediterranean, these quasi-mythical spaces retreated farther into the distance, but the farthest regions remained unknown and continued to accommodate the fantastic (Romm 1992).

This was not just a question of who, or what, might inhabit the most distant places: also at stake was the physical shape of the *oecumene,* the inhabited world, which was ultimately still determined by the old mythical conception of Earth surrounded by Ocean. Anybody wanting to give a complete overview of the world would always have to wrestle with mythical concepts of the *kosmos* and the question of the place of the *oecumene,* essentially of human beings, within it. Once Eratosthenes had calculated the size of the globe, it became clear that as much as three quarters of the earth were unknown and subject to speculation. Eratosthenes still assumed an outer Ocean surrounding the whole *oecumene* (Prontera 2014: 22–26). Ptolemy broke with that tradition, proposing a whole southern continent extending east from Africa and joining up with SouthEast Asia, making the Indian Ocean an inland sea. Rather than read this as a definite statement about large landmasses in the southern hemisphere, we should see it as a deliberate decision to do away with the ancient but entirely mythical certainty of Ocean encircling the world (Berggren and Jones 2000: 20–22). Ptolemy's work ostensibly is not concerned with myth: it offers a technical manual for mapmaking, followed by long lists of places with their coordinates; and yet, when it comes to fundamental ideas about the shape of the inhabited world, it is still quintessentially defined by its response to the mythical tradition.

## 2. Chorography, Mythography, and History

Chorography was the more detailed treatment of specific places and regions, in contrast to attempts to give overviews of the whole inhabited world (Ptolemy, *Geography* 1.1; Prontera 2011a). Most ancient geographical works, even Strabo's description of the whole world, engaged in this type of regional geography, and myths almost always appear in this context, since more detailed descriptions included elements of ethnography or cultural geography. At the same time, the boundaries between geography and history were fluid: historiography had begun with a strong geographical element in Herodotus's *Histories*, and later on, it was Polybius who emphasized the importance of this connection and included extensive geographical material in his work (Polyb. 12.25; Clarke 1999: 79–97). Since there was room for the past in most geographical works, myths could play their established role in defining the character and significance of specific places, and an author covering a large area could also trace the networks created by mythical traditions (Clarke 1999: 245–251).

Greek myths were from the very beginning closely linked to geography. The Homeric epics include many geographical details, with a particular focus on areas in mainland Greece, parts of Asia Minor, and the Greek islands. The catalogues of Achaean ships (Hom. *Il.* 2.484–760) and Trojan allies (Hom. *Il.* 2.815–877) list many place names and regions or tribes (Visser 1997). More details emerge within the narrative: for example, descriptions of landmarks and places in the Troad, details of Ithaca and its surrounding regions, and references to the topography of the southern Peloponnese. Crete also receives considerable attention. This information does not add up to a map of Greece or Asia Minor during one specific period, but the references are to actual places in the landscape, most of which could still be identified. These passages represent early Greek geographical writing, and the main catalogues do not contain a lot of mythological material, with the exception of a few genealogical details. Places and communities are listed in a loose topographical order, with occasional descriptive epithets: there is an affinity with early "cartographical" texts, such as the *periplous*, the description of coastal features and ports (Jacob 1991: 30–32; Engels 1999: 117).

## 3. LOCAL TRADITIONS

Greek myths were rooted in specific places, and they developed as part of a discourse between local traditions and greater mythical themes that connected local stories and helped create complex networks of tradition; these often echoed, albeit not in a systematic way, more tangible links between regions and communities (Hawes 2017: 5–12; Clarke 2017). First and foremost, every Greek city had a foundation story, and it was one of the crucial details one needed to know about a place. Although most of the communities around the Aegean could not recall a historical act of foundation, many of the Greek cities in the western Mediterranean and the Black Sea remembered a mother city and a founder who was buried in a central location. But at some stage, communities in the "Old Country" acquired foundation stories, too, and these reached back into mythical times, involving heroic, semi-divine figures operating in times before the Trojan War. Eventually, many of the colonies seem to have followed suit, and they, too, began to tell foundation stories that reached further back into the mythical past. As the Greeks encountered other peoples and cities, they began to tell stories about their neighbors' origins as well, and soon non-Greeks began to tap into this tradition, too, adopting Greek stories as part of their own mythical past. As a result, foundation stories became a kind of universal language throughout the Greek world and beyond, used to communicate the identities of individuals and their communities and underlining their links with a wider world (Malkin 1998: 5–6, 211–213, 216–221; Malkin 2005: 64–66; Hall 1997: 34–66, 58–73).

Local traditions went beyond just foundation stories; there were whole local genealogies of mythical kings, heroes, and heroines, complete with stories about memorable deeds, wars, family connections, and interactions with gods and heroes. Pausanias's standard introductions for individual regions or cities offer overviews of these local traditions, providing a basic outline of how a community presented itself to the outside world and offering a context for many of the local monuments and stories included in his description (Pretzler 2007: 76–78). From the archaic period, some mythographers were concerned with gaining an overview of local details and the links between them. Early genealogical works tried to give a systematic account of local mythical figures and their family connections across the Greek world. Since we are dealing with local dynasties, geography is a useful organizing principle, for example, in the *Catalogue of Women*, a work attributed to Hesiod but probably composed around the mid-6th century BCE. Other genealogical works and compilations of myths probably also created such supraregional overviews, for example, the *Great Ehoiai* and the *Melampodia* (West 1985: 1–11, 125–171; Hirschberger 2004). These works are likely to have influenced Hecataeus's *Periodos Gēs*, the first attempt to tackle a full description of the world, which probably defined regions with reference to mythical origin stories and genealogies (Clarke 1999: 59–62, Fowler 2013: 658–669).

## 4. Supraregional Traditions

Beyond their local community, most Greeks also thought of themselves as belonging to tribal groups; some were concentrated in one region, such as Boeotians or Arcadians, others spread wide over disparate areas, such as Ionians or Dorians. These groups, too, had a mythical past, usually going all the way back to an eponymous hero and putative ancestor: some, for example the Arcadians, claimed to be autochthonous, and their origin myths were firmly located in their own region, but most tribes told migration stories about how their ancestors replaced earlier inhabitants such as Pelasgians or Leleges (Fowler 2013: 84–100). The most significant upheavals were placed after the Trojan War, with Dorians (as Heraclidae staking an ancestral claim) invading the Peloponnese and displacing Achaeans and Ionians, and some Aeolians, Ionians, and Dorians moving to Asia Minor and founding the Greek cities there (Hall 1997: 56–65). In many places, these stories explained how the tribal map of the *Iliad* turned into the ethnic geography of the Classical period. These stories were seen as important, not least because some tribes had actual historical significance, and even in the Roman imperial period, they still defined local identities. Pausanias's *Description of Greece* demonstrates the extent to which these tribal myth-histories were embedded in local tradition and the memorial landscape: the introduction to the Achaean book includes a detailed narrative of the history of Ionians and Achaeans (Paus. 7.1–6), while the histories of a number of Peloponnesian cities start with complex origin myths and migration stories that end with the return of the Heraclidae (for instance, Paus. 2.12.3–13.2, 2.18.4–8, 3.1.1–7, 4.1–3).

There were also myths that involved heroes traveling and collaborating, providing supraregional connections between local traditions at certain points in the general mythical "timeline" (Clarke 2008: 106–109; 143–146). Writers describing whole regions would encounter parts of these stories in different locations and would need to clarify the connections. Strabo acknowledges the importance of these mythical links and provides an overview in his introduction (Strabo 1.3.2). The most prolific traveler, founder of cities, and general cause of upheaval in local myth-histories was Heracles. In parts of mainland Greece, Heracles changes the mythical "political" geography, essentially helping to reshape local traditions about pre–Trojan War "history" into the landscape we see in the *Iliad*. In the western Mediterranean, he or his travel companions became the founding heroes of many cities (Jourdain-Annequin 1989; Malkin 2011: 119–141). After Alexander's conquest, traditions about Heracles's journey to the distant East offered potential mythical connections for Asian communities with Greek aspirations. The story of the Argonauts became the major mythical theme for the whole Pontic region once the Greeks started to settle around the Black Sea during the archaic period. What is more, the crew of the Argo included a variable list of heroes from the entire Greek world, forging connections between local genealogies. Other stories brought teams of heroes together—for example, the hunt of the Calydonian boar. The biggest and most versatile set of travelers' stories is set after the Trojan War: the fall of Troy was a crucial event for Greek mythical geography, since it set in motion so many stories of displacement and new beginnings: in the *nostoi* tradition, many Greeks never got home at all or took a very long time to return, leaving new cities in their wake; Trojans fleeing their ruined home settled new places as well (Malkin 1998: 1–3). Most of Odysseus's adventures were set outside defined geography, but he, too, began to appear in local myths and, remarkably, also in the imagination of Etruscans and other Italic peoples (Prontera 1993: 387–388). These tales were decentralized and adaptable, yet at the same time, they offered a common framework where local stories could become part of a collective memory which was accessible not only to Greeks, but to some of their neighbors as well (Malkin 1998: 44–55).

# 5. MODES OF MYTHOGRAPHY IN GEOGRAPHICAL WORKS

Anyone writing geography who had some interest in local and regional details would have to decide how to deal with mythical traditions because they were so fundamental to the ways in which Greeks defined communities and how they thought about supraregional networks. Engaging with this material also meant dealing with inevitable contradictions and the fact that myths conceptualized space and connections between places very differently from geographers (Delattre 2017). Moreover, there were mythical stories everywhere, and people considered their local traditions as very significant. Geographers had to select what seemed relevant to their purpose. One crucial question is whether it was possible to present regional geography without any mythography at all. The answer is a qualified yes: the genre was flexible, but there were also good reasons to keep the stories in their places and include at least some mythical material.

It was possible to adopt a descriptive, quasi-cartographical approach to chorography. Ptolemy's focus on topographical data demonstrates this, but we also find it in the sparsest form of the *periplous*. It was possible to offer a plain list of places and landmarks, as we can see in large sections of Pseudo-Scylax's *Periplous*, but even here some places are defined by their mythical past (Shipley 2011: 15–16). Later authors who adopted the *periplous* format usually decided to include more mythical material in their works, for example, Pliny (Smith 2017) and Pomponius Mela (Smith 2016).

It was therefore possible within one geographical work to go from sparse references in some regions to dense, lengthy commentaries in others. Most ancient writers did not draw the line between myths and historical fact in the same way as we do today: details of the journeys of Heracles, Jason, and Odysseus are tentatively classed as history (Strabo 1.3.2.), even if implausible details might be considered mythical (Strabo 1.2.19). The Trojan War and the stories about migration in its aftermath, such as the colonization of Asia Minor by Aeolians, Ionians, and Dorians, and the return of the Heraclidae to the Peloponnese are regularly presented as part of local histories that seamlessly merge into accounts of events in the Classical and Hellenistic period (for instance, Strabo 8.7.1–3; see also Paus. 3.1.1–10.5, 7.6.3–5). Earlier migration stories back to the earliest pre-Greek peoples could be treated as factual history, too, even if there were clearly very complex disputes about them (Strabo 5.2.4, 7.7.1–2, 9.2.3, 12.8.4–7, 14.2.27). Not just Homer and other early poets, but also the classical Attic tragedians supply evidence for quasi-historical truth in relation to such stories (Strabo 1.3.20 discusses their quality as historical sources compared to Homer). Historians played a role in blurring the boundary between history and myth as well: both local and universal histories could start with what we would consider as myth and continue down to historical periods or even to the author's own day (Patterson 2013: 208–210). Ephorus, for example, served Strabo as a major source for the location of early pre-Greek peoples and migration stories, such as the histories of the Heraclidae (for instance, Strabo 8.5.4, 8.8.5, 10.3.2; Clarke 2008: 98–109).

# 6. STRABO AND MYTHOGRAPHY

Strabo's *Geography* is a universal work in seventeen books that attempts to describe the whole known world in considerable detail; it was composed during the later parts of the reign of Augustus or under Tiberius: Strabo lived from around 64 BCE to after 23 CE. This work demonstrates the flexibility of the genre in dealing with myth in the context of geography: coverage of mythical material in different regions varies and thus allows us to observe different approaches to mythography as part of geography.

Strabo's work contains the earliest known use of the word *mythographia* (Patterson 2013: 201; Strabo 1.2.35, 8.3.9). When Strabo talks about myth, he is usually referring to stories that relate incredible details (Strabo 11.6.2–4). In his introduction, Strabo emphasizes the usefulness of geography, particularly for those in power (1.1.17–18), but he states that a geographical work should also include theoretical material, in fields such as the arts (*technikē*), mathematics, and natural sciences (*physikē*), as well as history and myth. He contends that myths do not have much practical value, except perhaps through the moral lessons one might draw from them, but that they could still offer entertainment to those interested in the places where the stories were set. Strabo assumes that some men of action (*hoi prattontes*, by implication Strabo's intended readership) would enjoy myths, but not too many, because in the end, they will still prefer what is useful; and more generally, one should focus on the more trustworthy information (1.1.19).

Nevertheless, Strabo's work includes large amounts of mythical material (Patterson 2013: 207; 2017: 276). Any rules he may have set for himself limiting the space for mythography in his work are not just bent, but thoroughly broken when he reaches the parts of the Greek world to which the *Iliad* and *Odyssey* pay special attention (for a more detailed discussion of Strabo's Homeric geography, see section 7, "Strabo: Reading Homer as the First Geographer" below). Many myths recorded by Strabo deal with links between specific places and mythical heroes, particularly foundations, not just of cities, but also sanctuaries and cults (see the tables in Patterson 2017: 282–290). He also includes traditions that relate the migrations of tribal groups. Another crucial category are *aitia*, stories explaining aspects of local culture and peculiar names. In distant places, this includes stories about Greek heroes bringing aspects of their culture to strange peoples. The overwhelming majority of Strabo's myths are Greek, with just a few traditions of different origin: the most striking examples are the origin myths of some Italic people, such as the Hirpini, Samnites, and Picentini (Strabo 5.4.5, 5.4.12); the foundation story of Rome includes the usual mix of Greek and Italian traditions (Strabo 5.3.2–3), and we get a version of the story of Moses and the exodus from Egypt (16.2.35–9).

Given the scope of Strabo's *Geography* and the sheer number of places he mentions, we still have to acknowledge his very selective approach: many places remain without any reference to the mythical past, something worth noting in a Greek world so fundamentally defined by myths. This is not to dismiss Strabo as a mythographer—on the contrary, he clearly exploited the flexibility of the genre and made a deliberate decision to ration mythical material according to specific interests (Clarke 2017: 16–18; 2008: 140–150). The coverage of myths in the *Geography* varies from region to region: in parts of the world outside the reach of early Greek mythmaking, it is not very surprising that hardly any myths are included: there are more comparatively recent Roman foundation stories than mythical ones in Strabo's first few books, which cover western Europe. There are, however, also parts of the traditional Greek world where he allows little space for the mythical past, for example, in Sicily or in parts of Asia Minor (Trotta 2005; see also Clarke 1999: 264–270; Patterson 2017: 277–279); in some of these areas, Strabo prefers to define Greek cities with lists of recent intellectuals rather than by foundation stories or mythical genealogies (Engels 2005).

At one point, Strabo even presents himself as "not at all fond of myths" (Strabo 10.3.23: *hēkista philomuthountes*). But this statement is made in the context of justifying a long discussion that is unique in the *Geography*: he disentangles local traditions from Crete and Asia Minor, where the Curetes were either young men involved in cult activity or supernatural beings serving the gods (Strabo 10.3.7–22). As Strabo saw it, a discussion of the divine had to include early testimonies and myth, since the ancients chose to express their ideas through myth, and he was confident that it might be possible to arrive at some kind of truth by setting out all the available traditions (Strabo 10.3.23). This approach allows flexibility for the treatment of mythical material, leaving room for serious discussion without precluding criticism.

Strabo's critical attitude to myths and those who tell them is explicitly on show when he has to deal with material he considers untrustworthy. He dismisses myths that contradict geographical facts—for example, the idea that the Alpheus river flowed under the sea from the Peloponnese to Sicily to feed the fresh-water spring of Arethusa in Syracuse (Strabo 6.2.4) or various stories about Amazons and early conquests of India that had contributed to major confusion in the geography of Asia (Strabo 11.5.5). When he discusses reports of distant parts of the world, he labels details as mythical when he considers them ancient, false, or supernatural. In Strabo's mind, credibility is the crucial distinction between myth and history (Strabo 11.5.3; Lightfoot 2017: 253–254). Myths have their place, where they can inform us about ancient times and very ancient philosophical ideas, but mythical elements are misplaced in historical or ethnographical writing: Strabo concludes that one can trust heroic narratives presented by the epic poets and the classical tragedians more than the accounts of Ctesias, Herodotus, or Hellanicus (Strabo 11.6.3; Dueck 2005: 94–96).

Strabo often assumes that myths have been manipulated, and he approaches them with a great deal of skepticism: some local traditions are simply not credible (for instance, Strabo 5.1.9, 5.4.5, 7.7.12, 8.6.2). Sometimes, Strabo tries to explain how a story was fabricated, for example, when he links the story of Heracles's struggle against a shapeshifting Achelous with the frequently changing course of the river (Strabo 10.2.19); and the story of Geryon's herd is explained with a reference to the excellent grazing land around Gades (Strabo 3.5.4). Strabo is rationalizing myth in a time-honored fashion, but he also accuses others of "de-rationalizing" geographical facts to create mythical stories (see also Strabo 11.2.19 on the Golden Fleece). Much of Strabo's skepticism about mythical material is directed at the authors of his written sources. Experts on Homer resort to myth-telling to explain difficult passages and to demonstrate their cleverness (Strabo 13.1.69), poets embellish their works (Strabo 9.3.6, on Pindar), and even respectable historians do so on occasion (Strabo 9.3.11, on Ephorus). The risk is particularly great when historians believe that they must engage in flattery (for instance, Strabo 7.7.12: a local historian responding to regional pride); in Strabo's view, Alexander's campaign particularly inspired fantastical exaggerations to flatter the king (Strabo 11.5.5, 15.1.9, 15.2.7). In short, a universal geographer had to cope with many traditions about places and regions that were, at best, difficult to evaluate and sometimes too outlandish to be taken seriously.

# 7. STRABO: READING HOMER AS THE FIRST GEOGRAPHER

In all this chaos of local variants, purposeful manipulation, and treatments of mythical themes, Homer's epics stood out as the one literary source that most people accepted as the ultimate authority. There were disagreements over the exact interpretation of diffi-cult passages, and the identification of many of the places mentioned in the epics was contentious, but for geographers, the epics provided a whole collection of fixed data points to which much of the Greek mythical tradition was tethered in some way. Strabo cites Homer more than 700 times, compared to about 250 citations of all other kinds of Greek poetry (Kim 2010: 47; Dueck 2005: 87–92). He engages with a long tradition of Homeric scholarship, and many of the mythical details he presents without refer-ence to the epics are still indirectly concerned with Homeric geography. For example, when Strabo discusses early migrations, he often tries to explain how the ethnic "map" emerging in the *Iliad* came about, or how it changed into the picture familiar in the clas-sical texts. Strabo demonstrates two very different approaches to geography in the *Iliad* and *Odyssey*: in the introduction, he tries to gain an overview, with a lengthy general dis-cussion of Homer as a geographer, evaluating the poet's image of the world and the ge-ographical knowledge that emerges from the epics (Strabo 1.1.2–11; 1.2.3–40). In the rest of the *Geography*, he engages in Homeric geography as it had been practiced for a long time by then: he discusses details that refer to specific places and provides a geograph-ical commentary on relevant passages (Lightfoot 2017).

Ancient geographers thought that Homer's epics marked the beginning of their dis-cipline. Strabo (1.1.2) says in his introduction that his predecessors already considered Homer to be the founder (*archegētēs*) of the science of geography, and he paraphrases Eratosthenes, who saw the early history of the discipline as represented by Homer, followed by Anaximander and Hecataeus (Strabo 1.1.11). If a geographer wanted to focus on human geography, the *Iliad* and *Odyssey* had to be tackled, and there was an ongoing debate about the accuracy and trustworthiness of the geographical information Homer provided.

The epics inspired works that combined detailed literary commentaries with geog-raphy, comparing details mentioned by the poet with facts on the ground (Trachsel 2017; Pfeiffer 1968: 249–251, 257–261). Around the middle of the second century BCE, Demetrius of Scepsis wrote a commentary on the catalogue of the Trojan allies—thirty books on just over sixty lines (Strabo 13.1.45). A generation later, Apollodorus of Athens wrote twelve books on the *Catalogue of Ships*, which also drew on Eratosthenes's geographical work (Strabo 7.3.6). Most of what we know about the nature of these works is due to Strabo, who relies on geographical details in both commentaries, but also criticizes some of their interpretations. Some sections of the *Geography* are a commentary on Homeric geography in their own right (for instance, Strabo 8.3, 9.5, 13.1; Dueck 2000: 36–38). In the southwestern Peloponnese Strabo focuses on the problems with identifying the location of Nestor's Pylos (Strabo 8.3.24–29). He attempts to explain the *Odyssey*'s topography of Ithaca, neighboring islands, and the coast of the mainland nearby (Strabo 10.2). The most extensive discussion focuses on the Troad, where the *Iliad* supplies many topographical details relating to the raids and battles around Troy. The location of Homer's Troy was disputed, and Strabo contends that it was not located on the same site as the Ilium of his own day (Strabo 13.1.33–42). Other passages in Strabo's *Geography*, especially books 9 and 12, are organized with the Homeric catalogues in mind. The description of Thessaly (Strabo 9.5.4–22) is almost entirely a concise geographical commentary on the relevant section of the *Catalogue of Ships* (Hom. *Il.* 685–756).

It seems rather difficult to reconcile these lengthy passages expounding Homer with Strabo's stated aim of focusing on contemporary circumstances. In Elis and Messenia, Homeric geography differed considerably from those present-day circumstances. So why include a discussion of the ancient text at all? Strabo justifies this by appealing to the poet's fame and the central role he played in Greek education: every potential reader of the *Geography* had grown up with Homer and could be expected to know his works inside out (Strabo 8.3.3, 8.3.23). The epics may describe Greece in a distant past, but the ancient text remained an important part of the current landscape, at least in the mind of everybody with a Greek education (Clarke 1999: 248–249; Kim 2010: 81–83; Patterson 2013: 213). Strabo therefore aims to describe the current landscape in such a way that the facts on the ground do not contradict the details known from the epics (8.3.3). At the same time, he points out that some of the places listed in the *Iliad* no longer exist, but their ancient fame still justified inclusion in the description (for instance, 9.4.5, 9.5.5–8). As a result, parts of Strabo's mainland Greece appear to be almost devoid of contemporary features, while being overwhelmed by Homeric memories that were no longer part of the physical landscape but remained relevant in educated people's imaginations.

Discussions about the correct locations of specific Homeric places were considered important from the archaic period onward (Prontera 1993: 387–389). If the places in some passages could be identified, others raised fundamental questions about location. The *Odyssey* effectively abandons references to identifiable Mediterranean places as soon as it picks up Odysseus's story at Ogygia (Hom. *Od.* 5.1). The hero leaves "real geography" behind early on in the account of his adventures, in a storm that hits soon after the Ithacan ships leave Troy (Hom. *Od.* 9.81), and he returns to a known part of the world only when the Phaeacians finally bring him back to Ithaca (Hom. *Od.* 13.96; Fowler 2017: 244–250). Attempts to locate these "floating" episodes in the real world must have started early, possibly with Hesiod (Strabo 1.2.14), placing most of Odysseus's wanderings in the western Mediterranean (Prontera 2011b: 86–87; Malkin 1998: 1–3,

44–55). Although there was clearly room for debate about specific episodes, geographers usually assumed that the poet had specific places in mind. Various methods could be applied to identify these locations: Polybius preferred a rationalizing approach, which could account even for some of the fantastic monsters in Odysseus's narrative. For example, he thought that Homer's description of Scylla was connected with the behavior of dolphins and predatory fish when swarms of tuna passed by the coast of Sicily, and Charybdis reminded him of currents in the Strait of Messina. And while other commentators, including Strabo, assumed that part of Odysseus's journey should be located in the Ocean, outside the Pillars of Heracles, Polybius argued that there was room in the Mediterranean to get lost in a nine-day storm, and he backed up his argument with calculations of wind speed and distances (Polyb. 34.2–4, paraphrased in Strabo 1.2.15–18; Lightfoot 2017: 255–6; Kim 2010: 71–74). Crates of Mallus went further: he thought that scientific knowledge was encoded in the epics, for example, details about the northern Ocean and the shape of the continents. His map of the world was probably also based on Homer (Prontera 1993: 391–392; Schenkeveld 1976: 56; see Strabo 1.2.24, 2.5.10, 3.4.4). Strabo did not want to go that far, but he generally recognizes Homer as an important authority, who was committed to the truth, even if at times he chose to disguise it with mythical elements.

Eratosthenes's assessment of Homeric geography boldly disrupted the established ways of thinking about Homer and the meaning of poetry, with potential repercussions that went well beyond the context of geography. He assumed that the ancient poets wrote to entertain rather than to instruct their audiences (Strabo 1.2.3). This means that Homer never intended to set Odysseus's journey in specific places: the story is fictional, as are the places where it is set, and therefore entirely irrelevant for geography. In fact, not having to pay attention to a real-world setting allows the poet more freedom in developing some of the more fantastical episodes (Strabo 1.2.12; 1.2.19; Geus 2002: 264–267; Schenkeveld 1976: 55–56). As far as we know, this idea did not find many followers; at any rate, Strabo argued very forcefully against it. Too much was at stake: if geographers were to abandon the search for Homeric locations and treat the epics as fictional—essentially lies (there was no terminology to define the difference)—then Homer's position as foundation of Greek culture, education, and philosophy would be under threat (Lightfoot 2017: 251–253; Biraschi 1984).

Strabo uses the many traditional links between Odysseus's adventures and locations in Italy and Sicily to suggest that the poet did have specific places in mind, even if he did not identify them clearly (Strabo 1.2.12–14). Many of these connections had probably developed precisely because some of the vague locations in the *Odyssey* were there for the taking, so that this was a circular argument; but the locations of some of these stories had become such an established part of Greek tradition that it was impossible to recognize this (Biraschi 2005: 77–79). A more general defense of Homer's expertise and veracity could also draw on the more overtly geographical passages in the *Iliad* (Strabo 1.2.20), although this did not deal with the accusation of Apollodorus that Homer knew places in Greece very well and describes them accurately, but had little knowledge of places farther away, specifically Scythia (Strabo 7.3.6). In his introduction, Strabo discusses arguments about Homer's knowledge of the Black Sea, Egypt, and the Arabian Gulf (Strabo 1.1.10; 1.2.22–24; Kim 2010: 50–51). In this context, proof of Homer's knowledge of the western Mediterranean and other distant areas was important to defend his general credibility (Kim 2010: 71–77). The question comes up again when Strabo argues that Homer clearly knew Iberian peninsula, though he never mentions it explicitly (Strabo 3.2.12–13); when Strabo reaches a place named Odyssea in southern Spain, which invited questions about traces of Homeric heroes in the real world, he raises the more general topic of Homer as a source for scientific facts (3.4.3–4).

Engaging with Homer's geography was not just a matter of gathering geographical details for the description of regions. Strabo argues that Homer exhibits all the qualities a good geographer requires, and that the epics include the earliest attempts to record knowledge about the shape of the earth and large-scale geography. Strabo points out that Homer talks about Ocean circling the earth and mentions (albeit quite obliquely) the regions at the edges of the *oecumene* in all directions (Strabo 1.1.2–7). Strabo was strongly influenced by Hellenistic Stoicism (Dueck 2000: 62–69), which held that Homer was the source of all knowledge, but instead of taking this assumption for granted, he offers elaborate arguments to draw the image of a knowledgeable historian, geographer, and philosopher who sometimes disguises the truth he knows with poetic embellishment (Kim 2010: 50–53, 77–81). The dominance of the epics in Strabo's work is not due to some eccentric preference on the part of the author: his wrestling with various predecessors shows that by the Hellenistic period, Homeric exegesis had become a central concern of geography, so much so that even authors with mainly scientific interests, such as Eratosthenes, found it necessary to discuss the epics (Engels 1999: 115–120).

# 8. CONCLUSIONS

Mythography in ancient geographical writing demonstrates the fundamental role mythical traditions played in Greek thinking about the world and its human inhabitants. Much was at stake when geographers included myths in their work and chose to engage with the larger mythographical tradition. From fundamental thoughts about the shape of the world to deep-seated ideas about what it meant to be Greek and how Greeks related to other peoples, myths held whole worldviews together, and as such, they could belong to the genre of geographical writing. At the same time, geography was a field of knowledge in which the mythical tradition had to be confronted with observed facts in real places: here, geography stepped onto risky ground, particularly when the authority of Homer was under scrutiny. Past and present were often intertwined through the nexus of space, and competing data could spark vigorous debates about the stories of the heroic world and how relevant they were in explaining how the world of the later Greeks came to be. It is perhaps inevitable, then, that geographical writers attempting to make sense of the Greek world turned to mythography to help tease out the relationship between place, history, and myth.

## FURTHER READING

The study of Greek myths has been taking a distinctly spatial turn for some time now: ancient geographical writing has played a crucial role in these studies, which have in turn shed new light on links between ancient geography and mythography. Malkin has been offering crucial analysis of networks of mythical traditions from the Iron Age onward (for instance, Malkin 1998, 2005), culminating in his 2011 book on networks in the ancient Mediterranean. Hall (1997) demonstrated how myths developed in concert with the formation of ethnic and regional identities. Romm's (1992) seminal work discusses myths at the edges of the earth, on the boundary between geography and fiction. Recently Hawes (2017) brought together different perspectives on the ways in which mythical traditions are rooted in the landscape.

Clarke (1999, 2008) tackles the complexities of factoring time into the description of places and regions, both in historical and geographical texts, and more work has been done specifically on the treatment of the mythical past in geographical texts. Prontera (2011b) offers an overview; Clarke (2017), Delattre (2017) and Fowler (2017) tackle more specific problems for ancient authors who assessed and organized myths, including traditions that do not have a defined geographical setting.

Strabo's *Geography*, as the most substantial surviving example of the genre, has received special attention: Clarke (2008) discusses myths in Strabo, and more recently, Patterson (2013, 2017) has catalogued Strabo's main references to mythical stories and assessed how the ancient writer used this material. Strabo's emphasis on the Homeric epics and related traditions has also led to discussions of the links between geography and epic poetry and the long tradition, in antiquity, of scholarly treatises on this topic; for instance, Prontera (1993) and Kim (2010). On Strabo and Homer specifically, see Schenkeveld (1976), Biraschi (1984, 2005), and particularly Lightfoot's (2017) chapter in the *Routledge Companion to Strabo*.

## REFERENCES

Arnaud, Pascal. 2014. "Mapping the Edges of the Earth: Approaches and Cartographical Problems." In *The Periphery of the Classical World in Ancient Geography and Cartography*, edited by Alexander V. Podossinov, 31–57. Leuven: Peeters.

Berggren, J. Lennart, and Alexander Jones. 2000. *Ptolemy's Geography: An Annotated Translation of the Theoretical Chapters*. Princeton, NJ: Princeton University Press.

Biraschi, Anna M. 1984. "Strabone e la difesa di Omero nei Prolegomena." In *Strabone: Contributi allo studio della personalità e dell'opera*, vol.1, edited by Francesco Prontera, 127–153. Perugia: Università degli studi.

Biraschi, Anna M. 2005. "Strabo and Homer: A Chapter in Cultural History." *Strabo's Cultural Geography: The Making of a "Kolossourgia,"* edited by Daniela Dueck, Hugh Lindsay, and Sarah Pothecary, 73–85. Cambridge. UK: Cambridge University Press.

Clarke, Katherine. 1999. *Between Geography and History: Hellenistic Constructions of the Roman World*. Oxford: Oxford University Press.

Clarke, Katherine. 2008. *Making Time for the Past*. Oxford: Oxford University Press.

Clarke, Katherine. 2017. "Walking through History: Unlocking the Mythical Past." In *Myths on the Map: The Storied Landscapes of Ancient Greece*, edited by Greta Hawes, 14–31. Oxford: Oxford University Press.

Delattre, Charles. 2017. "Islands of Knowledge: Space and Names in Imperial Mythography." In *Myths on the Map: The Storied Landscapes of Ancient Greece*, edited by Greta Hawes, 261–280. Oxford: Oxford University Press.

Dueck, Daniela. 2000. *Strabo of Amasia: A Greek Man of Letters in Augustan Rome*. London and New York: Routledge.

Dueck, Daniela. 2005. "Strabo's Use of Poetry." In *Strabo's Cultural Geography: The Making of a "Kolossourgia"*, edited by Daniela Dueck, Hugh Lindsay, and Sarah Pothecary, 86–107. Cambridge, UK: Cambridge University Press.

Engels, Johannes. 1999. *Augusteische Oikumenegeographie und Universalhistorie im Werk Strabons von Amaseia*. Stuttgart: F. Steiner.

Engels, Johannes. 2005. "Ἄνδρες ἔνδοξοι or 'Men of High Reputation' in Strabo's *Geography*." In *Strabo's Cultural Geography: The Making of a "Kolossourgia"*, edited by Daniela Dueck, Hugh Lindsay, and Sarah Pothecary, 129–143. Cambridge, UK: Cambridge University Press.

Fowler, Robert L. 2013. *Early Greek Mythography*. Vol. 2: *Commentary*. Oxford: Oxford University Press.

Fowler, Robert L. 2017. "Imaginary Itineraries in the Beyond." In *Myths on the Map: The Storied Landscapes of Ancient Greece*, edited by Greta Hawes, 241–260. Oxford: Oxford University Press.

Geus, Klaus. 2002. *Eratosthenes von Kyrene: Studien zur helleistischen Kultur- und Wissenschaftsgeschichte*. Munich: C. H. Beck.

Hall, Jonathan. 1997. *Ethnic Identity in Greek Antiquity*. Cambridge, UK: Cambridge University Press.

Hawes, Greta, ed. 2017. *Myths on the Map: The Storied Landscapes of Ancient Greece*. Oxford: Oxford University Press.

Hirschberger, Martina. 2004. "Genealogie und Geographie: Der hesiodische *Gynaikon Katalogos* als Vorläufer von Hekataios und der ionischen *Historie*." *Antike Naturwissenschaft und ihre Rezeption* 14: 7–24.

Jacob, Christian. 1991. *Géographie et ethnographie en Grèce ancienne*. Paris: Armand Colin.

Jourdain-Annequin, Colette. 1989. "De l'espace de la cité à l'espace symbolique: Héraclès en Occident." *Dialogues d'histoire ancienne* 15: 31–48.

Kim, Lawrence Y. 2010. *Homer between History and Fiction in Imperial Greek Literature*. Cambridge, UK: Cambridge University Press.

Lightfoot, Jane L. 2017. "Man of Many Voices and of Much Knowledge; or, in Search of Strabo's Homer." In *The Routledge Companion to Strabo*, edited by Daniela Dueck, 251–262. London and New York: Routledge.

Malkin, Irad. 1998. *The Returns of Odysseus*. Berkeley: University of California Press.

Malkin, Irad. 2005. "Networks and the Emergence of Greek Identity." In *Mediterranean Paradigms and Classical Antiquity*, edited by Irad Malkin, 56–74. London and New York: Routledge.

Malkin, Irad. 2011. *A Small Greek World: Networks in the Ancient Mediterranean*. Oxford: Oxford University Press.

Patterson, Lee E. 2013. "Geographers as Mythographers: The Case of Strabo." In *Writing Myth: Mythography in the Ancient World*, edited by Stephen M. Trzaskoma, and R. Scott Smith, 201–221. Leuven: Peeters.

Patterson, Lee E. 2017. "Myth as Evidence in Strabo." In *The Routledge Companion to Strabo*, edited by Daniela Dueck, 276–293. London and New York: Routledge.

Pfeiffer, Rudolf. 1968. *History of Classical Scholarship: From the Beginnings to the End of the Hellenistic Age*. Oxford: Clarendon Press.

Pretzler, Maria. 2007. *Pausanias: Travel Writing in Ancient Greece*. London: Duckworth.

Prontera, Francesco. 1993. "Sull'esegesi ellenistica della geografia omerica." In *Philanthropia kai Eusebeia: Festschrift für Albrecht Dihle zum 70. Geburtstag*, edited by Glenn W. Most, Hubert Petersmann, and Adolf M. Richter, 387–397. Göttingen: Vandenhoeck and Ruprecht.

Prontera, Francesco. 2011a. "Geografia e corografia: Note sul lessico della cartografia antica." In *Geografia e storia nella Grecia antica*, edited by Francesco Prontera, 95–103. Florence: Leo S. Olschki Editore.

Prontera, Francesco. 2011b. "Sulle rappresentazioni mitiche della geografia greca." In *Geografia e storia nella Grecia antica*, edited by Francesco Prontera, 81–94. Florence: Leo S. Olschki Editore.

Prontera, Francesco. 2014. "Centre et périphérie dans les mappemondes grecques." In *The Periphery of the Classical World in Ancient Geography and Cartography*, edited by Alexander V. Podossinov, 13–29. Leuven: Peeters.

Romm, James S. 1989. "Herodotus and Mythic Geography: The Case of the Hyperboreans." *Transactions of the American Philological Association* 119: 97–113.

Romm, James S. 1992. *The Edges of the Earth in Ancient Thought: Geography, Exploration and Fiction*. Princeton, NJ: Princeton University Press.

Schenkeveld, Dirk M. 1976. "Strabo on Homer." *Mnemosyne* (Ser. 4) 29: 52–64.

Shipley, Graham. 2011. *Pseudo-Skylax's "Periplous": The Circumnavigation of the Inhabited World; Text, Translation and Commentary*. Exeter, UK: Bristol Phoenix Press.

Smith, R. Scott. 2016. "Between Narrative and Allusion: Mythography in Pomponius Mela's *Chorography*." *Polymnia* 2: 87–119.

Smith, R. Scott. 2017. "Myth and Mythography in Pliny's Geography, *Naturalis Historia* 3–6." *Polymnia* 3: 83–116.

Trachsel, Alexandra. 2017. "Strabo and the Homeric Commentators." In *The Routledge Companion to Strabo*, edited by Daniela Dueck, 263–275. London and New York: Routledge.

Trotta, Francesco. 2005. "The Foundation of Greek Colonies and Their Main Features in Strabo: A Portrayal Lacking Homogeneity?" In *Strabo's Cultural Geography: The Making of a "Kolossourgia"*, edited by Daniela Dueck, Hugh Lindsay, and Sarah Pothecary, 118–128. Cambridge, UK: Cambridge University Press.

Visser, Edzard. 1997. *Homers Katalog der Schiffe*. Stuttgart and Leipzig: Teubner.

West, Martin L. 1985. *The Hesiodic Catalogue of Women: Its Nature, Structure and Origins*. Oxford: Clarendon Press.

# CHAPTER 33

# MYTHOGRAPHER AND MYTHOGRAPHY

## Indigenous Categories? Greek Inquiries into the Heroic Past

### CLAUDE CALAME

To modern eyes, Greek mythography constitutes a distinct discursive genre if not a "literary genre" (see Pàmias in this volume).[1] While acknowledging that the Greek term came into use relatively late, the modern editor of the historiographers of the Greek heroic past does not hesitate to give his edition and detailed commentary of the few fragments that have come down to us the (misleading) title *Early Greek Mythography* (Fowler 2000, 2013). Still, neither *mythographos* nor *mythographia* is a term attested for that period (end of 6th to beginning of 4th c. BCE), when some scholars believe that we can first identify the spread of mythographical practices. So, neither *mythographos* as learned author nor *mythographia* as practice occurs before the Alexandrian period, before the appearance of the mythographical manuals as collections of narratives concerning the heroic past and traditions of the various Greek cities of the archaic and classical ages. Thus, the question is: What labels were given to those to whom we attribute the figure and function of a mythographer? What terms were applied to the products of their labor as they were working on a history of heroic time which, for us, belongs in the modern category of "myth?" Just as in the case of a *mythos*, which, up to the 5th century BCE, referred simply to a developed and argumentative speech act (*discours*) aimed at persuasion (more on this below), one should also examine the terms and indigenous categories corresponding to what we too quickly identify as *mythographer* and *mythography*.

---

[1] This chapter was translated by R. Scott Smith and Stephen M. Trzaskoma.

# 1. "Mythographers": A Late Classification

*Mythographos* first appears in our records, which are obviously very lacunose, in the 2nd century BCE, in Polybius (4.40.1–2). There, the Greek historian and politician associates mythographers with poets: none of their explanations of the current that flowed from the Euxine Sea and its silting up through alluvial deposits can hold up to real world observation (*hē kata physin theōria*). Aligning himself with Heraclitus (fr. 22 A 23 D.-K.) and diverging from his own predecessors (called *syngrapheis*, or "writers," that is, "prose-writers"), Polybius will earn the confidence of his contemporary listeners (*sic!*), and do so through the precision of his inquiry: *historia*, because *historeō*, as we will see, meant "inquire" since the time of Herodotus. Polybius likewise offers a similar use of *mythographos*, also in a geographical context, when discussing the Phlegraean Fields (3.91.7).

Before the 2nd century BCE, the only attestation of the word *mythographos* is found at the end of one of the *Unbelievable Stories* collected by Palaephatus, whose identity is not certain (see Koning, this volume). In discussing the story of the resurrection of Glaucus after his apparent death in a *pithos* full of honey and his revival by the seer that Minos put in the same tomb with him, Palaephatus (26) tells us the story of a real person named Glaucus who fell into a coma after having drunk to much honey. Because it is impossible for a man to come back to life, Palaephatus gives a rationalizing version of the story. He adds that this *mythos* has been subsequently shaped by the mythographers. He then gives a story about a different Glaucus (27) and calls it not *mythos* but *logos*: a story that is foolish. Could it be that here *logos*, even as a vain story, is contrasted with a myth, which would appear to be the specific domain of the mythographers? In fact, it is far from certain that both stories, corresponding to entries 26 and 27 in the text as transmitted to us, belong to the original collection, which is usually dated to the second half of the 4th century BCE (see Santoni 2000: 37–42; Koning, this volume). On the other hand, in the introduction of the collection (see Hawes 2014: 37–48), Palaephatus says that he is taking the stories (*ta legomena*) that he rationalizes from poets and logographers, without speaking of mythographers; he also calls these logographers *syngrapheis*, that is, "writers" or "composers." Similarly, in this same introductory text, he uses the verb *syngraphein* to describe his own narrative technique of reconstructing and rewriting: it is the result of his inquiring (*historēsas*).

We can add to this the fact that, through its Latin translation as *fabularum scriptor*, the term *mythographos* could be used for Herodotus in a Hellenistic treatise, erroneously attributed to Aristotle (fr. 248 Rose), that deals with the flooding of the Nile. The same could be true for a papyrus fragment, the author of which may be the geographer and historian Posidonius (*P.Oxy.* 4458; see Fowler 2000: xxvii n. 1). But as it happens, according to Aristotle, Herodotus is a *mythologos* (*GA* 756b7), a designation mixing *mythos* and *logos*.

As a generic term, in the plural *mythographoi* is used rather frequently by Diodorus Siculus a century after Polybius. For example, the historian attributes to a certain subset of mythographers a distinctive version of the episode of the descent of Theseus and Pirithous to Hades (4.63.4), as well as the hypothesis that Sicily was originally a peninsula (according to *hoi palaioi mythographoi* 4.85.3). As for the history of heroes who were made immortal, such as Heracles, Dionysus, or Aristaeus, this was the subject, according to Diodorus, of accounts transmitted both by historians and by mythographers (*logoi para tois historikois te kai mythographois*). Among the historians, Diodorus cites Euhemerus of Messene; he includes in the category of *mythologoi* (the term is doubtlessly taken from Plato; see *Resp.* 392d) Homer, Hesiod, and Orpheus—that is, poets who have fashioned stories (*mythoi*) on the subject of the gods that are full of marvelous elements. Mythographers are also associated with (ancient) poets by Dionysius of Halicarnassus (*Ant. Rom.* 1.13.2) when he discusses the origin of the indigenous Oenotrians. We will come back to this when we introduce the figure of Antiochus of Syracuse.

Moving forward in time, it is of course necessary to mention the famous preface that opens Plutarch's *Life of Theseus* (1.1–5). The biography of the great Athenian hero belongs to a chronological period too old to allow for an inquiry about the actions of the men, much less a credible account (*eikoti logōi*) about them. It will, therefore, be purified of *mythōdēs*, its fictional dimension, through the same work of inquiry (*historia*, a term employed three times in the dense text of the preface). When it comes to the marvelous elements of this heroic age, Plutarch not only associates mythographers with poets, but more than that, without inspiring any trust, he compares the "tragic tales" (*tragika*) told by these writers to the uninhabited and uncivilized regions that confront the investigators (*historikoi*) of geography when they come to the limits of the inhabited world (see Calame 2011: 73–76).

Thus, from the 2nd century BCE onward, "writers of myth" are writers of accounts and narratives related to an ancient past in the same way geographers are when they are dealing with remote regions.

# 2. LATE "MYTHOGRAPHY"

As for the noun *mythographia*, it is not found before Strabo in the 1st century CE (some elements of the history of the modern concept are given by Bremmer 2013: 55–56, with bibliography). In particular, when it comes to fabulous beings such as the Macrocephaloi, the Hemicynes, or the Pygmies, the geographer highlights the frequent confusion between that which belongs to the category of *mythikon* and that which falls into the category of *historikon* (1.2.35). Those who compose and write in prose (*hoi pezēi syngraphontes*) in the form of an inquiry (*en historias schēmati*) are compared to the poets such as Homer, Hesiod, and Alcman (the first *mytheuōn*, "telling a myth," the last *historōn*, "conducting an inquiry"—*sic!*). By writing in prose, the former avoid the impressions that might be left by something written in the form of a myth (*mythographia*). As a result, mythography is implicitly and paradoxically attached to poetry. And if prose writers weave tales related to obscure and unknown subjects, it is not through ignorance of reality, but to charm their public through the marvelous accounts they have fashioned. This is what Herodotus, Ctesias, Hellanicus (*FGrHist* 4 T 19 = test. 19 Fowler) and the writers of the *Indica* do. Theopompus also tells "myths" in his "histories," but recognizes them as such and explicitly admits this (see *FGrHist* 115 fr. 381). However, on the subject of the Epeans, the inhabitants of Elis in the Homeric *Catalog of Ships* (*Il.* 2.615–619), several versions concerning their relationship with the Eleans are in circulation, as Strabo again tells us (8.3.9). For example, according to Hecataeus (*FGrHist* 1 fr. 121 = fr. 25 Fowler), the Epeans helped Heracles gain mastery over Augeas and Elis. But the geographer goes on to say that these ancient writers (*archaioi syngrapheis*) relate (*legousin*) many things that do not correspond to reality; their disagreement is explained as a habitual falsification that is innate to "mythographies."

Turning to the verb *mythographein*, one of the few occurrences of the word is also found in Strabo (3.4.4). There, it is used in reference to Homer's account of Odysseus's travels (in epic and, consequently, poetic diction). Even if the poet has apparently situated the majority of the hero's stops beyond the Pillars of Heracles, it is because the material being inquired into (*ta historoumena*) is close to a fabrication (*plasma*), and for that reason, surprisingly, it does not lack credibility. Here we have epic poetry judged according to the criteria of geographical-historical inquiry, even if it is implicitly equated with "fabrications of our predecessors" (*plasmata tōn proterōn*). We may recall that, much earlier, these were rejected by Xenophanes when they recounted the battles of violent creatures like the Titans, the Giants, and the Centaurs (fr. 1.19–24 Gentili-Prato; see Calame 2015: 27–30, 81–86, especially for the usage of *plattein* "to fashion," in reference to the *mythoi* found in Plato).

# 3. ANCIENT INVESTIGATORS AND COMPOSITIONAL TECHNIQUES

From signifiers, however, it is necessary to move on to the signified. As a consequence, one has to move from the lexical realm, where terms that are morphologically associated with the same root exhibit their meaning, to the semantic realm, which includes the terms whose meaning is close despite being entirely unrelated morphologically.

From the point of view of their function, the authors we traditionally think of as mythographers—who thereby belong to the lexical realm of *mythographia*—are not designated by the term *mythographos*. To take but one example, Hecataeus, in the entry devoted to him in the *Suda* (s.v. *Hecataios e* 360 Adler), is represented as a *historiographos*. We recall, however, that Herodotus (2.143.1; 5.36.2; 5.125.1) regularly calls his colleague

Hecataeus a simple *logopoios*, a creator of stories or discourses, whereas he is put forward as the model of the *historikos* by Aelian (alongside Pythagoras as *sophos*, Olympos as *mousikos* and Homer as poet, *VH* 13.20). The same author (*VH* 9.23) describes Hecataeus as a *logopoios* in a passage where he includes the historiographer from Miletus among the poets and those who compose *archaioi mythoi*. Finally, Strabo, in the passage quoted above in connection with the word *mythographia* (8.3.9), includes Hecataeus among "the ancient writers" (*archaioi syngrapheis*). It will be recalled that, in the writings of Polybius (4.40.1), it is the word *syngrapheis* that encompasses, in the plural, the "mythographers" who were the predecessors of the historian himself on the question of the causes of the current that flows from the Black Sea.

*Syngrapheus* therefore is the most common word used to describe writers who are mythographers in modern name only. In the short treatise that he devotes to Thucydides, Dionysius of Halicarnassus classifies as *archaioi syngrapheis* not only Hecataeus, but also Eugeon of Samos, Charon of Lampsacus, Eudemos of Paros, and Acusilaus of Argos. These "ancient writers" or "composers" who predate Thucydides are said to have composed their investigations of the Greeks and barbarians, organized according to people and cities, based on oral traditions and on documents kept in temples or secular archives. Without a doubt, these investigations contain *mythoi*, but these are narratives that have long been given credence. Thus, they belong to an accepted tradition, to a tradition one believes in.

Among the different terms used of Hecataeus (Fowler 2000: 110, gives the complete list) to describe his "author-function" (to take on the concept developed by Michel Foucault), the rival of Herodotus never appears as a mythographer! When we turn to the practice of Latin authors, Hellanicus of Lesbos, who is nearly contemporary with Herodotus and Thucydides, is called *historiae scriptor*, precisely in association with these two historiographers (Aulus Gellius 15.23), while Jerome's translation of the *Chronicle* of Eusebius (*Ol.* 70.1, p. 107c Helm) makes him a *historiografus* alongside the *filosofus* Democritus and the *fysicus* Anaxagoras. On the Greek side, Hellanicus is considered a *historikos* (in particular in *Suda* s. v. *Hellanikos* e 739 Adler) or as an (ancient) *syngrapheus*, for instance, by Strabo (13.2.4), who likewise includes him among the *palaioi syngrapheis* (9.6.2), "the writers from the olden days." Dionysius of Halicarnassus, in turn (*Thuc.* 5.2), includes the same Hellanicus among the *archaioi syngrapheis* mentioned above. He places him on a list which, close in time to Thucydides, includes also Damastes of Sigeum, Xenomedes of Ceos, and Xanthus of Lydia. The historiographer from Lesbos is not considered a mythographer by later historians (for these indigenous descriptors of Hellanicus, see Fowler 2000: 147, 456–458, who, however, does not draw the logical conclusion from it). Here once again, there is no trace of *mythographos*.

When it comes to compositional and writing techniques, let us first recall that in the introduction to his inquiry, which takes form of a *sphragis*, Hecataeus classified his authoritative voice through the use of the verb *mytheisthai*: *Hekataios Milesios hōde mytheitai* (*FGrHist* 1 fr. 1a = fr. 1 Fowler). In the third person, as is appropriate when providing a "signature" (whether in poetry or prose), this verb is accompanied by a gesture of verbal *deixis* expressed through the demonstrative adverb *hōde*: "Hecataeus of Miletus tells *in the following way*." Thus designated, the written text of the inquiry—it must be remembered—is formulated in the following words not as an act of speech, but as an act of writing in the first person. This in turn is coupled with a gesture of *deixis* (*demonstratio ad oculos*): *tade graphō*, "I write what follows" (here and now). Presented as a real action of a performative kind, for which the narrating *ego* takes authorial responsibility in accordance with what he thinks is true (*hōs emoi dokei alēthea einai*), this act of writing is juxtaposed with the other Greek accounts that are for their part designated by the term *logoi*. These are accounts that seem laughable, to Hecataeus at least (see Calame 2011: 49–51).

What is more, we also have a "signature" from Antiochus of Syracuse, at the end of the 5th century BCE, in which the gesture of verbal *deixis*, which characterizes the speech that follows, is subordinated to the more technical term *syngraphein*: *tade synegrapse*, "he composed and wrote what follows" (*FGrHist* 555 fr. 2 = fr. 2 Fowler); among the ancient stories (*archaioi logoi*) the historiographer declares that he will reconfigure through writing only the most credible and corroborated ones. Dionysius of Halicarnassus on two occasions (*Ant. Rom.* 1.12.3 and 73.3) calls Antiochus a *syngrapheus*; Diodorus Siculus does the same (12.71.2). The verb *syngraphein* is the very same one with which Thucydides begins his account (1.1.1), thus characterizing his practice of written composition (*synegrapse* in the third person and in the aorist, as expected) with regard to the development of the "war that the Peloponnesians and Athenians declared on each other." Even if poets, like Theognis (19–26; see Calame 2004), also make frequent use of the technique of the "signature," by contrast, the early historiographers never invoke the authority of divine inspiration that the Muse represents. The authority of their voice is based on an act of writing that no longer depends on deified Memory, personified in the figure of Mnemosyne, but rather on their own judgment.

# 4. MYTHOGRAPHY AS A DISCURSIVE GENRE (*GENRE DISCURSIF*)?

But what about mythography as a potential (discursive) genre? As we know, the work of Hecataeus is given various titles: *Genealogies* (Athenaeus, Stephanus of Byzantium), *Inquiries* (*Historia(e)*, Stephanus of Byzantium, Strabo, Demetrius of Phaleron) and *Heroologies* (Harpocration). The essay on local history by Antiochus of Syracuse— "a very ancient writer" (*syngrapheus panu archaios*), according to Dionysius of Halicarnassus (*Ant. Rom.* 1.12.3)—is characterized by Pausanias (10.11.3) as a treatise on Sicily (*Siceliōtis syngraphē*) . The same written collection is characterized by Diodorus Siculus (12.71.2) as "an inquiry (*historia*) into Sicilian matters." This treatise is without a doubt distinct from the *Peri Italias*, the signature of which was mentioned earlier. As for Acusilaus of Argos, his biographer attributes to him *Genealogies* (*Suda*, s.v. *Acousilaos a* 942 Adler), which are classified as part of the generic category of *historia* by Ephorus (*FGrHist* 70 fr. 20). The point is that none of these titles explicitly attests a connection to a mythographical content, much less a mythographical genre. Even the denomination *genealogiai* does not correspond to a mythographical title.

Concerning the hypothesis of mythography as a genre, the situation is well illustrated by the fairly numerous testimonia that we have about the well-known Pherecydes of Athens. Called variously *historikos* (*historicus* in Latin), *historiographos*, and *genealogos* (according to the list of testimonia given by Fowler 2000: 272), and elsewhere *archaios syngrapheus* (by Dionysius of Halicarnassus *Ant. Rom.* 1.13.1, in a passage in which he is found alongside Antiochus of Sicily), Pherecydes in the notice of the *Suda* (s.v. Pherecydes *ph* 214 Adler = test. 1 Fowler) is said to have produced the first example of a *syngraphē* in prose (*pezōi logōi*). Usually called *Historiai*, elsewhere *Theogony*, this treatise, written in ten books, covers many great Greek lineages in genealogical narratives that sometimes descend from a divine or heroic founder to the present, such as the genealogy of the *Philaidae*, from which the Athenian Miltiades descends. The quotation preserved for us (*FGrHist* 3 fr. 2 = fr. 2 Fowler; see also Fowler 2013: 474–478) takes us through the genealogy of the great Athenian family, told in the narrative present tense, then the narrative aorist; its development leads us from the ancestor Philaeus, the son of Salaminian Ajax, down to Miltiades, the founder of the Chersonese. The genealogical account doubtlessly would have gone on to include Cimon, a politician, also in Athens, who was a contemporary of Pherecydes (for details, see the good study of Thomas 1989: 161–173). This case specifically concerns the Athenian past, but Pherecydes's general method in his *Inquiries* is to lead from a heroic founder up to the present.

The point is that it is not possible to speak of "mythography" either as a genre or even as a critical activity before the end of the 4th century BCE. We may, for instance, consider the *Tragodoumena* of Asclepiades of Tragilus (*FGrHist* 12 T2). A student of Isocrates like Ephorus and Theopompus, this rhetor worked in the school of Aristotle, which is not a coincidence when one considers the systematic nature of his criticism (see Pellizer 1993: 283–287). On account of this critical work, what we identify as mythography always involves an act of interpretation, even if only in the comparison of different versions transmitted by an extremely diverse tradition.

# 5. A "Mythographical Style"?

So, according to our ancient, native evidence, in the semantic field of what would be for us "mythography," we find neither mythographer as a function nor mythography as a genre, nor even mythography as a discursive form. What remains? The identification of a particular style according to our linguistic and analytical criteria? A distinctive register (Fowler 2006)? A factual style, along the lines of a summary, without the intrusion of anything like an enunciative point of view? Are we dealing with a "newly-minded style of mythography?" This is how Fowler (2013: 627–628) puts it in regard to the fragment of Acusilaus (*FGrHist* 2 fr. 22 = fr. 22, 56–83 Fowler) that recounts the union of Elatus's daughter, Caine, with Poseidon, then the transformation of the heroine by the god into an invulnerable man endowed with superhuman strength, who becomes the king of the Lapiths and, leading the war against the Centaurs, meets his death by the will of Zeus. This mythographical style of stories practically reduced to their plots and to the names and characteristics of their protagonists would be symptomatic of the "revolutionary implications of such fact-oriented works" (Fowler 2013: 628).

Still, this does not take into account a narrative manner that one finds particularly in Herodotus, though he is (incorrectly) excluded from Fowler's collection of fragments belonging to the supposed genre of early mythography. Certainly, the mythographical summaries that the investigator of Halicarnassus gives at the beginning of his *logos* (1.1–4) are ascribed to the *logioi* of the Persians: the abduction of Io, the daughter of the king of Argos, by the Phoenicians; the abduction of Europa, the daughter of the king of Tyre, by the Greeks; then the abduction of Medea, the daughter of the king of Aea in Colchis, again by the Greeks; and, finally, the taking of Helen by Alexander, the son of Priam, and thus the Trojan War, which becomes the beginning of the open hostilities between the Persians and the Greeks. This series of abductions involves repeated incursions across the border between Asia (represented by the Persians) and Europe (defended by the Greeks). This sequence corresponds to a series of violations of justice, enumerating as a result the causes of the future Persian Wars. Herodotus, when giving his own opinion (1.5.3–7.4), traces the origin of this hatred to the reign of Croesus, a king of Lydia from the dynasty of the Mermnadae, which assumed power after the murder of Candaules, descendant of a certain Alcaeus, son of Heracles. A detailed linguistic analysis would show that in this double account, the processes are very close to those of the "factual" style attributed to the "mythographers"—to which we will return. And yet Herodotus is not considered by modern scholars to be a mythographer.

In addition, if one compares Hesiod's poetic version of the genealogical account that sets out the descendants of Gaia and Ouranos (*Theogony* 132–138) with the mythographical version offered in the *Bibliotheca* attributed to Apollodorus (1.1–3), one will note that beyond some formal differences related to epic diction, the way that the narrative develops is fundamentally identical (Calame 2006a). The poet Hesiod narrates a genealogy in epic diction, just as much later, in prose, the mythographer Ps.-Apollodorus will.

# 6. "MYTHS": *ARCHAIA* AND *PALAIA*

Finally, there is the question of the indigenous terminology for what we identify as "myths," briefly, stories that recount the actions of protagonists who, as heroines and heroes, remain close to the gods. These heroic figures move through spaces that coincide, in general, with those of classical Greece, but in a time corresponding to an ancient period, a *pote* (then), which though chronologically vague, nevertheless often takes on a foundational significance. It has been said time and time again: the Greek term *mythos*, in its preclassical and classical usages, does not conform to that which we identify as a myth. *Mythos* corresponds to a discourse that is developed, elaborated, and designed to produce a result—namely, to carry conviction. Among the modes of argumentation that organize the logic and the utterance of a *mythos* (along with the corresponding practice of *mytheisthai*, "telling a *mythos*"), we find the recounting of a heroic story, with its exemplary value. Its relationship with the speaker's current and present circumstances is constitutive of the *mythos*. It is really only in Plato that the term *mythos* is employed—incidentally, in tension with *logos* (compare the uses of *mythologia* and *mythologein*)—to designate a story that, featuring gods and heroic figures, contains implausibilities and inconsistencies of a moral, not empirical, kind (see Calame 2011: 42–49, 256–262; 2015: 24–30).

In terms of the designation of the deeds of the heroic period, it is, paradoxically, Thucydides who gives us the answer. Just like Herodotus (Calame 2006), the historian of the Peloponnesian War designates the events of this heroic time of *to palai* as either *ta palaia* or *ta archaia*. It is not accidental that a scholiast used the term "archaeology" (literally, "speaking of beginning times") for the account at the beginning of Thucydides's work in which he presents the events that prefigured the political, economic, and military sway of contemporary Athens in the Aegean Sea basin: from the first steps Hellen took to unite the Greeks to the earliest naval battle between the Corinthians and Corcyreans, including the first conquest of the Cyclades through colonization by king Minos of Crete and, naturally, the Trojan War, with its principal protagonist, Agamemnon. Because these events from ancient times are transmitted through an oral tradition (understood as *mnēma*), and because they are known to us through the works of poets (such as Homer) or of logographers, who, anxious to seduce their public, embellish them, these stories must undergo the critical examination (*skopein*) of the author. Their fundamental historicity is, however, never in doubt in the remarks that Thucydides makes on the subject (1.20.1–21).

For this if no other reason, a number of passages from the "archaeology" of Thucydides, as well as the whole opening section of Herodotus's *Inquiry* that takes a "mythographical" form, would have deserved to be included in a collection of fragments of "mythographers." Moreover, in Plato's *Hippias Major*, the sophist from Elis uses the term *archaiologia* for the accounts about the heroes, people, and foundations of cities in ancient times (*to archaion*), which he uses to charm his public (285d = *FGrHist* 6 T 3 = 86 A 11 D.–K.). In a fragment cited by Clement of Alexandria (*Strom.* 6.15.1 = *FGrHist* 6 fr. 4 = fr. 86 B 6 D.–K.), Hippias declares his intention to compose (*poiēsomai*) a polymorphic account of his own, drawing equally on what can be found in the poets (for instance, Orpheus, Musaeus, Hesiod, and Homer) and in the treatises (*syngraphai*) of the Greeks and barbarians. Despite the fact that he is covering the heroic period, and is drawing on poetic sources for inspiration, Hippias is not a mythographer, but, by the standards of his own day, he is a logographer.

In addition, when it comes to signifiers, Dionysius of Halicarnassus (*Ant. Rom.* 1.28.3) uses the term *logos* for the partly genealogical account in which Hellanicus (*FGrHist* 4 fr.

4 = fr. 4 Fowler) describes the settlement of the Pelasgians in Italy and the foundation of Tyrsenia in Etruria. According to the same Dionysius (*Ant. Rom.* 1.13.1 and 3), Antiochus of Syracuse himself (*FGrHist* 555 fr. 2 = fr. 2 Fowler), in the *sphragis* presented above, uses *archaioi logoi* to describe the stories on which he draws to compose and write down his treatise (*synegrapse*) on Italy. It is the settlement of the Oenotri, mentioned earlier, that marks the beginning of this ancient time (*to palaion*). The eponymous hero of this ethnic group, Oenotrus, is likewise mentioned by Pherecydes of Athens (the *archaios syngrapheus*) in one of his many genealogical discussions (*FGrHist* 3 fr. 156 = fr. 156 and test. 6 Fowler). This earliest "mythographical" writing was inextricably tied, as we can see, to the form of genealogical accounts, such as that attested in poetic form in the Hesiodic *Catalog of Women*. The genealogical story develops from the form of the catalog (Delattre 2013: 105–110, 117–123; see also the important study of Jacob 1994). On the other hand, both the treatise of Hecataeus (frr. 3, 6, 7a, 9–12 Fowler) and that of Acusilaus (test. 1 Fowler) carry the title of *Genealogiae*! We will content ourselves with these two examples.

# 7. *MYTHOS* AND *LOGOS*: NO MYTHOLOGY

So, from neither the lexical nor the semantic point of view does mythography exist in classical Greece. There is also no mythology that would arise, simultaneously, in roughly the middle of the 5th century BCE. Based on an analysis of the uses of just the terms *mythos* and *logos* in context, there has been a recent attempt to reconstruct a contrasting dichotomy between *mythos* and *logos* (Fowler 2011; see also Calame 2015: 15–17). On this reading, even if the Greeks surely did not have the notion of a "mythical *mentalité*," and even if they did not recognize either a mythical kind of thought or a movement from myth to reason, still, with the help of the mythographers, they would have marked out a domain of mythology. This would have been opposed to *logos*, just as the fictive is opposed to factual: "The *mythos/logos* contrast, as one between imagination and reason, fictive and factual, is established in the 5th century and linked to critical inquiry in both history and philosophy in ways that correspond clearly to common understandings of 'myth' and 'reason' in Western tradition" (Fowler 2011: 66). Of course, during the 5th century BCE, the term *mythos* competed with other terms (among them *logos*!) to describe an account (regardless of its truth value). And, of course, the narrative content, which we moderns ascribe to that which we identify as myth, was understood in Greece by signifiers such as *archaia* or *palaia*. But the most salient consideration here is that *mythos* designates (in tragic poets, including Euripides, as much as in Homeric poetry) any persuasive discourse, sometimes but not always supported by a narrative.

The point is that mythography—and therefore "mythology"—is, for the period being considered, a nearly invisible genre or even a nonexistent one. The other point is that, in the context of their writing practices, the authors under discussion are never called mythographers. They do not consider themselves, nor do others consider them, to be such. In order to designate this practice of recording and composing in writing, the idea that seems to prevail is that of a spatiotemporal inquiry (*historia*), and to describe the practitioners themselves, the term *syngrapheus* is generally used. As far as this designation is concerned, take, for example, Xanthus of Lydia. This historiographer shows up in the long list that Dionysius of Halicarnassus (*Thuc.* 5.1) gives of *archaioi syngrapheis* who lived before the Peloponnesian War up to the age of Thucydides, contemporary with (when it comes to the most recent of them) Hellanicus of Lesbos and Xenomedes of Ceos. The latter is quoted extensively, in the form of elegiac couplets, by Callimachus (*Aetia* fr. 75, 54–55 Pfeiffer). Recounting the story of Acontius and Cydippe, the Alexandrian poet presents him as "the ancient (*archaios*) Xenomedes, who once made a complete record of everything having to do with the island (of Ceos) in a myth-telling record" (*eni mnēmei mythologōi*).

Here once again, we are faced with an arbitrary demarcation—and we should not forget this—prompted by the *ad hoc* definition of a putative Greek mythography that is supposed to be relevant as a prose genre for the so-called "Classical" period (late 6th c. to early 4th c. BCE).

# 8. Neither Myth nor History

In fact, from a temporal point of view, the attempt to demarcate a "mythical period" (Fowler 2000: xxix–xxx), which is marked off from a "historical period" by the Ionian migration and the return of the Heraclidae, is as arbitrary as it is insidious. There are two reasons for this.

First, such a delimitation already posed a problem in antiquity. To begin with, this is merely an inference that one reaches by assuming that Herodotus makes a distinction between a "time of mortals" and a "time of gods." Even if, in a passage that is continually adduced as evidence (3.122.2), Minos is pushed back before the so-called "human age" in contrast with the tyrant Polycrates of Samos, the king of Crete is not explicitly assigned to the "time of gods." This is especially true because Herodotus, when trying to reconcile Greek tradition with the long Egyptian chronology, has to reach back to the Trojan War and, in fact, even back to Heracles, thus calling upon figures belonging to the "time of heroes" (see Calame 2011: 65–66, with n. 71). But above all, the question of when history begins is treated very differently by those who came after the first historiographers. According to Diodorus Siculus (4.1.1–6), Ephorus, the student of Isocrates, in his attempt to write a universal history in the middle of the 4th century BCE, deliberately omitted the ancient mythologies (*tas palaias mythologias*) in order to start his inquiry with the return of the Heraclidae (*FGrHist* 70 T 8). Likewise, his contemporaries Callisthenes and Theopompus were said to have refrained from giving an account of these "old accounts" (*palaioi mythoi*). As for Diodorus Siculus himself, he explicitly devotes the first three books of his history to the mythologies of other peoples according to their investigations of the gods. Then he decides to begin his own history of the Greeks with Dionysus in accordance with the investigations of the Greeks into their "ancient times" (*archaioi chronoi*), which consist of the exploits of the most prominent heroes and demigods. For the poets and then the logographers of the preclassical period and the 5th century, the age of heroes ends either with the last sexual unions between gods and mortals, or with the Trojan War and the Returns to Greece (see Tosetti 2006; for Diodorus Siculus, see Saïd 2014).

Second, arbitrarily fixing the end of heroic time and thus the domain of "myth" at the return of the Heraclidae breaks the continuity that the Greeks perceived between what—for us—falls within the time of gods and heroes and what belongs to the time of mortals. Let us not forget that for Isocrates, in middle of the 4th century BCE, both the Trojan War and the Persian Wars depict *ta palaia*. In his *Panegyricus* (66–70 and 54–60) the praise of the present virtues of Athens and the exposition of its claims to hegemony take us not only through the discussion of the battles fought against Darius and Xerxes, but also through the battle against the Amazons, the daughters of Ares, and through King Erechtheus's fight against the Thracian king Eumolpus, the son of Poseidon. These *palaia* belong to the *patria*, without any distinction between the heroic past and recent history. What is more, *mythologein* is, by the act of narration, both explaining and legitimizing. Thus, in the speech written for the Spartan king Archidamus (16–24), Isocrates goes back precisely to the Return of the Heraclidae in the Peloponnese in order to justify the contemporary territorial claims of the Lacedaemonian king over Messenia (for bibliographic references to this topic see Calame 1998; see also Patterson, this volume).

# 9. From the Time of Origins to the Present

Be that as it may, when the first Greek logographers produced genealogical systemization, they chose a beginning, an origin, from both temporal and spatial points of view. This is true for Acusilaus, whom I have deliberately left out of the discussion for the most part until now (see the detailed study of Calame 2008). Variously called by those who cite him *historikos*, *historiographos*, and *archaios syngrapheus* (test. 1, 5, and 2 Fowler respectively), this writer puts at the beginning of his *Genealogies* a theogony. According to the testimony of Plato (*Symposium* 178ab = Acusilaus test. 6a Fowler), Chaos then Ge and Eros play a primordial role in it, just as in Hesiod's *Theogony*. As for the first mortal, this is Phoroneus, who will become the first king of Argos (fr. 23 a, b, c Fowler), ensuring the transition from the time of gods to that of heroes. To the temporal dimension of the genealogical account is joined a spatial dimension. This is embodied in the eponymous hero Argos, the son of the mortal Niobe and Zeus (fr. 25 Fowler); Acusilaus says that he was "born from the earth" (fr. 27 Fowler). The fact that the genealogical account focuses on foundational figures of the city of Argos and on its locale could lead one to think that it was elaborated until it reached the recent past or the present, especially when one considers a possibly analogous example of the Philaidae.

This is because this temporal line from the beginning of time up to the present also guides, as we have seen, the Athenocentric genealogy of the Philaidae as it is laid out by Pherecydes up to the recent relatives of Cimon, with the aim of establishing an order that is certainly ideological and political. Therefore, it is difficult to define Pherecydes as "the revolutionary who defined the genre of mythography" (Fowler 2013: 706). On this reading he would have inaugurated the "newly minded style of mythography" (Fowler 2013: 627) that one can likewise find in fr. 22 of Acusilaus. If Pherecydes "created the mythographical patrimony," if his *Inquiries* became the "first encyclopedia" and a "reference work" (Fowler 2013: 707), it is doubtless the result of later use of genealogical accounts in prose that often assume an etiological dimension. The few fragments we have, in all likelihood, reflect the successive reworkings of Pherecydes's *Histories*; these relate only indirectly to the original (Delattre 2013: 111–117; for the history of Thebes, see the good study of Berman 2013).

As we have seen, the argument of "just-the-facts style," does not allow us to escape Thomas's (1989: 173) conclusions about the method by which Pherecydes lays out the genealogy of the Philaidae: "The family's impressive service to Athens is incorporated and hints of its tyrannical connections omitted, in what is clearly a political statement as well as family tradition." There is hardly a need to mention the temporal continuity that we find in genealogical accounts that have a mythographical appearance and extend to the present (see also Jacob 1994: 193–199); for that is already what drives the poetic account of the successions of "the so-called ages of man" that Hesiod places at the beginning of the *Works and Days*. Insidiously called the "mythe des races," this account leads us from the period when mortals lived as gods (verse 112), through the period of the heroes of the Trojan War and the dispute over Thebes, up to the age of iron, in which the poetic "I" lives, that is, the here and now (verse 176). The entire poem is focused on trying to re-establish, under the control of Zeus, the state of justice that ought to prevail in the city (Calame 2006b: 85–142). This constant preoccupation with the relationship of the heroic past with the present and the current political situation is the same as that of Thucydides in the *Archaeology*; it is also often that of Herodotus. This is what provides the genealogical and historiographical account with its utility in any given historical, political, and cultural context. And it is through this that the accounts of the heroic past, continually refashioned, become "active myths" (see Patterson, this volume), first in the poems of the oral tradition, then in the production of historiographical writings, with their respective pragmatics. By this criterion neither Acusilaus nor Pherecydes, who are investigators and writers, is a mythographer in either the Hellenistic or modern senses of the word (Delattre 2013: 117–126).

Even if the writing of a genealogical account can, undoubtedly, appear factual and "impersonal"; nevertheless, this writing, on the one hand, is a vehicle for giving a correct genealogy, and, on the other, is characterized by a declarative orientation toward the present. According to Diodorus Siculus (12.71.2 = test. 3 Fowler), Antiochus of Syracuse laid out his *Inquiry* in nine books from the reign of Cocalus, the first legendary king of the Sicani, up to the congress at Gela in 424/423 BCE, when the cities of Sicily decided to form an alliance against the Athenians. The peculiar origin that Antiochus attributes to Metapontum is certainly polemical against Athens (as Fowler himself, 2013: 190, 633, recognizes).

Moreover, one would have to be quite adroit to identify in an uninterrupted chronicle like that offered by the *Parian Marble* any stylistic traits that would allow one to distinguish a mythical period from a historical one. The narrative and declarative thread of the chronicle covers in the same manner all the events that affected the political and cultural history of Athens from the reign of the primordial king Cecrops up to the moment that the inscription was dedicated in Paros in 264/263—including the reign of Minos, Demeter's involvement in Attica, the battle of Marathon, the death of Sophocles, and the beginning of Alexander's reign. One will note in this regard that the anonymous mythographical inscription known as the *Pride of Halicarnassus* adheres to the same logic. Based on the spate of publication generated by this new inscription from Salmacis, one recent study is able to conclude that "[ancient mythography] was not just an academic subject. It always served certain interests, be it local prestige, literary expertise or the acquisition of cultural capital" (Bremmer 2013: 72).

It is from this perspective of continuity between the heroic and human ages, pragmatically oriented toward the present, that Hellanicus's *Attikē Syngraphē* was written. The very few fragments that have come down to us of this first *Atthis* do mention Agraulos, the daughter of Cecrops (fr. *38 Fowler), the legendary king Mounychus (fr. 42 a and b Fowler) and Hippothoon, the son of Poseidon, the eponymous hero of the Attic tribe Hippothoontidae (fr. 43 Fowler). But this is not all. Thucydides himself (1.97.1) contrasts the detailed version that he offers concerning the rise in Athens' power before and then between the Persian Wars and the beginning of the Peloponnesian War with the inadequate and chronologically inexact summary that Hellanicus provides in his *Attikē Syngraphē*: that is the title that Thucydides gives to the treatise of his contemporary Hellanicus (*FGrHist* 4 fr. 49 Jacoby; see Hornblower 1991: 147–148; Hartog 2006: 66–74). The anachronistic modern distinction between myth and history arbitrarily suppresses the crucial evidence of the *archaiologia* of Thucydides compared to the one outlined by Hellanicus. It dismisses all reflection on the function and pragmatics of written treatises on the past of the Greek cities that belong—just as Herodotus's *logoi* do for human history and geography—to the vast number of critical and practical investigations and inquiries. Our witnesses for this are the Hippocratic doctors, for the physiological conception of humans; the sophists, for a critical reflection on language and rhetoric; and the so-called Presocratic philosophers, for cosmology and anthropology. In classical Greece, the inquiry into the heroic past of cities and of Greece could neither be conceivable nor understandable unless it was based on the historical, political, and cultural context and concerns of the present. It is never pure erudition.

Hypothesizing the existence of a Greek mythography in the classical period completely ignores the relationship of these forms of historiographical inquiry and composition with the various forms of poetic history; it ignores their strong relationships with the present context of their composition and performance, with the pragmatics it implies. To project onto them the later terms and concepts of *mythographer* and *mythography* negates their poetic function and pragmatics in the time and circumstances they were written for. This relationship, however, still seems well attested in the 1st century CE in an inscription from Amorgos (*IG* 12 (7), 273): the dedicatory text presents a certain Aristogenes as the "mythographer of Apollo and the Muses!"

## Further Reading

It is only with the greatest caution that one should use the edition and commentary of the fragments of the "Mythographers," collected by Robert Fowler under the doubly misleading title *Early Greek Mythography* (2000, 2013)—this, despite the remarkable philological accuracy of this work and the great value of his double commentary. First, there is no mythography constituted as such between the 7th and 5th centuries BCE; second, the notion of "early" ought to be abandoned. The handbook of Timothy Gantz, entitled *Early* (still!) *Greek Myth* (1993) is of great usefulness in this regard, since it shows the variety of forms, both poetic and prose, under which the stories that we identify as "myths" were told. When it comes to the stories about the age of heroes shaped and organized by the historiographers, such as Acusilaos and Pherecydes, according to their own individual narrative logic, one must consider both the forms of composition that were adopted and the circumstances surrounding the composition and their pragmatics (see my study, very limited, of 2008). In this regard the work of Charles Delattre (2013) shows one of the possible pathways. One will also find new perspectives in some of the essays collected by Trzaskoma and Smith (2013).

## References

Berman, Daniel W. 2013. "Greek Thebes in the Early Mythographic Tradition." In *Writing Myth: Mythography in the Ancient World*, edited by Stephen M. Trzaskoma and R. Scott Smith, 37–53. Leuven: Peeters.

Bremmer, Jan N. 2013. "Local Mythography: The Pride of Halicarnassus," In *Writing Myth. Mythography in the Ancient World*, edited by Stephen M. Trzaskoma and R. Scott Smith, 55–74. Leuven: Peeters.

Calame, Claude. 1998. "*Mûthos, lógos* et histoire: Usages du passé héroïque dans la rhétorique grecque." *L'Homme* 147: 127–149.

Calame, Claude. 2004. "Identités d'auteur à l'exemple de la Grèce classique: Signatures, énonciations, citations." In *Identités d'auteur dans l'Antiquité et la tradition européenne*, edited by Claude Calame and Roger Chartier, 11–39. Grenoble: Jérôme Millon.

Calame, Claude. 2006a. *Pratiques poétiques de la mémoire: Représentations de l'espace-temps en Grèce ancienne*. Paris: La Découverte. English translation: *Poetic and Performative Memory in Ancient Greece: Heroic Reference and Ritual Gestures in Time and Space*. Translated by Harlan Patton. Washington, DC: Center for Hellenic Studies, and Cambridge, MA: Harvard University Press 2009.

Calame, Claude. 2006b. "La fabrication historiographique d'un passé héroïque en Grèce classique: *Archaîa* et *palaiá* chez Hérodote." *Ktema* 31: 39–49.

Calame, Claude. 2008. "Les fonctions généalogiques: Acousilaos d'Argos et les débuts de l'historiographie grecque." *Europe* 945–946: 87–108.

Calame, Claude. 2011. *Mythe et histoire dans l'Antiquité grecque: La création symbolique d'une colonie.* 2nd ed. Paris: Les Belles Lettres.

Calame, Claude. 2015. *Qu'est-ce que la mythologie grecque?* Paris: Gallimard. English translation: *Greek Mythology: Poetics, Pragmatics and Fiction.* Translated by Janet Lloyd. Cambridge, UK: Cambridge University Press 2009.

Delattre, Charles. 2013. "Pentaméron mythographique: Les Grecs ont-ils écrit leurs mythes?" *Lalies* 33: 77–170.

Fowler, Robert L. 2000. *Early Greek* Mythography. Vol. 1: *Text and Introduction.* Oxford: Oxford University Press.

Fowler, Robert L. 2006. "How to Tell a Myth: Genealogy, Mythology, Mythography." *Kernos* 19: 35–46.

Fowler, Robert L. 2011, "Mythos and Logos," *Journal of Hellenic Studies* 131: 45–66.

Fowler, Robert L. 2013. *Early Greek Mythography.* Vol. 2: *Commentary.* Oxford: Oxford University Press.

Gantz, Timothy. 1993. *Early Greek Myth. A Guide to Literary and Artistic Sources,* Baltimore, MD: Johns Hopkins University Press.

Hartog, François. 2005. *Évidence de l'histoire: Ce que voient les historiens.* Paris: Éditions de l'EHESS.

Hawes, Greta. 2014. *Rationalizing Myth in Antiquity.* Oxford: Oxford University Press.

Hornblower, Simon. 1991. *A Commentary on Thucydides. Vol. I. Books I–III.* Oxford: Clarendon Press.

Jacob, Christian. 1994. "L'ordre généalogique entre le mythe et l'histoire." In *Transcrire les mythologies,* edited by Marcel Detienne, 169–202. Paris: Albin Michel.

Martin, Richard. 2013. "The 'Myth Before the Myth Began.'" In *Writing Down the Myths,* edited by Joseph F. Nagy, 45–66. Turnhout: Brepols.

Pellizer, Ezio. 1993. "La mitografia." In *Lo spazio letterario della Grecia antica,* vol. 1.2, edited by Giuseppe Cambiano, 283–303. Rome: Salerno Editrice.

Saïd, Suzanne. 2014. "Entre mythographie et histoire: Le traitement du mythe dans la *Bibliothèque historique* de Diodore de Sicile." In *Paradeigmata: Studies in Honour of Øivind Andersen,* edited by Eyjólfur K. Emilsson, Anastasia Maravela, Mathilde Skoie, 67–86. Athens, Greece: Norwegian Institute.

Santoni, Anna. 2000. *Palefato. Storie incredibili.* Pisa, Italy: Edizioni ETS.

Thomas, Rosalind. 1989. *Oral Tradition and Written Record in Classical Athens.* Cambridge, UK: Cambridge University Press.

Tosetti, Giovanni. 2006. "La dernière génération héroïque: Un parcours historico-religieux et sémio-narratif, d'Hésiode au ps.-Apollodore." *Kernos* 19: 113–130.

Trzaskoma, Stephen M., and Smith, R. Scott, ed. 2013, *Writing Myth: Mythography in the Ancient World.* Leuven: Peeters.

# PART IV

# MYTHOGRAPHY AND THE VISUAL ARTS

# CHAPTER 34

........................................................................................

# MYTHOGRAPHY AND GREEK VASE PAINTING

........................................................................................

## KATHRYN TOPPER

BEGINNING at least as early as the 7th century BCE, myths were popular subjects on Greek painted pottery. The choice of myths and the painters' treatments of them vary widely: at one end of the spectrum, we find moving depictions of Penthesileia's death (Munich, Antikensammlungen 2688; $ARV^2$ 879.1, 1673; *Paralipomena* 428; *Beazley Addenda*$^2$ 300; BAPD 211565) or the destruction of Troy (Naples, Museo Archeologico Nazionale 81699; $ARV^2$ 189.74, 1632; *Paralipomena* 341; *Beazley Addenda*$^2$ 189; BAPD 201724); at the other, we see lighthearted images of satyrs stealing weapons from the sleeping Herakles (Salerno, Museo Archeologico 1370; $ARV^2$ 188.67; *Paralipomena* 341; *Beazley Addenda*$^2$ 188; BAPD 201759) or caricatures of Odysseus and Circe (Oxford, Ashmolean Museum G 249; BAPD 680002). Whether any of these images can be classed as "mythographical"—that is, concerned with the systematization or interpretation of myths (Smith and Trzaskoma 2011)—is a more difficult question. There is no reason to expect this relatively scholarly textual genre to be reflected in a body of visual material that had its own, very different set of aims, but at the same time, it is not unreasonable to think that the modes of organizing information that would come to characterize mythography might be present in some of the Greeks' earliest visual treatments of myth. That question is the focus of this chapter.

It will be helpful to begin with certain preliminaries, the first of which involves the application of the term "mythography" to visual imagery. Whether we adopt a broad definition of mythography, as the narration of myth (Meliadò 2015: 1057), or a narrow definition, as the systematization or interpretation of mythological narratives (Smith and Trzaskoma 2011), we are applying to visual imagery an interpretive category that was developed to describe texts. This application depends on the metaphor of visual imagery as a type of language, a metaphor that has been fruitful for understanding some aspects of ancient art but is not equipped to explain everything about it.

The second preliminary point concerns the definition of "painted pottery" or "painted vase." These terms conventionally apply to a variety of decorated terracotta objects, ranging from wine cups to cosmetics boxes to wool-working implements, which were produced for a wide variety of contexts, including the symposium, the gymnasium, athletic and religious festivals, women's quarters, and the tomb. From a modern scholarly perspective, these objects are united by material, decorative style and technique, and sometimes iconography—thus they are all classified together as "painted pottery." In antiquity, however, they were primarily functional objects whose uses would contribute significantly to viewers' understanding of their imagery.

This chapter examines select examples of mythological vase paintings that share structural features with texts that were (or would eventually be codified as) mythographical. I start by considering the François vase (Florence, Museo Archeologico Etrusco 4209; *ABV* 76.1, 682; *Paralipomena* 29; *Beazley Addenda*$^2$ 21; BAPD 300000) and the so-called Heroines pyxis in London (London, British Museum E 773; *ARV*$^2$ 805.89, 1670; *Paralipomena* 420; *Beazley Addenda*$^2$ 291; BAPD 209970); these vases offer good examples of visual narrative and catalogue, organizational strategies that have parallels in the earliest Greek mythological literature. I then consider the pendant images on a famous skyphos by Makron (Boston, Museum of Fine Arts 13.186; *ARV*$^2$ 458.1, 1654; *Paralipomena* 377; *Beazley Addenda*$^2$ 243; BAPD 204681); this strategy, too, has parallels in ancient literature. I do not argue that the images on painted pottery are deliberately mythographical, as there is no evidence that the systematization and interpretation of myth was, for the vase painters, an end in itself. Their goals were quite different from those of later scholars, and to retroject the latter's aims onto them is to flatten a complex visual medium into one with a fundamentally literary agenda. Nevertheless, it is clear that as early as the archaic period, scenes of myth in vase painting shared structural features with the mythological poetry that would be described by later scholars as mythographical (Meliadò 2015: 1057).

# 1. Narrative and Catalogue: The François Vase and the "Heroines Pyxis"

The first two "mythographical" modes I consider are narrative and catalogue. By *narrative*, I mean any representation that includes both temporal sequence and change, regardless of the speed or order of events (see Ferrari 2003: 43–44, citing Barthes 1977: 101–104; Prince 1987; Todorov 1990: 27–38). By *catalogue*, I refer to the listing or juxtaposition of similar elements, as in the Homeric catalogue of ships (*Iliad* 2.494–759) or the Hesiodic *Catalogue of Women*. Both modes appear on the François vase, a large 6th-century Athenian volute krater discovered in a tomb in Chiusi. This unusually ornate vessel is adorned with 270 figures and 131 inscriptions, including two signatures each by the painter, Kleitias, and potter, Ergotimos.

The exterior of the krater is divided into registers, the top four of which contain the majority of the mythological decoration. The subjects on the obverse proceed from

FIGURE 34.1 The François Vase (obverse). Athenian black-figure krater. Signed by Ergotimos (potter) and Kleitias (painter), circa 570 BCE. Florence, Museo Archeologico Etrusco 4209. Photo Credit: Scala / Art Resource, New York.

the top, as follows: on the neck, the Calydonian boar hunt, with the funeral games for Patroclus below it; on the body, the wedding of Peleus and Thetis, and below that the ambush of Troilus by Achilles (Figure 34.1).

The wedding is the only subject to continue around the vessel to the reverse (Figure 34.2), where it sits atop a register depicting the return of Hephaestus to Olympus. Above the wedding, a Lapith centauromachy appears in the lower zone of the neck; in the register above that, Theseus leads the Athenian youths and maidens in the *geranos* dance as they arrive on Crete. The register below the mythological zone is decorated with an animal frieze that encircles the entire krater, and a geranomachy encircles the foot. On the exterior of each handle, Ajax carries the fallen Achilles from the battlefield in the lower zone, while a Potnia Thērōn figure occupies the upper zone; on the interior of the handle, a running gorgon hovers above the rim.

FIGURE 34.2 The François Vase (reverse). Athenian black-figure krater. Signed by Ergotimos (potter) and Kleitias (painter), circa 570 BCE. Florence, Museo Archeologico Etrusco 4209. Photo credit: Nimatallah / Art Resource, New York.

The François vase offers viewers a dizzying amount of visual information, and at first glance it is easy to mistake its selection of myths as random. As Andrew Stewart has demonstrated, however, the relationships among the mythological subjects in the four main decorative zones can be efficiently described using two terms—*syntagmatic* and *paradigmatic*—borrowed from the study of language. *Syntagmatic* relationships are those that involve combinations between elements within a system, such as words in a sentence. *Paradigmatic* relationships, by contrast, involve functional contrasts, or possibilities of substitution—within any given sentence, each word exists in a paradigmatic relationship to all the words that could be substituted for it (Culler 2002: 4–15).

As Stewart observed, these terms aptly describe the organization of mythological vignettes on the François vase (1983: 67–70). The four scenes on the obverse acquire significance in combination with one another and with the scenes of Achilles and Ajax on the handles. Together, these show key moments from the lives of Peleus and his son Achilles: the boar hunt, the wedding of Peleus and Thetis, the murder of Troilus, the funeral games for Patroclus, and, finally, the removal of Achilles's corpse from the battlefield. The fact that they are out of chronological sequence does not disqualify them from narrative status; it is generally understood that chronological order was less of a concern for ancient Greek and Roman viewers than for modern English-speaking ones (Small 1999), and this narrative flexibility gave artists leeway to take full advantage of the visual and spatial qualities of their media.

Stewart has argued compellingly that the design of the obverse is organized around the figure of Dionysus, who is situated at the center of the gods' procession in the wedding scene. Both his frontal face and the large amphora on his shoulder demand our attention; the latter is the only item to transgress the upper border, and it has been plausibly identified as the gold amphora in which Achilles's bones would eventually be buried along with those of Patroclus. This hypothesis is attractive insofar as it accounts for certain formal details, such as the evident heft of the vessel and the absence of a lid. Yet it also suggests a thematic unity with the two scenes closest to it: above, the games at Patroclus's funeral, and below, the murder for which Achilles would pay with his own life (Stewart 1983: 63–66).

The decoration on the reverse, like that on the obverse, is organized around the wedding procession. Here, however, the procession is not part of a larger narrative—that is, the vignettes are not related to one another by virtue of sequence and transformation. Instead, the arrangement is thematic, for each scene shows either a mythological wedding or the getting of a bride (Stewart 1983: 68; Hedreen 2011). As Stewart has put it, "The wedding theme is developed through comparison and contrast" (1983: 68), and together the scenes present a meditation on the varied natures of heroic and divine marriages.

This paratactic juxtaposition of similar elements is a well-known feature of archaic catalogue poetry, and it is increasingly being recognized in ancient visual art (Mangieri 2010; Bergmann 2017). About a century after the creation of the François vase, we see this arrangement adopted by a follower of Douris in a scene depicting the heroines of the mythological Argolid (Figure 34.3).

FIGURE 34.3 Athenian red-figure pyxis showing Argive heroines (rollout view). Attributed to a follower of Douris, circa 500–470 BCE. London, British Museum E 773. © Trustees of the British Museum.

The scene, which encircles the body of a pyxis, is at first indistinguishable from dozens of contemporary images showing women working wool, adorning themselves, or conversing with each other on a porch or in a courtyard (Ferrari 2002: 11–60). The inscriptions above their heads, however, identify them as Argive heroines. Iphigeneia stands in an open door, tying a fillet around her head, and Danae walks toward her with an open jewelry chest. Behind her, Helen sits in front of a wool basket, facing Clytemnestra, who holds a large alabastron in her extended right hand. Behind Clytemnestra, a pair of women stand facing each other between a column and the door from which Iphigeneia emerges. One extends a basket of fruit or wool to the other, and the name "Kassandra" floats in the space above them, although it is unclear to which woman it refers (Lyons 2008: 74–76; Mangieri 2010).

Although it is difficult to imagine a narrative in which the five women named on the pyxis would be at home together, Anthony Mangieri has observed that their lineup resembles a catalogue, a genre that could have genealogical import but that could also be organized around themes such as female virtue (Doherty 2006: 306; Mangieri 2010: 438). The specific pairings of women encourage reflection on what they have in common, as well as on the features that distinguish them. Danae and Iphigeneia, for example, are both condemned to death by their fathers; Danae survives, as do some versions of Iphigeneia, and their pairing on the pyxis invites consideration of their stories together. Iconographic details recall important themes and moments in their myths and help guide the comparisons: Iphigeneia's liminal position in the doorway underscores the theme of transition in both girls' stories, for both are sent to their deaths at the very moment when they should be married, and her act of binding her hair may also allude to the wedding (Mangieri 2010: 434). The small chest held by Danae, meanwhile, is an obvious allusion to the larger one in which she and the infant Perseus are imprisoned, and the necklace she delicately lifts from it resembles a small version of the golden shower we find represented on other 6th-century vases (Lyons 2008: 74–75).

The pairing of Helen and Clytemnestra is similarly loaded with meaning. Along with being sisters, they are both unfaithful wives, although Helen's position at the wool basket—the attribute *par excellence* of a virtuous woman (Ferrari 2002: 11–60)—may be a nod to the ancient ambivalence about her culpability in the Trojan War (on which see Blondell 2013). It is interesting, in any case, that the mirror and alabastron, items of female beauty and adornment, are more closely associated with Clytemnestra here than with Helen; it is as if each woman has been distanced from the feminine tools—textiles and adornment—with which she wields the greatest destruction. As for the remaining pair, the inscription does not clearly indicate which is Cassandra, nor is it obvious whether the basket carried by the woman on the left holds wool or fruit, although both would be suited to a scene like this (Lyons 2008: 74–75; Mangieri 2010: 436). Whatever the relationship between these women, their placement between Clytemnestra and Iphigeneia is surely significant—in addition to sharing a narrative connection, all three are known for their violent deaths.

Visual depictions of catalogues—and particularly catalogues of women—were not the sole province of vase painters in antiquity. Although the majority of surviving examples come from Roman art, and especially Roman painting (Bergmann 2017: 219–223), scholars have observed precedents for such works in Polygnotus's paintings in the Knidian Lesche at Delphi (Mangieri 2010: 440–441; Bergmann 2017: 210). The catalogue-like features of the images on the François vase and the Heroines pyxis, then, seem to have belonged to a larger tradition of visual mythological presentation that would continue to gather momentum in the Hellenistic and Roman periods.

## 2. PENDANT IMAGES AND THE ABDUCTION AND RECOVERY OF HELEN

The final compositional strategy I consider is the pairing of mythological images in a manner that highlights their associations and contrasts, thereby enhancing our understanding of both items in the pair. This use of *pendant* images has more often been studied in Roman art, especially in domestic wall paintings, where pendant associations are common (Brillant 1984: 53–89; Valladares 2005). Literary analogues to these visual pendants range from the doublets of archaic epic to groups of similes in Propertius to the parallel lives of Plutarch (Holliday 1993b: 185; Valladares 2005; Sammons 2013). While it is less common to speak of pendant relationships in Greek vase painting, we know that painters often took great care in coordinating the images on a single vase (Steiner 2007: 17–39), and experience with pedimental sculpture or pairs of monumental paintings in sanctuaries and other public settings would have made Greek viewers adept at parsing pendant relationships. The pendant framework, then, seems potentially productive for the study of vase painting.

A well-known skyphos by Makron in Boston offers a good example of pendant mythological images. On the obverse, Paris (labeled "Alexandros") leads Helen to the left, a small Eros hovering between them; Aeneas walks in front, and Aphrodite and Peitho bring up the rear (Figure 34.4).

On the reverse of the cup, Menelaus stands at the far right, about to draw his sword on Helen (Figure 34.5). She moves in terror toward Aphrodite, who stands behind her with arms outstretched. Kriseis and Kriseus (generally understood to be Chryseis and Chryses) observe quietly from the left. Priam sits under one handle, behind Menelaus, and a young boy stands under the other. With the exception of Eros and the boy, all the figures are identified by inscriptions.

Holliday has observed that "[a] pendant relationship functions effectively when the events depicted are believed to represent comparable states of affairs: The images exemplify analogous types" (1993b: 185). This is an apt description of the imagery on Makron's skyphos, which employs the iconography of weddings and abductions to portray Helen's departure and return, respectively. The structural similarity between weddings and abductions in Athenian iconography is as much a cliché in modern scholarship as it was

FIGURE 34.4 Athenian red-figure skyphos with abduction of Helen (obverse). Signed by Makron (painter) and Hieron (potter), circa 490 BCE. Height: 21.5 cm (8 7/16 in.); diameter: 39 cm (15 3/8 in.); diameter of mouth: 27.8 cm (10 15/16 in.). Museum of Fine Arts, Boston. Bartlett Collection—Museum purchase with funds from the Francis Bartlett Donation of 1912 13.186. Photograph © 2021 Museum of Fine Arts, Boston.

in antiquity, but the specific manner in which they are paired here is worth examining in greater detail.

While Makron is not alone in showing Helen as Paris's bride or her recovery by Menelaus as a violent pursuit, this is the only time the two episodes appear together on an Athenian vase. Their formal and thematic similarities—the direction of movement, the repetition of Helen and Aphrodite, and the framing of each group by a warrior with a large shield on one end and a woman with a small sprig on the other—create a sense of images that are in dialogue with one another, and they raise questions that drive at the heart of Greek anxieties about Helen. She is, as is often noted, a bride *par excellence*, and her " 'wedding' [to Paris] far overshadows her legitimate marriage to Menelaus in our sources" (Blondell 2013: 45). Yet Makron's image does not seem quite confident in the correctness of this wedding. Its typical bridal features—the veil and *stephane*, the procession, the female attendants, the clutching of the wrist, and the mediation of Eros—are marred by the Trojans' military dress, and the leftward movement of the procession is extremely unusual.

A similar ambivalence appears in the depiction of the recovery (Figure 34.5). The violence of Menelaus's gesture and Helen's evident fear are tempered by a composition that shares key features with maidens' abductions—namely, the female companions

FIGURE 34.5 Athenian red-figure skyphos with recovery of Helen (reverse). Signed by Makron (painter) and Hieron (potter), ca. 490 BCE. Height: 21.5 cm (8 7/16 in.); diameter: 39 cm (15 3/8 in.); diameter of mouth: 27.8 cm (10 15/16 in.). Museum of Fine Arts, Boston. Bartlett Collection—Museum purchase with funds from the Francis Bartlett Donation of 1912 13.186. Photograph © 2021 Museum of Fine Arts, Boston.

and the old man standing quietly at the side, implicitly sanctioning the proceedings. These formal similarities with abduction scenes give Helen's union with Menelaus an air of legitimacy, the latter's violent gesture notwithstanding, and the presence of Chryses and Chryseis is likewise noteworthy. Although their presence in this scene has been a source of bafflement to many scholars, Guy Hedreen notes that Chryseis shares with Helen the status of "object of a dispute that led to the loss of many lives . . . In this picture, then, Makron has included the two women who effected the deaths of the greatest number of Achaians and Trojans" (1996: 177). This thematic parallel extends to Chryses and Menelaus, both of whom had women taken from them, and the reunited Chryses and Chryseis function by turns as a parallel and a contrast to Helen and Menelaus.

No less than epic doublets or Plutarch's parallel lives, the pendant scenes on Makron's skyphos create meaning in juxtaposition. Each image raises questions about the other, forcing the viewer to contemplate the correctness of Paris's and Menelaus's actions, not to mention those of Helen herself. In this respect, the images belong to an interpretive tradition that intersects with the mythographical, although contributing to mythographical discourse was surely not the painter's intent.

## 3.  CONCLUSIONS

I have suggested in this chapter that vase paintings share narrative and rhetorical structures with texts that contributed to, or were appropriated into, the ancient mythographical tradition. Whether the images themselves can be considered mythographical depends on how restrictively one defines that term; the painters were certainly not concerned with the systematization and interpretation of myth as ends in themselves, but the examples considered in this chapter suggest that they expected viewers to be adept at the sort of narration and comparison that made mythographical thought possible.

Future investigations into the intersection of mythography and vase painting should proceed with two points in mind. First, any proposal that images are or can be mythographical relies implicitly on the metaphor of imagery as language, and it can therefore be guided by the large body of scholarship on linguistic—and especially narrative—structures in ancient art that has been produced since the 1980s (see "Further Reading"). This chapter has highlighted three structures—narrative, catalogue, and pendant—that are especially important to this undertaking, and it has been guided as much by the scholarship on linguistic and narrative structures in Greek and Roman art as by that on myth in vase painting.

The second point is that, for all its strengths, an approach that relies on the metaphor of imagery as language affords only a partial view of the mythological imagery on Greek painted pottery. This is particularly true of mythographical approaches, which privilege a seriousness that was often at odds with the painters' own approaches to myth. We see such a tension on the François vase, for example, where a strict focus on mythography might lead us to ignore features such as the battle of Pygmies and cranes encircling the foot. Unlike the majority of figures on the vase, neither the Pygmies nor the cranes are provided with inscriptions, and their presence is generally accepted as a comic footnote to the more serious proceedings above—"a parody . . . like the pseudoheroic Battle of Frogs and Mice, a commentary upon the tragicomedy of human pretensions," as Stewart has put it (1983: 70). The image is closely coordinated with the scenes in the upper register: the struggle between the small Pygmies and their avian foes is a comic deflation of the boar hunt above, with the bodies of the fallen hunter and dog echoed in those of the fallen Pygmies. The joke on the reverse is of a different nature; here the cranes are no doubt a reference to the *geranos*, or crane dance, in which Theseus leads the young Athenians on the neck. On other vessels, the humor takes a more visual turn, as in the tondo of a famous cup by Douris showing Jason vomited up by the serpent who guards the golden fleece (Vatican City, Museo Gregoriano Etrusco Vaticano 16545; *ARV*[2] 437.116, 1653; *Paralipomena* 375; *Beazley Addenda*[2] 239; BAPD 205162). This scene is clearly a play on the more common image of the vomiting symposiast who appears in other cup tondos (Shapiro and Cohen 2002), with Athena reduced to the role of the unfortunate attendant. Still other vases draw the drinker himself into the world of myth; we see this in the eye cups that blur the line between symposiasts and members of Dionysus's mythical *thiasos* (Hedreen 2007). In general, the vase painters' approaches to myth were wide-ranging and varied, and future discussions of their mythographical elements should proceed with this broader context in mind.

## FURTHER READING

The intersection of mythography and Greek vase painting has not been a topic of great interest to scholars, but those concerned with exploring it in the future will be aided methodologically by the studies of narrative in ancient art that were produced between the 1980s and the early 2000s. Although these studies are focused primarily on narrative, they concern themselves more broadly with the organization of visual information, and they are thus essential to anyone interested in the intersection between vase painting and textual or literary genres. Relevant works include Stewart (1983), Brilliant (1984), Holliday (1993a), Small (1999), Stansbury-O'Donnell (1999), Hedreen (2001), and Giuliani (2013). This work belongs to a larger conversation about the relationship between word and image in ancient art; in vase painting studies, the work of the Paris-Lausanne school remains an essential contribution—particularly Bérard (1989), who, along with his collaborators, has gone on to produce a large and significant bibliography. More recent contributions include Sourvinou-Inwood (1991), Steiner 2007), and especially Ferrari (2002).

As for depictions of myths themselves, there is no single comprehensive collection, although the multivolume *Lexicon Iconographicum Mythologiae Classicae* (Zurich, Munich, and Düsseldorf: Artemis Verlag, 1981–1999) remains an essential resource; the project is continued online at WebLIMC (https://weblimc.org). The Beazley Archive Pottery Database (https://www.beazley.ox.ac.uk/carc/pottery) is likewise essential and has replaced Beazley's physical volumes for many researchers. Novices to the BAPD should be warned, however, that search terms are not always consistent within the database—a search for "griffin," for instance, will not show any vase for which the sole identifying term is "grypomachy"—and the BAPD should never be used for statistical research without considerable care. As of this writing, the Trendall Research Center has an online presence (https://www.latrobe.edu.au/research/centres/trendall), but it has not yet replaced the physical catalogues of South Italian vase painting in user friendliness.

There are too many studies of individual myths and mythological figures on painted pottery to list here; readers will find many of them listed in the entries in *LIMC* and the BAPD. For vase paintings older than the 7th century BCE, there is often considerable debate about how to recognize mythological scenes; this issue is discussed in Snodgrass (1998), Langdon (2008), and Hurwit (2011). For later centuries, scholars have often assumed that the distinction between myth and non-myth is self-evident in vase painting, but Ferrari (2003) has rightly challenged this position.

Some mythological imagery is evidently associated with ritual, although the connections between the two are often poorly understood. Relevant studies include Sourvinou-Inwood (1988), Walsh (2009), Hedreen (2014), and Reitzammer (2016). These studies remind us that the mythological imagery on vases was often produced in dialogue with ritual performances, not texts, a point that anyone taking a mythographical approach to the imagery should keep in mind. It is also well established that vase painters frequently drew upon theatrical and other performances in highly nuanced ways when creating mythological imagery; see Green (1991), Hedreen (1992), and Taplin (1993, 2007).

## References

Barthes, Roland. 1977. "Introduction to the Structural Analysis of Narratives." In *Image-Music-Text*, trans. Stephen Heath, 79–124. New York: Hill and Wang.

Bérard, Claude, Christiane Bron, and Jean-Louis Durand, Françoise Frontisi-Ducroux, François Lissarrague, Alain Schnapp, et al., eds. 1989. *A City of Images: Iconography and Society in Ancient Greece*. Translated by Deborah Lyons. Princeton, NJ: Princeton University Press.

Bergmann, Bettina. 2017. "The Lineup: Passion, Transgression, and Mythological Women in Roman Painting." *EuGeStA* 7: 199–246.

Blondell, Ruby. 2013. *Helen of Troy: Beauty, Myth, Devastation*. Oxford: Oxford University Press.

Brilliant, Richard. 1984. *Visual Narratives: Storytelling in Etruscan and Roman Art*. Ithaca, NY: Cornell University Press.

Cohen, Beth, and H. Alan Shapiro. 2002. "The Use and Abuse of Athenian Vases." In *Essays in Honor of Dietrich von Bothmer*, edited by Andrew J. Clark, Jasper Gaunt, and Benedicte Gilman, 83–90. Amsterdam: Allard Pierson Museum.

Culler, Jonathan. 2002. *Structuralist Poetics: Structuralism, Linguistics and the Study of Literature*. 2nd ed. Routledge Classics 116. London: Routledge.

Doherty, Lillian. 2006. "Putting the Women Back into the Hesiodic *Catalogue of Women*." In *Laughing with Medusa: Classical Myth and Feminist Thought*, edited by Vanda Zajko and Miriam Leonard, 297–326. Oxford: Oxford University Press.

Ferrari, Gloria. 2002. *Figures of Speech: Men and Maidens in Ancient Greece*. Chicago: University of Chicago Press.

Ferrari, Gloria. 2003. "Myth and Genre on Athenian Vases." *Classical Antiquity* 22: 37–54.

Green, J. Richard. 1991. "On Seeing and Depicting the Theatre in Classical Athens." *Greek, Roman, and Byzantine Studies* 32: 15–50.

Guiliani, Luca. 2013. *Image and Myth: A History of Pictorial Narration in Greek Art*. Translated by Joseph O'Donnell. Chicago: University of Chicago Press.

Hedreen, Guy M. 1992. *Silens in Attic Black-figure Vase-Painting: Myth and Performance*. Ann Arbor, University of Michigan Press.

Hedreen, Guy M. 1996. "Image, Text, and Story in the Recovery of Helen." *Classical Antiquity* 15: 152–184.

Hedreen, Guy M. 2001. *Capturing Troy: The Narrative Functions of Landscape in Archaic and Early Classical Greek Art*. Ann Arbor: University of Michigan Press.

Hedreen, Guy M. 2007. "Involved Spectatorship in Greek Art." *Art History* 30: 217–246.

Hedreen, Guy M. 2011. "Bild, Mythos, and Ritual: Choral Dance in Theseus's Cretan Adventure on the François Vase." *Hesperia* 80: 491–510.

Hedreen, Guy M. 2014. "The Artificial Sculptural Image of Dionysos in Athenian Vase Painting and the Mythological Discourse of Early Greek Life." In *Approaching the Ancient Artifact*, edited by Amalia Avramidou and Denise Demetriou, 267–280. Berlin and Boston: De Gruyter.

Holliday, Peter J., ed. 1993a. *Narrative and Event in Ancient Art*. Cambridge, UK: Cambridge University Press.

Holliday, Peter J.. 1993b. "Narrative Structures in the François Tomb." In *Narrative and Event in Ancient Art*, edited by Peter J. Holliday, 175–197. Cambridge, UK: Cambridge University Press.

Hurwit, Jeffrey M. 2011. "The Shipwreck of Odysseus: Strong and Weak Imagery in Geometric Art." *American Journal of Archaeology* 115: 1–18.

Langdon, Susan H. 2008. *Art and Identity in Dark Age Greece, 1100–700 BC*. Cambridge, UK: Cambridge University Press.

Lyons, Claire. 2008. "Objects of Affection: Gender and Genre on Some Athenian Vases." In *Papers on Special Techniques in Athenian Vases*, edited by Kenneth Lapatin, 73–84. Los Angeles: J. Paul Getty Museum.

Mangieri, Anthony F. 2010. "Legendary Women and Greek Womanhood: The Heroines Pyxis in the British Museum." *American Journal of Archaeology* 114: 429–445.

Meliadò, Claudio. 2015. "Mythography." In *Brill's Companion to Ancient Greek Scholarship*, vol. 1, edited by Franco Montanari, Stephanos Matthaios, and Antonios Rengakos, 1057–1089. Leiden: Brill.

Oakley, John H., and Rebecca H. Sinos. 1993. *The Wedding in Ancient Athens*. Madison: University of Wisconsin Press.

Prince, Gerald. 1987. *Dictionary of Narratology*. Lincoln: University of Nebraska Press.

Reitzammer, Laurialan. 2016. *The Athenian Adonia in Context: The Adonis Festival as Cultural Practice*. Madison: University of Wisconsin Press.

Sammons, Benjamin. 2013. "Narrative Doublets in the Epic Cycle." *American Journal of Philology* 134: 529–556.

Small, Jocelyn P. 1999. "Time *in* Space: Narrative in Classical Art." *Art Bulletin* 81: 562–575.

Smith, R. Scott, and Stephen M. Trzaskoma. 2011. "Mythography." In *Oxford Bibliographies Online*. Oxford: Oxford University Press.

Snodgrass, Anthony. 1998. *Homer and the Artists: Text and Picture in Early Greek Art*. Cambridge, UK: Cambridge University Press.

Sourvinou-Inwood, Christiane. 1988. *Studies in Girls' Transitions: Aspects of the Arkteia and Age Representation in Attic Iconography*. Athens, Greece: Kardamitsa.

Sourvinou-Inwood, Christiane. 1991. *Reading Greek Culture: Texts and Images, Rituals and Myths*. Oxford: Oxford University Press.

Stansbury-O'Donnell, Mark. 1999. *Pictorial Narrative in Ancient Greek Art*. Cambridge, UK: Cambridge University Press.

Steiner, Ann. 2007. *Reading Greek Vases*. Cambridge, UK: Cambridge University Press.

Stewart, Andrew. 1983. "Stesichoros and the François Vase." In *Ancient Greek Art and Iconography*, edited by Warren G. Moon, 53–74. Madison: University of Wisconsin Press.

Taplin, Oliver. 1993. *Comic Angels and Other Approaches to Greek Drama through Vase-Painting*. Oxford: Clarendon Press.

Taplin, Oliver. 2007. *Pots and Plays: Interactions between Tragedy and Greek Vase-Painting of the Fourth Century B.C.* Los Angeles: Getty Publications.

Todorov, Tzvetan. 1990. *Genres in Discourse*. Cambridge, UK: Cambridge University Press.

Valladares, Hérica. 2005. "The Lover as Model Viewer: Gendered Dynamics in Propertius 1.3." In *Gendered Dynamics in Latin Love Poetry*, edited by Ronnie Ancona and Ellen Greene, 206–242. Baltimore, MD: Johns Hopkins University Press.

Walsh, David. 2009. *Distorted Ideals in Greek Vase Painting: The World of Mythological Burlesque*. Cambridge, UK, and New York: Cambridge University Press.

......................................................................................................

# CHAPTER 35

# MYTHOGRAPHY AND ROMAN
# WALL PAINTING

......................................................................................................

## ELEANOR WINSOR LEACH[†]

FROM the Roman Republic into late antiquity, painted representations of mythological persons and events enjoyed a strong presence in Roman visual culture in public and private buildings. By historical and geological accident, the remains of settlements buried by the Vesuvian eruption of 79 CE have given us the best-preserved repertoire of these. They are located mostly in structures identifiable as houses and offer a visual complement to our written records of myth. In this chapter, I will explore ways in which we may consider pictorial content in light of mythographical intellectual trends.

Myths in their essential form are narratives with plots, but they can be referenced and recalled to mind by the mere mention of an important character or event, for instance, "Jason and the Golden Fleece." Analogously, their painted representation comprises a form of visual shorthand in which a part represents the whole. A present-day illustrator producing images to accompany a moment in a story has two choices: either to include every detail of that event on the page or else to provide a free interpretation, perhaps to capture an atmosphere or mood. Some like it one way, some the other, but in either case, the audience for the illustration has the written text with which to compare. Such is not the case in ancient mythological paintings (with a few Homeric and Vergilian exceptions). For most ancient painters and viewers, most stories exist only in memory. Thus, when some feature of a painting seems to reference a story that we recognize, its focus requires a recollection of the fuller narrative context to give it meaning. Accordingly, any assemblage of moments from the same story invites a retelling and a reconnecting of links in its narrative chain that the viewer independently must supply. In this way, our reconstructive encounter rather resembles the technique of mythographers in summarizing myths.

Actually, as will be seen in our repertoire of still extant decorative installations, this kind of episodic continuity is rare. The majority of rooms with mythological assemblages display single narrative moments that at first glance seem unrelated. Should we take these for random decoration or look for some programmatic rationale to make sense of them? Or again, what if the figures in a painting are readily identifiable—gods or heroes as they may be—and yet their painting does not obviously seem to represent a version of their story as we know it? Where do we go from here? Can mythography be of any assistance? For an answer we may look at such differences among texts as Smith and Trzaskoma (2007: x–xiv) have shown to characterize two or more versions of one and the same plot in Ps.-Apollodorus's *Library* and Hyginus's *Fabulae*. Add additional variants, and more differences will appear. And so, to return to shorthand nomenclature such as "Story of Jason," we can recognize that there is no single definitive version of a myth. Long histories of transmission have played upon an inherent flexibility that, in the case of visual representation, is available to patron's choice or painter's imagination.

Such variations will form the substance of this chapter. For sake of clarity, its overall structure will follow a chronological course from the Republic through the early empire. Several myths will recur in different contexts with differences that demonstrate their flexibility. Discussions of format will figure because format affects the way in which a story can be told. Like the details of a written narrative, those of a painting will give their own version of a myth.

## 1. PAINTING BEFORE ROME

Mythological painting is not an exclusively Roman phenomenon. The 2nd-century CE travel writer Pausanias in his *Description of Greece* sees the works of many Greek painters, which he describes in abundant detail. Among Roman writers, the Elder Pliny in his *Natural History* bears vicarious witness to some Greek examples in accordance with an historical trajectory. He often mentions the names of famous artists in connection with their best-known subjects and their particular locations. Some of these are single subjects, primarily gods or heroes. So, Parrhasius painted Theseus and also groups of heroes in conversation: Meleager, Hercules, Perseus, Aeneas, Castor and Pollux; Telephus with Achilles, Agamemnon, and Odysseus—some quite improbable within mythological chronology (*NH* 35.70–71). Where multiple paintings in one location treated the same subject, they could do so through multiple lenses, as, for instance, in the Athenian Theseion, where the titulary hero was represented in multiple panels (Paus. 1.17.2–3). In other cases, the combination of subjects might seem to be primarily thematic. Among the most celebrated displays of this kind was the Athenian Stoa Poikile of the 5th century BCE, displaying the works of the master painters Polygnotus, Micon, and Panaenus but mentioned only by topic (*NH* 35.57–59): Iliupersis, Marathon, and Amazonomachy. Within this mixture of history and mythology, battles are certainly the theme. Thus, Micon's *Iliupersis* might reveal several interconnected moments in succession or else combine several within one comprehensive frame, as in Polygnotus's *Lesche* of the Cnidians at Delphi (Pollitt 1990: 127–141). Only in two instances of his historical listing does Pliny give us any indication of the composition alongside the content (see discussion of Timanthes' Iphigenia painting in section 6).

Elsewhere we do find descriptive passages (*ekphraseis*), some based on presumably existing compositions and others purely fictional. On the side of the real are epigrams paying tribute to an actual artist's subject or skill. Thus, Pliny notes that the Aphrodite of Apelles was made famous by Greek epigrams, while nine different poets celebrated Timomachus of Byzantium's rendition of Medea, all of them remarking on her expression of divided feelings as she contemplates the murder of her children (Gutzwiller 2004; Gurd 2007. For the epigrams, see *Anth. Pal.* 16.135–141 and 143). On the fictive side, both poetry and prose offer *ekphraseis* of paintings, some very detailed and some involving interpretive intervention, of which the most extensive is the coverlet on the marriage couch of Peleus and Thetis in Catullus 64, a figured tapestry rather than a painting, but the pictorial value is the same (McNally 1985; Elsner 2007c). Here the narrator not only brings Ariadne to life but gives her a voice with which to tell her own story as well.

A passage from Petronius's *Satyricon* involves a personal, subjective, and emotional reaction. When Encolpius, the novel's protagonist, enters a *pinacotheca* that is stocked with masterpieces by great classical painters, he compares the images to his own situation (Petron. *Sat.* 83):

> Here an eagle was bearing the boy of Ida up to the sky; here a fair-skinned Hylas warded off an impudent Naiad. Apollo cursed his murderous hands and decorated his unstrung lyre with a newly sprung flower. Amidst these faces of painted lovers, I cried out as if all alone: "So, love affects gods as well! Jupiter, in his very own sky, could not find something to love, but at least he harmed no one in his eagerness to sin on earth. The Nymph who ravished Hylas would have kept her love under control if she had believed that Hercules would come to stop her. Apollo revived the ghost of the boy as a flower. All these divinities gained embraces without contest.

Encolpius is, of course, no art historian, and the gallery is imaginary, but the scenes he mentions are both formulaic and evoke a personal response, reflecting one in an array of potential interactions with art. The point is not his aesthetic discrimination but, rather, the subjectivity that causes him to select three paintings depicting the homoerotic domination of mortals by gods. Even so, he only responds to the aspects that interest him. He is unconcerned with the melancholy fates of the mortals, focusing only on the elements that are relevant to his own situation. Another viewer giving fuller accounts of the stories might be less ready to align his sympathies with the gods.

# 2. REPUBLICAN FIRST CENTURY: THE ODYSSEY FRIEZE

Let us turn to our visual record. In the repertoire of the mid-Republic, which gives our first evidence for painting of any kind, there were virtually no figurative paintings, but at about the middle of the 1st century BCE, there appears a narrative frieze with labels depicting scenes from the *Odyssey*, including the Laestrygonians, Circe, an Underworld scene, and the Sirens (von Blanckenhagen 1963; Lowenstam 1995). Located within the opulent district of the Esquiline Hill, its context might be either public or private but was certainly designed for an audience of high culture. It is tempting to coordinate this installation with Vitruvius's short passage on wall painting that mentions such pictorial subjects as the battles of Troy and "wanderings of Ulysses with landscape backgrounds" (*De Arch.* 7.5.2). The emphasis on wanderings and landscape backgrounds suggests the kind of sequential continuity that a frieze might involve.

In the actual Esquiline frieze, episodes unfold in groups of two or three frames, beginning with the landing of Ulysses's comrades and their interview with the Laestrygonian princess near the shore. In the succeeding frames, the giants first swarm to attack, and second, having already sunk some ships, carry Greek corpses to the shore. A concluding half frame shows Ulysses's ship already under sail. With this comes a shift in the viewpoint from which we experience the story. Until now, we have followed its progress as if through the eyes of Ulysses, but hereafter happenings in the house of Circe, the Underworld, and the Sirens' cliff include Ulysses as a participant. Nothing precisely comparable exists elsewhere in the extant repertoire, although a frieze of Trojan War scenes from the Casa del Criptoportico in Pompeii is sometimes cited for comparison. For a literary parallel of roughly comparable date, we may think of *Aeneid* 1 and its succession of Trojan War scenes that Aeneas discovers within the Carthaginian Temple of Juno, but more broadly, of course, the selection of different pieces of a larger mythical narrative is an underlying principle of a mythographical frame of reference.

## 3.  FROM FRIEZES TO PANELS

Sometime about the mid-1st century BCE, complex illusionistic architectonic designs are replaced with large-scale panel paintings on individual walls. Hypothetically, we may consider this new fashion to be a Roman counterpart to the celebrated masterpiece paintings of the Greek artists, which must have been of similar dimensions. One spacious enclosure in the Villa Imperiale in Pompeii features three episodes from the myths of Crete: on the rear wall, a heroic Theseus with a decapitated Minotaur at his feet; to the left, he abandons the princess Ariadne; and on the right, Daedalus, the maker of the labyrinth, has lost his son Icarus in flight. Perhaps we might think of the Athenian Theseion as model. Here as in other places, the mounted panels on each wall are distinguished by elegant housings of columns called *aediculae* (little shrines). Once inaugurated, this architectonic fashion persists throughout the history of representation and may be considered as the mark of what we call the "picture gallery." Even when the same subject is involved, the change from frieze representation to panels disrupts straightforward sequence and poses a new challenge to the viewer: to supply the connections from background knowledge.

Because few locations for the early Augustan period remain intact, we have no reliable estimate of the full extent of this large-scale panel format. The Casa del Citharista in Pompeii contains sets of rooms so decorated; the so-called House of Livia on the Palatine features a room where two extant paintings depict moments from the story of Io's transformation and the love of Polyphemus for the sea nymph Galatea, perhaps an allusion to Theocritus *Idyll* 11. For each, the central theme depicts a significant moment at the heart of the story. In the one panel, Argus guards the nymph Io, small horns sprouting on her head, as Mercury steals in from behind. Viewers aware of the myth will know the subterfuges the god will use to put the watchman to sleep and rescue the maiden—a composition that not only provides background but invites looking ahead: Argus will be beheaded and Io, in a cow-like form, will swim to Egypt. The companion picture of Polyphemus shows the one-eyed giant, driven by Eros, wading into the sea while nymphs cluster mockingly nearby. No such scene figures in Theocritus's poem, where only one nymph hears the Cyclops's love song. Here the painter has seen the ridiculous incompatibilities in a story whose helpless obsession can, all the same, seem even touchingly sympathetic in its literary embodiments. As to the choice of the two particular subjects, common ground is not immediately apparent unless we want to think of Juno's sentinel, the monster Argus, as enamored of the woman he is set to guard.

## 4. CONTINUOUS NARRATIVE

In the late Augustan and early Julio-Claudian years, the custom of grouping framed pictures three or four to a room continues but on a wholly altered scale of representation and narrative technique, and their subjects offer intimate links with tragic plots that, ultimately, could derive from tragic texts or performance, but also from mythographical summaries (see Meccariello, this volume, for the latter). The paintings come, in one instance, from a decorated villa on the slopes of Vesuvius (von Blanckenhagen 1990), but also from the center of Pompeii (Dawson 1944; Leach 1988). Generally speaking, fully realized natural settings dominate, forming backgrounds for small active figures, and the same personages often appear several times within the same frame, challenging the viewer to recognize a sequential order of actions and thus to impose a narrative interpretation upon the scene. Two good instances are representations of the myth of Actaeon, who appears in several such panels (Leach 1981), and Dirce, whose story appears in two (Leach 1986). These are both Theban stories, so the viewer might think of their wooded backgrounds as Mt. Cithaeron, but they might also recall the stage. In the examples of the former, Actaeon is depicted encountering the goddess Diana bathing naked in a woodland stream. In Ovid's literary version (*Met.* 3.143–255) she is surrounded by nymphs but in the paintings is dramatically alone. However, individual painters can present nuanced details to inspire an interpretive response from the viewer, for instance, to discern whether Actaeon's transgression was accidental or deliberate (*Met.* 3.142: "For what crime did a mistake hold?").

For instance, in the Casa del Frutteto the sighting seems quite possibly accidental and guiltless, as the hunter emerges from a rocky pass with one arm raised as much to indicate surprise as intention. The bathing goddess kneels at the edge of a stream and gestures toward Actaeon. Her attention fixes on the canine attack at the center of the painting. By contrast, the scene in the Casa di Epidius Rufus (preserved only in a line drawing), the sighting is certainly deliberate, as Actaeon peers in a direct gaze on the naked goddess. A second stage of action shows her dressed and energetically rushing at the hunter while urging on the dogs. The setting mingles natural and human worlds, and Actaeon might seem to have attempted to save himself by flight toward a villa building in the background as Ovid puts the impulse into his mind (*Met.* 3.204–205).

No such ambiguities plague the images of Dirce and Antiope in the Casa di Giulio Polibio (Leach 1986; see Franklin 1990 for a likely counterpart in the Casa del Marinaio, preserved in only its lower half). Central to this myth is the punitive binding of Dirce beneath the hooves of a bull, a tale quite popular with artists, whether on wall painting or monumental sculpture (see the famous version in the Naples Archaeological Museum). But the version in the Casa di Giulio Polibio is the only continuous version of the myth, featuring four stages of action. It is tempting to connect it with Euripides's *Antiope*, the plot of which can be tentatively reconstructed from numerous fragments, as well as from mythographical summaries (Hyg. 8, Apollod. 3.42–43 and schol. Ap. Rhod. 4.1090). The painting's "narrative" approach invites comparison both with literary versions, including Propertius 3.15, and mythographical texts that offer summaries.

The composition consists of four scenes taking place in the wilderness around a shrine of Dionysus, which is set in the center. The background perhaps suggests Cithaeron, where Antiope gave birth to and exposed her sons, Zethus and Amphion, who were then found and raised by a herdsman (as the above sources agree). In the upper-left corner we encounter a figure of just this herdsman, who raised the twins on Cithaeron; in Euripides, he gives the prologue, providing the background that is presumably incorporated in our mythographic accounts. Moving counterclockwise, there next appears a troupe of Bacchantes (compare Hyg. 8); here Antiope is identified by her raised hands, while Zethus and Amphion are already laying hands on Dirce. The two scenes conflate two stages of the story since in our sources the twins are initially resistant to the pleas of this unknown woman (Prop. 3.15.36–37; Hyg. 8), and the recognition scene between mother and sons certainly would have been a prominent feature of Euripides's play.

One would expect that the painting would next depict the binding of Dirce to the bull (Prop. 3.15.37–38; Hyg. 8), but the next narrative step shows Dirce already bound and being dragged by the bull, the most frequently depicted scene in static versions of the myth. Finally, the narrative concludes with the figure of Amphion seated on a rock in the upper-right hand register, playing the lyre that would build the walls of Thebes—a continuation of the myth that presumably went beyond the narrative arc of the tragedy (but see Propertius 3.15, where Amphion is said to sing *paeans* from the cliffs after punishing Dirce). Even so, with its four distinct stages of action, this is the fullest of all continuous narratives, but the effect is not to make the painting more erudite and obscure but the opposite: the performative sequence is open to viewers who had encountered the play itself, or perhaps an elegaic or mythographical version of the same material.

Theater and painting diverge because the latter frequently shows actions that spectators of the former would not have seen in that context but had heard in a prologue or messenger speech. For instance, viewers of Ennius's *Andromeda* would not have witnessed Perseus swooping down from the clouds (Enn. *Andr.* fr. 117–118 Jocelyn), as is depicted in two paintings in the Villa Boscotrecase and the Casa del Sacerdos Amandus. Ovid, however, places the scene luridly before our eyes (*Met.* 4.707–740). By contrast, viewers would have perhaps remembered the negotiation scene between Perseus and Andromeda's father, Cepheus, though the version in the Amandus painting includes a much larger cluster of armed attendants, as if to intimate Cepheus's duplicity in his promise of Andromeda's hand and Perseus's ensuing battle against a rival suitor. Distinctive differences like this show that artists and owners were not bound to a text or one approach; consider the different versions of Icarus's death in the Casa del Frutteto and the Casa di Sacerdos Amandus (von Blanckenhagen 1968), where the latter enhances the dramatic moment by depicting the rowing crews pointing upward in excitement.

In spaces where we encounter multiple paintings—for instance, the Perseus episode and the Daedalus episode in the Casa di Sacerdos Amandus—it is a natural question whether the combinations or selections of subjects are simply random choices by the patron or painter or were designed to provoke the viewer's discovery of interactive cross-referencing. While they are less obviously related than the three Cretan images mentioned earlier, these disparate story lines can, through compositional similarities, be discovered to highlight certain aspects of their themes, as, for instance, in the case of the Perseus and Polyphemus panels in the Villa Boscotrecase, where the central crags framing their principal figures emphasize their obvious settings, but also highlight the shared motif of romantic attraction with sinister intimations of violence looming behind. When these same two subjects recur in the new ensembles of the Frutteto and the Sacerdos Amandus, which are most likely of later date, a few changed details enlarge on their relationship. Not only has Daedalus been added to the group, but also, in the Sacerdos Amandus, a large figure image of Hercules receiving the golden apples from the Hesperides. Now all four components show images of ventures beyond customary boundaries that have varied outcomes. The success of Perseus contrasts with Daedalus's failure, and the Cyclops also goes outside his element in longing for the sea nymph. We will consider these connections more fully with a more complete case study, the Casa di Giasone, next.

# 5. CASA DI GIASONE (HOUSE OF JASON)

Although during this mid- to late-Augustan period continuous narrative appears to be the favored mode, one roughly contemporaneous set of pictures in Naples taken from two rooms of the Pompeian Casa di Giasone favor the portrayal of individual moments over narrative compositions (Zevi 1964). Background similarities unite the subjects very clearly in one group of three panels, and there is an open or partially open doorway at the center of each. Within these architectural frameworks, the scenes themselves depict moments of social interaction having troubled love stories as the focus, each one depicting a different stage of its affair. A seated Paris is the object of Helen's gaze; but because there is no visible communication between the two and an Eros stands in the doorway between them, perhaps this is the inception of love. Phaedra, by contrast, is already in the grips of her passion for Hippolytus, for the nurse holds in her hand the tablet and stylus for writing the fateful letter accusing him of attempted rape. In the doorway is an unidentified female attendant, who may be the one to carry the letter to its addressee. Finally, a seated Medea seemingly has come to a point of decision but is not yet able to raise her eyes to the boys themselves. The open doorways at the rear of each scenario may remind us of the stage but might also allude to the open-endedness of the decisive moment.

Thus, it might seem that we are looking at a mythical sequence of exempla as typical of mythographical works as of Roman poetry. In terms of the latter, one can point especially to Propertius 1.3, which starts with a catalog of sleeping heroines who serve as models for a sleeping Cynthia—faint as Ariadne on the empty seashore, free as Andromeda after her release from the rocks, or weary as a maenad in a grassy meadow exhausted from the dance (see a different catalog at 1.15). Similarly, these images, by their locations in small rooms, must surely be intended to elicit just such associative ramifications of comparison and contrast in the conversations between a host and his guests.

From a second pendant room opening off the peristyle of the house, come three images whose landscape settings are the thematic opposite of the three doorway scenes. Each features a single centrally located tree whose clear reference to the identity of the principal figures reinforces the story line—an oak tree for Zeus in the deception of Europa and a poplar in the scene of Hercules and Nessus. What the viewer can supply here is a journey across water—the sea and a river—following in consequence of each scene's dramatic interaction. Both scenes are also connected through instances of deception and the participants' moods related to the journey: the bull turns a complicitous eye to the viewer (Europa seems quite willing), while Nessus bows low before Hercules with a gesture that might seem to be indicating the measure of the water to be crossed (a nervous Deianira stands stiffly clutching her infant). The third scene, with architecture and a more developed perspective, is more difficult to identify, but I would suggest that the combination of a Pan figure holding his pipe and a long-robed lyre player are the contest of Pan and Apollo, with seated nymphs as the judges.

## 6. Early to Late Imperial

From these "traditional" formats, difficult to place in relative chronology, we turn to the full-blown compositions of the late Neronian period, and especially the Flavian decade.

Because of the serious damage done by the earthquake of 62 CE, and the subsequent need for restoration, these years are the most abundant for the production of painting. This proliferation suggests a lively industry, with painters moving rapidly from house to house as they were called upon by numerous patrons. For some of the most popular painters, trajectories have been traced by a scholar who observed certain characteristics of detail: the shapes of ears, or knees, or even toes (Richardson 2000). These observations are useful to our social understanding of practice in revealing not only individual specializations, but also the number of painters who might have been employed within the several rooms of a given house.

We thus have two distinctly opposite modes of composition calling forth wholly different responses from the viewer: first, small panels with one to three figure compositions that more often present actors than actions and, second, large multifigured compositions that dramatize the events they depict before our eyes. For the most part, the smaller compositions are static; figures either seated or standing allude to their myths through identifiable properties or attributes. Almost a majority of the subjects are erotic, employing an Eros to signify lines of attraction or desire, and a lens into the broader narrative. For example, from the Casa di Meleagro we encounter a seated Ganymede, identifiable by his Phrygian cap, with an eagle emerging, heralded by an Eros, as well as a solitary Ariadne awakened to Theseus's departure, her deserting lover's sails visible at the horizon, and an Eros weeping over the scene. For the most part, these small compositions, many of which exist still in situ, are located in modestly sized chambers, which does not preclude their function as conversation pieces. However, in the same house we can see a paratactic series of seven such panels filling the inner walls to make a genuine *pinacotheca*, but the thematic logic of their selection is hard to deduce.

No person is likely to approach these unobtrusive renderings of familiar topics with questions about their derivation from any specific literary source. When seeming duplicate or multiple versions occur, as with Ariadne or Perseus, we may take them to constitute a tradition of their own. The same is not true of the large-scale dramatic compositions that decorated principal rooms of some of the more opulent houses of Pompeii, upon which their discoverers were eager to confer value through some manner of connection with the lost masterpieces of classical Greece. Particularly strong in the later 18th and 19th centuries, this impulse carried with it the implicit assumption that anything produced in Rome could only be derivative and inferior—most notably expressed by Wincklemann, whose belief was rooted in Greek cultural superiority (see Mattusch 2011: 83, letter 30). To be fair, Wincklemann's views were themselves shaped by ancient sources, such as Pliny's *Natural History*, which highlighted famous Greek works. When discoveries in Pompeii and Herculaneum coincided with this ancient testimony, it was easy to fall in line with the idea that every Roman work of art was based on a (better) Greek masterpiece. As present-day scholars now acknowledge, such assumptions are problematic, and connections are in no way so simple (for a similar view of sculpture, see Perry 2005). Let us consider, as a case study, one of the most famous paintings from Pompeii, the sacrifice of Iphigenia, which was once housed in the Casa di Poeta Tragico.

Among the most celebrated of classical Greek masterpieces was the *Sacrifice of Iphigenia at Aulis*. We are fortunate to have the testimony not only of Pliny, but also of Cicero, Quintilian, and Plutarch, with some variations in detail. On this basis we can be fairly certain that the picture was visible in Rome. Attributing this painting to Timanthes, who was contemporary with Parrhasius, Pliny describes the grieving audience of Greeks as Iphigenia stands at the altar, focusing on the detail that the artist depicted Agamemnon veiled, whom "he was unable adequately to portray" (*NH* 35.74–75; trans. Rackham). Although Pliny calls the painting celebrated in oratory, the mentions of it we have occur in texts about oratorical theory. Cicero invokes this painting in his description of degrees of grief (*Orator* 74). Quintilian's comment adds that the spectator is left to supply the emotional content for him- or herself (2.13.13). In veiling Agamemnon's figure Timanthes may well have followed the text of Euripides's drama, in which Agamemnon hides his eyes and tears with his robe as Iphigenia approaches the altar.

When we turn to the Pompeian wall painting, there are important differences. Pliny's description positions Iphigenia at the altar to await her doom in a manner more suggestive of her dignity in Euripides, but in the painting, she is being carried between Menelaus and Odysseus, bundled like a sack of laundry. It is hard to see "indications of grief" on the faces of these two or Calchas, yet the veiled figure can only be Agamemnon, whose sorrow the artist was unable to depict. From this inclusion, we might conjecture that the fame of Timanthes's painting might have made it a matter of common knowledge, or perhaps even that Cicero's description did serve as a model, but there is no warrant for considering that the owner or painters were attempting to reproduce the composition itself. Far from being a "free copy," this is more likely to be the effort of the painter to supply a requested topic, and when we remember that the six paintings in the adjoining atrium were Iliadic in theme, the choice of this critical moment that prefaced the sailing of the Greek fleet makes perfect sense. Comparable discrepancies can be seen between Pliny's brief description and another Troy-themed painting, the apprehension of Achilles on Scyros, which is best reserved for discussion in context.

## 7. Ensembles in the Casa dei Dioscuri

Romans did not waste their largest and presumably most expensive paintings on hidden chambers of the house. Without making value judgments, we can say that these striking pictures organized the hierarchy of domestic spaces by their placement where they were available to be seen by the greatest number of persons, in accordance with Vitruvius's statement (*De Arch.* 6.5.1) that public areas are those to which all persons are admitted. With an interest in the strategic employment of domestic spaces as carriers of self-representation, scholars have come to consider the totality of painting not as a series of random acts but as a deliberate unity, either with the goal of attaining thematic coherence or of demarcating sight lines. Passing over the much-discussed Casa dei Vettii

(Clarke 1991: 209–244), the Casa di Poeta Tragico (Bergmann 1994), and the Casa del Menandro (Lorenz 2014), we will consider the assemblage that once decorated the fully excavated Casa dei Dioscuri. Because of the quality of its several paintings but also their stylistic differences, Richardson (1955) chose this house as the anchor for his study of individual painters' characteristic marks.

The owners of the house, the Nigidii Vaccae, are well documented as prosperous tradespersons, bronze merchants who had brought their business from Capua to Pompeii. That their occupation gave them no embarrassment can be seen from their signature public donations. Both the Stabian and Forum baths have inscribed bronze benches and braziers whose legs were of bovine shape, but their domestic decorations also were of a nature to proclaim their pride of position, with even some subtle allusions to their transfer of place. For example, in the entrance corridor, the Dioscuri, patrons of sailing and of trade, are prominently displayed with their horses. We might think of them as small statues installed as protectors of the house and its enterprises. Continuing into the atrium, one encounters similar images of Ceres, Bacchus, Saturn, and Jupiter as one navigates around the central forest of columns. Stylistically similar to the two Dioscuri of the entrance way, these may be understood to simulate a set of statues placed on consoles around the walls.

Coming to the tablinum, one can scarcely help being dazzled by the large-scale figure paintings on opposite walls depicting two moments in the life of Achilles: his enraged response to Agamemnon's demand for Briseis, when he is checked by Minerva's hand, and, on the opposite wall, his apprehension on Scyros, which has a very different kind of composition. This is the picture that Pliny attributes to Athenion (*NH* 35.134): "Achilles in the guise of a maiden at the moment of detection by Ulysses, a picture containing six figures," but this panel has seven and perhaps two more at the left-hand edge. Achilles is at the center of the action, his hand on the shield that reveals his masculine identity with Odysseus and Diomedes on either side, each grasping an arm. Other figures look on in dismay, including Deidamia and Lycomedes, but the conspicuous figure is Achilles: enveloped in a floating cloud of gauzy fabric, his glance turned obliquely away in what seems to be embarrassment. Achilles is not just dressed in feminine garments, but his body, too, is rendered softly effeminate, especially his full and rounded legs and thick ankles. Looking from this Achilles to the very different one who is drawing his sword in the companion piece, we may recall that the common element in both episodes is the hero's relationship with a woman, but the two stages of action show transferal and the assertion of identity (on Achilles in Roman literature and art, see Cameron 2013). Would it be possible to apply this idea to the house owners who had put off their Capuan allegiance to adopt a Roman one?

Three smaller rooms surround the atrium, one with paintings still in situ. This is a small, high-ceilinged room of unusual blue color, whose two extant paintings show a close thematic relationship: Myrrha already half-metamorphosized into a tree, attended by nymphs as she gives birth to Adonis through her bark, and Scylla, the daughter of Nisus, who has cut her father's talismanic purple lock. The two incidents are based on troubled relationships between daughters and fathers, though of different sorts.

Whether by a coincidental process of association or a deliberate echo, the two are close together in Ovid's *Metamorphoses* (Scylla 8.11–151; Myrrha 10.298–518). Certainly, this room gives abundant ground for conversation, and might therefore serve as a triclinium, but not for any large group.

For an ample setting for hospitality, we turn to the peristyle, entering under a landscape image of Pan who is recoiling in distaste from the hermaphrodite he has just uncovered. One might wonder how this very frivolous subject might accord with the dignified decorations of the atrium, but perhaps it is a deliberate marker of a change of atmosphere from the sober to the more recreational, as expected of a peristyle. The decoration of this area, however, is not at all light-hearted. At the one end was its grand dining room, once revetted in marble plaques—one of very few Pompeian rooms so opulently furnished. This vantage point offers prospects in two directions: a window on the right side opens on the smaller peristyle decorated with garden paintings; and through the large doorway down the line of the peristyle across its two water basins to the piers at the far end, which carried a singular decoration in simulated bronze work: tall tripods surrounded by figures representing the deaths of Niobe's children. On the one side, Diana shoots down the girls, and, on the other, Apollo shoots down the boys. Because the material is bronze, we might take it for a signature item representing the craftsmanship of which the family-owned workshops were capable. The piers framing the prospect at closer range pair two traditional topics that are identifiably the work of the same painter: Perseus releasing Andromeda, and Medea hesitating before her children. These have literary analogs, but what do these initially disparate seeming subjects have to do with each other, or with the tripod decoration that they frame? Medea's filicide may furnish a keynote; for Andromeda's plight would never have occurred had not her mother boasted of her beauty, while Niobe's offspring also suffer in consequence of a mother's egotistical boast. Thus, all three of these stories place guilt on the mother, in contrast with the sinfulness of children we saw in the small blue room with its dysfunctional father-daughter relationships. Just as Richardson demonstrated with respect to the variety of its painters and its range of subjects, the movement from the obscure to the familiar Casa dei Dioscuri bespeaks its owner's cultural discrimination in its mythological—or mythographical—selection.

## 8. PHILOSTRATUS'S FICTIVE TOUR GUIDE

Thus far we have encountered mythological arrangements in domestic spaces that may place interactive demands on the viewer. Moving two centuries forward, we can see an example of interaction between viewer and the picture gallery vividly realized in the *Imagines* by the Elder Philostratus, a major intellectual figure of the Second Sophistic. Mythography in these books presents itself in the form of an oral discourse, a guided tour of a collection of painted panels assembled on five terraces of a seaside Neapolitan villa. Whereas a few of these paintings present natural scenery, and a few others are still lifes, the majority are mythological panels and can be visualized as large-scale figures engaged in actions that are significant within the contexts of their myths, which is to place them within the same genre of composition as the Flavian examples previously discussed. But these descriptions turn tables on the spectator, for instead of being challenged to decipher painted actions from his own resources of knowledge, he has this decipherment thrust upon him as the speaker builds the image figure by figure, gesture by gesture before his eyes.

In his preface, Philostratus outlines the power of painting for not only its technical merits but also its ability to evoke emotion, and proposes to take his main addressee, a young boy of ten years, through the interpretation of several paintings. Thus, the reader is not the primary recipient of this exposition, but stands, instead, as an affiliate listener, for the discourse has an immediate double audience built in: first, a young boy who is the son of the house where the paintings are located, and second, a crowd of Neapolitan ephebes who have pursued the rhetor as would-be disciples, keen to learn interpretation of painting as a principle of his art.

As this process unfolds, interpretation can be seen in two aspects: one whenever certain images bear some resemblance to literary embodiments of their subjects; and the other as the rhetor Philostratus infuses the subjects with an active life, sometimes simulating their thoughts, sometimes discerning their purpose, and often spilling over the confinement of a picture frame to draw the depicted actions into the larger contexts of their myths. In other words, the rhetor actually recreates the subjects he describes. To consider how this works for the viewer, we can look at two aspects of the discourse: first, at the rhetor's direct intervention in his narrative with expressions of personal impression or opinion, and second, at his interruption of the descriptive process with forms of direct address.

The latter most often engage the young boy who is standing in the forefront of the gathering as primary designated audience. As the rhetor says, "My boy," he gives the discourse a spatial dimension that sometimes serves as little more than a reminder of his presence, but sometimes relates directly to his qualifications as a listener. Thus, the desertion of Ariadne by Theseus is introduced as a tale often heard from a nurse that makes old women weep (1.15). More often, these interventions incorporate a later stage of *paideia*, as in the opening panel, where the rhetor asks the boy if he noticed that the painting represented a scene from the *Iliad*, the descent of the fire god on Scamander (*Imag.* 1.1 on *Il.* 21). When the rhetor turns to the courtship of Amymone by Neptune, he first paints the Homeric image of the sea god's angry rush through the waves before softening the glance turned upon the maiden, who is nonetheless afraid. And then, as in deference to his hearer's childhood innocence, he gestures toward the remainder of the narrative but leaves out any lurid details concerning what happens in the bridal chamber (1.8).

Many more such interventions, however, are prefaced by a general injunction to "look," calling attention to some details of the representation such as the horses of the charioteers in the race of Pelops and Oenomaus and the beauty of Pelops himself as cherished by Neptune (1.17). Sometimes, however, more complex engagement is solicited, as when in regarding the image of Amphion, we are asked to look closely first at the construction of the musician's lyre, but then at the open lips of the singer to imagine words he must be using—"no doubt a hymn to Earth"—as stones run together at his sound (1.10). Finally, in the way of intervention are the rhetor's moments of dialogue with his characters, as when he tries vainly to enlighten Narcissus concerning the deception of the pool that gives back his image. Does he expect, the rhetor asks, the pool to enter into conversation (1.23)? At such moments, so far has the rhetor entered into the fiction of the painting that he appears to have carried himself beyond boundaries.

Given the impression of realism in Philostratus's discourses, one can question how reliably this assemblage of individual images represents the state of painting in its time—that is to say, two centuries after the destruction of Pompeii. Chronologically, the question is unanswerable because the images themselves are said to be an eclectic gathering representing some of the finest artistic skills and thus could include both new and old. In this respect the collection is more revealing of a state of reception than of current artistic practice. All the same, one aspect that goes beyond our known repertoire is the range of subjects, for alongside such familiar overlapping themes as Ariadne, Narcissus, Amymone, Perseus, and the freeing of Andromeda, where the painting seems to have selected the same dramatic moments as those we already know, such seemingly singular inclusions as Semele, Memnon, Glaucus Pontius, Amphiaraus, and Antigone may well transform literary moments into new visual form.

Aspects of selection and composition, however, show us a quite different species of dramatic action, one that is amplified by the addition of depictions of separate or sequential stages of the narrative at points before or after (or even both) the main action. While Daedalus in his workshop applies all his artistry to the wooden cow, Pasiphae roams outside by the pasture, caught up in her passion for the bull (*Imag.* 1.16). The education of Achilles also offers two complementary phases of his life with the centaur Chiron (2.2), one that recalls the tender tutorial bond between teacher and pupil in the music lesson in the Herculaneum basilica; the other, a wild outdoor scene where the pupil gallops with his master. Such representations must logically exceed the probable compass of a single panel, unless, of course, we want to understand them as versions of continuous narrative. Finally, there are subjects whose actions may seem to exceed the possibilities of painted representation, especially when the image engulfs the canvas in conflagration, as with the fiery roll of Hephaestus over Scamander (1.1), the birth of Dionysus from his mother's fiery death (1.14), or the plunge of Phaethon (1.11). Another sort of example is the opening of the earth and the descent of Amphiaraus into the underworld (1.27). Such depictions differ from those in which the rhetor himself appears to be creating the action, as when he sets the Theban stones moving to Amphion's lyre (1.10). Here the supernatural or improbable constitutes the essence of the image itself. Given the obvious fictional quality of these images, we may come to understand the generally fictional character of all that, in achieving the rhetor's celebrated truth in painting, might seem to have carried both himself and his viewer into another world.

## FURTHER READING

The relationship of mythological paintings to mythography or mythographical impulses has not been explicitly explored, but many studies offer insight into the organization, choice, and thematic or aesthetic relationships among the paintings. Even so, most of the work on mythological wall paintings is couched in architectural and art historical studies, which are offered below as a starting point for future work.

For full-scale overviews of Roman wall painting, see Ling (1991); Mazzolini (2004); Croisille (2005); Lorenz (2008); La Rocca, Ensoli, Tortorella, and Papini (2009); and Pappalardo (2009). For a general survey of Pliny's chapters on painting, see Isager (1991). For wall painting in Pompeii, there are a number of useful surveys starting with the venerable but still useful Mau (1902); but see also Reinach (1922), including line drawings of now-lost paintings; Dawson (1944); Thompson (1960, 1961); De Carolis (2001); Leach (2004); Hodske (2007); and Bragantini (2009). There have also been important specialized studies of wall painting in individual buildings, much of which is mythological in nature: Zevi (1964); Bergmann (1996) on the Casa di Giasone; Clarke (1991, esp. 209–244) on the Casa dei Vettii; Peters (1993) on Casa di Marco Lucrezio Frontone; Barringer (1994) on the Macellum; Bergmann (1994) on the Casa di Poeta Tragico; and Ling and Ling (2005) and Lorenz (2014), both on the Casa di Menandro. Also of interest are explorations of individual myths in different spaces: von Blanckenhagen (1968); Ling (1979); and Coralini (2001).

Of late, several essays on the viewer experience have appeared that lend insight into how viewers might "read" artistic programs. Elsner's work on viewership is essential (esp. Elsner 1995, but also 2000, 2007b, and 2007c). In addition, see Platt (2002); Lorenz (2007); and Newby (2011). For Philostratus's *Imagines*, which offers an ancient view of explaining and interpreting paintings, see Lehmann (1941); Leach (2000); Elsner (2007a); and, especially, the collection of essays in Bowie and Elsner (2009), including Dubel (2009) and Newby (2009). Of course, connected with viewership are self-representation and the rhetoric of space, for which see Leach (1988); Trimble (2002); and Perry (2002, 2005).

## REFERENCES

Barringer, Judith. 1994. "The Mythological Paintings in the Macellum at Pompeii." *Classical Antiquity* 13: 149–166.

Bergmann, Bettina. 1994. "The Roman House as Memory Theater: The House of the Tragic Poet." *Art Bulletin* 76: 225–256.

Bergmann, Bettina. 1996. "The Pregnant Moment: Tragic Wives in the Roman Interior." In *Sexuality in Ancient Art*, edited by Natalie Boymel Kampen, 199–218. Cambridge, UK: Cambridge University Press.

Bowie, Ewen, and Jaś Elsner, eds. 2009. *Philostratus.* Cambridge, UK: Cambridge University Press.

Bragantini, Irene, and Vittoria Sampaolo. 2009. *La Pittura Pompeiana.* Naples: Electa.

Cameron, Alan. 2013. "Young Achilles in the Roman World." In *Writing Myth: Mythography in the Ancient World*, edited by Stephen M. Trzaskoma and R. Scott Smith, 253–288. Leuven: Peeters.

Clarke, John. 1991. *The Houses of Roman Italy 100 B.C.–A.D. 250: Ritual, Space and Decoration.* Berkeley: University of California Press.

Coralini, Antonella. 2001. *Hercules domesticus: Immagini di Ercole nelle case della regione vesuviana (I secolo a.C–79 d.C).* Naples: Electa.

Croisille, Jean-Michel. 2005. *Le Peinture Romain.* Paris: Picard.

Dawson, Christopher M. 1944. *Romano-Campanian Mythological Landscape Painting.* Yale Classical Studies 9. New Haven, CT: Yale University Press.

De Carolis, Ernesto. 2001. *Gods and Heroes in Pompeii.* Translated by Lori-Ann Touchette. Los Angeles: J. Paul Getty Museum.

Dubel, Sandrine. 2009. "Colour in Philostratus' *Imagines.*" In *Philostratus*, edited by Ewen Bowie and Jaś Elsner, 309–321. Cambridge, UK: Cambridge University Press.

Elsner, Jaś. 1995. *Art and the Roman Viewer: The Transformation of Art from the Pagan World to Christianity.* Cambridge, UK: Cambridge University Press.

Elsner, Jaś. 2000. "Making Myth Visible: The Horae of Philostratus and the Dance of the Text." *Mitteilungen des Deutschen Archäologischen Instituts, Römische Abteilung* 107: 253–278.

Elsner, Jaś. 2007a. "Philostratus Visualizes the Tragic: Some Ecphrastic and Pictorial Receptions of Greek Tragedy in the Roman Era." In *Visualizing the Tragic: Drama, Myth, and Ritual in Greek Art and Literture: Essays in Honour of Froma Zeitlin*, edited by Chris Kraus, Simon Goldhill, Helene P. Foley, and Jaś Elsner, 209–337. Oxford: Oxford University Press.

Elsner, Jaś. 2007b. "Viewer as Image: Intimations of Narcissus." In *Roman Eyes: Visuality and Subjectivity in Art and Text*, edited by Jaś Elsner, 132–176. Princeton, NJ: Princeton University Press.

Elsner, Jaś. 2007c. "Viewing Ariadne: From Ekphrasis to Wall Painting in the Roman World." *Classical Philology* 102: 20–44.

Franklin, James L., Jr. 1990. *Pompeii: "The Casa del Marinaio" and Its History.* Rome: L'Erma di Bretschneider.

Gurd, Sean A. 2007. "Meaning and Material Presence: Four Epigrams on Timomachus' Unfinished *Medea.*" *Transactions of the American Philological Association* 137: 305–332.

Gutzwiller, Kathryn. 2004. "Seeing Thought: Timomachus' Medea and Ecphrastic Epigram." *American Journal of Philology* 125: 339–386.

Hodske, Jürgen. 2007. *Mythologische Bildthemen in den Häusern Pompejis: Die Bedeutung der zentralen Mythenbilder für die Bewohner Pompejis.* Ruhpolding, Germany: Verlag Franz Philipp Rutzen.

Isager, Jacob. 1991. *Pliny on Art and Society: The Elder Pliny's Chapters on the History of Art.* Translated by Henrik Rosenmeier. London: Routledge.

Jocelyn, Henry D. 1967. *The Tragedies of Ennius: The Fragments.* Cambridge, UK: Cambridge University Press.

La Rocca, Eugenio, Serena Ensoli, Stefano Tortorella, and Massimiliano Papini, eds. 2009. *Roma: La pittura di un impero.* Milan: Skira.

Leach, Eleanor Winsor. 1981. "Metamorphoses of the Acteon Myth in Campanian Painting." *Mitteilungen des Deutschen Archäologischen Instituts, Römische Abteilung* 88: 307–328.

Leach, Eleanor Winsor. 1986. "The Punishment of Dirce: A Newly Discovered Painting in the Casa di Giulio Polibio and its Significance within the Visual Tradition." *Mitteilungen des Deutschen Archäologischen Instituts, Römische Abteilung* 93: 157–182.

Leach, Eleanor Winsor. 1988. *The Rhetoric of Space: Literary and Artistic Representations of Landscape in Republican and Augustan Rome.* Princeton, NJ: Princeton University Press.

Leach, Eleanor Winsor. 1992. "Polyphemus in a Landscape: Traditions of Pastoral Courtship." In *The Pastoral Landscape*, edited by John Dixon Hunt, 63–88. Washington DC: National Gallery of Art.

Leach, Eleanor Winsor. 2000. "Narrative Space and the Viewer in Philostratus' *Eikones*." *Mitteilungen des Deutschen Archäologischen Instituts, Römische Abteilung* 107: 237–252.

Leach, Eleanor Winsor. 2004. *The Social Life of Painting in Ancient Rome and on the Bay of Naples*. Cambridge, UK: Cambridge University Press.

Lehmann, Karl. 1941. "The *Imagines* of The Elder Philostratus." *Art Bulletin* 23: 16–44.

Ling, Roger. 1979. "Hylas in Pompeian Art." *Mélanges de l'École française de Rome* 91: 773–816.

Ling, Roger. 1991. *Roman Painting*. Cambridge, UK: Cambridge University Press.

Ling, Roger, and Lesley Ling. 2005. *The Insula of the Menander at Pompeii II: The Decorations*. Oxford: Oxford University Press.

Lorenz, Katharina. 2007. "The Ear of the Beholder: Spectator Figures and Narrative Structure in Pompeian Painting." *Art History* 30: 665–682.

Lorenz, Katharina. 2008. *Bilder machen Räume: Mythenbilder in pompeianische Häusern*. Berlin: De Gruyter.

Lorenz, Katharina. 2014. "The Casa di Menandro in Pompeii: Rhetoric and the Topology of Roman Wall Painting." In *Rhetoric in Roman Art*, edited by Jaś Elsner and Michel Meyer, 183–210. Cambridge, UK: Cambridge University Press.

Lowenstam, Steven. 1995. "The Sources of the Odyssey Landscapes." *Echos du monde classique: Classical Views* 39: 193–226.

Mattusch, Carol C., ed. 2011. *Johann Joachim Winckelmann: Letter and Report on the Discoveries at Herculaneum*. Los Angeles: J. Paul Getty Museum.

Mau, August. 1902. *Pompeii: Its Life and Art*. Translated by Francis W. Kelsey. 2nd ed. New York: Macmillan.

McNally, Sheila. 1985. "Ariadne and Others: Images of Sleep in Greek and Early Roman Art." *Classical Antiquity* 4: 152–192.

Mazzolini, Donatella, Umberto Pappalardo, and Romano Luciano. 2004. *Domus: Wall Painting in the Roman House*. Los Angeles: J. Paul Getty Museum.

Newby, Zahra. 2009. "Absorption and Erudition in Philostratus *Imagines*." In *Philostratus*, edited by Ewen Bowie and Jaś Elsner, 322–342. Cambridge, UK: Cambridge University Press.

Newby, Zahra. 2011. "Displaying Myths for Roman Eyes." In *A Companion to Greek Mythology*, edited by Ken Dowden and Niall Livingstone, 265–281. Chichester, UK: Blackwell.

Pappalardo, Umberto. 2009. *The Splendor of Roman Wall Painting*. Los Angeles: J. Paul Getty Museum.

Perry, Ellen. 2002. "Rhetoric, Literary Criticism, and the Roman Aesthetics of Artistic Imitation." In *The Ancient Art of Emulation: Studies in Artistic Originality and Tradition from the Present to Classical Antiquity*, edited by Elaine K. Gazda, 153–172. Ann Arbor: University of Michigan Press.

Perry, Ellen. 2005. *Aesthetic of Emulation in the Visual Arts of Ancient Rome*. Cambridge, UK: Cambridge University Press.

Peters, Willem J. Th., ed. 1993. *La casa di Marcus Lucretius Fronto e le sue pitture*. Amsterdam: Thesis Publishers.

Phillips, Kyle M. 1966. "Perseus and Andromeda." *American Journal of Archaeology* 72: 1–23.

Platt, Verity. 2002. "Viewing, Desiring, Believing: Confronting the Divine in a Pompeian House." *Art History* 25: 87–112.

Pollitt, Jerome J. 1990. *The Art of Ancient Greece: Sources and Documents*. Cambridge, UK: Cambridge University Press.

Reinach, Salomon. 1922. *Répertoire de peintures Grecques et Romaines*. Paris: Éditions Ernest Leroux.

Richardson, Lawrence, Jr. 1955. *Pompeii: The Casa dei Dioscuri and Its Painters*. Memoirs of the American Academy in Rome 23. Rome: American Academy.

Richardson, Lawrence, Jr. 2000. *A Catalog of Identifiable Figure Painters of Ancient Pompeii, Herculaneum, and Stabiae*. Baltimore, MD: Johns Hopkins University Press.

Smith, R. Scott, and Stephen M. Trzaskoma. 2007. *Apollodorus' "Library" and Hyginus' "Fabulae": Two Handbooks of Greek Mythology*. Indianapolis, IN: Hackett.

Thompson, Mary Lee. 1960. "Programmatic Painting in Pompeii: The Meaningful Combination of Mythological Pictures in Room Decoration." Diss. New York University.

Thompson, Mary Lee. 1961. "The Monumental and Literary Evidence for Programmatic Painting in Antiquity." *Marsyas* 9: 36–77.

Trimble, Jennifer F. 2002. "Greek Myth, Gender and Social Structure in a Roman House: Two Paintings of Achilles at Pompeii." In *The Ancient Art of Emulation: Studies in Artistic Originality and Tradition from the Present to Classical Antiquity*, edited by Elaine K. Gazda, 225–248. Ann Arbor: University of Michigan Press.

von Blanckenhagen, Peter H. 1963. "The Odyssey Frieze." *Mitteilungen des Deutschen Archäologischen Instituts, Römische Abteilung* 70: 100–146, pls. 40–53.

von Blanckenhagen, Peter H. 1968. "Daedalus and Icarus on Pompeian Walls." *Mitteilungen des Deutschen Archäologischen Instituts, Römische Abteilung* 75: 106–143 and pls. 27–47.

von Blanckenhagen, Peter H., and Christine Alexander. 1962. *The Paintings from Boscotrecase*, with an Appendix by Georges Papadopulos. Heidelberg: F. H. Kerle.

von Blanckenhagen, Peter H., and Christine Alexander. 1990. *The Augustan Villa at Boscotrecase*. With Joan R. Mertens and Christel Faltermeyer. Mainz, Germany: P. von Zabern.

Zevi, Fausto. 1964. *La Casa Reg. IX.5.18–21 a Pompei e le sue pitture*. Rome. L'Erma di Bretschneider.

# CHAPTER 36

......................................................................................................

# RETELLING GREEK MYTHS
# ON ROMAN SARCOPHAGI

......................................................................................................

## ZAHRA NEWBY

MUCH of this handbook is concerned with the ways that myths were retold and interpreted in literary sources, but myths were also communicated through visual means, and art often tells its own versions of these stories and plays off against literary, theatrical, oral, and mythographical traditions.[1] This chapter will focus on the mythological narratives that decorated Roman sarcophagi of the 2nd to 3rd centuries CE and consider how they might be read and understood in relation to the wider framework of mythography.

As this handbook shows, mythography can be broadly divided into two types: *systematic* mythography, which collects and organizes myths into coherent accounts, and *interpretative* mythography, which seeks to explain myths by rationalizing them or by reading them as allegories of philosophical or ethical truths. How do mythological sarcophagi fit within this framework, and what sorts of mythography do they offer? In fact, though it is not discussed in these precise terms, this question lies at the heart of a debate over the significance of mythological sarcophagi that took place in the 1940s between two eminent historians of religion, Franz Cumont and Arthur Darby Nock. Cumont (1942) read the myths that appear on sarcophagi as complex allegories for the fate of the soul after death. Nock's (1946) review of Cumont rejected his eschatological interpretations and argued that the primary aim was to assert the classicism and culture of the deceased. In mythographical terms, Nock favored a systematic, narrative view of the sarcophagi, whereas Cumont suggested an interpretative, allegorical one. Where, then, does modern scholarship place them?

It is important, perhaps, to start with a caveat. Mythological sarcophagi are not primarily mythographic, because their primary focus is not on myth per se, nor do they

[1] I would like to thank the editors for inviting me to contribute to this handbook, and for their thoughtful critiques which have improved this chapter. All errors remain my own.

aim to retell myth for its own sake. Rather, their use of myth must be seen within the funerary context of the images; here myth is deployed, among a range of other options, because of the opportunities it afforded both to remember particular qualities of the deceased and to alleviate the grief of the bereaved. Yet with this important fact in mind, it is still useful to think about mythological sarcophagi within the wider framework of mythography. Just as individual mythographers arranged their material to best suit their own purposes (whether systematic or interpretative), so, too, we can see the artists of mythological sarcophagi as involved in a process of selection, organization, and interpretation by which the mythological stories were chosen, depicted, and reinterpreted in ways that suited the needs of their purchasers.

The funerary context in which these images functioned means that, on a general level, they inherently belong to the "interpretative" branch of mythography, reinterpreting myths to say something about the human, nonmythological realm. Yet much of this interpretation remains external to the image itself: it lies within the thought processes of the craftsman who depicted the image, the patron who selected it, and the viewers who saw it and made the connections to the deceased or their own sense of grief, or both. We can use other sources (such as funerary literature, rhetoric, or epitaphs) to try to recreate these thought processes and set the parameters for possible and likely reactions, but it is important to remember that this level of interpretation is distinct from that of the sarcophagus imagery itself. At a visual level, we can find imagery that spans the whole range from systematic to interpretative mythography, depending on how the myths are depicted, the number of scenes included, and the placing of particular myths together to create specific sorts of links.

## 1. THE SCOPE OF THE MATERIAL

Mythical stories appear in funerary contexts from the earliest periods, on vases as well as sarcophagi. A sarcophagus dated to the late 6th century BCE, found in the Troad, was decorated with the sacrifice of Polyxena, perhaps as a fitting gesture of homage to the man buried within (Neer 2012; Draycott 2018). Mythological episodes also appear on Etruscan sarcophagi and, especially, on cinerary urns in the Hellenistic period (van der Meer 2004; Brilliant 1984: 43–52). However, the 2nd and 3rd centuries CE saw an explosion of interest in the depiction of mythological stories in the funerary sphere, particularly on the marble sarcophagi produced in the workshops of Rome and Athens.

Stone sarcophagi were produced all over the Mediterranean world in the Roman imperial period. Three major centers of production were based at Rome, Athens, and Dokimeion in Asia Minor, but there were also numerous other local workshops (Russell 2013: 256–310). Sarcophagi roughly divide into three main types: garland, frieze, and columnar, and mythological scenes can feature on all of these—in the vignettes above garland swags, as we see on the Theseus and Ariadne sarcophagus discussed below, or in statuary figures placed within columnar arcades, which can sometimes collectively present a narrative, as on sarcophagi featuring the Labours of Heracles (Jongste 1992: 109–124). The majority of mythological narratives, however, appear on frieze sarcophagi.

Frieze sarcophagi were produced in large numbers by workshops based in the city of Rome, and in lesser numbers by the workshops in Athens. Generally speaking, they were less common in Asia Minor, where columnar and garland sarcophagi were more popular, though one exception is discussed at the end of this chapter. Sarcophagi from Rome sometimes carry nonmythological scenes, such as hunting scenes, philosophers, or biographical scenes, but myth was a very popular option, particularly from the 2nd to mid-3rd centuries. The Attic frieze sarcophagi are almost exclusively mythological in subject matter, though the themes that were chosen and their depiction differ significantly from those of the sarcophagi produced at Rome. A much smaller range of myths are depicted (around 20, in contrast to around 50 at Rome: Ewald 2004: ills. 1 and 2; see also Ewald 2018), and they tend to favor single synoptic scenes rather than continuous narration. Another difference is the absence of portrait heads. From the late 2nd century CE, mythological figures frequently sport portrait features on sarcophagi produced in Rome, but not on those from Athens.

Of the surviving sarcophagi produced in Roman metropolitan workshops that we might broadly call "mythological," over two-thirds are decorated with generic depictions of a mythological realm, incorporating scenes of Erotes, marine creatures, or members of the Dionysiac *thiasos* (Zanker and Ewald 2012: 111–173). The rest, however, are decorated with narrative scenes drawn from around fifty different myths. During the earliest stages of production, a number of different myths appear on sarcophagi, either in vignettes above the swags on garland sarcophagi, or in frieze form (Junker 2005–2006). By the middle of the 2nd century, however, this experimentation had settled down, and though a number of different myths are still represented, they can mostly be seen as fitting into one of a limited range of themes, stressing either the violence of death, heroism, or marital *concordia* (Zanker and Ewald 2012). Scenes of sudden deaths or abduction include the rape of Persephone, but also the deaths of the Niobids, the death of Creusa, and the rape of the Leucippidae. Scenes of manly heroism, such as those found on the Meleager hunting sarcophagi, are complemented by the appearance of other hunting heroes in the myths of Adonis or Hippolytus, as well as in scenes of Heracles's Labours. The third major theme, that of marital devotion, can be expressed through the myth of Endymion, as well as in other mythological unions, such as those of Dionysus and Ariadne or Achilles and Penthesilea, or, in different form, by the myths of Alcestis and Laodamia, which combine expressions of grief at the death of the loved one with praise of conjugal loyalty. Here myth is used to discuss themes that resonate with the funerary context, and to offer analogies for human experience.

By the early 3rd century, sarcophagi seem to have become less narrative and more prone to excerpt particular elements, or to alter them to stress a specific interpretation of the myth, tying it closely to the individual being commemorated, sometimes through the addition of portrait features (for discussions linking this to the so-called demythologization, or *Entmythologisierung*, of sarcophagi, see Zanker and Ewald

2012: 249–260; Borg 2014: 237–240). In contrast, the desire to retell a narrative is much more pronounced on 2nd-century sarcophagi, particularly those which use contin-uous narration, where a series of different chronological episodes from a myth are presented next to one another. This change from narrative to excerption has been re-lated to a gradual increase in what is called *interpretatio Romana*, the process by which Greek myths were refigured and selectively represented to stress particular Roman values (Blome 1992, discussed by Bielfeldt 2005: 20–22; also Lorenz 2011: 309–311; Borg 2018: 170–173). While excerpted images often seem to privilege a particular reading of the myth above others, narrative retellings, too, could allow for interpretative responses to their myths, though as noted, at the level of the viewer, rather than embedded within the image itself.

# 2. From Systematic to Interpretative: Theseus on Two Roman Sarcophagi

To see how these different levels of narration, symbolism, and interpretation play out, I focus on a number of examples that map onto some of the different mythographical approaches. I start with two representations of the myth of Theseus, which show how visual retellings could vary from systematic or narrative to interpretative (Blome 1992).

Among the earliest sarcophagi produced in Rome is a garland sarcophagus, now in the Metropolitan Museum in New York City, dating around the 130s CE, showing the myth of Theseus and Ariadne (Fig. 36.1; Herdejürgen 1996: no. 23). In scenes running from left to right, the front of this sarcophagus depicts three episodes from the life of Theseus: Theseus receiving the thread from Ariadne, his victory over the Minotaur, and his abandonment of Ariadne. The three scenes chosen represent the key details of the myth, as it is also told in Hyginus (*Fab.* 42–43), and the reading from left to right encourages us to recall the chronological narrative of the myth.

This is one of the clearest examples of what we might call a "systematic" retelling of the myth, sticking closely to its core elements and depicting them in forms that are already well established in the visual tradition. Yet the choice of this myth in a funerary con-text suggests that it held meaning beyond the simple desire to retell the myth. Indeed, myths on sarcophagi often seem to be used as *exempla* of particular human values or experiences (Newby 2016: 273–319; Borg 2018). A funerary consolation by Statius written around thirty years earlier than this sarcophagus includes Theseus as a mythological paradigm for the beauty of the deceased youth (*Silvae* 2.6.25–6), while in Hyginus's the-matic lists "Theseus . . . whom Ariadne loved" appears in a list of handsome men (*Fab.* 270). This sarcophagus contained a skeleton of a man aged between thirty-six and fifty-five years (McCann 1978: 25); the choice of Theseus to decorate the chest may have been

**FIGURE 36.1.** Garland sarcophagus showing the myth of Theseus and Ariadne. New York, the Metropolitan Museum of Art, inv. 90.12a, b. Photo: www.metmuseum.org.

prompted by the desire to celebrate the deceased through comparison to a beautiful and courageous hero of Greek myth.

While the central scene establishes Theseus as a heroic figure noted particularly for his defeat of the Minotaur, the flanking scenes situate him in a more emotional context. To the left Ariadne is shown acting as a helpmate to the hero, mapping onto the visual prototype of the supportive wife that appears elsewhere on both mythological and "real life" sarcophagi. Theseus's departure through a doorway can also be read as an allegory for death, while the scene at the opposite end, in which he departs as Ariadne sleeps, has resonances with funerary epigrams and poems in which the bereaved imagine meeting their lost relatives in their dreams (*CIL* 6.18817; Statius, *Silvae*, 3.3.203–204). Theseus's departure here adds a bittersweet note, warning that such reunions can only ever be fleeting.

Here, a narrative depiction of the myth can also be seen to hold a funerary message, elevating the man buried inside by its rhetorical paradigm of the vigorous hero whose death tears him away from his loving wife. It is important to stress that this interpretative reading rests with the viewer rather than the relief itself. The narrative retelling allows us to see various resonances in the myth, from which we can select those most relevant to the funerary context. Some of these actually change the myth's core meaning by turning Theseus's abandonment of Ariadne into a metaphor for death, but the visual depiction itself sticks fairly closely to the traditional story.

The rewriting of Theseus's abandonment of Ariadne as a metaphor for bereavement is made much more explicit on a mid-3rd-century sarcophagus now in Cliveden, Buckinghamshire (Fig. 36.2; Zanker and Ewald 2012: 405–408, documentation no. 36). Here the front of the sarcophagus shows three scenes. To the left we see Theseus surrounded by his companions in a form that evokes scenes of other mythological

**FIGURE 36.2.** Frieze sarcophagus showing Theseus and Ariadne. Cliveden, UK. Photo: http://arachne.uni-koeln.de/item/objekt/4816.

heroes, such as Hippolytus embarking on the hunt, and suggests his physical prowess. In the middle, we see Theseus in his ship, departing from the sleeping Ariadne, and at the far right, he stands with his foot on the head of the defeated Minotaur.

There are some elements of the traditional myth here in the presence of the Minotaur and the boat, but this is not a systematic retelling of the myth such as that found on the garland sarcophagus. There is no clear sense of narrative order, and most strikingly, the heads of Theseus and Ariadne have been given portrait faces. An inscription on a lid that has been linked with the sarcophagus includes a dedication from a mother to her son, Artemidorus, who died shortly after his seventeenth birthday (*CIL* 15.4062). If the lid did belong to this sarcophagus, which seems likely, it suggests that Artemidorus was here equated with the beautiful and heroic Theseus through the use of portrait features, while the older features on the face of Ariadne would be those of his mother. A mother's grief is here compared with the grief of the abandoned Ariadne.

The same kind of distortion of the mythological "facts" to suit a new interpretation can be seen in a late 3rd-century sarcophagus in the Museo Nazionale Romano showing Hippolytus standing between the seated figures of Phaedra and Theseus (Fig. 36.3; Zanker and Ewald 2012: 348–350, documentation no. 18). Both Hippolytus and Phaedra are given roughed out faces, suggesting they were intended to evoke the person buried within and a bereaved relative. The pairing of Phaedra with Theseus, who does not appear on the earlier Hippolytus sarcophagi, presents them as proud parents, rather than lustful stepmother and irate father, and indeed the tablet brandished by Hippolytus seems to act more as a proclamation of his own *paideia* than the fateful letter left by Phaedra in Euripides' retelling of the myth (Euripides, *Hippolytus* 856-996).

In these two later sarcophagi we can see that the original details of the myths have receded in favor of a new interpretation. The erotic love stories are elided to focus instead on Theseus and Hippolytus as emblems of *virtus* and *paideia*, while the women who loved them turn from lovers to mothers, offering extreme metaphors for the grief

**FIGURE 36.3.** Sarcophagus showing Hippolytus between Phaedra and Theseus. Rome, Museo Nazionale Romano, inv. 112444. Photo: Felbermeyer, D-DAI-ROM 61.1417.

of bereavement. While earlier narrative versions of the myths provided the material for such interpretations, they operated in a more creative, open-ended fashion, providing mythological exempla that could be woven into a rhetorical encomium about the virtues of the deceased and the grief of the bereaved. The refocusing of these myths in the later sarcophagi suggests a concern to limit their messages to a particular focus and eliminate the aspects of the myth that did not suit that purpose.

# 3. THEMATIC GROUPINGS

In addition to the systematic retellings of myths that we find in mythographic texts, some also include separate lists of myths that group them together into particular categories, as at the end of Hyginus's *Fabulae*. Hyginus's groupings of dutiful children, faithful women, or close friends (*Fab.* 254, 256–257) can be compared with the thematic approach to historical exempla that we find in texts such as Valerius Maximus's *Memorable Doings and Sayings*. Although Valerius lists mostly examples from Roman history, there is some overlap between the two authors in both approach and detail. Thus, despite some differences in names, both Valerius and Hyginus include among their examples of pious children Cleobis and Biton and the daughter who suckled her father, Mycon, to save him from starvation (Valerius Maximus, *Memorable Doings and*

FIGURE 36.4.  Front of a sarcophagus showing the Rape of Persephone. Florence, Uffizi inv. 86. Photo: Singer, D-DAI-ROM 72.120.

*Sayings* 5.4 [ext.] 1, 4; Hyginus, *Fab.* 254). Hyginus includes Theseus and Pirithous in a list of loyal friends, whereas Valerius lists them only to reject their claims in favor of Roman exempla (Hyginus, *Fab.* 257; Valerius Maximus, *Memorable Doings and Sayings* 4.7.4). While Roman writers are often scathing about the exemplary power of figures from Greek myth as opposed to the role models offered by Roman history (for instance, Livy Preface 10), Hyginus's compilation of myths according to similar ethical categories shows that mythological figures could also be seen as exempla of the virtues esteemed in Roman society. Indeed, this is precisely the way we see myths being used on the sarcophagi.

While most sarcophagi choose to focus on a particular individual myth, a few put a number of analogous myths together as exempla of the same underlying value. This can be seen on a sarcophagus in the Uffizi Museum in Florence (Grassinger 1999: no. 81). The front of the sarcophagus is decorated with a scene of the Rape of Persephone, a powerful metaphor for the suddenness of death and the pain it leaves behind (Fig. 36.4). On the two short sides, however, scenes from two different myths were chosen. These showed, on the left, Hermes leading a draped female figure toward a rocky arch (Fig. 36.5), and on the right, Heracles leading another draped female out from a similar rocky arch (Fig. 36.6).

Comparison with other visual sources and the details of the myths leads us to identify these women as Laodamia, on the left, who chose to die to be reunited with her husband Protesilaus, and Alcestis, on the right, who despite her willingness to die in place of her husband, was restored to him by the hero Heracles. The three myths

FIGURE 36.5. Left short side of a Persephone sarcophagus showing Hermes and Laodameia. Florence, Uffizi inv. 86. Photo: Singer, D-DAI-ROM 72.127.

FIGURE 36.6. Right short side of a Persephone sarcophagus showing Heracles and Alcestis. Florence, Uffizi inv. 86. Photo: Singer, D-DAI-ROM 72.126.

**FIGURE 36.7.** Sarcophagus with myths of Mars and Rhea Silvia and Selene and Endymion. Vatican, Museo Gregoriano Profano inv. 9558. Photo: Rossa, D-DAI-ROM 74.535.

on this sarcophagus all share a link with the Underworld and suggest that while death can tear a person away from their loved ones (Persephone), it can also reunite them with those who have gone before (Laodamia). Yet the pairing of Laodamia and Alcestis also suggests another theme, that of the loyal wife who out of love for her husband will willingly meet her death. These two women appear in funerary epitaphs as examples of loyal wives (for example, *IG* 14.607; *CIL* 10.7563.78) and on Hyginus's list of faithful women (*Fab.* 256), and they frequently appear in funerary art (Newby 2011: 194–199; 2016: 240–254). Mythological sarcophagi are part of a wider general culture that was prepared to see mythological figures as moral exempla and to use them to praise the dead.

Hyginus occasionally inserts Roman figures into his mythological lists, putting Lucretia into his list of faithful women, and Romulus and Remus into those who were suckled by animals (*Fab.* 256, 252; see Smith and Trzaskoma 2007: xlviii-xlix; Fletcher, this volume). A similar thematic pairing of Greek and Roman myths can be seen in an early 3rd-century sarcophagus in the Vatican that puts together the story of Mars and Rhea Silvia with that of Selene and Endymion (Fig. 36.7; Sichtermann 1992: no. 99). Typologically, the myths are very similar as they both involve gods visiting sleeping mortals. The myth of Selene and Endymion is one of the most popular themes for sarcophagi and can be read as having a number of funerary resonances, evoking the un-dying love between the couple and Endymion's enduring youth and beauty, as well as the potential for everlasting life. We can see the sleeping Endymion either as the deceased, with death euphemistically compared to sleep, or as the bereaved, who is reunited with their lost love through their dreams (Koortbojian 1995: 63–113).

This multiplicity of messages was tied down on some sarcophagi by the addition of portrait features to either Selene or Endymion, or sometimes to both (Newby 2011: 205–209). On this sarcophagus the faces of Selene and Endymion are restored, but those of Mars and Rhea Silvia both wear portrait features, equating them with the individuals buried within. The woman's hairstyle dates to the early Severan period, while the man's is later, suggesting that she may have died first and that her husband commissioned the sarcophagi to express his enduring love for her and hope for reunion in death. The typological pairing with Selene and Endymion allows the myth of Mars and Rhea Silvia to evoke ideas of enduring love, which are not integral to the myth itself, and to present the deceased man in the model of the father of the Roman people, Mars. Here a Roman myth takes on some of the erotic connotations of Greek myths, while also keeping its power as a founding myth of the Roman state.

# 4. East-West Retellings of the Trojan War

We have seen how sarcophagi can systematically retell individual myths, sometimes selecting and combining myths as examples of particular thematic categories. On some occasions the visual retellings change the underlying myth quite extensively, turning Ariadne and Phaedra into embodiments of the grief of a bereaved mother rather than a wife or lover. Yet even when the visual retelling adheres more closely to the usual version of the myth, we can see the potential for interpretative readings that see the myths as allegories for the afterlife or expressions of grief and bereavement. Here I want to look at how the retellings of myths could vary depending on where they were produced and purchased, by focusing on three different retellings of events from the Trojan War.

A group of Attic sarcophagi show the scene of the ransoming of Hector, as seen on a sarcophagus found in a tomb near Igoumenitsa in Northern Greece (Fig. 36.8; Rogge 1995: no. 12). Priam kneels before the grieving figure of Achilles to the right, while in the center and left foreground the body of his son is shown still lashed to Achilles's chariot. Behind Hector's body is the wagon piled high with a ransom of Trojan treasure. This retelling closely corresponds with the version given in *Iliad* 24 and repeated in summary form in Hyginus *Fab.* 106 and Ps.-Apollodorus, *Epitome* 4.8. The overall effect of the representation is to evoke the world of Homeric heroism, where warriors die in battle, and to reinforce the importance of proper burial. The reference to Homer was probably a significant factor in the popularity of this scene. In Roman times, Athens could be seen as the cultural storehouse of all that was great about ancient Greece, and the sarcophagi seem to reflect and export this ideal of a Greek cultural identity based on the most important myths of the Greek past (Ewald 2004, 2018). This version of Greekness was not

FIGURE 36.8. Attic sarcophagus showing the ransoming of Hector. Ioannina Archaeological Museum inv. 6176. Photo: von Eickstedt, D-DAI-ATH-1993/266.

only for Athenians but reached an audience across the Mediterranean: in addition to this example from northwest Greece, others have been found in southern Greece, Asia Minor, and Tyre, as well as at Athens itself (Rogge 1995: 20–22).

By contrast, a sarcophagus from Ostia also retells the events from the last third of the *Iliad*, but with a different emphasis (Fig. 36.9; Grassinger 1999: no. 27). This unusual piece is generally accepted as being the product of a Roman metropolitan workshop; despite similarities with the later Attic sarcophagi, it shows clear iconographic parallels with other Roman products, such as the *Tabulae Iliacae*, which justifies seeing it primarily as a Roman creation (Giuliani 1989; Grassinger 1999: 43–48, contra Rogge 1995: 71–72).

Rather than the single episode favored on the Attic sarcophagi, the Ostian piece shows four separate scenes taken from the narrative of the Trojan War. To the right of the main chest Achilles sits at the deathbed of his companion Patroclus in a scene that has iconographical parallels with other mythological and "vita humana" death-bed scenes (see Lorenz 2011 on Meleager sarcophagi). The mythological death is related to the human situation of the bereaved mourning the loss of their loved one. To the left, we see Achilles's response to Patroclus's death, his rearming as he rejoins the fighting at Troy. Yet the scene can also be read at a generic level as a representation of an archetypal warrior preparing himself for battle and taking leave of his relatives. In this sense, as Giuliani (1989: 37) noted, we can read the front as two representations of the typical

**FIGURE 36.9.** Sarcophagus with scenes of Hector, Achilles, and Patroclus. Ostia Museum inv. 43504. Photo: Ministero dei Beni e delle Attività Culturali e del Turismo.

warrior: preparing for war on the left and being mourned in death on the right. While narratalogically the hero and the deceased are actually different people here (Achilles and Patroclus), visually, we can read them as being the same man; indeed, the fact that the arming man's face is obscured by his helmet encourages this ambiguity, since we cannot determine his identity by seeing whether he wore a beard (as Patroclus) or is beardless (as Achilles). This whole scene thus acts as a representation of heroic valor and the honor and grief such a hero deserves in death, besides alluding to the events of the *Iliad*.

If the scenes on the chest can be seen as both narrative and generic depictions, the lid returns specifically to the Homeric narrative. Here we see two scenes of the body of Hector: at the left, tied to the back of Achilles's chariot and, at the right, as it is being washed in preparation for burial following his ransom by King Priam. In the left-hand scene Hector is shown tied by his hands to Achilles's chariot, in contrast to the usual visual representations of the mutilation of his body, which show him tied by his feet. While the *Iliad* 22.396–398 specifies that Hector was tied by his feet, *Iliad* 24.14–16, where Hector's body is dragged around Patroclus's tomb, as here, is less precise. We should not, in any case, assume that the artist was working with a text of Homer at his elbow. Rather, the depictions of myths on sarcophagi probably relied on a variety of sources: the general oral tradition, retellings in the theatre and pantomime, and the long-standing visual representation of these scenes in art. Here, artistic concerns probably induced the artist to vary that tradition; positioned in this way, the body provides a symmetrical pendant to the scene opposite, where the corpse is being prepared for burial. Though here, too, we can seek out a literary source (*Il.* 24.582–590 has Achilles instructing his servants to clean Hector's body before it is to be released to Priam for burial), the scene also has an artistic function, providing a complement to the scene below and pairing the scene of grief with one of ritual washing.

Taken as a whole, then, this sarcophagus shows that tension between narrative and symbolic meaning that is so characteristic of Roman mythological sarcophagi. We may recall the Homeric narrative, but it is depicted in terms that encourage the viewer to see it as a clear analogy for the life of the deceased and the grief he leaves behind. This is not a consistent parallel narrative, since applying the myth to the deceased requires some chopping and changing of models—at one point, he is like Achilles, preparing for war, the next like Patroclus, or even Hector, being mourned and prepared for burial. Yet this is consistent with the flexibility with which we find mythological models being used in funerary consolations, or indeed in mythographical lists, where the same mythological story or figure could be used to represent a number of different categories.

My third example is a sarcophagus held at the Rhode Island School of Design, originally found in Rome (Fig. 36.10; Waelkens 1982: 35–36, no. 6; Van Keuren, Gromet, and Herz 2009: 163–167; Strocka 2017: 76–77). Dated to around 155–160 CE, it is made from Dokimeion marble and belongs to the small group of Dokimeion frieze sarcophagi, many of which were produced for export. The sarcophagus front shows the death of Hector. To the left are two warriors fighting—the beardless Achilles and the bearded Hector—and in the middle we see the dragging of Hector's body around the walls of

FIGURE 36.10. Sarcophagus with the death of Hector. Rhode Island School of Design Museum, 21-074. Photo: Erik Gould, courtesy of the Museum of Art, Rhode Island School of Design, Providence.

Troy, preceded by the goddess Athena and watched by the aged Priam. To the right is the seated figure of a mourning woman, Hector's wife Andromache. She seems isolated, lost in her grief, the cause of which is depicted before her.

This is the only surviving depiction we have of this particular version of the story, though a similar scene is shown in a drawing of a Roman sarcophagus known in the 16th century (Grassinger 1999: cat. 29). Though this sarcophagus was produced in Asia Minor, the unusual iconography seems particularly tailored to Rome. It is notable that this version tells the story primarily from the Trojan side, perhaps to chime with Rome's Trojan ancestry.

The seated Andromache is the dominant figure, drawing us to interpret the myth through its effect on her. At the other end of the frieze, the bearded figure of Hector challenges Achilles, Hector's outstretched arm giving him a greater sense of vigour and heroism. The imagery calls us to applaud Hector's heroism and bewail the effect his loss has on his grieving widow Andromache. We see a similar focus on Hector in Hyginus's summary of the *Iliad* at *Fabulae* 106, which is, tellingly, entitled (though we do not know when), *Hectoris Lytra* ("The Ransoming of Hector"). Here, Hyginus describes Achilles dragging Hector's body around the walls of Troy, diverging from the Homeric account in which Achilles drags the body away from Troy and back to the Greek camp, thus instead following a tradition we can also find in Vergil, *Aeneid* 1.483, and in Euripides, *Andromache* 107–108. The city walls that appear on this sarcophagus might also be a reference to this alternative account.

The Hector and Andromache who appear so prominently on this sarcophagus can perhaps be read as archetypes for the Roman couple who bought the sarcophagus, whose heroism and grief are exalted by this comparison to the mythological figures of Hector and Andromache. Plutarch's *Life of Brutus* 23 includes a comparable anecdote of Brutus's wife Portia, who is said to have wept upon seeing a painting of Andromache taking leave of Hector because of the similarity to her own position. Here, the concentration on Andromache as the archetype of a grieving wife seems designed to appeal to a Roman taste for celebrations of marital love and devotion through mythological analogy, though it achieves this through a figural type that was also popular on other Asia Minor sarcophagi.

## 5. CONCLUSIONS

Mythological sarcophagi portrayed their subjects in a number of ways, sometimes presenting a single synoptic scene; at other times, presenting a more detailed narrative representation through the use of continuous narration. The appearance of a variety of different myths according to broader thematic categories can be likened to the lists that also appear in Hyginus, as well as to a rhetorical culture of the time that encouraged the presentation of historical or mythological figures as exempla of various virtues. Mythological sarcophagi selected from the wider corpus of myths those that could be particularly related to the funerary context, but individual retellings could also vary between more narrative versions, where the funerary message was left open for the viewer or purchaser to create, to those where the funerary symbolism was more explicitly conveyed by the use of particular visual techniques, such as adding portrait features, or by displaying comparable mythological stories together. Both types of sarcophagi, however, show the pervasive power of Greek myth in the Roman period as a means to think with and as a shared cultural language that could be adapted to suit both individual and societal concerns.

## FURTHER READING

The primary catalogues of mythological sarcophagi are those contained in the German corpus, *Die antiken Sarkophagreliefs*, begun by Robert (1897–1919), partly updated by Koch (1975) on Meleager; Sichtermann (1992) on Apollo–Graces; and Grassinger (1999) on Achilles–Amazons. For a comprehensive overview of all sarcophagi, Koch and Sichtermann (1982) is still useful. See Rogge (1995) and Oakley (2011) on the Attic sarcophagi and, for Asia Minor sarcophagi, the helpful overview and bibliography in Koch (2011), with Strocka (2017) on the Dokimeion sarcophagi. Zanker and Ewald (2012) provides an excellent interpretative study of the mythological sarcophagi.

For discussions of the allegorizing interpretations of mythological sarcophagi offered by Cumont (1942) and their rejection by Nock (1946), see Balty (2013). In recent decades, Koortbojian (1995) and Zanker and Ewald (2012) have shifted the focus to the analogies to the lives of the deceased that the myths presented and the consolation mythological stories offered to the bereaved families. The exemplary character of Roman mythological sarcophagi and their comparison to other forms of funerary commemoration are discussed in Newby (2014; 2016: 228–319; see also Borg 2018). On the contexts in which sarcophagi were viewed, see Meinecke (2014). The vibrancy of sarcophagi studies in current scholarship is shown in a number of excellent collections: Elsner and Huskinson (2011); the 2012 edition of the journal *RES, Anthropology and Aesthetics* (no. 61/62); and Galinier and Baratte (2013). Older views that located the iconographical origins of sarcophagi in illustrated manuscripts or picture books (for example, Weitzmann 1959; Schefold 1976) are now rejected in favor of more fluidity whereby artists could draw from a wide range of visual sources (for example, Jongste 1992: 13–31). However, there remains room for a comprehensive analysis of the visual and verbal sources from which sarcophagi artists drew, to complement a new focus on the practicalities of production (Russell 2013).

## REFERENCES

Balty, Jean-Charles. 2013. "Franz Cumont et l'Interprétation Symbolique des Sarcophages Romains, à près de Soixante Ans des *Recherches*." In *Iconographie funéraire romain et société: Corpus antique, approaches nouvelles?*, edited by Martin Galinier and François Baratte, 7–27. Perpignan, France: Presses Universitaires de Perpignan.
Bielfeldt, Ruth. 2005. *Orestes auf römischen Sarkophage*. Berlin: Reimer.

Blome, Peter. 1992. "Funerärsymbolische Collagen auf mythologischen Sarkophagreliefs." *Studi Italiani di Filologia Classica* 10: 1061–1073.

Borg, Barbara. 2014. "Rhetoric and Art in Third-Century CE Rome." In *Art and Rhetoric in Roman Culture*, edited by Jaś Elsner and Michal Meyer, 235–255. Cambridge, UK: Cambridge University Press.

Borg, Barbara. 2018. "No One Is Immortal: From Exemplum Mortalitatis to Exemplum Virtutis." In *Wandering Myths: Transcultural Uses of Myth in the Ancient World*, edited by Beate Dignas and Lucy Audley-Miller, 169–208. Berlin: De Gruyter.

Brilliant, Richard. 1984. *Visual Narratives: Storytelling in Etruscan and Roman Art*. Ithaca, NY: Cornell University Press.

Cumont, Franz. 1942. *Recherches sur le symbolisme funéraire des Romains*. Paris: P. Geuthner.

Draycott, Catherine. 2018. "Making Meaning of Myth." In *Wandering Myths: Transcultural Uses of Myth in the Ancient World*, edited by Beate Dignas and Lucy Audley-Miller, 23–70. Berlin: De Gruyter.

Elsner, Jaś, and Janet Huskinson, eds. 2011. *Life, Death and Representation: Some New Work on Roman Sarcophagi*. Berlin and New York: De Gruyter.

Elsner, Jaś, and Michel Meyer, eds. 2014. *Art and Rhetoric in Roman Culture*. Cambridge, UK: Cambridge University Press.

Ewald, Björn. 2004. "Men, Muscle and Myth: Attic Sarcophagi in the Cultural Context of the Second Sophistic." In *Paideia: The World of the Second Sophistic*, edited by Barbara Borg, 229–275. Berlin and New York: De Gruyter.

Ewald, Björn. 2018. "Attic Sarcophagi: Myth Selection and the Heroising Tradition." In *Wandering Myths: Transcultural Uses of Myth in the Ancient World*, edited by Beate Dignas and Lucy Audley-Miller, 23–70. Berlin: De Gruyter.

Galinier, Martin, and François Baratte, eds. 2013. *Iconographie funéraire romain et société: Corpus antique, approaches nouvelles?* Perpignan, France: Presses Universitaires de Perpignan.

Giuliani, Luca. 1989. "Achille-Sarkophage in Ost und West: Genese einer Ikonographie." *Jahrbuch der Berliner Museen* 31: 25–39.

Grassinger, Dagmar. 1999. *Die antiken Sarkophagreliefs XII: Die Mythologischen Sarkophage 1 Achill, Adonis, Aeneas, Aktaion, Alkestis, Amazonen*. Berlin: Mann.

Herdejürgen, Helga. 1996. *Die antiken Sarkophagreliefs VI. 2. Stadrömische und Italienische Girlandensarkophage: I. Die sarkophage des ersten und zweiten Jahrhunderts*. Berlin: Mann.

Jongste, Peter. 1992. *The Twelve Labours of Hercules on Roman Sarcophagi*. Rome: L'Erma di Bretschneider.

Junker, Klaus. 2005–2006. "Römische mythologische Sarkophage: Zur Entstehung eines Denkmaltypus." *Mitteilungen des Deutschen Archäologischen Instituts, Römische Abteilung* 112: 163–187.

Koch, Guntram. 1975. *Die antiken Sarkophagreliefs XII: Die Mythologischen Sarkophage 6. Meleager*. Berlin: Mann.

Koch, Guntram. 2011. "Sarcofagi di età imperiale romana in Asia Minore: Una sintesi." In *Roman Sculpture in Asia Minor*, edited by Francesco D'Andria and Ilaria Romeo, 9–29. *Journal of Roman Archaeology* Supplement 80.

Koch, Guntram, and Hellmut Sichtermann. 1982. *Römische Sarkophage: Handbuch der Archäologie*. Munich: Beck.

Koortbojian, Michael. 1995. *Myth, Meaning, and Memory on Roman Sarcophagi*. Berkeley: University of California Press.

Lorenz, Katharina. 2011. "Image in Distress? The Death of Meleager on Roman Sarcophagi." In *Life, Death and Representation: Some New Work on Roman Sarcophagi*, edited by Jaś Elsner and Janet Huskinson, 309–336. Berlin and New York: De Gruyter.

McCann, Anna. 1978. *Roman Sarcophagi in the Metropolitan Museum of Art*. New York: Metropolitan Museum of Art.

Meinecke, Katharina. 2014. *Sarcophagum posuit: Römische Steinsarkophage im Kontext*. Sarkophag-studien 7. Wiesbaden: Franz Philipp Rutzen.

Neer, Richard. 2012. "'A Tomb Both Great and Blameless': Marriage and Murder on a Sarcophagus from the Hellespont." *RES: Anthropology and Aesthetics* 61–62 (spring–autumn): 98–115. https://www.jstor.org/stable/23647823.

Newby, Zahra. 2011. "In the Guise of Gods and Heroes: Portrait Heads on Roman Mythological Sarcophagi." In *Life, Death and Representation: Some New Work on Roman Sarcophagi*, edited by Jaś Elsner and Janet Huskinson, 189–227. Berlin and New York: De Gruyter.

Newby, Zahra. 2014. "Poems in Stone: Reading Mythological Sarcophagi through Statius' Consolations." In *Art and Rhetoric in Roman Culture*, edited by Jaś Elsner and Michal Meyer, 256–287. Cambridge, UK: Cambridge University Press.

Newby, Zahra. 2016. *Greek Myths in Roman Art and Culture: Imagery, Values and Identity in Italy, 50 BC–AD 250*. Cambridge, UK: Cambridge University Press.

Nock, Arthur Darby. 1946. "Sarcophagi and Symbolism." *American Journal of Archaeology* 50: 140–170.

Oakley, John. 2011. *Die attischen Sarkophage: III: Andere Mythen*. Berlin: Mann.

Robert, Carl. 1897–1919. *Die antiken Sarkophagreliefs III: Einzelmythen*. Berlin: Mann.

Rogge, Sabine. 1995. *Die attischen Sarkophage. I: Achill und Hippolytos*. Berlin: Mann.

Russell, Ben. 2013. *The Economies of the Roman Stone Trade*. Oxford: Oxford University Press.

Schefold, Karl. 1976. "Bilderbücher als Vorlagen römischer Sarkophage." *Les Mélanges de l'École française de Rome—Antiquité* 88: 759–814.

Sichtermann, Hellmut. 1992. *Die antiken Sarkophagreliefs XII: Die Mythologischen Sarkophage 2. Apollon-Grazien*. Berlin: Mann.

Smith, R. Scott, and Stephen Trzaskoma. 2007. *Apollodorus' "Library" and Hyginus' "Fabulae": Two Handbooks of Greek Mythology*. Indianapolis, IN: Hackett.

Strocka, Volker M. 2017. *Dokimenische Säulensarkophage: Datierung und Deutung*. Bonn: Dr. Rudolf Habelt GmbH.

van der Meer, L. Bouke. 2004. *Myths and More on Etruscan Stone Sarcophagi (c. 350–c. 200 BC)*. Louvain: Peeters.

Van Keuren, Frances, L. Peter Gromet, and Norman Herz. 2009. "Three Mythological Sarcophagi at the RISD Museum: Marble Provenances and Iconography." In *Asmosia VII: Actes du VIIe colloque international de l'ASMOSIA*, edited by Yannis Maniatis, 159–173. Athens, Greece: Bulletin de Correspondence Hellénique Supplément 51.

Waelkens, Marc. 1982. *Dokimeion: Die Werkstatt der repräsentativen kleinasiatischen Sarkophage, Chronologie und Typologie ihrer Producktion*. Berlin: Mann.

Weitzmann, Kurt. 1959. *Ancient Book Illumination*. Cambridge, MA: Harvard University Press.

Zanker, Paul, and Björn Ewald. 2012. *Living with Myths: The Imagery of Roman Sarcophagi*. Translated by Julia Slater. Oxford: Oxford University Press.

# PART V

## CHRISTIAN MYTHOGRAPHY

# CHAPTER 37

## MYTHOGRAPHY AND CHRISTIANITY

### JENNIFER NIMMO SMITH

## 1. CONTEXT

CHRISTIANITY, beginning with Joseph's registration in Bethlehem of Judaea, had always engaged with the Graeco-Roman world, if on its own terms (van Nuffelen 2011: 22, 217–219). Its writings, from Paul's letters onward, were written in *koine*, the Greek of the Eastern Roman Empire, into which an earlier version of the Hebrew Bible was translated from the late 3rd century BCE. The Septuagint played a vital part in preserving the identity of Hellenized Jews and in forming the New Testament (Rajak 2009; Law 2013). Paul, a Hellenized Jew of the Diaspora, was born in Tarsus, in Cilicia, and educated in rabbinical studies in Jerusalem. Knowing both Hebrew and Aramaic, he often used citations of and references to the Septuagint, with its other Greek versions, in his letters. His powerful eloquence (Cameron 1991: 33) has raised questions about whether he had training in classical culture (Hock 2003) in addition to a contemporary Hellenistic Jewish education (Hengel 1991: 54–62; Donaldson 2001: 1077). His citation from the classical poet Aratus, "for we are also his (God's) offspring" (Acts 17:28), however, was balanced by warnings against philosophy in Colossians 2:8; "myths" were proscribed in his and Peter's letters. The long-standing philosophical theme of the "two ways" is nevertheless found in Matthew 7:13–14 (Rochette 1998: 106 n. 12) and a possible influence from Euripides's *Bacchae* is suggested in Acts (MacDonald 2013).

First-generation Christian converts, then, who had attended both the general and more specialized courses of the Hellenistic educational system in the East and West alike (see Smith and Trzaskoma, this volume, on education), used this as common ground to defend and promote their new faith from the 2nd century on, in a world of many idols (Watts 2015: 17–36). Trained as they were in grammar and rhetoric, they could supplement Paul's attacks on idolatry in Romans with detailed lists of examples; they developed arguments of their own based on their knowledge of classical and Hellenistic history and literature and the long-standing debates of philosophers on the nature and even the existence of the divine (Whitmarsh 2015).

They were also convinced that the Olympian gods and heroes—the foundational figures of a mythological system that served as the basis of Greek and Roman cults, history, and literature (Burkert 985: 1–9)—had originally been humans and were deified for performing deeds that benefited mankind. This *euhemerism*, to use the modern term, is named after Euhemerus of Messene (late 4th–early 3rd c. BCE), although his *Sacred History* was written to explain the origins of religion and cults without any satirical or atheistic intent (Winiarczyk 2013). Euhemerism (see Hawes, this volume, "Rationalizing and Historizing") was an attractive interpretative strategy. Based on the idea that Zeus was but a mortal who had been deified because of his civilizing deeds, it served as a convenient method for denying pagan gods divine status—a theory that influenced the later account of the origin of idols in the Wisdom of Solomon, 14:12–31 (2nd c. BCE on), where a father's grief caused a commemorative statue of his dead son to become worshipped as a god (Horbury 2001: 664). Euhemerus's work exists only in fragments collected by Eusebius from Diodorus Siculus; the Latin Christian Lactantius preserved fragments of a Latin translation made by Ennius (Winiarczyk 1991: T10). Some Christian writers knew of him only as an atheist.

Another key principle was that the learning of Greek was dependent on the Hebrew Bible because of the priority of the Jews. This notion had been promoted by Hellenistic Jews from the 2nd century BCE and by Josephus (1st century CE; see Goodman 1999: 48), and it is possibly mentioned in the works of the Jewish philosopher Philo of Alexandria (15 BCE–50 CE; see Runia 1995: 60–61). The Christians developed the theory to establish the priority of their faith (Droge 1989: 47–48 n. 115; Ridings 1995: 24–28; Boys-Stones 2001: 80, 179–181). Related to this theme is the later argument that Christians were justified in making careful use of pagan learning (the so-called spoiling of the Egyptians) in their religious studies (Beatrice 2007; Allen 2008).

Some also adopted Philo's frequent use of allegory in interpreting the scriptures (Runia 1993). This well-known ancient, classical, and Hellenistic interpretative approach—saying one thing while meaning another—could be and was very controversial, despite its employment by Paul in his explanation of the relationship between the Old and New Covenants, in Galatians 4:24 (Pépin 1976: 249; Barclay 2001: 1162–1163; Edwards 1999a: 68–69; on allegory in general, see Ramelli, this volume). Other rhetorical tropes included personification, long found in the Old Testament, as well as in classical literature.

Christian writers used a variety of terms to describe those whom they sought to convert: Greek speakers (although, from 212 CE onward, all were Romans) were called "Greeks/Hellenes" or "gentiles," "polytheists" or "those from outside;" those who spoke Latin were known as "gentiles" or, with contempt "the profane." Tertullian acknowledged that Greeks could be counted among Romans "in regard to their superstition" (*To the Gentiles*, 1.8.11–12), but he could also (*On the Crown* 11.1) contrast a *paganus* (civilian) with a *miles* (Christian soldier) (Lane Fox 1986: 31; Salzman 2008: 186–192; Shorrock 2011: 3–8). He described non-Christian literature as "secular" (*On the Crown* 7.3). The term "pagan" occurred regularly in Latin from the mid-4th century, and I employ it here, unless Greek religion and philosophy are specifically mentioned, for non-Christian and non-Jewish believers in general (Cameron 2011: 314–332; but see Versnel 2011: 24 n. 3). The nomenclature of Greek or Roman deities used in the chapter will follow the linguistic practice of the individual writers.

# 2. CHRISTIAN WRITERS: A CHRONOLOGICAL SURVEY

One of the first Christian writers to address the question of myth was the Athenian philosopher Aristides (2nd c. CE), whose work survived in later Greek and in Syriac and Armenian versions (Grant 1988: 36–39, 195 n. 32; Pouderon 2005: 121–125). Aristides's simple but effective (as a rallying cry to Christians, at least) *Apology* was presented first to Hadrian, and then to Antoninus Pius. It rejected the barbarian belief that idols, elements, natural phenomena, and especially mortal men of the past, formed from the earth and with all their human failings, were gods. A general account of the cruelty, immorality, jealousy, and incestuous behavior of the Homeric gods preceded a detailed, formulaic set of statements and rhetorical questions about each of them in turn, points that recurred, in different presentations, throughout Christian polemic. This Christian account of the Olympian gods reflected Aristides's own learning and the rationalizing Homeric scholarship of the Hellenistic philosophical schools. He described the sacrifice of children to Cronos, who devoured his own, and his castration by Zeus (instead of Uranus by Cronos) before imprisoning him in Tartarus. How could a god devour his own children and be mutilated and imprisoned? He listed Zeus's well-known metamorphoses into many forms to seduce women and a boy, Ganymede, and his many children by these women—how could it be acceptable for a god be an adulterer, homosexual, or a parricide? Hephaistos was criticized for having an occupation and being lame; Hermes, for being a magician, thief, greedy, deformed, and an interpreter; Asclepius's skill as a doctor could not save him from death. The evils the Greeks attributed to their gods could only lead to corrupt and evil behavior by men.

Another convert, Justin Martyr, born in Samaria, taught in Rome, where he was martyred between 165–168 CE. He wrote two apologies in Greek, addressed to the Roman emperor Antoninus Pius. The first began with an appeal to reason (*logos*; also, Greek: "a word"; see John 1.1–5), which demanded that "all who are truly pious and philosophers . . . should respect the truth." After condemning all the Greek deities as demons (*Apol.* 1.5.3, 2.10.6, with possibly the first Christian reference to Pl. *Ti.* 28c; Geffcken 1907: 174–175), as Socrates himself had, he gave a selection of myths about Zeus and his sons similar to that of Aristides, but with the aim to establish parallels between Christianity and paganism. The Christians' morality and virtue, now that they no longer believed in such gods, was emphasized (Knust 2006: esp. 89–94), although later, in

*Apology* 2, he cited Xenophon's well-known account of Heracles's encounter with Virtue and Vice at the fork in the road to emphasize the importance of moral choice among both pagans and Christians (*Apol.* 2.11.6–8). Taking further analogies from Hermes (the messenger of the gods), the conception of Perseus, and the divine healer, Asclepius, he argued that what he said about Christianity was true because it had been predicted in prophecies and episodes in the Old Testament (*Apol.* 1.31–53), composed long before any works of the Greek writers. His chronology had great influence on his successors (Droge 1989: 49). Aspects of the myths—for example, Dionysus's discovery of wine, Bellerophon's flight on Pegasus, Perseus's virginal birth, and Asclepius's raising of the dead—were, in fact, copied from these prophecies (54).

Tatian, another Christian convert, born in Assyria, who had known Justin in Rome, took up the theory. In his *Oration to the Greeks*, he showed more admiration of the barbarians than did Aristides, for he attributed all the discoveries of Greek civilisation to them (*Ad Gr.* 1–2), and he criticized the Greeks, first, for their different dialects, and then for the contradictions within their philosophies. In his selection of the Greek deities, which, following Justin (8.3–5), he described as demons, he sarcastically focused on their differences: Rhea promoted castration, whereas Aphrodite was married; Artemis was a magician, Apollo, a healer; Athena and Asclepius divided the drops of Medusa's blood, the first for murder, the other for healing. He alone identified the omphalos at Delphi as Dionysus's tomb (though the latter was said to have been buried on Mount Parnassus) and he mockingly echoes the initiates' cry at Eleusis (*Orphicorum Fragmenta I (XXIII)*; compare *Orphicorum Fr.* 74; see Burkert 1985: ch. 6.1.4). Tatian lists more absurdities: Were the heavens empty before the catasterisms of Erigone's dog, Artemis's scorpion, Chiron, half the Argo, and Callisto's bear? Why were some *not* elevated to the heavens (9)? Then there are the absurd metamorphoses of the gods, including an otherwise unknown one in which Rhea changes into a tree (10). Tatian's diatribe ended with chronological proofs of the priority of Moses from Greek evidence about the Trojan War, including from Herodotus (29–31), and then from Chaldaean, Phoenician, and Egyptian historians, and lists of Argive and Attic kings (36–41).

Athenagoras of Athens addressed his *Plea for the Christians* to Marcus Aurelius and Commodus, "conquerors . . . and, more than all, philosophers," in 177 CE, to persuade them that the accusations of atheism, Thyestean meals, and incest against the Christians were unjust. He dismissed the Greek poets' and philosophers' opinions about the gods as conjecture, in comparison with the divinely inspired revelations of the prophets (*Leg.* 4–7). In ch. 17, he stated that the Greek gods were mere men whose names and genealogies had been invented, first by Orpheus, then by Homer, Hesiod, and Herodotus. With details from one of the Orphic theogonies (West 1983: 6, *Orphicorum Fr.* 69–89; Herrero de Jáuregui 2010: 167–171, 385–387) he described how a three-headed dragon, created from water and mud, emerged and produced an egg, from which, in turn, came Uranus and Ge, the parents of the Fates, the giants with a hundred hands, the Cyclopes, and Argos, who rebelled against their father. When Uranus sent them down, bound to Tartarus, Ge then bore the Titans. In another passage, he described their monstrous and ridiculous forms and their deeds: Cronus's and Zeus's mutilation and imprisonment of their respective fathers, Cronus's murder of his children, and Zeus's taking the shape of a dragon and raping Rhea when she fled from him as a dragon, and his fathering of Dionysus on Persephone, again as a serpent. Was there any reverent or worthy reason in such accounts for their divinity? Who could believe that the firstborn god of all could father a serpent? Further proofs of the Olympian gods' human passions showing that they could not be divine were presented in an elegant dialogue in 21 (Zeegers-Vander Vorst 1972: 320 n. 2). In ch. 32, he returned to Zeus's incest with his mother, sister, and daughter, behavior far worse than that of Thyestes, and compared it with the chastity and self-control of the Christians.

The *To Autolycus* of Theophilus, bishop of Antioch from 169 to 177, was written after 181 CE in three books and is framed as a conversation with a pagan friend. As in other texts already discussed, the first two books contain brief accounts of the gods as nothing more than deified dead men (1.8, 2.7, the latter pointing to a genealogy by Satyrus that traced a line from Bacchus to Ptolemy Philopator). In book 3, after rejecting all Greek poetry, history, and philosophy for its inconsistency and internal contradictions (3.3), Theophilus arraigns both Cronus and Zeus for devouring their children, and denounces the latter's incest and immorality, with reference to Chrysippus (*SVF* 2.1071–1075; Grant 1970: 110). This is followed by attacks on Jupiter Latiaris, Attis, and Antinous, among others (3.8). Theophilus's chronology proved the priority of Christian scriptures, with evidence from Plato, Josephus, the Old Testament, and a list of Roman rulers up to the death of Marcus Aurelius (3.27).

Clement of Alexandria (around 150–215), another convert, displayed a wide range of literary information about pagan mythology. His *Exhortation to the Greeks* was intended to call well-educated pagans to Christianity by a lengthy attack on the origins and rites of the mystery cults, in particular, and the general belief in pagan gods. Using a sustained comparison of the power of music in both pagan and Christian texts, he attributed the musical influence Amphion, Arion, and Orpheus exerted over nature and mankind to demons, who through them enticed men to idolatry and the celebration of crimes. He contrasted this with the "new song" (Ps 33.3 and elsewhere) of "his [bard]" (Christ) which brought forgetfulness of all ills (Homer, *Od.* 4.22) in 1.1–3. Whereas Athenagoras described the (Orphic) beginnings of the pagan gods, Clement gave detailed (and equally polemical) information about the mystery cults of Aphrodite, Deo, Demeter, Dionysus, the Corybantes, and Persephatta and their founders, foundation myths, rites, and sacred objects (2.12–22). The systematic, alphabetic arrangement of his material (and its similarities with earlier evidence of Orphic beliefs), led to the identification of its source as a handbook, derived from a Hellenistic Orphic theogony (Riedweg 1987: 120; Herrero de Jáuregui 2007, 2010). Clement's description of the fate of Dionysus, for example, is well-known: he is lured away from his guardians with toys and apples by the Titans, who then tear him apart and cook the fragments, except the heart, which is saved by Pallas Athene, until Zeus, lured by the smell, blasts the Titans with a thunderbolt and entrusts Apollo with the burial of the remains near Delphi; so, too, the account of how Baubo ended Demeter's mourning with her obscene gesture. Clement summed up these mysteries as those of atheists, celebrated in honor of gods who did not exist, as Euhemerus and others whom the pagans denoted atheists had recognized (2.23; Winiarczyk 1991: T20). Clement's account of the myth of Orpheus casts Orpheus as a poet and a hierophant of a "theology of idols," who later recanted, as Theophilus had noted (7.74, Bernabé OF 377 [III]; Herrero de Jáuregui 2010: 347), and he may have deliberately omitted Orpheus's descent into Hades in search of Eurydice and his death by violence to avoid an unacceptable parallelism with Christianity (Herrero de Jáuregui 2010: 247–248). Dionysus's descent to Hades and the salacious result of his safe return are, however, described in detail, with the reason for the *phalloi* set up in his honor at the rites in Halymous in Attica (2.34). Clement's later work, the *Miscellanies*, a collection of his notes for Christian converts, reproduced Tatian's chronology and also owed much to his pre-Christian studies in philosophy and the exegetic techniques of Philo (Runia 1993: 132–156).

The Latin Christian Tertullian (active around 160–240) was brought up a pagan in Roman Carthage, where he received an excellent education in both Latin and Greek (Barnes 1985: 187–210; Rives 1995: 274; Dunn 2004: 3–11). Soon after his conversion he wrote *To the Gentiles*, which rebuked the pagans for their unjustified contempt for the Christians. In book 1, he mocked the pagans' praise of Homer, who had lined the gods up against each other like gladiators in his poems, in which he described the wounding of Venus, the enchainment of Mars, and Jupiter's tears over the death of his son, Sarpedon, and the list of Jupiter's previous love affairs when he was overtaken by desire for Hera. The second book discussed Roman gods and heroes, with much reference to the lost antiquarian work *On Divine Matters* of M. Terentius Varro (116–127 BCE), of which Tertullian had made his own abridgment (2.1.8; Cardauns T3; see Rüpke 2005). Tertullian dismissed Varro's threefold division of cults into philosophical, mythic, and civic—the philosophers could not agree; the poets were untrustworthy; and the people were confused and spoiled for choice. The Egyptian people had even chosen to worship animals, and the man they deified as the god Serapis was merely Joseph, as the ears of corn on his headdress showed.

At 2.9, with contemporary relevance (Price 1999: 124–126), Tertullian criticized the heroes the Romans worshipped for their nobility: the great hero Aeneas had been wounded in action and, worse, deserted his country; Romulus had founded a city, but he killed his brother and captured the Sabine maidens by guile. And why was the god of dung deified? Laurentia was nothing more than a prostitute (10). Varro's set of Roman gods, who attended every stage of life, from conception to adulthood and marriage (11), was savagely ridiculed, as were the varying opinions about Saturn, who committed incest and was a parricide and, as expected, a mere mortal (12.5–16). In the *Apology*, composed as Truth's formal defense statement before magistrates, he repeated his previous attack on the vile behavior of pagan gods described by the poets (14.2–15.4); and at ch. 19, he claimed that Moses and the prophets predated all the history and the culture of "your literature." Christ's pure incarnation was contrasted with Jupiter's incestuous and adulterous unions in various disguises (21).

Origen (185–254 CE), the biblical scholar and exegete, was the son of a Christian teacher of rhetoric, Leonides, who was martyred in Alexandria in 202: Origen himself died of his injuries after being tortured during the persecution under Decius in 254, in Tyre. The references to his "predecessors" in matters of allegorical scriptural exegesis in his works are taken to refer to Philo and Clement (Runia 1993: 182–183; see Ramelli, this volume, on Origen's importance). He first, in *Philocalia* 13, which is part of a collection of his writings associated with Gregory of Nazianzus and Basil of Caesarea (Elm 2012: 22, n. 23), encouraged the careful use of secular learning for Christians.

Eusebius, the ecclesiastical historian, theologian, and bishop of Caesarea (313–339 CE), and the Christian converts Arnobius and his pupil Lactantius, teachers of rhetoric in Sicca, in Roman North Africa, lived through the persecution of 303–311 and beyond. At the request of his local bishop, either during or well after the persecution, Arnobius composed *Against the Gentiles* in seven books to prove that his conversion was genuine (Simmons 1995; Edwards 2004; 2015: 33–39). He argued his case with the passion and breadth of learning of Tertullian, providing proof after proof from secular literature and philosophy, including the standby texts of Euhemerus (as he noted, translated into Latin by Ennius, *Adv. Nat.* 4.29; Winiarczyk 1991: T21), Cicero, and Varro in witty, sarcastic prose. Among Eusebius's many hostile mentions of the pagan gods, his juxtaposition of two myths stands out—a well-known local one from Rome, the story of Numa Pompilius's tricking Jupiter into accepting an onion, hair, and a small fish for a human head (Ov. *Fast.* 3.285–398), and the vivid description of the origins of the Phrygian cult of Attis (Bremmer 2004: 543–546; Alvar 2008: 64–68). He spared no detail in describing Jupiter's unsuccessful attempt to rape the Great Mother, the monster his semen engendered from the desolate rock, how Liber arranged the monster's self-castration, the subsequent birth of Attis, and the frenzied rites of the Phrygians (5.5–7). The briefer account of the other mystery cults (18–22) either owed much to Clement or was derived separately from a similar source (Herrero de Jáuregui 2010: 153–155). Eusebius is as outspoken as Clement about Dionysus's encounter with Prosymnus (28). His rejection of allegorical interpretation is absolute.

Lactantius, Arnobius's pupil, was summoned to teach rhetoric in Nicomedia under Diocletian, and was there converted to Christianity (Edwards 1999b; 2015: 20–28). He composed the *Divine Institutes*, also in seven books, though neither he nor Arnobius showed any knowledge of each other's work, out of indignation at the criticisms of Christianity made by pagan philosophers (Digeser 2012) and the persecution, after 303. The intellectual background he and Arnobius shared, however, stood them both in good stead. Lactantius intended his work to be an exposition of the truths of Christianity rather than an apology like Tertullian's. He wrote it in a discursive, Ciceronian style, with well-educated pagan readers in mind, and illustrated each point he made with careful references to both Latin and Greek authorities alike. Book 1, for example, which investigated the nature of pagan gods, began with his proof of the unity of the divine, drawn from the revelation of the prophets, but hastily laid aside to concentrate on passages from the poets Orpheus, Vergil, and Ovid about the creation of the world. The philosophers, he stated, dissented in the details but were basically in agreement, as were Hermes Trismegistus, the Judaeo-Christian Sibylline verses (which he associates with Varro's Sibylline Books), and the oracles of Apollo (Bowen and Garnsey 2003: 16–21;

Lightfoot 2012: viii–x, 81–93). There follows a by-now familiar polemic—a lively and satirical account of the crimes and inadequacies of the mortal gods and their cults, and he provides as many implicit or explicit parallel exempla for each episode as he can find. The inventors of these "silly superstitions" were men as well, he stated, Euhemerus (again, through Ennius: Winiarczyk 1991: T65) or Melisseus of Crete (from the commentary of Didymus on Pindar) and firmly dated, with reference to Theophilus, to 1800 years earlier.

Lactantius's enthusiasm for Vergil did not stop him from vigorous criticism of "pious Aeneas," who slaughtered even those who were begging him for mercy (5.10); in especial, his use of *Eclogue* 4, again with evidence from the Sybils, to show faint but true intimations of a golden age to come (7.24.11–12), however, had much influence on later Christian writings (Bowen and Garnsey 2003: 18).

Eusebius wrote the *Evangelical Preparation* to inform and encourage new converts to Christianity, both Jewish and gentile (Kofsky 2002: 76; Edwards 2015: 3–19), in the light of Constantine's conversion. Much is owed to his use of source material in his citations (Johnson 2014: 26–28). His account of Greek "theology" in book 2.1–51, however, was a skillfully summarized and modified adaptation of the mythology in Diodorus of Siculus's *Library*, books 3 and 4, to present a "formidable attack on paganism" (one not intended by Diodorus; see Inowlocki 2006: 91). He also preserved Diodorus's account of Euhemerus and copied in Clement's account of the mystery cults. Book 10 collected a set of similar extracts, from Clement and Tatian among others, to prove that though the Greeks had acquired most of their learning and polytheistic religion from the barbarians, it was from the Hebrews alone that their philosophers had learned of the worship of a supreme god (he had already established their priority to the Greeks in his *Chronicon*: see Barnes 1981: 106–120; Burgess 1997; Johnson 2014: 86–89).

In the mid-4th century, the Sicilian Julius Firmicus Maternus, a well-educated former lawyer and author of an eight-volume defense and explanation of astrology (around 334–337), wrote *On the Error of Profane Religions* as a Christian (Kahlos 2009: 87–93). He continued the earlier Christian attacks on pagan beliefs in mystery religions with great vehemence (Edwards 2015: 308–312) and called on the emperors, Constantius II and Constans, to ban pagan cults, based as they were on the deaths of mortals. In one euhemeristic account he described the murder of Liber, the son of Jupiter, the king of Crete, by the Titans at Juno's instigation and explained that they had cooked and eaten his body to hide the evidence of their crime and that Jupiter had preserved his heart (saved by Minerva) in a statue that was thereafter worshipped by the Cretans in sacred rites, including omophagy (*Err. Prof. Rel.* 6). The abduction of Proserpina by Pluto in Sicily turned the escape to Hades into a suicide and murder by drowning when Pluto, when he saw a hostile band in pursuit, drove his chariot into a deep lake; to comfort Demeter, the locals of Henna invented the story that her daughter had been carried off by the "king of the underworld" (7.4)—the first in a series of misinformation leading Demeter to sail to Greece to find her, with gifts of corn, for which she and her daughter were deified (7). In an imagined conversation, the sun, in an attack on solar worship, complained that he was identified as Osiris, Attis, and the Cretan Liber, and thus either castrated or murdered, then cooked in a pot or roasted in seven pieces on seven spits (8). The other mysteries, as in Clement and Arnobius, are linked with adultery, prostitution, and murder. Firmicus also listed the sins of the gods that encouraged men to commit adultery, incest, theft, murder, treachery, and cannibalism, in slightly less detail than his predecessors (12), and he identified Serapis in Alexandria as Joseph, the (great-grand-) child (*pais*) of Sara (13).

The restoration of pagan sacrifice and religion by the Emperor Julian between 361–363 ended with his death, and the legislation prohibiting the appointment of anyone who was not convinced of the moral value of classical literature to a state teaching post (his "teaching law"; *Cod. Theod.* 13.3.5) was soon reversed. Gregory of Nazianzus (330–389 CE), the son of a Christian mother, whose conversion of her pagan monotheistic husband, Gregory the Elder, resulted in the latter's appointment to the bishopric of Nazianzus, refashioned traditional antipagan arguments against Julian's beliefs (Demoen 1996; Elm 2012, with Kaldellis 2007: 154–165) in Sermons 4 and 5 (364–365 CE). His account of the "theology" of Orpheus in 4.114, like Clement's, transferred Baubo's gesture to the ritual of Demeter (*Orphicorum Fr. III*, 395 and added, or possibly invented, an otherwise unknown verse about Zeus (*Orphicorum Fr. III* 848). Pagan rites were contrasted with Christian ceremonies in *On Baptism* (39) in 381 CE, and pagan myths used in commemoration of his friend and fellow student in Athens, Basil of Caesarea, (43). Basil had less affection than Gregory for Athens (Rubenson 2006: 119–132), but his letter to young men, *On the Value of Greek Literature*, showed that his studies there had not been forgotten (Pelikan 1993: 176; Perrot 2012: xxx–liii). Basil's younger brother, Gregory of Nyssa, also praised the careful use of pagan learning (*Life of Moses*, 115), as did Jerome (Hagendahl 1958: 325–326), the great biblical scholar and translator of Origen and Eusebius, who had met Gregory of Nazianzus in Constantinople in 381.

By 392, the Emperor Theodosius I had banned all pagan sacrifices, public and private, and pagan cults. But the sack of Rome by the Arian Goths in 410 caused some Christians in the West to voice doubts about their faith. Augustine, bishop of Hippo in Africa (395–430 CE), the converted son of a Christian mother and a pagan father, who had been educated in Carthage and was a professor of rhetoric in Milan before his conversion (Brown 1967), began his great work of reassurance for the faithful and a call to conversion for those who were as yet uncommitted, the *City of God*, in 412/413. He completed it in 425, four years before the Vandals invaded Africa and laid siege to Carthage. In books 1–10, Augustine refined and expanded on the traditional themes of Christian polemic, with reference to Vergil's *Aeneid* for the Roman gods. For example, how could the Romans believe that gods who had "defaulted" from Troy would save Rome (*De Civ. D.* 1.3)? Why was Troy destroyed by the Greeks when it worshipped the same gods as the Greeks? Why was Paris's adultery punished but that of Venus with Anchises condoned (3.3)? Mention is made of Euhemerus's careful research before repeating the story of the guardian of Hercules's temple and his bet, "a disgraceful story" (6.7.4–5). Then there are the rites of Juno in Samos, of Ceres and her search for Proserpina, of Venus and Adonis, and Cybele and Attis, and the self-castration of the Galli, all more disgusting than any performance on the stage (6.7.6). Augustine considered that Varro knew of Attis's fate but chose not to mention it or the behavior of the Galli, lately seen with powdered faces and pomaded hair, extorting contributions from local shopkeepers in the streets of Carthage (7.25–26, Cardauns T 267). Their self-mutilation made Cybele's worship far worse than that of Jupiter with his sexual excesses and of Saturn, who swallowed his children. At 18.2–22, the first part of his chronology of Rome, based on Eusebius's *Chronicon* (as translated and continued by Jerome; Barnes 1981: 112–120), he included additions from Varro, and expanded on the Euhemeristic criticism of the pagan gods within it, already attacked in the earlier part of his work (O'Daly 2007: 184–195). He also, with reference to Lactantius, approved of the testimony of the Sibyl against false gods, and about the birth of Christ (23). In ch. 37, the statement that the "theological" poets Orpheus, Linus, Musaeus, and others preceded the Hebrew prophets (as noted in the *Chronicon*) is followed by the dating of Moses, and above all, Abraham, to before the Greeks (O'Daly 2007: 189).

In the East, the bishop and church historian Theodoret of Cyr (393–466 CE) was born a Christian in Antioch and used the extensive learning he had acquired in its schools (Millar 2007) in *A Cure for Hellenic Maladies*, an early work (around 420) addressed to well-educated pagans. It comprises twelve well-organized books and might have been intended as a manual (Papadogiannakis 2012: 139). Although much of his material against pagan beliefs and cults is drawn, without attribution, from Clement and Eusebius (Papadogiannakis 2012: 132–140), he interweaves them with great skill into his arguments. His accounts of the immoral behavior of the gods, for example, with the obscene details of the mystery cults, are not collected in a single book but repeated in various contexts (Halton 2013: 11). Vestiges of some cults even remain: locals still swore by Heracles, a man deified despite his immorality, which caused his death, and ceremonies were held in secret to Asclepius, another mortal, whose statues were coiled in a snake as a symbol of the curative powers of medicine (8.15–23). The phallic rites of Dionysus, son of Semele, already mentioned in book 1, were "passed over in silence" (8.24).

Such rites were not described by Nonnus of Panopolis (active 450–470 CE) in his forty-eight-book epic, the *Dionysiaca*, on the mythological exploits of Dionysus, who also composed the *Paraphrase of St. John the Divine* in the same meter (Chuvin 2014: 3–20; Agosti 2012: 367; Livrea 2003: 447–455). Such a work is undeniable proof that an interest in a modified version of mythography was felt to be compatible with Christianity, where polemic against Dionysus was so consistently featured.

Pseudo-Nonnus, the author of the early 6th-century *Commentaries on Sermons* 4, 5, 39 and 43 of Gregory of Nazianzus, showed a more down-to-earth association between Christianity and paganism. Originally anonymous, he was first identified as an "Abbot Nonos," in a slightly later hand, on the title of *Commentary* 39 in a 10th-century manuscript of the *Sermons*; but the subsequent association with Nonnus of Panopolis could not stand, in view of the very great disparity in learning and language between the texts (Nimmo Smith 1996; Accorinti 2016:37). As the collection and explanation of the *historiae* mentioned by St. Gregory (in *Sermons* 4 and 5, 39, and 43) show, his commentaries explain far more than myths. For the term *historia* is used to describe the account or story behind every historical, literary, mythical, or philosophical reference (Nimmo Smith 1992: 5 n. 17; Cameron 2004: 90–93). He established his aims in the

Proem to 4, which categorized the sermon as a denunciation, *stēliteutikos logos*, rather than an invective, *psogos*, "because it treats mainly of the actions (of the subject) with some comparisons" rather than the usual encomiastic topics of birth, upbringing, and actions (which Gregory, in fact, included), but led to an explanation for the use of stone or bronze markers (*stēlai*) upon which the noble or evil deeds of benefactors or of public enemies were engraved and displayed. He continues: "So much then for the theme (hypothesis), and as for the stories, we shall describe them in the best terms we can." It is followed by ninety-seven numbered paragraphs, each of whose titles cites the subject of each comment (some of which are multiple). There are thirty-five in *Com.* 5, twenty-four in *Com.* 39, and eighteen in *Com.* 43. Over half of these refer to classical literature, mythology, and pagan religion. All are written in a plain, repetitive style but make use of cross-references to avoid excessive repetition. His attitude to the pagan gods and their rites is, on the whole, dispassionate, even about the *phalloi* of Dionysus in 4.38 and 5.19, although at 39.2 he mentions "some most foolish Greeks" in the mountains of Caria, who still mutilated themselves in obedience to the Phrygian rites. He repeated Gregory's attribution of Baubo's obscene gesture to Demeter, and his mockery of an "Orphic" verse in 4.77. Only Zeus is alleged to be a man, and not a god, firstly in 5.25, because of his tomb in Crete, and secondly, in 39.1, because of "a common story, with which the holy Gregory agrees." His views on magic and demons are described elsewhere (Nimmo Smith 2006).

The *Commentaries* became popular and were translated into Syriac, Armenian, and Georgian. They were added to other scholia and commentaries on Gregory's works, taken over in full by Cosmas of Jerusalem (675–752 CE) in his *Commentary on the Poetry of Gregory of Nazianzus* (Lozza 2000; Nimmo Smith 2019), where the biblical references are also explained, and excerpted in the *Suda* (10th c. CE).

Fulgentius the Mythographer is now generally accepted as a different author from the anti-Arian Bishop Fulgentius of Ruspe in Africa, 468–533 (Hays 2003, 2013; Wolff 2008). Four interconnected works are attributed to him, the *Mythologies*, *The Exposition of the Content of Virgil according to Moral Philosophy*, *The Explanation of Obsolete Words*, and *On the Ages of the World and of Man*, a lipogrammatic history in twenty-three chapters, of which the first fourteen, A–O, survive (Hays 2004; Whitbread 1971). It is clear from these works that Fulgentius was a well-educated Christian with a wide knowledge of secular literature, both of the past and of his time, and a lively interest in languages, his native Libyan, Latin, Greek, and Hebrew. His works were previously dated to the late 5th to early 6th centuries; the present mid-6th-century date is not universally accepted (Wolff 2008; Wolff and Dain 2013: 10).

Book 1 of the *Mythologies* begins with a long, allusive, comic, and carefully structured prologue (Wolff and Dain 2003, 12–15), in which Fulgentius twice rejects mythological themes, first in preference to philosophy (3.16–4.7), and then—but after an invocation to the Muses and their arrival (7.5–8)—to expose them "so that once the fictional invention of lying Greece has been buried we might recognize what mystic meaning we ought to grasp within these stories" (11.16–18; see Albu 2009; Selent 2011: 53). Although the Muse Calliope mocked Fulgentius, she visited him in his bedchamber that night, accompanied by Thalia, Satyra, and Philosophia, to inspire him "with the higher doctrines of philosophy, not those from which poetry, tragedy, satire and comedy are derived" (15.1–6; see Relihan 1988). Calliope's first account was therefore of the origin of idols, derived from an otherwise unknown account of Diophantus of Lacedaemon (on Diophantus's sources, see Baldwin 1988; Hays 1996). A certain Syrophanes in Egypt set up an image (*eidolon*) of his dead son to which his slaves made offerings to avoid punishment ("with an appearance of grief," *eidos dolou*, 16, 17–18 an explanation employing an etymological approach, as is common in Fulgentius) rather than in worship. The next twenty-one chapters of book 1, beginning with Saturn, and, indeed, those in books 2 (sixteen chapters) and 3 (twelve chapters), all follow a similar formula: first Greek and Latin etymologies, followed by the story presented with allegories and rationalizing explanations, with frequent references to sources or citations, or both.

The Olympian gods, with their attendants and descendants, came first in book 1: the accounts increase gradually in length and complexity of the exegesis, and several several focus on the number three: 1.4 (Neptune), 1.6–1.9 (Cerberus, Furies, Fates, and Harpies). Chapter 15 described the nine Muses as representing, with Apollo, the ten organs of speech, the ten strings of his lyre, and the ten strings of a psaltery in the Bible. Fulgentius added his own explanation of the Muses as stages of learning and knowledge, using his own or accepted etymologies for their names. Chapter 22 ended the book with the fable of Admetus and Alcestis: "[W]hile there is nothing better than a kindly wife, there is nothing more cruel than a hostile one." Admetus is explained as a mind "prone to fear," *ad* (to), *metus* (fear), a purely Latin etymology, which is why he wished to marry Alcestis, her name being derived from *alkē*, Greek for "boldness." Her boldness in dying for him is rewarded when Hercules, representing virtue, brings her back from the dead (Hays 1996).

In book 2.1, the threefold theme continues as the three goddesses, in the judgment of Paris, are for the first time (Seznac 1953: 89) allegorized in detail as the three types of life described by philosophers: *contemplative* (Minerva), *active* (Juno), and *sensual* (Venus). Vices of various kinds were exposed in the rest of the book from Juno onward (Albu 2009: 200), and the book ends with the love of the Moon, or Proserpina, the goddess of the lower world, for the sleeping Endymion (2.16).

Book 3 described love affairs, adulterous, incestuous, or disgraceful (as of the elderly Berecyntia's passion for her young lover Attis, 3.5), of which only that of Cupid and Psyche (ch. 6), fully euhemerized, has a happy ending. Musical theory and the difficulty of analyzing its effects are discussed in chapter 9, on Marsyas and Apollo, and in chapter 10, where Orpheus (*oreafone*, "matchless sound") finds Eurydice ("deep judgment") again in Hades but loses her with a backward look. The last fable (ch. 12) describes the descent of Alpheus (*aletias fos*, "the light of truth") to the lower world in pursuit of Arethousa (*arete isa*, "the nobility of equity"), prepared for *the Exposition of the Content of Virgil* to come.

Confronted with a mass of information, Fulgentius applied a clear organizational principle with an inventive interpretative approach. He also included steadily increasing references (tacit and overt) to Christianity. His robust accounts of the sexual mores of the gods and heroes are found in the Fathers before him, and were applied, as by them, to those "with ears to hear."

## FURTHER READING

The Christian writers are best read for themselves, in text or translation, with their editions (see "References") and the studies of them, both earlier (such as Hagendahl 1958) and more recent (Barnes 1981; Simmons 1995; O'Daly and Herrero de Jáuregui 2007; Papadogiannakis 2012; Johnson 2014). Excellent publications, such as Bernabé (2005–2007), Cardauns (1976), Demoen (1996), Winiarczk (1991, 2013), and Zeegers-Vander Vorst (1972), compare and contrast the details of their polemics; more general studies (Lane Fox 1986; Droge 1989; Ridings 1995; Runia1993; Kahlos 2009; and Whitmarsh 2015) discuss the context of their works. For specific accounts of non-Christian religion, see Burkert (1985), West (1983), Lightfoot (2012), Cameron (2011), van Nuffeln (2011), Edwards (2015), and Watts (2015).

## LIST OF SOURCES AND WORKS CITED

### Primary Texts and Translations

Abbreviations: ANF: Ante-Nicene Fathers; CCSG: Corpus Christianorum Series Graeca; CCSL: Corpus Christianorum Series Latina; SC: Sources Chrétiennes.

Aristides' *Apology*: Bernard Pouderon, ed. *Aristide, Apologie*. SC 470. Paris 2003; tr. ANF 2.

Arnobius of Sicca: August Reifferscheid, ed. *Adversus Nationes libri VII. Corpus Scriptorum Ecclesiastorum Latinorum* 4. Vienna: C. Gerold, 1875; trans. George E. McCracken. *The Case against the Pagans*. 2 vols. Westminster, MD: Newman Press, 1949.

Athenagoras: Miroslav Marcovich, ed. *Legatio pro Christianis*. Berlin 1990; tr. ANF 2.

Augustine of Hippo: Bertrand Dombart and Alfons Kalb, eds. *De Civitate Dei*. Leipzig: Teubner, 1928–29; CCSL 47, 48, 1955; tr. Henry Bettenson. *St Augustine. The City of God against the Pagans*. St. Ives: Penguin, 1984.

Basil of Caesarea: Fernand Boulenger and Arnaud Perrot. *Basile de Césarée. Aux jeunes gens. Comment tirer profit de la littérature grecque*. Paris: Les Belles Lettres 2012; tr. Roy J. Deferrari and Martin R. P. McGuire. *St Basil, Letters*. 4 vols. Loeb Classical Library. Cambridge, MA: Harvard University Press, 1926–1934; Nigel G. Wilson, ed. *On the Value of Greek Literature*. London: Duckworth, 1975.

Clement of Alexandria: Miroslav Marcovich, *Clementis Alexandri Protrepticus*. Brill: Leiden, 1995. Claude Mondésert, ed. *Clément d'Alexandrie, Le Protréptique*. 2nd ed. SC 2. Paris 1949; tr. ANF 2; George W. Butterworth, *Clement of Alexandria*. Loeb Classical Library. Cambridge, MA: Harvard University Press, 1999.

Cosmas of Jerusalem: Giuseppe Lozza. *Cosma di Gerusalemne, Commentario ai Carmi di Gregorio Nazianzeno*. Naples: M. D'Auria, 2000.

Eusebius of Caesarea: Karl Mras, ed. *Eusebius Werke, Band 8: Die Praeparatio Evangelica*. Berlin: Akademie Verlag, 1954–1956; tr. Edwin H. Gifford, *Eusebius: Preparation for the Gospel*. Oxford: Clarendon Press, 1903.

Firmicus Maternus: Robert Turcan, ed. and tr. *L'Erreur des religions païennes*. Paris: Les Belles Lettres, 1982; tr. Clarence A. Forbes. *Firmicus Maternus: The Error of Pagan Religions*. New York: Newman Press, 1970.

Fulgentius: Rudolf Helm, ed. *Fabii Planciadis Fulgentii V. C. Opera*. Stuttgart: Teubner, 1970; translations: see Whitbread 1971 and Wolff and Dain 2013 in "Secondary Sources."

Gregory of Nazianzus: Jean Bernardi, ed. *Discours* 4 and 5 (SC 309, Paris 1983); *Disc.* 39 (SC 358, 1990); *Disc.* 43 (SC 384, 1992); tr. (*Sermons* 4 and 5) Charles W. King. *Julian the Emperor: Containing Gregory Nazianzen's Two Invectives and Libanius' Monody, with Julian's Extant Philosophical Works*. London: G. Bell and Sons, 1888. For *Sermons* 39 and 43 see *Nicene and Post-Nicene Fathers: Cyril of Jerusalem, Gregory Nazianzen*, series 2, vol. 7 (1893).

Justin: Denis Minns and Paul Parvis. *Justin, Philosopher and Martyr: Apologies*. Oxford: Oxford University Press, 2009.

Lactantius: Eberhard Heck and Antonie Wlosok, ed. *L. Caelius Firmianus Lactantius. Divinarum Institutionum Libri Septem*. Vol. 1. Munich and Leipzig: Teubner, 2005; Vols. 2–3, Berlin and New York, 2007, 2009; Vol. 4, Berlin and Boston, 2011; Anthony Bowen and Peter Garnsey. *Lactantius. Divine Institutes*. Liverpool. Liverpool University Press, 2003.

Origen: *Philocalia*. SC 226 (Paris: 1976, ed. Éric Junod), SC 302 (1983, ed. Marguerite Harl); tr. ANF 4.

Orphic Material: Albertus Bernabé, ed. *Poetae Epici Graeci Testimonia et Fragmenta Pars II: Orphicorum et Orphicis Similium Testimonia et Fragmenta*. 3 vols. Munich: K. G. Saur, 2004–2007.

Pseudo-Nonnus: Jennifer Nimmo Smith, Sebastian P. Brock, and Bernard Coulie. *Pseudo-Nonniani in IV Orationes Gregorii Nazianzeni Commentarii*. CCSG 27. Turnhout: Brepols, 1992; tr. Jennifer Nimmo Smith. *A Christian's Guide to Greek Learning. The Pseudo-Nonnus Commentaries on Sermons 4, 5, 39 and 43 by Gregory of Nazianzus*. Liverpool: Liverpool University Press, 2001.

Tatian, *To the Greeks*: Miroslav Marcovich, ed. *Tatiani oratio ad Graecos, Theophili Antiocheni ad Autolycum*. Berlin and New York: De Gruyter, 1995. Molly Whittaker, ed. and tr. *Tatian: Oratio ad Graecos and Fragments*: Oxford: Clarendon Press, 1982.

Tertullian: Jan G. Ph. Borleffs, ed. *Ad Nationes* (CPL 2), Eligius Dekkers, ed. *Apologeticum* (CPL 3). In *Tertulliani Opera I*. CCSL 1. Turnhout: Brepols, 1954; tr. ANF 11–13.

Theodoret: Pierre Canivet, ed. and tr. *Théodoret de Cyr. Thérapeutique des maladies helléniques*. Paris: Éditions du Cerf, 1958; tr. Thomas Halton. *Theodoret of Cyrus: A Cure for Pagan Maladies*. New York: Newman Press, 2013.

Theophilus: Robert M. Grant, ed. *Theophilus of Antioch. Ad Autolycum*. Oxford: Oxford University Press, 1970.

Varro: Burkhart Cardauns, ed. *M. Terentius Varro. Antiquitates Rerum Divinarum*, I *Die Fragmente*, II, *Kommentar*. Mainz: Akademie der Wissenschaften und der Literatur.

## Secondary Sources

Accorinti, Domenico. 2016. "The Poet from Panopolis: An Obscure Biography and a Controversial Figure." In *Brill's Companion to Nonnus of Panopolis*, edited by Domenico Accorinti, 11–53. Leiden: Brill.

Agosti, Gianfranco. 2012. "Greek Poetry." In *The Oxford Handbook of Late Antiquity*, edited by Scott Fitzgerald Johnson, 361–404. Oxford: Oxford University Press.

Albu, Emily. 2009. "Disarming Aeneas: Fulgentius on *Arms and the Man*." In *The Power of Religion in Late Antiquity*, edited by Andrew Cain and Noel Lenski, 21–30. Farnham, UK: Ashgate.

Allen, Joel S. 2008. *The Despoliation of Egypt in Pre-Rabbinic, Rabbinic and Patristic Thinking*. Leiden: Brill.

Alvar, Jaime. 2008. *Romanising Oriental Gods: Myth, Salvation and Ethics in the Cults of Cybele, Isis and Mithras*. Translated and edited by Richard Gordon. Leiden: Brill.

Baldwin, Barry. 1988. "Fulgentius and His Sources." *Traditio* 44: 37–57.

Barclay, John. 2001. "I Corinthians." In *The Oxford Bible Commentary*, edited by John Barton and John Muddiman, 1108–1133. Oxford: Oxford University Press.

Barnes, Timothy D. 1981. *Constantine and Eusebius*. Cambridge, MA: Harvard University Press.

Barnes, Timothy D. 1985. *Tertullian: A Historical and Literary Study*. Rev. ed. Oxford: Oxford University Press.

Beatrice, Pier F. 2007. "The Treasures of the Egyptians: A Chapter in the History of Patristic Exegesis and Late Antique Culture." *Studia Patristica* 39: 159–183.

Boys-Stones, George R. 2001. *Post-Hellenistic Philosophy. A Study of Its Development from the Stoics to Origen*. Oxford: Oxford University Press.

Bremmer, Jan. 2004. "Attis: A Greek God in Anatolian Pessinous and Catullan Rome." *Mnemosyne* 57: 534–573.

Brown, Peter. 1967. *Augustine of Hippo*. London: Faber and Faber.

Burgess, Richard W. 1997. "The Dates and Editions of Eusebius' *Chronici Canones* and *Historia Ecclesiastica*." *Journal of Theological Studies* 48: 471–504.

Burkert, Walter. 1985. *Greek Religion*. Translated by John Raffan. Cambridge, MA: Harvard University Press.

Cameron, Alan. 2004. *Greek Mythography in the Roman World*. Oxford: Oxford University Press.

Cameron, Alan. 2011. *The Last Pagans of Rome*. Oxford: Oxford University Press.

Cameron, Averil. 1991. *Christianity and the Rhetoric of Empire*. Oxford: Oxford University Press.

Chuvin, Pierre. 2014. "Revisiting Old Problems: Literature and Religion in the *Dionysiaca*." In *Nonnus of Panopolis in Context: Poetry and Cultural Milieu in Late Antiquity*, edited by Konstantinos Spanoudakis, 3–20. Berlin and Boston: De Gruyter.

Demoen, Kristoffel. 1996. *Pagan and Christian Exempla in Gregory Nazianzen*. Turnhout: Brepols.

Digeser, Elizabeth DePalma. 2012. *A Threat to Public Piety, Christians, Platonists and the Great Persecution*. Ithaca, NY: Cornell University Press.

Donaldson, Terence L. 2001. "Introduction to the Pauline Corpus." In *The Oxford Bible Commentary*, edited by John Barton and John Muddiman, 1062–1082. Oxford: Oxford University Press.

Droge, Arthur J. 1989. *Homer or Moses? Early Christian Interpretations of the History of Culture*. Tübingen: Mohr Siebeck.

Dunn, Geoffrey D. 2004. *Tertullian*. London: Routledge.

Edwards, Mark J., ed. 1999a. *Ancient Christian Commentary on Scripture, New Testament VIII: Galatians, Ephesians, Philippians*. London: IVP Academic.

Edwards, Mark J. 1999b. "The Flowering of Latin Apologetic: Lactantius and Arnobius." In *Apologetics in the Roman Empire: Pagans, Jews, and Christians*, edited by Mark Edwards, Martin Goodman, and Simon Price, 197–221. Oxford: Clarendon Press.

Edwards, Mark J. 2004. "Dating Arnobius: Why Discount the Evidence of Jerome?" *Antiquité Tardive* 12: 263–271.

Edwards, Mark J. 2015. *Religions of the Constantinian Empire*. Oxford: Oxford University Press.

Elm, Susanna. 2012. *Sons of Hellenism, Fathers of the Church: Emperor Julian, Gregory Nazianzus and the Vision of Rome*. Berkeley: University of California Press.

Geffcken, Johannes. 1907. *Zwei griechischen Apologeten*. Leipzig: Teubner.

Goodman, Martin. 1999. "Josephus' Treatise *Against Apion*." In *Apologetics in the Roman Empire: Pagans, Jews, and Christians*, edited by Mark Edwards, Martin Goodman, and Simon Price, 45–58. Oxford: Clarendon Press.

Grant, Robert M. 1988. *Greek Apologists of the Second Century*. London: SCM Press.

Hagendahl, Harald. 1958. *Latin Fathers and the Classics. A Study on the Apologists, Jerome and other Christian Writers*. Gothenburg, Sweden: Acta Universitatis Gothoburgensis.

Hays, Gregory. 1996. "Fulgentius the Mythographer." Diss. Cornell University.

Hays, Gregory. 2003. "The Date and Identity of the Mythographer Fulgentius." *Journal of Medieval Latin* 13: 163–252.

Hays, Gregory. 2004. "'Romuleis Libicisque Litteris': Fulgentius and the 'Vandal Rennaissance.'" In *Vandals, Romans and Berbers: New Perspectives on Late Antique North Africa*, edited by Andrew H. Merrills, 101–132. Aldershot, UK: Ashgate.

Hays, Gregory. 2013. "Fulgentius the Mythographer?" In *Writing Myth: Mythography in the Ancient World*, edited by Stephen M. Trzaskoma and R. Scott Smith, 309–333. Leuven: Peeters.

Hengel, Martin. 1991. *The Pre-Christian Paul*. With Roland Deines. Translated by John Bowden. Philadelphia: Trinity Press International.

Herrero de Jáuregui, Miguel. 2007. "Las fuentes de Clem. Alex. *Protr.* II.12–22: Un tratado sobre los misterios y una teogonía órphica." *Emerita* 75: 19–50.

Herrero de Jáuregui, Miguel. 2010. *Orphism and Christianity in Late Antiquity*. Translated by Jennifer Ottman and Daniel Rodriguez. Berlin and New York: De Gruyter.

Hock, Ronald F. 2003. "Paul and Greco-Roman Education." In *Paul in the Greco-Roman World: A Handbook*, edited by J. Paul Sampley, 198–227. Harrisburg, PA: Trinity International Press.

Horbury, William. 2001. "The Wisdom of Solomon." In *The Oxford Bible Commentary*, edited by John Barton and John Muddiman, 650–667. Oxford: Oxford University Press.

Inowlocki, Sabrina. 2006. *Eusebius and the Jewish Authors: His Citation Technique in an Apologetic Context*. Leiden: Brill.

Johnson, Aaron. 2014. *Eusebius*. London: I.B. Tauris.

Kahlos, Maijastina. 2009. "The Rhetoric of Tolerance and Intolerance: From Lactantius to Firmicus Maternus." In *Continuity and Discontinuity in Early Christian Apologetics*, edited by Jörg Ulrich, Anders-Christian Jacobsen, and Maijastina Kahlos, 79–95. Frankfurt: Peter Lang.

Kaldellis, Anthony. 2007. *Hellenism in Byzantium: The Transformations of Greek Identity and the Reception of the Classical Tradition*. Cambridge, UK: Cambridge University Press.

Knust, Jennifer Wright. 2006. *Abandoned to Lust, Sexual Slander and Ancient Christianity*. New York: Columbia University Press.

Kofsky, Aryeh. 2002. *Eusebius of Caesarea against Paganism*. Leiden: Brill.

Lane Fox, Robin. 1986. *Pagans and Christians*. St. Ives: Penguin.

Law, Timothy M. 2013. *When God Spoke Greek*. Oxford: Oxford University Press.

Lightfoot, Jane L. 2007. *The Sibylline Oracles*. Oxford: Oxford University Press.

Livrea, Enrico. 2003. "The Nonnus Question Revisited." In *Des Géants à Dionysos: Mélanges de mythologie et de poésie grecques offerts à Francis Vian*, edited by Domenico Accorinti and Pierre Chuvin, 447–457. Alessandria, Italy: Edizioni dell'Orso.

MacDonald, Dennis R. 2013. "Classical Greek Poetry and the Acts of the Apostles: Imitations of Euripides' *Bacchae*." In *Christian Origins and Greco-Roman Culture*, edited by Stanley E. Porter and Andrew W. Pitts, 463–496. Leiden: Brill.

Millar, Fergus. 2007. "Theodoret of Cyrrhus: A Syrian in Greek Dress?" In *From Rome to Constantinople: Studies in Honour of Averil Cameron*, edited by Hagit Amirav and Bas ter Haar Romeny, 105–125. Leuven: Peeters.

Nimmo Smith, Jennifer. 1996. "Nonnus and Pseudo-Nonnos: The Poet and the Commentator." *ΦΙΛΕΛΛΗΝ: Studies in Honour of Robert Browning*, edited by Costas N. Constantinides, Nikolaos M. Panagotakes, Elizabeth Jeffreys, and Athanasios D. Angelou, 281–299. Venice: Istituto ellenico di studi bizantini e postbizantini di Venezia.

Nimmo Smith, Jennifer. 2006. "Magic at the Cross-Roads in the Sixth Century." In *Byzantine Style, Religion and Civilisation: In Honour of Sir Steven Runciman*, edited by Elizabeth M. Jeffreys, 224–237. Cambridge, UK: Cambridge University Press.

Nimmo Smith, Jennifer. 2019. "The Reception of the 'Catalogue of Inventors' in Gregory of Nazianzus' Sermon 4,107–109, in Pseudo-Nonnus' Commentary on Sermon 4 and Beyond: An End or a Beginning?" In *The Literary History of Byzantium, Editions, Translations and Studies in Honour of Joseph A. Munitiz SJ*, edited by Bram Roosen and Peter Van Deun, 333–356. Turnhout: Brepols.

O'Daly, Gerard. 2007. *Augustine's City of God: A Reader's Guide*. Oxford: Oxford University Press. (Original work published in 1999).

Papadogiannakis, Yannis. 2012. *Christianity and Hellenism in the Fifth Century Greek East: Theodoret's Apologetics against the Greeks in Context*. Washington DC: Center for Hellenic Studies.

Pelikan, Jaroslav. 1993. *Christianity and Classical Culture*. New Haven, CT: Yale University Press.

Pépin, Jean. 1976. *Mythe et allégorie: Les origines grecques et les contestations judéo-chrétiennes*. Paris: Aubier.

Pouderon, Bernard. 2005. *Les apologistes grecs du IIᵉ siècles*. Paris: Les Éditions du Cerf.

Price, Simon. 1999. "Latin Christian Apologetics: Minucius Felix, Tertullian and Cyprian." In *Apologetics in the Roman Empire, Pagans, Jews, and Christians*, edited by Mark Edwards, Martin Goodman, and Simon Price, 105–129. Oxford: Clarendon Press.

Rajak, Tessa. 2009. *Translation and Survival: The Greek Bible of the Ancient Jewish Diaspora*. Oxford: Oxford University Press.

Relihan, Joel C. 1988. "Fulgentius, *Mitologiae* 1.20–21." *American Journal of Philology* 109: 229–230.

Ridings, Daniel. 1995. *Attic Moses: The Dependency Theme in Some Early Christian Writers*. Gothenburg, Sweden: Acta Universitatis Gothoburgensis.

Riedweg, Christoph. 1987. *Mysterienterminologie bei Platon, Philon und Klemens von Alexandrien*. Berlin: De Gruyter.

Rives, James B. 1995. *Religion and Authority in Roman Carthage from Augustus to Constantine*. Oxford: Oxford University Press.

Rochette, Bruno. 1998. "Héraclès à la croisée des chemins: Un *topos* de la littérature gréco-latine." *Les études classiques* 66: 105–113.

Rubenson, Samuel. 2006. "The Cappadocians on the Areopagus." In *Gregory of Nazianzus: Images and Reflections*, edited by Jostein Børtnes and Tomas Hägg, 113–132. Copenhagen: Museum Tusculanum Press.

Runia, David T. 1993. *Philo in Early Christian Literature: A Survey*. Minneapolis, MN: Van Gorcum.

Runia, David T. 1995. "Why Does Clement Call Philo 'The Pythagorean'"? In *Philo and the Church Fathers: A Collection of Papers*, edited by David T. Runia, 54–76. Leiden: Brill.

Rüpke, Jörg. 2005. "Varro's *Tria genera theologiae*: Religious Thinking in the Late Republic." *Ordia Prima* 4: 107–129.

Salzman, Michele R. 2008. "Pagans and Christians." In *The Oxford Handbook of Early Christian Studies*, edited by Susan Ashbrook Harvey and David G. Hunter, 186–202. Oxford: Oxford University Press.

Seznac, Jean. 1953. *The Survival of the Pagan Gods: The Mythological Tradition and Its Place in Renaissance Humanism and Art*. Translated by Barbara F. Sessions. Princeton, NJ: Princeton University Press.

Shorrock, Robert. 2011. *The Myth of Paganism: Nonnus, Dionysus and the World of Late Antiquity*. Bristol: Bristol Classical Press.

Simmons, Michael B. 1995. *Arnobius of Sicca, Religious Conflict and Competition in the Age of Diocletian*. Oxford: Oxford University Press.

Selent, Doreen. 2011. *Allegorische Mythenerklärung in der Spätantike: Wege zum Werk des Dracontius*. Rahden, Germany: Verlag Marie Leidorf.

van Nuffelen, Peter. 2011. *Rethinking the Gods: Philosophical Readings of Religion in the Post-Hellenistic Period*. Cambridge, UK: Cambridge University Press.

Versnel, Hank S. 2011. *Coping with the Gods: Wayward Readings in Greek Theology* (= *Religions in the Graeco-Roman World*. Leiden: Brill.

Watts, Edward J. 2015. *The Final Pagan Generation*. Oakland: University of California Press.

West, Martin L. 1983. *The Orphic Poems*. Oxford: Oxford University Press.

Whitbread, Leslie G., tr. 1971. *Fulgentius the Mythographer*. Columbus: Ohio State University Press.

Whitmarsh, Tim. 2015. *Battling the Gods: Atheism in the Ancient World*. New York: Alfred A. Knopf.

Winiarczyk, Marek, ed. 1991. *Euhemeri Mesenii Reliquiae*. Stuttgart: Teubner.

Winiarczyk, Marek. 2013. *The Sacred History of Euhemerus of Messene*. Translated by Wittold Zbirohowski-Kościa. Berlin: De Gruyter.

Wolff, Étienne. 2008. "Vergil and Fulgentius." *Vergilian Society* 54: 59–69.

Wolff, Étienne, and Philippe Dain, eds. 2013. *Fulgence Mythologies*. Villeneuve d'Ascq: Presses du Septentrion.

Zeegers-Vander Vorst, Nicole. 1972. *Les citations des poètes grecs chez les apologistes chrétiens du II siècle*. Leuven: Bibliothèque de l'Université Bureau du Recueil.

# CHAPTER 38

............................................................................................................

# BYZANTINE MYTHOGRAPHY

............................................................................................................

## BENJAMIN GARSTAD

THIS chapter is concerned with the original contributions of Byzantine authors to the literature on myth, but it must be remembered, as we consider what these authors were reading and the sources of their works, that the literate public in the Byzantine period potentially had access to most of the Greek mythography that has been discussed in the preceding chapters of this handbook—even some awareness of a few of the Latin works—and it is thanks to the efforts of Byzantine scribes that these mythographic works are preserved for us.[*] If the Byzantines failed to produce a systematic handbook of myth like that of Apollodorus, it is because they could avail themselves of Apollodorus's work itself, and did. Their interest in mythography was a result of the form and content of Byzantine education. From the acquisition of basic literacy to the appreciation of the classical literary canon and the appropriation of examples of rhetorical eloquence, Byzantine education continued on the model inherited from antiquity and depended on a recognized body of staple works, primarily Homer, but also much of the rest of poetry on mythical subjects (see Smith and Trzaskoma, this volume, on education). Dionysius Thrax, whose grammar was not supplanted as an elementary textbook until the 12th century, inculcated a knowledge of mythology as basic to the reading of literature. So, mythography remained necessary and meaningful to, at least, the upper echelons of the Byzantine public, which were always more literate than their counterparts in the West, and especially, to the administrators of Church and State, whose prospects for advancement might depend on a display of fluency and erudition that included a familiarity with the classics of a bygone era. Perhaps because of the careerist motives of many of its readers and writers, Constantinople was the center of the production and presentation of much mythographical material. But myth was also imbibed by readers in the context of a society that was permeated by the presence of the Church and its teachings.

[*] I am grateful to Eric Cullhed, Adam Goldwyn, and William Hutton for their invaluable assistance in preparing this chapter.

Some counterpoise, if not reconciliation, was sought between traditional culture and upbringing, *paideia*, and Christian doctrine. Perhaps the most renowned prescription along these lines, simply because of its authorship, was St. Basil the Great's (died 379) *To the Youth* or *On Greek Literature*. Inasmuch as the pursuit of virtue is the path to heavenly rewards, Basil urges his audience to avail themselves of every example of and exhortation to virtue at their disposal. The best guide to eternal life is the Sacred Scriptures, but the young are unready for their profundity and should prepare themselves by reading profane literature, just as one looks first at the sun's reflection in the water before peering at the sun itself. Basil's watchword is discrimination: select what fosters virtue and discard what impedes it. He instructs his readers to be especially sure to ignore what the poets have to say about the gods, not only their multiplicity, but also their violent discords and shameful sexual conduct. But he tells them to ignore such contamination just as Odysseus stopped up his ears and passed by the Sirens! Zeus may disport himself little better than a beast, but Odysseus is held up as a model; arriving naked on Phaeacia, he was nevertheless clothed with virtue. In a manner that will recur in Byzantine mythography, the poets, with the ambivalent myths they retail, are classed alongside the historians, orators, and philosophers as authors who praise virtue and so speed the soul to salvation. Byzantine authors were often happy to mine myth for morally instructive lessons, as Basil counsels, but the student of mythography is fortunate that, by and large, they rejected his injunction to discard the insalubrious stories of the gods.

A more constructive, and ultimately more influential, approach to divine myth was taken by Eusebius of Caesarea (260/265–339). In the opening books of his *Praeparatio Evangelica,* he outlines what he calls the "theologies," or accounts of the gods, of various nations. These are abridgments and quotations of what a number of historians had to say about the gods; Philo of Byblos produced an ancient Phoenician history written by Sanchuniathon, and the rest are derived from Diodorus Siculus's *Bibliotheca*: the account of Egypt in the first book, Dionysius Scytobrachion's fanciful history of the Atlanteans, and the *Sacred Inscription* of Euhemerus. These "theologies" disagree among themselves in detail—implying a certain criticism—and Eusebius dismisses each in turn, but they all agree on his critical apologetic point, that the error of polytheism, wherever it is found, is the worship of idols of dead men. The accounts of the gods included in the *Praeparatio Evangelica* are Hellenistic historicizing narratives, and while they take the pantheons of different nations for their casts of characters, their relation to traditional myth is severely attenuated. In his *Chronicle* Eusebius pursues a similar apologetic point, demonstrating that Moses is older than, not only the pagan poets, but also the pagan gods, but still adheres closer to traditional myth, turning the happenings of myth into the events of history. So he can indicate when, for instance, the dispute between Poseidon and Athena over the land of Cecrops was adjudicated (484 years after the birth of Abraham), when Zeus abducted Europa to Crete (585 years from Abraham), and when Perseus slew Dionysus in battle (720 years from Abraham). The intervals between the running columns of regnal years in the *Chronicle* are, indeed, full of mythological information. And despite the *Chronicle*'s essentially biblical orientation, the Fall of Troy (835 years after Abraham) is treated as a watershed moment; there is a clear break in the text and the various chronologies are recalibrated at this point. The same features established by Eusebius, the historicity of mythological events and the pivotal importance of the Trojan War, are to be found throughout the Byzantine chronicle tradition that he did so much to inaugurate, although in distinct, rather than imitative forms.

The most distinctive, and apparently most pervasive, Byzantine interpretation of the gods of myth was found in the chronicles and was a narrative centered on the figure of "Picus, who is also Zeus." The earliest surviving versions of this narrative, which must precede both of them, are in two 6th-century works: the lost Greek original of the *Excerpta Latina Barbari* and the chronicle of John Malalas, but it is not certain when and by whom the so-called Picus-Zeus narrative was first written, though it is surely a Christian composition. This account traces the careers and migrations of a whole line of kings who were taken for gods, from its origin in Assyria, where Cronos first practiced kingly rule and the dynasty continued until Sardanapalus, to Italy, where first Cronos and then his son Picus-Zeus established themselves in the wild West, and then to Egypt, where "Faunus, who is also Hermes" finds his way and becomes king, to be followed by his descendants Hephaistos and Helios. The so-called gods are taken as historical figures; this is clear not only from the historiographical context in which the narrative is found, but also from its implication from the outset in the legendary history of Assyria traceable to Ctesias of Cnidos. The multiple names of the god-kings and their movements from one country to another allow a relatively small number of characters to account for the mythical figures of many nations. The narrative eschews any mention of demons, with whom the pagan gods had been associated in Christian literature since the time of Justin Martyr (died around 165), but gives definite ages and reign lengths to its characters, thus offering an account of the gods in the form of history that was fit for inclusion in the chronicles (though its indefinite relation to other events allowed it to be variously placed in time). Otherwise, its details were largely a combination of the features of a long-standing profane critique of myth and the arguments of Christian apologetic. The deified men are said to be named for the planets, which might explain their deification but also undermines any real identification between them and the "visible gods"—the heavenly bodies. They seem to be taken for gods mostly because they were kings and inventors of arts and craft, though their role as philanderers and magicians explicitly contributed to the process, revealing as well the nefarious characters who came to be worshipped as gods. These features probably originated in the context of a polemic against a vital paganism, but they were admirably well suited to an ongoing response to a continued reading of myth.

The Picus-Zeus narrative is not the only treatment of mythical subjects in Malalas's chronicle; indeed, his first five books are largely a satisfyingly representative selection of well-rounded versions of various myths that tend to stick much closer to their originals, while still being suitably adapted to serve a historian's purposes and interspersed with chronological computations from Adam and renditions of biblical stories. Perseus, for example, worked magical spells over the severed head of a simple country girl and used it to paralyze his enemies in battle, overthrew Sardanapalus, and made himself king of Assyria, establishing the Persian fire cult (2.11–13). Pentheus was at odds with his bastard cousin, Dionysus, who had come to Thebes with an army wanting a share of the rule, but his mother Agave reconciled them, inadvertently allowing Dionysus to ambush and behead Pentheus; so, they say Agave beheaded her son (2.14). Oedipus made a name for himself by defeating Sphinx, a horrid looking peasant woman "with big breasts," who led a robber band that harassed travelers in the vicinity of Thebes; he tricked her, infiltrated her gang, and killed her. Instead of meeting at a crossroads by the ineluctable workings of fate, Oedipus brings about the death of Laius in a manner reminiscent of the biblical rivalry of Saul and David: jealous of the popular adulation Oedipus's success won him, Laius unleashed the army on the citizenry—could a mythographer before the massacres of Theodosius and Justinian have imagined such a scenario?—and was killed in the ensuing civil strife. The dowager queen Iocaste selected Oedipus to rule in her late husband's stead, all unawares that he was her son (2.17). The strands that connect myth to the spiritual reality of a latter day are obvious when on their quest the Argonauts receive an oracle concerning Mary, the Theotokos, and behold a vision of the archangel Michael; the temples they founded in commemoration, it is noted, have become appropriately dedicated churches (4.8–9).

Most of Malalas's fifth book is devoted to an account of the Trojan War and its aftermath; it is as remarkable for its intricate composition as for its fulsomeness, and stresses those aspects not covered by Homer. The opening chapters describe the upbringing of Paris and his crime, the massing of the Greek army and its departure from Aulis, the preliminary attacks on Trojan allies and plundering raids—when Achilles alienates himself from the army by secretly withholding Briseis from the general distribution of plunder—and then give a series of sketches of the leading figures at Troy. These sketches are not so much pen portraits as the clipped and impersonal stuff of a personnel dossier or a police blotter, for example: "The ardent lover of the preceding [Achilles] was Patroclus; he was heavy set and strong, middling in stature, with dirty blonde hair, a ruddy complexion, a fine face, and good eyes; he was nobly born, a mighty warrior, with a sedate character and a fine beard." All of this material is attributed to Dictys of Crete, making Malalas the fullest witness to the Greek text of this author, the early existence of which is vouched for by meager papyrus fragments, as is the catalogue of Greek ships that follows. Then there is a painfully sparse notice covering everything from the landing of the expedition to the plundering of the Phrygian kingdom, the death of Priam and Hecuba, and the sack of their kingdom, as well as a calculation of the length of "the kingdom of Ephesus" from its foundation, all in only a few lines.

The details of the Fall of Troy are delivered in the context of the division of the spoils and the dispute over the Palladion, as Ajax and Odysseus make speeches presenting their respective cases with reference to their deeds—needless to say, Odysseus's speech is much longer! The case is still unresolved when Ajax is mysteriously stabbed to death in the night; Odysseus flees, and his wanderings are described at length. Sisyphus of Cos is cited as a source for the adventures of Odysseus, but he is described as a companion of Teucer and so can probably be connected to much of the following narrative. The account returns to Troy; Diomedes and Agamemnon depart, leaving Pyrrhus to perform the obsequies for Ajax, whose brother Teucer arrives shortly thereafter. In gratitude, Teucer tells Pyrrhus about his father's heroics, relating Hector's death not in single combat, but in an ambush set by Achilles; his fateful meeting with Polyxena at the ransoming of Hector's body; the arrival and defeat of, first, Penthesileia and the Amazons, and then Memnon and the Indians (or Ethiopians); and the treacherous slaying of Achilles in the grove of Apollo. The last of the heroes leave for home at this point, and Malalas relates that Homer found Sisyphus of Cos's eyewitness account of Troy and wrote the *Iliad* and Vergil wrote up the remainder, and that Dictys's work was discovered much later. But the story of Troy does not really end until Malalas has related the wanderings of Orestes and Iphigeneia over his own home turf of the future site of Antioch.

Such elaboration was not necessarily the norm in the formative period of the Byzantine chronicle tradition. The *Excerpta Latina Barbari* offers only a brief note on the Trojan War, misunderstood by the Latin translator, who mistook "Ilium" (*hē Ilios*) for "Helios" (*hēlios*) (1.7.1): "In the days of Eli the priest, the ruin of Sun City (*solis exterminatio*) was accomplished by the Achaeans, among whom are mentioned Agamemnon and Menelaus and Achilles and all the other Danaans, concerning whom Homer, the scholar and writer set out the history." But if the *Excerpta* represents a dead end in terms of the transmission of material, Malalas is the fountainhead of a long and vibrant tradition of Byzantine chronicles. As Treadgold (2007) has pointed out, there is nothing to indicate that Malalas's chronicle was at all popular, especially in comparison with the histories of his classicizing contemporaries Procopius and Agathias. But as a succession of world chronicles from Adam updated and effectively replaced Malalas's original composition, each instantiation absorbed and adapted material, not least on myth, which had first been included in his chronicle, if not directly, then at second or third hand. By such recycling or ingestion into a series of chronicles, some form of Malalas's rendition of myth remained perennially before the Byzantine reading public, and through translation it exerted an influence throughout the eastern cultural sphere, the so-called Byzantine Commonwealth and beyond.

For the better part of a millennium Byzantine chroniclers felt free to modify and rearrange Malalas's material, but their handling of myth was, with few exceptions, recognizably derived from what we find in Malalas. In the *Chronicon Paschale* up to the reign of Heraclius (610–641), much of the earlier treatment of myth is taken over but it is set apart as a separate block, excluded from the painstaking chronology that characterizes the rest of the chronicle, and there is no account of the Trojan War. John of Nikiu, an eyewitness to the Arab invasion of Egypt, wrote his chronicle in Greek, but it was translated, first into Arabic and then into Ethiopic, so that the coverage of myth that survives in a garbled and abbreviated form in the Ethiopic text got a wide airing. George the Syncellus (died after 810) set out to correct the errors and miscalculations of Eusebius, and one of his express purposes in doing so was to demonstrate that Moses is, indeed, older than Zeus and all the figures of Greek myth, so there is plenty of mythological material in the miscellaneous notes interspersed between stretches of archaic king-lists, but it goes back to the lost Greek text of Eusebius's *Chronicle* and represents rather earlier sources than Malalas. Malalas's treatment of myth does find a place in the synoptic historical overture running from Adam to Alexander's successors that begins the chronicle of George Hamartolos ("the Sinner," or George the Monk; covering to 842), which was translated into Old Georgian and Church Slavonic, inspiring the Slavonic chronicle tradition including the famous Nestor, and formed the basis of numerous later works. One of these was the chronicle of Symeon the Logothete, of which there are numerous versions under different names; rather than a sequence of narratives, they present a continuous series of chronological notices strung together, in which characters and events from myth are inextricably woven into the mainly biblical subject matter. In the 12th century George Cedrenus gave accounts of various mythical figures, from Cronos to the sons of Oedipus, as a digression on the patriarch Phalek; he approached the Picus-Zeus narrative from three different angles, adding a brief snapshot of Dionysius Scytobrachion's account of the gods under another head. Otherwise, his treatment of myth comes ultimately from Malalas, including a protracted account of the Trojan War.

If the chronicles already mentioned may be seen as milestones or links in a chain, the *Synopsis Chronike* of Constantine Manasses, probably written between 1145 and 1148, was one of the foremost works of Byzantine literature. More than a hundred surviving manuscripts and an influential Bulgarian translation attest to its immense popularity. The appeal may have lain in the patronage of the *Sebastocratorissa* Irene, but more likely it was the composition in verse, which made it highly readable and easy to memorize, or even the selection and arrangement of the contents, which includes generous helpings of what we would call myth, but Manasses considers history. Manasses reduces the Picus-Zeus narrative to its most salacious aspect, the incestuous marriage of Ninus and Semiramis, and does not involve Perseus in the demise of Sardanapalus, following instead Ctesias and Diodorus Siculus. But he gives lengthier treatment to the Trojan War than to any other topic and vows at the outset that he will not follow the version of Homer, who distorted things; he proves as good as his word. He accepts the variant according to which Proteus detained Helen in Egypt but the Greeks nevertheless made war on Troy for the sake of plundering its wealth. Achilles withdrew from battle because of Odysseus's deceitful judicial murder of Palamedes but returned because of the death of Patroclus. Priam appealed to David for military aid but was refused; the Jewish king was either preoccupied with wars against the gentiles or afraid to expose his susceptible subjects to the heathen and idolatrous Greeks. Otherwise, the course of events is recognizable from Malalas. Manasses's treatment of Aeneas deals mostly with prophecy, appropriately enough since the Byzantines saw Old Rome as an anticipation of their own "Roman Empire." In addition to the profusion of copies of his own work in circulation, Manasses had followers, Michael Glykas in the 12th century and Joel the Chronographer in the 13th, who availed themselves of material on myth from the chronicle tradition that Manasses had neglected; even the most popular writer could not expunge the accumulated weight of the mythography going back to Malalas.

The accounts of the mythical period we find in the chronicles were not confined to one genre but seem to represent the common Byzantine understanding of the gods, heroes, and myths. This is indicated by the appearance of material we can trace back to Malalas in various entries in the magisterial lexicon of around 1000, the *Souda*, a work as broadly comprehensive as it was widely recopied and diffused. The Picus-Zeus narrative works itself into not only the discussion of *Pēcus* but also the entries "Egypt" and "Hephaistos." "Ares" is treated as a word for iron or war and in grammatical terms, but also appears as a name for the Assyrian king "Thourras," who was named after the planet Mars. The Macedonian kings of that name are treated under the heading "Perseus," but "Medusa" produces a more or less complete rendition of Malalas's account of the hero Perseus. Literate Byzantines were familiar with Sophocles's plays, but "Oedipus" is discussed in terms of the historicized version in the chronicles. Despite the extensive entry on Homer, perhaps the longest in the whole work, the narrative under the heading "Ilium" sets up the Trojan War very much as the chronicles do. Even the description of the game "Tavla" and its invention by Palamedes goes back to Malalas. If encyclopedias represent a society's intellectual consensus, then what we might consider an idiosyncratic interpretation of myth as history had an unassailable place in Byzantium's view of the past it studied so sedulously.

If, however, a reader's purpose was to gain an overview of the traditional stories, not to discover the historical truth that stood behind them, the Byzantine era produced, and Byzantine society maintained, at least one suitable resource more congenial to aesthetic sensibilities than a lexicon. The *Dionysiaca* of Nonnus of Panopolis (5th c.) is an epic poem on the wine god, but it is also a veritable encyclopedia of mythology, comprehending within its forty-eight books narration of or allusion to practically every story told by the old poets. Nonnus displays the reverential rivalry characteristic of Byzantine engagement with Homer, but his delight in exhaustive catalogues and variant versions belies something of a pedantic intent. The description of Eros's quiverful of arrows, for instance, becomes a list of Zeus's seductions of mortal women, including Alexander's mother Olympias (7.110–135). There is also a catalogue of youths beloved by gods (10.250–264) and of the love affairs of Naiads and fountain goddesses (40.535–573). Having told the story of Dionysus's invention of wine, Nonnus immediately turns to give "another, older report" of the origin of wine (12.292–397). Likewise, he gives two different versions of the parentage of Beroë, the patroness of Berytus/Beirut (41.143–229). The naval battle in book 43 seems to involve every deity associated with the sea, and Nemesis poses her question to Artemis so as to catalogue the enemies of the Huntress, with the significant exception of Actaeon (48.392–413). If Nonnus's gorgeous—not to say overwrought—epic failed to lay out a plain survey of mythological knowledge, it at least indicated most every character and story that a literate person might be expected to know.

Epic poetry was not the only art form that offered information on myth. There were many mythological subjects, mostly characters from the Trojan War and several deities, among the statues that decorated the Zeuxippus Baths in the middle of Constantinople, along with images of Greek and Roman historical figures, athletes, poets, philosophers, and even historians. The eclectic assortment of subjects recalls the varied teachers of virtue St. Basil recommended to his readers, and the combination of myth with history and philosophy that was characteristic of the Byzantines' handling of their literary heritage as a whole. These statues themselves could be taken as an instruction on myth—a profane parallel to the use of icons as teaching tools in the Byzantine Church—but the series of poems describing some eighty of them, written by Christodorus of Coptos in the reign of Anastasius I (491–518), constitute a real mythographical document, much as the representations of paintings in the *Eikones* of the two Philostrati do. Some of Christodorus's descriptions are rather superficial appraisals of appearance only, his treatment of a statue of Helen (168–170), for instance. But others manage to at least imply rich and dramatic narratives, as when he depicts Auge as a disheveled rape victim (138–143) or the bitter and treasonous sentiment of Helenus against Priam and Troy (155–159). He gives a statue of Homer the longest description by far (311–350).

The Zeuxippus Baths were destroyed by fire in 532, but the Byzantines continued to look to the statuary that graced their city for mythological information. This is evident from the *Patria of Constantinople*, four books on civic lore and monuments compiled in the late 10th century and surviving in more than sixty manuscripts. Drawing on material from John Lydus (6th c.), a number of statues are identified as those of certain gods and goddesses by their attributes, and then the attributes are discussed as indicative of the character of each deity (2.3–13): the statue with the lyre is Apollo, and they give him a lyre because he is the sun, the harmony of everything (2.4). These descriptions presume an almost complete ignorance of myth. A similar illiteracy seems to prevent the compiler and his source, the *Parastaseis Syntomoi Chronikai*, from adjudicating between the popular suppositions that a giant equestrian statue from Antioch depicts either Joshua or Bellerophon (2.47). But the description of a statue group of Perseus and Andromeda, despite setting their story in Iconium, sticks closer to traditional myth than does the version in Malalas. While Malalas (2.11) presents Andromeda as a consecrated priestess raped by Perseus, who uses Medusa's head as a magical battle talisman, the *Patria* depicts her offered as a sacrifice to a dragon and rescued by Perseus, who slew the beast with the Gorgon's head, rather (2.85). Statues of mythical subjects were, nevertheless, supposed to be invested with roughly appropriate magical qualities; one of Aphrodite was said to reveal unchaste women who came near it by compelling them to lift their skirts and expose themselves (2.65). The *Patria* also depends on the 6th-century Hesychius of Miletus to develop the character of Byzantium's eponymous founder Byzas, the son of Ceroessa (daughter of Io and Zeus) and Poseidon, who, in typical heroic fashion, defeated wild beasts and marauding barbarians, and to adjust the site of one of the Labours of Heracles, the breaking of Diomedes's horses, from the usual Abdera to the confines of Constantinople, the Zeuxippus, to be precise.

John Tzetzes (12th c.) wrote not as an avocation, but as a profession. His income from commissions for writing, supplemented by some teaching, was precarious, as attested by his regular complaints of poverty. It is telling that a writer who had to cultivate an appeal to highly literate audiences and to solicit commissions from those who would appear to be tasteful and discriminating concentrated so assiduously on mythological topics and ancient poetry. In his *Antehomerica*, *Homerica*, and *Posthomerica*, Tzetzes briefly sketches respectively the events before, during, and after the *Iliad*—all the while offering insults to a certain Isaac and his wife, who preferred charity to lepers over literary patronage—and while he is familiar with good poetic sources such as Quintus of

Smyrna and Tryphiodorus, he also reveals a dependence on the account of the Trojan War found in the chronicles and on his favorite method of interpretation, allegory. He explains his allegorical method in the *Exegesis of the Iliad*, an elementary commentary intended for schoolchildren: there is rhetorical allegory, describing mundane matters in poetic language; physical allegory, when myth really speaks of the weather or the constitution of the world; and mathematical allegory, which discusses astronomy and astrology in mythical terms. The gods may be allegorized in five different—and not necessarily mutually exclusive—ways: physically, as elements of the cosmos or weather conditions; psychologically, as character traits or impulses; "pragmatically" in two ways, as kings or philosophers; and astronomically, as planets.

Tzetzes employs these methods in his *Allegories of the Iliad* and *Allegories of the Odyssey*. The first begins with a lengthy prologue describing the events leading up to the opening of the *Iliad* and the appearances of the principal characters, obviously derived from Malalas and the chronicle tradition. For its first fifteen books Tzetzes enjoyed the patronage of the Empress Irene (*née* Bertha von Sulzbach); thereafter, the work was subsidized by a Constantine Cotertzes, and the change in patrons makes for a difference in tone and content. The earlier portion offers a paraphrase summing up the action of each book and more straightforward interpretations of details, perhaps as a concession to the limited Greek of the German-born empress. Chryses, for example, is presented as a sorcerer and astronomer, and Hera's sending Athena from heaven to restrain Achilles in his argument with Agamemnon is interpreted as the prudence of the soul coming from the head, which has the spherical form of the heaven. That those born under the sign of Venus are saved from danger and are desirable to others explains Aphrodite's actions for the benefit of Paris in book 3. The allegory in the later portion is denser and more complicated. On book 18, for instance, Tzetzes enumerates five different senses in which the sea, Thetis, is the mother of Achilles and explains how Hephaestus and his smithy indicate the origins and arrangement of the universe, before giving surprisingly short shrift to the rich symbolism of Achilles's shield. The *Allegories of the Odyssey* work along the same lines, regularly interpreting Zeus as Destiny (*Heimarmene*) and the inspiration of the Muse as the poet's knowledge, but presume a greater familiarity with the Homeric text than the work on the *Iliad*, and so proceed at a faster pace.

Tzetzes also wrote a *Theogony* on the basis of Homer and Hesiod, which included a catalogue of the heroes at Troy, and commentary material on Hesiod, Aristophanes, Lycophron, Oppian, and the tragedians, in addition to a collection of self-revelatory letters. His masterpiece, however, was the *Histories* (or *Chiliades* for its arbitrary division into books of a thousand lines each), a miscellaneous collection of engaging and improving stories that happily combines mythological, historical, and biblical material in a way that by now should be familiar. In handling myth in the *Histories*, Tzetzes cites authorities like Apollodorus and Palaephatus and tends to look for the pragmatic reality under the poets' flowery rhetoric. Without so much as mentioning metamorphosis, he interprets Hyacinthus and Narcissus by saying that flowers and trees, and even stars, have been named for love of such youths (1.254–256), and explains the frequent appearance of Zeus in myth by indicating that since the world began, kings have been called Zeus (1.474).

Eustathius of Thessalonica (around 1115–1195/6), amid an impressively extensive and diverse oeuvre, wrote commentaries on the Homeric epics, or, rather, selections and summaries of the scholarship on Homer, as his chosen title *Parekbolai* implies, much lengthier than the poems of Tzetzes. These were also the fruit of work in the classroom, though Eustathius taught as an adjunct to a successful career in church administration, but they often have rather different interests. Eustathius seems chiefly concerned with Homer as a rhetorical model, noting points of grammar, how the meaning of words changed over time, and useful exempla. He also elucidates the epics with reference to his present reality, connecting the reader to the Homeric world and imbuing it with a particular vividness. He did not shy away from mythological topics, but he only discussed them enough to clarify what Homer said. He was critical of those who attempted to apply an allegorical interpretation to every line and phrase in Homer, but he also insisted that a text might be understood on two levels and did not hesitate to employ allegory himself, speaking of it as a "cure (*therapeia*) of myth," though one perhaps inadequate to its task: he balks at "measuring out the great sea of myth with the dipper of allegory." Eustathius may not have made much of an original contribution to Byzantine mythography, but his commentaries remain valuable for preserving scraps of now lost works and for demonstrating how the Byzantine curriculum made the study of myth obligatory to a thorough scholar and teacher, even if his real interests lay elsewhere.

The Trojan War was a matter of enduring interest to the Byzantine world. Isaac Comnenus the Porphyrogenitus (1093–after 1152), the son of Alexius I (reigned 1081–1118), has been identified as the author of a brief twofold treatise that proposes to make up for Homer's omissions, covering the events from Heracles's sack of Troy through the life of Paris and the Fall of Troy to the departure of the victorious Greeks, and to give descriptions of the principal characters at Troy. The structure and details, as well as the historical treatment and even the chiding of Homer for his deficiencies, are all familiar from the chronicles, their obvious source, and little about the work is original, but it is remarkable that its composition should have been considered a fit undertaking for a prince of the blood. The fascination with Troy survived the cultural disruption that marked the Latin conquest of 1204 and the establishment of bilingual courts by the new Frankish overlords of Greece. These rulers and patrons brought with them a taste for chivalric romance that was satisfied by poets working in the vernacular of their domains. Some of these poems were likewise on imported themes and characters, while others attempted to embrace traditional poetic subjects. In the anonymous *Tale of Achilles* (of uncertain date), the hero is named Achilles and rules the Myrmidons, and his boon companion is Patroclus, but otherwise, the story has nothing to do with the Trojan War, taking its cue instead from the vernacular romance *Digenes Akrites*. The later *Tale That Happened at Troy* (*Diēgēsis genamenē en Troiāi*, sometimes called a "Byzantine Iliad") adheres closer to recognizable sources, especially Constantine Manasses, but still takes substantial liberties. The first half of the poem concerns Paris and begins with his birth and the baleful prophecy that accompanied it, but the attempts to forestall it are borrowed from the myth of Perseus; Paris is cast adrift in a chest and secluded in a tower, but after being shipwrecked and taken in by monks he insinuates himself into Menelaus's house in a monk's habit and seduces Helen. Once the Greeks set out to recapture her, the emphasis shifts to Achilles and the standard elements of the Trojan War, including the treacherous slaying of Achilles and the grief it causes. Constantine Hermoniakos composed his *Metaphrasis of the Trojan War*, commissioned by John II of Epirus (reigned 1323–1335), in twenty-four books like the *Iliad*, but it covers the whole course of events from the Judgment of Paris to the blinding of Polymestor, as well as an initial biography of Homer. Hermoniakos knew the text of Homer and quotes from the *Iliad* but also drastically summarizes its plot and elides some parts, especially when the pagan gods play a role; he depends to a greater extent on Tzetzes's *Allegories of the Iliad* and Manasses's *Chronike Synopsis*. The anonymous *War of Troy* (probably also 14th-century), by contrast, reveals no awareness of either Homer or the Byzantine chronicle tradition; it is rather a translation of Benoit de Ste. Maure's *Roman de Troie*, but at over 14,000 lines it is also the longest of the Greek chivalric romances and appears to have had a considerable influence on the genre. The appearance of a work so dependent on western literature might be taken to indicate a decline in the indigenous mythological tradition but could rather be the sign of a mythographical culture that was robust enough to welcome and absorb new material.

The Trojan War was not the only matter of myth to receive attention in the later stages of Byzantine culture, and vernacular poetry was not the only medium in which it was discussed. John Pediasimos (around 1250–1310/1314), who held the office "Consul of the Philosophers" in Palaeologan Constantinople, wrote on a variety of topics, from geometry and medicine to the marriages allowed by canon law, but one of them was the *Labours of Heracles*. This short treatise is a paraphrase of Apollodorus's treatment of the subject (*Bibl.* 2.72–126). It never strays very far from the text of Apollodorus, but it shows evidence of intelligent engagement and reworking. Pediasimos's work demonstrates that western influence was not pervasive, that myth had not altogether sunk to the level of folklore but was still a topic of scholarly inquiry and discussion for dedicated intellectuals, and that Byzantine scholars continued to depend on the best ancient texts in their study of mythography until the end of the period.

The last days of Byzantium saw mythological knowledge, which had been retained as something of an antiquarian curiosity and aid to the study of literature, repurposed for what were perhaps intended to be religious services. The philosopher George Gemistus Plethon (around 1360–1452) sought to reinvigorate the Greek nation by reviving not only the ideals, but also the political forms of Classical Antiquity. To this end he wrote the *Book of Laws*, which prescribed prayers, hymns, and sacrifices to Zeus and the rest of the Olympian pantheon. After Plethon's death the sole copy of the *Laws* was delivered into the hands of George Scholarius, an old philosophical opponent of Plethon, now the Patriarch Gennadius. Amid the devastation caused by the Turkish capture of Constantinople, Gennadius was appalled to read, in addition to the pagan liturgy, of God referred to as Zeus and of a trinity of Creator, World-Mind, and World-Soul. With some regret, Gennadius had the book burned, and so it survives only in fragments, some from the pen of Plethon himself. Before we rush to consider Plethon the last ember of ancient Hellenism or the first spark of Greek neopaganism, however, we should heed Wind's (1968: 244–245) caution that there are several good reasons for thinking that Plethon's contemporaries considered him an unimpeachable exponent of Christian orthodoxy and that the ceremonies set forth in the *Laws* were nothing more than "a secular sort of initiation, probably not more extravagant or sinister than the academic initiations in Rome which aroused clerical suspicion under Pius II because of their ritual paraphernalia."

The gods and heroes of myth were generally understood as historical figures in Byzantium. It was essential not only to deny the divinity of the objects of pagan cult, but also to insist on the reality, in some sense, of the subjects of so much literature that was still read. It can come as no surprise, then, that the chronicle tradition bulks so large in a discussion of Byzantine mythography; it is in records of the remote past that the curious would naturally seek some accounts of the people and events of myth. Even beyond the chronicles, the indiscriminate mingling of myth and history, as well as philosophy, was characteristic of Byzantine literature. This is because the value of mythology, like that of history and philosophy, was seen to be didactic as much as diversionary. The lessons of myth, though, often had to be teased out of their ridiculous or profane repositories, and the Byzantines were adept at employing allegory to draw insights out of poetry that enlightened their readers and would no doubt have surprised the original poets. Such a concern with understanding myth, and so undertaking the work of mythography, remained important in Byzantine society because Homer, fountainhead of myth, remained fundamental to Byzantine education.

## FURTHER READING

As far as I am aware, there is no single survey covering the topic of mythography in Byzantium. Nor is there any entry on "myth" or "mythography" in such a comprehensive reference work as the *Oxford Dictionary of Byzantium*. There are, however, extensive and detailed treatments of many aspects of the subject in numerous studies devoted to the authors and works, and they appear in the bibliography, along with some annotations.

## BIBLIOGRAPHY

Note: Sources in this list are grouped and presented in the same order one meets them in the chapter discussion.

*St. Basil, To the Youth*

Wilson, Nigel G., ed. *Saint Basil on the Value of Greek Literature*. London: Duckworth, 1975. English translation: Padelford, Frederick M. *Essays on the Study and Use of Poetry*, 99–120. New York: Henry Holt & Co., 1902.

## Eusebius of Caesarea

*Preparation for the Gospel* (especially books 1 and 2), edition and English translation: Gifford, Edwin H. *Eusebii Pamphili Evangelicae Praeparationis Libri XV.* 2 vols. Oxford: Clarendon Press, 1903.

Eusebius' *Chronicle* itself is lost, but an edition of Jerome's Latin translation, the earliest surviving version may be found in: Fotheringham, John K., ed. *Evsebii Pamphili Chronici Canones Latine vertit, adavxit, ad sua tempora prodvxit S. Evsebius Hieronymvs.* London: Humphrey Milford, 1923.

## John Malalas

Edition: Thurn, Johannes, ed. *Ioannis Malalae Chronographia.* Berlin: Walter de Gruyter, 2000. English translation: Jeffreys, Elizabeth, Michael Jeffreys, and Roger Scott, trans. *The Chronicle of John Malalas.* Melbourne: Australian Association for Byzantine Studies, 1986.

Treadgold, Warren. "The Byzantine World Histories of John Malalas and Eustathius of Epiphania." *International History Review* 29 (2007): 709–45.

*Excerpta Latina Barbari*, edition and English translation: Garstad, Benjamin. *Pseudo-Methodius, Apocalypse: An Alexandrian World Chronicle.* Cambridge, MA: Harvard University Press, 2012.

## The Picus-Zeus Narrative

Jeffreys, Elizabeth. "The Chronicle of John Malalas, Book I: A Commentary." In *The Sixth Century: End or Beginning*, edited by Pauline Allen and Elizabeth Jeffreys, 52–74. Brisbane: Australian Association for Byzantine Studies, 1996.

Garstad, Benjamin. "The *Excerpta Latina Barbari* and the 'Picus-Zeus narrative.'" *Jahrbuch für Internationale Germanistik* 34 (2002): 259–313.

Garstad, Benjamin. "Joseph as a Model for Faunus-Hermes." *Vigiliae Christianae* 63 (2009): 493–521.

Garstad, Benjamin. "The Account of Thoulis, King of Egypt." *Byzantinische Zeitschrift* 107 (2014): 51–76.

Garstad, Benjamin. "Euhemerus and the *Chronicle* of John Malalas." *International History Review* 38 (2016): 900–929.

## Malalas on Myth and the Trojan War

Hörling, Elsa. "Mythos und Pistis: Zur Deutung heidnischer Mythen in der christlichen Weltchronik des Johannes Malalas." Diss. Lund University, 1980.

Reinert, Stephen. "The Image of Dionysus in Malalas' Chronicle." In *Byzantine Studies in Honor of Milton V. Anastos*, edited by Speros Vryonis, 1–41. Malibu, CA: Undena Publications, 1985.

Garstad, Benjamin. "Perseus and the Foundation of Tarsus in the *Chronicle* of John Malalas." *Byzantion* 84 (2014): 171–183.

Goldwyn, Adam J. "John Malalas and the Origins of the Allegorical and Novelistic Traditions of the Trojan War in Byzantium." *Troianalexandrina* 15 (2015): 23–49.

Goldwyn, Adam J. "The Trojan War from Rome to New Rome." In *Miscellanea Byzantina I*, edited by Przemysław Marciniak, 9–34. Katowice, Poland: University of Silesia Press, 2016.

### *The Byzantine Chronicle Tradition on the Primeval Ages and the Mythological Period*

Jeffreys, Elizabeth. "The Attitudes of Byzantine Chroniclers towards Ancient History." *Byzantion* 49 (1979): 199–238.

Adler, William. *Time Immemorial: Archaic History and its Sources in Christian Chronography from Julius Africanus to George Syncellus*. Washington, DC: Dumbarton Oaks, 1989.

On the individual authors, see the entries for each in Warren Treadgold, *The Early Byzantine Historians*. London: Palgrave Macmillan, 2007; and Treadgold, *The Middle Byzantine Historians*. London: Palgrave Macmillan, 2013. Texts (and some translations) of those mentioned may be found as indicated:

*Chronicon Paschale*, edition: Dindorf, Ludwig, ed. *Chronicon Paschale*. 2 vols. Bonn: Weber, 1832.

John of Nikiu, English translation: Charles, Robert H. *The Chronicle of John, Bishop of Nikiu*. London: Williams & Norgate, 1916.

George the Syncellus: Mosshammer, Alden A., ed. *Georgii Syncelli Ecloga Chronographica*. Leipzig: B. G. Teubner, 1984. English translation: Adler, William, and Paul Tuffin. *The Chronography of George Synkellos*. Oxford: Oxford University Press, 2002.

George Hamartolos: de Boor, Carl, ed. *Georgii Monachi Chronicon*, 2 vols. Leipzig: B. G. Teubner, 1904.

Symeon Logothetes: Wahlgren, Stephan, ed. *Symeonis Magistri et Logothetae Chronicon*. Berlin: Walter de Gruyter, 2006.

George Cedrenus: Tartaglia, Luigi, ed. *Georgii Cedreni Historiarum Compendium*. 2 vols. Rome: Bardi Edizioni, 2016.

Constantine Manasses: Lampsidis, Odysseus, ed. *Constantini Manassis Breviarium Chronicum*. 2 vols. Athens, Greece: Institutum Graecoromanae Antiquitatis, 1996. English translation: Yuretich, Linda. *The Chronicle of Constantine Manasses*. Liverpool: Liverpool University Press, 2018.

Michael Glykas: Bekker, Immanuel, ed. *Michaelis Glycae Annales*. Bonn: Weber, 1836.

Joel the Chronographer: Iadevaia, Francesca, ed. *Cronografia compendiaria*. Messina, Italy: EDAS, 1979.

### *Souda*

Edition: Adler, Ada, ed. *Suidae Lexicon*. 5 vols. Leipzig: Teubner, 1928–1938. There is an electronic version, with English translations, on the website the Suda On Line: https://www.stoa.org/sol. See especially the entries for: Ἄρης (A 3852), Αἰγαῖον (Αι 23), Αἴγυπτος (Αι 77), Ἥφαιστος (H 661), Θοῦλις (Θ 415), Θούρρας (Θ 417), Ἴλιον (I 320), Ἰώ (I 453), Μέδουσα (M 406), Μεταλλεῖς (M 704), Ὅμηρος (O 251), Πῆκος (Π 1500), Τάβλα (T 7), Οἰδίπους (Οι 34), Φαῦνος (Φ 148).

### *Nonnus of Panopolis*

Edition and French translation: Vian, Francis, et al., eds. *Nonnos de Panopolis: Les Dionysiaques*. 18 vols. Paris: Les Belles Lettres, 1976–2006.

Text and English translation: Rouse, William H. D. *Nonnos. Dionysiaca*. 3 vols. Cambridge, MA: Harvard University Press, 1940.

Accorinti, Domenico, ed. *Brill's Companion to Nonnus of Panopolis*. Leiden: Brill, 2016.

Liebeschuetz, Wolfgang. "The Use of Pagan Mythology in the Christian Empire with Particular Reference to the *Dionysiaca* of Nonnus." In *The Sixth Century: End or Beginning?* Edited by Pauline Allen and Elizabeth Jeffreys, 75–91. Brisbane: Australian Association for Byzantine Studies, 1996.

### Christodorus of Coptos

The *Description of the Statues* of Christodorus of Coptos constitutes book 2 of the *Greek Anthology*. Edition and English translation: Paton, William R., revised by Michael A. Tueller. *Greek Anthology I*, 83–145. Cambridge, MA: Harvard University Press, 2014.
Kaldellis, Anthony. "Christodoros on the Statues of the Zeuxippos Baths: A New Reading of the *Ekphrasis*." *Greek, Roman and Byzantine Studies* 47 (2007): 361–383.

### Patria of Constantinople

Edition and English translation: Berger, Albrecht. *Accounts of Medieval Constantinople.* Cambridge, MA: Harvard University Press, 2013.

### For the sources of the *Patria*

Edition and English translation: Cameron, Averil, and Judith Herrin, eds. *Constantinople in the Early Eighth Century: The "Parastaseis Syntomoi Chronikai."* Leiden: Brill, 1984.
Kaldellis, Anthony. "The Works and Days of Hesychios the Illoustrios of Miletos." *Greek, Roman and Byzantine Studies* 45 (2005): 381–403.
Braccini, Tommaso. *Bisanzio prima di Bisanzio: Miti fondazioni della nuova Roma.* Rome: Salerno Editrice, 2019.

### John Tzetzes

The edition of the Homeric summaries is quite old: Jacobs, Friedrich, ed. *Ioannis Tzetzae Antehomerica Homerica et Posthomerica.* Leipzig: Weidmann, 1793, but English translations of the *Antehomerica* (https://archive.org/details/TzetzesANTEHOMERICA), *Homerica* (https://archive.org/details/TzetzesHOMERICA), and *Posthomerica* (https://archive.org/details/TzetzesPOSTHOMERICA) are available on the Internet.
*Exegesis of the Iliad*: Papathomopoulos, Manolis, ed. Εξήγησις Ιοάννου Γραμματικού του Τζέζου εις την Ομήρου Ιλιαδα. Athens, Greece: Ακαδèμια Athènôn, 2007.
*Homeric Allegories*, edition and English translation: Goldwyn, Adam J., and Dimitra Kokkini. *John Tzetzes. Allegories of the Iliad.* Cambridge, MA: Harvard University Press, 2015, and *John Tzetzes, Allegories of the Odyssey.* Cambridge, MA: Harvard University Press, 2019.
*Histories*: Leone, Pietro L., ed. *Ioannis Tzetzae historiae.* Napoli: Libreria Scientifica Editrice, 1968. English translation online at Internet Archive: https://archive.org/details/TzetzesCH ILIADES.
Hunger, Herbert. "Allegorische Mythendeutung in der Antike und bei Johannes Tzetzes." *Jahrbuch der österreichischen byzantinischen Gesellschaft* 3 (1954): 35–54.
Goldwyn, Adam J. "Theory and Method in John Tzetzes' *Allegories of the* Iliad and *Allegories of the* Odyssey." *Scandinavian Journal of Byzantine and Modern Greek Studies* 3 (2017): 141–171.

## Eustathius of Thessalonica

*Iliad* commentary: van der Valk, Marchinus, ed. *Commentarii ad Homeri Iliadem.* 4 vols. Leiden: E. J. Brill, 1971–1987.

*Odyssey* commentary: Cullhed, Eric. *Eustathios of Thessalonike, Commentary on Homer's Odyssey: Volume I on Rhapsodies A-B.* Uppsala: Uppsala Universitet, 2016. This is the first volume of a project, in collaboration with S. Douglas Olson, that intends to present new editions and English translations of Eustathius's complete commentary on Homer.

Browning, Robert. "Homer in Byzantium." *Viator* 6 (1975): 15–33.

Pizzone, Aglae. "Audiences and Emotions in Eustathios of Thessalonike's Commentaries on Homer." *Dumbarton Oaks Papers* 70 (2016): 225–244.

## Treatments of Trojan Material

Isaac Comnenus: Hinck, Hugo, ed. *Polemonis Declamationes,* 57–88. Leipzig: B. G. Teubner, 1873.

*Tale of Achilles*: Hesseling, Dirk C., ed. *L'Achilléïde byzantine.* Amsterdam: J. Müller, 1919.

*Tale that Happened at Troy*: Nørgaard, Lars, and Ole L. Smith, eds. *A Byzantine Iliad.* Copenhagen: Museum Tusculanum, 1975.

Constantine Hermoniakos: Legrand, Émile, ed. *ΙΛΙΑΔΟΣ ΡΑΨΩΙΔΙΑΙ ΚΔ'. La guerre de Troie: Poème du XIVe siècle en vers octosyllabes par Constantin Hermoniacos.* Paris: J. Maisonneuve, 1890.

*War of Troy*: Jeffreys, Elizabeth, and Manolis Papathomopoulos, eds. *Ο ΠΟΛΕΜΟΣ ΤΗΣ ΤΡΟΑΔΟΣ (The War of Troy).* Athens, Greece: Morphotiko Hidryma Ethnikes Trapezes, 1996.

Beaton, Roderick. *The Medieval Greek Romance.* 2nd ed. London: Routledge, 1996.

Nilsson, Ingela. "From Homer to Hermoniakos: Some Considerations of Troy Matter in Byzantine Literature." *Troialexandrina* 4 (2004): 9–34.

## John Pediasimos

Edition and French translation: Levrie, Katrien. *Jean Pédiasimos: Essai sur les douze travaux d'Héracles.* Leuven: Peeters, 2018.

## George Gemistus Plethon

*Book of Laws*, edition and French translation: Alexandre, Charles, ed. *Pléthon. Traité des lois.* Paris: Firmin Didot, 1858. English translation: Woodhouse, Christopher M. *George Gemistos Plethon: The Last of the Hellenes,* 322–356. Oxford: Clarendon Press, 1986.

Anastos, Milton V. "Pletho's Calendar and Liturgy." *Dumbarton Oaks Papers* 4 (1948): 183–305.

Wind, Edgar. *Pagan Mysteries in the Renaissance.* London: Faber & Faber, 1968.

# CHAPTER 39

# MYTHOGRAPHY IN THE LATIN WEST

## BENJAMIN GARSTAD

THE motivation for writing mythography in the Middle Ages in western Europe remained much the same as it had been in antiquity—that is, to explain the mythological allusions and the stray references to the characters and events of myth that peppered any literary work. The need for mythography was, no doubt, more acute in the medieval era, as the Latin literary canon being read in schools remained the same, but its mythological underpinnings were ever further from the lived experience of its readers. Two of the changes that made the Latin Middle Ages what they were added a couple of imperatives to the work of the mythographer. On the one hand, the bilingualism in Greek and Latin that had been the common attribute of the educated Roman came to be a rarity as the teaching of Greek in the West faltered and failed. So, the mythographer had to set out the basics of Greek literature and vocabulary necessary to an understanding of, for example, the story of Achilles or the elements of the Greek name for Venus. On the other, the triumph of Christianity made it necessary to render the gods of the ancients innocuous and make it clear that they were false gods, usually by explaining them as deceased men whose deeds were misunderstood and inflated. Thus, a religious impulse was added to the rationalizing tendency of Palaephatus and the historical speculation of Euhemerus.

The basis for medieval western mythography was the treatment of the gods and myth in Latin patristic literature, which was at least as widely read as the school texts that necessitated an understanding of myth. Here the reader could find not only the basic contentions of the Church in regard to paganism and explanations of the gods as dead men, but also valuable mythological details. Tertullian, the earliest Christian author in Latin (about 160–about 240), proposed to prove the humanity of all the gods by establishing that their common forefather was a man. To this end, he offered the indications of Saturn's residence in Italy, culled from myth and antiquities, as evidence that he was indeed a man (*Ad Nat.* 2.12.26–29, *Apol.* 10). This argument, along with the brief account of Saturn in Italy, is taken over into the slightly later *Octavius* of Minucius Felix (*Oct.* 21.4–10). In his short treatise *De Idolorum Vanitate*, Cyprian (about 200–258) laid out the lineaments of the Christian understanding that the gods were deceased kings, whose images had been set up as memorials, but whose worship was perpetuated by crafty demons; the evidence was offered in the form of references to myths that were about not only the deification of mortals but also the manual labor undertaken by the gods, and their births and graves. Other apologists, Arnobius of Sicca (wrote about 295), Firmicus Maternus (about 343–350), and the anonymous author of the *De Execrandis Diis Gentium* (disputedly attributed to Tertullian but dated to as late as the 6th century), provided plentiful mythological material in their refutations of paganism, although the manuscript tradition of these authors would indicate that their readership in the Middle Ages was decidedly limited.

Far more influential were the works of Lactantius, Eusebius (by way of Jerome), and Augustine. The first book of the *Divinae Institutiones* (303–313) of Lactantius was concerned with the worship falsely offered to the pagan gods, and the second, with how this worship originated. Both books make ample reference to the more scandalous myths about the pagan gods and quote extensively from Euhemerus's account (in Ennius's Latin translation) of the gods as ancient human kings. In Jerome's translation of the *Chronicle* of Eusebius of Caesarea (380–382) the gods and heroes of myth are treated as historical figures and dates are assigned to their careers. Augustine takes over this historical rendering of myth in its eighteenth book, but the preponderant interpretation of the gods in his *City of God* (413–426) is a combination of euhemerism, maintaining that the gods were once human beings, and diabolism, holding that the cults of dead men were overtaken and fostered by demons (see esp. *De Civ. D.* 7.18, 27, 34).

Medieval mythography was also informed by the standard works of literary and cultural scholarship that were preserved from antiquity, such as Cicero's *De Natura Deorum* and Servius's commentaries on the works of Vergil.

The first and arguably most influential of the medieval mythographers was Fulgentius, who goes under the names of Fabius Planciades Fulgentius and Fabius Claudius Gordianus Fulgentius. He wrote in North Africa sometime between 550 and 642, most likely, shortly after 550. He has been identified with Fulgentius, the bishop of Ruspe (468–533), and though Hays (2003; see also "Fulgentius Bibliography" website in bibliography) has conclusively shown this identification to be false, the confusion can only have added the luster of pontifical sanctity to his memory. In addition to the *Mitologiae*, which commands our attention, Fulgentius also wrote the *Expositio Virgilianae Continentiae*, an elucidation of the *Aeneid* with moral overtones; the *Expositio Sermonum Antiquorum*, on archaic words; and the *De Aetatibus Mundi et Hominis*, an unfinished history of the world in fourteen books, each of which refrains from using a successive letter of the alphabet (the *Super Thebaiden*, an allegorical reading of Statius, was also ascribed, falsely, to Fulgentius but actually written much later). All attempts to discover something about the life of Fulgentius must depend on the internal evidence of his works and thus run the risk of reading too much into possible hints and mistaking literary imposture for personal information. The subjects of his works suggest the interests of a schoolmaster, but Fulgentius tends to imply that his days in the classroom were long behind him; there were, moreover, plenty of amateur authors who took an interest in learning and education in his day. He speaks of retirement to his country estate, but this may reflect a literary commonplace rather than his actual circumstances. He also refers to a wife, who may have existed as no more than a metaphorical opponent to his proffered mistress, Satire.

The *Mitologiae* opens with a lengthy prologue in which Fulgentius professes to be treating a topic of no interest to the practical or the powerful, and then, in an encounter with the Muse Calliope, determines not to simply relate the fictions of myth but to expose deviations from the truth and impose an allegorical reading on them. True to his word, in the three books that follow, Fulgentius offers, along with details of depictions and an indication of the common attributes of some gods and heroes, short rehearsals of various tales. But unlike Hyginus's *Fabulae*, for instance, these are not straightforward retellings of the stories, and they often assume some previous knowledge on the reader's part. Fulgentius retells his myths in order to subject them to an etymological dissection and allegorical interpretation and to extract from them an improving moral lesson. He brings to his task an apparent knowledge of Greek, but not one that inspires in him any respect for the Greeks; he contrasts Greek lies (the literal sense of a myth) with Roman truth (his interpretation). Fulgentius also displays a knowledge of otherwise unattested sources and similarly unattested quotations from known authors, but even allowing for access to a larger body of still extant works, it is hard to avoid the suspicion of fabricated citations. The Christian orientation of the *Mitologiae* is evident in stray remarks and contributions to the moral edification found in myth. And while Fulgentius has practically none of the apologists' argumentative intent, he still begins his treatment of myth with an account of the origins of idolatry (*Mit.* 1.1).

Fulgentius's knowledge of myth is generally sound, but there are occasionally remarkable errors. For instance, he has Saturn, rather than Caelus, castrated to engender Venus (*Mit.* 1.2, 2.1), an error that is frequently perpetuated in the medieval tradition. More representative of Fulgentius's approach, however, is his treatment of Bellerophon (*Mit.* 3.1). He briefly tells the story and then proceeds to explain each of its elements from the meaning of the Greek behind the names and with numerous references to Homer, Menander, Virgil, and Epicharmus. Bellerophon, from *buleforunta*, is good counsel opposed (*antion*) to Antia's lust. He slays the Cymera (Chimaera), the *cymeron* (*kyme* + *eron*) or "wavering of love" as it were, which is depicted with three heads to represent the three stages of love, beginning, completion, and ending, because good counsel defeats lust. Often, though, Fulgentius does not actually recount a myth and simply addresses himself to mythic characters on their own. For instance, he explains the nine Muses (*Mit.* 1.15) both, on the basis of their number, with the addition of Apollo to make ten, as the various parts of the body that produce speech, here with reference to a number of Greek authorities, and, from the meaning in Greek of their names, as the successive stages of learning from desiring instruction to passing it along competently.

Fulgentius's involved and challenging style has elicited comment from modern critics. Little as it may be to today's taste, it should be remembered that Fulgentius's was a bravura performance in his own day, much admired and imitated by those who were able in the Middle Ages, especially the Carolingian period. Indeed, Fulgentius exerted an enormous influence on medieval scholarship, which persisted into the Renaissance and beyond, and few of the authors we shall discuss do not depend upon him in one way or another. Of particular note are the efforts of Baudri of Bougueil (Baldric of Dol; d. 1130) to render the *Mitologiae* into over a thousand lines of Latin verse and the work of John Ridewall, who drew on a plethora of sources, but acknowledged his debt to Fulgentius in the title of his *Fulgentius Metaforalis* (about 1331), which identified the heathen gods with virtues.

Another seminal treatment of myth for the Middle Ages was not a discrete work, but rather a chapter in Isidore of Seville's (about 560–636) encyclopedic *Etymologiae* or *Origines*. Isidore attempts a comprehensive understanding of the world by tracing the roots of the words for all of the things in it. The heathen gods have their place in his work inasmuch as they have been given names and occur in human discourse. Very few of the etymologies found in Isidore are his own; rather, they were gleaned from a lifetime of reading. Isidore's great service was to collect them in one place under appropriate headings and his original contribution was the selection and arrangement of his material, which conveys its own message. His discussion of the pagan gods (*Etym.* 8.11), for instance, begins by asserting that the Graeco-Roman gods were once men who after death came to be worshipped for their merits, sketches the origins of idolatry and the meaning of words associated with it, explicates such words as demon, Devil, Satan, and Antichrist, and then discusses the Semitic gods mentioned in the Old Testament. Before they are ever discussed in detail, consequently, the gods are understood from a decidedly Christian perspective that does not need to be repeated constantly: the so-called gods are mortal and their idols, memorials to the dead; their worship is cultivated by fallen angels who entice men to sin, and they have the same essence as the grotesque alien gods opposed by the prophets of old.

When Isidore turns to discuss each of the gods in turn, he begins by saying that the myths try to draw a connection between the names of the gods and physical causes and the origins of the elements, but that these are poetic fictions intended to enhance the reputation of shameful men (*Etym.* 8.11.29). Nevertheless, these physical allegories are the explanations that Isidore will present in the course of his discussion of the gods without any overt contradiction. And he tends to present as many as he can find, instead of choosing one over another. In addition to their names, Isidore also discusses the attributes of the gods, their habits and spheres of interest. For instance, Saturn holds a scythe to signify an association with agriculture, the cyclical nature of time, or knowledge, because it is sharp on the inside (*Etym.* 8.11.32). Mars is an adulterer because, as god of war, he is faithless to warriors (*Etym.* 8.11.51). And Mercury is god not only of speech, but also of commerce because speech goes between buyers and sellers, and of thieves, because speech deceives the minds of listeners (*Etym.* 8.11.45–47). Myths as stories do not occur very often, and when they do it is to bolster an interpretation of Isidore's, whether apologetic or simply explanatory. He says that according to the poets Prometheus first created human beings, because he was actually the first to make likenesses of them out of clay (*Etym.* 8.11.8). And Isidore briefly relates the story of Apollo defeating the serpent Python in order to explain his epithet Pythius (*Etym.* 8.11.54–55).

The combination of apologetic concerns and disinterested scholarship in Isidore's approach is seen in his treatment of Jupiter (*Etym.* 8.11.34–36). The name of Jupiter (*Iovis*) comes from "helping" (*a iuvando*) and Jupiter as if it were *iuvans pater* ("helping father"). Isidore notes that he is called "Jupiter the Best" (*Iuppiter Optimus*) but insists on the irony of this title on account of his sexual excesses. There follows a brief catalogue of Jupiter's seductions with rationalizing explanations of his transformations. He is imagined to have been a bull because he carried off Europa in a ship with a bull for a figurehead. Likewise, he is thought to have seduced Danae with a shower of gold because he bribed her with gold; an eagle in the case of Ganymede because he raped/ snatched him; a serpent because he crept about, and a swan because he sang. Isidore ends by saying these are less figures of speech than they are crimes when made plain, and by deploring that the gods were thought to be so much worse than men were expected to be. Perhaps more typical, since free of polemics, is Isidore's explanation of Vulcan (*Etym.* 8.11.39–41) as fire, his name from *volans candor* ("flying brilliance") or *volicanus* since he flies through the air and fire comes from the clouds. Homer is cited for the fall of Vulcan, a story that came about because lightning falls from the air. Vulcan is thought to be born from Juno's thigh because lightning comes from the lower parts of the air. He is lame because fire is not straight but seems crooked in appearance and movement. He is the inventor of the smithy because fire is necessary for the working of metals.

The space devoted to the gods and myth in the *Etymologiae* may be small, but its importance lies in the incalculable influence Isidore exerted on the general learning of the Middle Ages. The traces of this influence can be found in all sorts of literature, from biblical glosses to vernacular poetry. It is no less evident in the dictionaries and encyclopedias that were written in more direct imitation of Isidore. The discussion of the gods in the encyclopedic *De Universo* of Rabanus Maurus (776 or 784–856), one of the leading scholars of the Carolingian era, is essentially a verbatim repetition of the passage in the *Etymologiae*. Although the *Historia Scholastica* of Peter Comestor (died about 1179) follows the biblical text very closely, it also includes brief accounts of the gods as historical figures, which owe as much to Eusebius as to Isidore. Vincent of Beauvais, in his discussion of the origins of idolatry in the *Speculum Historiale* (about 1244), cited Isidore and Peter Comestor, as well as Cicero and the Pseudo-Clementine literature, to prove that the gods were deified men. Roger Bacon referred to Augustine, Isidore, and the Venerable Bede in his *Opus Maius* (about 1268) to demonstrate that the patriarchs and prophets who had received divine revelation, and so the fullness of philosophy, had preceded the pagan philosophers, among whom he counts the gods and heroes of myth.

Mythography and allegory enjoyed something of a reciprocal relationship throughout the Middle Ages. Already in Fulgentius and Isidore, as well as in such standard medieval reading as the *Saturnalia* of Macrobius and Martianus Capella's *Marriage of Philology and Mercury*, there are abundant examples of the idea that the surface meaning of stories hid a deeper meaning, that the representations of the gods and their deeds as reported by myth could offer potent images of the physical universe, moral instruction, and philosophical truth. These allegorical interpretations are among the explanations offered by mythographers. But in their enthusiasm for discovering hidden truths, the allegorists often neglected to make the story of the myths they were interpreting plain; the earlier ones assumed such basic knowledge on the part of their readers. So, it fell to the mythographers to lay out clearly the myths alluded to by the allegorists. And while the allegorists offered their interpretations seemingly haphazardly, as suited the purposes of their own compositions, the mythographers organized them according to genealogical relationships and the dictates of myth itself.

Theodulf of Orleans (about 750–821) considered it the duty of the wise man to transform the lies of poets into truth and discover what their images stand for, such as Hercules representing virtue or Cacus theft, or all the attributes of Cupid representing the tortures and deceits of love. Remigius of Auxerre's (841–908) commentary on Martianus Capella tried to explain the complicated allegory of the *De Nuptiis*'s first two books, applying different kinds of interpretation, including the allegorical, to the mythological figures found there, and was exploited especially by the Third Vatican Mythographer. John of Salisbury (about 1115–1180) reminds us that allegory appealed in part to the scholar's arrogance, for he urged the interpretation of myth because it hides secret teachings that are unrecognized by the common rabble. The allegorical tradition culminated in the French verse *Ovide Moralisé*, which discovered in the racy tales of the *Metamorphoses* all the lessons of virtue and biblical knowledge necessary to equip a circumspect Christian and was soon rendered in Latin to become the fifteenth book of Pierre Bersuire's (1290–1362) *De Fabulis Poetarum*, the *Ovidius Moralizatus*.

The appearance of stories of the gods in the Middle Ages was not restricted to works of learned erudition. They were also to be found in the ongoing efforts of clerics to combat paganism, whether the lingering superstitions of peasants or the beliefs of the unconverted on the frontiers of Christendom. Despite the no doubt changing complexion of the paganism encountered, the response seems to have continued to be in terms of Graeco-Roman myth. Caesarius of Arles (about 470–542) urged his flock not to call the days of the week by the names of the pagan gods, since by doing this, he said, they gave honor to disreputable men and women, who were born during Israel's sojourn in Egypt. Likewise, Martin of Braga (about 520–580) attempting to weed out the vestiges of paganism in his see, declared in the *De Correctione Rusticorum* that, after a period when men worshipped the heavenly bodies and elements of nature, demons assumed the names of evil men and women and arrogated worship to themselves. The names are, of course, those of the pagan gods and their wickedness is demonstrated by a brief catalogue of crimes easily recognizable from mythology. Demons continue to infest the world, Martin asserted, and men still call upon them, even naming the days of the week after them. According to Gregory of Tours (about 540–594), when Clothilda set about to persuade her husband Clovis (reigned 481–511) of the error of his pagan ways, she insisted that his gods were idols with the names of dead men and substantiated her point by referring to Saturn's flight before his son, the unspeakable and incestuous philandering of Jupiter, and the sorcery of Mars and Mercury. Scholars may suggest that this recreation of domestic proselytizing is more compatible with the conception of paganism held by Gregory and his learned audience than it is with the realities of Frankish religion, but it is consistent with most of the other early medieval responses to paganism, which discuss Graeco-Roman gods.

Daniel of Winchester (died 745) advised Boniface (680–754) in his missionary efforts among the Saxons and Frisians not to dispute the divine genealogies the pagans offered him, but to take them as the starting point of his preaching. If the gods were born from the intercourse of men and women, like men, they were men, and if they had a beginning, so did the world. Such genealogies were a feature of both Graeco-Roman and Germanic myth, and it is hard to say which Daniel and Boniface had in mind. We should not assume that, just because this was intended as practical advice, it was some distinctly Saxon myth. An anonymous contemporary homilist included a denunciation of the Graeco-Roman gods with a smattering of details in his outline of Christian history, although he was so unfamiliar with myth as to take Venus for a man. Perhaps most remarkably, when in the 11th century Ælfric (about 995–about 1020) and Wulfstan (died 1023) wrote in English and opposed themselves to the paganism of the Scandinavians, they gave an account of the heathen gods that began on Crete, mentioned the cannibalism of Saturn, the fornication of Jupiter, and the theft and deceit of Mercury, and gave the gods their Latin names. They do note that the Danes call Jupiter Thor and Mercury Odin but correct their error in thinking that Jupiter (Thor) was the son of Mercury (Odin)—it was the other way around. The myths of the Greeks and Romans, since they were in fact a history of dead men, were more authoritative than the living paganism of the Scandinavians against which Ælfric and Wulfstan inveighed.

For the most part, however, mythology was dealt with in the Middle Ages not as the target of refutation, but as part of the learning of the ancients. Readers of ancient texts needed to know in full the stories that were briefly alluded to and have their obscure points clarified. They also had to be provided with an edifying interpretation of those apparently silly or salacious stories. These needs were satisfied by collections of the fables of the Greeks and Romans. The most significant of these are the three works that go under the name of the Vatican Mythographers. The designation is the result of three distinct, but related, works being published together by Angelo Mai in 1831 on the basis of texts he had found in the Vatican Library. These mythographies share interests and intent, as well as a number of sources, and the later ones borrow from the earlier, but each is very much its own work and exhibits significant differences from the others.

The so-called First Vatican Mythographer was once thought to have written in the 7th or 8th century, but more recent investigation has uncovered the use of Remigius of Auxerre (841–908) as a source and a consequent redating to sometime between 875 and 1075. The text contains no indication as to the author's identity. He included 229, mostly brief, entries in three books; the second book ends with a note that as the first book had one hundred tales, so will the second, suggesting that the third book, with only twenty-nine, might have been left unfinished. Book 1 begins abruptly with Prometheus and proceeds to Minerva and Vulcan, and there is no apparent order to the entries, although stories with common characters or that deal with the same event occur together. Book 3 (3.201) commences with a genealogy of the gods and heroes that attempts to integrate much of the miscellaneous material found throughout the various entries by following various lines, and it might be a belated effort to impose some kind of organization on the work as a whole. The entries themselves give synopses of stories from Greek and Latin mythology, as well as Greek and Roman history, indeed stories of any kind likely to be the subject of allusion in classical literature. The mixture is a salutary reminder that for the Middle Ages myths were supposed to preserve historical truth, however corruptly, and the accounts of classical history had something of the quality of fable. Many, if not most, of the entries are merely descriptive or narrative, offering an explanation intended to spell out the story behind a stray reference or name. Some include interpretations, mainly rationalizing, reducing the supernatural and unnatural to the misunderstood mundane, but there are also etymological and moral interpretations; all of them give evidence of attentive reading, rather than originality. There are entries that, instead of discussing a single character or story, provide summary plots of the *Aeneid*, or rather a potted history of Aeneas (2.199), the *Iliad* (3.206), and Apuleius's story of Cupid and Psyche (3.226). The mythographer owes obvious, if unacknowledged, debts to Servius, the *scholia* on Statius, Hyginus (through intermediaries), and Fulgentius. The First Vatican Mythographer survives in a single manuscript, which indicates a limited readership and audience, but he did exert an influence on the Second Vatican Mythographer, at least.

The Second Vatican Mythographer, like the First, is anonymous, and we can say little more about his date than that, based on the evidence of influence, he must have written later than the First. His material is rather better organized, within the limitations of the subject. He begins with a brief discourse on the invention of fables and the actual origin of the gods, which is largely taken from Isidore. Then he treats Saturn, Jupiter, and the other chief gods, followed by myths of lesser deities and heroes. Interspersed among these fables are a few historical anecdotes that are ultimately derived from Herodotus (84 Cleobis and Biton; 217 a garbled version of the story of Croesus) and Livy (236–239). Perhaps most remarkably, a notice on the drainage works of Julius Caesar (184) is included in the midst of several entries on Hercules, perhaps recalled by the interpretation of the hero's defeat of the Lernaean Hydra as a land reclamation project (188)—another reminder of the mingling of myth and ancient history in the medieval imagination. There is perhaps a more consistent effort to provide interpretations for the stories than in the First Vatican Mythographer, but there remain many instances where the story is simply told without explanation. The Second Mythographer can produce obscure mythological details, which can provide a seemly unity to apparently disparate tales, like the necklace of Gorgons' eyes, the accursed heirloom of the house of Cadmus (99), or surprising variants to well-known stories, such as an alternate version of the origins of the Trojan War as revenge for the rape of Hesione, with a guiltless Helen (227). But he is not always the master of his material; he knows, as Fulgentius apparently did not, that Saturn castrated his father, Caelus, but the explanation he provides for the birth of Venus depends on the error that it was Saturn who was castrated (40). As in the First Mythographer, some entries are elaborated according to the dictates of literary works. The entry on Peleus and Thetis (248), for instance, traces the events of the Trojan

Cycle from Discord's intervention at the marriage feast to the sacrifice of Polyxena at Achilles's tomb, but it gives pride of place to those incidents that make up the action of the *Iliad*. This purely narrative entry is followed by one giving a physical allegory of certain elements of the story. Eleven manuscripts of the Second Mythographer survive, as compared to the one of the First, suggesting a relatively larger readership and influence.

In some manuscripts the work of the Third Vatican Mythographer is credited to Alberic of London, who has been identified with a Canon Alberic, whose name appears in the charters of Saint Paul's Cathedral from about 1160. Alberic's name is stricken out in some instances and replaced with "Nequam." This Nequam has been identified with Alexander Neckam (1157–1217), abbot of Circencester, polymath, and prolific author. Seznec (1981: 170–171) has suggested that Alberic of London, Alexander Neckam, and the Third Vatican Mythographer are all the same person, but there is no agreement on the matter. At least we have a workable date of around the latter half of the 12th century for the composition of the text. The Third Mythographer has a reputation for better style and exhibiting more personality than the other two. While his Latin may be superior, most of the supposed indications of character are actually derived from his sources. The quip that the rapacious life represented by Juno was anciently led by a few tyrants, but now by everyone (11.22), for instance, is taken from Fulgentius (*Mit.* 2.1). The Third Mythographer begins with an account of the origins of idolatry (also taken from Fulgentius) and polytheism, and then states his, largely unfulfilled, intention to refute the errors of antiquity. Rather he gives a masterful display of antique lore and undertakes to extract as much insight and utility as possible from his erudition. He organizes his material into fifteen lengthy chapters on the principal gods and heroes. He is not composing a story collection like the other two Mythographers, but he still covers a great deal of the same material and connections are signaled by the inclusion of a treatment under a certain heading. Mars, for example, is dealt with in the chapter on Venus. The Third Mythographer also makes the discussion of myth an opportunity for lengthy digressions on such arcane and subtle subjects as the nature of the soul and the afterlife (6.5–30), sacrificial ritual (6.30–35), augury (11.12–16), and astrology (15.1–12). The result is an impressive compendium of miscellaneous learning in which one often loses sight of the myths at its core. The Third Mythographer makes use of a wide variety of sources: the canonical poets, Horace, Vergil, Ovid, Lucan, and Statius, as well as Lucretius, and the *Narrationes* ascribed to Lactantius Placidus, Servius, Macrobius, Martianus Capella, Fulgentius, and Remigius of Auxerre's commentary on Martianus. The Third Mythographer enjoyed considerable popularity well into the Renaissance under different names, such as the *Liber Ymaginum Deorum*, the *Scintillarium Poetarum*, and the *Poetarius*. We know that Petrarch owned a copy of what he called the "Poetarius Albrici." Some two centuries after Alberic, the *Liber Ymaginum*, a set of illustrations with descriptions, was composed on the basis of his work.

The Vatican Mythographers were not alone in collecting and explaining mythological material as the Middle Ages progressed, but they do seem to have been more comprehensive and, certainly the Second and Third Mythographers, more widely circulating exponents of mythography. Another compendious work of mythography is Conrad of Mure's *Fabularius*, completed in Zurich in 1273, which begins with a metrical gene-alogy of the gods and then offers a thorough dictionary of mythology, although once again the distinction between mythology and ancient history is not strictly observed. Similar efforts are briefer or survive in only a few manuscripts, or a single one, or not at all. The later 12th-century *Liber de Natura Deorum* or Digby Mythographer, for in-stance, is represented by a lone manuscript and never achieved much influence; the my-thographer often shows more interest in narrative than interpretation and depends on the common list of mythological sources, including Alberic, as well as the mysterious Theodontius.

The work of the shadowy Theodontius is lost but exerted enormous influence through those who borrowed from it. Theodontius appears to have produced his work at some time between the composition of the Servius *auctus*, an identifiable source, in the 7th or 8th century and Bernard of Utrecht's commentary on Theodulus, written between 1076 and 1099, which exploits Theodontius. Most of the fragments are characteristic of medieval mythography, inasmuch as they apply natural and historical allegory to myths and attempt to derive some philosophical insight from them. Theodontius's most im-portant contribution to the mythographic tradition was the introduction of the figure of Demogorgon as the progenitor of all the gods; in this he seems to have been propagating an error based on a misreading of *demiourgon* in the *scholia* on Statius. In addition to the Digby Mythographer and a few other stray signs of influence, Theodontius was known to Paolo da Perugia (died 1348). It was in Paolo's lost *Collectiones* that Boccaccio found the material he derived from Theodontius and so gives us our clearest indications of the lost mythographer. The brief surviving works on myth by Paolo da Perugia, the *Genealogia Deorum*, and by Barlaam of Calabria bring us up to the immediate sources of Boccaccio and remind us that his watershed of mythography, the *Genealogie*, is the product of a continuous tradition.

Genealogies of the gods and collections of stories were not the only means by which Greek and Roman myth were conveyed to the Middle Ages. The Trojan War was one of the most popular subjects of history and romance throughout the period. There are innu-merable examples of nations and cities tracing their origins back to the refugees who fled from Troy, as Vergil did for the Romans in the *Aeneid*. Among the most famous are the accounts of the origin of the Franks found in such early sources as Fredegar (658) and the *Liber Historiae Francorum* (727), which relate that they were one of the groups scattered from Troy and only after long wanderings by the Sea of Azov and the Danube did they come to the Rhine, whence they entered the pages of history. Geoffrey of Monmouth (died 1155) likewise found the earliest of his kings of Britain in Brutus, a descendant of Aeneas who led a band of Trojan exiles in search of a new homeland. Snorri Sturluson (1179–1241) even traced the line of the Norse gods back to Priam in the *Prose Edda*.

But the consequences of the Trojan War were not narrated as often as the war itself. On the basis of Dictys of Crete, Dares of Phrygia, the *Ilias Latina*, and lesser-known sources like that represented by the Rawlinson *Excidium Troie*, as well as the *romans d'antiquité* collected by Jean Bodel (about 1165–1210) as the *matière de Rome*, Benoît de Sainte Maure (died 1173) wrote his lengthy poem, *Le Roman de Troie*, between 1155 and

1160. Benoît's French poem was rendered into Latin prose by the Sicilian Guido delle Colonne (Guido de Columnis) as the *Historia Destructionis Troiae* (about 1287), and in that form was more often adapted by other authors and exerted even greater influence.

The works of Benoît and Guido give an exhaustive account of the Trojan War from the expedition of Jason and the Argonauts up to the death of Ulysses, which might be hard for a reader of the *Iliad* to recognize. It is not simply that the story has been enlarged, altered, and rearranged, but that Hector and Achilles and the rest appear under the guise of knights jousting on their destriers and paying court to ladies. Hector and the other Trojans, moreover, acquit themselves rather better on the field of battle than their Homeric counterparts and Achilles even acknowledges Hector as the better warrior; all of this would suit a western audience readier to identify with the Trojans than the Greeks. Hector, after all, not Achilles, was destined to be found amongst the Nine Worthies.

The elaboration of the story of Troilus and Briseis (Boccaccio's Criseida) was Benoît and Guido's most important contribution to the tradition of the Trojan War. Before their writing Troilus was a negligible character, unassociated with a tragic love story, but the story worked up by Benoît and transmitted by Guido was to provide material for the likes of Boccaccio (*Il Filostrato*), Chaucer (*Troilus and Criseyde*), Henryson (*Testament of Cresseid*), and Shakespeare (*Troilus and Cressida*). Guido also includes (in Book 10) a digression of a more familiar mythographic stamp, which specifically refers to the authority of Isidore, outlining the origins of idolatry, the principal gods of the ancients, and the demonic inspiration of their cults. The Trojan Cycle returned to Greece with all of its medieval trappings and anti-Homeric bias when Benoît's *Roman de Troie* was translated into Greek political verse around 1350.

There were a number of other treatments of the Trojan War in Latin verse from the middle of the 12th century on. Simon Chèvre d'Or (Simon Aurea Capra) wrote an *Ylias* based on the *Excidium Troie* and the *Aeneid* at some time in the 12th century. Joseph of Exeter wrote the so-called *De Bello Trojano*, probably between 1182 and 1189, principally on the basis of Dares Phrygius. The *Anonymi Historia Troyana Daretis Frigii* also seems to have been written before the end of the 12th century. And Albert of Stade (died about 1265) wrote his *Troilus* with the same broad coverage as Benoît and Guido, from Jason to the return of the Greek heroes.

The Trojan War was also the subject of several vernacular romances and histories. One of the earliest of these was the Middle High German *Liet von Troye* of Herbort von Fritzlâr, written about 1190–1200 as a shortened version of Benoît's *Roman*. The Old Norse *Trójumanna saga* from the early 13th century was based on Dares, with revisions from the *Ilias Latina* and the *Aeneid*. Segher Dieregotgaf and Jacob van Maerlant produced Dutch versions of Benoît, the *Trojaensche Oorlag* and *Istory van Troyen* respectively, in the 13th century. Konrad of Würzburg's (died 1287) *Trojanischer Krieg*—unfinished at forty thousand lines!—augmented Benoît with material from the *Excidium Troie* or other obscure sources. In the 14th century the *Historia Troyana Polimétrica*, a Spanish prose composition with inserted poems, translated and amplified (especially in the poems) Benoît and Leomarte's *Sumas de Historia Troyana* was based on Guido and other sources. The 14th century also saw the appearance of the English *Seege or Batayle of Troy*, the Italian *Istorietta Trojana* and *La Fiorita* of Armannino Giudice, and even a Bulgarian *Trojanska Priča*.

Statius's repute in the Middle Ages as a rival to Vergil ensured that there was a "matter of Thebes" alongside the "matter of Troy," but it never enjoyed the latter's popularity. The anonymous French *Roman de Thèbes*, written around 1150–1155 (but certainly before the *Roman de Troie*), was based on an abridgement of Statius's *Thebaid*. As in Benoît's poem, the supernatural is eschewed and the protagonists follow the conventions of knightly combat and courtly love. Hue de Rotelande, writing in the 1180s, seems to have borrowed little more than the names in the *Roman de Thèbes* for his *Ipomedon* and *Protheselaus*, typical medieval romances with practically no relation to classical myth. But Boccaccio's *Teseida*, Chaucer's *Anelinda and Arcite* and *Knight's Tale*, and Lydgate's *Siege of Thebes* exhibit rather more substantial debts to the *Roman de Thèbes*.

We might end by noting the suggestion that one of the most popular and pervasive medieval literary phenomena, the Arthurian legends, are actually retellings of Greek and Roman myth in disguise. Lewis (1932) proposed that Chrestien de Troyes's sources, the *contes d'aventure*, were garbled and vulgarized postclassical versions of various classical myths and that the Celtic element in the stories of Arthur was nothing more than a thin veneer of names and settings. More recently, Anderson (2004) has argued that the Arthurian material preserves obscure strains of Arcadian myth and the legendary history of Lydia, articulated in antiquity and again throughout the Middle Ages, but leaving the interval rather hazy. But since the *matière de Bretagne* was not recognized in the Middle Ages as a rendition of classical mythology, whether it was or not, it may have no place in a discussion of the tradition of Greek and Roman mythography.

## Further Reading

Two works must guide those who would like to begin a further investigation of mythography in the medieval West. One, Seznec (1981), a learned and wide-ranging examination of the place the pagan gods found in the culture and learning of the Christian society of the Middle Ages, may be dated, but has aged well on account of the great erudition it displays so lightly and the lucid exposition of a mass of often dense and confusing material. Jane Chance's three-volume survey (1994–2015) is somewhat more comprehensive and brings the bibliography up to date.

## Bibliography

This bibliography, with annotations, has been arranged into sections that follow the course of the discussion in the chapter.

### Abbreviations

CCSL = Corpus christianorum, Series latina
PL = *Patrologia Latina*

## General

Seznec, Jean. *The Survival of the Pagan Gods: The Mythological Tradition and Its Place in Renaissance Humanism and Art*. New York: Bollingen Foundation, 1953; repr. Princeton, NJ: Princeton University Press, 1981.

Chance, Jane. *Medieval Mythography*. 3 vols. Gainesville: University Press of Florida, 1994–2015.


## Fulgentius

Edition (with *Super Thebaiden*): Helm, Rudolf, ed. *Fabii Planciadis Fulgentii V. C. Opera*. Leipzig: Teubner, 1898; repr. Stuttgart: Teubner, 1970.

English translation: Whitbread, Leslie G. *Fulgentius the Mythographer*. Columbus: Ohio State University Press, 1971.

French translation and Helm's text (without apparatus) of the *Mitologiae*, with extensive notes: Wolff, Étienne, and Philippe Dain. *Fulgence. Mythologies*. Villeneuve d'Asc, France: Presses Universitaires du Septentrion, 2013.

Hays, Gregory. "The Date and Identity of the Mythographer Fulgentius." *Journal of Medieval Latin* 13 (2003): 163–252.

A comprehensive annotated electronic 'Fulgentius Bibliography' is maintained by Gregory Hays at https://uva.theopenscholar.com/gregory-hays/fulgentius-bibliography.


## Isidore of Seville

Edition: Lindsay, Wallace M., ed. *Isidori Hispalensis Episcopi Etymologiarum sive Originum Libri XX*. 2 vols. Oxford: Clarendon Press 1911.

Spanish translation (with Latin text): Oroz Reta, José, and Manuel-Antonio Marcos Casquero, trans. *Etimologías: Edición bilingüe*. Madrid: Biblioteca de autores cristianos 1993.

The *Auteurs latins du Moyen Âge* series of Les Belles Lettres is producing new editions with translations in various languages of individual books of the *Etymologiae*, but Book 8 has not yet appeared.

English translation: Barney, Stephen A., W. J. Lewis, J. A. Beach, and Oliver Berghof, trans. *The Etymologies of Isidore of Seville*. Cambridge, UK: Cambridge University Press, 2006.

MacFarlane, Katherine N. "Isidore of Seville on the Pagan Gods (Origines 8.11)." *Transactions of the American Philosophical Society* 70 (1980): 1–40.

The influence of Isidore upon later writers is to be found in Rabanus Maurus: *PL* 111.426–436; Peter Comestor: *Historia libri Genesis* 39, 40, 64, 67, 70, 76, 86 (*PL* 198.1089–1090, 1109–1111, 1112, 1116–1117, 1124); Vincent of Beauvais: *Speculum Historiale* 1.102; Roger Bacon: *Opus Maius* 2.9–10.


## Allegorical Tradition

Brisson, Luc. *How Philosophers Saved Myths: Allegorical Interpretation and Classical Mythology*. Translated by Catherine Tihanyi. Chicago: University of Chicago Press, 2004.

Theodulf of Orleans: *Carm.* 5.1 (*PL* 331–333).

Remigius of Auxerre: Lutz, Cora E., ed. *Remigii Autissiodorensis commentum in Martianum Capellam*. 2 vols. Leiden: Brill, 1962–1965.

John of Salisbury: *Entheticus* 175–196 (*PL* 199.969).

*Ovide moralisé*: de Boer, Cornelis, ed. *"Ovide moralisé": Poème du commencement du quatorzième siècle*, 5 vols. Amsterdam: J. Müller, 1915–1938; repr. Wiesbaden: Martin Sändig, 1966–1968.


## Clerical Opposition to Paganism

Caesarius of Arles: *Sermo* 193.4 (*CCSL* 104: 782–786).

Martin of Braga: *De correctione rusticorum* 6–9.

Gregory of Tours: *Historia Francorum* 2.29.

Daniel of Winchester to Boniface: Boniface, *Epistula* 23 (*Monumenta Germaniae Historica, Epp. sel.* 1: 39–40).

Anonymous Gallic homilist: see Levison, Wilhelm. *England and the Continent in the Eighth Century*, 302–314. Oxford: Clarendon Press, 1946.

Ælfric: Pope, John C., ed. *Homilies of Ælfric: A Supplementary Collection*, 2.667–724. Oxford: Oxford University Press, 1967–1968.

Wulfstan, *De falsis deis*: Bethurum, Dorothy, ed. *The Homilies of Wulstan*, 221–224. Oxford: Clarendon Press, 1957.

Johnson, David F. "Euhemerisation versus Demonisation: The Pagan Gods and Ælfric's *De falsis diis*." In *Pagans and Christians: The Interplay between Christian Latin and Traditional Germanic Cultures in Early Medieval Europe*, edited by Tette Hofstra, Luuk A. J. R. Houwen, and Alasdair A. MacDonald, 35–69. Groningen: Egbert Forsten, 1995.

Garstad, Benjamin. "Barbarian Interest in the *Excerpta Latina Barbari*." *Early Medieval Europe* 19 (2011): 3–42, esp. 10–11, 37–38.


## The Vatican Mythographers

Edition of First and Second Mythographers: Kulcsár, Péter, ed. *Mythographi Vaticani I et II*. Turnhout: Brepols 1987.

Edition of the First Mythographer with French translation and notes: Zorzetti, Nevio, ed. and Jacques Berlioz, trans. *Le premier Mythographe du Vatican*. Paris: Budé 1995.

The best, though not satisfactory, edition of the Third Mythographer remains Bode, Georg H., ed. *Scriptores rerum mythicarum Latini tres Romae nuper reperti*. Celle: E. H. C. Schulze, 1834; repr. Hildesheim: Georg Olms, 1968.

French translation, with extensive commentary: Dain, Philippe. rev. François Kerlouégan. *Mythographe du Vatican I*. Besançon/Paris: Annales Littéraires de l'Université de Besançon/ Les Belles Lettres, 1995. Dain, Philippe. *Mythographe du Vatican II* Besançon/Paris: Presses universitaires Franc-Comtoises/Les Belles Lettres, 2000. Dain, Philippe. *Mythographe du Vatican III*. Besançon: Presses universitaires de Franche-Comté, 2005.

English translation of all three Mythographers: Pepin, Ronald E. *The Vatican Mythographers*. New York: Fordham University Press, 2008.


## Conrad of Mure

Edition: van de Loo, Tom, ed. *Conradi de Mure Fabularius* (*CCCM* 210). Turnhout: Brepols, 2006.

## Digby Mythographer

Allen, Judson Boyce. "An Anonymous Twelfth-Century 'De Natura Deorum' in the Bodleian Library." *Traditio* 26 (1970): 352–364.

Brown, Virginia. "An Edition of an Anonymous Twelfth-Century *Liber de natura deorum.*" *Medieval Studies* 34 (1972): 1–70.

## Theodontius

Landi, Carlo. *Demogòrgon*. Palermo: Edizioni Sandron 1930.

Pade, Marianne. "The Fragments of Theodontius in Boccaccio's *Genealogie Deorum Gentilium Libri.*" In *Avignon and Naples: Italy in France—France in Italy in the Fourteenth Century*, edited by Marianne Pade, Hannemarie R. Jensen, and Lene W. Petersen, 149–166. Rome: "L'Erma" di Bretschneider, 1993.

Schwertsik, Peter. "Un commento medievale alle 'Metamorfosi' d'Ovidio nella Napoli del Trecento: Boccaccio e l'Invenzione di 'Theodontius.'" *Medioevo e rinascimento* 26 (2012): 61–84.

## Trojan Cycle

Benoît de Sainte-Maure, *Roman de Troie*, edition: Constans, Léopold, ed. *Le Roman de Troie par Benoit de Sainte-Maure*, 6 vols. Paris: Firmin-Didot, 1904–1912.

Excerpts of Benoît with modern French paraphrase: Baumgartner, Emmanuèle, and Françoise Vielliard, eds. *Benoit de Sainte-Maure, Le Roman de Troie*. Paris: Livre de poche, 1998.

Guido delle Colonne, edition: Griffin, Nathaniel E., ed. *Guido de Columnis, Historia destructionis Troiae*. Cambridge, MA: Medieval Academy of America, 1936.

English translation: Meek, Mary E., trans. *Historia Destructionis Troiae*. Bloomington: Indiana University Press, 1974.

Keller, Wolfram R. *Selves and Nations: The Troy Story from Sicily to England in the Middle Ages*. Heidelberg: Universitätsverlag Winter, 2008.

*Excidium Troiae*: Atwood, Elmer Bagby, and Virgil K. Whitaker, eds. *Excidium Troiae*. Cambridge, MA: Medieval Academy of America, 1944.

*Anonymi Historia*: Stohlmann, Jürgen, ed. *Anonymi Historia Troyana Daretis Frigii*. Ratingen, Germany: A. Henn, 1968.

Joseph of Exeter: Bate, Alan K. *Joseph of Exeter, Trojan War I–III*. Warminster, UK: Aris and Phillips, 1986.

Medieval Greek *War of Troy*: Jeffreys, Elizabeth M., and Manolis Papathomopoulos, eds. *Ο ΠΟΛΕΜΟΣ ΤΗΣ ΤΡΟΑΔΟΣ (The War of Troy)*. Athens, Greece: Morphotiko Hidryma Ethnikes Trapezes, 1996.

Eisenhut, Werner. "Spätantike Trojaerzählungen: Mit einem Ausblickauf die mittellateinische Trojaliteratur." *Mittellateinisches Jahrbuch* 18 (1983): 1–28.

Graus, František. "Troja und trojanische Herkunftssage im Mittelalter." In *Kontinuität und Transformation der Antike im Mittelalter*, edited by Willi Erzgräber, 25–43. Sigmaringen, Germany: Thorbecke, 1989.

Garstad, Benjamin. "Barbarian Interest in the *Excerpta Latina Barbari.*" *Early Medieval Europe* 19 (2011): 3–42, esp. 18–23.

## Theban Cycle

Battles, Dominique. *The Medieval Tradition of Thebes: History and Narrative in the OF "Roman de Thèbes," Boccaccio, Chaucer, and Lydgate.* London: Routledge, 2004.

## Arthurian Material

Lewis, Charles Bertram. *Classical Mythology and Arthurian Romance.* London: Humphrey Milford, 1932.
Anderson, Graham. *King Arthur in Antiquity.* London: Routledge, 2004.

.....................................................................................

# CHAPTER 40

# MYTHOGRAPHY AND THE RECEPTION OF CLASSICAL MYTHOLOGY IN THE RENAISSANCE, 1340–1600

.....................................................................................

## JON SOLOMON

DEVELOPMENTS in the reception of classical mythology from the late medieval period to the Renaissance shared much the same profile as that of other artistic genres and intellectual disciplines. Moving across blurred chronological lines, artistic subject matter and output formats continued along familiar paths as bodies of knowledge continued to expand, especially with the infusion of Greek scholars from Southern Italy and Constantinople, and there was a manifold increase in consumption after the installation of numerous printing presses in the latter half of the 15th century. Interestingly, the introduction of ancient Greek literature for many decades remained within the confines of the urban academic centers and royal or aristocratic courts governed by enlightened patrons, but the printing press almost immediately brought literature and academic studies to a much more general audience and turned a select few of the latter into standard handbooks. More specifically, by the mid-14th century, Italian humanists had begun regularizing scholarly access to classical mythology, synthesizing in a mythographical manner the ancient and medieval traditions in widely distributed Latin works that would serve as guides to poets, artists, clergy, and scholars for nearly two centuries.

The Benedictine monk Pierre Bersuire (Petrus Berchorius), for instance, effectively supplanted the late medieval allegorical tradition, which was represented in the first few decades of the 14th century by Giovanni del Virgilio's commentaries on Ovid (*Allegorie, Esposizioni*) and the *Ovide Moralisé*, the anonymous 70,000-line Old French translation and allegorical exegesis of Ovid's *Metamorphoses*, themselves the culmination of at least two centuries of medieval Ovid commentaries (McKinley 2001: 89–113). Bersuire's Latin *Ovidius Moralizatus*, included as the fifteenth and penultimate book of his *Reductorium*

*Morale* of 1342, updated his original recension of a few years earlier by incorporating allegorical interpretations from the *Ovide Moralisé*, given him by Philip de Vitry, and John Ridewall's (Joannes Ridevallus) more recent *Fulgentius Metaforalis*, as well as supplemental mythological information from the Third Vatican Mythographer (Fumo 2014). Despite incorporating such recent sources, Bersuire's *Ovidius Moralizatus*, like many of the subsequent compendia, offered paraphrases of Ovid's mythological narratives and literal, natural, historical, and spiritual allegorizations, a methodology derived ultimately from Arnulf of Orléans. He represents Saturn, for instance, as the first among the planets, the concept of time, the king of Crete, and a symbol of evil.

In Avignon, Bersuire had become acquainted with Petrarch, whose Latin epic *Africa* (3.138–264) provided the literary inspiration and mythological material for the introduction to Bersuire's treatise known separately as *De Formis Figurisque Deorum* (Reynolds 1971: 18–19). Here, Bersuire allegorized the major gods and their attributes as well as such lesser groups as the Fates and the Harpies. As an independent treatise *De Formis Figurisque Deorum* was disseminated throughout Europe and became one of the most popular mythological works of the period, helping to establish subsequent Renaissance iconography. Ironically, it was later attached to the *Ovide Moralisé* tradition (Pairet 2011: 83–87; Lord 2011: 270–275).

Including his *Africa* of the early 1340s, much of Petrarch's scholarly output was derived primarily from Latin historical sources, and his epic poem and his contemporary *De Viris Illustribus* were originally designed to celebrate ancient Roman military and civic heroes as models for moral instruction, much as did the works of Petrarch's immediate predecessors in Avignon, Guglielmo de Pastrengo and Giovanni Colonna (Witt 2009; Ross 1970). Neither had included mythological characters in their versions of *De Viris Illustribus*, but in the first part of Pastrengo's *De Originibus*, an alphabetically arranged list of founders, discoverers, and inventors, he included Apollo and Asclepius (medicine); the Argonauts (sailing); Atreus (eclipses); Cadmus (Greek letters); Chiron (Artemisia); Daedalus (building materials); Mercury (magic, the lyre, the cithara), the lawgivers Lycurgus, Minos, and others; and several other mythological personages.

By the early 1350s, Petrarch had adopted a universalistic scope typical of the period, incorporating in his expanded second recension biographies of not only biblical and quasi-historical ancient Near Eastern figures but also Jason and Hercules. Petrarch's biography of Jason, at fewer than a thousand words, was relatively brief. Citing and quoting Valerius Flaccus and Justin, Petrarch substitutes historical context for mythical narrative: the voyage of the Argo is the first in history; two of the men associated with Jason were the eponymous ancestors of the kingdoms of Media and Armenia; and several comparisons between Jason and Alexander highlight the latter as the subsequent conqueror of the East. Even more to the point, his slightly longer biography of Hercules begins with the sentence, "It is an easy matter to tell stories (*fabulas*) about Hercules, but very difficult to construct a history (*ystoriam*)." The biography depends on the tradition that there were numerous historical men named Hercules who were illustrious for their wisdom or their military exploits or feats of strength. Thereafter, Petrarch focuses his narrative on the geographical range of Hercules's travels (drawing from Servius on *Aeneid* 8.564 and 1.741).

Inspired by Petrarch's collection of biographies but expanding the mythological selections considerably, Giovanni Boccaccio in the early 1360s incorporated more than three dozen biographies in his *De Mulieribus Claris*, including the Eastern Semiramis and Dido and such female figures as Camilla, Lavinia, and Rhea Ilia thought to belong to the early period of Roman history. Whereas Bersuire's introduction had allegorized the Olympian divinities Venus, Diana, Minerva, and Juno, as well as Ops (Opis), the wife of Saturn, Boccaccio omitted Diana but wrote short (300–600 words) biographies of a range of mythical women, categorizing most of them as queens—for example, Ceres, "Goddess of the Harvest and Queen of Sicily"—maidens, wives, or daughters. He arranged them in their perceived chronological order, beginning with Eve, Semiramis, Opis, and Juno and ending with the Homeric Clytemnestra, Helen, Circe, and Penelope. As in Petrarch's biographical collection of famous men, and as was appropriate for the theme of his own *De Casibus Virorum Illustrium*, Boccaccio featured only a single divinity (Saturn), four mythological figures (Cadmus, Thyestes, Atreus, Theseus), and two Homeric kings (Priam, Agamemnon) among his nearly two hundred entries.

Boccaccio's *Allegoria Mitologica*, written in the early 1330s and preceding both Bersuire and Petrarch's mythological works, was a relatively brief Latin synthesis of the biblical and Ovidian creation accounts. Much more ambitious and influential was his *Genealogia Deorum Gentilium*, which he wrote and edited from the 1350s until the time of his death in 1375. The work contained mythological narratives and exegeses of 723 mythological personages ranging, again, according to the traditional chronology but now arranged genealogically, from the post-ancient Demogorgon and the primordial concepts of Eternity, Chaos, Strife, the Arcadian Pan, the Fates, Pronapides's celestial Polus, and Phyton (1.1–1.7), to Earth and her offspring (1.8–1.13) and Erebus and his (1.14–2.1), through to extended divine and heroic lineages ending with Alexander and Scipio, whose divinity Boccaccio denied, thus clearly delineating the difference between mythologically divine and historical human characters, despite human claims to divine lineage. Because of the genealogical framework, Boccaccio was constrained not to write individual entries on otherwise well-known mythological characters who were not of divine lineage, for instance, Pyramus and Thisbe. But he often included non-pedigreed mythological personages and creatures in the entries on pedigreed characters; for instance, Jocasta appears in the entries on Laius, Oedipus, and Antigone, all descendants of Agenor, Belus, Epaphus, and the first Jupiter (2.69–74), and the *Odyssey*'s Lotus Eaters appear in the entry on Neptune's son Polyphemus (10.14). Including groups like the Sirens (7.20), Centaurs (9.27), and Muses (11.2), as well as mothers, spouses, and unnamed siblings and beasts, Boccaccio arranges discussions of approximately a thousand mythical beings within his encyclopedic scope.

He used over 220 ancient and medieval Latin sources, citing and quoting such poets as Ovid, Vergil, Lucan, and Statius hundreds of times, and following Cicero's *De Natura Deorum* in distributing the euhemerizing mythological information about the Olympian gods to multiple individuals who had such names as Jupiter, Mercury, or Venus. He also used a number of Greek sources, derived for the most part indirectly from Latin sources. One of these was the *Chronica* of Eusebius, via Jerome, which Boccaccio cited frequently to help confirm the historicity of the traditional mythological chronology. In addition, when Boccaccio was a student in Naples in the 1330s, Paolo da Perugia, head librarian at the Angevin court of Robert the Wise and author of the nonextant mythological *Collectiones*, provided him with an abundance of Greek material supplied by the Calabrian Greek Barlaam. Boccaccio also gained access to the relatively obscure Greek Arcadian tradition provided by the lesser-known Theodontius (Pade 1997; Schwertsik 2012). To gain access to Homer, Boccaccio sponsored and housed the Calabrian Greek Leontius Pilatus (Leonzio Pilato), who rendered translations of the Homeric epics for him, thereby introducing sources in the ancient Greek language into Renaissance scholarship (Pertusi 1964). Boccaccio quotes over forty Homeric passages in Greek, albeit with minor but ubiquitous orthographical errors. He also cites Homer in approximately two hundred passages, some for narrative detail such as the *kestos* Aphrodite/Venus wears in *Iliad* 14.214–217, others to fill out unique genealogies, especially in book 6 on the lineage descended from Dardanus (the sixteenth child of the second Jupiter), where, for instance, citing *Iliad* 20.237–238, Boccaccio lists Lampus, Clytion, and Hicetaon as the sons of Laomedon.

Like Bersuire, Boccaccio allegorizes the planetary gods, but Boccaccio's exegeses represent a wider variety of methodologies and source types. For his entry on Saturn (8.1), for instance, he initially cites the *Sacred History* and Ennius in Lactantius's *Divine Institutes* (1.11–14), all within a euhemeristic, historical framework, specifying that Saturn was a human who glorified his origins by claiming Uranus and Earth as his father and mother. He cites Cicero (*Nat. D.* 2.63) for the etymology of his name, "saturated in years" (*quod saturetur annis*), his great age accounting not only for his depiction as an old man but also the fable that he devoured and vomited out his children, since over time the earth destroys and reproduces its fruits. He cites Macrobius's *Saturnalia* (1.7.31) to account for Saturnian rites being transformed from human sacrifice to the symbolic use of wax figurines of humans. He cites Lactantius Placidus's commentary on Statius's *Thebaid* (8.44) to explain that Jupiter banished Saturn not to the nether regions but to Italy. And he cites Albumasar's *Introduction to Astronomy* (7.9) while explaining that as a sad, old man Saturn had a cold, dry complexion and foul breath, was melancholic, gluttonous, and avaricious, was a significator of agricultural work, and moved slowly to reflect the relatively lengthy orbital period of the planet Saturn.

Both in manuscript and printed form, and translated into French and Italian, Boccaccio's comprehensive and learned *Genealogy* would remain a widely disseminated compendium of Greco-Roman mythology well into the 16th century. More immediately, Coluccio Salutati, humanist and the chancellor of Florence, commissioned an alphabetical index of Boccaccio's treatise, and during the three decades following Boccaccio's death compiled his own lengthy mythological treatise on the labors of Hercules, *De Laboribus Herculis* (Ullman 1951; Morreale 1954). Also citing a plethora of ancient sources, like Boccaccio in the final two books of the *Genealogy*, in the first of four books he justified the study of ancient Greek and Latin literature by maintaining that it expressed theological truths unknown even to the ancient poets. Following the tradition that leads from Seneca's two morally contradictory Hercules dramas to Petrarch's brief biography and Boccaccio's account in the *Genealogy* (13.1), where he identifies thirty-one Herculean labors and parerga, Salutati's second and final recension of the treatise examines forty-three Herculean labors and parerga and concludes, in the fourth book, with an allegorical interpretation of the mythological *katabases* of Orpheus, Amphiaraus, Perithous and Theseus, Aeneas, and Hercules. Unlike Boccaccio's *Genealogy*, however, Salutati's work had little subsequent influence (Chance 2015: 363–395).

In the first decades of the 15th century, writers from the English Chaucer to the Franco-Italian Christine de Pizan borrowed from both Ovid and Boccaccio. Chaucer, it has been proposed, met with Boccaccio in Italy in 1372/1373, or if not, he was well versed in Boccaccio's writings, evidenced most clearly perhaps in his *Troilus and Criseyde*. In addition, such major works as *The Canterbury Tales*, structurally modeled after Boccaccio's *Decameron*, as well as *The House of Fame*, *Parlement of Foules*, and *The Legend of Good Women*, incorporate Greco-Roman pagan divinities for imagery or as allegorical figures and allude to or even paraphrase several Greco-Roman mythological stories, often as moral exempla. Some of the women he features also appeared in some of the works discussed thus far—namely, Boccaccio's Thisbe (in *De Mulieribus Claris*), Vergil's Dido, Seneca's Medea, Catullus's Ariadne, Statius's Hypsipyle, Ovid's Hypermnestra, and Livy's Lucretia, many of these also addressed by authors from Ovid to Dante. Moving on chronologically, three dozen of the biographies of mythological women in Christine's *Le Livre de la Cité des Dames* (1405), including the early Roman figures, derived directly from Boccaccio's *De Mulieribus Claris*, and nearly two dozen of them appear as well in her *L'Épistre de Othéa a Hector* (1400) (Chance 2015: 206–362). In contrast, even though his poem specifically treats contemporary subjects and secular themes, John Gower filled his *Vox Clamantis* (1381) with Ovidian allusions, and the controlling figure in the prologue of his *Confessio Amantis* (1390) is Venus. John Lydgate translated Guido delle Colonne's *Historia Destructionis Troiae* and greatly expanded the English sector of the Trojan War tradition in his *Troy Book*, and then he did the same for the Theban tradition in his *Siege of Thebes* (1422) (Fewer 2004).

Library collections of Greek manuscripts in Venice, Rome, and other Italian cities expanded considerably during these decades, and a few previously inaccessible works essential for the study of Greco-Roman mythology, such as Plutarch's *Life of Theseus*, were rendered into Latin for the first time. However, most of the mid-15th-century humanist scholarship concentrated on Greco-Roman historical prose, rhetoric, and other nonmythological genres and subjects, engendering more scholarly accumulation than artistic output (Celenza 1997). Beginning in the 1470s, a number of versatile artists and intellectuals at the Florentine court of Lorenzo de' Medici applied some of this recently accumulated knowledge to an innovative set of classicizing works. The Latin *Silvae* of Poliziano (Angelo Ambrogini) featured extended hexameter tributes to Vergil (*Manto*) and Homer (*Ambra*), and after studying Theocritus's and Vergil's pastoral works, Poliziano penned his *Orfeo* in Italian and established the pastoral drama as a staple of

Renaissance celebratory theatrical and literary production. The Florentine Platonic Academy included Poliziano as a member, and it was led by Marsilio Ficino, whose third book of *De Vita* (1489) features the pagan gods as archetypes. Artists associated with the Medici court re-established mythological subject matter as an alternative to religious paintings and portraits of aristocrats. Antonio del Pollaiuolo painted and sculpted several works depicting Hercules, long a public symbol of Florence, while Sandro Botticelli executed allegorical works, such as the *Birth of Venus*, *Primavera*, and *Mars and Venus*, inspired in part by the Academy's Neoplatonic tenets.

This efflorescence of mythological works was patronized by the aristocratic dynasties in a number of northern Italian cities. Poliziano's *Orfeo* was written in Ferrara and performed in Mantua (Pirrotta and Povoledo 1982: 44). The aptly named Duke Ercole I of the d'Este court at Ferrara sponsored the groundbreaking public performances of Plautus's *Amphitryon* (1487) and Niccolò da Correggio's Ovidian *Cefalo* (Brand 1995; Lavin 1954). Shortly after, the *editio princeps* of Apuleius's *Metamorphoses* in 1469 led to Niccolò's subsequent dramatic adaptation and a Ferrara production of the story of Cupid and Psyche (Gaisser 2008: 185–196). In 1493 Ludovico Sforza in Milan sponsored the performance of Baldassare Taccone's *Danae*. Many of the same Italian aristocrats also patronized painted mythological panel and fresco cycles (for instance, Giulio Romano's Sala dei Giganti at the Palazzo Te in Mantua), some of them connected directly with literary and dramatic adaptations, for example, Bernadino Luini's Cephalus and Procris cycle at the Casa Rabia in Milan. However, although Italian, French, and English dramatists experimented with translations and adaptations of Greek and Senecan tragedy—most notably, Sperone Speroni's dramatization of Ovid's letter from *Canace* (1546) and Gian Giorgio Trissino's *Sofonisba* (1515/1524), the latter along with Giambattista Giraldi Cinthio's *Orbecche* (1541) by design featuring historical protagonists—these plays, intended as reading texts, were rarely performed (Charlton 1946: xxix–xci). By the end of the century, Orsatto Giustiniani's translation of Sophocles's *Oedipus Tyrannus* was the celebrated inaugural production at Palladio's Teatro Olimpico in Vicenza in 1585, but even this important production failed to inspire a consistent schedule of revivals (Burian 1997; Di Maria 2005).

In contrast, newly conceived pastoral themes and settings flourished throughout the 16th century, led by Jacopo Sannazaro's *Arcadia*. Written in Italian, Sannazaro's work successfully synthesized scholarship, prose style, and poetic imagery. It captured the imagination of a readership fascinated by the concept of ancient fields and woods filled with mythological denizens and appreciative of literate prose punctuated with atmospheric poems and songs. Originally contemporary with Poliziano's *Orfeo*, *Arcadia* first circulated in manuscript form until Sannazaro revised the work and published it in 1504. It appeared in dozens of editions throughout the century and inspired other authors to recreate their own literary versions of Arcadia, several of which were very well received in other countries—for instance, Jorge de Montemayor's *Diana* (1559) in Spain, the two versions of Philip Sydney's *Arcadia* written in England in the 1570s and 1580s, and Honoré d'Urfé's *L'Astrée* (1607) in France.

Following works like Cinthio's *Egle* (1545) and Agostino Beccari's *Sacrifizio* (1555), the principals of which included the likes of Pan, satyrs, and nymphs, two Italian pastoral dramas achieved international distribution during the last few decades of the 16th century. Tasso's *Aminta* (1573) popularized two nymphs named Silvia and Dafne, the former a chaste devotee of Diana, the latter no longer chaste. *Aminta's* mythological narrative motifs include Silvia bathing in a spring à la Diana and later losing her veil, causing Aminta to attempt suicide, much like Thisbe and Pyramus. The plot of Giovanni Battista Guarini's very successful *Il Pastor Fido* (1590) resolves in a marriage between descendants of Hercules (Silvio) and Pan (Amarilli), and as in Ovid's tale of Cephalus and Procris, Silvio mistakes a lurking lover for a wild animal and wounds her. Similarly, the prologue of Isabella Andreini's *Mirtilla* (1588) consists of a dialogue between Venus and Cupid (Amore). And the moon goddess Cynthia, Neptune, and Bacchus play guiding and variously interpreted allegorical figures in John Lyly's inventive English pastorals *Endimion*, *Gallathea*, and *Midas*. Like Poliziano's *Orfeo*, many commissioned court productions included musical numbers or interludes, and the period was replete with *intermedi*, *entr'actes*, and masques that featured mythological characters and subjects in Arcadian-style settings that were populated with nymphs and shepherds and usually overseen by stereotyped depictions of pagan divinities.

Following their medieval predecessors, who had not yet acquired a knowledge of Greek, Renaissance authors continued the tradition of adapting the ancient mythological epic genre, but now in vernacular languages. In 1460, Raoul Lefèvre devised a number of new characters and episodes for his *Histoire de Jason*, and his *Recoeil des Histoires de Troyes* (1464) included extended passages on Jupiter and Saturn, Perseus, and Hercules. During the next decade, William Caxton printed an English translation of the latter, *Recuyell of the Histories of Troy*, and this was just a few years before he printed the first English translation of Ovid's *Metamorphoses*. The creation of an epic in French decasyllables by Pierre de Ronsard helped to demonstrate the viability of the language. Appropriately, Ronsard's *Franciade* was a foundation epic recounting the myth of Francus (that is, Astyanax), who leaves Andromache and Helenus in Epirus, while he goes off to fulfill his destiny and become the founder of France. Like Odysseus and Aeneas, he is involved in a shipwreck, and when he lands in Crete, he encounters two sisters, partly modeled after Ariadne and Phaedra, one of whom, Clymène, turns out to be his Dido, dying near the end of the third book (Sommers 1983; Knape 2007). Ronsard began the project in the 1540s and revised it for three decades, completing only four of the projected twenty-four books.

The two influential epics produced in Italy during the 16th century, Ludovico Ariosto's *Orlando Furioso* (1532) and Torquato Tasso's *La Gerusalemme Liberata* (1581), refurbished techniques, characters, and narrative motifs established by Homer and Vergil. Near the outset of *Orlando Furioso*, Ariosto introduces Discord, the personified goddess who had helped instigate the Trojan War, and the final lines clearly echo those of the *Aeneid*. In between, Ariosto inserts episodes that are dependent on classical myths involving the Harpies, Cyclops, and Perseus and Andromeda (17.45, 10.92, 33.108). Also, there are throughout references to Hector's sword and armor, which Orlando wears, and at one point (18.184), the Saracen Medoro prays to the triple-goddess aspect of Diana (Shapiro 1983). Astolfo's metamorphosis into a talking myrtle bush on the island of Alcina (6.28–56) has a long classical pedigree from which Tasso (13.40–51) drew as well (Verg. *Aen.* 3.13–68; Ov. *Met.* 8.742–776; Dante, *Inf.* 13.22–108). Tasso's evil instigator is the Fury Allecto, and his satanic Armida transforms unwary humans, as did her ancient prototype Circe. Moreover, Armida's enchantment of Rinaldo very much resembles the initial stages of the romance between Dido and Aeneas. Such set passages as the invocation to the Muses and the catalogue of funereal trees (3.72–76) as well as two elaborate ancient mythological and historical ecphrases (16.2–7; 17.62–83) are classical in form (compare Verg. *Aen.* 1.453–493; 8.626–738). In the very first canto of the *Gerusalemme Liberata* Tasso offers a version of Homer's catalogue of ships (*Il.* 2.494–877), and in the third Erminia's survey of the Crusaders from atop the walls of Jerusalem recalls Helen's survey above Troy (*teichoscopia, Il.* 3.154–242).

Boccaccio's and Bersuire's works provided standard sources for the frequent allusions and comparisons to mythological characters and stories that continued to pervade European poetry and scholarly prose throughout the 15th and early 16th centuries, whether for the Florentine Platonists, the English Ricardian poets, the French Pléiade, or Erasmus (for instance, *De Copia* 3). They were supplemented by the repeated publication of a number of ancient and medieval works, particularly allegorical and iconographical works such as those authored by Fulgentius, Palaephatus, Macrobius, and Martianus Capella, and the information supplied by the Third Vatican Mythographer (Seznec 1953: 224–226; Pepin 2008: 7–11). But these would now, in the middle of the 16th century, be supplemented and ultimately replaced by a succession of books that were more comprehensive and had access to all the Greek mythological sources—including Hesiod, Pindar, most of the Attic tragedies, Apollonius, and Pausanias and a few Byzantine sources such as Maximus Planudes and John Tzetzes—that had been identified, edited, and published since the era of Petrarch and Boccaccio. Relatively late arrivals were the two important ancient mythological collections generally known as Hyginus's *Fabulae* (1535) and Ps.-Apollodorus's *Bibliotheca* (1555; Seznec 1953: 219–256).

As a student at the advent of the century, Lilio Gregorio Giraldi compiled his treatise on the Muses, *Syntagma de Musis*, published in 1507, and then in a second edition in 1511. As in his more mature work, Giraldi allocated the results of his research mostly to delineations of *cognomina* used by poets—that is, such alternate group names and epithets as Camoenae, Parnassides, Pierides, and Castalides, offering predominantly etymological and geographical information, citing and quoting ancient authorities, and criticizing his scholarly predecessors, thereby setting the precedent for the subsequent crop of mythologists (Enenkel 2002: 44–49). Over these next decades, which included an extended stay in Rome to examine ancient Roman artifacts, Giraldi continued his research, and in 1548 he published his magnum opus, *De Deis Gentium Historia* (Enenkel 2002: 10–27). In his dedication to Duke Ercole II of Ferrara, Giraldi explains that his scope will comprise religion and mythology of all ancient cultures, but the Greco-Roman material consumes sixteen of the seventeen sections (*syntagmata*) in the treatise. Very much unlike Boccaccio's genealogical arrangement, each of those chapters is dedicated to a single divinity or thematic group of divinities. *Syntagma* 3, for instance, treats Juno, Hymenaeus, and Thalassius, and *Syntagma* 13 treats Venus, Cupid, the Graces, Adonis, and Vulcan. For each divinity he defines the meaning and etymology of their name and their many *cognomina*, and in addition to discussing the geographical locations and sacred rites associated with these many names, Giraldi also incorporates ecphrases of many visual works of art associated with them and their characteristic divine attributes. Although Giraldi does not offer his own allegorical interpretations, his is nonetheless a voluminous work. The first edition contains approximately 11,000 quotations and citations from 473 ancient and medieval authors, a little more than twice the number Boccaccio cites. But despite Giraldi's ambitious historical scope, his focus on the history of religion prevents him from including many of the nondivine characters described by Boccaccio. Although Giraldi's *De Deis Gentium Historia* was seldom reprinted and never translated into a vernacular language, it did provide essential source material for Cartari and Conti.

During this first half of the century, several other works treating the pagan gods and myths appeared, although they were of smaller scope or included mythological names only as part of a larger philological framework, as in Robert Estienne's *Dictionarium Nominum Propriorum*. These included general works on classical literature like the *Antiquarum Lectionum* (1516) of Lodovico Celio Ricchieri (Caelius Rhodiginus) and the *Genialium Dierum* (1522) of the Neapolitan Alessandro Alessandri (Alexander ab Alexandro) as well as the *Theologia Mythologica* (1532) of the German Georg Pictor (Georgius Pictorius), the latter focusing again on the iconographical aspects of the pagan divinities (Mulryan and Brown 2006: 1.xxv–xlvi; Hawkins 1981: 55; Seznec 1953: 228). *De Cognominibus Deorum Gentilium* (1541) by Julien de Havrech (Julianus Aurelius) paralleled Giraldi's work in focusing on ancient religion and assigning each of the major gods to individual chapters that delineate their *cognomina* in detail, although here the male Olympian gods are assigned to the first book; the female Olympians, to the second, and lesser or terrestrial gods such as Janus, Saturn, Pluto, Bacchus, and Sol, to the third (Enenkel 2002: 32–34).

The works by Cartari and Conti were much more widely distributed and influential. Unlike most of his predecessors, Vincenzo Cartari chose the Italian language for the text of his *Imagini colla sposizione degli dei degli antichi* (*Images Depicting the Ancient Gods*) (1556), but like Giraldi and his contemporaries, Cartari focused on the iconography of Greco-Roman gods, and as the subtitle outlines, "the idols, rites, ceremonies, and other matters relating to the religion of the ancients." He devotes an introduction and fifteen individual chapters primarily to the Olympian gods. Although the succession of gods does not proceed in a traditional arrangement (1, Saturn; 2, Apollo; 3, Diana; 4, Jupiter; 5, Juno; and 6, the Great Mother), a detailed list of contents containing approximately 1600 names and abundant marginal subtitles make the lengthy text more user-friendly. In each chapter, Cartari includes brief discussions of subsidiary mythical beings. The chapter on Pluto, for instance, contains entries on Rhadamanthys, Aeacus, and Minos, Proserpina, Cerberus, the Furies, Harpies, the rivers of the Underworld, the Chimaera, the Parcae, Charon, and Vergil's list of evils (*Aen.* 6.273–281), as well as relevant

Underworld stories about Hercules, Theseus, and Orestes. Most of the entries are both descriptive and interpretive and employ historical and natural perspectives. The Chimaera, for instance, is a mountain in Lycia, and Minos represents remorse for one's sins. Beginning with the 1571 second edition, which Cartari himself had supervised, Cartari's book gained a much broader audience with the addition of eighty-five etchings by Bolognino Zaltieri. By the end of the century, the expanded work had been reprinted several times and translated into Latin, French, and English.

Natale Conti (Natalis Comes) brought this period of mythological compendia to a peak with the publication of his Latin *Mythologiae* in 1567. His organizational method is quite different from those of his predecessors. His ten chapters included individualized thematic essays divided by religious topics and mythological geography, and in each he investigates a variety of pagan mythological figures and events, including sacrificial rites associated with the gods. His expressed purpose is to reveal the natural and philosophical truths hidden in the fables and imagery, still echoing Boccaccio and Bersuire, although he does not cite them and claims (1.1) that he is the first to do so. His selection of sources is unique for the period, however, since he relies on, in addition to the traditional corpus of Latin poets and Cicero, such Greek authors as Pindar (Chapter 5 begins with a discussion of the four panhellenic games), Aristotle, Theophrastus, Theocritus, Nicander, Pausanias, Plutarch, Lucian, and Tzetzes, and he even inserts some of his own Latin and Greek poems (for instance, 2.10). Not nearly so closely associated with visual imagery as the contemporary, predominantly iconographic studies, and amplified with Geoffrey Linocier's essay on the Muses (*Mythologiae Musarum Libellus*), Conti's learned and variegated discussions provided literary source material for Edmund Spenser's *Faerie Queene* (1590) and Francis Bacon's *De Sapientia Veterum* (1609), in which each of the chapters specifies a particular mythological figure, as well as works by Ronsard, Lope de Vega, and John Milton. It endured as a standard reference until the late 18th century, when a new aesthetic preferred mythological narrative to allegory and other traditions of medieval interpretation (Mulryan and Brown 2006: xxxvi–xliii; Starnes and Talbert 1955: 11–28, 85–97, 341–343).

The renewed northern Italian fascination with ancient mythology literally spilled out into the streets on February 21, 1565, as Florentines watched the Masquerade of the Genealogy of the Gods of the Pagans (*Mascherata della genealogia degli dei de' gentile*), a parade of twenty-one floats dedicated to pagan characters. That their main source was the genealogical treatise of Boccaccio, a Florentine, is clear from the title and the cart representing the mysterious Demogorgon and from contemporary texts (Pierguidi 2007). The parade was part of the wedding celebration of Giovanna of Austria and Duke Francesco, son of Cosimo I, who had already commissioned Benvenuto Cellini's bronze sculpture of Perseus holding the head of Medusa, which is still displayed in the Loggia dei Lanzi. The celebration included performances of Francesco d'Ambra's Italian comedy *La Cofanaria*, which parodied the story of Cupid and Psyche, and the accompanying *intermedi* represented "the chorus of the ancient fables of the Greeks" while promoting cultural chauvinism: descending from the top of the proscenium, the Muses sang about how their beloved Hellenic Mount

Parnassus had been occupied by the Turks, compelling Apollo to transfer the Muses to Mount Fiesole. Venus rides in a gilded, jeweled chariot pulled by two white swans, accompanied by the three Graces and the Hours, all observed by Jupiter, Juno, Saturn, Mars, Mercury, and other Greco-Roman gods. Similarly, in a 1583 Florentine production Boccaccio's Demogorgon sang a duet with Eternity (*GDG* 1.1; Seznec 1953: 221–222). And three years later, the inaugural of the Uffizi Theater included five scenes populated by several dozen Olympian, terrestrial, and maritime gods, followed by a pastoral afterpiece (Nagler 1964: 58–69).

Despite the influence of Giraldi, Cartari, and Conti, characters and dynamic moments from Ovid's *Metamorphoses* remained a regular option for painters as well. Whereas Venetian artists, for instance, employed pagan mythological imagery for a variety of purposes ranging from academic allegory to the glorification of the Venetian empire, six of the seven erotic mythological paintings Habsburg King Philip II commissioned from Titian in the 1550s and 1560s depicted *Danae, Venus and Adonis, Perseus and Andromeda, The Rape of Europa, Diana and Actaeon*, and *Diana and Callisto* (Nichols 1999: 231; Brundin and Treherne 2009: 136). Titian, who along with Cartari belonged to the Venetian Accademia dei Pellegrini, founded in the 1550s, painted several versions of Venus and Adonis, and in the subsequent decades before the close of the century other well-known renderings were executed by Paolo Veronese, Annibale Carracci, and the Flemish Bartholomeus Spranger, the latter two roughly contemporary with the narrative poem by the young, English William Shakespeare (Volpi 1996: 10–12). With the maturity of Shakespeare, the introduction of opera, and promulgation of trompe l'oeil painting, the Baroque period would bring fresh approaches and new international developments into the legacy of Greco-Roman mythology.

## FURTHER READING

There is no specific standard collection or reference work for the study of the Renaissance mythological tradition, although Seznec (1953), Starnes and Talbert (1955), and Highet (1949) provide traditional introductions and overviews, and the work by Grafton, Most, and Settis (2010) contains dozens of relevant articles, with bibliography, and is accessible online.

For the late medieval Ovidian commentary tradition, see Coulson and Roy (2000), McKinley (2001); Pairet (2011), Lord (2011), and Fumo (2014). For the *Ovidius Moralizatus* of Petrus Berchorius, see de Boer (1915–1938) and Reynolds (1971).

For specific chapters on the major authors of the humanistic period, see Chance (2015). For Petrarch and his immediate predecessors Pastrengo and Colonna, see Ferrone (2012), Witt (2009), Bottari (1991), and Ross (1970). For Boccaccio, see Solomon (2011); on Theodontius, see Pade (1997), Schwertsik (2012, 2015); and on Leontius, see Pertusi (1964). For the 16th-century mythological compendia of Cartari and Conti, see Mulryan (2012), Mulryan and Brown (2006), Volpi (1996), and Enenkel (2002). For the Florentine masquerade, see Pierguidi (2007).

For the later poetic tradition, see Fewer (2004), Brundin and Treherne (2009), Hawkins (1981), Sommers (1983), Knape (2007), Ford (1997), and Shapiro (1983). For staged Renaissance works, see Celenza (1997), Bregoli-Russo (1997), Burian (1997), Pirrotta and Povoledo (1982), Nagler (1964), Brand (1995), Lavin (1954), and Di Maria (2005). For the transmission of Apuleius and Seneca, see Gaisser (2008) and Charlton (1946). For the visual tradition, see Nichols (1999), Dunlop (2009), and Corretti (2015).

## References

Bottari, Guglielmo, ed. 1991. *Guglielmo da Pastrengo: De Viris Illustribus et De Originibus.* Padua: Antenore.

Brand, C. Peter. 1995. "The Renaissance of Comedy: The Achievement of Italian 'Commedia Erudita.'" *Modern Language Review* 90: xxix–xlii.

Bregoli-Russo, Mauda. 1997. *Teatro dei Gonzaga at Tempo di Isabella d'Este.* New York: Peter Lang.

Brundin, Abigail, and Matthew Treherne. 2009. *Forms of Faith in Sixteenth-Century Italy.* Aldershot, UK: Ashgate.

Burian, Peter. 1997. "Tragedy Adapted for Stages and Screens: The Renaissance to the Present." In *The Cambridge Companion to Greek Tragedy*, edited by Patricia E. Easterling, 228–234. Cambridge, UK: Cambridge University Press.

Celenza, Christopher S. 1997. "Parallel Lives: Plutarch's 'Lives,' Lapo da Castiglionchio the Younger (1405–1438) and the Art of Italian Renaissance Translation." *Illinois Classical Studies* 22: 121–155.

Chance, Jane. 2015. *Medieval Mythography.* Vol. 3: *The Emergence of Italian Humanism, 1321–1475.* Gainesville: University Press of Florida.

Charlton, Henry B. 1946. *The Senecan Tradition in Renaissance Tragedy.* Manchester, UK: Manchester University Press.

Corretti, Christine. 2015. *Cellini's Perseus and Medusa and the Loggia dei Lanzi: Configurations of the Body of State.* Leiden: Brill.

Coulson, Frank T., and Bruno Roy. 2000. *Incipitarium Ovidianum: A Finding Guide for Texts Related to the Study of Ovid in the Middle Ages and Renaissance.* Turnhout: Brepols.

de Boer, Cornelis, ed. 1915–1938. *Ovide moralisé.* 5 vols. Amsterdam: J. Muller.

Di Maria, Salvatore. 2005. "Italian Reception of Greek Tragedy." In *A Companion to Greek Tragedy*, edited by Justina Gregory, 428–432. Malden, MA: Wiley-Blackwell.

Dunlop, Anne. 2009. *Painted Palaces: The Rise of Secular Art in Early Renaissance Italy.* University Park: Pennsylvania State University Press.

Enenkel, Karl A. E. 2002. "The Making of 16th-Century Mythography: Giraldi's *Syntagma de Musis* (1507, 1511 and 1539), *De Deis Gentium Historia* (ca. 1500–1548); Julien De Havrech's *De Cognominibus Deorum Gentilium* (1541)." *Humanistica Lovaniensia* 51: 9–53.

Ferrone, Silvano, ed. 2012. *Francesco Petrarca: De viris illustribus.* Florence: Le Lettere.

Fewer, Colin. 2004. "John Lydgate's *Troy Book* and the Ideology of Prudence." *Chaucer Review* 38: 229–245.

Ford, Philip. 1997. *Ronsard's Hymns: A Literary and Iconographical Study.* Tempe, AZ: Medieval and Renaissance Texts and Studies.

Fumo, Jamie C. 2014. "Commentary and Collaboration in the Medieval Allegorical Tradition." In *A Handbook to the Reception of Ovid*, edited by in John F. Miller and Carole E. Newlands, 119–126. Chichester, UK, and Malden, MA: Wiley-Blackwell.

Gaisser, Julia H. 2008. *The Fortunes of Apuleius and the "Golden Ass": A Study in Transmission and Reception*. Princeton, NJ: Princeton University Press.

Grafton, Anthony, Glenn W. Most, and Salvatore Settis, eds. 2010. *The Classical Tradition*. Cambridge, MA: Harvard University Press.

Hawkins, Peter S. 1981. "From Mythography to Myth-Making: Spenser and the Magna Mater Cybele." *Sixteenth Century Journal* 12: 50–64.

Highet, Gilbert. 1949. *The Classical Tradition: Greek and Roman Influences on Western Literature*. New York: Oxford University Press.

Knape, Joachim. 2007. "Epic." In *Brill's New Pauly*, vol. 2, edited by Manfred Landfester, 197–202. Leiden: Brill.

Lavin, Irving. 1954. "Cephalus and Procris: Transformations of an Ovidian Myth." *Journal of the Warburg and Courtauld Institutes* 17: 260–287.

Lord, Carla. 2011. "A Survey of Imagery in Medieval Manuscripts of Ovid's *Metamorphoses* and Related Commentaries." In *Ovid in the Middle Ages*, edited by James G. Clark, Frank T. Coulson, and Kathryn L. McKinley, 257–283. Cambridge, UK: Cambridge University Press.

McKinley, Kathryn L. 2001. *Reading the Ovidian Heroine: "Metamorphoses" Commentaries 1100–1618*. Leiden: Brill.

Morreale, Margherita. 1954. "Coluccio Salutati's 'De Laboribus Herculis' (1406) and Enrique de Villena's 'Los Doze Tranajos de Hercules' (1417)." *Studies in Philology* 51: 95–106.

Mulryan, John, trans. 2012. *Vincenzo Cartari's "Images of the Gods of the Ancients": The First Italian Mythography*. Tempe, AZ: Arizona Center for Medieval and Renaissance Studies.

Mulryan, John, and Steven Brown, eds. and trans. 2006. *Natale Conti's "Mythologiae."* 2 vols. Tempe AZ: Arizona Center for Medieval and Renaissance Studies.

Nagler, Alois M. 1964. *Theatre Festivals of the Medici, 1539–1637*. New Haven, CT and London: Yale University Press.

Nichols, Tom. 1999. *Tintoretto: Tradition and Identity*. London: Reaktion Books.

Pade, Marianne. 1997. "The Fragments of Theodontius in Boccaccio's *Genealogie deorum gentilium libri*." In *Avignon and Naples: Italy in France—France in Italy in the Fourteenth Century*, edited by Marianne Pade, Hannemarie R. Jensen, and Lene W. Petersen, 149–166. Rome: L'Erma di Bretschneider.

Pairet, Ana. 2011. "Recasting the *Metamorphoses* in Fourteenth-Century France: The Challenges of the *Ovide Moralisé*." In *Ovid in the Middle Ages*, edited by James G. Clark, Frank T. Coulson, and Kathryn L. McKinley, 83–107. Cambridge, UK: Cambridge University Press.

Pepin, Ronald E. 2008. *The Vatican Mythographers*. New York: Fordham University Press.

Pertusi, Agostino. 1964. *Leonzio Pilato fra Petrarca e Boccaccio*. Venice and Rome: Istituto per la Collaborazione Culturale.

Pierguidi, Stefano. 2007. "Baccio Baldini e la 'mascherata della genealogia degli dei.'" *Zeitschrift für Kunstgeschichte* 70: 347–364.

Pirrotta, Nino and Elena Povoledo. 1982. *Music and Theatre from Poliziano to Monteverdi*. Translated by Karen Eales. Cambridge, UK: Cambridge University Press.

Reynolds, William D. 1971. "The *Ovidius Moralizatus* of Petrus Berchorius: An Introduction and Translation." Diss. University of Illinois at Urbana-Champaign.

Ross, W. Braxton. 1970. "Giovanni Colonna, Historian at Avignon." *Speculum* 45: 533–563.

Schwertsik, Peter R. 2012. "Un comment medieval alle 'Metamorfosi' d'Ovidio nella Napoli del Trecento: Boccaccio e l'invenzione di 'Theodontius.'" *Medioevo e rinascimento* 26: 61–84.

Schwertsik, Peter R. 2015. *Die Erschaffung des heidnischen Götterhimmels durch Boccaccio: Die Quellen der Genealogia Deorum Gentilium in Neapel.* Paderborn: Wilhelm Fink.

Seznec, Jean. 1953. *The Survival of the Pagan Gods: The Mythological Tradition and Its Place in Renaissance Humanism and Art.* Translated by Barbara F. Sessions. Princeton, NJ: Princeton University Press.

Shapiro, Marianne. 1983. "Perseus and Bellerophon in Orlando Furioso." *Modern Philology* 81: 109–130.

Solomon, Jon. 2011/2017. *Giovanni Boccaccio: Genealogy of the Pagan Gods.* 2 vols. Cambridge, MA: Harvard University Press.

Sommers, Paula. 1983. "Phaedra, Ariadne and the 'Franciade': Ronsard's Motif of the Two Sisters." *Romanische Forschungen* 95: 117–123.

Starnes, DeWitt T., and Ernest W. Talbert. 1955. *Classical Myth and Legend in Renaissance Dictionaries in Their Relation to Classical Learning of Contemporary English Writers.* Chapel Hill: University of North Carolina Press.

Ullman, Berthold L. 1951. *Coluccio Salutati: De Laboribus Herculis.* Zurich: Thesaurus Mundi.

Volpi, Caterina. 1996. *Le immagini degli dèi di Vincenzo Cartari.* Rome: De Luca.

Witt, Ronald G. 2009. "The Rebirth of the Romans as Models of Character." In *Petrarch: A Critical Guide to the Complete Works*, edited by Victoria Kirkham and Armando Maggi, 103–111. Chicago: University of Chicago Press.

# Index

*For the benefit of digital users, indexed terms that span two pages (e.g., 52–53) may, on occasion, appear on only one of those pages.*

Figures are indicated by *f* following the page number